GREAT BRITAIN
AND THE WAR OF 1914–1918

EUROPE IN THE TWENTIETH CENTURY

Each of these books is available as a Beacon Paperback

Great Britain and the War of 1914–1918

SIR LLEWELLYN WOODWARD

*Fellow of All Souls College
and formerly Professor of Modern History
in the University of Oxford
Professor Emeritus at the Institute for
Advanced Study, Princeton, N.J.*

BEACON PRESS   BOSTON

Contents

PART III

The Western Front in 1915 and 1916: difficulties of the Coalition: death of Lord Kitchener

PART IV

The war at sea to the autumn of 1916

PART V

Great Britain and President Wilson's proposals for bringing the war to an end, 1914–1917: the entry of the United States into the war

PART VI

Lloyd George becomes Prime Minister: the Allied offensives of 1917: mutinies in the French army

PART VII

The establishment of the Supreme War Council: the Western Allies and Russia after the Bolshevik revolution

PART VIII

The last two years of the war at sea

PART IX

The war in the air

PART X

The German western offensives, March–June, 1918: Allied and German war aims: the defeat and surrender of Germany

PART XI

The Western Allies and the Bolsheviks

PART XII

The organisation of British resources for total war

PART XIII

The Peace Settlement with Germany

Editor's introduction
by Stephen R. Graubard

Europe in the Twentieth Century

Most historians, until quite recently, looked with suspicion on their professional colleagues who thought to investigate near-contemporary events. Although there was never anything like agreement on the matter, it was generally assumed that the requirements of objective scholarship could not be satisfied by historians who chose to write about their own times. The argument seemed compelling that those who undertook such tasks would always be operating with essentially incomplete archives, particularly in the diplomatic and political fields, but in other areas as well.

When the charge of incomplete documentation was refuted by those who insisted that the historian of twentieth-century happenings was in fact rarely hampered by a lack of materials, but was, on the contrary, generally overwhelmed by their abundance, having at his disposal incomparable documentation of kinds available to the historian for no other period, the argument shifted to a questioning of whether the historian could ever be objective in judging his own times.

The idea that objectivity was possible, but not to be expected of the historian concerned with near-contemporary events, spoke of a bias that owed a great deal to the nineteenth-century German school of history, perhaps best exemplified by von Ranke. The monographic tradition, with its emphasis on facts, supposedly neutral, and with its injunction to avoid judgments, particularly value judgments, still enjoyed currency in the early part of the twentieth century. R. G. Collingwood, in *The Idea of History*, probably did as much as anyone to discredit the notion that the historian was capable of taking himself out of his materials, or that his principal purpose should be the discovery and recording of value-free facts. Once the historian's role in shaping his materials was admitted, it became difficult to argue that what the historian did when he approached the events of the sixteenth century differed significantly from what he did when he set out to study the twentieth. Clearly, the distinction of a particular historical work was the only meaningful criterion for judging its acceptability; there was no intrinsic reason why research on twentieth-century subjects should result in work inferior in any way to what was realized when other periods were investigated.

The acceptance of contemporary history as a legitimate field of inquiry by professional scholars was slow, but once accomplished, it contributed to the creation of a literature that was soon recognized to have distinction and importance. There were, however, marked differences between the reception of these works and of those written by scholars who preferred to concentrate on earlier periods. To put the matter in purely commercial terms, scholarly studies of twentieth-century events competed in a market still dominated by popular books. For almost every imaginable twentieth-century theme, there was generally available a book written by someone who saw the possibility of finding a mass market for his work. The quality of these popular studies was of course uneven: some were original in very important respects; many were well written; a few were scarcely more than popularizations of scholarly works; the greatest number, perhaps, claimed no merit except that they offered amusement for those who wished to be entertained by lively narrative. In any case, because there was a mass market for such books, they were quickly reissued in inexpensive paperback editions and found their way into university course syllabi and onto the shelves of personal libraries.

Happily, Gresham's Law does not always operate, at least not with respect to books. Many publishers resisted the temptation to publish only popular studies of contemporary themes, showing in their selection of books on the twentieth century the same fastidiousness that they demonstrated when they chose a title for some period for which popular taste was less in evidence. The American reading public has been well served in having many excellent scholarly works on twentieth-century subjects issued in paperback editions. Nevertheless, important titles still exist only in hard covers, and one of the principal purposes of the Beacon Press paperback series, *Europe in the Twentieth Century,* is to make such works available.

Great Britain and the War of 1914–1918

Sir Llewellyn Woodward's *Great Britain and the War of 1914–1918* opens with an unusual statement; the author writes: 'This book is a short account — the essential facts and a running commentary — of the part taken by Great Britain in the First World War. I have written it because, with one exception, the war histories which I have read do not answer to the questions I would put to them'. This is in many ways a remarkable assertion. How can it be that a literature already so vast, on which historians — professional and amateur — have expended such effort for well over fifty years, should have produced only a single work that satisfies? Is it possible that so many have labored in a field and that only one work, having to do with the military aspects of the war, should answer a particular historian's needs? For those who go no further in the book the remark may appear immodest; for those who are disposed to go on, it will be found to be eminently fair. This book resembles no other on the subject; its originality derives in part from the self-confidence that permits the author to open his work in the way that he does.

Scholarly study of World War I is filled with anomalies. Many of the best books deal almost entirely with either military *or* political issues. While such a division might have been justified for earlier wars, it is peculiarly inappropriate for the 1914–1918 holocaust, where the fighting front was so inextricably tied to what happened at home. The war provoked deep passion among those who wrote about it, a sentiment that seems scarcely to diminish with the passage of time. After 1945, for example, a whole spate of books appeared that might reasonably be called 'donkey' studies. They elaborated a single theme, already presaged in certain of the political biographies and autobiographies of the interwar period. For these historians, the World War I story was simple: the armies were badly led; the officers were unsuited to their tasks; they ordered the maiming and killing of hundreds of thousands of innocent soldiers in unnecessary military combat. Many of these works, highly emotional in content, were dominated by an unstated pacifist sentiment. They contrasted markedly with the books that dealt with the home front; these, again, were of many kinds. In the 1920's, the Carnegie Endowment for International Peace supported research into how the various belligerents managed to operate their economies in the midst of Armageddon. These works were monographic, of very varied quality, rarely of a kind that would generate debate. Beginning at the same time, a larger number of books began to appear, which provided in varying degrees information about wartime politics. If the Generals were men with feet of clay (with intelligences of not markedly different substance), many of the politicians emerged as Machiavellian, or, worse still, as indecisive bunglers. Neither the military nor the civilian heads of state enjoyed very fair treatment at the hands of many who chose to write about them. Needless to say, there were always numerous apologia (often written by the subjects themselves) to counteract this hostile historical record. Still, the overwhelming number of books were critical, some to the point of insult.

Sir Llewellyn Woodward's work belongs to a very different tradition. His chief purpose is objectivity. There are few heroes to be found in the book and no villains. Yet, there is a remarkable candor about it. When one compares Woodward's description with that available elsewhere, one is impressed by the judiciousness of the remarks made. The author seeks not so much to excite his reader's fancy as to make him aware of what he may not know. Thus, for example, in writing about Haig, there is none of the conventional emphasis on his Presbyterian self-confidence, but there is no concealing his very real inadequacies. Woodward is blunt: 'Haig's career before 1914 was that of an efficient officer enjoying the advantages of wealth, high social position, and the important "connexions" which had always been of considerable help in securing military promotion'. Why, later, was he unsuited to his task? Not, according to Woodward, because he was stubborn or a fool. Rather, because he was a cavalry officer, who surrounded himself with others of the same kind, and the war was not a war suited for officers with such training. Engineers and artillery officers would have done better. Also, Haig's failure to consort with able civilian leaders is thought by Woodward to have been significant. His remoteness from the front, the absence of first-class ability in his entourage — all played a role in limiting his understanding of the options that existed. This does not prevent Woodward from saying that with all his shortcomings he was probably the ablest British commander to be found among the small circle of high officers. There was never a thought of going outside that circle in making an appointment; this would have been deemed improper.

The judiciousness that Woodward shows when dealing with the military is equally evident when he turns to the politicians. David Lloyd George is not a 'mystery', a 'wizard' whose Welsh obfuscations need to be penetrated. Again, there is measure in everything that Woodward says about him. He understands that his method of conducting business did not make him a dictator. His small War Cabinet was not an agency controlled by himself, ready to do his bidding. Woodward is categorical when he writes: '. . . the charge of improvisation which later historians have made against his government is unfair, except indeed as far as the conduct of a war requires continual adaptation to events'. Lloyd George is in no sense Woodward's hero, but he is not disposed to accept the judgments — so frequently adverse — that others made of the Prime Minister. Woodward's views on the motives for Keynes' attacks on all the Allied leaders are well worth pondering.

There is an immense independence reflected in this work. It is not simply the independence of an individual who refuses to repeat the common judgments of a particular individual. More important, perhaps, is the fact that Woodward understands the interrelations between events. There was not a military front, a naval front, a home front, and a diplomatic front. Each impinged on the other. The great requirement of the war was organization. Asquith's failure, Woodward tells us, his 'extrusion' — to use Woodward's wonderful term — was caused by the fact 'that most of the Conservatives, including Bonar Law, wanted to keep Asquith as an insurance against the instability of Lloyd George, and at the same time to make large changes in organisation. The second stage came when the Conservatives found — partly through Asquith's own action — that they could not get these changes unless they accepted Lloyd George as Prime Minister'. The author recognizes that the manner of getting rid of Asquith was not entirely commendable; as he says: 'The change, when it came, was brought about by methods not creditable to the parties concerned, though it is difficult to see how a certain amount of backstairs intrigue could have been avoided'. What is significant for Woodward is not what Beaverbrook and others expended such effort to narrate in the minutest detail — how one Prime Minister was exchanged for another — but how one system of organizing for the war gave way to another. For all his interest in personalities, Woodward never loses sight of the essential; he is never unaware of what is happening to institutions.

This, then, is the unique character of the work. In only one sense is it a narrative of the war. Beyond that, it is a remarkably judicious account of how one of the major belligerents came to change itself to accommodate to the harsh requirements of Armageddon. The work is dispassionate; there is no preaching. It offers an unrivaled example of the kind of interpretation that is possible even on contested historical issues. This is its originality; beyond that, there is a willingness to look not at what an earlier generation thought to be significant about the war, but what, with the perspective of half a century, can now be seen to have been significant.

Introduction

This book is a short account – the essential facts and a running commentary – of the part taken by Great Britain in the First World War. I have written it because, with one exception, the war histories which I have read do not answer the questions I would put to them. The exception is C. R. F. M. Cruttwell's *History of the Great War*, written over thirty years ago, and covering all the battle-fronts. My purpose is both narrower and wider. Narrower in the sense that, although I must obviously view the war as a whole, I have concentrated upon the British part in it; wider in that I have tried to take account not only of the fighting, but of domestic matters such as the political and economic organisation of Great Britain for war, the extension of state control, the problems set by shortages of shipping and food. I have also carried the story beyond the military defeat of Germany and her Allies to the armistice of November 11, 1918, the Peace Conference, and the Treaty of Versailles. In order to explain why neither of the European belligerent groups would agree to bring the war to an end earlier by a 'peace without victory', I have had to say a good deal about British and German war aims, and the discussions with President Wilson.

I have mentioned Cruttwell's book by name because I think it the most profound study of any war in modern times. I do not mean that there are no other good books. The official histories of British naval, military, and air operations are on the whole very good, though they, and especially those dealing with the Western Front, are too often a defence of the strategy of the British High Command. Anyhow these histories are necessarily so very long and detailed – thirty volumes for military operations alone – that the ordinary reader cannot cope with them. The memoirs and other writings of the senior British commanders shew, often painfully, their limitations. Churchill's *The World Crisis* is a brilliant but not an objective book. Other experts on military affairs, notably Sir Basil Liddell Hart, have taught me a great deal. It is curious that there should be no comprehensive history, though there are some excellent monographs, on what has been called, with some exaggeration, the 'home front'. Lloyd George's *War Memoirs* and *The Truth about the Peace Treaties* are untrustworthy and thus fail to do him justice. Lord Beaverbrook's revelations about the struggles for power among the leading politicians are valuable at their own level, in spite of their reduction of the government of England to a series of ignoble intrigues. Lord Hankey's two volumes on *The Supreme Command, 1914-1918*, are of greater permanent importance.

Like most other writers on the Great War, I have found it hard to resist the temptation to include too much. In order to avoid encumbering and slowing down the tempo of my narrative I have made great use of footnotes. It is possible to read my book – I have tried the experiment – without looking at any of these notes, but they gave me, and I hope may give others, an opportunity to notice interesting and not irrelevant details which I should otherwise have had to leave out.

Inevitably, when I had finished writing the book, I felt that it was not, and could not be the book I would like to have written. The history which I would like to have written would have been distilled from the 'case-histories' of many millions of soldiers, records personal and unique, infinite in their variety, but with a basic likeness for the fighting men of every country. Shakespeare in some of his historical plays (John Bates in *Henry V*), Tolstoy in *War and Peace*, Thomas Hardy in *The Dynasts* have come near to such multiple, symbolic representation. I am not foolish enough to imagine myself in this rare company. The only 'case-history' with which I could deal would be my own, but I came out of the war very lightly; my greatest burden for most of the time was not exposure to immediate danger but long frustration and accidie. In retrospect I can even regard my four years of military service as a hateful discipline, but none the less a discipline. However, this hypothesis is of interest only to myself. If I mention now shortly some of my personal reactions of fifty years ago I do so only to make clear what my presuppositions and prejudices were and still remain.

I was twenty-four when the war broke out. Hitherto, without knowing it, I had lived too much in and with my books. After leaving Oxford in 1913, I was fortunate enough to win several awards which, together, allowed me to plan four years of travel and research in Europe. I did not look beyond these four years. I arranged to spend the first of them in Paris. For the second year I decided to go to Germany, and for the third year to Russia. I had no plans for the fourth year. It interests me now to think that I never had any thought of going to the United States. While I was in Paris I was asked to coach the son of a transatlantic family (the mother was English) who spent most of their time in France and Italy. I liked them, and they were very kind to me. They invited me to spend August and part of September with them at Vallombrosa. From Vallombrosa I intended to go to Munich for a term, or perhaps for the academic year 1914–15.

The war thus cut directly across my plans and not merely my plans, but all my interests, hopes, and wishes. It happened (I need not explain why so odd a thing – for me – should have happened) that on the day of the assassination of the Archduke Francis Ferdinand I was staying at a large, cosmopolitan hotel in the Black Forest. My host was an Englishman, partly of German descent, in the diplomatic service. We were having tea on the terrace of the hotel when the head waiter came round telling everyone that the Archduke and his wife had been murdered. I remember that people got up from their tables and talked in little groups. There was one group of Russians. To me the news meant nothing more than another political assassination in the Balkans. My host said at once that there was likely to be a European war and that England would be involved in it. Another of his guests, a very charming and clever Bavarian woman, agreed with him. I was bewildered at all this excitement, and did not like to shew my ignorance by asking too many questions.

About a week later I came back leisurely to England by a cross-country journey, from Freiburg to Mulhouse, and thence by Besançon, Autun, Nevers, and Orleans to Paris. Already there was some activity on the vast empty sidings along the branch line into Alsace from the main Freiburg–Basel railway. I remember the steel rails shining in the afternoon sunlight. When I entered French territory I was surprised to be asked to give some proof of my identity (passports were, of course, not needed for travel in France or Germany in those days). I had sent my luggage, except for one bag, directly from Germany to London, so I had nothing about me to shew who I was. The frontier official asked me where I was going to spend the night; I said truthfully that I had no idea. This satisfied him and I continued on my way.

After packing up a few things in Paris I took the night boat from Dieppe to Newhaven. There may have been some political excitement in Paris; if so, I did not notice it. I went to Oxford for my first weekend in England. This would have been (I think) the weekend of July 18–20. On Sunday night I was asked to dinner in St John's senior common

room (the long vacation had begun and the Fellows were not dining in
hall). By this time I was a little curious that no one in England in my
hearing had even mentioned the event, or any possible consequences of
the event which had so much disturbed the groups of Europeans at tea
in the Black Forest. I did not venture to ask what my hosts in St John's
thought about it (I suspect that only two of the Fellows present thought
about it at all). It would have seemed ridiculous to suggest at dessert on
this quiet Sunday evening that a European war might break out in a
fortnight. I accepted a friend's invitation to stay with him for a few
days in the Cotswolds. Then I would go to Vallombrosa.

When the war came I did not go to Vallombrosa. Like most of my
Oxford contemporaries and school friends I tried to join the army. A
doctor who examined me at a recruiting office hesitated about my heart;
he told me to take a holiday and to present myself again later. At my
father's advice (my father was a civil servant at the Admiralty. He had
no 'top-level' information but always expected an Anglo-German
war, and was sure, when it came, that it would be a long one) I went
back to Oxford in order to apply for a commission through the
OTC.

I began my military training in the familiar Oxford University Park.
I was, however, now disturbed in my mind. I could not feel sure that
Great Britain had been right to come into the war. I disliked my
military instruction. It was very elementary, yet I could not evade the
fact that I was being taught to kill men. I should never be very efficient
at the job, but to kill men would be the intention of my will. Could I
be satisfied that, behind the appeals to patriotism and duty, the background of the war was not just another squabble over markets? Was
not England enmeshed in the same political selfishness as Germany,
less crudely and boastfully, but caught up in the same predatory social
system? Anyhow why should we interfere in what was primarily an
Austro-Russian dispute over areas of political influence in south-
eastern Europe? What claim had society upon me to help in getting it
out of the political impasse into which it had blundered? Above all,
would I be justified in killing Germans? Killing was murder, whatever
the recruiting slogans might say about my King and Country needing
me.

I was more than once on the point of withdrawing my application
for a commission. If I had done so, I would have tried to find some
non-combatant work such as stretcher-bearing or mine-sweeping. No
one could have been less qualified for either employment, and my

motives for considering them were far from noble. I just did not want to be thought afraid of risking my skin in the army. I had, in fact, no cause to be afraid, because at that time (in spite of my father – and Lord Kitchener) I did not believe that the war would go on long enough for me to take part in it as a trained soldier.

This mood lasted for about six weeks. I had been in Germany several times before July, 1914. My longest visit was only for a month, but one did not have to stay for a month in the country to realize the extraordinary collective arrogance of the German people, and, in particular, of the officers and non-commissioned officers of the German army. The university professors and students at Bonn, where I spent my month, were tiresomely full of talk about the coming war in which the British 'colonies' would 'rebel', and the German navy sink the British fleet. I found, casually, that one professor of church history bought and studied the current British navy lists. I could not imagine a Canon of Christ Church giving me details of the armament of the latest German 'Dreadnoughts'.[1] Other foreign students – not only the English – were as astonished as I was over this preoccupation with war and conquest. A later generation is inclined to disbelieve accounts of pre-1914 Germany given by young Englishmen like myself. The well-known earlier comment by the Socialist Bebel – 'the people are still drunk with victory' – is also discounted as coming from a German who was 'up against' most of his countrymen. One could hardly accuse the Chancellor Bethmann-Hollweg of political anti-Germanism. Bethmann-Hollweg in the spring of 1915 admitted to Valentini, the head of the Emperor's private civil Cabinet, that he could do nothing to damp down the widespread demand for annexationist war aims: 'The psychology of our people has been so much poisoned by boasting during the last twenty-five years that it would probably become timid if we were to prohibit it.'

Militarism was a very real and very unpleasing phenomenon. The behaviour of the German armies in Belgium did not surprise me. I would have expected as much from the students and from more than one of the professors in Bonn. The decisive argument with me, however, was not the abruptness with which the ordinary 'decent' German would fall back into barbarism. My argument was simply that of Socrates; if you have enjoyed the benefit of the laws of your country,

[1] It is, however, only fair to say that one of the officers who instructed me in the OUOTC was an Anglican clergyman (and the kindest and least aggressive of men).

you must not refuse obedience to them even when you think they are mistaken and when it is to your personal advantage to evade or disobey them. The fact that I found this argument decisive, and that I did not ask myself what a Christian ought to do shews how deeply the Greek and Latin which I had read at school and the university had entered into my thinking. I found no answer to the argument of Socrates. I thought of it in Flanders when I was first ordered to take action – in fact I took the action on my own initiative in accordance with general instructions – to fire on some German soldiers against whom individually I had no grievance or sense of wrong. I did not regret my decision at any time during the war. Fifty years later, having gone over the argument with myself again and again, I am perhaps less sure that I was right, but, on balance, taking everything into account, I still think that, having accepted the benefit of the laws, and having indeed enjoyed privileges open only to a small minority, I had a duty to do what the state asked of me.

I mention my own case because I think that very many of my friends and contemporaries felt as I did, though they may not have put the matter to themselves in the same words. I have often wondered whether we should have come to the same conclusion if we had known how long-drawn and terrible the war would be, and how many others younger than ourselves would be engulfed in it. I have never been able to answer this question. In this simple form it is indeed unanswerable. There are three different questions: (1) who was responsible for the outbreak of the war? (2) should Great Britain have taken part in it? (3) should the western Powers have made a real attempt to end it in the latter part of 1916 or early in 1917 in terms of a compromise peace?

Anyone who follows closely the course of events leading to the outbreak of the war can hardly avoid concluding that the major responsibility – not the sole responsibility – lay with Germany and Austria-Hungary, and, after these two Powers, more with Russia than with France, and least of all with England. Obviously, if the central Powers could have foreseen their defeat they would not have provoked the war. They expected victory; there is no evidence that they would have drawn back at the last moment even if they had not been caught up in their own mobilisation plans. The German and Austro-Hungarian military leaders had convinced themselves that a European war would come sooner or later; they wanted to use what they thought the best opportunity for it, that is to say, to fight it when Germany was at her greatest military strength in relation to France and Russia. It is not true to say that the war broke out accidentally, and that given more time and greater skill in negotiation it would have been avoided. The Germans, in particular, if they had been willing to do so, could have called off the war before it was too late.

The answer to the second question – the question of British participation in the war – was stated very clearly by Grey and others and needs no repetition. Self-preservation as well as the defence of international agreements compelled us to take part. If we had stood aside, our position as a great Power, whatever the result of the war, would have been disastrous. Anyhow, leaving aside self-interest, I think still that we were morally justified in resisting the Germans. With a German victory in the war Europe would have been darker even than it is today. Grey, who thought that this war (as Chamberlain thought about the second war) might bring about general ruin, would none the less have spoken as he did about the entry of his country if he could actually have foreseen the extent and ultimate reverberation of the calamities which would follow.

Once the war had begun there was no practical way of ending it on terms short of a complete victory for one or other of the belligerent groups. Neither side could accept President Wilson's idea of a compromise peace, a 'peace without victory'. Behind Wilson's idea lay the fallacy that each Power could return to its previous standing as though nothing had happened. Such a return to the *status quo* was not possible; the changes brought about by battle in the European and, one might say, the world balance of power could not be ignored after the first few weeks of fighting. German war aims remained annexationist until the very hour of military defeat. Ludendorff and Hindenburg were talking as late as August, 1918, about the transfer of the Briey–Longwy area of France to Germany and of the precise degree of servitude which it would be necessary to impose upon Belgium. At the end of 1917 the Germans had shewn in their treatment of eastern and south-eastern Europe the kind of terms which they would impose upon the west. From their own point of view the German high command had no option. A compromise peace, which did not allow them to display tangible fruits of victory, would not have seemed to the German people worth the sacrifices of the war, and would have shaken the military-autocratic system of government in Germany. A victorious peace, on the other hand, would give this regime enhanced prestige, and fasten its control upon the German people as well as upon the rest of Europe. Wilson himself recognised at last that there was no hope of general security as long as Germany was controlled by a military oligarchy. As for Germany's chief ally, there could be for the Habsburgs only complete victory or complete defeat. Either the German-Magyar domination of the Slav nationalities must be re-established or the empire would collapse.

On the side of the western Powers – the German bid for a rapid victory having failed – a 'compromise' peace would have given Germany the opportunity to recover from her military mistakes, and, at a suitable moment of her own choosing, to recommence the war. There would be no real peace in Europe, no end to the piling up of armaments, while the character of the German government remained unchanged, and the country was as strongly placed as ever for a resumption of aggressive war.

Thus, however much one detested the slaughter and suffering, there was nothing for it but to go on, and to go on until victory. One might not share the popular belief in a much better world after the war, but at least the world would not be under the stifling domination of German force.

If I did not think it possible to end the war by any means short of inflicting heavy defeat on the enemy, I never lost confidence that, even with the generals we had to accept because we had no better ones, we should not lose the war. We were, however, trying to win it in the crudest way at least as far as our land forces were concerned. Looking back at my own angry reflexions on our commanders, I can see that I was a considerable prig, intellectually intolerant, and affected by a half-realised class jealousy; I disliked the social code of many regular officers (not all – my own colonel in France was an admirable exception), their assumptions of superiority, their standards of value, but the reasons for my dismay, on finding myself inside the army, went beyond a criticism of military arrogance – after all, I had seen a much more unpleasing state of things in Germany. What alarmed me was the lowness of professional competence among the higher ranks. From Kitchener downwards these commanders just did not know how to set about their task of winning the war. No one doubted their personal courage, their discipline, their coolness in difficult moments, their power of endurance. Their trouble was lack of imagination and 'free intelligence'. After the first few months of the war the problem before them, in its simplest form, had been to find a means of protecting their men against machine gun and rifle fire while they were crossing the area between their own and the enemy trenches. The experience of recent warfare, in Manchuria and the Balkans, ought to have made the high command aware earlier of this problem and of the impossibility of solving it without some new form of mechanical aid. The War Office, to use a loose but convenient designation of the whole senior directing body, had at its disposal in Great Britain some of the best engineering talent in the world. The senior officers never took the initiative in consulting this talent or in providing the engineers with the means for experiment on a large scale in order to solve this new military problem. If the cavalrymen who cluttered up the high places in the military command had been as eager and co-operative in experiment as the pilots and designers of aeroplanes, the waste of life in futile attacks on the Western Front might have been avoided, just as, conversely, if the small number of enthusiasts responsible for the development of military aircraft had been as slow, unimaginative, and unhelpful as the General Staff shewed themselves towards the development of the tanks, we should have been continuously outmatched in the air.

Kitchener said of the military position after the introduction of trench warfare, 'this is not war', yet it was the war he was fighting, and his first duty ought to have been to look for a way of meeting the new conditions. Owing to the lack of an intelligent professional approach, therefore, the soldiers fell back after the summer of 1916, upon the doctrine of 'attrition', wearing the enemy down by attacks, general or local, which in fact weakened the attackers as much as the defenders. This plan, if one can call it a plan, did result in victory, but the victorious generals nearly destroyed European civilisation by the methods which they employed to save it. Fortunately for the Allies the enemy generals were equally obtuse. I can see now that the routine-mindedness of military men had deeper causes than I thought at the time and that it was not fair to put the whole blame upon the army commanders, individually or collectively, for their mental illiteracy. English society had taken no trouble to ensure that its armed defence would be directed by men as able as those who managed its civil affairs. The intellectual requirements for entrance into the army were far below those laid down for entrance into the higher branches of the civil service. One of my Oxford colleagues said to me in 1919, when I was complaining of the low mental level of our military leadership, that the army was 'run by pass men'. The English people had been willing to allow this dangerous state of things. They could not complain of the consequences when they had left the fate of a generation in the hands of a custom-bound clique which would never have been permitted to take over the management of any other important department of state or of a great business. Even so, the last word remained, in war as in peace, with civilian Ministers. Asquith described Kitchener as 'the only soldier with brains since Wolseley', yet he did nothing to encourage Kitchener to apply new ideas to a new situation. Churchill and Lloyd George indeed realised the facts: Churchill was discredited, somewhat unfairly, by the failure at Gallipoli; Lloyd George had neither the moral strength nor the mastery of detail which would have enabled him to dominate the military chiefs. He realised their helplessness before the problem set to them; he could not get rid of them, since he had no better candidates to put in their places, and, after the missed opportunities of 1915, he did not suggest a feasible alternative to their concentration upon a disastrous strategy.

I remembered gloomily that this kind of thing had happened before, not of course exactly, but after the manner in which historical situations recur. The western Roman Empire had disintegrated because the cultivated classes in society left the profession of arms and the duties of defence to hired barbarians, and gave them little help from mechanical devices. Barbarians fought barbarians with similar weapons and similar tactics, and the western Empire came to a squalid end. We took our barbarians from within our own society, but the result could well be the same.

From the autumn of 1916 I was in a state of angry depression. I was a totally insignificant part of a vast, ill-directed machine. As the months passed my feelings of inner insubordination became more intense, but there was nothing I could do about them. The odds were that, before the war ended, I should be killed uselessly, as thousands of better people than myself had already been killed. This was not what I had meant by my Socratic ideas of obedience to the laws because I had benefited from them. At least about one thing I had no illusion. The war had to be won, and as it would have to be won by those who were directing it or by other professionals of the same plodding type, the end would be one of mutual exhaustion in which the moral standards of the victors as well as the defeated would be dangerously lowered. Our own much-praised propaganda organisation seemed to be doing a good deal to lower these standards. In the autumn of 1916 I was sent to Salonika. One of my 'bottle-washing' jobs there was to hand out material from London to the local Greek newspapers. I remember a disgusting sentence, transmitted by wireless from the propaganda office: 'Our men are enjoying killing Germans in the spring sunshine.'

The instruments which we were using, the methods by which we were trying to uphold the freedom and high culture of Europe were all the time dragging us down. When would this *dégringolade* end? What were the prospects for western civilisation? There was much talk at this time of 'a war to end war', about the spirit of comradeship in the trenches, the debt owed to the fallen. I did not regard such talk as insincere, but I could not imagine how a change for the better, a great regeneration could come out of this mass slaughter. We should have avoided a greater calamity; that would be all. I did not even expect so grim a conflict for power to be the last of its kind. War was not the way to end war. The Allies would win; after their victory there would be much fiercer hatred between nations, not merely the superficial xenophobia of every large group for every other large group, or the *nouveau riche* type of nationalist arrogance which had taken hold of the Germans, but a hatred based in the Allied countries on the havoc Germany had caused and the savagery with which she had fought the war, and based in Germany on the bitter consequences of defeat, thwarted ambition, and loss of status. The Great Powers had managed their affairs unwisely before 1914; were they likely to shew more wisdom after the strain of a war in which their best citizens had been killed and their accumulated resources gone to waste? There would be far less mutual trust, less, not more co-operation, and less chance of a lasting peace because the Germans would never acknowledge what they had done and never accept the loss of their dominant position in Europe.

Alas I could find little reason to hope for better relations between Englishmen and Englishmen. The most unselfish would have given their lives. Those who had known and loved them would never forget them. For a time there would be a general sense of sorrow, but it could not be lasting. It meant little to say that the dead would be held in everlasting remembrance. How could they be remembered by those to whom they would be only names on countless memorial stones? Few people in 1914 had thought about the young soldiers killed in the Crimean war. Even the South African war memorials had no personal significance to the generation twenty years younger than myself. If I lived to be an old man, I should find that only the contemporaries of my youth were really moved by the thought of the losses in the battle of the Somme. As for the 'comradeship of the trenches' which was positive and remarkable during the war, I did not see how such a relationship could be preserved in the scramble and competition of the modern industrial system to which the soldiers would return.

During these dismal years, if I had been consistent with my own past, I should have turned for consolation to religion and poetry. Before 1914 I had thought of taking Orders; I had observed even then that I was continually postponing the date of doing so, and I think it certain that, war or no war, I should not have felt able to commit myself to the beliefs which, however lightly they seemed to fall upon some clergy-men, an ordained minister of the Church of England bound himself publicly to hold and to teach. Nevertheless in 1914 I was a practising Anglican; four years later I still had not broken altogether with the practice of religion, but I had drifted away from it. The sacraments had lost meaning for me; the creeds had become antique formulae. I did not suppose that the problem of reconciling the goodness of God with the existence of evil, pain, and unmerited suffering had been set for the first time by the war, or that defensive war – the *bellum justum* of the lawyers – was necessarily incompatible with Christian teaching. I agreed with William Temple that, although Great Britain was morally bound to declare war on Germany in 1914 and to fight on until victory, the war itself shewed 'the un-Christian principles which had dominated the life of western Christendom, and of which the Church and the Nations had need to repent'. I could subscribe also to Temple's other comment that, for the first time since the Emperor Constantine, war was regarded by large numbers of Christian Europeans as marking the collapse of Christianity, and that responsibility for the outbreak of a particular war was being assessed in terms of moral guilt. This change of attitude was largely the result of the slow permeation of western thought by Christian ideas. On the other hand it was not difficult to put aside the crude conclusions of a number of clergy that the suffering brought by the war was a divine judgment on national sins, general or particular. (Drunkenness, sabbath-breaking, even the disestablishment of the Welsh church were put forward as sins calling for Divine chastisement upon the whole nation.) Temple rightly described this view as 'sheer superstition'. I could not, however, accept his own interpretation of the value of suffering as a form of purgation. Now that I am old, I should not reject this idea; indeed I find consolation in it. I would not, however, apply it in the case of suffering inflicted haphazard upon innocent and guilty by other human beings. I have mentioned the first time I directed the firing of guns with the purpose of killing Germans. I could not regard myself as having acted in order to give these Germans a chance of purgation through suffering.

It might be true, as Scott Holland wrote, that 'if only the world had been Christian, it would not be at war', but this fact did not reconcile the coexistence of an omnipotent and merciful Providence with the misery of the innocent. It was no argument to say that the frightful tale of injustice would be set right in another state of being outside time. Why permit the evil things to happen at all? No doctrine of free will, no theory of Christian redemption provided a solution.

I was only one among many thousands who put these questions, in one form or another, without finding an answer. With few exceptions the clergy of the Established Church did not help us to find an answer. The Church of England, as would-be reformers put it, was 'not organised for a crisis'. Since the Tractarians the Anglican clergy had imitated the example of other callings in a movement to raise their own professional standards and status. They had done so with unfortunate consequences. They had indeed professionalised themselves, but in so doing they had lost touch with an increasing number of the laity. They had reintroduced sacerdotal procedures and practices which had ceased to be part of the tradition of the English people. They had dressed them-selves up in forgotten uniforms, copes, mitres, chasubles, and what not without realising how little meaning these marks of status had for the ordinary church-goer. Tennyson had summed up the movement long ago, before the revival of ritual and ceremonial had reached its present pitch, when he wrote (in *Maud*) about hearing 'the snowy-banded, dilettante, delicate-handed priest intone'. What did it matter how many candles were lit on an altar, whether this altar were of wood or stone, if the foundation and fabric of Christian doctrine were crumbling under the pressure of modern linguistic, historical, and anthropological research? What had these hieratic figures, cocooned in their finely-stitched embroideries, to do with good and evil as the common man saw good and evil in a real world?

If I broke or drifted away from the Church of England, I could not join any other religious body. The Roman Catholic Church, since the Council of Trent, and earlier, had worked out dogmatic and devotional fantasies which seemed to me absurd. The Protestant non-conformists were a historical survival. The only one of these bodies likely to appeal to me was the Society of Friends, but I never could make out what they did or did not believe. In any case, in the immediate context of the war, their attitude towards military service was irritatingly confused, and I was too much of a prig myself not to be aware very quickly of any element of priggishness in others.

During this time I read, as far as I could get hold of it, the literature

of imagination written during the war. Before 1914 the poetry which
moved me most had been of a traditional kind. I did not dislike the
mildly contemplative verse which Edward Marsh published in his anth-
ologies of 'Georgian' writers. Most of the writers had been brought up,
as I was, in the long-established discipline of Greek and Latin. Most
of them lived, as I had lived, in the less industrialised half of England,
where the countryside had only begun to change from the Victorian
pattern; the garden of Somersby Rectory, described in *In Memoriam*,
the 'full-foliaged elms' and 'large leaves of the sycamore', were
familiar to me. Hardy, Yeats – the Yeats of 1900 and the dedication
to 'The Shadowy Waters' – Francis Thompson, Bridges, and Masefield
were the ruling contemporary poets. Walter de la Mare, Rupert
Brooke, and half a dozen others seemed likely to dominate the next
twenty years without any startling change. I had come across – no one
who read the literary journals could fail to do so – certain new and
noisy figures; Ezra Pound, the Vorticists, *et hoc genus omne*. When I was
living in Paris I learned a great deal about Marinetti and his friends. I
had agreed with the judgment of the new weekly paper, the *New Statesman*, about the so-called Vorticist movement. A reviewer in this paper
described Pound as unconvincing: 'when he is comprehensible, he is
usually silly; when he is incomprehensible, he would not, I suppose be
found less silly by anyone who had the key to his cypher'.[1] As for
Marinetti, the *New Statesman* in July, 1914, seemed to me to put the
matter simply: 'Signor Marinetti's glorification of war, violence, and
cruelty is like Kipling at fourteen writing in a school magazine, if you
could imagine Kipling emancipated from religion and belief in British
law and order . . . The whole thing is a display of penny fireworks . . .
Art is not a diffusion of life into wavy lines and dots and dashes but the
opposite.' Again, in this ill-fated July of 1914, I had thought a reviewer
in the *New Statesman* right in saying that Pound's Provençal poems
reminded him of an American tourist sending home picture postcards
of the places he had seen on his travels.

I could document my own perplexities and anger from the changes
in the poetry of the war years between 1914 and the latter part of 1916.
There were some good poems written in the early part of the war.
They were not, or most of them were not, written out of personal experience of the fighting. The theme of Thomas Hardy's 'In Time of

---

[1] Rupert Brooke, in the *Cambridge Review*, had reviewed Pound more favourably: 'when he has passed through stammering to speech and when he has more
clearly recognised the nature of poetry, he may be a great poet'.

the Breaking of Nations' is the order and continuity of life, not the disorder and catastrophe of battle; the poem was written in 1915, but Hardy, in his august manner, was remembering something he had seen in Cornwall over forty years earlier during the Franco-Prussian war, when he had heard the news of the battle of Gravelotte. A. E. Housman's 'Epitaph on an Army of Mercenaries' had as its background the war of movement, the line of battle of the old regular army, not the slaughter in the trenches. Rupert Brooke's war poems belong to the period before the Gallipoli landings; Brooke died while war was still an adventure to him and his friends. Wilfred Grenfell was killed in action in 1915; his strangely noble poem 'Into Battle' also belongs to the time before mass killing had become a dreadful routine. The change came after the battle of Loos, the failure at Gallipoli, and, above all, after the holocaust on the Somme.

The horrors of the 'war of attrition', repeated again and again by the commanders to whom all the Great Powers had handed over the destiny of youth, stunned and deafened the imagination. The personal anguish was beyond description. Writers as different as Yeats and Kipling have remarked that such emotional distress stifled the writing of poetry and turned men's minds away from it. In Kipling's words:[1]

> What man hears aught except the groaning guns?
>   What man heeds ought save what each instant brings?
> When each man's life all imaged life outruns
>   What man shall pleasure in imaginings?
> So it has fallen, as it was bound to fall.
> We are not, nor we were not heard at all.

The background of 1914 and the first nine months of 1915 were so very different from that of the later war years that there is no unity between the two periods. Furthermore there was now a dividing line between contemporaries; those who had fought in the war and those who had not done so. The poems of those who had seen war for themselves became short, violent protests against the monstrous situation into which the soldiers of all the belligerent nations had been thrust. Wilfred Owen, Siegfried Sassoon, and Robert Graves could not use the poetic conventions of the so-called 'Georgians' to describe the appalling

[1] I have seen these words quoted recently, in regard to the failure of the poetic imagination to compass the dreadful experience of modern war. I cannot remember who quoted them, and in what context; they seem to me to apply to both wars.

facts of battle. One can notice the transition in Sassoon's writing from

> Ring your sweet bells; but let them be farewells
> To the green-vista'd gladness of the past
> That changed us into soldiers

to

> O German mother dreaming by the fire,
> While you are knitting socks to send your son
> His face is trodden deeper in the mud.

Wilfred Owen's 'Futility' is perhaps even closer to the Georgian language, and is yet an age away in substance.

> ... Was it for this the clay grew tall?
> O what made fatuous sunbeams toil
> To break earth's sleep at all?

So to me, in the last years of the war, the futility, inevitable, outrageous in its necessity, overshadowed everything. I use the words 'inevitable' and 'necessary' because I still thought that a German victory would fasten on Europe chains from which there would be no hope of release except after even greater misery. If I did not expect a much better world to come out of it, at least, though at far too heavy a cost, our victory would have removed the threat of a mindless European tyranny.

Then, almost as an anti-climax, the war ended. After being let out of hospital and pronounced fit for 'light work', I assisted a temporary section of the Foreign Office in preparing for publication a number of handbooks for the use of the British Delegation to the Paris Confer-ence. These books were in general very good. I wrote only one of them. I have reason to think that Balfour read the handbooks – I know that he read my small contribution. I doubt whether Lloyd George even looked at the title-pages. I respected my colleagues in this work. I liked their hopefulness, though, as the weeks and months passed, we began to realise the difference between putting forward the most admirable proposals and getting agreement on them. I found it an extraordinary thing to be listening again to the talk of people of first-class ability; I still felt a strange and immeasurable difference between the majority who had not seen war at first hand and those who, like Wilfred Owen, had watched the light fall at dawn on the body of a dead soldier.

As I have said, I never expected a satisfactory peace settlement. Europe had been torn apart with such savagery that reconciliation must be far distant, I did not think the treaty of Versailles too severe. Germany had survived the war as a united Reich. I had assumed, rightly, as it turned out, that the Germans would forget the terms which they had intended to fasten on their enemies, and that they would cry out against everything likely to lessen their own chances of regaining the military status which they had lost by defeat. I could see no advantages – only great risks – in a generosity which from the British point of view would have been at others' expense, and which would have met with no response from Germany. I never shared the Russian Bolshevist dream of a world revolution in the supposed interest of the proletariat. Such a revolution was most improbable, but, if it had spread over Europe, the result might have been chaos; there was a limit to the capacity of western society to hold together. The Bolshevist revolution was based upon implacable hatred; the only revolution which would have had a chance of success (and, remembering the history of the Crucifixion, one could not put this chance very high) must have been based upon compassion and forgiveness, notions which Marx and Lenin in their intellectual pride never envisaged.

Throughout this time I was tired and unwell. I had been in military hospitals for nearly eight months in 1918, and was very ill again for a short time during the influenza epidemic. After July, 1918, when I came back to England in a hospital ship from Malta, I was not personally unhappy – the very reverse, in fact, because I was with my wife whom I had married while in England on short leave in 1917. We had parted at the gate of Southampton Docks on a September evening uncertain whether we should ever meet again. When she came to me after my disembarkation at Avonmouth, I could hardly believe my immense good fortune. We were together. I was sure that I should slowly get well again. I expected the war to end before the winter. I could think of plans for the future. I was still young and could look forward to a reasonably good job, though I did not know what this job would be.

My good fortune continued when, after a pleasant but extremely fatiguing three months in the summer of 1919 as a schoolmaster, I was elected to a fellowship at All Souls. This fellowship left me to choose my profession. I think that, if I had been offered some literary or publishing work, I should have taken it, but I did not know any literary men in London or elsewhere, or how to set about trying to establish myself as a writer. I also doubted whether I could earn a living from the kind of books which I hoped to write. A College tutorship would give me a quiet sufficiency, and time outside my teaching. So I stayed on in Oxford. I have never regretted my choice. I enjoyed the tutorial hours with my pupils. I wrote a good deal, and always in the way I wanted to write and on the subjects I wanted to write about. Within a year or so I realised how wise I had been not to have given up my independence for a more competitive existence, and especially so because I began to find myself out of sympathy with nearly all post-war writing. My failure to see more than newfangledness where others acclaimed originality at first bewildered me, until I discovered that the study of history, though in some respects a danger to the imagination, at least freed one from the tyranny of contemporary fashion. I could remember the French saying about a majority which was built up in time – *qui se compte par générations.* I should say now that, fundamentally, the reason for my distaste for contemporary moods and styles was that, although I had ceased to be a believing Christian (I still attended my college chapel as an act of ancestral piety) I went on reasoning in Christian terms and my judgments were according to Christian standards of value. At all events, I was sure that the only hope for the future of the world lay in accepting the Christian virtues of compassion and humility. I kept in mind two sentences of a non-Christian writer, Anatole France: *il faut mépriser les hommes avec allégresse,* and *les grands écrivains n'ont pas l'âme basse.* I did not find many signs of gentleness or nobility in English post-war writing. The favourable reception given to Lytton Strachey's *Eminent Victorians* shocked me because Strachey distorted and even suppressed facts in his attempt to 'debunk' heroic action. Keynes' reckless condemnation of Wilson, Lloyd George, and Clemenceau seemed equally overdrawn for literary effect. Aldous Huxley made living people into puppets, and seemed to enjoy his own cruelty to them. James Joyce's almost incredible detachment from personal emotion – *Ulysses* seemed to me to shew neither pity nor any sense of distress – left him, for all his virtuosity, without more healing power for his contemporaries than one would expect from a diagnosis of humanity undertaken by a scientist on a distant planet. D. H. Lawrence was, for me, the most remarkable of the younger writers who did not go to the war. He was physically as well as mentally unfit for military service, and, as his letters shew, unable to give a coherent explanation why the war affected him as it did. Sometimes he treated it merely as an interference with his freedom of action and choice. He wrote in December, 1914, that he was 'glad of this war' . . . 'it kicks the pasteboard bottom in of the usual "good" popular novel'. At the end of January, 1915, he felt 'hopeful now about the war'. We should 'all rise again from this grave – though the killed soldiers will have to wait until the last trump'. Lawrence looked forward to a new community 'wherein the struggle shall not be for money or for power', though he did not suggest reasons why a most deadly contest for power should have this happy conclusion. Then the mass slaughter, and his own private anxieties – financial troubles aggravated by the suppression of his novel *The Rainbow* – played on his nerves and made him think that he would find 'freedom' in America. As the months passed, this nervous anger against a hostile world became almost hysterical; he talked about a society based on honesty and love, and yet railed against the folly and mediocrity of the nations who would compose it. Finally, exasperated, depressed, and ill, he lost hope in everyone and everything. In November, 1918, he began to 'despair altogether about human relationships . . . one may just as well turn into a sort of lone wolf and have done with it'. Under the nagging pressure of his own poverty the ideal of a new community disappeared. He cadged for money, looked for a legacy to his wife which would enable him 'to *get out*, out of England, – really, out of Europe . . . I feel caged, somehow, and I *cannot* find out how to earn enough to keep us, and it maddens me.' In November, 1919, Lawrence managed to go, not 'out of Europe' but to Italy. His health improved; he was rather less harassed for money, yet of the hopes of a new society regenerated by the experience of war, nothing remained. For me, and others who had admired his insight, there was in his later work no coherent philosophy, and, alas, less artistic power.

This lack of coherence in the work of my contemporaries alarmed and depressed me almost as much as the lack of compassion. I could recognise little in the new experiments, especially in painting and sculpture, which did not signify a deep and general disorder concealed under much pretentious talk. I remember some sentences written in the *New Statesman* by J. C. Squire in January, 1920 – I have a copy of them now – which expressed very clearly my own dismay:

> Posterity may detect (in the changed mode of imaginative response) something more important than we can clearly see. It is not for nothing that, to an extent not foreseen in the early days of Marinetti, a section of artists, in all countries from France to Nicaragua, are running amok, inuring us to every kind of lunacy and incomprehensibility, and threatening an atmosphere which may powerfully affect those who grow up into it. However foolish

we may think it, the disease is too general to be ignored, and it has subcutaneous connexions with the general state of the European soul and mind. Underlying literature, as all other human activities, is philosophy, systematised or vaguely assumed, and it may be that we are here and now in the middle of a critical battlefield, of a conflict between beliefs and working assumptions which to some of us mean security, vigour, and health, and beliefs or disbeliefs, passions and manias which might, were they to spread, mean the death of ordered civilisation and of literature with it.

At this time the forces of anarchy, or so I thought them, in western civilisation were strengthened at least temporarily by the hypotheses reached in the new science of psychology and the practical study of psychoanalysis. These hypotheses, or firm conclusions as they were popularly taken to be, seemed to deny the humanist assumption of man as a rational creature, capable, in a favourable environment, of almost endless improvement, self-improvement as well as mastery of his surroundings. The exploration of the depths of personality began largely with the observation of abnormal cases, but Freud and his fellow-workers found to their surprise that explanations which fitted the behaviour of disordered minds and personalities applied also to the behaviour of so-called normal people. The conscious attitudes and values of human adults appeared to be determined to a large extent by experiences which dated back to early childhood and could be analysed in terms of suppressed infantile sexuality.

These views had reached England before 1914. They had been received at first with bewilderment. An English translation of Freud's *The Interpretation of Dreams* was published in 1913. The publishers stated that the sale of the book was 'limited to members of the medical, scholastic, legal and clerical professions'. One reviewer, after describing Freud's views very fairly, called the book 'a remarkable collection of data, however rickety the theory based on them seems to be'. Other critics were harsher; a French professor of psychology, after hearing Freud lecture in Paris, described the lecture as 'une mauvaise plaisanterie'.

Once these theories had come into wide circulation, they were bound to have a disintegrating effect. They were a fountain of compassion for those who used them in their art of healing. At the same time they might well appear, especially to readers untrained in the critical examination of concepts, to destroy the moral and intellectual bases of western civilisation. They offered, at least on a superficial reading,

neither hope nor any ground for stability to a society almost strained
to breaking-point by the external havoc and emotional devastation of
the war. They could be used to justify, if such a term applied, the
wilder experiments already being made in art and letters.

Such a situation in which traditional values were overturned was not
new in western society. I remembered once again the end of the western Roman Empire. In the fifth century a Roman poet, sailing past the
island of Capraria after it had been given over to a monastery, wrote
of the place 'Squalet lucifugis insula plena viris',[1] but he did not mean
by this invasion of what seemed to him a degrading superstition that
the citadel of human personality had been undermined and brought
to ruin.[2] In any case a new stability was regained, after a time of sordid
confusion, largely by the efforts, in modern jargon, of a dedicated
élite within the Christian church. There was now no likelihood of such
a Christian revival. Outside the church there was not merely no intellectual or moral élite, no single, dominant body with the artistic
skill and imaginative strength to rebuild the ruins into which the ideas
of human progress and of the nobility of human beings had fallen.
The writers of imagination who had fought in the war and survived
had to meet this crisis; the hackneyed term is unsuitable to describe the
general desiccation of the streams of poetry. They had to meet it as
individuals because their older contemporaries were of little help and
their juniors, who had not shared in the experience of the war, were
inclined to retire into private and often savagely ironic commentaries
of their own. H. G. Wells continued to write a great deal; already in
an essay of 1911 he had argued for the use of the novel as a general
medium of discussion in an age of vanishing certainty, but his own
work took on more and more the character of bare statements of
social and political facts; his analysis was too rapid, and often too
superficial (as in his *Outline of History*) to give satisfactory answers.
Bernard Shaw, at the height of his reputation, might have used the

---

[1] 'The island is squalid with men who run away from the light.'

[2] Francis Thompson, whose poetry, apart from *The Hound of Heaven*, fell into
eclipse between 1914 and 1919, had come near to expressing the new ideas in
An Anthem of Earth

> Thou dost this body, this enhavocked realm,
> Subject to ancient and ancestral shadows;
> Descended passions sway it; it is distraught
> With ghostly usurpation, dinned and fretted
> With the still-tyrannous dead; a haunted tenement,
> Peopled from barrows and outworn ossuaries.

theatre as the great Athenian tragic poets and Aristophanes had used it over two thousand years earlier, but Shaw was not Aristophanes, and the English stage was not the Greek theatre. Shaw himself, in his preface to *Heartbreak House*, written during the war, pointed out that economic and social conditions in war-time made the playing of serious drama almost impossible. The theatres were filled with audiences who wanted nothing but light entertainment.

I am writing of things which happened nearly fifty years ago, though, as so often with the old, they are very clear to me, clearer than many events of the late 1940s. I can remember how odd it seemed to me that, suddenly, I neither understood nor sympathised with the new fashions in imaginative writing. I continued to think of the barbarians infiltrating into and finally overthrowing the high civilisation of the western Roman Empire. When I read the bits and pieces of recondite learning, the quotations and echoes from earlier poets in *The Waste Land* – Desmond MacCarthy likened them to collector's pieces carefully arranged in the window of an expensive shop – I was reminded of a cameo of Augustus in the treasury of Aachen cathedral, preserved for its rich associations and framed in a barbarian setting. When I looked at the latest modes in painting I thought of the curious forecast made by the Abbé Lamennais over a century ago about an atheist society falling into ruin in spite of its immense material achievements: 'Reason will decay before men's eyes. The simplest truths will appear strange and remarkable, and will scarcely be endured.'

I am not so absurd as to claim that my judgment in these matters was right. Indeed I know that most people with a better claim to judge works of imagination think me altogether wrong. I am merely recording that the experience of the first war left me with a conflict of views about the nature of things which I have not been able to decide because the evidence for each of the two views has seemed, paradoxically, to be valid in its own field and yet finally incomplete. On the one hand I have observed the bleak indifference of time and chance, the negation of values in a universe without justice or compassion or hope or the possibility of lasting good. The only judgment to be passed on such a spectacle is in Housman's words:

> For men at whiles are sober,
>   And think by fits and starts,
> And if they think, they fasten
>   Their hands upon their hearts.

On the other hand there has remained with me an inexplicable (that is to say, I find no way of explaining it) sense of the unity and goodness of life. This deep confidence has not been a fugitive mood, a piece of wishful thinking or defence mechanism, a death wish or the like. It has had nothing to do with my physical health. It is not an inference from my own observation or that of others on the processes of living. The visible, countable evidence, as I have said, is mainly the other way.

It may be said 'What has all this personal record to do with writing a history of the war of 1914–18? Why trouble others with my perplexities?' Again I may be mistaken, but I think it essential that anyone attempting to write the kind of history, or, as I have called it, running commentary, which cannot be compiled equally well by computing machines ought to set out his philosophy. I think this to be especially necessary for a historian of war. No one has put the case more directly, in the case of war, than John Ruskin, though I could quote a curiously similar statement by Bismarck during the Franco-Prussian war. In 1865 Ruskin gave a lecture on 'War' to the cadets of the Royal Military Academy, Woolwich. He published the lecture, with an introduction, in his book *The Crown of Wild Olive*. In this introduction he wrote of the

> difficulty of knowing whether to address one's audience as believing, or not believing, in any other world than this. . . . And the more I thought over what I had got to say, the less I found I could say it, without reference to this intangible or intractable question. It made all the difference in asserting any principle of war, whether one assumed that a discharge of artillery would merely knead down a certain quantity of once living clay into a level line, as in a brickfield; or whether, out of every separately Christian-named portion of the ruinous heap, there went out, into the smoke and deadfallen air of battle, some astonished condition of soul,[1] unwillingly released.

In this year 1967 I would put the question in a less simple form, but it would be the same question.

[1] Ruskin's words 'some *astonished* condition of soul' have a parallel in the prayer of a French nun of the later seventeenth century; 'Et, à l'heure de ma mort, soyez le refuge de mon âme *étonnée*.'

The outbreak of war: the BEF: deadlock on the Western Front and disquiet at home

CHAPTER I

The immediate origins of the war

The Great War of 1914–18 arose out of a political situation in which the Powers of Europe were divided into two groups, roughly equal in military strength. Germany and Austria-Hungary were in one group, with Italy as a somewhat doubtful ally; France, Russia, and Great Britain were in the other group. France and Russia, like Germany and Austria-Hungary, were linked by a treaty of alliance; Great Britain, though aligned with France and Russia, was not bound by any military convention with them, and retained full freedom of decision in the event of a war. Military conversations, however, had taken place between the British and French to arrange common action if the two Powers were together involved in war with Germany. In 1912 the French moved most of their fleet from the Channel and the North Sea to the Mediterranean; the move implied collaboration with Great Britain at sea, but again an exchange of letters with the British Government disclaimed any mutual commitment. Naval conversations were also held with Russia; for geographical reasons these conversations were less important than those with France. Nevertheless, as time passed, and the Germans tried to break the Anglo-French and Anglo-Russian *ententes*, a feeling grew up, especially in France, that Great Britain was committed, morally as well as by self-interest, to come to the assistance of France if she were attacked by Germany.

The aim of Grey's foreign policy had been to lessen the tension between the two Continental military alliances. These efforts seemed to have succeeded in the crisis brought about by war in the Balkans in 1912–13. Servia, Greece and Bulgaria had combined to get rid of what remained of Turkish sovereignty in Europe. They defeated Turkey, but quarrelled over the spoils of victory. Servia[1] gained in territory, and would have gained more if Austria-Hungary had not refused to allow

---

[1] Until the outbreak of war in 1914 the Cyrillic characters in the name 'Servia' were translated in this manner in Great Britain. After the outbreak of war the transliteration 'Serbia' came into general use in England.

her to establish herself on the Adriatic coast. Austria-Hungary objected
to the aggrandisement of Servia because this southern Slav state
favoured the predominance of Russian influence in the Balkans; an
enlarged Servia would therefore block the way to Austro-Hungarian
and German control of the Balkan peninsula and the routes through
it to the Near and Middle East. For Austria-Hungary Servian expansion would have even more serious domestic consequences.
Austria-Hungary had already assumed full sovereignty over the
former Turkish provinces of Bosnia and Herzegovina, most of whose
inhabitants were Slav. Servian nationalist ambitions envisaged a greater
Servian kingdom including Bosnia-Herzegovina and possibly other
Slav areas under Austro-Hungarian rule. Such a kingdom would have
meant the disruption of the multi-national Habsburg Empire whose
collapse seemed anyhow probable after the death of the Emperor
Francis Joseph.[1]

If Austria-Hungary could not allow the Servian threat to her
political cohesion, Germany could not allow the break-up of Austria-
Hungary. In the years before 1914 Germany had made the blunder, and
worse, of arousing the fears of the three Powers, France, Russia, and
Great Britain by an aggressive policy. France had never been reconciled to the loss of Alsace-Lorraine in 1871; Russia was alienated by the
eastward expansion of German influence through the Balkans and
along the line of the German-controlled Baghdad railway – an expansion which cut across the age-long efforts of Russia to reach
Constantinople and these same Middle Eastern regions. Great Britain
had been disquieted by German competition in shipbuilding openly
directed against the naval predominance which was vital to an island
state without a large army and dependent for her existence upon seaborne trade.

Since Austria-Hungary could not permit further expansion by
Servia, and since Russia could not permit Servia to be weakened, since
Germany had to uphold the existence of Austria-Hungary as a Great
Power, and since France was pledged to support Russia against Germany and Austria-Hungary, and Great Britain could not allow the
defeat of France and Russia without grave danger to herself, the peace
of Europe depended upon the degree of restraint shewn by the Servian
nationalists and by the political and military leaders of Austria-Hungary. In the latter part of the Balkan war Austria-Hungary would have
attacked Servia if Germany had promised support. Until the summer

[1] Francis Joseph was 84 in 1914.

of 1914 Germany continued on the whole to restrain rather than encourage her ally.

A change in German policy then brought about the calamity of general war. What was the reason for this change? It has been alleged that, apart from the need to assist her only sure ally in Europe, Germany had planned war for the autumn of 1914 as a means of establishing world hegemony, and that she used the Austro-Servian crisis as a convenient pretext for her attack. There was an important body of opinion in the Reich utterly confident of German military superiority and hoping to impose a German pattern upon the rest of Europe. The Emperor William II, unstable, boastful, and yet fundamentally unsure of himself, seemed at times to share these pan-German ambitions while publicly disclaiming them. They found support among the armed forces and in many financial and business circles. The mood of the German people was arrogant, sharp, and given to applaud methods of bullying and blackmail. There is, however, less reason to suppose a deliberate plan to wage aggressive war for political ends (as the elder Moltke had described the Prussian war of 1866 against Austria)[1] than to regard Germany, for all her outward show of confidence, as nervous of encirclement and attack by other Powers. The German people were unlikely to see in the policy of their rulers a reason for the distrust in which their country was held. If, then, the Germans thought war inevitable, they had better choose their own time for it, and fight while they were still in a position to overwhelm their enemies.

In the autumn of 1914 Germany was at her maximum strength against France and Russia. On the naval side she had completed the widening of the Kiel canal which enabled her to move in safety the largest capital ships between the Baltic and the North Sea. On land Russia and to a certain extent France were in the middle of plans of military organisation which in a short time would add greatly to their military strength. Germany had taken in 1913 an exceptional financial measure for military purposes; she had raised a special levy of 1000 million marks.[2] She could not easily repeat this measure in peace-time.

[1] 'A war not fought out of necessity to meet a threat to our existence, not called into being by public opinion. It was a war recognised by the government as necessary, a war long planned, quietly prepared for, and fought not for acquisition of land or increase of territory, but for an ideal end – for predominance and power (für ein ideales Gut, für Machtstellung), Moltke, *Gesammelte Schriften*, iii. 426.

[2] A contemporary equivalent would be about £300,000,000. It has been alleged that the German Government took steps, with a view to the outbreak of war, in

Moltke,[1] the Chief of Staff, had cause to say, in June, 1914: 'The sooner things boil over, the better for us.' Four months earlier Conrad von Hoetzendorf, Austro-Hungarian Chief of Staff, had written to Moltke: 'What are we waiting for?'

There is another factor of which account must be taken. The nation states of Europe in 1914 have been described retrospectively as existing in an 'international anarchy'. Such was not the view of contemporaries. There was no super-national authority in Europe, dictating, in Hobbes' words, 'articles of peace', but the relations between the Great Powers had become more orderly, and, at least apparently, subject to an agreed law during the course of the nineteenth century. International law might still be described as 'the measure of conscience of the stronger', yet there seemed to be a greater awareness of the danger which a general war would cause to the interlocked interests of civilised states and also a growing sense of revulsion against the moral evil of war as such, and a movement of public opinion away from the older view that aggressive war was a legitimate instrument of policy. This saner attitude, however, had not developed evenly among the Great Powers. The relevant consideration here is not that the more backward states were backward owing to some innate 'wickedness' or that the more advanced states had among their citizens a larger share of moral virtue. Different attitudes to war persisted and were of sinister importance; they were due much more to the fact that the nations of Europe, and different classes within nations, were at different stages of political maturity. For historical reasons the two western Great Powers, Great Britain and France, had responded more quickly to the conditions and possibilities of the Industrial Revolution. They were genuine parliamentary democracies. They had learned, neither completely nor uniformly, but on an average throughout all classes, that, owing to technological progress, the centuries of poverty and scarcity might be brought to an end, and that war was no longer necessary to secure the minimum requirements of good living. Germany might also have learned these lessons, but her political development had been retarded by the failure of the liberal elements in the country to bring about national unity

---

the spring and summer of 1914 to increase the national gold reserve by getting German banks to call in foreign debts. It is not without significance that heavy guns ordered in Germany (and paid for by the Belgian Government) for the defence of Antwerp were not delivered in the summer of 1914.

[1] Nephew of the elder Moltke.

in the critical years 1848–9. National unity had been achieved by Bismarck who held to the ideas of the most backward governing class in Europe outside Russia – the class of Prussian landowners. Bismarck fashioned the political institutions of the German Reich in a form which ensured political control to this backward minority. They in turn imposed their standards, judgments, and values upon a docile and prosperous middle class, and to a large extent, upon the German people as a whole. Germany was the only Great Power in which effective public opinion was less liberal in 1914 than it had been two generations earlier. The wealth created by the German population, and its vast productive potential were therefore at the disposition of a governing class out of touch with the best thought and most intelligent hopes of the age. In this submission of the German people to 'the traditional mentality of poverty-haunted border robbers' lay the deeper reasons for the ill-starred willingness of Germany to accept the risks of provoking a European war in 1914. The attitude of the German military party in the early summer of that year can be seen clearly in the report of Colonel House[1] whom President Wilson had sent to Europe at the end of May, 1914, to discuss with European Governments the possibility of a peace pact. House found in control of German policy a 'military oligarchy', determined upon war, and even ready to depose the Emperor in favour of the Crown Prince if he resisted their designs.

At this dangerous moment in international politics, on June 28, 1914, the Archduke Francis Ferdinand, heir to the Emperor Francis Joseph, was assassinated at Sarajevo in Bosnia. The murderer and his associates were members of a Servian secret society which aimed at detaching Bosnia-Herzegovina from Austria-Hungary. The Archduke, violent and unpopular with the ruling authorities, was believed to favour the so-called trialist solution of the nationalist problem of the Habsburg Empire, that is to say, the grant of self-governing institutions to the southern Slavs as co-partners with the ruling German and Magyar nationalities.[2] There is no evidence that the Servian Government had anything to do with the assassination, but they had allowed an open campaign of propaganda on Servian territory against Austria-Hungary, and had not prevented their own officials from taking part in it.

[1] See below, pp. 210–11.
[2] This trialist solution was disliked by the Austro-Hungarian authorities, who feared its effects on the rest of the Empire, and by the Serbian nationalists, who thought that it might weaken the force of the nationalist movement.

The Austro-Hungarian Government seized the occasion to deal 'once and for all' with Servian incitements to disruption. They knew the risk that Russia would strongly oppose their action, and that, before they started measures which might lead to war they must be sure of German support. On July 5 therefore the Emperor Francis Joseph sent a letter to William II by special envoy saying that Austria intended to deal severely with Servia and might go as far as partitioning the country. Similar information was given to the German Foreign Office. William II at first answered cautiously; later, without waiting to consult Bethmann-Hollweg, the German Chancellor, he agreed that Austria should 'march into Servia at the present time, which is all in our favour'. William asked the Minister of War whether the German army was 'ready for all contingencies'. The Minister answered (not unexpectedly) 'yes', and the Chancellor, on his return to Berlin later in the day, agreed with the Emperor that Austria must decide for herself what to do, and that Germany must not desert her.

William II seems to have thought that neither Russia nor France would intervene. He did not mention England, and indeed had no reason to do so. If Russia and France did not resort to war, there could be no question of English intervention. On the other hand William took account of the possibility of war. He did not, as is sometimes said, merely give Austria a free hand to do what she thought fit; he knew that she intended military action, and might go as far as a partition of Servia. In promising German support he had no need to order special military preparations. German plans of mobilisation were ready to the last detail. Moreover for Germany mobilisation meant war. The mobilised German armies would not stand passively on the frontiers awaiting events. The German strategic plan for victory against France and Russia envisaged a rapid invasion of Belgium, the overthrow of France in a lightning campaign before the Russians had completed their slow process of mobilising and begun to advance westwards. While the mass of the German armies was moving towards the French frontier, a special force would secure a road into Belgium and France through Liège, and other troops would occupy Luxembourg. This plan could not be changed at short notice. Once it was set in motion by a mobilisation order, war would follow.[1] William II therefore merely assured himself that the military chiefs were ready to put the order into effect. He also consulted the head of Krupps. Baron Krupp von Bohlen told him that his firm had sufficient material 'for a long

[1] For this so-called Schlieffen plan, see also below, p. 32.

time' – a 'long time' being the short war which would bring a German victory on two fronts. The naval chiefs also took their precautions. Admiral von Spee in the Pacific was warned that England was a possible enemy if France and Russia were drawn into the war.

The Austro-Hungarian governmental machinery moved with its usual slowness – too slowly for the Germans who wanted a *fait accompli* which would anticipate Russian attempts to prevent the disruption of Servia. Austria did not send an ultimatum to Servia until July 23. Meanwhile, on the plan to localise the war, they (and the Germans) tried to influence European opinion. The Austro-Hungarian Embassy in London was instructed to write to important people who might support the case against Servia. After an article of July 16 in *The Times* warning Austria, the Ambassador asked Wickham Steed, the foreign editor, to lunch, and suggested that he should 'use his influence' in the British press to make the position of Austria understood. Steed warned the Ambassador that an attack on Servia would at once bring in Russia and that, if the war then became general, Great Britain would certainly intervene.

For the first few days after the assassination Grey and the Foreign Office do not seem to have been seriously alarmed about possible consequences. Prince Lichnowsky, the German Ambassador, came back from leave on July 6. He told Grey that he had found 'anxiety and pessimism' in Berlin; that Austria intended 'to do something' and might take military action against Servia. There was some feeling that 'trouble was bound to come', and that it would be better not to hold Austria back but to 'let the trouble come now rather than later'. Lichnowsky hoped that, if 'trouble' came, Great Britain would use her influence to mitigate feeling in St Petersburg. Grey answered that he was disturbed by what the Ambassador had said, and that he would like to talk over matters later with him.[1] Grey then spoke to the Cabinet, whose members were dismayed by the prospect of another acute crisis in European affairs at a time when Great Britain was occupied with a grave situation in Ireland. On July 9 Grey mentioned to Lichnowsky the Anglo-French and Anglo-Russian naval and military conversations. He explained that these conversations had not resulted in any binding agreements. He added that, 'if Austrian action with regard to Servia kept within certain bounds, it would . . . be comparatively easy to

[1] *British Documents on the Origins of the War* (henceforward referred to as B.D.), Vol. XI, No. 32.

encourage patience at St Petersburg; but there were some things that
Austria might do that would make the Russian Government say that
the Slav feeling in Russia was so strong that they must send an ulti-
matum or something of that sort'.[1] On July 20 Grey again warned
Lichnowsky that Austria should keep her demands within reasonable
limits. Grey said that he 'hated the idea of a war between any of the
Great Powers, and that any of them should be dragged into a war by
Servia was detestable'.[2]

The Austrian Note to Servia of July 23 demanded an answer within
forty-eight hours. The Servian Government was required to disavow
all propaganda against Austria-Hungary, to suppress the Servian
nationalist societies, hold a judicial enquiry into the events of the
assassination, and allow 'organs of the Austro-Hungarian Government'
to assist on Servian territory in searching out the guilty parties and
putting an end to the subversive movement. The German Government,
although the Foreign Minister, von Jagow, pretended otherwise,[3]
knew the general nature of the Austrian demands before the Note was
sent and approved of the ultimatum. Grey described the Note to the
Austrian Ambassador on July 24 as 'the most formidable document'
which he had ever seen 'addressed by one State to another that was
independent'.[4] The Austrian Government did not want Servia to accept
the terms. They intended war, and hoped only that Russia would not
intervene, though the Russian Government had already said that they
would not allow an attack upon Servia. Grey did not think that a war
between Austria and Servia could be localised. He said to the Austrian
Ambassador on July 24 that he felt 'great apprehension' for the peace
of Europe and that he must consult with other Powers to see what
might be done. He had pointed out at his previous interview that the
possible consequences of the situation were 'terrible'. If as many as four
Great Powers . . . were engaged in war, the expenditure in money and
the interference with trade would bring about 'a complete collapse of
European credit and industry. In these days, in great industrial States,
this would mean a state of things worse than that of 1848, and irrespective of who were victors in the war, many things might be com-

[1] B.D., No. 41.

[2] B.D., No. 68.

[3] Jagow was given the actual text of the Note nearly twenty-four hours before
the time of delivery. If the German Government had regarded any change in the
text as desirable they could easily have notified Vienna, but they sent no comment
before the Note was delivered.

[4] B.D., No. 91.

pletely swept away'. Grey advised the Austro-Hungarian Government to enter on a direct exchange of views with Russia.[1]

In accordance with the procedure agreed between the German and Austro-Hungarian Governments the German Ambassador on July 24 asked Grey to assist in localising the Austro-Servian dispute. Grey was certain that it could not be localised. He told Lichnowsky that, in view of the character of the Austrian Note and of the short time-limit, he could do nothing to influence Russia. He suggested that Austria should be asked to prolong her time-limit. Instead of accepting the German-Austrian proposal that Great Britain should invite Russia to stand aside while Austria crushed Servia, Grey thus wanted Germany to restrain Austria from making her attack. He said that Germany, France, Italy, and Great Britain should work together at Vienna and St Petersburg in favour of moderation, but that Germany alone could influence Austria to postpone military action.[2]

The Servian reply to the Austrian Note accepted nearly all the Austrian demands. The Servian Government was unwilling to allow Austrian representatives to take part in an enquiry into Servian complicity in the murder of Francis Ferdinand or to assist in the suppression of the Servian nationalist movement. They offered, however, to submit the whole of the dispute to the Hague Court. The Austrian Government, not having received a full acceptance of the terms, ordered their Minister to leave Belgrade at once.

On hearing from the Austrian Ambassador on July 25 that the Austrian action at Belgrade was 'not an ultimatum, but a *démarche* with a time-limit', and that if Servia did not comply with the Austrian demands, a breach of diplomatic relations, and military preparations, but not actual operations would follow, Grey said to Lichnowsky that the situation would soon be that both Austria and Russia would have mobilised. The only chance of peace would be for the four Powers to join in asking both Austria and Russia not to cross their frontiers until

---

[1] *B.D.*, No. 86. Grey's forecast of European revolution following economic collapse was especially relevant to conditions in Austria-Hungary, but the fear of a general collapse was continually present in Grey's mind. See below, p. 20. One may contrast Grey's own statements of his anxieties with William's II view that Grey deliberately brought on the war in order to destroy German trade.

[2] *B.D.*, No. 99. The German reply to Grey's proposal was that they had 'passed it on' to Vienna, but that Count Berchtold appeared to be away, and that as the Austrian ultimatum expired 'today' (25th) there no longer seemed any chance of postponement. Lichnowsky sent two telegrams urgently asking that Grey's proposal should not be rejected.

there had been time for them (the four Powers) to suggest a settlement. Grey repeated his fear that an Austro-Russian conflict might mean a general war; Great Britain had no binding commitments, but could not remain indifferent to developments in Europe.[1] Lichnowsky told the German Foreign Office that, if Germany refused the British proposal for mediation, she would probably force Great Britain to the side of France and Russia.

On July 26 Grey, remembering the success of the Ambassadors' Conference in London during the Balkan crisis of 1912-13, proposed[2] a conference of Great Britain, France, Germany, and Italy; the four Powers would invite Austria-Hungary, Servia, and Russia to suspend all military operations pending the result of the conference. Sazonov, the Russian Foreign Minister, said that he would prefer direct Austro-Russian negotiations, but that, if this plan failed, he would agree to Grey's proposal. France and Italy accepted the proposal. Germany rejected it on the ground that she could not agree to bring Austria before a European tribunal in regard to her policy towards Servia.[3] The German Chancellor knew that the other three Powers would not agree to his own proposal to allow Austria a free hand. The Russian suggestion of direct negotiations also came to nothing because Count Berchtold, the Austro-Hungarian Foreign Minister, avoided seeing the Russian Ambassador in Vienna until July 28 and then told him that the proposal for discussing Austro-Servian relations was unacceptable and in any case came too late because Austria had already decided to declare war on Servia on July 28.

★　　★　　★

[1] B.D., No. 116 and Die Deutschen Dokumente zum Kriegsausbruch (henceforward referred to as D.D.), Nos. 180 and 179.

[2] B.D., 139-40. The proposal was actually sent out by Nicolson, Permanent Under-Secretary at the Foreign Office, with the approval of Grey, who was away from the office on July 26. Nicolson, and Tyrrell, Grey's private secretary, in transmitting the proposal to Lichnowsky, warned him that there was no chance of localising the dispute. If Great Britain and Germany succeeded in saving the peace of Europe, Anglo-German relations would be 'placed on a secure footing for all time. If we do not (succeed), then everything is uncertain.' On the other hand the Emperor and his Chancellor seem to have felt reassured on July 26 by a telegram from Prince Henry of Prussia claiming that he had been told by King George V that 'we (Great Britain) shall try all we can to keep out of this and to remain neutral'. In fact, King George had said: 'I don't know what we shall do. We have no quarrel with anyone, and I hope we shall remain neutral. But if Germany declares war on Russia, and France joins Russia, then I am afraid we shall be dragged into it'.

[3] B.D., Nos. 185 and 249. D.D., No 248.

Austria had declared war sooner than she had at first intended; she would not be ready to invade Servia until August 12, but she wanted by her *fait accompli* to put a stop to efforts at mediation between herself and Servia. The crisis had now reached the acute stage which Grey had foreseen. The declaration of war on Servia would not bring a withdrawal of Russian opposition. The Russians were not bluffing. They would not tolerate what they (and, for that matter, Austria) regarded as a decisive blow to Russian influence in the Balkans. Since Austria had taken the initiative in military measures, the chances of avoiding a European war had diminished because the General Staffs of the Continental armies were tied to their time-tables of mobilisation; Germany, in particular, with her plans for a rapid campaign against France, could not afford to lose a day. Grey was also right in saying that Germany alone could stop Austria. So far from attempting to do so, Germany had been urging Austria not to delay, and was dismayed to hear that military operations would not begin for another fortnight. The German refusal to agree to Grey's proposal for a conference, that is to say, the refusal to recognise that the Austro-Servian dispute was almost certain to lead to a European war if Austria were not held back, therefore left Germany as well as Austria-Hungary with a heavy share of responsibility for the outbreak of the war. On July 27 Grey had told Lichnowsky that the Servian reply to the Austrian Note shewed that Russia was exercising a moderating influence on Servia, and that Germany should do the same with Austria. Grey also said that, if Austria persisted in her present course and Germany supported her, 'without any reference to the merits of the dispute', but merely because 'she could not afford to see Austria crushed, just so other issues might be raised that would supersede the dispute between Austria and Servia, and would bring other Powers in and the war would be the biggest ever known'.[1] Lichnowsky had no doubt about Grey's meaning. He telegraphed to Berlin that, if Austria tried to 'crush' Servia, England would 'place herself unconditionally on the side of France and Russia'.[2] There was also an important fact which would have impressed the German authorities more than Lichnowsky's reports. On the morning of July 27 the British press announced officially that the

[1] *B.D.*, No. 176.

[2] *D.D.*, No. 265. Grey said in the House of Commons on July 27 that, if the dispute ceased to be between Austria-Hungary and Servia, and became one in which another Great Power was involved, 'it can but end in the greatest catastrophe that has ever befallen Europe at one blow: no one can say what would be the limit of the issues that might be raised by such a conflict'.

fleet, which was about to disperse after manœuvres, would remain concentrated.

For a short time now there was a chance that Germany might not follow Austria on her reckless course. The Emperor William, who had approved of Austrian action when he expected it to be rapid, and thought that it could be localised, now began to realise the risks which he was allowing Germany to run. On reading the text of the Servian reply to the Austrian Note, he suddenly concluded that this reply was 'a great moral victory for Austria', and that 'every reason for war disappears'. He proposed on the morning of July 28 that Austria should be content with the occupation of Belgrade as a guarantee that Servia carried out her promises.

Bethmann-Hollweg waited until the late evening before transmitting this suggestion to Vienna (thus ensuring that it did not arrive before the Austrian declaration of war on Servia). He pointed out that, if Austria refused every suggestion for mediation, she would have the responsibility put on her for the outbreak of a European war. He recommended that she should consider repeating that she did not intend to annex Servian territory, and that she would be satisfied with the occupation of Belgrade and other places as a guarantee of the 'complete fulfilment' of her demands (not, as William II had suggested, the fulfilment of the promises in the Servian reply). Bethmann-Hollweg knew before he sent his telegram that Austria intended to hand over parts of Servia to Bulgaria and probably other parts to Albania. He told the German Ambassador in Vienna to avoid giving the impression of holding Austria back; Germany merely wanted to ensure that, if a war broke out, it would be fought under the best possible conditions for the two Central Powers.[1]

The final stage on the road to catastrophe now began with the inevitable Russian answer to the refusal of Austria to discuss with Russia her action against Servia and her declaration of war on July 28. The Russians, on hearing of the declaration of war, decided to order on the following day a mobilisation against Austria, but not against Germany. The political advantages of this partial mobilisation were obvious, but the Russian military authorities disliked it because it would interfere seriously with the general mobilisation which they now thought unavoidable. The Tsar was persuaded with great difficulty on the night of July 29 to order general mobilisation. He countermanded the order before it was sent out because he believed that he had more hopeful

[1] D.D., No. 323.

news in a personal message from William II. He replied to this message with a suggestion that the dispute should be referred to the Hague Court – a proposal which the Germans thought merely absurd.

On hearing (July 29) of the Russian order for partial mobilisation Grey told Lichnowsky that he thought mediation between Austria and Russia not impossible although it was too late to prevent all Austrian military operations against Servia. Grey proposed, on lines similar to William II's plan (of which Grey knew nothing), that Austria, after occupying 'Belgrade and other places' should agree not to advance further, 'pending an effort of the Powers to mediate between her and Russia'. Grey also warned Lichnowsky even more definitely that, if Germany and France came into the war, 'the issue might be so great that it would involve all European interests'. Great Britain might then have to decide very rapidly whether British interests required her intervention. Grey said that he was putting the facts in the form of a private statement because he did not want to leave himself open to the charge that the friendly tone of his conversations had misled Lichnowsky or the German Government into believing that 'we should not take action, and to the reproach that, if they had not been so misled, the course of things might have been different'.[1] William II now had no doubt about British intervention. After his fashion he regarded Grey's words as evidence of secret plotting. 'England reveals herself in her true colours at the moment when she thinks we are caught in the toils. This means that we are to leave Austria in the lurch.'[2]

Bethmann-Hollweg also could have no doubts. Moreover, in addition to Lichnowsky's report, the Chancellor now had information that neither Italy nor Roumania was likely to take the Austro-German side. At this late hour Bethmann-Hollweg made a more genuine attempt to get direct talks between Austria and Russia, but he never went as far as insisting on them, and his messages to Vienna give the impression that he was still concerned mainly with trying to fix on Russia the responsibility for the war which he now thought certain. Finally, Bethmann-Hollweg surrendered to the German military pressure and

[1] B.D., Nos. 263, 284, 285, 286.

[2] D.D., No. 368. William II's attitude of mind had little significance at this time except to shew his unfitness for the responsible office which he held. He now convinced himself that 'the whole war is plainly arranged between England, France, and Russia for the annihilation of Germany'. He was particularly violent against England, and thought that he could trace the machinations of Edward VII in the 'plot' against Germany. 'Edward VII after his death is none the less stronger than I am.' D.D., No. 401.

let matters take their course. He telegraphed during the night of July 29–30 to the German Ambassador repeating the proposal for a halt in Belgrade and for opening conversations with Russia on this basis. He told the Ambassador of Lichnowsky's report, and pointed out that a refusal of Austria 'to enter into an exchange of views with St Petersburg would be . . . a serious mistake, for that is just what would provoke the armed intervention of Russia . . . We are ready to fulfil the obligations of our alliance, but must refuse to be drawn into a world conflagration lightheartedly by Austria and without regard to our advice.[1] Even so the Chancellor did not advise Austria to give up her plan of invading Servia, though he knew that this step alone would be likely to prevent full Russian mobilisation. In any case Berchtold had already asked Germany to warn Russia that further measures of mobilisation on her part would lead to German mobilisation. Bethmann-Hollweg had sent a message in this sense in the early afternoon of July 29.[2] Berchtold could therefore feel sure of his ally and need make no concessions. He agreed to allow the Austrian Ambassador at St Petersburg to begin conversations with the Russian Foreign Minister, but the Ambassador was merely to explain that Austria intended only a temporary occupation of Servian territory; there was to be no real discussion of the Austrian demands. As for the proposal for a 'halt in Belgrade' Berchtold had not sent an answer; he explained that, owing to the absence of Count Tisza, the Hungarian Minister President, no answer could be expected until July 31.[3]

In the evening of July 30 Bethmann-Hollweg instructed the German Ambassador at Vienna to urge the Austrians once again to accept the 'halt in Belgrade' proposal. The Chancellor cancelled this telegram before midnight.[4] He had given way to the demands of the General Staff. The General Staff could not allow the situation to drag on while the Russians and French took steps which would make their mobilisation easier. In the afternoon of July 30 Moltke had recommended

---

[1] D.D., Nos. 396 and 397.   [2] D.D., Nos. 342 and 378.

[3] It would have been possible to have communicated with Tisza by telephone. In fact, Conrad and Berchtold, with the Emperor's approval, had decided in the afternoon to reject a formula put forward by Sasonow and revised by Grey to the effect that 'if Austria, having occupied Belgrade and neighbouring Servian territory, declares herself ready in the interest of European peace to cease her advance and to discuss how a complete settlement could be arrived at', he (Grey) hoped that 'Russia would also consent to discussion and suspension of further military preparations, provided that the other Powers did the same', B.D., No. 309: Conrad von Hoetzendorf, F., *Aus meiner Dienstzeit*, iv, 149–52.

[4] D.D., Nos. 441 and 450.

Conrad to decline Grey's proposals and to mobilise at once against Russia. The *casus foederis* with Germany would then have arisen, and Germany herself could order full mobilisation. In Moltke's words, 'A European war offers the last chance of preserving Austria-Hungary.'[1]

Russia decided upon general mobilisation during the evening of July 30; Austria took a similar decision, subject to formal German agreement. The Russian mobilisation notices were published on the morning of July 31, and the Austrian just after midday. German mobilisation, as Moltke had said, was bound to follow. Austrian and Russian mobilisation would not automatically mean war. German mobilisation would bring with it the invasion of Belgium; Moltke had drawn up and given to the German Foreign Office on July 26 an ultimatum to be presented, when the time came, to the Belgian Government.

Grey indeed had little hope that war could be prevented. On the night of July 29–30 he had received a message from Bethmann-Hollweg which he (Grey) described as shewing that 'we were henceforth to converse upon how we should conduct ourselves in war, no longer how war could be avoided'.[2] The German Chancellor was merely attempting once again (though he could hardly have hoped to succeed) to get English neutrality. He promised, on condition of such neutrality, that Germany would make no territorial demands on France, though he would give no assurance about the French colonies. Germany would also promise the territorial integrity of Belgium after the war, provided that Belgium had taken no hostile action against her.[3] Grey had been astonished at the combination of naïveté and cynicism in this proposal. He answered that the proposal could not 'for a moment be entertained', but added that, if Great Britain and Germany worked together to preserve the peace of Europe in the present crisis, he would try to bring about some arrangement by which 'Germany could be assured that no hostile or aggressive policy would be pursued against her or her allies by France, Russia, or Great Britain, jointly or separately'.[4] On the morning of July 31 Grey made another direct appeal to Germany. He said to Lichnowsky that 'if Germany could get any reasonable proposal put forward which made it clear that Germany and Austria were

---

[1] Conrad, iv, 152. Moltke had told Conrad that he did not expect English neutrality. Bethmann-Hollweg telegraphed to the German Minister at Stockholm on July 30 that England was expected to enter the war on the Franco-Russian side, *D.D.*, No. 406.

[2] Grey, *Twenty-Five Years*, i, 326.

[3] *B.D.*, No. 293.   [4] *B.D.*, No. 303.

striving to preserve European peace, and that Russia and France would be unreasonable if they rejected it', he would 'support it at St Petersburg and Paris and go to the length of saying that, if Russia and France would not accept it, His Majesty's Government would have nothing more to do with the consequences; but, otherwise, . . . if France became involved . . . we should be drawn in'. Grey's idea of a reasonable proposal was that the four Powers should 'offer to Austria that they would undertake to see that she received full satisfaction of her demands on Servia, provided that they did not impair Servian sovereignty and the integrity of Servian territory'. The four Powers would guarantee to Russia that the Austrian demands would be kept within these limits. All Powers would suspend military operations or preparations.[1]

The Germans answered Grey's last appeal by saying that they had sent a communication to Russia and must await the Russian reply. This communication was an ultimatum. On getting news of the Russian mobilisation order – the Germans already knew that the Austrians were issuing a similar order – the German Foreign Office telegraphed to Russia an announcement proclaiming a state of 'immediate danger of war'[2] and warning Russia that, if she did not suspend every military move against Germany and Austria-Hungary within twelve hours, Germany would mobilise. A note of a similar kind was sent to the French Government, with an additional sentence that for Germany mobilisation meant war. The French Government was asked to declare within eighteen hours whether they would remain neutral in a German-Russian war. The German Ambassador in Paris was instructed to demand that, if the French gave a promise of neutrality, they should hand over the fortresses of Toul and Verdun to Germany as pledges for the period of the war.[3]

The Germans did not wait for an answer from France or Russia before beginning their mobilisation. The German order was issued in the afternoon of August 1. French mobilisation was ordered on this

[1] *B.D.*, No. 340.

[2] 'Kriegsgefahrzustand', a state of imminent danger of war, was a technical term denoting the taking of all measures preparatory to war short of mobilisation.

[3] Since the French Government made no offer of neutrality (their reply was that France would act in accordance with her interests), the Ambassador did not have to carry out this instruction to ask for pledges of neutrality. The fact that the Germans intended to put forward such a demand was not generally known until 1918. The reason for such an impossible request was that the Germans wanted to be sure of a French refusal. French neutrality, even for a few weeks, would have upset the German military plans for a rapid campaign in the west before turning eastwards against Russia.

same afternoon. The French General Staff had been pressing for it earlier. Joffre, the French Commander-in-Chief, warned his Government on July 31 that every day's delay would mean losing territory to the depth of fifteen to twenty kilometres. The French Government gave instructions that their troops should be kept ten kilometres back from the frontier; Germany, who could not wait, would thus have to declare war on France.

The purpose of the French withdrawal was to convince British opinion that France was not the aggressor. Grey needed no convincing. He thought of a European war, not as William II imagined him to be thinking, in terms of a long-planned opportunity to achieve the destruction of Germany, but as a terrible evil which might cause the destruction of Europe. His whole policy had been directed towards bringing about general appeasement. Nevertheless he regarded British intervention as necessary in British interests if France were drawn into the war. The war had arisen out of a question of little concern to Great Britain, but once the four Great Continental Powers were engaged in it, the issue would become one of European predominance, and, if Germany and Austria were victorious, British interests would be in extreme danger. If, on the other hand, France and Russia won without British aid, they would be unlikely to shew much consideration for a nation which, in their view, would have repudiated its obligations. It was true, again, that Great Britain had no binding commitments with France, but, as Eyre Crowe[1] wrote in a memorandum of July 31 to Grey:

> The Entente has been made, strengthened, put to the test and celebrated in a manner justifying the belief that a moral bond was being forged. The whole policy of the Entente can have no meaning if it does not signify that in a just quarrel England would stand by her friends. This honourable expectation has been raised. We cannot repudiate it without exposing our good name to grave criticism.[2]

Grey himself felt this moral obligation though he did not regard it as extending to a situation in which France was acting in accordance with the terms of the Franco-Russian alliance. Grey told the French Ambassador as late as August 1 that it was 'most unreasonable to say that, because France had an obligation under an alliance of which we did not even know the terms, therefore we were bound, equally with her

[1] Assistant Under-Secretary of State in the Foreign Office.   [2] *B.D.*, No. 369.

by the obligation in that alliance, to be involved in war'.[1] Grey indeed was so much concerned with the possibility of an economic collapse in Europe that he would have regarded the maintenance of neutrality, if he had thought it possible on other grounds, as a means of preventing European anarchy. He told Cambon on July 31 that 'the commercial and financial situation was exceedingly serious; there was danger of a complete collapse that would involve us and everyone else in ruin; and it was possible that our standing aside might be the only means of preventing a complete collapse of European credit in which we should be involved. This might be a paramount consideration in deciding our attitude.'[2]

Later in this same conversation Grey said that 'the preservation of the neutrality of Belgium might be, I would not say a decisive, but an important factor in determining our attitude'. Grey realised that, from the point of view of British interests, the neutrality and independence of Belgium were vital matters, irrespective of the other issues involved.[3] Moreover the question of Belgium had nothing to do with Russia and could be considered apart from the Austro-Russian and Austro-Servian disputes. On July 31 Grey put a formal question to the French and German Governments whether, in the event of war, they would respect Belgian neutrality. The French answered that they would respect it, provided that it was not violated by any other Power. The

[1] B.D., No. 447.

[2] B.D., No. 367. Grey was defending to Cambon the British refusal to promise intervention on the side of France, but he was expressing a view which he really held. Crowe argued against this view in his memorandum of July 31 (B.D., No. 369): 'The systematic disturbance of an enemy's financial organisation and the creation of panic is part of a well-laid preparation for war . . . The panic in the city has been largely influenced by the deliberate acts of German financial houses, who are in at least as close touch with the German as with the British Government, and who are notoriously in daily communication with the German Embassy.' Crowe regarded commercial opinion as 'generally, timid, and apt to follow pusillanimous counsels'.

Grey's fear of an economic collapse can be seen in his speech to the House of Commons on August 3, when he told the House that 'If we are engaged in war, we shall suffer but little more than we shall suffer even if we stand out. We are going to suffer, I am afraid, terribly in this war, whether we are in it or whether we stand aside.' Grey does not at this time seem to have thought that Great Britain would be involved in a vast military effort. He regarded her own position as assured by her fleet, but did not think she could escape from very severe losses from a general European collapse of credit.

[3] Great Britain, as a signatory of the treaty of 1839 guaranteeing Belgian neutrality, had a right, though not in all circumstances an obligation to go to war in defence of the treaty.

Germans said that they could not give an answer without disclosing their plan of campaign. It has been said that, if Great Britain had stated earlier and definitely that she would take the side of France and Russia in a war against Austria and Germany, the latter would have compelled Austria to accept the British proposals for securing a peaceful settlement. Apart from Grey's clear and frequent warnings in the earlier stages of the crisis, the Germans were left in no doubt, after July 28, when there was still time to call a halt, that Great Britain would be drawn into a war. It is also clear that the German military authorities would not have been deflected from their course if they had been given a formal notice of British intervention. The General Staff – and the Chancellor – had accepted the Schlieffen plan with its political implication of a violation of Belgian neutrality which made British intervention more than likely, but this intervention would not be a decisive factor in a campaign involving the rapid defeat of France and the German occupation of the Channel coast from Brest to Antwerp.[1] The Germans did not intend to risk their fleet in an unnecessary battle at sea; a British blockade, in a short war, would not be more than a temporary nuisance. The British Expeditionary Force, if it ever reached the battle line, would be defeated in company with the immensely larger French army.

From Grey's point of view an announcement, while peace and war was still in the balance, that Great Britain would intervene on the side of France and Russia was dangerous, since it might lead Russia to refuse to agree to the reasonable demands of Austria that Servia should put an end to the use of her territory for anti-Austrian activities. In any case Grey was in no position to promise intervention since the Liberal Cabinet were not in agreement about it. A majority – about two-thirds – of the Cabinet believed that Great Britain could and should remain neutral. Lloyd George took this view on economic grounds. Opinion in the City, partly, as Crowe pointed out, under German influence, was for neutrality. Morley thought that a European war might lead to the dislocation of 'order', and that a Russian victory would be a danger to civilisation. The British Cabinet indeed alone of the European Governments was taken almost completely by surprise at the sudden emergence of a crisis. Grey himself was not without responsibility for this remarkable ignorance of the unstable condition of Europe after the Balkan war. Grey himself admitted later that he should have given more attention to the problem of the future of the

[1] See below, p. 32.

multi-national Habsburg Empire, and for that matter, Asquith can be criticised on more general grounds. Grey had never been much concerned with educating opinion in his own party or in the country on the realities of international politics. He was not even sure, on taking office, whether the Foreign Secretary would find it compatible with his departmental duties to sit in the House of Commons.[1] Grey did not like making speeches; he found the social side of his office distasteful, and, like Asquith, paid little attention to the press. The left wing of his party was extremely suspicious of Russia, and much more favourable to Germany than German opinion was to England. The Liberal party was by tradition inclined to isolationism, and more interested in social questions than in questions of foreign policy. The education of most Englishmen gave them no instruction or interest in contemporary European affairs; there were no centres of information and discussion, such as the Institute of International Affairs in the years after 1919, for the dissemination of knowledge and the development of an instructed opinion. Englishmen in general were probably less informed in 1914 about tensions in Europe than they had been in the period between Waterloo and the Franco-Prussian war.

All the Great Powers except Great Britain had taken their decisions by August 1. The German declaration of war on Russia was made in the early evening of that day. The German declaration of war on France was delayed (in the hope that France would declare war on Germany)[2] until 6.15 p.m. on August 3. Meanwhile at daybreak on August 2 German troops, in accordance with the German time-table of mobilisation and attack, entered Luxembourg.[3] In the evening of August 2 the German Minister in Brussels presented the German ultimatum to Belgium, with a time-limit of twelve hours. The reply was that Belgium would defend her rights. King Albert of Belgium telegraphed to King George V asking for diplomatic support, and, on the morning of August 4, after German troops had invaded Belgian territory, the Belgian Government appealed for French, British, and Russian help in the country's defence.

By this time the British Government had decided upon immediate

[1] Parl. Deb., 4th ser., H. of C., vol. 152, cols. 803–4. Grey's predecessors for nearly forty years had sat in the House of Lords. Grey thought that the House ought not to accept 'the doctrine that it is impossible for the Secretary of State for Foreign Affairs to be a member of the House of Commons'.
[2] On August 2 the French Government withdrew the order to their forces to keep ten kilometres from the frontier, though they were still forbidden to advance beyond it.   [3] Some German troops had already crossed into Luxembourg.

intervention. They had reached this decision by stages. On August 1 the Cabinet authorised Grey to tell Lichnowsky that the violation of Belgian neutrality would have a very strong effect upon British public opinion. When Lichnowsky asked whether Germany would remain neutral if Belgian neutrality were preserved, Grey would give no promise. Lichnowsky then enquired whether Great Britain would remain neutral if Germany agreed to respect the integrity of France and her colonies. Grey again refused any promise.[1] On the same day Grey also refused a French appeal for British intervention. He promised, however, to ask the Cabinet to consider giving a pledge to defend the north coast of France against a German naval attack.[2]

On August 2, after the news of the German entry into Luxembourg had reached London, the Cabinet decided that Grey should assure the French Government that, if the German fleet came into the Channel or through the North Sea 'to undertake hostile operations against French coasts or shipping, the British fleet would give all the protection in its power'.[3] In fact the Germans had no intention of sending their fleet into the Channel or the North Sea, but the French Ambassador realised that this promise was decisive for Great Britain. He has recorded his relief at Grey's statement in the words: 'A great country does not wage war by halves. Once it decided to fight the war at sea, it would necessarily be led to fighting it on land.'

Nevertheless the Cabinet had still to resolve whether it would go beyond the promise of limited intervention. Asquith, Grey, Haldane, and Churchill, who thought it necessary to go the whole way, were supported by a letter received during the morning of August 2 from

[1] *B.D.*, No. 448. A curious misunderstanding between Grey and Lichnowsky occurred on August 1. Grey asked whether Germany would agree to remain neutral, and not to attack France, if Great Britain also agreed to remain neutral, and to secure the neutrality of France. Lichnowsky understood this question to refer to German neutrality towards France and French neutrality towards Germany in a Russo-German war. Grey has stated that he meant German neutrality in a war between Austria and Russia. Lichnowsky telegraphed his interpretation of Grey's proposal to Berlin, where William II took it as a definite proposal which would imply the end of the Triple Entente. The Emperor now wanted Moltke to concentrate the German forces solely against Russia. Moltke had to point out the impossibility of changing German war plans at short notice. A later message from Lichnowsky corrected the misunderstanding. It is still not altogether clear how such a misunderstanding could have arisen. The most likely explanation is that both Grey and Lichnowsky were affected by the strain and anxiety of these days during which both men were trying to find a solution which might prevent the outbreak of general war.

[2] *B.D.*, No. 447.   [3] *B.D.*, No. 487.

the Unionist leaders, Lansdowne and Bonar Law, offering the full backing of their party for all measures in aid of France and Russia.[1] The Prime Minister was now assured, in the event of a split in the Cabinet, of an adequate parliamentary majority for a coalition in favour of intervention.

Moreover the anti-interventionist party began to waver, now that a German invasion of Belgium was certain. In the evening of August 2 the Cabinet decided that a substantial violation of Belgian neutrality would be a *casus belli*. Morley and Burns resigned at once; Simon and Beauchamp resigned on the following day, but withdrew their resignations.

In the afternoon of August 3, after the Belgians had rejected the German ultimatum, Grey spoke strongly in the House of Commons in favour of intervention. He explained that Parliament was free to decide on the question; there were no binding commitments to France and Russia except the promise given on the previous day to protect the French coasts and shipping. Grey spoke of the British *entente* with France, and left it to the judgment of the House to decide how far Great Britain was morally bound to come to the assistance of the French. He then turned to the Belgian question. Here he gave his view that Great Britain was bound to honour her obligations and to respond to a Belgian appeal. Grey's speech carried the great majority of the House. On August 4 Asquith announced to Parliament that the Germans had invaded Belgium. The German Government had appealed to Great Britain to allow this violation of an international treaty as an act of necessity. The British reply was an ultimatum with a time-limit expiring at midnight.[2]

[1] Asquith knew on August 1, from a conversation of Churchill with F. E. Smith, that he could count upon Unionist support. A few days earlier he could not have been altogether certain. Bonar Law was then doubtful whether his party would be 'unanimous or overwhelmingly in favour of war' except for the defence of Belgian neutrality. Grey, *Twenty-Five Years*, i, 337.

[2] At an interview with the British Ambassador after the delivery of the British ultimatum, Bethmann-Hollweg made a lengthy set speech in English in which he accused Great Britain of going to war 'just for a word "Neutrality", a word which in war-time had so often been disregarded, just for a scrap of paper'. *B.D.*, No. 671. Bethmann-Hollweg had described the invasion of Belgium as an act of political necessity. Within a few weeks, when he was still expecting a rapid German victory, he drew up a confidential memorandum in which he laid down that Belgium could not be given back her independent status but must remain in political, economic, and military vassalage to Germany. The particular degree of servitude which he proposed from time to time to fasten on Belgium is a remarkable measure of Bethmann-Hollweg's changes of view about German chances of victory. See below, Chapters 15 and 27.

The British Expeditionary Force: the first four months of the war on the Western Front

The British Regular Army, at the outbreak of the war, consisted of some 250,000 officers and men with the colours, and about 200,000 men in the Army Reserve and Special Reserve. In addition there were about 250,000 men in the Territorial Army. The existence of the latter, and the fact that a well-equipped expeditionary force was ready for immediate use was due in large measure to the organising ability of Haldane as Secretary for War between 1906 and 1911 but some at least of the administrative and other changes which made Haldane's work possible had been initiated before the Liberal Government took office.

The South African war, like the Crimean war nearly half a century earlier, had shown the inadequacy of British military organisation. After preliminary enquiries a committee under the chairmanship of Lord Esher[1] was appointed to consider the various proposals for re-improvement. Balfour had already taken the important step in 1902–3 of setting up an Imperial Defence Committee.[2] The Committee, which included non-Cabinet members, had only advisory functions, but did much to work out plans for co-ordinating the activities of the departments of State in the event of war.[3]

---

[1] Reginald Baliol Brett, 1852–1930, 2nd Viscount Esher; his mother was Alsatian, and his wife the daughter of the Belgian Minister in London. Esher was not a man of first-class ability, and never held an important office (he refused the Secretaryship of State for War and the Viceroyalty of India), but had great political influence – especially on army reform – through his personal friendship with King Edward VII, King George V, and many leading statesmen, Unionist and Liberal. It was said of him that he had 'all the axes, with none of them to grind'. A less friendly criticism was that, although he liked the indirect exercise of power, he refused to take the responsibilities of office.

[2] The idea of such a committee had been suggested to Balfour by the First Lord of the Admiralty (Lord Selborne) and the Secretary of State for War (Brodrick). A Cabinet Defence Committee existed, but was concerned mainly with estimates.

[3] The Esher Committee recommended that the Imperial Defence Committee

The Esher Committee recommended the abolition of the post of Commander-in-Chief, and the establishment of an Army Council, with four military and two civil members, and of a General Staff on the lines of those of the Continental armies. From the point of view of organisation for war this latter requirement was essential. A Royal Commission had proposed it in 1889-90. The opposition of the Duke of Cambridge,[1] who was then Commander-in-Chief, was to be expected; unfortunately Campbell-Bannerman, Secretary of State for War in the Liberal Administration of 1892, also disliked the plan because he thought that a General Staff might be tempted to plan 'possible operations in possible wars' against the neighbours of Great Britain. The Unionists had done nothing to put the recommendation into effect, and the senior officers of the army were content to leave things as they were. Hence at the most critical period of the South African war the War Office had practically no comprehensive studies of the military resources of any foreign countries, and no combined plan of operations – naval and military – in the event of war with a Great Power.

The Unionist Government accepted the recommendations of the Esher Committee. They formed an Army Council which began in a leisurely way to deal with the question of a General Staff. One of the tasks of the Committee of Imperial Defence and Army Council was to reconsider existing assumptions about the purpose and duties of the army. Until the South African war the accepted view had been that the army had to find men first for the defence of the British Isles, and then for the defence of India and of fortresses and coaling stations abroad. Subject to these requirements the policy of the government in a European war would be 'to aim at being able' to send abroad two army corps, but 'the probability of the employment of an army corps in the field in any European war is sufficiently improbable to make it the primary duty of the military authorities to organise our forces

---

should have a permanent secretariat. This secretariat under the direction of Colonel (later Lord) Hankey was the nucleus out of which the Cabinet secretariat developed. See also below, p. 41, note 1.

[1] The Duke of Cambridge was a cousin of Queen Victoria. The Queen appointed him Commander-in-Chief in 1856 because Wellington had recommended eight years earlier that the post should be held by a member of the royal family. (Esher once commented that the navy was a 'constitutional force' and the army a 'royal force'.) The Duke was a stupid man, who disliked any change in the army as Wellington had left it. The Queen always supported her cousin, and the Duke refused to resign until in 1895 the Prime Minister insisted upon his removal.

efficiently for the defence of this country'.[1] In March, 1901, Brodrick, as Secretary for War, said that we must be prepared to send two (he later mentioned three) army corps abroad. In 1904, however, Arnold-Forster – Brodrick's successor at the War Office – regarded India as 'our only possible place of contact with a great European army'. Balfour, at this time, also agreed that 'the whole trend of circumstances in the East' was to make us 'a Continental Power conterminous with another Continental Power', and that this was 'the dominating circumstance' which we had to take into account in framing our Army estimates. In the spring of 1905 Balfour still regarded the 'frontier of India' as the danger-point for military operations.

The general position, however, was rapidly changing. The defeat of Russia by Japan had made a Russian threat to India less likely – if it ever had been likely.[2] The persistence and increasing *tempo* of German naval construction – and the anti-English propaganda by which it was supported – suggested that the danger-point for Great Britain might be much nearer than India; the first Moroccan crisis and the attempt of Germany to break the Anglo-French *entente* confirmed this view. The question of British military intervention in Europe thus became of immediate importance. In August, 1905, Balfour asked the General Staff to report how long it would take to land two British army corps in Belgium; even so the Committee of Imperial Defence do not seem to have considered any general military plan, and the civilian Ministers still assumed that British support of France would be mainly naval. Fisher had begun to make plans of his own, without consulting the War Office, though he appears to have had some discussion with the French naval attaché (and, through him, the French Ministry of Marine). These plans and discussions also had not gone very far, but Fisher was known to favour landing a force on the coast of Pomerania.[3]

[1] These words are taken from the report of a committee under the chairmanship of Earl Stanhope in 1891. The wording is clumsy and obscure, but the intention is clear. The two schools of thought – those who regarded the navy as sufficient defence against invasion, and those who believed that an invasion, or at all events a large-scale destructive raid, was possible – were known respectively as the 'blue water' and the 'bolt from the blue' schools.

[2] The Anglo-Russian agreement of 1907 seemed to remove any threat to India.

[3] Fisher was obsessed with this plan (see below, p. 177), and kept to it in spite of the obvious fact that modern means of communication, allowing a very rapid concentration of resistance, had destroyed all chance of success for a raid of this kind. Fifty years earlier, in the second Schleswig-Holstein crisis, Bismarck had been asked what he would do if the British army invaded the Schleswig-Holstein

Haldane had the problem of an expeditionary force thrust upon him even before the Liberals had won the general election of 1906. Grey told him on January 13 of a conversation three days earlier with the French Ambassador. The Ambassador had asked him what Great Britain would do if the French – as they feared – were attacked by Germany in the summer. The Prime Minister authorised 'non-committal' Anglo-French and Anglo-Belgian staff conversations[1] in which the British representatives said that Great Britain would be able to send an expeditionary force of 105,000 officers and men to France within thirty-two days. The Committee of Imperial Defence thought this military estimate an exaggeration. On their view the largest available force would not have been above 80,000, and the mobilisation and transport of the force would have taken at least two months.

Haldane's problem was to provide for an expeditionary force larger and more efficiently organised for rapid mobilisation and transport than the numbers already available. He had also to secure that this force

---

peninsula. His answer was that he would send the Prussian police to arrest it. Fisher's idea in 1914 was that, after destroying the German fleet, the British navy should land a Russian army on the Pomeranian coast.

[1] These, and later conversations of a similar non-binding kind, have been criticised on two grounds: (i) that they took place not only without the approval but even without the knowledge of the Cabinet as a whole, and (ii) that, although they were expressly described as 'non-committal', they implied or at all events went too far towards implying that, in the event of war, the British Government would send assistance to France on the lines discussed. For these criticisms, see also above p. 3.

Whether or not the criticisms are valid, it was unfortunate that at least during the autumn of 1905 the Committee of Imperial Defence had not worked out a co-ordinated plan for British strategy in the event of a Continental war. Such a plan would almost certainly have included sending immediate help to the French or Belgians in the form of an expeditionary force. On the other hand the emphasis of British officers (especially General Wilson, Director of Military Operations) in close touch with the French on this form of assistance had unfortunate results. If the British Government had been able to make it clear to the French that the despatch of an expeditionary force to France was only a part of the general strategy which they would develop in the event of a long war, they would have left themselves more free to use, for example, their traditional method of amphibious warfare. Unless they safeguarded themselves in this way, they were surrendering their strategic freedom of action to the French General Staff, of whose plans they knew surprisingly little. Once they had made this surrender, they were unlikely to regain the initiative; even after they had built up an immense army, they would see it engulfed in French plans, while the French would measure the British contribution to any joint Allied effort solely in terms of the size of the British army in France.

could be adequately maintained, and that, when it was out of the country, there were enough trained men left behind to meet a sudden raid (on the assumption that no enemy invading force larger than 70,000 could escape the watchfulness of the navy).[1] Haldane had to convince two opposite types of critic: the left wing of his own party whose main interest in military matters was to cut down expenditure, and the section of the Conservatives who supported Lord Roberts' or other plans for universal service. The supporters of compulsory service organised much propaganda, but never convinced more than a small minority of their fellow-countrymen. In 1912 the General Staff had themselves reported on military grounds against any change in the voluntary system.[2] Haldane met the financial critics within his own party by explaining that, if there were a clear idea of the purpose of the army, it would be possible to save money by cutting down expenditures not relevant to this purpose.[3] He followed Balfour in assuming that the navy protected the country against large-scale invasion. He told the House of Commons on March 8, 1906, that 'if the Army is not wanted for home defence, then its size is something which is capable of being calculated'. He based his own calculation on the size of the expeditionary force which – in addition to the garrisons in India, Egypt, and a few other areas – the army might have to provide. The figures for the expeditionary force – some 5500 officers and 154,000 men[4] – were taken as a maximum number which could be transported rapidly. There was a certain amount of special pleading in

[1] See note at end of this Chapter.

[2] They regarded a change-over in the British military system as unwise during a period of unrest on the Continent, and thought that it might be interpreted as preparation for an aggressive war and might provoke 'preventive' retaliation. Haldane, *Before the War*, pp. 174-5. Haldane took the unusual step of getting Sir Ian Hamilton, who was then Adjutant-General, and Mr (later Sir) Charles Harris, a senior official at the War Office, to write a book (published in 1910) entitled *Compulsory Service*, setting out the arguments against Lord Roberts' proposals.

[3] One small instance of such wasteful expenditure was the maintenance of a number of forts on the North Downs though for many years they had been regarded as useless for the defence of London against an invader.

[4] One cavalry and six infantry divisions. See also below, p. 32. An infantry division was about 18,000, or, including base details, about 20,000 strong. The infantry, artillery, train, and ambulances of a division on the march occupied about 15 miles of road. A cavalry division occupied about $11\frac{1}{2}$ miles. The Expeditionary Force, if aligned on one road, would have stretched from London to Bath. According to Colonel Repington (see below, p. 80) Haldane proposed the title 'Striking Force'. Repington suggested 'Expeditionary Force' as less likely to 'alarm' the left-wing Liberals.

this argument. The figure of the expeditionary force could have been doubled – that is to say, the first 200,000 could have been transported at once, and another 200,000 could have been sent later. The 'size of the army', in effect, depended upon the amount of money which a Liberal government thought fit to allow to it.

Haldane worked out his plans with great skill. He had military backing from a group of younger officers, including Haig, and, although his Conservative predecessors gave him no help – Arnold-Forster attacked his proposals – he could reckon on powerful support from Esher. In addition to providing an expeditionary force, Haldane also reorganised the old Second Line of defence by the creation of a Territorial Army. The Territorial Army was divided into fourteen divisions arranged on a county basis, and a reserve of officers was secured by the formation of Officers' Training Corps at the public schools and universities. Haldane's appeal to local patriotism, and, in particular, to the support of the upper middle and upper classes brought some criticism from the left. Ramsay MacDonald described the county Territorial Associations as 'like an introduction or footnote to Beaconsfield's novels', but the plan worked, and the only alternative to it – some form of compulsory service – would have met with much stronger opposition. Although their obligations were limited to home defence, there was no doubt that, in the event of war, a high proportion of 'Territorials' would volunteer for service abroad. The 'Second Line' would thus provide a reserve for the reinforcement of the regular divisions sent abroad as well as a nucleus of cadres for training recruits.

It is a curious sign of Haldane's concentration on the task in hand – and of Asquith's lack of drive in co-ordinating the work of different Departments – that there was no agreement at the highest level with the Admiralty about the use to which the expeditionary force might be put. Fisher told the Imperial Defence Committee in the autumn of 1908 that the despatch of an expeditionary force to France, if Great Britain were involved, with France, in war against Germany, would be a grave blunder because the force would certainly be captured. Fisher argued that British military action should be limited to coastal raids (he mentioned his own Pomeranian project), the recovery of Heligoland, and the garrisoning of Antwerp. Asquith merely moved the adjournment of the Committee; Fisher was near to retirement and his successor was likely to be readier to accept the military plan. After the appointment of Sir A. K. Wilson as First Sea Lord, Asquith did nothing to ensure that the military and naval views were reconciled. Hence, when at the Agadir crisis in August, 1911, the Committee of Imperial Defence again discussed plans, Sir A. K. Wilson was found to be supporting Fisher's previous view. Haldane insisted on a change, and the Admiralty agreed to protect a landing west – but not east – of Calais. At this time also the Belgians began to fear that an agreement with Great Britain or France would become known to the Germans and would be regarded by them as a breach of Belgian neutrality. The Belgian Government therefore informed the British Government that a landing or other entry into Belgium, except at Belgium invitation, would be resisted as a hostile act.

The lack of any detailed scheme of action – other than one of general co-operation with the French – was shewn at the outbreak of war. The British Cabinet and General Staff still knew nothing, officially, about the French military plans. The General Staff, in the 'non-committal' military conversations with the French, had made contingent arrangements for a landing, but there was extraordinary vagueness on the British side. On August 2 Asquith noted that 'the despatch of the Expeditionary Force to help France is at this moment out of the question, and would serve no object'.[1] Three or four days later when the British Ministers met to discuss whether the Force should be despatched, and where it should go, its Commander-in-Chief, Sir John French, argued at first in favour of Antwerp in order to strengthen the Belgian army and threaten the Germans with an attack in flank. The Cabinet, however, decided to keep to the arrangements made with the French.[2] The French welcomed the British divisions as a reinforcement to their left flank without realising how decisive this reinforcement would be. They had not anticipated a German attack in such strength through Belgium. When the attack came they underestimated its speed and violence. Their own plan was also offensive – an attack in Lorraine on either side of Metz which would breach the German line and dislocate a German advance through Belgium. This plan had been adopted without reference to the British Expeditionary Force – the French indeed had not been able to count upon British support.

Even if they had wanted to do so, the Germans could not have changed their military plans after the entry of Great Britain into the war.

[1] Asquith, *Memories and Reflections*, ii, 9.

[2] French's Antwerp plan was hardly possible at this stage, since (i) the naval arrangements had been based on the assumption that no landing would take place east of Calais, and (ii) the approach to Antwerp by sea was through Dutch waters.

German observers had formed a good opinion of the British army, but regarded it as too small to affect the strategic decision on their western front. The German High Command did not ask the navy to try to interfere with the transport of the British Expeditionary Force across the Channel; they did not expect the force to be transported so quickly, that is to say, in time to affect the encircling movement of the German armies.[1] The German plan, devised by Count Schlieffen,[2] involved the invasion of Belgium; after passing Brussels the right wing, especially strengthened, would turn south-west and advance rapidly to the west of Paris. It would then move to the south-east, and, with other armies which had wheeled on a smaller axis, would drive the French into Switzerland, or towards other German forces in Lorraine. If this movement succeeded, the British divisions would fall into German hands with the defeat of the French. For a similar reason the Germans did not divert troops to capture the Channel ports.

Four divisions of the Expeditionary Force landed in France between August 9 and August 17, and moved forward from their main base at Le Havre to the agreed area of concentration between Le Cateau and Maubeuge.[3] They were engaged at once, and henceforward were fighting or marching almost continuously until mid-November. The battles of these months were very different from the expectations either of the French or the Germans. The pre-war plans of campaign went wrong on each side. The French offensive in Lorraine was defeated, and the Germans, though they came near to carrying out Schlieffen's grand design, did not destroy the French armies. The failure of the German enveloping movement was due partly to the unexpected presence of the B E F in their path, and partly to the neglect of the High Command to subordinate all other dispositions to the strengthening of their right wing. They did not reduce the strength of this wing,[4]

[1] In any case an attempt at interference on a large scale against overwhelming British naval predominance would have been contrary to the plans of the German naval staff. The Germans expected the British landings to take place at Ostend or Calais and were surprised to meet the British force at Mons.

[2] Chief of the German General Staff from 1891 to 1905. For criticism of the plan see G. Ritter, *Staatskunst und Kriegshandwerk*, ii, Chapter 9.

[3] The fifth division was sent on August 20; a sixth arrived on September 16, and a seventh landed at Zeebrugge on October 6–7. An eighth, formed like the seventh, mainly from troops brought back from oversea stations, was in France by November 3. Two Indian divisions arrived in France in October.

[4] The German High Command, however, out of over-confidence, made the mistake of sending on August 25 two corps from the 1st army (on the extreme right) to the Russian front.

but they reinforced their left wing in the hope of a 'double' envelop-ment – a 'pincer' grip encircling almost the whole of the French forces. They also gave up Schlieffen's plan to go west of Paris; they turned south-east again in the hope of destroying the French and British.

The result was that the German outflanking force was itself out-flanked from the west by an improvised French army supported on the east by the BEF.[1] This second stage of the fighting began on September 5, and lasted only until September 13. During these days the Germans retreated from their furthest point of advance; they drew back across the Marne and the Ourcq to the Aisne. The German retreat was an orderly one; it might not have been so if Sir John French had realised what was happening, and had moved the BEF forward more quickly. Once the Germans had reached the Aisne they were in a very strong position from which the Allies could have dis-lodged them only by a wide turning movement from the west. There were no troops available for a movement of this kind.

Thus both the Germans and the French were disappointed. The German failure was the more ominous, since the High Command had calculated on a short war.[2] On the other hand, the French, though their armies had escaped destruction, had lost nearly a tenth of their country, including four-fifths of the coal mines, nearly all the iron resources, and most of the industrial production of the north. For the next two months each side tried to regain the initiative by outflanking the other in the open country between the Oise and the sea. During this third phase of the war of movement the British army was brought back to its original position on the left of the French. Owing to the complicated marches and counter-marches since mid-August it had become wedged between two French armies; the return to the left flank was made in order to shorten its route of supply.[3] Sir John French's insistence on this move turned out to be of the greatest importance. Neither he nor Joffre realised at this time that the Germans were intending the heaviest possible drive towards the Channel ports. The attack began after the reduction of Antwerp. The Germans were compelled to turn aside to

[1] The Germans did not allow sufficiently for the excellent French railways which made possible a rapid move of troops from east to west behind the front.

[2] Molke was quietly replaced by Falkenhayn after the battle of the Marne.

[3] On August 29 during the critical period of the first German advance the British base had been changed from Le Havre to Saint Nazaire. Such was the freedom of movement secured by British sea power that by September 5 all men, horses, and stores had been moved from Rouen and Le Havre. The base was trans-ferred again to Le Havre and Rouen in the latter part of October.

take Antwerp since the Belgian field army – still 65,000 strong – was sheltering behind its fortifications. It is difficult to understand why the Allies did not make an earlier attempt to save this fortress – the obvious bastion for their left flank and for the defence of the Channel ports. In spite of the rapid fall of Liège and Namur, they overestimated the time which Antwerp could hold out, though they knew – or should have known – that for ten years past[1] the Belgians had not regarded the forts as proof against 6-inch shells and that their armament was old and insufficient. The Allies hoped that their own armies in their outflanking movement would reach Antwerp before the Germans. Churchill, indeed, had tried to persuade Kitchener early in September to send British territorial divisions to the place. Only too late – when the German attack had begun, and the Belgian Government had decided to leave for Ostend and to withdraw the field army in the direction of Ghent – the British and French military authorities offered to send over 50,000 troops to assist in the defence. A force of some 12,000 – consisting of British marines and two untrained naval brigades – actually reached the city. Their presence, rather than any material help which they could give, encouraged the Belgians to prolong resistance for another five days.

These five days were of great value to the Allies. Antwerp fell on October 10; the first divisions of the British Expeditionary Force to reach Flanders from the Aisne had not begun to detrain at Abbeville until October 8. Even so, neither the French nor the British High Command grasped the position. They continued hopefully the last phase of their outflanking attempts without even knowing that they themselves were about to be attacked in greatly superior strength. The attack came very near to success on October 31 when the Germans broke through the line of the 1st British division south-east of Ypres, but were driven back by a counter-attack. Again on November 11 a German thrust was met at a critical point by an improvised body, including cooks and transport drivers.

French as well as British troops took part in the defence of Antwerp. It is necessary to remember the smallness of the British Expeditionary Force in relation to the seventy French and seventy-two German divisions on the Western Front. This British force, however, had an importance far exceeding its size. The presence of the British divisions on the French left flank had slowed down the first German drive at the

[1] This fact had become clear after the Japanese had destroyed similar fortifications at Port Arthur.

height of its success; the German commander von Kluck admitted later that the British resistance prevented him from taking Paris. Similarly the British advance across the Marne compelled the Germans to withdraw their extended right wing and to begin a general retreat to the Aisne. The transfer of the British force to the left in October again turned the scale in favour of the defence at the time of the last German drive before the winter.

In each case the decisive contribution of the Expeditionary Force was due to its location and the courage and efficiency of the regimental commanders and men rather than to the strategic ability of its Commander-in-Chief. Sir John French would have withdrawn his whole force behind the Seine during the retreat if Kitchener had not crossed to France on the night of August 31–September 1, and, with the authority of Asquith, Churchill, and Lloyd George, insisted on the maintenance of contact with the French armies.[1] The advance to the Marne was at Joffre's request, and was slower than it need have been owing to French's failure to take full advantage of his opportunity. On October 26, three days before the German thrust to secure the Channel ports, French forecast that the Germans 'were quite incapable of making any strong and sustained attack'.

Fortunately the tactical handling of brigades and battalions, and, above all, of companies, batteries, and platoons, was outstandingly good. The men of the regular British army so much astonished the enemy that he was always overestimating their numbers. A more resolute advance by the Germans might have broken the thin line of resistance in the battle for the Channel ports, but the German commanders could not believe that so few men could fight for so long with such determination; the attackers faltered and hesitated to push their advantage home because they mistook the main force for an outpost system and suspected hidden reserves which in fact did not exist. Earlier the Germans are said to have conjectured from the rapidity and accuracy of British rifle fire that each battalion had more than its actual complement of two machine guns.[2]

[1] There is not, as has sometimes been said, an analogy between French's proposed withdrawal and the action of Gort on May 25, 1940, in ordering a withdrawal to the sea. It is also wrong to infer that the order of the British Government of which Kitchener informed French in fact put Joffre in command of the BEF.

[2] In 1909 the British Army School of Musketry at Hythe had recommended that each battalion should have six machine guns. The recommendation was rejected for financial reasons. The School then decided – as the only alternative –

This predominance against heavy odds was paid for by heavy casualties. At the end of November the survivors of the battalions of the original Expeditionary Force which had fought from the first retreat to the battle of Ypres averaged about one officer and thirty men. It is an exaggeration to say that the old British regular army disappeared in this fighting. The High Command remained, though many staff officers were killed. There were few units which had not suffered so heavily that their identity was almost submerged in the arrival of new drafts. The staff and senior command of the new armies – not in all respects to their advantage – thus continued to be in the control of 'regulars' and there were enough non-commissioned officers to provide an invaluable nucleus for these armies. Nevertheless, as a compact, highly trained instrument, the British army of 1914 was required to sacrifice itself in defeating the German plans for a short war; the courage, skill and discipline with which it fulfilled its duty have never been surpassed.[1]

NOTE TO CHAPTER 2

The defence of Great Britain against invasion

The despatch of the greater part of the regular army overseas had been based on the assumption that the navy could prevent an enemy force larger than 70,000 from landing in Great Britain. Two divisions of the

---

to give special training in order to increase the rate of fire of every man with a rifle. Contrary to the general British view, the Germans began the war with roughly the same proportion of machine guns to their infantry, but they had organised the machine gunners in companies which, by acting together, often gave the impression of a larger total number of guns per 1000 men.

[1] The British casualties on the Western Front to the end of November, 1914, were as follows: killed, 842 officers and 8631 other ranks; wounded, 2097 officers and 37,264 other ranks; missing (including prisoners) 688 officers and 40,432 other ranks. These casualties included those of the Indian Corps. The greater number of casualties were among the infantry (originally 84,000) of the first seven divisions of the Expeditionary Force.

Unnecessary hardship was caused in the first days of the fighting owing to the strict adherence to pre-war regulations by the Royal Army Medical Corps. There were no motor ambulances in the advanced zone and only one at the British Military Hospital at Versailles. An offer by the British Red Cross to send 200 motor ambulances had been refused. An offer of 1000 nurses who might have been stationed on the lines of communication was also refused. Kitchener accepted the Red Cross offers as soon as he heard of them. The American hospital in Paris also provided much help.

Expeditionary Force were, however, held back until Territorial units were considered fit to replace them as an adequate protection against raids. In January, 1916, a conference of naval and military officers was held to review the whole question of the strength of the Home Defence Forces. The conference came to the view that the Germans could reckon on transporting and landing 160,000 men – ten divisions – on the east coast from south of the Wash to Dover, and that the navy might not be able to interfere with the landing effectively for twenty-four hours. The Admiralty accepted these conclusions and the War Office could hardly dispute them. The conclusions, however, required the maintenance of more than 160,000 men in the British Isles, since obviously there would have to be a certain dispersion of the home defence force. Sir John French, who became Commander-in-Chief at home after leaving the Expeditionary Force, asked for a field force of 230,000 men, and 220,000 for 'sedentary' duties, i.e. garrisoning ports and other 'vulnerable points', and anti-aircraft defence. After the rebellion of 1916, an additional 50,000 men were required to provide against internal disturbance in Ireland.

It was not possible to meet these demands in 1916. After the battle of Jutland the naval position was more favourable to Great Britain, but the general estimate of an invading force of 160,000 remained unchanged. Two divisions were withdrawn from home defence early in 1917 and sent to France. At the end of the year the situation had then altered in two respects. The task of finding men for service abroad had become even more pressing, while the difficulties of invasion – from the enemy point of view – had increased. With the entry of the United States into the war there were greater naval resources for discovering and dealing with an enemy convoy. The development of minefields meant that an invading convoy would be delayed by minesweeping, or limited in its direction of approach; a great improvement and extension of air reconnaissances also reduced the chances of surprise. The Admiralty were now willing to lower their figures for a raiding force from 160,000 to 70,000; the War Cabinet therefore reduced by 40,000 the active Home Defence Force.

CHAPTER 3

Trench warfare on the Western Front: failure of the High Command to deal with an unexpected situation

From mid-November, 1914, trench warfare extended along the whole Allied line. Already, before the end of September this type of war had been general between the Aisne and the Swiss border, but each army had regarded it as temporary or local while a decision was being reached in the outflanking movements further north. When these movements failed, there was nothing for it but to dig in on the lines reached from the Aisne to the North Sea. The weather prevented any further attacks on a large scale. From this time until March, 1917, the front lines did not move as much as ten miles in either direction. In any case, each of the belligerents was coming to the end of his resources of ammunition. The common civilian view – not only in Great Britain – had been that, if only for financial reasons, a war between the Great Powers would be short. The General Staffs of the Continental armies had taken the same view for military reasons; the Germans had planned for a rapid victory since they could not otherwise be sure that their victory would be decisive. The French had also based their plans on a rapid offensive. The British General Staff could hardly have held out against this almost unanimous opinion even if they had tried to do so. Their own judgment may be seen in the estimate which they made of the munitions likely to be required by the Expeditionary Force. This estimate provided for four great battles, each of three days, during the first two months of hostilities.[1]

Kitchener – and Haig – thought otherwise, but they had not been closely concerned, in the years immediately before the war, with the larger strategical questions affecting the employment of the Expeditionary Force. In any case, their ideas of a long war had been in terms of the prolongation of 'open' warfare, and not of two armies facing

[1] See also below, pp. 461–2.

each other, month after month, over barriers of trenches extending from the sea to the Jura. The use of the term 'trench' rather than 'siege' warfare had unfortunate consequences on the minds of the British commanders, since British manuals of tactics regarded trench warfare as little different from 'open' war of the old style in which the objective of the infantry was to clear a passage for the cavalry.[1] On the other hand the analogy with siege warfare could not be pressed too far. The trench lines, from 1915 onwards, were more elaborate, and extended in greater depth than the defences of a fortress. Furthermore, once a sizable breach had been made in the defences of a fortress, the place would fall. A besieged garrison had to hold its ground or surrender, whereas a breach in the continuous line of trenches, unless it were both very wide and very deep, might result only in the withdrawal of the enemy to another prepared position in the rear. Thus the process of advance would be a series of minor steps repeated again and again.

Whatever term might be applied to this unexpected development in the war, neither side was fully equipped or trained for it. The Germans were better able to adapt themselves rapidly to it because they had prepared their troops more adequately for the assault of fortifications, and had learned more lessons from a study of the Russo-Japanese and Balkan wars.[2] Thus they had heavy siege guns, mortars, searchlights, grenades, pistol lights, periscopes, and other requirements of siege warfare, though not in sufficient quantity to meet the need of trench fighting over a long period on the whole Western Front. If this situation had not led to such tragic consequences, and to such prolonged suffering and waste of life in all the belligerent armies, there would have been almost an element of comedy in the bewilderment of the professional soldiers. Kitchener's comment to Grey shewed his surprise: 'I don't know what is to be done. This isn't war.' Sir John French was equally naïve: 'I cannot help wondering why none of us realised what the modern rifle, the machine gun, motor traction, the aeroplane, and wireless telegraphy would bring about.'

Sir John French did not get far in his analysis of the problems set by these new instruments of war. The first problem was to devise some means of armoured protection for infantry attacking across an area protected by wire entanglements and covered by the rifle and machine-gun

[1] See B. H. Liddell Hart, *Through the Fog of War*, p. 243.
[2] Especially the successful resistance of the Turks on the Chatalja lines outside Constantinople.

fire of an entrenched enemy.[1] No admiral in the twentieth century would have sent wooden ships against an armoured battle squadron, yet during 1915, and to a large extent throughout the war, the leading professional soldiers of Europe allowed their attacking infantry to cross zones of fire with less protection than their predecessors of the seventeenth century had available for themselves against a very much weaker defence. The second problem involved the exploitation of victory after a breach had been made in the enemy's defence system. This exploitation meant, in effect, a sudden return to open warfare, but not in the conditions envisaged by the textbooks.[2] It meant moving up and bringing into action large numbers of guns, and passing through the gap in the defences large masses of infantry (cavalry were unsuited for the purpose) over broken ground devastated by shell fire and still dominated by the enemy's heavy artillery. Until the last stages of the war the High Command neither solved nor even fully understood this second problem; for too long they did not give urgent consideration to the possibility of using mechanical devices to help in the solution of the first problem. There was indeed no easy answer. Nevertheless the solution should not have seemed beyond the reach of the greatest engineering nation of the world. The charges against the military authorities are not so much that they refused mechanical devices when they were actually put into their hands (though some commanders, not including Haig, were absurdly prejudiced in this respect),[3] but that they did not grasp from the first the problems with which they were faced and insist that their solution should receive the highest priority, and also that, when they were given new weapons, they did not realise the need to think out new tactics for their exploitation. The development of aircraft during the war is in remarkable contrast with the lack of practical imagination on the part of the high authorities responsible for the conduct of the fighting on the ground.

There is less excuse for this failure of imagination because new methods of protecting an attacking force against rifle and machine-gun fire were being explored in Great Britain, though not by the General

[1] General Sir Ian Hamilton, in his evidence to the Royal Commission on the war in South Africa, alone referred to the great difficulty likely to be met in future wars in attacking across a bullet-swept zone. He suggested giving the infantry steel shields on wheels.

[2] See C. R. F. M. Cruttwell, *The role of British strategy in the Great War*, p. 48, and J. Terraine, *Douglas Haig*, pp. 144-5.

[3] Robertson, after the battle of the Somme had reached its third month, described the tanks as 'a somewhat desperate innovation'.

Staff. These new methods were based on two assumptions: (i) that the development of the internal combustion engine had provided means for propelling an armoured vehicle across country (armoured trains were already known but, by definition, ran only on rails); and (ii) that the recently invented caterpillar tractor might solve the special problem of getting these 'self-propelled' armoured vehicles over broken ground. The notion of 'land-cruisers' was not new; H. G. Wells had already imagined them in a novel. There had been more than talk about them. In 1911 an invention had been submitted to the Austro-Hungarian military authorities and rejected by them. Two years later a German inventor had given a demonstration of a 'land-cruiser'. Fortunately for the Allies, the machine did not work. Caterpillar tractors were actually in use for the transport of heavy guns in 1908. In 1912 an Australian engineer sent to the War Office a design for an armoured vehicle which anticipated and to some extent surpassed the plans adopted during the war. The design was put aside because the War Office had no occasion for its use. No more attention was given to it.

The occasion arose, with grim suddenness, in the early winter of 1914. If, at this stage, the matter had been taken up with the resolution shewn nine years earlier by Admiral Fisher in the design and building of an 'all big gun ship', the war might have been shortened, and hundreds of thousands of European lives might have been saved. In the case of the 'Dreadnought', however, the impulsion came from above, whereas the proposals resulting at long last in the 'tanks' were made to the leading military authorities and not by them. In October, 1914, Major E. D. Swinton, a soldier of imagination, and, like Kitchener, an engineer, was at GHQ as an official press representative. He knew of the American Holt tractor. He suggested to GHQ the idea of an armoured machine-gun destroyer which could be driven through wire and across trenches. Swinton also spoke to Lieutenant-Colonel Hankey, secretary of the Committee of Imperial Defence,[1] and made other attempts, most of them unsuccessful, to interest the military authorities in his plan. In January, 1915, he persuaded the Director of Fortifications and Works – the senior post in the Royal Engineers – to set up an informal

[1] Hankey, owing to his 'key' position on the Committee of Imperial Defence, and still more, owing to his alert mind and remarkable organising ability, was throughout the war, and the Peace Conference, a kind of 'universal secretary' who did much to bring order and general over-all supervision into the multifarious war organisations. For Hankey's own account (which, though invaluable, is not distorted by undue modesty) of his work, see his book, *The Supreme Command*, 1914–18, 2 vols, 1961.

committee. The committee observed the trials of a Holt tractor dragging a truck loaded to represent the weight of an armoured fighting vehicle. They regarded the results as disappointing, and gave them no further consideration. Meanwhile Hankey had circulated Swinton's suggestion, with other proposals, to the War Council.[1] Churchill, who read the memorandum, had already asked Rear-Admiral Bacon in October, 1914, to get the Coventry Ordnance Works (of which Bacon was chairman) to adapt for the crossing of trenches a tractor designed to haul 15-inch howitzers. On January 5, 1915, Churchill wrote to Asquith urging the necessity for experiments. Asquith passed the letter to Kitchener. Kitchener handed it to Major-General von Donop, Master-General of the Ordnance, with orders that experiments should be carried out. The War Office did not try Bacon's machine until May, 1915. It then, like the Holt tractor, failed in its tests. For a time nothing more was done about the various projects. Von Donop took little interest in the experiments; he thought that all of them would fail, and did not regard it as his duty to assist in overcoming the causes of failure.

Churchill, however, was undertaking more researches. Before the end of January, 1915, he sanctioned the formation of a 'landships committee' and paid for their experiments out of Admiralty funds. He consulted the Director of Naval Construction, and had experiments made in secret by the Armoured Car Division of the RNAS. They were handicapped because they did not know the requirements of the army; an attempt to elicit these requirements from GHQ brought no answer. Early in June, however, after the collapse of the British attack at Festubert, Swinton submitted another memorandum to GHQ proposing 'armoured, caterpillar-drawn machine-gun destroyers' which would cross 'no-man's land' between the British and German trenches. Later in the month French sent Swinton's memoranda (Swinton had supplemented his proposals with more detail) to the War Office. French suggested consultation with 'some experienced firm' about the possibility of constructing machines on Swinton's plan. Swinton pointed out that the manufacturers so consulted should be told exactly what the machines would be expected to do. He suggested that they should be capable of crossing an 8-foot gap and climbing a parapet 5 feet high. The War Office now got into touch with the Admiralty

---

[1] See below, p. 62. The memorandum is printed in Hankey, op. cit., i, 244–50. For an excellent account of the various proposals out of which the 'tanks' finally emerged, see B. H. Liddell Hart, *The Tanks* (1959), vol. i, Ch. 2.

Committee, which henceforward became a joint naval and military body. Churchill was no longer at the Admiralty, but as a member of the War Committee he used his influence to extend and speed the experiments. In the latter part of July Swinton came home from France to be (in Hankey's absence) acting secretary of the Dardanelles committee. In this key place he was able to steer the experiments in the right direction. The result was that the first completed machine was given an official trial at Hatfield on February 2, 1916, in the presence of Kitchener, Robertson, Balfour, and Lloyd George. The tests were successful. Lloyd George was enthusiastic; Kitchener was not satisfied, and came away before the performance was over. On his way home, he is said to have told Robertson that he had deliberately depreciated the machines because otherwise he was afraid that their existence could not be kept secret.[1] At all events the War Office ordered forty 'tanks'. Swinton persuaded them to raise this figure to a hundred.

There was still little sense of urgency in the War Office and the High Command over the matter. The invention was regarded as a possible auxiliary 'gadget', not as an immense step to victory. The first machines for training were not ready until June, 1916; Haig then wanted to bring them into action without delay. In spite of appeals from Swinton, who had been given charge of training, and in spite of the views of the tank officers themselves – and of Lloyd George – that the secret of its existence should not be given away until the new weapon could be used in large numbers, and until there had been longer study of the technical conditions of its use, Haig insisted on employing the forty-nine tanks available on the Somme battlefield on September 15.[2] He was sufficiently impressed with the result to order 1000 tanks. The Army Council cancelled the order. Lloyd George at once intervened to restore it.

It has been suggested, in excuse for their slowness in applying easily available talent and resources, that in 1914 and the early part of 1915 the military authorities at home were fully occupied with the critical work of supplying munitions; that – in spite of Kitchener's 'long-term' plans – they still expected the war to end in 1915 or 1916, and could not give

[1] Liddell Hart (op. cit., p. 50) doubts whether Kitchener really had this precaution in mind, since he talked about the machines later in disparaging terms to the designers. He seems to have been afraid that the machines would be 'shot up' on a battlefield. The non-committal term 'tank' had been used by their inventors in December, 1915.

[2] See below, pp. 153-4. Only thirty-six tanks actually reached the starting-point of attack.

much thought or divert existing resources to an invention which might not work and, anyhow, could not affect the issue for a good many months. Even if there had been an adequate employment of engineering skill in other fields, this excuse would hardly have been valid. It was not valid at all in another matter which could have been settled far more rapidly. Within the first few weeks of war the military authorities should have realised that the provision of steel helmets would prevent a large number of head wounds, especially those caused by shrapnel bursts in the air. The British military authorities did not draw this obvious inference. The French, however, began to issue helmets to their infantry in the spring of 1915. The British GHQ asked for samples for trial, and were given some 500 at the end of July, 1915. They did not regard the French helmet as adequate, and started experiments in England. A sample was sent to France early in September and GHQ then ordered 50 per battalion. 3500 were received by the end of October, 1915. After further experiments a new pattern was put into manufacture at the end of November. 140,000 had reached France by March, 1916. It was soon found that the number of head wounds fell to less than a quarter of the previous average. GHQ then asked for an accelerated supply, and a million helmets were delivered by July, 1916.

A third example of military dilatoriness was the delay in taking up the Stokes mortar. This instrument was invented by Mr Wilfrid Stokes in January, 1915. The military authorities twice pronounced it dangerous, though they did not themselves set about improving it or producing something better; the trench mortars in use in 1915 were regarded by the infantry as most unreliable.[1] Six months passed before the attention of Major Foulkes, the officer in charge of experiments in chemical warfare in France, was drawn to Mr Stokes' invention.[2] At his suggestion the mortar was adapted to meet the War Office objections, and, in August, 1915 – seven months after the inventor had submitted his idea to the War Office – the first order for 1000 mortars was placed.[3]

[1] The British army had no trench mortars at the outbreak of war. The War Office had rejected a proposal made in 1906, in the light of experience during the Russo-Japanese war, to devise some kind of mortar for the support of infantry.

[2] A divisional officer who had disagreed with the official view, brought a model to France. Haig was impressed with it and ordered further research.

[3] A small Experimental Section of the Royal Engineers formed in June, 1915, did useful work in dealing with inventions and improvements connected with trench warfare. This section was later in close touch with the Ministry of Munitions, but was not officially recognised, and did not receive an 'establishment', until October, 1918. The light automatic Lewis gun came into use in July, 1915.

CHAPTER 4

The higher direction of the war: Asquith and Kitchener

Although the professional soldiers must be blamed primarily for the lack of imagination and initiative in the face of the new problems of trench warfare, it is fair to remember that the Prime Minister and his Cabinet colleagues were responsible to the nation for the conduct of the war, and that, except for Churchill and, fitfully, Lloyd George, the civilian Ministers took little care to ensure that the military authorities were exploring every mechanical aid to victory at the lowest cost in human life.

The Liberal administration in office at the outbreak of war had been elected in December, 1910, on domestic issues, without reference to foreign or military policy. The British electorate had been evenly divided between the two great parties,[1] each of which had secured the same number of seats. The Liberal majority in the House of Commons had been provided by forty-two Labour members and eighty-four Irish nationalists. The Unionists had promised, on August 2, their 'unhesitating support' of the Government if it decided to go to war on the side of France and Russia. This promise had been of value to Asquith in bringing over the doubtful members of his Cabinet to his own policy during the last hours of peace. Asquith indeed appears to have had in mind the possibility of a coalition if the neutralists had been strong enough to break up the Government. Once this danger was over, there was no immediate need and no demand for a coalition. The Liberals had no wish to suggest it; the Unionists at this time would have been most unwilling to join it. Party feeling in the spring and summer of 1914 had been so high that Liberals and Conservatives, Home-rulers and Unionists, could not have worked well together as Ministers.

[1] Liberals, 272, Unionists, 272. (The term 'Unionist' applied between 1886 and 1914 to the coalition of Conservatives and Liberal 'Unionists' who left the Liberal party in opposition to Gladstone's Home Rule Bill. The term 'Conservative and Unionist' was still in use in 1914, but there was no longer any real distinction between the Unionist and Conservative sections of the party.)

F. S. Oliver[1] wrote to Milner on August 5, 1914: 'The conduct of the war by a Government which has so messed and misconceived our domestic situation is not a thing in which I can have supreme confidence.'[2]

The Unionists in Parliament, however, supported Government measures for the prosecution of the war; the Government agreed to set aside controversial legislation, that is to say, the promotion of controversial measures not essential to the attainment of victory, but the Unionists thought that the Liberals took advantage of the informal party truce by putting the Home Rule bill on the Statute book, with a suspensory act delaying its operation until after the war, and a promise that the Government would not use force for the coercion of Ulster. The Unionists anyhow found the party truce unsatisfactory. The situation in the Commons was in many respects as though a coalition existed; on the other hand the Unionists were told little of the Government plans, and their mildest criticisms were resented. The fact that they did not attack the Government openly (as the Liberals had done during the South African war) gave a public impression of acquiescence and even of responsibility for decisions or delays in which they had no part.

In view of their attitude immediately before the outbreak of war, the Labour party was for a time bewildered by events. Grey's speech of August 3 convinced the majority of Labour opinion in the country, but left the party executive in some confusion. On August 5 the executive described the war as due to 'Foreign Ministers pursuing diplomatic politics for the purpose of maintaining a balance of power'. They criticised Grey's policy of *ententes* and said that he had committed the honour of the country to the support of France before the House of Commons had had time to consider the situation. The Labour movement had opposed the policy which had produced the war, and would now concentrate on the restoration of peace and on mitigating destitution while the war lasted. This statement said nothing about winning the war, but it was not a refusal to take a part in it. On the evening of August 5 a majority of Labour members refused to accept MacDonald's proposal that he should speak in the Commons against the Prime Minister's motion for a war credit of £100,000,000. MacDonald then resigned his leadership of the party.[3] He described Grey as 'a menace to

[1] See below, p. 155.

[2] Sir E. Wrench, *Alfred, Lord Milner*, p. 294.

[3] MacDonald and four Liberals – Norman Angell, E. D. Morel, Charles Trevelyan, and A. Ponsonby – formed in 1914 a 'Union of Democratic Control'

the peace of Europe for the last eight years'. He shifted his ground a little as time passed, but remained inconsistent. In July, 1915, he admitted that 'those who can enlist, ought to enlist', yet he would not shew himself on a recruiting platform. Snowden described him as 'dancing around the mulberry bush'.

On August 29 the Parliamentary Labour Party agreed to support recruiting though the executive of the ILP had advised its branches to have nothing to do with it, and had issued a manifesto to the effect that in 'forcing this appalling crime upon the nations, it is the rulers, the diplomats, the militarists who have sealed their doom'. Two months later a majority of Labour members and the Parliamentary Committee of the TUC produced a counterblast to this manifesto. The rift between the minority and majority continued; the minority was divided between a pacifist and what might be called an anti-capitalist revolutionary section. The two sections coalesced only in blaming Great Britain and her Allies for the outbreak of war.[1] As the war went on, the debate about its origins faded out, and was replaced by another debate about the future peace terms; here again there was an opportunity to evade the more urgent matter of winning the war.

With the Conservatives unwilling to attack the Government, and the Labour members in disarray, there was no regular and organised parliamentary Opposition. This lack of opportunity for serious debate on the direction of the war – together with an unimaginative military censorship which concealed information without doing much for military security – gave an unfortunate importance to attacks upon ministerial policy in the press and therefore to a few great newspaper proprietors. Northcliffe, who owned *The Times* as well as the *Daily Mail*, was the most influential and probably the ablest of this small group of men whose intellectual powers and judgment fell far short of the position they had acquired almost accidentally, and for reasons which had nothing to do with their understanding of public affairs. As time passed, Northcliffe became pathologically unbalanced. He was always imprisoned within the closed circle of ideas accepted by the public he

---

with a programme for a more democratic control of foreign policy after the war, and some kind (unspecified) of international organisation to secure disarmament and world peace. Henderson also joined the Union.

[1] A review in the *New Statesman* on February 27, 1915, described an ILP pamphlet on 'How the War came' as shewing that there was 'neither honesty nor intelligence in the pacifist cause'.

was addressing – the *Daily Mail* represented his own mentality. Northcliffe had occasional flashes of insight; in general he did not know what he wanted, if indeed he wanted anything more than to exercise 'influence' and to be known as exercising it. The attitude of the leading politicians towards these newspaper owners differed according to temperament. Asquith, whose faults did not include shoddiness, despised and ignored them until he was forced to take them into account. Lloyd George, who never neglected anyone or anything likely to be of service to him, used the opportunities which the newspaper proprietors offered, but was not afraid to quarrel with them. Bonar Law was generally indifferent, though he happened to be on terms of close personal relationship with Sir Max Aitken, who later became one of them. Balfour, who did not read newspapers, characteristically took care that someone else should read them for him. Churchill, in 1915, was so indignant at the ill-mannered machinations of the ill-mannered 'press lords' – holders of power without responsibility[1] – that he proposed to Asquith the transformation of *The Times* into a 'British Gazette' under official control.

At first the day-to-day direction of the war was left to the Prime Minister and the heads of the service departments, while the Committee of Imperial Defence became a kind of War Council for a number of questions of policy – including home defence. There were no precedents within living memory for the conduct of a great European war; even so, it soon became clear that a Cabinet of over twenty members could not 'direct' anything. One may sympathise with Kitchener's well-known comment that it was 'repugnant to him to have to reveal military secrets to twenty-three gentlemen with whom he was barely acquainted', but the Cabinet could not control or even discuss the war adequately unless they knew these secrets, and Kitchener, who combined in practise the duties of Secretary of State for War and Chief of Staff, did not make matters easier, because, secrets or no secrets, he was clumsy and inexperienced in explaining a plan or a situation to a committee. In November, 1914 – surprisingly late – Asquith set up a special Cabinet Committee for the conduct of the war. This committee, which took over many of the functions of the Imperial Defence Committee, was known as the War Council, and consisted of the Prime Minister, the Secretaries of State for War, Foreign Affairs,

---

[1] Baldwin, a good many years later, used these words about them, with the comment 'the privilege of the harlot through the ages'.

and India, the First Lord of the Admiralty, and the Chancellor of the Exchequer. Balfour, who had been a member of the Imperial Defence Committee from its foundation was asked to join the Council. Lord Haldane and Admiral Sir A. K. Wilson joined it in January, 1915, and other experts were called in when necessary. The new War Council was still too large, and again, owing to Kitchener's secretiveness, spent too much time in argument. There was unnecessary duplication of business because the Cabinet continued to discuss questions which should have been left to the decision of the Council. Hankey, who was the Council's Secretary, has described it as 'a supplement to the Cabinet for exploring some of the larger questions of policy rather than an instrument for the day to day conduct of the war'.[1]

The machinery of direction, if it may be so called, was improved by the appointment of committees for special purposes, notably for the supply of munitions. Nevertheless there was increasing public disquiet over the management of affairs. The successful defence of the west, although at great cost in lives and territory, against the first German onrush was forgotten; the consequences of this German failure could

[1] Hankey, op. cit., i, 238-9. Hankey's examination of the merits and defects of the Council is the most authoritative judgment on its work. He points out that the Council did not meet at regular intervals or work to a fixed agenda. Thus there was no meeting between the end of March and May 14. The Council did not ask for written memoranda or appreciations of the factors involved in a plan or situation from the departments most concerned, the Admiralty, War Office, and Foreign Office. This criticism applied to the departments themselves; the Admiralty did not give the War Office their own detailed appreciation of the problems of a naval attack on the Dardanelles. The Prime Minister, who received all important Foreign Office telegrams, was not sent, as a matter of routine, copies of important telegrams regarding military operations. One of the reasons for the withholding of information was a desire for secrecy. There was, however, far too much leakage of information. Anyone concerned with the security arrangements before the North African landings in 1942 can read only with astonishment the fact that Miss Violet Asquith, who was then under twenty-eight, was told by Churchill, and allowed to divulge to Rupert Brooke and his friends information that the Naval Brigade was to sail to the Dardanelles.

Miss Asquith was the Prime Minister's daughter; she might feel sure that her own close friends would not pass on information, but she knew nothing of the skill with which enemy agents could extract and piece together facts which those who revealed them had no intention of disclosing. On a lower social scale, and in much less discreet company, the table talk recorded by the egregious Colonel Repington in his diary shews the extent of gossip in certain circles in London. Kitchener's secretiveness was increased because he could hardly be unaware of this gossip. Haig, if he wished to talk at table on confidential matters with a guest at GHQ, would have the doors of the room locked after the mess servants had brought in the dishes.

not yet be seen. It was becoming clear that, in spite of the optimism of Sir John French, Kitchener's estimate of a three years' war might not be incorrect. Against this depressing prospect there were a number of major and minor mistakes which critics attributed, not without reason, to a defective and vacillating conduct of the war.

Criticism of the Government became, inevitably, criticism of the Prime Minister, though at this stage the Conservatives would not have accepted any other Liberal than Asquith. Asquith's patriotism, courage, and strength of nerve were never in doubt, but the judicial temper which served him well in peace, was unsuited to the conduct of a war. His handling of the Irish question before August, 1914, had shewn a certain indecision and refusal to face facts. As a national leader he had nothing of the fire and imagination of the elder or the younger Pitt. In his Cabinet he was too ready to allow matters requiring rapid decision to drag on, and to continue peace-time methods of leisurely discussion. Lloyd George complained that Asquith was 'treating the war as if it were Home Rule or Welsh Disestablishment',[1] and that he 'dealt with questions not as they arose, but as they were presented to him – always, essentially the judge'.

Asquith indeed might have been a better, though not an ideal Prime Minister in time of war if his main task had been to guide and restrain a brilliant but impetuous military commander. Lord Kitchener, who became Secretary of State for War on August 6, 1914, was neither brilliant nor impetuous, and needed a Prime Minister different in temper from Asquith. Thus the combination of the two men, however close and confident their mutual relations, did not produce the qualities likely to lead to victory.

The choice of Kitchener as Secretary of State was due in part to an absurd newspaper clamour against Haldane, on the supposed ground of German sympathies. Obviously the Prime Minister, who had taken over the War Office at the time of the Curragh trouble in Ireland, could not continue to combine it with the general direction of the Government. There was much to be said – apart from the unjust attacks on Haldane – for choosing a soldier of great reputation and experience who was well known to the whole Empire. It is also more than doubtful whether any civilian Minister – even Haldane – would have been able to convince his colleagues at once that they must prepare for a long war. In spite of a certain coarseness of feature Kitchener's

---

[1] Lord Riddell, *War Diary*, pp. 65 and 118. Haldane also complained about Asquith's indolence. B. Webb, *Diaries, 1912–14*, June 14, 1915.

appearance was in his favour; his tall figure, his ice-blue eyes,[1] finely shaped head, and strong, determined look, even his aloofness of manner, gave confidence. He was not too old.[2] He was sympathetic to the French; he had joined as a volunteer, while on holiday from Woolwich Academy, the French *Gardes Mobiles* in the Franco-Prussian war.[3] He received a commission in the Royal Engineers in 1871. He could speak French and German, but was not regarded even as shewing 'promise' in other subjects. One reason for his backwardness may have been poor health. He grew stronger and tougher in a hot climate. His early career was in the Near East away from regimental duty on special survey work in Palestine and Cyprus. From 1882 to 1885 he was mainly with the Egyptian army. In 1886 he became Governor of the Eastern Sudan. In 1892, owing largely to Cromer's influence, he was appointed Sirdar of the Egyptian army. He spent four years in preparing this army for active service and between 1896 and 1898 carried out, at small cost to his own forces, the reconquest of the Sudan. He was Commander-in-Chief in South Africa during the latter part of the South African war and in India (where he established a Staff College) from 1902 to 1909. In 1909 he was made a Field-Marshal, and two years later, succeeded Cromer in Egypt. Morley, who was Secretary of State for India during the latter part of Kitchener's command there, admired his judgment and ability, and described him as a 'curious personality, not attractive in manner, but (with) a kind heart buried away somewhere' and with 'inner tastes . . . much more artistic than military'.[4] A less friendly comment on Kitchener was that 'he was never seen to address or even notice a private soldier'.

Kitchener's strong point was organisation. He had won his Egyptian

---

[1] They were affected in later years by long exposure to desert glare and sandstorms.

[2] Horatio Herbert Kitchener was born in Ireland, of English parents, in 1850. His father, Colonel Kitchener, was of a roving disposition, with unconventional ideas about the education of his children. Until 1863 they were taught at home. The family then settled in Switzerland, where Kitchener went first to a French and later to an English school. He worked from 1866 to 1868 under a military coach in London before entering Woolwich as a cadet.

[3] The family had moved from Switzerland to Dinan in France. Kitchener did not take part in the fighting, but nearly died of pleurisy and pneumonia. Churchill has suggested that Kitchener's distrust of the British Territorials was due to his association of the name with the inefficient French 'Territoriales' of the Franco-Prussian war.

[4] Throughout his life Kitchener was a firm High Churchman, and much interested in Biblical archaeology.

victories by careful and deliberate planning. When he had been asked before the battle of Atbara how he proposed to attack, his answer was that he had brought his army 1500 miles and fed it, and that he now expected his generals 'to do the rest'. His training and service had been in the Royal Engineers, and he knew little of tactics. His methodical wearing down of the enemy in the South African war had been mainly a matter of organisation. None the less he had a certain 'intuition' of war; he guessed more clearly than the French General Staff the German plans in 1914. His belief that the war would last at least three years set the scale for the mobilisation of British resources even though he did not always act on his own conclusions. If he was partly responsible for the chances missed at Gallipoli, he was also opposed to making a great attack in France in 1915, before the British armies were fully equipped and trained.

Kitchener's merits outweighed his shortcomings, but these short-comings were serious. Except for the South African war and the years of his command in India, his active life had been spent in the Levant and the Sudan. He knew little of English conditions and of politics.[1] He had worked with men of great ability who had recognised his talents. As a young man he had impressed Gordon. Cromer had the highest opinion of him. On the other hand he had quarrelled with Curzon, the only politician of first rank with whom he had come into close contact. Curzon in 1901, after three months' experience of Kitchener, had remarked on his inability to listen to the other side of a case. 'I never met so concentrated a man. He uses an argument. You answer him. He repeats it. You give a second reply even more cogent than the first. He repeats it again. You demolish him. He repeats it without alteration a third time.'[2]

Kitchener's civilian colleagues found this concentration not merely irksome but dangerous. They were unable to get from him the facts or the judgments which they required before making up their minds. Kitchener, like Haig, could express himself clearly on paper; he was less good at putting his views before a committee. In any case, he was

---

[1] He once asked J. A. Spender whether the *Daily News* was a Liberal or a Conservative paper. In the early part of the war, when he was complaining that the army could not get sufficient meat supplies, he proposed an embargo on meat exports. His colleagues in the Cabinet had the greatest difficulty in making him aware of the facts of an entrepôt trade.

[2] Three months later Curzon's comment was that he was doing his best 'to govern this remarkable phenomenon', but that it was harder to govern Kitchener than to govern India. Sir Philip Magnus, *Kitchener*, p. 203.

never very willing to give information. As Grey wrote later, 'Kitchener did not realise that general responsibility must be shared with the Cabinet, and strategic responsibility with the most independent and expert military brains, organised on a general staff and working with him.'[1] Consequently the Ministers tended to regard him with impatience; impatience developed into suspicion, and suspicion into something like intellectual contempt. Asquith almost alone retained confidence in him, and described him as 'the only soldier with brains since Wolseley'.

Kitchener's position was a difficult one. He was occupying a Cabinet office normally held by a civilian, but neither he nor anyone else could forget that he was also a Field-Marshal. His own comment 'I am put here to conduct a great war, and I have no army' reveals more than his judgment on the unpreparedness of the country. He assumed that he was 'conducting the war'. Neither his Cabinet colleagues nor Sir John French, Commander-in-Chief in the field, took this view. On his visit to France to prevent French from withdrawing his army behind the Seine Kitchener had angered him by appearing at his headquarters not in civilian clothes as Secretary of State for War, but in uniform which emphasised his seniority as a Field-Marshal. At home Fisher at the Admiralty resented the fact that, while Kitchener was a member of the Cabinet, he (Fisher) had to state his views through Churchill.

Kitchener's unwillingness to share responsibility might appear inconsistent with his other habit of leaving subordinates to carry out his orders – orders which were more often verbal than written – but in fact there was no contradiction. It would have been better if Kitchener had interfered more in the matter of general supervision – for example, in the sphere of the department of the Master-General of Ordnance; he had no time to do so because he did not use subordinates in his own proper work. He had always been too much his own Staff Officer. When he took over the War Office, he did nothing to correct the blunder which had allowed the greater number of senior staff officers to go with the Expeditionary Force to France. Hence he could not cope with the problems which faced him. The result was that, first, the control of munitions was taken from him, and then Sir William Robertson was brought back from France as Chief of the Imperial

[1] Grey, *Twenty-Five Years*, ii, 246. Kitchener said to Hankey in September, 1915, that the Ministers could not keep secrets. He added: 'If they will only all divorce their wives, I will tell them everything.' Hankey, op. cit., i, 221. There was good reason for this comment.

General Staff on terms which practically removed from Kitchener the control of operations. Kitchener could not but realise this evidence of disappointment and distrust; he still failed to see that he was himself largely to blame. He complained that 'they (the politicians) want to use my name and deprive me of authority', yet he had not even allowed himself time, or provided himself with the means of understanding the conditions of the 'new warfare'. Haig recorded a visit to Kitchener at the War Office on July 14, 1915:

> We spoke about the nature of the operations in Flanders. Kitchener seemed to me very ignorant of what is being done, and how trenches are attacked, and how bombarded. He admitted that the nature of the modern lines of defence was quite new to him, and he said he 'felt quite at sea on the subject'. I respected him for being so honest. As regards Artillery, he did not know the term 'counter-battery', or how some guns were told off to deal with hostile infantry and some with the hostile guns.[1]

In January, 1915, Curzon summed up in a memorandum to Lansdowne the Conservative disquiet over the higher direction of the war by the Liberal Administration:

> We are expected to give a mute and almost unquestioning support to everything done by the Government; to maintain patriotic silence about the various blunders that have been committed in connexion with the War. . . . The Government are to have all the advantages, while we have all the drawbacks of a Coalition. They tell us nothing or next to nothing of their plans, and yet they pretend our leaders share their knowledge and their responsibility . . . I do not think this state of affairs can continue indefinitely, both because the temper of our party will not long stand it, and because, in the interests of the nation, the position is both highly inexpedient and unfair.[2]

Curzon did not want a coalition; he thought that it would be even more embarrassing to the Conservatives. Lansdowne, Bonar Law, and

[1] This ignorance of the conditions in which the war was being fought had a serious indirect effect on the training of the first 'new armies'. About the date of this conversation between Kitchener and Haig, the writer was attending a month's course for junior field artillery officers at the army gunnery school on Salisbury Plain. The instruction given at the course was good, but it dealt almost entirely with the use of artillery in open or semi-open warfare, and was of little value to the officers concerned when, less than two months later, they found themselves in the Ypres salient.

[2] Lord Newton, *Life of Lord Lansdowne*, pp. 446–8.

Walter Long agreed with Curzon. Lansdowne wrote to Bonar Law: 'We can scarcely leave matters where they are.' Thus, unless there were a sudden and resounding military victory, a political crisis over the higher direction of the war was certain. There was no such victory. Instead, the coincidence of failures on the Western Front and at Gallipoli with an outburst of public impatience at the apparent failure to provide sufficient ammunition for the BEF in France compelled Asquith to agree to a coalition Administration.

PART II

The war outside the Western Front:
British attacks on Turkey:
formation of the first Coalition Ministry

CHAPTER 5

The expedition to Gallipoli: hesitation and delays: the naval attempt to force the Straits: the first landings and the failure to advance

At the end of 1914, after open warfare had come to an end on the Western Front, the British Government could have put forward to the French a claim to a greater share in deciding the future strategy of the war. The British navy had safeguarded the transport of a large force to France, and had enabled the French to concentrate their fleet in the Mediterranean and thereby to secure their communications with North Africa. The British navy had also driven the enemy from the oceans; after the victory of the Falkland Islands, only one German light cruiser, the *Dresden*, was active against Allied shipping. The German High Seas Fleet was in its home ports. The submarine menace was far less severe than in the later periods of the war, and there was no naval reason against landing an expeditionary force anywhere outside the range of German coastal fortifications.

Kitchener had decided at once, on taking over the Secretaryship of State for War, to plan for a war lasting at least three years, and to form a new army of seventy divisions, while keeping up the strength of the existing Regular Army and the Territorial Force. He asked on August 7 for 100,000 volunteers, and obtained them within a few days. By mid-September the number was 500,000. For a time the War Office had to slow down the intake of recruits in order to allow for organising the accommodation, clothing, feeding, and training of this larger number.[1] A month later, when it was clear that the war would last longer than had been commonly expected, a new recruiting drive was

[1] This organisation was not carried out at first with much efficiency. For example, no large contracts for boots were arranged until nearly five weeks after the outbreak of war; meantime the French army authorities had placed orders in England for a million pairs, while the War Office had done nothing either to prevent workers in the industry from enlisting or to provide substitute labour. See also below, Chapters 30 and 31.

begun. Before the end of February, 1915, another 500,000 men had been recruited, and more were continuing to come in. The Territorial Force, which was below establishment on the outbreak of war, soon made up its deficit, and at the end of the year was double its original strength; most of the men who joined it undertook to serve, if required, outside the United Kingdom.[1] Canada, Australia, and New Zealand also promised contingents at the outbreak of war, and sent larger numbers than they had offered – 30,000 sailed from Canada on October 3, and another 30,000 from Australia, with nearly 8500 from New Zealand, later in October when a naval escort was available.

There was also no doubt that British wealth and manufacturing capacity could sustain a long war, secure American credits and, while the navy kept open the routes of supply, make good to France the industrial resources lost to the German invaders. It would therefore have been possible for the British Government, if they had produced a plan, at least to have chosen the field of action most appropriate to their resources. From the Allied point of view the most promising field of action was against Turkey. Turkey had entered the war, suddenly, on October 28, 1914, with a naval attack on Odessa, but the pro-German sympathies of the Young Turks, and especially of their leader Enver Pasha, were well known. The British and French Governments had information, in the first week of August, of a secret treaty, signed on August 1, 1914, by the Turks and the Germans providing for Turkish belligerency in the case of war between Germany and Russia. The entry of the *Goeben* and *Breslau* into Turkish waters[2] provided further evidence of the course which Enver had decided to take. The Turks thought that they had more to gain from a German than from an Allied victory, which, in Turkish eyes, meant a victory for Russia. The alternative to joining the Germans would have been to play for safety by obtaining guarantees from the side of the Entente in return for neutrality.

Apart from their own rashness of temper, the Young Turks were unlikely to choose this alternative. They had been impressed by confident German propaganda and, in spite of the failure of the German army to win a quick decision in the west, expected a German victory. Moreover their entry into the war might make a great contribution to

[1] Twenty-three Territorial battalions went to the Western Front in 1914. Three divisions left for India, and one for Egypt to replace units of the Regular Army.

[2] See below, pp. 170-172.

this victory. They would cut off Russia from access to the Mediterranean for trade and supplies, and compel the British and French to divert troops to Egypt and the Russians to fight in the Caucasus. They would open a way – if (as was likely) Bulgaria could be brought into the war on the German side – for German forces to reach the Persian Gulf. Their support of Germany might cause serious unrest among the Moslem subjects of the Entente Powers.

For all these reasons the Entente Powers – France and Russia as well as Great Britain – had a direct interest in dealing as rapid and as heavy a blow as possible against Turkey. British sea power offered an opportunity for striking at any one of the vulnerable points of the Turkish Empire without employing a dangerously large number of troops – 'dangerously large' in the sense that Great Britain and France could not afford to weaken themselves in the west.[1] The British and French, obviously, had to provide against a renewal of the German offensive on the Western Front. On the other hand the Germans could not bring their whole force, or anything like it, to the Western Front until they had secured themselves against Russia. Even on an unfavourable estimate of Russian powers of resistance, a very strong German concentration in the west was hardly possible before the autumn of 1915; meanwhile the Allies would have a superiority more than sufficient for defence, and increasing as the months passed and the new British armies began to take the field. This superiority was not in itself adequate for a complete victory on the Western Front in 1915; the supply of munitions and other material would not yet allow an offensive on a sufficiently large scale, or so the Allies should have reckoned.

Kitchener indeed did reckon in this way. He wanted a general Allied offensive in the west to be postponed until 1916 when the new British armies would be fully trained, and the supply of material of war very greatly augmented. To the argument that, if the Russians were defeated in the summer of 1915, the Germans could return westward in overwhelming strength, it could well be said that an Allied diversion elsewhere than on the Western Front would be the easiest and least costly way of preventing a possible Russian defeat, and also of compelling the Germans to send troops to the assistance of Austria-Hungary. Such a diversion might shake or even destroy Turkish fighting power,

---

[1] From the Russian angle, as will be seen, the position was different. A British or French attack would divert Turkish forces from the Caucasus and thus allow the Russians to keep larger forces on their own fronts against Germany and Austria-Hungary.

and encourage Greece, Roumania, and possibly Bulgaria to join the Allied side. It was also likely to bring Italy into the war against Austria-Hungary and Germany.

Unfortunately the British Government considered too many plans and did not concentrate decisively and urgently on any one of them. At the end of December, 1914, Colonel Hankey's memorandum[1] had been circulated to the members of the Council at the direction of the Prime Minister. This memorandum pointed out that, unless we could devise some new method for capturing trenches protected by barbed wire and machine guns, we could not break the deadlock on the Western Front, and must therefore look elsewhere. Hankey suggested striking at Germany through her Allies, and especially through Turkey. If we could take Constantinople, we should open a way to supply Russia with munitions, receive from her large quantities of wheat,[2] and release some 350,000 tons of shipping.

Almost at the same time Lloyd George wrote a paper suggesting that the British army should be moved from France (with the exception of a large reserve to be stationed near the coast) and that it should be used for an attack, with Serbian co-operation, on Austria from Salonika or a port such as Ragusa on the Dalmatian coast, together with a subsidiary landing on the coast of Syria to cut Turkish lines of communication with Egypt. Lloyd George hoped for Roumanian and Greek support. He suggested that preliminary steps, such as the collection of transport, could be taken at once before a final decision about the operations. Lloyd George's memorandum was written in terms likely to arouse military opposition, and was not supported by anything more than a superficial study. He ignored, for example, the German advantage of 'interior lines' of communication and the limited capacity of Salonika and other ports. It was therefore easy to raise technical objections to the plan, and by his almost contemptuous language about the operations of the previous months on the Western Front Lloyd George invited hostile criticism.[3]

On the other hand Kitchener was doubtful. He was baffled by a kind of warfare which he did not understand, and could see no answer to the

---

[1] See above, p. 42.

[2] These imports would lead to an improvement in Russian credit.

[3] Galliéni and other influential French generals also proposed an attack from Salonika, but in the direction of Constantinople, and thence along the Danube. They regarded the co-operation of the Balkan states as certain since no one of them could risk isolation.

problem set by it. Neither he nor the Cabinet gave much thought to the proposal to employ new methods to capture trenches. Kitchener wrote to Sir John French on January 2, 1915, that the French staff were probably as much perplexed as ourselves now that they were faced with 'trenches that render attack only a waste of men for a few yards of quite worthless ground'. Kitchener told Sir John French that the 'feeling [in England] was gaining ground that, although it is essential to defend the line we hold, troops over and above what is necessary for that service could be better employed elsewhere'. He added: 'the question of *where* anything effective can be accomplished opens a large field and requires a good deal of study'.

Kitchener asked for the views of Sir John French's staff. If the General Staff had remained at the War Office on the outbreak of war, or if Kitchener had built it up again during the first five months of the war, he might have had reasoned and impartial advice. Sir John French and his headquarters staff were unlikely to look with favour on any plan which would divert reinforcements from themselves. French answered that with sufficient men and munitions he could break through the German lines, but that, if the Germans brought back the bulk of their armies to the west, he would need the strongest possible force to resist an attack.[1] He therefore did not recommend a diversion; if an expedition were sent anywhere, the best place would be Salonika. He regarded an attack on Turkey as unlikely to produce decisive results against Germany. He repeated the views which he had previously expressed that the best plan of all would be an attack in the west, in combination with the fleet, to drive the Germans out of Zeebrugge and Ostend.

This latter plan had already been opposed by Joffre.[2] It was not at once rejected in London, but Joffre's opposition continued, and in any case the attack would have to be made mainly over waterlogged and difficult country, without cover, in which entrenching was hardly

---

[1] On December 28, 1914, he had assured the Cabinet that the French High Command considered that they had sufficient troops to deal with any German attack on the Allied line, and that they did not expect such an attack. His later estimate did not contradict this assurance, since on December 28 he was considering only the immediate future.

[2] Joffre therefore described French's plan as a 'mouvement excentrique', i.e. as unlikely to serve his (Joffre's) main purpose of liberating French territory. He did not realise the strategic importance to Great Britain of gaining the naval bases on the Belgian coast. Moreover at this time he underrated the offensive power of the British army. For Joffre's plan, see below, p. 133.

possible. Kitchener did not favour the Salonika proposal, though he regarded it as less impracticable than an expedition based on a port in the Adriatic. He thought that, owing to the risk of Austrian submarine attack, a landing in the northern part of the Adriatic should not be undertaken unless the heavily defended naval base of Pola had been destroyed. A landing at Ragusa was out of the question. The Austrians could easily wreck the port; even if they failed to do so, the hinterland was extremely difficult, and the roads few. Salonika was a better port; the Allies could use it, however, only if the Greeks joined them. The communications leading into Serbia were scanty; there was a single line of railway, which was vulnerable to destruction by raid unless it were protected by a fairly large force.

The argument about Salonika was not decisive, but already, on the day of Kitchener's letter to Sir John French a new factor appeared in the situation. The British Ambassador at St Petersburg telegraphed to London that the Russian forces in the Caucasus were being threatened by a Turkish enveloping movement; the Grand Duke Nicholas could not send them reinforcements, and had asked the Chief of the British Military Mission whether Lord Kitchener could arrange for some naval or military demonstration to draw Turkish troops away from the Caucasus front. This appeal turned out to be unnecessary; the Russians already knew on January 3, 1915 – though they did not report the fact – that the Turkish plan had failed. The Turks, though they had shown remarkable courage and enterprise, had been unable to sustain an attack in mountain country 500 miles from their base at Konia.

Kitchener, before this Russian appeal reached him, had come to favour an attack at Alexandretta. A British light cruiser had carried out demolitions there without opposition on December 18,[1] but the navy regarded the harbour facilities as inadequate. Kitchener accepted this opinion,[2] and now thought that the only place at which a demonstra-

---

[1] This operation had led to one of the oddest incidents in the war. The landing party, after destroying the railway line north of the town, had ordered the destruction of military stores and of the only two railway engines in the place. The Turks agreed to blow up the engines if the British would provide the explosives. They refused, at first, to allow the British landing party to carry out the work. Finally they agreed on the condition that the British torpedo-lieutenant in charge of the explosives should be rated temporarily as a Turkish naval officer. On these terms a party of Turkish cavalry went to fetch the engines which were duly blown up.

[2] He accepted it somewhat too easily, in view of the ability of the navy soon afterwards to maintain the supplies of the Gallipoli expedition in far more unfavourable conditions.

tion might have any effect would be the Dardanelles. With the approval of Grey and Churchill – though without consulting the Prime Minister or the General Staff – he replied to the Russians through the Foreign Office that we would make a demonstration; we were, however, unable to do anything on a scale likely to induce the enemy to withdraw troops from the Caucasus. On the following day, January 3, Lord Fisher, who had seen the telegram from Russia, wrote one of his impetuous letters to Churchill suggesting an attack on Turkey, with 75,000 trained British troops, and another 25,000 Indians. At the same time the Greeks were to be persuaded to land at Gallipoli, the Bulgarians to attack Adrianople, and the Roumanians to join the Russians and Serbs in an attack on Austria-Hungary.

This fantasy was on a level with Fisher's other ideas about a landing in the Baltic; there was no possibility of finding 75,000 'regular' troops. The proposals for a Balkan coalition took no account of Greco-Bulgarian jealousies. Nevertheless Fisher had made one concluding comment of the greatest importance. He suggested that a squadron of 'obsolete' battleships could force the passage of the Dardanelles. This plan was not altogether wild. The advantages of getting through the Dardanelles were so very obvious that the operation would already have been carried out if the military and naval authorities had thought it feasible. Before the war the General Staff and the Admiralty had examined the possibility of such an operation. In a memorandum of December, 1906, to the Committee of Imperial Defence, they had advised against unaided naval action; the General Staff had been unwilling to recommend the operation even as a joint naval and military affair. The Admiralty, however, had stated that, although the cost would be heavy, a joint operation might succeed. The Committee of Imperial Defence had then decided that the risks were too great and that the operation should not be tried unless, for general reasons, it was essential to attempt it. At the beginning of September, 1914, Churchill, while Kitchener was away in Paris, asked the CIGS to examine, jointly with the Admiralty, the possibility of seizing the Gallipoli peninsula with the help of a Greek army, and then bringing the British fleet into the Sea of Marmora. The General Staff now thought that the operation would not be impossible, but that it would require 60,000 men and a good number of siege guns. Even after Turkey entered the war, there was no possibility of carrying out an attack of this kind since, unless they could get Bulgarian co-operation, the Greeks were unwilling to attack the Turks. On November 3, 1914, the Admiralty, without consulting the Cabinet, ordered a short bombardment of the outer forts of the Dardanelles. They admitted later that this order was a mistake, since it put the enemy on the alert. The Turks were greatly alarmed, and now paid more attention to German advice that they should strengthen the minefields and inner defences of the peninsula and the straits.

The purpose of the bombardment was merely to discover the range of the fortress guns. The operation succeeded within twenty minutes – mainly by two lucky shots – in reducing the fort of Sedd-El-Bahr (at the entrance to the channel).[1] This achievement, which caused more damage than any of the later attacks, seemed to throw doubt on the established view that, even with improved methods of observation, warships were unable to deal adequately with land forts. Furthermore, as Fisher realised, it suggested a use for the considerable number of 'pre-Dreadnought' British and French battleships and cruisers. These ships were unsuited for service with the main fleets or (owing to their comparatively slow speed) for patrol work in areas especially vulnerable to submarine attack. They were, however, heavily armed, and might well be employed against the Turkish forts. Moreover, while the army was extremely short of ammunition, the navy had used far less than they had expected.

On November 25 Churchill had mentioned to the War Council the desirability of capturing the Gallipoli peninsula by a combined operation, but there were no troops available to support a naval attack or to follow it by an advance on Constantinople. Churchill now took up Fisher's proposal for using the older ships, though Fisher himself had made it only as part of a scheme involving military operations on a large scale. On January 3 Churchill telegraphed to Vice-Admiral Carden, who commanded a squadron sent to blockade the Dardanelles,[2] asking whether he thought it possible to force the Straits 'by ships alone', that is to say, by the older battleships. Churchill stated that the 'importance of the result would justify severe loss'.

Carden replied on January 5 that in his opinion the Dardanelles could

[1] The length of the Dardanelles passage is about 41 miles. The width varies from 1600 yards to 4½ miles. The 'narrows' between Chanak and Kilid Bahr are 14 miles from the entrance. See map 5.

[2] The Admiralty had at first proposed – wisely – to give this appointment to Admiral Limpus, who had been Chief of the British Naval Mission to Turkey, and knew more than any other British officer about the Turkish fleet and the Gallipoli defences.

not be 'rushed', but that 'they might be forced by extended operations with large numbers of ships'. On January 7 and 8 the War Council considered the various projects already suggested to it. They regarded the Adriatic proposals as impracticable and decided against the Zeebrugge plan. A landing at Salonika depended upon Greek collaboration, and could also be ruled out for the time. Kitchener gave his opinion that a combined operation against the Dardanelles deserved more study, but that it would require 150,000 men. He now inclined to think that the Germans were intending to attack on the Western Front; he therefore advised that until after this attack no troops should be moved from the west. The War Council accepted Kitchener's judgment. They resolved that the main theatre for the British army should be the Western Front as long as the French required our support, but that, if the defeat of the expected German attack showed that no advance was possible in the west, British troops should undertake operations elsewhere. A sub-committee of the Council, including Kitchener, Lloyd George, Balfour, and Churchill, was set up to consider and prepare plans for such operations.

The War Council had not discussed the feasibility of naval action unsupported by an army at the Dardanelles. Before their next meeting, on January 13, Churchill had received more details from Admiral Carden. Admiral Carden's plan, which was approved, and largely drawn up by his staff, was an attack in four stages: (i) reduction of the forts at the entrance to the Dardanelles; (ii) destruction of the inner defences as far as Kephez Bay (where the channel narrowed before widening again at the entrance to the Narrows proper between Kilid Bahr and Chanak); (iii) reduction of the forts at the Narrows; (iv) clearing the minefield and reduction of the defences beyond the Narrows.[1] Admiral Carden thought the operations might take a month.

[1] The outer and intermediate forts before the Narrows were the least difficult obstacles. The main problems were set by (i) the minefields, especially in the entrance to, and passage of, the Narrows; (ii) mobile guns and howitzers defending the minefields against sweeping, and assisted at night by searchlights. Until the mines were swept ships could not stand in close enough to detect and overwhelm this defence, but the mines could not be cleared while the mine-sweepers were under heavy fire at fairly close range. The trawlers used for sweeping were manned by fishermen with little training for their work; their vessels could move only slowly against the strong current through the Straits from the Sea of Marmora. If the whole operation had been properly studied, combined naval and military action would have been seen as necessary from the start, i.e. a force strong enough to deal with the mobile guns would have been landed to co-operate with the naval attack.

If in the early stages they proved too difficult, they could be regarded merely as a demonstration, and broken off. Fisher raised no objection to this plan; he proposed indeed that the new battleship *Queen Elizabeth*, armed with 15-inch guns, should carry out her gunnery tests by firing at the Dardanelles forts.[1]

Churchill expounded the plan to the War Council on January 13. The Council now showed its lack of resolution. Kitchener again told them that for some months no troops would be available. He did not on this account oppose a naval operation at the Dardanelles. The Council were attracted by the immense possibilities which might follow a successful entry into the Sea of Marmora. They were also reassured by the statement that, if necessary, the operation could be broken off. They resolved that the Admiralty should consider promptly the possibility of effective action in the Adriatic at Cattaro or elsewhere, with a view (*inter alia*) to bringing pressure on Italy to enter the war, and should 'also prepare for a naval expedition in February to bombard and take the Gallipoli peninsula, with Constantinople as its objective'.

This resolution was no credit to the eminent men who drafted and accepted it. The Adriatic plan, as a large-scale operation, had already been discarded; it was not clear what was meant by 'effective action'. A bombardment, without a landing, would have little effect on the general position of Austria-Hungary. The second half of the resolution was even more dangerously worded. A naval expedition could 'take' neither the Gallipoli peninsula nor Constantinople. It might smash the Dardanelles forts, but there was no reason to suppose that its arrival off the Golden Horn would cause the Turks to surrender. The fleet could hardly go to the extreme step of compelling this surrender by the bombardment of Constantinople, and indeed, if the Turkish army had been withdrawn, and the city thereby left an 'open town', a bombardment would have been contrary to international law.[2] In any case, without a military occupation of the Gallipoli peninsula and the expulsion of the Turkish forces, the Turks would continue to hold both sides of the Straits and would therefore be able greatly to hamper, if not to prevent, supplies from reaching the fleet. No one appears to have raised the pertinent question whether it would be possible to break off

---

[1] A decision had already been taken that the ship should undertake her gunnery tests in the Mediterranean.

[2] The only Turkish gun and rifle factory was in a suburb of the city, and the only shell and small arms factory just outside it.

the operation, except at the earliest stage, without loss of prestige and serious diplomatic consequences in the Balkans.

Even so, the Council was not agreed about the meaning of its own resolution. The Prime Minister thought he had sanctioned merely the 'preparation' of an expedition. Churchill took the view that the Council had approved of a 'principle', with 'general knowledge' of the method by which it was to be put into effect. Lord Crewe and others considered that they had approved of the operation, subject to any change owing to unforeseen conditions. Fisher and Admiral Wilson had left the Council room before the resolution was read out. The confusion of mind and lack of direction were also shown by the fact that at this meeting of January 13 the Council changed, or rather 'half-changed' its mind over Sir John French's plan for an attack along the Belgian coast. French had come to London to press this plan. The Council agreed that preparations should be made for it, but gave no final decision.

Churchill, therefore, in telling Admiral Carden that his plan was approved in principle, and in ordering a closer study of the proposed attack on the assumption that the principle was settled, went beyond the view of the Prime Minister and some at least of his colleagues. Churchill committed them further when he wrote to the Grand Duke Nicholas on January 19 that 'it has been determined to attempt to force the Dardanelles by naval force. . . . It is our intention to press the matter to a conclusion.'

On January 20 Churchill suggested to Kitchener that a landing should be made at Alexandretta at the same time as the attack on the Dardanelles; if the latter attack had to be called off, it would appear to have been merely a feint to cover the landing on the coast of Asia Minor. The Admiralty wished to begin the bombardment on February 15. Kitchener answered that he would have no troops available on that date. This answer was consistent with his earlier statements. Meanwhile Fisher was beginning to doubt the feasibility of the whole plan. He would not give up his Baltic project; he had opposed a reconsideration of the Zeebrugge plan on the ground that the operation might well cause the loss of ships' crews. This same argument applied even more strongly to the risk of losses in the Dardanelles. The old ships were of little value, but if they were blown up, their officers and men would be lost and could not be replaced.

The War Council met again on January 28. Kitchener said that the naval attack was of vital importance, and that its success would be equivalent to a successful campaign by the new armies. Churchill repeated that the naval Commander-in-Chief believed that the operation could be carried out and that it would take three weeks or a month. He said that the ships were already on their way. At this point in the discussion Fisher almost resigned, but was persuaded by Kitchener, and later by Churchill, to give his 'reluctant' consent. As he explained afterwards, it was extremely difficult for him, in view of the general attitude of the Council, 'to forbid, before it had been tried, an experiment on which rested so many sanguine hopes'. At a second meeting of the War Council on January 28, final approval was given to the naval operation, and, again, Constantinople was stated, vaguely, to be its ultimate objective.

If the enterprise had now been pushed ahead with determination, it might have succeeded. Once more the British Government failed to concentrate on a single plan. The sub-committee appointed by the War Council on January 8 had reported in favour of a landing at Salonika as the best method of helping the Serbs. The latter had defeated a second Austrian attack in December, 1914, but at great loss to themselves; there was doubt whether they could resist another invasion.[1] The question of providing the necessary forces for an operation outside the Western Front had also changed. Joffre had finally rejected Sir John French's Zeebrugge plan; it was therefore unnecessary to send Sir John French the reinforcements – four divisions – required for this purpose. The French High Command were, however, as unwilling as Kitchener and Sir John to move troops from France or even to give up a claim on the four divisions. After much discussion the British and French Commanders-in-Chief agreed to allow two of the promised divisions to be withdrawn from France in March.

On February 9 the War Council heard that Bulgaria had accepted a loan from Germany. This fact showed that Bulgaria was likely to enter the war on the German side;[2] the need to help Serbia thus became more

[1] Such an attack was unlikely in mid-winter, or, in any case, while the Austro-Hungarian armies were deeply engaged against Russia.

[2] The Foreign Office made great efforts to keep Bulgaria from entering the war on the German side, but it is very doubtful whether anything less than a decisive success at the Dardanelles would have won Bulgaria over to the side of the Entente Powers. King Ferdinand of Bulgaria – 'Foxy Ferdinand' – was German; he wanted and expected a German victory. Moreover after the Balkan wars of 1912-13 Bulgaria had claims against her neighbours, and especially against Serbia and Greece. She wanted a port on the Aegean and parts of Macedonia. Greece would not allow her to take Kavalla, and Serbia would not give up Monastir. In spite of the almost hopeless position of their armies in the event of a Bulgarian as well as another Austrian attack (probably with German help) the

urgent. After more discussion with the French it was agreed that, if Greece would join the Allies, one French and one British division would be sent to Salonika. This offer was too small to satisfy the Greeks, though they were willing to accept it if Roumania could be induced to come into the war. Owing to the Russian retirement on their south-eastern front Roumania would certainly refuse. Hence, after February 15, when the Greek reply was received, the Salonika project was again deferred.

Nearly three weeks had passed since the decision to attack the Dardanelles; the naval bombardment was soon to begin. The War Council, which had accepted Kitchener's view that no troops could be spared for Gallipoli, had found meanwhile that two divisions were available, though they had proposed to use them not to support and follow up the forcing of the Dardanelles, but on another enterprise. Naval opinion, however, was becoming more doubtful of the chances of success without the assistance of troops. If, as it was now seen, troops were available, they should be sent to Gallipoli. In any case it was realised – too late – that unless the Turkish field army were driven from the peninsula, the Straits would still be impassable by any vessels other than heavily armoured ships of war.

These arguments impressed the War Council. It is hardly credible that they had not been considered earlier. On February 16 the Council decided to prepare a military force; the 29th Division – the only available 'regular' division – was to sail, if possible, within nine or ten days to Mudros. Arrangements were to be made for further support, if required, from Egypt. This force was to be 'available in case of necessity to support the naval attack on the Dardanelles'.

What was meant by 'support'? Were the troops to land before, during, or after the reduction of the forts? Were they to land if the naval operation was not successful? If a large body of troops were

---

Serbian Government persisted in refusing all except very minor concessions, although Great Britain and France had promised the Serbians large territorial increases at the expense of Austria-Hungary. The Allies also offered their good offices after the war in persuading Greece to give up Kavalla in return for territorial compensation in Asia Minor. At the beginning of September, 1915, the Serbian Government, under protest, finally offered a small section of Macedonia to Bulgaria after the war. The Bulgarians, however, while they were negotiating with the Allies, had already sent a special envoy to Berlin to sign a convention with the Central Powers. This convention was signed on September 6. See also below, p. 88.

collected in the neighbourhood of the Dardanelles, would it be possible, without the most damaging effect upon Allied prestige, to break off the operation? Since the troops could not arrive for a month, was it not advisable to postpone the naval bombardment? Not one of these questions was given adequate consideration. The General Staff was not asked to work out preliminary plans for the use of the troops, or even told, officially, until March 11, that large military operations were to be undertaken at the Dardanelles.[1]

On February 19 Kitchener again changed his mind. He said that, owing to the grave news from Russia,[2] he was once more afraid that the Germans would be able to mass troops in the west. He could not therefore allow the 29th Division to go to the Dardanelles, but suggested that the Australian and New Zealand divisions in Egypt might be sent, and might reach the Dardanelles more quickly. These divisions were short of equipment and ammunition; Kitchener also overlooked the obvious fact that the transports to take the divisions in Egypt to Mudros would have to come from Great Britain.

Kitchener refused to give way about the 29th Division. He still thought in terms of a naval reduction of the forts, and believed that, if the fleet reached the Sea of Marmora, the Turks would have to evacuate the peninsula, since they might otherwise be cut off at the Isthmus of Bulair. Nevertheless Kitchener asked General Birdwood,[3] commander of the Australian and New Zealand force, to report on the number of troops required. Meanwhile the naval bombardment had begun. With the support of Kitchener, Grey, and Churchill, the War Council now decided that failure would have disastrous effects, and that, if naval action alone did not succeed, the army must be used. Lloyd George agreed about the consequences of failure, but thought that the army might be better employed elsewhere in the Near East, and not necessarily at the Dardanelles. His argument might have carried more weight if he had been able to suggest an alternative operation which was immediately practicable.

The naval attack had opened on February 19. In spite of bad weather a certain amount of success was obtained, and, until the end of February, small parties of marines were able to land and to blow up the guns in the

[1] It is even more astonishing that although the CIGS (Lieutenant-General Sir J. W. Murray) was present at all the meetings of the War Council, he made no comment at them, gave no instructions to his subordinates to work out any plans, and was not asked to do so by Kitchener.

[2] I.e. successful German and Austrian attacks on the ill-equipped Russians.

[3] Birdwood had served as Kitchener's Military Secretary in India.

abandoned forts of the outer defences.[1] From the begining of March the Turks began to put up entanglements and to construct trenches. Moreover the naval bombardment was having less effect on the inter-mediate defences. The operation, however, had already produced one important political consequence which might well have had a decisive result on the Gallipoli enterprise and thereby on the whole course of the war. On March 1 Venizelos proposed that the Greeks should enter the war at once, and should land three divisions on the Gallipoli peninsula. On the following day the Russian Government told the Russian Minister at Athens and the Russian Ambassadors in London and Paris that 'in no circumstances' could they 'allow Greek forces to participate in the Allied attack on Constantinople'. This veto – due to Russian fears that the Greeks might claim Constantinople for themselves – caused King Constantine and the Greek general staff to reject Venizelos' proposal. Within eleven days the Russians had secured from Great Britain and France a secret promise of Constantinople if they fought the war to a successful end. By their veto of March 2 they had ruined their own chances of fighting the war to a successful end, and had negotiated away the Tsarist regime.

General Birdwood reported to Kitchener on March 4 and 5 that he did not expect the fleet to master the Straits without a military landing, and that a large force would be needed. For a time Kitchener still thought that the navy would get through the Straits, and that the army would be required only to hold the Isthmus of Bulair after the Turks had evacuated the peninsula. On March 9 Admiral Carden decided that he could do no more until his air service was reinforced.[2] In view of Birdwood's report and of the delay in the naval operation Kitchener now realised that the land force would have to be large. He agreed on March 10 to send the 29th Division, but the transports to carry it had gone to Egypt to take the Australian and New Zealand divisions. No other ships were available until March 15. Preparations were made

[1] A party of thirty men moved about unopposed at the point where, two months later, the 29th Division lost 3000 between landing and nightfall.

[2] Until the end of March, 1915, the navy had only eight machines for reconais-sance at the Dardanelles. Two were aeroplanes which could not be used for lack of a suitable landing ground; six were seaplanes which could take off only in smooth water and had to fly low owing to their weak engines. There were no trained observers; wireless communication and air photography had not yet been much developed and the maps of the peninsula were inaccurate. Kitchener had refused to send military machines when the operations were purely naval. Good air photographs of the Turkish defences were, however, available before the landings.

for the embarkation of the division.[1] General Sir Ian Hamilton was appointed to command what was now becoming an expeditionary force of considerable size.

Sir Ian Hamilton was sixty-two years old. The greater part of his military career had been in India, where Roberts had noticed his abilities, and taken him on his staff. He was chief of a British military mission with the Japanese army in the field during the Russo-Japanese war, and thus had experience of 'modern' war. Kitchener had thought of substituting him for French as Commander-in-Chief of the BEF in October, 1914. It is doubtful, however, whether, in spite of his ability, he was really fitted for high command. He was too optimistic, and not strong enough in character to assert his authority and to get sufficient 'drive' from less competent subordinates.

Hamilton left London on March 13 without a complete staff. He was given long and somewhat vague instructions, but no definite plan. No plans indeed had been made for using the army now being assembled. Kitchener continued to hope that only minor operations would be necessary.[2] The commander of the army arrived on March 18 in time to watch from a light cruiser the heaviest of the naval assaults. The bombardment, once again, was fairly successful, but two old British battleships and one French battleship were sunk by mines; another French battleship ran ashore and the British cruiser *Inflexible* – a modern ship – was disabled. It was assumed at the time that these mines were floated down from above the Narrows. In fact they were on a line of mines running parallel to the Asiatic shore, and therefore undetected in the sweeping operations which had dealt with mines laid across the Straits. The risk of further loss was much less than was supposed. The Turks had a reserve only of twenty mines, and had

[1] These preparations again showed the dangers of Kitchener's methods of over-centralisation, and also the lack of elementary information in the Intelligence section of the General Staff. Kitchener was told by General Maxwell, Commander-in-Chief in Egypt, that pack transport would be necessary, since there appeared to be no suitable roads on the peninsula. Kitchener did not pass on this message. The 29th Division had been equipped with 3-ton motor lorries for service in France. On enquiry at the War Office whether these lorries would be of use at Gallipoli the Intelligence section replied that they did not know.

[2] Hamilton's instructions were headed 'Constantinople Expeditionary Force'. He asked Kitchener to choose a less ambitious title 'in order to avoid Fate's evil eye'. Kitchener was unable to provide Hamilton with anything more than a few old books on the Turkish army and a map which turned out to be inaccurate. The War Office did not know how many enemy troops were on the peninsula or the names of the Turkish or German commanders.

fired most of their ammunition. Another attack might well have completed the destruction of the forts, but on March 22 Admiral de Robeck (who was in command of the fleet owing to the illness of Admiral Carden) decided that he could not get through to the Sea of Marmora without the help of the army. Hamilton agreed with him, and the two commanders telegraphed that the landing of the troops would have to be undertaken 'in the teeth of strenuous opposition'.

Thus, instead of a naval attack opening the way for the army, the army was now to come to the assistance of the fleet. Churchill thought that the fleet should make another attempt, but the Admiralty supported the views of de Robeck and Hamilton. The War Council could hardly reject the considered judgment of their experts. On March 16, Hankey had written a memorandum for the Prime Minister calling attention to the difficulty of a landing when all chance of surprise had been lost. Hankey pointed out that combined operations needed the most careful preparation, and that the War Council ought to assure themselves that the details had been thoroughly worked out. He included a list of questions upon which it was desirable 'to cross-examine the naval and military authorities', and ended with a warning that unless these and other questions had been fully thought out,' 'it is conceivable that a serious disaster may occur'.[1]

On March 19, though the War Council were still expecting the naval attack to succeed, the Prime Minister asked Kitchener whether a scheme for a landing had been worked out. Kitchener's answer was that there was not enough information at home for the preparation of a detailed scheme, and that the work would have to be done on the spot. The Prime Minister and his colleagues accepted this reply, though it did not meet the large points raised in Hankey's memorandum.[2]

---

[1] According to Hankey as late as April 6 Churchill's view was that there would be no difficulty in landing on the peninsula. (Hankey, op. cit., i, 300). On April 19 Hankey thought Churchill 'extraordinarily optimistic'.

[2] e.g. the supply of boats, lighters, and tugs, and the provision of landing piers, pontoons, etc. In fact, no arrangements were made at home for supplying tugs and lighters, and the supply was limited to the craft which the authorities could buy locally at Mediterranean ports. The material for improvising piers was also obtained and made up locally. The Expeditionary Force, which needed a large number of technicians and skilled workers, was given no more than the usual divisional field companies of engineers. The transports carrying the 29th Division were hastily loaded in England, without reference to the possibility of a landing on hostile territory. Hence they had to be unloaded, sorted out, and reloaded in Alexandria. The ammunition of the 29th Division's ammunition column was not even

The War Council finally committed themselves on March 27 to the views of de Robeck and Hamilton. The landings at Gallipoli were not made until April 25. The delay was inevitable because the preparations of which Hankey wrote had not been made. Even if the invading force had been marshalled earlier, the weather in April was so bad that a landing could not have been carried out, or the troops supplied, on open beaches.[1] The month's respite, however, was invaluable for the Turks and their German advisers. The Turks had been thoroughly frightened at their narrow escape on March 18, and had decided on March 24 to put their forces at the Dardanelles under the command of General Liman von Sanders. Liman arrived at Gallipoli on March 26. He decided at once to reorganise the whole defence scheme; during the four weeks before the landing he constructed elaborate defence lines – including wire under the water at likely points.[2] He also trained the Turkish troops in bombing and rifle fire and in the manœuvres required for rapid concentration. Against these enemy preparations the landing force had little protection during their dangerous move from the transports to the shore. There is no excuse for one official refusal which cost many lives. Admiral Fisher had been preparing large flat-bottomed boats, each with a carrying capacity of 500 men, for his projected Baltic scheme. These boats had steel-plated sides and decks and were proof against bullets and shrapnel. Some, though not all of them, were ready in March, 1915. Hamilton heard of them by chance through one of his staff. He could not ask directly for them, because their preparation had been kept secret, but he enquired whether the Admiralty could supply them. Kitchener answered that they could not be provided, and Hamilton accepted this reply.[3]

Even with the chances against them, the landings might have succeeded. The plan was to land at five different points on the southern end of the peninsula. Two of them were on beaches where an attack

---

located until this work of resorting had gone on for a week. In general the expedition was fitted out not for trench but for mobile warfare.

[1] Although the weather was unusually bad, the War Council and their military advisers should have known much earlier that March and April were normally unsettled months in the Aegean area, and that continuous spells of fine weather could not be reckoned on until the beginning of May.

[2] There are only small tides, and therefore no appreciable changes in the high-water lines in the Aegean. For the landing beaches, see map 5.

[3] These lighters, known as 'beetles' from their black-painted sides and the projecting arms of their landing ramps, were sent out later for the landing at Suvla Bay.

would certainly be expected. At one of them – Y beach – there was no opposition; the troops were sitting around while to the south of them their comrades, after heavy losses, were barely able to hold narrow strips of land. Commodore Keyes, who was de Robeck's Chief of Staff, at once suggested that the reserves should be sent to Y beach. He repeated this advice later in the day, but Hamilton would not interfere with the plans of his divisional commander further south, although obviously the situation could be judged only by a commander who knew what was happening on all the beaches. The easternmost landing also met with little opposition and if advantage had been taken of these two opportunities, the Turks might have been attacked from the rear.

Meanwhile the Australian and New Zealand Army Corps had been given a separate objective. After landing some ten miles north of Y beach they were to push eastwards and to cut the Turkish communications. Owing to insufficient allowance for the strong northerly current up the coast they were put ashore about a mile too far north at points where the broken nature of the ground made progress inland especially difficult. The 'Anzacs' nearly succeeded, but were held along a line of about $1\frac{1}{2}$ miles nowhere more than 1000 yards from the shore.

In spite of the superb efforts of the troops engaged, Hamilton's forces on May 8, the fourteenth day after their landing, had suffered heavy casualties and made little progress. Under better tactical direction the attacks on May 6, 7, and 8, over a three-mile front, might have succeeded, but the High Command still did not understand that a daylight advance, without the strongest artillery preparation, against unlocated machine gun positions was an impossible task for the bravest of men.[1]

The British Government had now to decide what they would do. They could withdraw from the peninsula and abandon the campaign, but only with serious political consequences. They could send large reinforcements, and make another attack on the Turkish positions; the reinforcements, however, were needed in France if the policy of attack on the Western Front were to be continued. Kitchener, in view of the Russian defeats in Galicia, thought that the Germans would be able to

[1] The infantry, in the fighting of May 6–8 at Gallipoli, was supported by 15,500 rounds of shell fire (mainly field gun shrapnel, but including heavier shells from naval guns). The artillery had very little help from air observation during this engagement.

bring troops to the west and might even attempt an invasion on the east coast of England while the country had sent nearly all its fully trained and equipped men overseas. A third plan would be to provide reinforcements sufficient to maintain the strength of Hamilton's army, and to add a division to it.[1] Although a grand attack would not be possible, the army might hope to make progress slowly. Hamilton himself had indeed suggested this plan in a telegram of May 10 to Kitchener. The War Council discussed these different possibilities on May 14.[2] They asked Kitchener to enquire how many divisions Hamilton would need for a rapid decision, that is to say, for a large-scale attack. Hamilton replied on May 17 that, if the Russians could land an army corps on the shores of the Bosphorus, and if Greece or Bulgaria declared war on Turkey, he would need two divisions; otherwise he would want four. A political crisis at home now occupied the minds of the Prime Minister and his colleagues. For three weeks no decision was taken about Gallipoli; during this time the Turks, far from 'getting demoralised', were strengthening their defences.

On May 9, the day after the failure in Gallipoli, three corps of the British army in France attacked the German lines at Aubers Ridge. The offensive was supported by 600 guns, firing 80,000 rounds. The attack – at a cost of over 11,500 casualties – was beaten back. It was abandoned at nightfall, and not resumed. The artillery had not enough shells for another heavy bombardment; in any case there would have been little chance of gaining more than a local success. If the guns and shells, and the additional divisions had been at Gallipoli, the course of the war might well have been altered.

[1] This division had already been promised to Hamilton.

[2] A fourth plan advocated by Keyes was an immediate resumption of the naval attack. Keyes argued that most of the guns protecting the minefields would have been removed to assist the Turkish field army. (This, in fact, was the case.) Admiral de Robeck, however, with the agreement of the Admiralty, thought that the risks to the army if the fleet suffered further heavy losses, were too great. Three battleships were lost during the next month; it is unlikely that there would have been heavier losses if an attempt had been made to get through to the Sea of Marmora. In June and July there was heavy but inconclusive fighting on the Helles front; British casualties in these all too familiar attempts to send men against machine guns were about 16,000; the Turks suffered more heavily in their attacks but were more easily reinforced.

CHAPTER 6

The political crisis of May, 1915, and the formation of the first Coalition Ministry: unsuccessful attacks at Gallipoli: the evacuation of the peninsula

On May 14 Admiral Fisher, who had become increasingly uneasy over the risks involved in further naval action at the Dardanelles, agreed reluctantly to send four cruisers and some smaller craft to join the fleet there. Next morning he received from Churchill, for discussion or formal approval, an order considerably increasing the amount, in ships and material, of these reinforcements. Fisher at once resigned in his usual dramatic way. He left a note at the Prime Minister's house and then disappeared from the Admiralty without mentioning an address, although he took care to see Lloyd George and to give him a message for Bonar Law suggesting that the House of Commons should discuss his reasons for resignation, and warning all and sundry that a great national disaster was 'very near' at the Dardanelles. He also made it clear that he was totally opposed to Churchill's policy, and could not work with him.[1]

At this same time public opinion was suddenly alarmed by reports of a grave shortage of shells on the Western Front owing – so it was alleged – to the incompetence of the Government.[2] Every soldier was aware that there was not enough ammunition. The astonishing fact is that, in spite of the narrow limits of supply, Sir John French should have contemplated any attacks. Kitchener had told French on January 9, 1915, that it was impossible to maintain a supply of shells on the scale which he (French) considered necessary for an offensive, and that, unless he could accumulate a sufficient reserve, he would be unwise 'to embark on extensive offensive operations against the enemy's trenches'.

[1] Fisher, tracked down to the Charing Cross Hotel (near the Admiralty), and ordered back to his post by Asquith, proposed impossible conditions for the withdrawal of his resignation. He refused to serve under Balfour and demanded almost absolute powers for himself. Asquith, in writing to the King, said that Fisher's attitude shewed signs of 'mental aberration'.

[2] For the action taken (down to the establishment of the Ministry of Munitions) to increase the supply of guns and ammunition, see below, Chapter 30.

Kitchener pointed out that the duration of an attack could not be determined in advance, and that the effect of bringing it to an end, owing to a shortage of ammunition, before the objectives had been secured, might result 'in a serious reverse'. French had taken too little notice of this warning when he attacked in March, yet, after the failure at Neuve Chapelle and the heavy fighting at Ypres, he attacked again at Aubers Ridge and Festubert in May. He even assured Kitchener on April 14 that 'with the present supply of ammunition' he would have 'as much as his troops will be able to use on the next forward movement'.[1] He repeated this assurance on May 2. In spite of these assurances French, after the defeat of his attack at Festubert, gave an interview to Colonel Repington (the military correspondent of *The Times*) and sent two officers from his personal staff to London to see Lloyd George, Northcliffe,[2] the Conservative party leaders, and others in order to stir up a campaign against Kitchener. Repington knew nothing of French's statement of May 2. He had already telegraphed on May 12 to *The Times* that 'the want of an unlimited supply of high explosive shells was a fatal bar to our success'. French did not see this telegram before it was sent, though he told Repington that he approved of it. *The Times* published the telegram on May 14 and commented in a leading article that 'British soldiers died in vain on Aubers Ridge on

---

[1] French later denied that he had given Kitchener any such assurance. It is, however, most unlikely that Kitchener would have reported it to the Prime Minister in a letter of April 14 if he had not been certain of French's words. Moreover French's written statement of May 2 contained the words 'the ammunition will be alright'. French, who, as usual, was over-confident, may have wanted to convince Kitchener, who remained more than doubtful, that an offensive was justified; he may therefore have continued to ask urgently for an increase in the supply of ammunition while at the same time asserting that he had accumulated enough for the proposed attack.

Lloyd George (*War Memoirs*, i, 201) accuses Kitchener of concealing information about the shortage of shells from him even when he was chairman of the Treasury Munitions Committee (see below, p. 465). There seems no doubt that Lloyd George did not know the facts. Repington was astonished at his ignorance. It may well be that Lloyd George had not asked Kitchener for information; Kitchener, in view of his unwillingness to impart military information to his civilian colleagues, and in view of his distrust of Lloyd George, was unlikely to have volunteered information unless he had been asked for it. Kitchener had said in the House of Lords on March 15 that the output of war material 'is not only not equal to our necessities but does not fulfil our expectations, for a very large number of our orders have not been completed by the dates on which they were promised'. Parl. Deb., 5th Ser., H. of L., vol 18, col. 721.

[2] Northcliffe had earlier suggested to French that he should bring pressure on Kitchener and the Cabinet not to divert troops and munitions to the Dardanelles.

(May 9) because more shells were needed. The Government, who have so seriously failed to organise adequately our national resources, must bear their share of the grave responsibility.'

This charge was the more alarming to the public because the Prime Minister, on the strength of Kitchener's report that Sir John French had enough ammunition, had stated in a speech at Newcastle on April 20 that there was no shortage. It is characteristic of Asquith, whatever his short-comings as Prime Minister, that he did not defend himself, as he easily could have done, by quoting Kitchener's letter of April 14.[1] Northcliffe, however, weakened the effect of his criticism of the Government by directing a personal attack against Kitchener. Kitchener still held popu-lar confidence, and the Ministers, including Lloyd George, who were exasperated by his methods and now doubtful of his fitness for his post, had no other soldier to put in his place. The storm over the munitions

[1] Asquith did not make this letter public until June, 1919. There was also some answer to the special charge that the War Office had neglected the production of high explosive shell. Before the war British 18-pr. field artillery was supplied entirely with shrapnel; 4·5 field howitzers had high explosive shell, but only to the extent of 30 per cent of their total supplies. Early in September, 1914, the War Office took up the question of providing high explosive for the 18-prs. Opinion at GHQ was divided, but on the whole favoured some explosive shell for these guns if they could be provided without interfering with the supply of shrapnel. In October 1000 high explosive shells were sent to France for 18-prs. French reported favourably on them, and asked that 50 per cent of the ammunition for the field guns should be of this type. He lowered the percentage to 25 a week later, and increased it again to 50 at the end of December. The demand raised the question whether machinery used in the production of shrapnel could be adapted to the manufacture of high explosive shells; the process of adaptation was estimated at ten weeks. At this time the total monthly production was about 45,000 shells, whereas the expenditure in France from the outbreak of war had been 385,000. The War Office decided not to interfere with the production of shrapnel, but to give additional orders for high explosive. They secured promises for over 480,000 high explosive shells by May 15, 1915. Only 52,000 were de-livered by this date. In the early months of 1915 there was no unanimity that high explosive was better than shrapnel for cutting wire. Experiments by French in January supported the view that shrapnel gave better results. Shrapnel cut the wire into small pieces, whereas high explosive, with the fuses then available, broke it, but left it as an entanglement. At Neuve Chapelle the results expected from shrapnel were generally obtained. The Germans, however, also noted these effects, and put up walls in front of their wire to catch the shrapnel bullets or sunk the wire in shallow pits. After Neuve Chapelle French asked that the proportion of high explosive should be reduced to 30 per cent. With the improvement in the German defences, the demand for high explosive again became more urgent, but the need was more for heavy guns firing these shells, since field guns could not destroy the newer type of defence. By 1917 a new high explosive shell, bursting on graze, was introduced.

shortage might therefore have blown over. Fisher's resignation was another matter. Curzon wrote that the Government had been 'kicked over by old Jack Fisher'.[1] Churchill – the political renegade – was at this time even more disliked and distrusted by the Conservatives than Lloyd George. Bonar Law warned Asquith that the Unionist party would vote against him if he supported Churchill against Fisher. Bonar Law also saw Lloyd George. Lloyd George realised that, if the Conservatives overthrew the Ministry, they would not include him in their Cabinet, and that the only way to keep his place was to secure a national Coalition. He therefore told Asquith that he would resign unless such a coalition were formed. Asquith agreed to some extent with the distrust of Churchill, at all events as First Lord of the Admiralty. He also saw that the alternative to bringing Conservatives into his Cabinet and making a change at the Admiralty was a debate in Parliament which might enforce his resignation, and would certainly have a bad effect upon national unity.[2]

The Coalition was announced on May 19, and the Ministers nominated during the following week. Asquith kept most of the higher offices in Liberal hands. He insisted that Grey should remain Foreign Secretary, and that McKenna should be Chancellor of the Exchequer. Kitchener, who was regarded as outside party, though he was known to be Conservative in sympathy, continued as Secretary for War. Lloyd George became Minister of Munitions, and Balfour First Lord of the Admiralty. Churchill was moved – downwards – to the Chancellorship of the Duchy of Lancaster, though he remained a member of the 'inner committee' directing the war. The Conservatives foolishly refused to accept Haldane; they also asked for the inclusion of Carson as Attorney-General. Asquith tried to counterbalance the effect of Carson's appointment on Irish Nationalist opinion by giving office to Redmond, but Redmond thought it 'politically impossible' for him to accept the offer. Arthur Henderson, with the reluctant assent of his party, joined the Ministry as President of the Board of Education.[3]

[1] Lord Ronaldshay, *Life of Lord Curzon*, iii, 125.

[2] Otherwise Asquith agreed only with reluctance to a coalition, and did not think that it would strengthen the Government.

Curzon's description of the Coalition as a 'big experiment dictated by forces almost outside personal control' is a good summary applicable not only to the formation of the government but to the later change from Asquith to Lloyd George as Prime Minister. Ronaldshay, id., iii, 123.

[3] In October, 1916, Henderson became Paymaster-General. This office kept him in the Cabinet; he had no administrative responsibilities, but acted as adviser on Labour questions.

Three other members of the Labour party were given junior offices. Bonar Law, who might well have claimed a more important post, became Colonial Secretary, with the understanding that he would be one of the Ministers controlling the direction of the war.[1]

The Coalition Cabinet at once set up a new committee – known at first from its main task as the Dardanelles Committee – to consider what decisions to take about the Gallipoli compaign. The members of the Committee, under Asquith's chairmanship, were Balfour, Crewe, Curzon, Lloyd George, Grey, Kitchener, Lansdowne, Bonar Law, McKenna, and Selborne.[2] At its first meeting on June 7 the Committee had before it two memoranda. One of the two had been written by Kitchener on May 28. Kitchener began with a reference to the general principles adopted six months earlier that the Western Front and the safety of the British Isles were the first considerations in British strategy, but that, if no decision could be obtained on the Western Front, operations might be carried out elsewhere. He then repeated the three possible courses of action mentioned on May 14,[3] and recommended the compromise plan of sending a moderate reinforcement to Gallipoli and hoping for a gradual advance. The other memorandum, written by Churchill, argued against an Allied offensive in the west, regarded a German offensive as unlikely, and proposed to give Hamilton large reinforcements at once.[4]

In spite of his memorandum of May 28 Kitchener seems to have been influenced by Churchill's arguments. At the meeting of the Committee on June 7 he came down in favour of sending Hamilton the four divisions for which he had asked. One had already left for the Aegean.[5]

[1] Bonar Law told Redmond that he had agreed to join the Ministry because the alternative was a general election. This election might have resulted in a majority for the Conservatives, and within a short time 'there would have been an ordinary party opposition in the House of Commons, with effects most disastrous to the country'.

[2] The work of the Committee was limited at first to the Gallipoli campaign, but (as Hankey foresaw) this campaign could not be dealt with in isolation. The First Sea Lord and the CIGS, however, did not attend as regular members until September. Carson became a member of the Committee in August.

[3] See above, p. 77.

[4] The general line of argument was similar to that of Churchill's memorandum of June 18. See below, p. 84.

[5] This division was needed to make good existing deficiencies. The Committee regarded the three other divisions as required for an offensive. Hamilton calculated in a similar way. Hence in reckoning divisions on June 7, three not four were taken as the 'additional' divisions.

Owing to the difficulty of finding transports, the last of the other three were not expected to arrive at Mudros before August 20. After the meeting Churchill argued strongly in favour of sending another two divisions. On June 11 he suggested a landing on the Bulair isthmus in order to cut off the Turkish supplies. Kitchener telegraphed to Hamilton for his opinion on this plan. Hamilton replied unfavourably; the arrival of German submarines had made it impossible to give sufficient naval protection to the transports and supply ships as far north as Bulair. Churchill then wrote again to Kitchener, and on June 18 drew up a second memorandum. He argued that even if the whole force at the Dardanelles were moved to the Western Front, it would still be impossible to make a decisive break-through in 1915. On the other hand the capture of Constantinople would ensure that Russia would remain in the war; the Balkan States would also be likely to join the Allies. Hence in 1916 the Allies would have the numerical predominance required to 'wear down' the enemy. Otherwise they might not have this superiority.

Churchill's argument ingeniously showed the Dardanelles expedition not as an expensive diversion but as a preliminary and useful step towards 'salving' Russia and, later, undertaking a successful offensive in the west. Kitchener continued to accept this view. It was agreed that the three additional divisions promised on June 7 could arrive more quickly if they were sent in the three liners *Aquitania*, *Mauretania*, and *Olympia*. Kitchener was even ready to send a larger force. He assumed at the time – after the Boulogne Conference[1] – that there would not be an autumn offensive in France. Hamilton had already been offered a fourth division. On June 28 he was offered a fifth. A week later Kitchener realised that, in spite of the British arguments in favour of delay, the French were insisting upon an early offensive on the Western Front, with full British co-operation. Nevertheless he kept to his latest decision that the strongest reinforcements should go to the Dardanelles where alone an immediate victory could be gained, and a way opened for close contact with the Russians.

Unfortunately this decision to strike with all available resources at Gallipoli came too late. Even with the use of the most rapid transport, Hamilton would not get the full reinforcement which he needed so very urgently until the second week in August. His men were always under fire – the so-called 'rest areas' were shelled – and were suffering heavily from sickness as well as from battle casualties. There was little

[1] See below, p. 131.

or no shade against the intense heat, and never enough water.[1] Dust and flies caused continuous discomfort and spread disease. On the other hand the Turks were being strongly reinforced. Moreover Kitchener made one blunder which had the gravest consequences. The three new divisions were to be sent out as a corps to Gallipoli. Hamilton asked for an experienced corps commander from France, and mentioned Lieutenant-General Sir Henry Rawlinson or Major-General Sir S. Byng. Kitchener refused to ask French to spare them. He pointed out that both these officers were junior in rank to Lieutenant-General Sir Bryan Mahon, who had trained one of the three divisions and was taking it to Gallipoli. He was unwilling to invite Mahon to serve under a corps commander junior to himself.

Owing to this routine punctiliousness Kitchener could find only one general senior in rank to Mahon who was available and fit for service at Gallipoli. This single candidate was Lieutenant-General the Hon. Sir Frederick Stopford. Stopford was sixty-one years old; he was a careful soldier, and well liked, but had never commanded a force in battle.[2] Hamilton gave way to Kitchener's insistence, and, unwisely, assigned to Stopford a task requiring skill, quickness, and determination as well as experience of fighting conditions. Stopford had none of these qualities; his mismanagement of the troops under his command lost the opportunity of victory which came, for the last time, in the August offensive. Hamilton was very confident that with the reinforcements he would succeed. The Turks and their German advisers were also fairly well aware that there would be another British attempt to break through their defences. Any doubts which they might have felt were removed by a speech which Churchill delivered at Dundee on June 5. Churchill pointed out that Kitchener had not agreed to the Gallipoli campaign without considering it in relation to other demands on the British army; the struggle would be heavy, but victory would come in the end.

Liman von Sanders interpreted this speech to mean that he must expect another attack. He decided, wrongly, that the attack would take the form of a landing somewhere between Enos and Besika Bay. In fact Hamilton planned a surprise landing at Suvla Bay, north of the 'Anzac' landings; this landing would coincide with an attack from the Anzac

[1] The Turks had an excellent water supply on the Gallipoli heights. One German general has recorded his view that, without it, the physical resistance of the Turks would have broken down.

[2] During the South African war he had been Military Secretary to Sir Redvers Buller, and had returned with him to England. In 1914 he was given command of a home defence army.

positions. The troops from Suvla Bay would move quickly to the high ground surrounding their points of landing, and would link up with the Anzac forces in an advance to the Dardanelles above the Narrows.

The plan was admirable, though insufficient allowance was made for the difficult ground – a tangle of ravines and spurs – over which the Anzac forces had to attack. The Turks were taken unawares at Suvla Bay; an immediate advance to the heights would have led to a decisive victory. Unfortunately the commander at Suvla Bay was General Stopford. He dallied and muddled, wasted invaluable time, and thus allowed the Turkish reinforcements, whom he could easily have forestalled, to get first to the key positions.[1] No single act of incompetence had such far-reaching effects on the history of the war. The whole of Hamilton's plan was ruined, and an attack which began with high hopes on the night of August 6–7 ended four days later in disaster. Not one of the objectives had been gained or held, and in this failure 25,000 casualties had been incurred.[2]

Hamilton continued his attempts to retrieve the position, but, in spite of intense courage on the part of his British, Australian, and New Zealand troops, he merely increased his losses. On August 17 he had to admit in a telegram to Kitchener that his *coup* had so far failed' and that he needed immediate replacements to the number of 45,000 and another 50,000 new men. Even this calculation was subject to the provision that the Turks did not bring up large reinforcements. Thus the attempt to bring the Gallipoli campaign to a quick conclusion had collapsed.

What were the Dardanelles Committee and the Cabinet to do? Commodore Keyes continued to argue that the navy could save the situation. He thought that the Turks were not expecting a naval attack. The fleet now had more mine-sweepers, and much better air observation; the mobile guns which had harassed the mine-sweepers had probably been removed to assist the army. Hence Keyes estimated that at least half of an attacking force would get through and that a squadron

[1] Stopford arrived off Suvla Bay during the night of August 6–7; he did not go ashore until the afternoon of August 8, when the opportunity to advance had been lost.

[2] The disaster was worse owing to the inadequate arrangements for taking the sick and wounded off the peninsula. Hamilton must share the blame with the army medical authorities in England for this unnecessary addition to the suffering of the troops; the authorities in England were slow, after the decision to send large reinforcements to Gallipoli, in providing hospital ships and launches, but Hamilton was also late in asking for them.

in the Sea of Marmora could compel the Turks to retreat owing to shortage of supplies. Admiral Wemyss, who was Admiral de Robeck's second in command, agreed with Keyes. Although Admiral de Robeck himself did not think that the plan would succeed, he ordered Keyes to submit detailed proposals. On the other hand he told the Admiralty that he regarded the plan as a 'grave error'.

Churchill would have accepted this plan, but the Admiralty refused to act against Admiral de Robeck's judgment. At the same time the Dardanelles Committee did not feel sure that, even with the large reinforcements for which he asked, Hamilton would succeed. In any case these reinforcements could not easily be found because at this time Kitchener was convinced that the British Government must acquiesce in Joffre's plan for an autumn offensive; this offensive would require all the available British support. Hence the Dardanelles Committee decided to send only about 25,000 men to Hamilton. Suddenly, however, the French seemed to have changed their minds.

There had been throughout 1915 a strong and influential section of opinion in France favourable to an expedition in the eastern Mediterranean and the postponement of an offensive in the west. The expensive and disappointing results of the western attacks in the spring and early summer led to increasing discontent, and, before Hamilton's offensive in August, the French Government was considering the despatch of large forces to capture Constantinople if the British Expedition was unable to do so.[1] Joffre himself was willing to allow troops to be sent from France, but only after his own offensive had taken place. If, as Joffre expected, the offensive succeeded, he could be sure that all other plans would fall into the background. Meanwhile a political intrigue in France was also influencing the military decisions of the government.

In the month of June a group of dissatisfied politicians wanted to supersede Joffre by General Sarrail, a 'political general' on the Republican left. Joffre dismissed Sarrail from the command of the Third French army on July 22. Sarrail's friends then tried to get him an independent position. He was offered the command of the French force at the Dardanelles, but this force was only an army corps. Sarrail's friends therefore continued their intrigues to persuade the Government to form a new army to serve in the Mediterranean. After the failure of Hamilton's offensive the French began to study a plan for sending Sarrail and the new army, when it had been formed, to the Asiatic side of the Straits.

[1] See also above, p. 62, note 3.

Joffre still refused to allow any French troops to leave France before the end of September. The Germans, however, had realised the grave danger to them if the Dardanelles were forced, and the very small margin by which this danger had been averted. They now decided to secure their position in Turkey and the Balkans by an attack on Serbia[1] for which they could buy, at Serbian expense, the help of Bulgaria. On September 22 Bulgaria began to mobilise. Venizelos, who was in office again, asked for Allied support to enable Greece to fulfil her promises under a military convention with Serbia. This convention applied in the case of an attack by Bulgaria on either state. Under the terms of the convention the Greeks had agreed to supply an army of 90,000 and Serbia an army of 150,000. The Serbs could not now provide this force. Venizelos, however, offered on behalf of Greece to enter the war if the Allies would provide it. The French Government agreed at once to do so. The British Government were less willing, but could hardly refuse without a serious disagreement with the French, though they doubted whether an adequate force could be found in time to prevent the Germans from overrunning Serbia and the Bulgarians from cutting off the Serbian retreat. It was impossible, indeed, to send more than a small force immediately, and this force could come only from Gallipoli. Hence on September 25, the day of the opening of the Loos offensive, Kitchener telegraphed to Hamilton that two British divisions, and, probably, one French division must be withdrawn from the Dardanelles, and sent to Salonika. The Allied landings at Salonika began on October 5.

At the insistence of the French, the Allies, having failed to give adequate support to one Mediterranean expedition which might have succeeded, were now committed to another expedition which was

---

[1] It is not to the credit of the Allies that they had taken no steps, after the Serbs had defeated the Austrians, and inflicted heavy losses on them, to try to strengthen the Serbian army against an inevitable third attack, probably with German support. On the other hand (i) there were insuperable practical difficulties in providing adequate reinforcement without at least the co-operation of Greece, (ii) success at Gallipoli would have made all the difference to the attitude of Greece and probably of Bulgaria and Roumania, and (iii) the Serbian chances of resistance were less after the heavy defeats of Russia in Galicia in the summer of 1915; these defeats also affected the Bulgarian and Roumanian view of the Allied chances of winning the war. It remains true, however, that the British High Command, obsessed with the idea of a break-through on the Western Front, tended to write off the defeat of Austria as a Russian responsibility, or, after the entry of Italy into the war, as a joint responsibility of Russia and Italy. See also above, p. 70, note 2, for the relations between Bulgaria and other Balkan States.

almost certain to fail in its primary purpose. There would have been
little chance of saving Serbia even with the assistance of the Greeks.[1]
King Constantine of Greece, however, repudiated the offer of assistance
and Venizelos resigned. The fact that the Allies were sending troops to
Salonika from Gallipoli implied that they had given up hope of forcing
the Straits. The general situation thus suggested to the King that
Germany would win the war.[2] On October 7 the Dardanelles Committee decided to ask for the joint advice of the Admiralty War Staff
and the General Staff. Their advice was that no more troops should be
sent to Salonika. The General Staff merely echoed the views of French
and Haig. They recommended a continuance of the offensive in France;
otherwise they were in favour of sending more troops to Gallipoli.
They thought that a force of six British and two Indian divisions from
France would be enough to capture the peninsula, and that this force
should be sent to Egypt for organisation under a new commander. The
First Sea Lord, Admiral Sir Henry Jackson, added a note strongly
opposing the Salonika diversion, and pointing out that delay in resuming the attack at the Dardanelles might end in disaster.

The Dardanelles Committee, as they had done so often, postponed a
decision. Seven weeks had now gone by since Hamilton's appeal for
reinforcements. Winter was approaching; it would soon become very
difficult either to land a new army at Gallipoli or to withdraw the
existing force. It was also thought that, probably in the early part of
December, the Turks could receive guns, ammunition, and, if necessary, officers and men from Germany.[3] The French were wholly
against the abandonment of Salonika; the alternative, though the
British Government hesitated to face it, was the abandonment of
Gallipoli. On October 11 the Dardanelles Committee agreed to send an
'adequate and substantial force' to Egypt 'without prejudice to its final
destination'. They wanted another opinion on the choice between
Gallipoli and Salonika, and resolved that an officer of high rank – they

[1] The General Staff had already recommended on military grounds that no
British troops should be sent to Salonika.

[2] The King, with his German connexions, would have come down on the
German side after the earlier refusal of the Russians to accept Greek collaboration
in attacking the Turks (see above, p. 73), but Greece depended upon supplies
which the British and French navies could cut off.

[3] In fact, owing to the damage done to the railway through Serbia, the bad
roads from Constantinople to the Peninsula, and the remarkable activities of
British submarines in the Sea of Marmora, the Germans were able to send very
little heavy material to the Turks before the evacuation. Rail communication
between Germany and Constantinople was not restored until January 15, 1916.

suggested Kitchener or Haig – should be sent to the Mediterranean to advise on the use of the 'adequate and substantial force'.[1] Meanwhile Kitchener asked Hamilton for an estimate of the probable losses in an evacuation of the peninsula. Hamilton replied that he might lose half of his force.

On October 14 the Dardanelles Committee met again. They considered that Hamilton should be recalled, and that a new commander should survey the problem. Hamilton's recall was, on the whole, desirable. The Committee seem to have been influenced by very unfair criticism made by Stopford, who had been sent back to London, and by attacks on the army (other than the Australians) and its commanders by an Australian journalist. On the other hand the Committee had some reason for mistrusting Hamilton's judgment, and for thinking that the troops under his command must also have lost confidence in him. The new commander, Sir Charles Monro, was, however, known to be in favour of concentration on the Western Front, and was no more likely than Hamilton to produce an unbiased report. Monro indeed, before leaving England, had made up his mind that, if the evacuation of Gallipoli were practicable, it should be carried out.

Monro arrived in the Aegean on October 28. To a certain extent the situation was already more clear, or, rather the choice of action had become more limited. The unsuccessful offensive in France had been abandoned; the decision to remain at Salonika had been taken. Bulgaria, as had been expected, declared war on Serbia on October 14, and on October 23 Bulgarian forces cut the railway from Salonika to Nish. Although it was now evident that an Allied force of a sufficient size could not possibly reach Salonika in time to save Serbia, the French insisted even more strongly on sending reinforcements to the place. Joffre came to London on October 29 to try to persuade the British Government. He made it known that, in the case of a British refusal, he would resign his command and hinted that the French would act

[1] Sir E. Carson resigned at this time from the Government on the ground that they were not sending adequate help to Serbia. With the Prime Minister's permission he read his letter of resignation to the House of Commons. The letter was published in *The Times* on November 3, 1915. It included the following passage: 'I could understand a policy of limiting all our actions to the Western theatre, and using all our resources there (which is, I think, in reality what the War Staff suggests). . . . But to send an army to Egypt to await action which may or may not be possible on the report of a General to be sent to Gallipoli seems the most futile and hesitating decision that could be come to.' Thus the Germans, and the Turks, were given valuable information of British intentions.

independently. In view of this extreme pressure, the British Government agreed to reinforce Salonika on the understanding that, if communications could not be opened up with the Serbian army, the Allied forces would be withdrawn.

The divisions which were to be held for a time in Egypt had thus to go to Salonika and not to Gallipoli. There remained only the possibility of another naval attack on the Straits. Admiral de Robeck allowed Keyes to come to London in order to put his plan to the Admiralty, but the Admiral himself was still opposed to the scheme, and, once again, the Dardanelles Committee had an opportunity to delay a decision. They were now waiting for Monro's report. Kitchener did not give Monro much time. He telegraphed on October 29 that he wanted an early answer to the main question, 'namely, leaving or staying'. Monro spent one day, and only one day, on a visit to the three Gallipoli positions: Helles, Anzac, and Suvla Bay. He reported on the following day – October 31 – in favour of evacuation. It is fair to say that, before his arrival, the General Staff of the Expeditionary force had prepared a memorandum for his use. The memorandum made no recommendations, but pointed out that another large-scale attack could not safely be made until the spring, and would then require 250,000 men; that, in the meantime, a reinforcement of two divisions was essential to safeguard the ground already held, and that, including winter losses, the total number of reinforcements needed for victory would be about 400,000.

Monro's report reached London just before the Dardanelles Committee was transferred into a new and smaller War Committee[1], with more power to take decisions on matters requiring immediate action. Churchill, who had remained strongly in favour of Keyes' plan, and against evacuation, was not a member of the new committee. The first business of the committee was to consider Monro's report. Kitchener was not at this time in favour of evacuation, but, in view of the promises to the French, he could not provide more troops for Gallipoli. Even if he could have found the troops, there were no ships to transport them. He was now inclined to support Keyes' plan, with an addition of a landing near Bulair to cut off the peninsula when the fleet had reached the Sea of Marmora. The War Committee asked him to go out to Gallipoli and judge for himself whether Monro was right in suggesting evacuation.[2]

[1] See below, p. 156.
[2] Kitchener was distressed at the thought of the losses which he expected during the withdrawal. He told the Prime Minister before he left England: 'I

Kitchener left England on November 4. He had already heard from General Birdwood that a landing at the base of the peninsula was impracticable. Before he started from London he also found that the Admiralty had decided against a naval attack except in co-operation with a new attack by the army. Thus there seemed no alternative to evacuation. After his arrival at Mudros Kitchener came reluctantly to this conclusion. In order to lessen the dangerous effect of withdrawal upon Moslem opinion, and to secure the defence of Egypt, when the Turkish army at Gallipoli was free to go elsewhere, Kitchener proposed a landing at Ayas Bay, opposite Alexandretta. This proposal[1] was strongly opposed by the French who, for political reasons, did not want British troops near Syria. The Admiralty did not think the harbour facilities adequate or safe against submarine attack. The War Office would have had difficulty in finding the necessary troops. Finally General Birdwood pointed out that all the available small craft would be needed for the evacuation of Gallipoli and that it would be absurd to take large numbers of them away for a landing 900 miles off. Kitchener's first report, though on balance in favour of evacuation, had not been decisive. The question of withdrawal from Gallipoli was linked with the situation at Salonika and this situation in turn depended to a considerable extent on the attitude of the Greek King. Kitchener went to see King Constantine on November 19. Whatever his personal wishes, and ultimate expectations of a German victory, the King continued to realise that he could not go into the war on the German side without putting all his ports and all Greek seaborne trade and shipping at the mercy of the Allies. It was therefore not surprising that he decided to remain, at least for the time, an unfriendly neutral, and that, in spite of previous threats, he did not interfere with the Salonika force. None the less the maintenance of this force had made it impossible to provide adequately for the Gallipoli army. Kitchener therefore

---

pace my room at night, and see the boats fired at, and capsizing, and the drowning men.' He knew also that there was increasing distrust of his own control at the War Office, and that a very considerable body of opinion in the Cabinet regarded his mission to the Mediterranean as a step to getting him out of office. He said of this mission: 'Perhaps if I lose a lot of men over there, I shall not want to come back.'

[1] It has been recently argued (R. Rhodes James, *Gallipoli*, pp. 330–1) that the Ayas Bay plan was put forward to Kitchener merely to make it easier for him to agree to evacuation. This plan, however, had been proposed earlier; if there had been sufficient resources available at the end of 1915 or early in 1916, and the French had not objected to it on political grounds, it might well have been attempted. See note 1 at the end of this chapter.

telegraphed on November 22 definitely in favour of evacuating Sulva and Anzac but retaining, at least for the time, the position at Helles. On the following day the Prime Minister replied that the War Committee were in favour of total evacuation.

Kitchener sailed for England on November 24. Since he knew that the policy of withdrawal had been practically accepted, he gave orders that all surplus stores should be taken away at once. Unfortunately the first stores to be re-embarked at Suvla were those which had most lately arrived. These latest arrivals included winter clothing, which, by an absurd error of judgment, was returned to Mudros. Hence, when a severe blizzard struck the peninsula on November 27, and was followed by two nights of exceptionally severe frost, the troops in the exposed position at Suvla had to meet it in their light summer clothing, and suffered 5000 cases of frostbite; 200 men were frozen to death or drowned in the trenches.[1]

The decision on evacuation was not taken until December 7. The delay was due partly to a last-hour appeal from Admiral Wemyss, who had succeeded Admiral de Robeck as naval commander at the Dardanelles, in favour of Keyes' plan for naval action, partly to Kitchener's own last-minute hesitation, partly to a division of opinion in the Cabinet. Curzon, in particular, argued that, if it were physically possible to hold the peninsula, the attempt should be made; withdrawal would not mean an economy of man-power, since it would be necessary to send strong reinforcements to all points, including Egypt, where the Turks might attack. Once again, also, the Salonika question came into the matter. On December 4 the Prime Minister, Balfour, and Kitchener met Briand (now Prime Minister), Joffre, Galliéni, and French naval representatives at Calais. The British representatives pointed out that the condition of British participation in the Salonika expedition had not been fulfilled. Serbia could not be saved, and the best course now was withdrawal. The Conference agreed, but the French Government asked on the next day that the decision should be reversed. On December 7 the Russian Government telegraphed in favour of remaining at Salonika.[2]

A withdrawal from Salonika, in order to reinforce Gallipoli, would have meant a break with the French on an issue of major policy. Earlier

[1] The trials of the men on the other beaches were severe, but there was more shelter than at Suvla.
[2] It was not known at the time that this Russian telegram was sent at the request of the French.

in the year – before their plans had gone wrong – the British Government might have insisted on their right of decision. Even now they could have insisted if their own commander in France, in spite of the lessons of 1915, had not been in favour of Joffre's main plan of an offensive in the west. They gave way, however, to the French argument (which masked, as before, a great deal of internal political intrigue) that it was necessary to hold Salonika in order to 'encourage' Roumania and to keep Greece from joining the enemy and thus allowing him submarine bases in Greek ports, though it remained clear that Constantine would not risk the destruction of these ports. Finally the Admiralty, supported by Admiral de Robeck, who was back in England after giving up his command, was unwilling to risk the loss of more ships when even the forcing of the Dardanelles seemed unlikely to lead to the capture of Constantinople. Even on December 7 the Cabinet postponed one part of their decision. They ordered the evacuation of the Suvla and Anzac positions, but, for the time, decided to retain Helles. It was fairly obvious for military reasons that Helles could not be held long in isolation; on December 24, before the formal decision had been reached, Robertson[1] instructed General Birdwood to make all his preparations to leave.

The evacuation of the Suvla and Anzac beaches was carried out with remarkable skill, and completed on the nights of December 19/20. The weather was favourable; the Turks did not know what was happening until after the last shipload had left. Between December 8 and this last night 83,000 officers and men, 186 guns, nearly 2000 vehicles, and 4695 horses and mules were taken off. On the final night there were no casualties at Suvla, and every animal, gun, and wagon was brought away. At Anzac, two men were wounded; a few worn-out guns were left behind, after destruction, and less than 100 transport animals could not be taken on board. The evacuation of Helles on January 8–9 was in some respects an even more astonishing feat. The Turks had every reason to expect it;[2] the weather was less good, but once again 35,268

[1] Robertson took over his duties as CIGS on December 23.

[2] The Turks might anyhow have been on the watch more carefully for the earlier evacuation. The question was openly discussed in London and as early as October 14 Lord Milner advised in the House of Lords that the Government should consider 'withdrawal from an enterprise the successful completion of which is now hopeless'. (See also above, p. 90, note 1, for Carson's letter of resignation). On November 18 Lord Ribblesdale, after saying – again in the House of Lords – that it was common knowledge that Monro had reported in favour of evacuation, asked whether Kitchener had been sent out to give a second opinion

officers and men, 127 guns, 328 horses and mules were brought off without casualties. Five hundred mules had to be shot, and nearly 1600 vehicles were abandoned. The weather conditions indeed turned out to be in favour of the British, since the Turks assumed the sea to be too rough to allow any embarkation.

So ended a campaign which cost the Allies over 250,000 casualties; 43,000 British, Australian, and New Zealand officers and men were killed, missing, or prisoners of war, or had died of wounds and disease. The Turkish losses were heavier. The Turkish army, which fought well at Gallipoli, never recovered from these losses, and, to that extent, the Gallipoli campaign prefaced the way for Allenby's victories in Palestine. Nevertheless the evacuation was not a victory, but the last stage in a defeat, and a defeat which, by greater forethought, resolution, and ability on the part of the military and civilian authorities in control of the war, might have been avoided.

NOTE I

The proposed landing at Alexandretta in 1915

A landing at Alexandretta had been suggested at the end of 1914 not only by Lloyd George, but by General Maxwell. Alexandretta (Iskanderun) on the east side of Ayas Bay (at the head of the Gulf of Iskanderun) was an important point on the line of Turkish communications. The Baghdad railway was originally planned to run through it, but the course had been changed, for strategic reasons, to go inland from Tarsus and to reach Aleppo through the Amanus mountains. The main tunnels through the mountains were not completed at the outbreak of war. There was also a gap north of Tarsus in the Taurus mountains. Troops and supplies therefore had to cross these mountains by road, and either (i) take the line from Tarsus to Alexandretta, and thence go by road to Aleppo, or (ii) continue on the main line to the Amanus mountains, go by road for some twenty miles across the mountains above the unfinished tunnels, and then rejoin at Islahiya the completed line to Aleppo. The Alexandretta route was much the easier of the two. The Amanus road was not fit for wheeled traffic – especially in winter – until 1916. In any case an Allied expedition landing in Ayas

---

or to carry out the withdrawal. Fortunately the Germans and Turks assumed that these questions had been arranged to hide the preparations for another British attack.

Bay could have cut the Tarsus–Amanus line west of the junction for Alexandretta.

The difficulties in the way of finding transport and equipment were serious but not insuperable. The submarine threat in the Mediterranean was not yet severe; a landing at Alexandretta would have lessened the number of troops necessary for protecting Egypt and the Canal, and made it difficult for the Turks to send reinforcements and supplies to Mesopotamia. In November, 1915, Kitchener telegraphed to Asquith from Mudros in favour of the plan. He thought that a force of eight divisions in all would be sufficient. The General Staff in London, however, held to the view that a diversion of this kind would have no effect in weakening Germany. They produced arguments that the force would have to hold a perimeter of fifty miles, and must therefore be at least 160,000 strong in infantry; that the wastage would be about 20 per cent monthly for the first three months, and then 15 per cent; that the Turks could easily concentrate a larger army against the expedition. The Admiralty was also doubtful whether enough lighters and small craft could be found at least until the Gallipoli and Salonika forces had been withdrawn. They also doubted whether the harbour facilities were adequate or safe against submarine attack. Kitchener answered these criticisms. He pointed out – with the support of Monro – that a surprise landing would not be opposed by more than 5000 men and that it would take the Turks a week to assemble even 15,000 troops. He kept to his estimate of eight divisions, or 150,000 men, since most of the front was protected by a wide river which large bodies of men could cross only at certain points.

The decisive factor, on the British side, was the persistent belief that concentration on the Western Front would lead to a break-through in 1916. Even if this illusion had been dispersed, the plan would probably have foundered, since the French raised the strongest objections to it unless the expedition were mainly French, and under French command. The French military attaché in London delivered a note to the CIGS on November 13, 1915, that the 'moral and political position of France' in the Levant would have to be considered, and that 'in order to avoid any subsequent misunderstanding' the French view should be taken into account. Since the French Government were unable to mount the expedition themselves, this veto ended the matter.

NOTE 2

The Salonika expedition

Until the last two months of the war the history of the Salonika
expedition was as depressing as its origins. The enemy had no motive
for making an effort to dislodge the Allied forces. From the German
point of view there was considerable profit in using Bulgarians and
Turks – with a small amount of German assistance (mainly technical) –
to immobilise in one of the unhealthiest areas of Europe 300,000 Allied
troops whose supply ships offered good targets for submarine attack.

As in the other distant expeditions, the troops suffered from administrative incompetence. The French – having landed first – not unnaturally took for their own use the best sites and buildings. The British 10th
Division – coming from Gallipoli – arrived mainly in drill (i.e. cotton)
uniforms and shorts, and, although a certain number of serge uniforms
great coats, and blankets were issued, the supply – even five weeks after
the first landing on October 5 – was insufficient; in November the
division advanced in this ill-provided state into the mountainous
hinterland, where it met the blizzard which was usual at this time of the
year.[1] Tents were sent without tent poles; 500 mules arrived in a
transport on October 7, without picketing pegs or ropes, and with few
nosebags. The expedition suffered from the fact that, at first, nearly all
its stores came from Egypt, where it was assumed that Salonika, being
in Europe, could be treated as though it were a port on the Riviera.
Warm underclothing, ordered for the winter, did not arrive until the
end of March. The Salonika command asked for sun helmets; they
waited until February 1916 to do so, in spite of local warnings of the
Macedonian summer heat, but the Director-General of Medical
Services in Egypt thought them unnecessary, and throughout the first
summer the supply was inadequate. Macedonia was known to be one
of the worst malarial regions in Europe; a sufficient supply of mosquito
nets was not requested until February, 1916. The Egyptian authorities
again cut down the numbers, and throughout the first summer the
supply was far below the requirements.[2]

[1] For the effect of this storm at Gallipoli, see above, p. 93.

[2] The Salonika authorities also asked for fire-extinguishers. There was always
a danger of fire in the overcrowded city, the docks, and the surrounding camps
during the dry summer months when a strong wind – known locally as the
Vardar wind – might blow for three days on end. The first answer from Egypt
to the request was 'Why are fire-extinguishers required?' In 1917 a great part of
the city was destroyed by a fire (for which the Allied Expeditionary Force was
not responsible).

For some time after the unsuccessful attempt to enter Serbia, there was no question of an offensive from Salonika. The British Command, not without reason, distrusted Sarrail, and the War Office was hoping, in vain, for an opportunity to persuade the French to evacuate the place. In May, 1916, the Greeks handed over to the Bulgarians the strong Fort Rupel a few miles up the narrow gorge through which the river Struma passes into Bulgaria.[1] The British army on this front thus had to face an almost impregnable mountain barrier if they were to advance. In August an attack by Sarrail to contain Bulgarian forces in order to help the Roumanians[2] was both costly and useless, since the Roumanian armies were defeated in a quick, relentless German attack to which the Bulgarian contribution was only incidental. Another attempt, in April, 1917, to advance up the Vardar valley failed with heavy loss, though Sarrail had talked of Sofia as his distant objective. Further fighting in May was no more successful.[3]

After these futile attempts at the impossible, no offensive was attempted until September, 1918. By this time Sarrail had left Salonika. The French and British commanders, Franchet d'Esperey and Milne, believed that the Bulgarians were now near to collapse. The War Office and the Supreme War Council at Versailles were unconvinced. Lloyd George insisted that the attack should be made. The offensive opened on September 15. The British attacked in the same difficult area as before. Their attack failed, but it drew off the enemy's reserves, and the Serbs – trained in mountain warfare – and French were able to break the enemy resistance. The Bulgarians had had enough of the war. Within a fortnight the Bulgarian Government signed an armistice, and their army went home.

[1] This act was regarded at the time by the Allies as one of treachery. The Allies, however, had agreed with the Greek Government in December, 1915, that, if Anglo-French troops remained on Greek soil, the Greek army would neither assist in attack nor hinder an advance of the Central Powers.

[2] Roumania declared war on Austria-Hungary on August 27, 1916, after the most anxious calculation whether she would be on the winning side. If she had come to a decision a few weeks earlier, the help of the Roumanian armies might have been enough to enable the Russians under Brussiloff to inflict a decisive defeat on Austria-Hungary before the Germans could interfere.

[3] At this time the only manuals of instruction on the use of artillery in attack possessed by the Salonika army dated from before the battle of the Somme.

CHAPTER 7

The expedition to Mesopotamia: mismanagement and disaster: the fall of Kut: recovery: the capture of Baghdad

The expedition to Gallipoli was wrecked by hesitant and divided counsels, delays, and bad leadership at critical moments, but if it had succeeded, the effect on the general course of the war must have been immense. A victory in Mesopotamia[1] could not have had such far-reaching strategic consequences. The only justification for sending troops to an area remote from the main areas of fighting was the need to protect the oil works and pipe line at Abadan and to demonstrate to the Arabs of Mesopotamia and the sheiks of the Persian gulf region who were under British protection that they would have British support against Turkey. The safeguarding of the oil supplies was indeed the original purpose of the expedition, though after the Turkish declaration of war the British Government extended the objective to the occupation of Basra. Since the small force required was to come from India, the War Office readily left the immediate control of it to the Government of India, and, in Great Britain, to the India Office, though the latter had no organisation suited for the remote control of a war.

The War Office knew little about Mesopotamia. They had previously shared with the General Staff in India the responsibility for collecting military information about it, but they had no plans for a possible campaign there, and did not even possess good maps of the area. The Government of India also had no plans and no good maps. The Indian army was not prepared for an expedition on any considerable scale. The British army in India had remained since about 1858 about 75,000 strong, and the Indian army (with British officers) about 160,000 strong. The duties of both armies were, primarily, the

---

[1] The western name 'Mesopotamia' for the area covering roughly the Turkish vilayets of Basra, Baghdad, and Mosul goes back to the Hellenistic age, but had no local significance in the nineteenth century. The local name for the lowland area of the Tigris and Euphrates basins was, and is, Iraq. See Map 8.

maintenance of internal security, the defence of the frontiers against hostile tribes and border states, and the defence of India in the event of war with a Great Power. Russia was the only Great Power likely to threaten India, and, after the Anglo-Russian convention of 1907, a Russian attack was improbable. Hence the equipment of the army had been severely cut down. The field army had no aeroplanes, no wireless, no motor transport, and little telephone equipment. The hospital and medical services were under establishment. Haig, when Chief of the General Staff in India, had written a strong memorandum on the unpreparedness of the army, but Morley, as Secretary of State, had limited annual military expenditure and had forbidden the 'dispersion' of effort over 'matters in Tibet, Persia, the Persian Gulf, etc.'

The use of part of the Indian army for service outside India in a grave emergency was not, however, excluded, though the War Office in December, 1912, had made only leisurely enquiry about the amount of aid which India could provide. They did not send their letter until July, 1913. A reply from the Government of India did not reach the War Office until after the outbreak of war. In September, 1914, Kitchener had asked that thirty-nine of the forty-two British infantry battalions in India should be replaced by territorial battalions from Great Britain.

The expeditionary force of one division sent to Basra was therefore as large as the Indian military authorities could spare without considerable risk. The climate of Basra was one of the worst climates in the world. The day temperature ranged from a maximum of about 114 degrees between May and August to a minimum of about 80[1] in January. Most of the world's epidemic diseases were to be found there. The few scattered towns between Basra and Baghdad were little more than filthy agglomerations of low-grade Arabs. Communications were determined – and limited – by the rise and fall in the level of the Tigris and Euphrates whose waters had never been properly controlled during the centuries of incompetent Turkish rule. The seasons of high water were normally from early January to March, followed by a further rise, due to the melting of the distant mountain snows, between April and June. In low water the channel between Basra and Kut – 385 miles in the winding course of the Tigris, and only about 180 in a direct line – was from five to six and half feet deep some seventy-five miles from Basra, and twice or even four times as deep in the high floods. The channel was uncertain, with many shoals; along the 'narrows',

1 The night temperature in winter fell to about twenty-three degrees.

extending for twenty-eight miles, two vessels could not pass unless
one of them was banked in. The countryside was flooded at high water;
there were no railways south of Baghdad, and no roads, only trails
which became impassable in the rains and often disappeared under the
floods. The flies were a continual plague except in winter. Mirages –
a real obstacle to military observers – and sand haze added to the
difficulties of campaigning.[1]

The occupation of Basra was easy, but the miserable town of 30,000
people, with an adjacent suburb, had no landing quays. Ocean-going
steamers which could cross the bar of the Shatt-al-Arab discharged their
cargoes into native boats. There were also few warehouses. An army
landing at the place was hardly better off, and in some respects worse
off than the British army of the Crimea when its sole port of supply
was the small quay at Balaclava. From the outset indeed the Mesopotamian campaign was a grim historical repetition of the errors made
in the first Crimean winter, though unfortunately these errors were not
as quickly remedied as they had been sixty years earlier.[2] Thus the loading of ships bound for Basra was carried out haphazardly at Bombay.
The cargoes were not always known, and little care was taken to ensure
that orders were properly fulfilled. Firewood, for example, which
could have been cut into bundles, was sent in large logs. In one instance
a ship laden with heavy material and plant was supplied with a derrick
and crane for unloading – there were no cranes at Basra – but the crane
was at the bottom of the ship with the cargo on top of it. Unloaded
steamships began to accumulate at Basra; at one time there were forty
of them in a line stretching for eight miles.

The first duties of the command in Mesopotamia, the Government
of India, and, in the final control, the India Office and the British
Cabinet should have been to ensure that Basra – the only port – had
adequate facilities, and to provide sufficient water transport of shallow
draught before any move was made upstream from the base. Neither
of these elementary tasks was carried out. In December, 1915 – over

[1] One problem – showing the unforeseen difficulties of a land campaign in a
totally insanitary country – was to secure the safety of the transport animals from
the endemic animal infections. For a long time there were only three veterinary
officers with the force at Basra. Their measures to prevent the spread of diseases
included the establishment of a free animal clinic.

[2] As late as November, 1916, Gertrude Bell wrote from Basra to Sir Valentine
Chirol of 'a colossal, far-reaching, inefficiency and incompetence. Since the
Crimea, I don't think there has been such a campaign.' E. Burgoyne, *Gertrude
Bell, 1914–26*, ii p. 42.

a year after the occupation of Basra – Sir George Buchanan, Chairman and Senior Engineer of the Rangoon Harbour Trust, was sent to advise on the organisation of the port. He was coldly received by the local military authorities and, until he made personal representations at Simla, had little scope for action.[1]

The shifts, confusion, and delays in the provision of river craft were even more inexcusable. The responsibility must be shared between General Nixon,[2] the military authorities in India[3] and England, and – again – the Cabinet. The problem, at every stage in the campaign, could have been stated in simple terms. A division, or brigade, needed so many tons of supplies daily; the distances over which the supplies were to be transported were known, and there was enough information about the river levels at different seasons to estimate the maximum draught required for the river shipping. Additional steamers were essential for special work – including hospital ships. No operations north of Basra should have been undertaken until sufficient craft had been assembled, from time to time, for the purposes in view. Nixon is primarily to blame for not estimating or stating his requirements with sufficient definiteness, and for failing to insist that these requirements would have to be met before he could move far from his base. His foolish confidence that, when he reached Baghdad, he would find everything he needed only made matters worse. He had first to reach Baghdad; in any case, before his arrival, the Turks could have destroyed, sunk, or rendered useless every steamer on the river. On the other hand the Government of India, and the authorities in Great Britain, could have made – roughly – for themselves the detailed calculations with which Nixon failed to supply them. In the last resort,

[1] Sir George Buchanan, *The Tragedy of Mesopotamia* (1938), p. 31.

[2] General Sir John Nixon–a cavalry officer–had commanded the Northern Army in India. He was given command of the Mesopotamian Expeditionary Force in March, 1915.

[3] Sir Beauchamp Duff, Commander-in-Chief in India, never visited Mesopotamia. No senior member of his staff went there in 1914. The minority report of the Mesopotamia Commission (see below, pp. 112–113), after summing up the shortcomings and lack of co-operation and drive on the part of the Government of India, concluded: 'It would appear that, in fact, the Army Administration in India was jealous of the Army at home; they wished to retain the magnitude of their command; they felt they were neglected, "out of the picture", and they determined, perhaps unconsciously, to be obstructive.' It is difficult not to accept this criticism. It should be added that it is not a criticism of the fighting value of the Indian army, or of the excellent relations in this army between regimental officers and men.

the Cabinet should not have sanctioned an advance unless they were sure that adequate transport had been supplied.[1] The army and marine authorities in India were also vague and inefficient. The first of a number of steamers ordered by Nixon in July, 1915 – the order was for too few and was sent too late – did not reach Basra until May, 1916. The failure to provide hospital ships was not less disgraceful. Until July, 1915, there was only one hospital ship to take sick and wounded from Mesopotamia and also from East Africa to Bombay. In Mesopotamia itself there were no hospital ships for river working. A proposal to build a light railway from Basra to Nasiriya in August, 1915, was turned down on grounds of expense.

After the occupation of Basra, the military authorities in India rightly rejected a wild suggestion that a brigade might be sent to seize and occupy Baghdad. They agreed, however, that the British force might advance as far as Qurna at the junction of the Tigris and the Euphrates. The force would then hold the whole of the navigable water to the Persian Gulf and the fertile area between Qurna and the sea. If Arab support were forthcoming, an advance might be made to Baghdad. Qurna was occupied without much difficulty in the first week of December, 1914. This dirty little town – believed by the Arabs to be the site of the garden of Eden! – was protected by dykes from inundation during the flood season. Early in February, 1915, the waters were rising in the neighbourhood, and most of the troops were withdrawn. Meanwhile a Turkish army which had come from the Euphrates valley was easily defeated in an attempt to recapture Basra.[2]

There had been much discussion between the War Office, the Government of India, and the commander in Mesopotamia whether another advance should be made as far as Amara on the Tigris or Nasiriya[3] on the Euphrates. On the other hand, when Nixon was

[1] The Prime Minister could not have been expected to supervise the details of the Mesopotamian campaign, but it is evidence of Asquith's lack of drive in the conduct of the war that he did not assure himself that this essential problem was being properly dealt with. The Viceroy of India was hardly less to blame for not taking more care to discover and remedy the shortcomings of the Indian military and marine authorities.

[2] The first stage of the fighting was watched, from a distance, outside Basra by a crowd carrying gifts and prepared to welcome the Turks whom the population expected, owing to their superior numbers, to win the battle.

[3] The reason put forward for an advance to Nasiriya was that at this point a channel from the Tigris joined the Euphrates. In fact this channel could be used for navigation only in high flood, and even then only to a point thirty miles distant from Nasiriya.

appointed to the command of the Mesopotamian force, he was instructed to submit plans not only for the occupation of the Basra vilayet, but for 'a subsequent advance to Baghdad'. He was told that the occupation of the Basra vilayet meant going as far as Amara and Nasiriya. Sir Beauchamp Duff said later that in asking for plans for the occupation of Baghdad, he was merely taking measures in view of 'possible eventualities'. Nixon, however, assumed that he was being instructed to open an offensive, and that the instructions about Baghdad meant a change in policy. Nixon did not think it necessary to enquire whether his interpretation was right. He might well have done so, since the instructions also required him to report on the 'adequacy and suitability of the river gunboats and transport now en route, namely:—two Nile gunboats, armament not yet known,[1] seven paddlers from the Irrawaddy Flotilla Company', and a few other small craft. The Nile gunboats sank on their passage through the Red Sea; the paddlers were found to be of too deep a draught to go above Qurna in the months of low water.

Nixon had no adequate knowledge of the strength of the enemy, and no aeroplanes[2] with which to make a reconnaisance of their positions. He advanced in the hottest season of the year, when he knew that his water transport was insufficient, and that the low water period was soon to begin. He captured Amara on June 4 and Nasiriya on July 25, only to discover that the occupation of the latter was unnecessary, at all events, until the rivers rose some six months later. Most of the casualties of his force were from sickness.

In these circumstances – and with the unlikelihood of getting reinforcements and adequate river craft – an advance beyond Nasiriya or Amara should have seemed even less practicable than at the time when Nixon was given his instructions. The argument that an enemy force at Kut threatened both Nasiriya and Amara had already been shown to be unfounded, and an advance to Kut would add over 150 miles to the lines of communication when the army was already short of men and transport. Nixon, however, was thinking not only in terms of

[1] It is remarkable that the Indian Command had not found out, before they accepted the despatch of the ships, what was the armament of the gunboats and the draught of the paddlers.

[2] A few machines – unsuited to the climate – were provided at the end of August, but only three aeroplanes and two converted seaplanes were available for the battle of Kut. None of these machines had a reliable compass for reconnaissance work. A few more aeroplanes reached Townshend before the attack on Ctesiphon.

holding Kut but of moving on to Baghdad. The Government of India agreed with an advance to Kut, but still disapproved of an attempt to reach Baghdad. Within a short time, however, the Viceroy, Lord Hardinge, suggested to the India Office that the capture of Baghdad would impress opinion in the Middle East, and would offset British failure at the Dardanelles. On the other hand, Hardinge did not recommend the plan unless reinforcements could be provided from Egypt or the Western Front.

General Townshend, who was given command of the force sent to occupy Kut, also had in mind a possible entry into Baghdad, if only to take away the British women and children in the city. Kut was captured – with heavy losses to the Turks[1] – at the end of September, but the Turks were able to make an orderly retreat to a prepared position at Ctesiphon. An attempt to pursue them before they had recovered from their defeat was impossible owing to difficulties of navigation; there was not enough land transport, and the few steamers available took twenty-four hours to get through two miles of river above Kut.

From this time the expedition fell into disaster. Once again the division of responsibility between the Cabinet, the War Office, the India Office, and the civil and military authorities in India hindered rapid, well-informed, and effective decisions, and once again also all the authorities concerned evaded the simple calculation that disaster would be certain if the number of river boats were not sufficient, with a margin for losses, repairs, and unexpected demands. The authorities in turn found a decision about an advance difficult because the commanders in Mesopotamia were not in agreement. Townshend, though vain and over-confident of his own military talent,[2] was more cautious than Nixon. Townshend, whose force consisted roughly of one division,[3] warned Nixon that the capture and occupation of Baghdad would need two divisions, exclusive of troops on the lines of communication. Nixon was too eager to assume that every chance would turn out favourably. He did not allow for the reinforcements which the

[1] The British and Indian casualties were much less heavy, but amounted to nearly double the number expected by General Townshend. Once again the wounded suffered severely owing to the insufficient medical and transport arrangements. They were carried down from Kut in the empty supply ships – including those which had brought up horses and mules.

[2] Townshend had an odd liking for a comparison between his own tactics and those of Napoleon.

[3] The force was tired from over-exertion, and had suffered heavy losses in fighting and from sickness.

Turks would be able to concentrate before Townshend was ready to advance. He counted upon a promise of two Indian divisions from France within an estimated time-table of two months, although past experience should have shown him that such promises were always too hopeful. In any case he did not take proper account of the time which it would take to move large reinforcements from Basra to Kut. Above all he had failed to make any real improvement in Basra – after the place had been in occupation for a year – or to face squarely the question of river transport – how much river tonnage was essential, and how much he was likely to receive within a given time.

The shortage of river steamers and tugs worked cumulatively in creating a shortage of land transport. At the time of Townshend's advance to Ctesiphon there were some 2000 mules and many carts at Basra, but no steamers for transporting them. Townshend was also without oxen for moving his heavy guns. In any case, owing to the delays in the concentration and advance of the force caused by lack of transport, the possibility of an advance by land was limited, since heavy rain was almost certain soon after the end of October. When at last, Townshend opened his attack on Ctesiphon, the Turks had had time to bring in one of their best divisions. Nixon still did not 'believe a word' about the strength of these reinforcements. An air reconnaissance on November 21 – the day before the attack – had disclosed the presence of this new division, but the pilot had been forced down and captured by the Turks. A second reconnaissance flight – with an untrained observer – failed to notice any change at Ctesiphon.

The attack on Ctesiphon, though made with great courage, was a failure. The Turkish first lines were captured at a cost of 4500 casualties out of the attacking force of 12,000. Townshend had not the resources to continue the assault against superior numbers. He therefore retired to Kut. Once again the medical arrangements were inadequate; Nixon's expectation of bringing the wounded to Baghdad had grim consequences.

The situation was now most serious. The capture of Baghdad might have countered the lowering effects on British prestige of the failure – soon to be followed by evacuation – at Gallipoli. Any hope of positive Arab support had been given up; more active hostility was now likely. The long-range repercussions of defeat might reach Persia, Afghanistan, and India. Thus, once begun, the attempt to reach Baghdad could not be abandoned without danger. It was therefore necessary to send stronger forces, and to support them with a better transport organisation. These reinforcements, and the river ships required for them, could not arrive for several months. Meanwhile immediate measures were needed to relieve Townshend whose depleted army had been surrounded in a none too secure position at Kut.

It might have been wiser to have ordered Townshend, in spite of the utter fatigue of his men, to have moved below Kut before the Turks had invested the place. Every mile downstream lessened the difficulties of supply and relief, and increased the difficulties of the enemy. The General Staff in India – the Commander-in-chief had still not visited Mesopotamia to see conditions for himself – thought it doubtful whether Townshend could hold out long enough, that is to say, until mid-January, when a relieving force was likely to arrive. They expected that the Turks would receive reinforcements enabling them to spare about 20,000 men to oppose this force. Nixon telegraphed to Townshend on December 2 – the day before the retreating force reached Kut – that he must decide for himself whether to stay there or move lower down the river. In other words, Townshend had permission to continue his withdrawal. Through a mistake of a staff officer, Townshend was not given this telegram until December 4. He had meanwhile decided to stay at Kut owing to the exhaustion of his men and the difficulty of moving the large quantities of supplies accumulated in the place. He now thought it too late to withdraw even if he had wished to do so.

After this decision had been taken, Townshend made the grave error of miscalculating the length of time for which his supplies would last, and once more Nixon, in this all important matter, did not insist upon detailed information. Townshend telegraphed on December 7 that he had sixty days of rations for his men, and thirty days' supply of fodder. He did not say whether he was cutting down daily rations, and did not make any cuts until January 22. He also did not take account of the large stores of grain accumulated by merchants in the town,[1] or – until too late – of the use of his transport animals for food. On January 25 he telegraphed that, by using his horses and mules as food, he could hold out for another eighty-four days.[2] If this possibility had

[1] Townshend's reason for keeping all genuine householders of Kut and their families – over 5000 people – in the place was that if he had turned them out, the women and children would have died of cold and starvation. There is no evidence that he could not have sent them immediately downstream with sufficient supplies to prevent a calamity of this kind.

[2] He explained that he had not felt justified in killing the transport animals until he knew that there was no immediate hope of relief. This explanation, however,

been known earlier – it is almost incredible that Nixon did not make more careful enquiries – the relief expedition under General Aylmer need not have made such desperate haste. The force would then have been larger and better supplied, and might have avoided the desperate frontal attacks which cost heavy casualties only to end in failure.

As matters were, General Aylmer's task was almost impossible. The Indian reinforcements promised from France arrived piecemeal, and without their staffs and medical units. Nixon had said that he did not need the staff. The force consisted largely of units not previously known to one another, and all without experience of Mesopotamian conditions. The equipment was insufficient, and much of it – from India – antiquated. There were no heavy howitzers, anti-aircraft guns, trench mortars, or Very lights, and not enough machine guns. In a country where bridging was essential General Aylmer had at first only one company of engineers.[1] Only two aeroplanes were available for artillery work. Once again there were not enough medical supplies, and the situation was made worse because one large consignment was left behind at Basra owing to a mistake of an officer who had been told to bring it up to the front. Even if there had been more troops and more supplies, the additional river transport had not arrived to take them up-stream. On January 21 when severe fighting had begun for the relief of Kut, some 10,000 men and twelve guns at Basra could not be sent forward because there was no transport for them.

The defeat of this heterogeneous, ill-provided and hastily collected force was not surprising. Only after he had decided that for a time no further advance was possible General Aylmer heard that there had

---

makes his earlier estimate of total resources all the more absurd. There were difficulties in persuading the Indian troops to eat horsemeat, although messages were sent from their religious leaders in India giving them full dispensation to do so. Their scruples might have been overcome earlier if they had had no alternative ration. When he realised that relief was delayed Townshend requisitioned stores of local merchants amounting to nearly 1000 tons of barley – some of this belonged to the firm of Messrs Lynch who would certainly have made no objection if the supplies had been taken earlier.

[1] In November, 1915, Nixon had asked for fifty pontoons from India. Only twenty-three had reached Basra by the middle of January, 1916. Native boats had to be used: at a critical time a bridge put across the Tigris, consisting mainly of these boats, collapsed in a high wind and thus prevented a move to outflank the defence which might otherwise have brought about a Turkish defeat and the relief of Kut. The outflanking move had to be abandoned for frontal attacks which failed with heavy loss.

been no urgent reason for risking an immediate attack and that Townshend could hold out for another twelve weeks.[1]

A second attempt at relief was made on March 8–10. The planning and execution of this attack (though not the courage and endurance of the troops) are open to question; a chance of taking the main Turkish defence by surprise was missed. General Aylmer had been reinforced, but, owing to the lack of transport, some 12,000 infantry, twenty-six guns, 2000 mules, and a large number of carts did not reach the fighting area by March 8. The shortage of howitzers was still serious, the infantry was still without trench mortars, and many battalions had only two machine guns. On March 11 there were only thirty-seven steamers and tugs capable of towing sixty-eight barges with an average daily delivery of 300 tons, whereas the requirements in tonnage were at least half as much again. A third attempt to relieve Kut also failed. It was delayed by floods, and by the usual transport shortage. For a time the relieving force had only about a week's rations in hand and once more the movement of reinforcements had to be stopped in order to bring up food. This third attack came very near to success; the position might have been different if Townshend had thought it possible to make a diversionary sortie from Kut. Finally, after a last effort on April 22, the tired troops could get no further. Townshend surrendered on April 29, after the Turks had rejected a fantastic offer[2] of £2,000,000 and forty guns if the force were allowed to retire on parole.

Some 12,000 prisoners were taken. The cruel and incompetent treatment of these prisoners, and especially of the rank and file, was typical of the dismal history of the Ottoman Empire. Nearly 70 per cent of the British prisoners died; the losses among the Indian troops – other than Moslems, who were given special treatment – were also very high. For a long time the Turks refused to allow neutral observers to inspect their prison camps.[3] After the fall of Kut neither the British nor the Turks were capable of large-scale action. The season of high floods and great

[1] General Nixon had resigned his command early in January, 1916. He was succeeded by Lt-General Sir Percy Lake, Chief of Staff in India.

[2] This offer was a grave political error. It was authorised by the Cabinet, who indeed doubled the original proposal of £1,000,000. Sir Percy Cox, the Chief Political Officer with the expedition, strongly opposed the offer (which seems to have originated from Townshend). The facts of the offer and of its refusal were used throughout the Middle East and elsewhere as material for anti-British propaganda.

[3] The United States Ambassador at Constantinople, and, after the American entry into the war, the Netherlands Ambassador made great efforts, ultimately with some success, to improve the harsh lot of the prisoners.

heat had begun; the heat was unusually severe and prolonged, and the troops still suffered immense and unnecessary hardships owing to the lack of transport. From the end of August, 1916, the position began rapidly to improve. There were more steamers, the port installations at Basra were much better, and adequate arrangements were made for the transport of the sick and wounded.

General Lake, whose health was suffering from the climate and from overstrain, was recalled in August, and was succeeded by Major-General Sir F. S. Maude.[1] Maude was much abler than his predecessors, and had ample warning from their mistakes. He did not attempt an advance until he had sufficient troops, transport, and supplies, and until his men had recovered from the appalling conditions which they had been enduring. He thereby lost three months of good weather, but there was no sensible alternative. Anyhow, the fall of Kut had not been followed by the disastrous political consequences which had been feared; there were no repercussions in India.

At the end of December, 1916, Maude was ready to attack. After hard fighting his troops turned the enemy out of their defences at Kut by February 24, 1917, and chased them for three days until a halt was necessary for bringing up supplies. On March 5 Maude resumed his advance. He drove the enemy out of their last position, and entered Baghdad on March 11. The Turks destroyed many installations, including an important German wireless station, and the Arabs and Kurds did much looting in the short time before the British forces marched in, but very large quantities of material – railway workshops, ice-making plant, pipes, pumps, cranes, and other heavy equipment – were taken almost intact.

For the rest of the month Maude consolidated his position. Apart from the immediate effect upon Arab opinion, the capture of Baghdad was timely, since the Russian military collapse and political confusion were soon to have serious repercussions in the Caucasus and Persia, and indeed throughout the Middle East. Maude's future plans depended to a large extent upon a Russian advance. There was still considerable hope that the Russians might reach Mosul, but until the situation was clearer, a British move beyond the limits of the vilayet of Baghdad would have been imprudent.

It was not long before the hopes of Russian co-operation faded.

---

[1] Maude was born in 1864. He had served in France in 1914, commanded a division at Gallipoli, and taken an important part in the evacuation of Suvla and Helles.

Colonel Richardson, liaison officer with the Russian force in Persia, reached Baghdad early in April. His view was that the Russians could not continue effective operations against the Turks. With the increasing disorganisation of the Russian army there seemed a danger that the Turks might be able to bring some 120,000 men and 300 guns from the Russian front in an attempt to recover Baghdad. Hence Maude decided to limit his operations to the capture of Samarra at the north end of the railway from Baghdad. In any case the summer floods would soon have made fighting almost impossible.

For a short time the Russian army appeared to be rallying, at least against the Austrians, but after the failure of the 'Kerensky' offensive,[1] there was little hope of improvement. The British defeat at Gaza[2] also made it more likely that the Turks would concentrate a large force against Maude's army. Early in June the War Office had information that the Germans were preparing a strong force to collaborate with the Turks.[3] This German plan did not come off. The supply difficulties were very great. The Turks and Germans did not get on well together; the Germans complained of Turkish inefficiency, and the Turks of German highhandedness.[4]

Early in October it became clear that Falkenhayn's attack was being abandoned, and the Turkish reinforcements diverted to Syria. Early in November the Turks were driven out of Tigrit on the Tigris and beyond the Baghdad–Samarra railway. General Maude died of cholera on November 18. He had been the most successful British general hitherto on any of the war fronts; at his death the Mesopotamian force was secure against any attack likely to be made against it. General Marshall, who was in command of one of the army corps, succeeded him as Commander-in-Chief. Marshall was instructed to carry on an 'active defence' and warned that he might be asked to give up a part of his force. An Indian division was in fact withdrawn to Egypt in December. Except in providing a diversion to draw off enemy forces from Syria, Baghdad was now a 'dead end'. A new situation

---

[1] See below, p. 306.   [2] See below, p. 118.
[3] General Falkenhayn and a staff of German officers began preparations in Turkey during June for the offensive.
[4] An immense explosion of munitions at Haidar Pasha railway station (the railway terminus on the east side of the Bosphorus) delayed the German-Turkish preparations which were already behind schedule. Falkenhayn earlier seems to have had doubts about the plan. Mustapha Kemal was strongly against it, and thought that the Germans were merely using up Turkish resources in their own interests.

arose with the collapse of Russia and the Bolshevist Revolution, but distances and difficulties of communications were a great obstacle. The Allied fears of a possible enemy drive across Caucasia, Persia, and the Caspian to Afghanistan and India as well as Allied hopes of keeping large areas of the Russian Empire out of the hands of the Bolshevists were not realised.[1]

NOTE

The Mesopotamia Commission

The Government of India, and the General Staff in India and Mesopotamia had done their utmost, by means of a censorship more rigid than on any other front, to conceal the unnecessary sufferings of the troops. This policy only made matters worse, since it could not be effective for long in hiding the facts, and gave an impression of indifference which, especially in regard to General Nixon, was not the case, and also suggested that the authorities concerned were totally without excuse.

Soon after the transfer (in February, 1916) of the direction and management of the expedition to the War Office, the government of India sent two commissioners to enquire into the medical arrangements in Mesopotamia. The terms of enquiry were later widened, and a third commissioner added. The War Cabinet, however, realised that a limited 'departmental' enquiry of this kind would not satisfy public opinion; they appointed a commission in London, under the chairmanship of Lord George Hamilton, to enquire into the expedition as a whole. The Commission was a strong one; it examined about a hundred witnesses, including Sir Beauchamp Duff, but, for reasons of expense and also in order to avoid delay, did not go to Mesopotamia or India, and therefore did not examine the Quartermaster-General in India or any of his staff, though those officers were directly responsible for the transport arrangements.

The findings of the Commission were severe. Nixon, and, after him, Lord Hardinge, Sir Beauchamp Duff, the Military Secretary of the India Office, and Austen Chamberlain, the Secretary of State for India, were mentioned by name as the high authorities chiefly responsible for the grave errors. The Commissioners stated that 'looking at the

---

[1] For British operations in the region of the Caucasus and the Caspian see below, Chapter 29.

facts, which from the first must have been apparent to any administrator, military or civilian, who gave a few minutes' consideration to the
map and to the conditions in Mesopotamia, the want of foresight and
provision for the most fundamental needs of the expedition reflects
discredit upon the organising aptitude of all the authorities concerned'.[1]

On the other hand, the Commissioners pointed out that the shortcomings in the armament and equipment of the expedition 'were the
natural result of the policy of indiscriminate retrenchment pursued for
some years before the war by the Indian Government under instructions from the Home Government, by which the Army was to be
prepared and maintained for frontier and internal use'.

The report of the Commission was published in June, 1917. There
was a considerable demand in the more popular sections of the press
for the punishment of some of the persons censured. Nixon had already
retired. Duff had been replaced when he left India to give evidence
before the Commission. Hardinge's term of office had expired, and
Austen Chamberlain resigned though, in fact, he was less responsible
than Kitchener who knew the general condition of the Indian army.[2]
The House of Commons did not come to any definite decision on a
proposal to set up a judicial enquiry to consider the allegations against
individuals. On August 1 the Army Council stated that they had asked
the officers concerned to submit written explanations of the statements
in the report. The Council would then consider action in each case.
No action was taken. General Nixon must have explained himself
satisfactorily to the Army Council, since in 1920 he was made a
GCMG.

[1] The minority report was even more severe.
[2] Hardinge, who had returned to the Foreign Office, also resigned, but Balfour,
as Foreign Secretary, would not accept his resignation.

CHAPTER 8

Egypt, Palestine, and Syria, 1915–1918

There is a certain oddness in the facts that, while British forces were engaging the Turks in Gallipoli and Mesopotamia, no attempt was made to advance into Palestine and Syria from the well-provided base in Egypt, and that the defence of the Suez Canal was organised on, or rather behind the Canal itself. One reason was that the British could not be altogether sure that they would not have to deal with serious internal trouble in Egypt. Kitchener, as British Agent and Consul-General in Egypt (and *de facto* ruler of the country) from 1911 to 1914, had continued the economic and administrative reforms which had saved Egypt from bankruptcy and improved the position of the peasantry without satisfying the political discontent of an increasingly vocal part of the population. Kitchener, like most officials in Egypt, did not regard the country as ready for independence; it must be said that they made little effort to prepare Egyptians for the termination of British control either by developing higher education or by training men for the senior administrative posts. Kitchener's own measures to lighten the peasants' burden of debt were well meant, but brought forward without much consideration of the reactions of the intended beneficiaries.[1]

There was also the risk, or certainty of trouble in the western desert from an ambitious tribal leader, the Senussi, and his similarly named followers. The Senussi had taken the Turkish side in the Italian cam-

---

[1] For example, Kitchener set up government depots where the fellahin could get accurate information about cotton prices when selling their crops. He also established at these depots offices of the Post Office Savings Bank where the peasants could deposit the proceeds of their sales. In fact the fellahin could get three times the rate of interest by private lending, and were not inclined to parade their wealth by leaving it in a public institution of which the local custodian was almost certain to be a gossip. When the Government invited the local authorities to put pressure upon the peasantry to deposit money in the banks, many peasants thought it prudent to obey and borrowed sums at 9 per cent from local money-lenders to earn 3 per cent in the banks. See P. G. Elgood, *Egypt and the Army*, p. 35–6.

paign of 1911–12 in Cyrenaica. They were more anti-Italian than pro-Turkish; the Italian occupation of the coast line of Cyrenaica had cut off their trade with Tripoli and Constantinople. They would probably have remained neutral after 1914 in return for a British subsidy, but, with the entry of Italy into the war, they accepted Turkish and German offers of arms and money. In the autumn of 1915 they began to attack Egyptian frontier garrisons. Some garrisons deserted to them. The British authorities seem to have been unnecessarily afraid that the fellahin might rise *en masse* in support of the invaders. In fact, the Egyptians were not inclined to welcome invaders from anywhere; Kitchener, remembering his campaign against the Mahdi, took the Senussi too seriously. The main difficulty was one of catching and pinning down an elusive enemy, ably led, until his capture, by Ja'far Pasha, an Arab from Baghdad. Ja'far, on hearing of the Turkish atrocities in Syria against the Arabs, joined the Arab rebels under the Sherif of Mecca.[1]

Sir John Maxwell, Commander-in-Chief, and the British military authorities might have been less disturbed about the possibility of civil disturbance in Egypt after the readiness of the Egyptians to do what they were asked to do at the outbreak of war. The Khedive, Abbas Hilmi, was openly anti-British; his general incompetence made him harmless except for intrigue. He was in Constantinople at the outbreak of war, and stayed there; in December, 1914, the British Government announced his deposition and the substitution of a British Protectorate for the Turkish suzerainty over Egypt. Egypt was already in a state of war; the Council of Ministers on August 5, obediently yielding to British pressure, had issued a declaration to this effect. The Turks had tried then and later to stir up disaffection, but Egyptians, however much they might wish to assert their independence, saw no advantage in exchanging one form of direct foreign control for another. The declaration of a Protectorate thus made, for the time, little practical difference. The British authorities, however, made a serious mistake in stating that Great Britain would undertake the defence of Egypt without calling for Egyptian aid. In fact, during the course of the war the British Government needed a great deal of Egyptian co-operation, and, to their unpopularity, insisted on getting it. Compulsion was used to secure enough men for an Egyptian Labour Corps, and later, for a Camel Corps. This exercise of superior power was the more intolerable

---

[1] Ja'far Pasha received a CMG for his services and later became Prime Minister of Iraq.

(it was one of the chief causes of the rebellion of 1919) because it fell upon a country which had little or no interest in the war as such. The Egyptians had almost no ocean shipping; the Suez Canal, which was under long lease to a foreign company and regulated by an international Convention, was itself hardly a part of Egypt, since it passed through desert country and lakes on the edge of the Sinai peninsula some eighty miles east of Cairo and the Nile.[1]

British military experts did not think a Turkish attack upon the Canal impracticable, though the crossing of the Sinai desert was a severe difficulty. The shortest route – along the narrow coastal strip – was not possible for vehicles, but some distance inland there were hard tracks over a broad limestone plateau with adequate watering places for about 5000 men and 2000 camels. The Turks might have done more damage if they had limited themselves to guerrilla raids across this plateau in order to block the canal from the eastern side. They did not, however, have many mines, and – more important – Djemal Pasha, the Turkish commander in the area of Syria and Palestine, believed that the arrival of a Turkish force on the banks of the canal would start a rebellion in the form of a Holy war in Egypt.

With this purpose in view, a Turkish force of about 20,000 strong, capably organised by a German Colonel Kress von Kressenstein, advanced to the Canal early in February, 1915. The attack was completely defeated, and the enemy force might have been destroyed if the British command had not made pursuit impossible by failing to arrange measures for the transport of water into the Sinai peninsula for the supply of their own counter-attack. No other Turkish expedition reached the eastern bank of the Canal. General Maxwell still exaggerated the chances of an enemy attack, but early in 1916 his successor,[2]

[1] See map 9.

[2] The arrival in Egypt of the greater part of the army from Gallipoli had resulted in a somewhat ludicrous superfluity of staff officers. There were for a time three different organisations in Egypt: (1) Maxwell's command of what was known as 'the force in Egypt', (2) the Mediterranean Expeditionary Force including the army from Gallipoli. In December, 1915, General Sir Archibald Murray was sent from England to command the MEF, and given the responsibility for the defence of the Canal; (3) a so-called 'Levant Base' controlling transport and co-ordinating supplies for all the expeditionary forces in the Mediterranean and Middle East. In March, 1916, the War Office put an end to this administrative confusion by recalling Maxwell, disbanding the Levant Base as a separate entity, and giving the sole command in Egypt to Murray. The MEF was now renamed the Egyptian Expeditionary Force. Even so the size of Murray's staff (662 in all early in 1917) at Cairo was a by-word among those who were not

General Murray, recommended that the defence of Egypt should be secured by the occupation of El Arish and Kossaima on the southern outskirts of Palestine. The Turks would then be unable to cross the Sinai peninsula. The first step was an advance to the oasis of Qatiya, about twenty-five miles east of Qantara, the British military base at the northern end of the Canal. A light railway was begun to Qatiya and cavalry pushed out in the area beyond it. A Turkish raid took the British (somewhat unnecessarily) by surprise and for a time regained Qatiya, but the advance continued. In August, 1916, Kress made a more determined attack on the British positions at Romani, north of Qatiya, at the point reached by the railway. The attack was a complete failure, but once again there were no adequate arrangements for pursuit and Kress managed to get away. No other attempt was made to stop the British advance; in December, 1916, El Arish – a place with an abundant water supply – was reached, and mounted troops went on another twenty miles or so to Rafa, half-way between El Arish and Gaza.

What was to be done with this large, well-equipped army, including Australian and New Zealand troops of high calibre as well as British and Indian brigades? Lloyd George, now Prime Minister, had always believed in defeating the Turks. He wanted a victory somewhere to offset the failure on the Somme and the German successes against Russia and Roumania. He did not order Murray to take the offensive in Palestine; he reminded him that his 'primary mission' was the defence of Egypt, but suggested that he should make 'the maximum possible effort' during the winter.

Murray replied by asking for two more divisions. He cannot have expected to get them, and in January, 1917, was ordered to send back one of his divisions for the next campaign in France; an advance into Syria and Palestine would have to be postponed until later in the year. Murray, however, decided that he could improve the chances of rapid success in the autumn by taking the fortress of Gaza at the entrance to Palestine. The Turkish defence was now better. The Germans had done a great deal to improve communications behind the front, and the British had come a long way from their main base in Egypt. The Germans also had air superiority. They wisely kept their subordinate fronts, including Palestine, supplied with a few of the most recent type

---

members of it. At the time of greatest confusion a parody of the Athanasian Creed describing the staff ('And yet there is not one commander-in-chief but three commanders-in-chief', etc.) had a popular circulation among the fighting units.

of aircraft and were therefore able to exercise air control for all essential purposes over the less powerful British machines used before the end of 1917.

Murray attacked Gaza on March 26. The enemy were expecting an attack, but at the end of the day the attackers had broken into the town. Owing to bad staff work,[1] the troops were withdrawn during the night. Next day it was too late to bring them back. Murray sent a misleading account of this disastrous failure to the War Office. He understated his own casualties, multiplied threefold those of the enemy, and gave the impression that the operation had been 'most successful'. Not unnaturally, the War Office took him at his word and recommended him to go on. He made a second attempt on Gaza three weeks later – a frontal attack against positions now much strengthened – though, if he had waited he might, like Allenby, have turned the defences by an attack through Beersheba. This second attempt was heavily defeated, and in June Murray was recalled to England. General Sir Edward Allenby took his place. Allenby had gained, on the whole, a good reputation in France. He was a cavalry general, but with a mind more open than most of his fellows to the conditions of siege warfare. He had immense vitality and determination, and was popular with his troops; he lived with them, and not in the far-off luxury of Cairo. He took up his command when the Turks were becoming dispirited, war-weary, and anxious to get rid of German control and the exploitation of Turkish resources for German ends. The Arab revolt, begun by the Sherif of Mecca in June, 1916, was another embarrassment to Turkey. Sherif Hussein Ibn Ali of Mecca ruled over the northernmost of the three regions – the Hejaz, Asir, and the Yemen – bordering the Red Sea. The Turks exercised hardly more than a nominal authority, outside the few towns, over these large but mainly desert areas. After the outbreak of war the two southern regions were almost entirely cut off from communication with Turkey by the British control of the Red Sea. A railway ran from Damascus to Medina, some 250 miles north-north-east of Mecca. Hussein wanted to get rid of Turkish suzerainty and to revive the long-fallen Arab Empire, including in a new State Arabia, Syria, and Iraq. The British

---

[1] Especially a failure to send at once to Advanced Headquarters south of Gaza Turkish wireless messages (intercepted and decoded in Cairo) describing their position as desperate. Success on the first day of the attack was necessary because the attacking force could not be provided with food and water for more than twenty-four hours.

Government welcomed his opposition to the Turks, and began negotiations with him in the autumn of 1915, but, partly owing to French interests in Syria, would not promise more than an independent Arabia and parts of Syria.[1] Hussein's plans of revolt were hurried on by news of Turkish massacres of Arab leaders in Syria and by the despatch of 3000 Turkish reinforcements (to be followed by a German mission) along the Hejaz railway to Medina.[2] The German mission never reached Medina, and went back to Syria. The Arab rebels, already supplied with British arms, took Mecca and the seaport of Jeddah, and besieged Medina. They could not capture the place or prevent a detachment from the garrison setting out to recover Mecca. At this point the British authorities in London considered sending an Indian brigade to support the rebels. Murray and his advisers thought the plan unwise. In any case, before it was put into effect, T. E. Lawrence, a young archaeologist on the staff of the Arab Bureau – an organisation set up in Cairo to deal with relations with the Arabs – had reached the camp of Feisal, a younger son of Hussein, outside Medina. Lawrence realised at once that the Arabs ought not to attempt to

[1] Between December, 1915, and May, 1916, Sir Mark Sykes and M. Georges Picot, a French diplomat, drew up an agreement, which was accepted by their respective Governments, and also by the Russian Government, delimiting the respective interests of the three Powers in relation to an independent Arab State or Federation. The agreement dealt primarily with four areas: (1) the vilayet of Adana and the coastal strip of Syria west of the line Aleppo–Homs–Damascus, (2) Mesopotamia south of Baghdad, with access to the ports of Haifa and Acre, (3) and (4) an area bounded on the west by a line from Damascus to the lake of Tiberias, the Jordan valley, and the Dead Sea, and extending thence west and south to Gaza and Akaba. The eastern boundary ran from Rowanduz on the Persian frontier to Mesopotamia. The cities of Aleppo, Homs, and Damascus were included in the area. Areas (1) and (2) were to be respectively under direct French and British administration (after consultation with an Arab State or Federation). Areas (3) and (4) were to be given to an independent Arab State or Federation. Area (3) – the northern half – would be under French influence, and area (4) – the southern half – would be under British influence, that is to say, if the Arab State or Federation asked for foreign advisers, these advisers would be French in the northern and British in the southern half. Palestine was to be under a special regime. Russia was to receive the Turkish provinces of Erzerum, Trebizond, and Tiflis.

This agreement, embodying the maximum which the French would concede to an independent Arab State or Federation, was not known to the Sherif of Mecca or to the Italian Government until it was published by the Bolsheviks, though both the Sherif and the Italians suspected some Anglo-French arrangement, and indeed could guess its terms without much difficulty.

[2] Under German leadership they might have been able to make a surprise attack on Aden.

capture strongly fortified places or attack Turkish regular forces; they should limit themselves generally to cutting Turkish communications and spreading the revolt among the tribes up to the Damascus area. This plan was quickly adopted by Feisal; he moved to the north of Medina and thus compelled the Turks to give up their attempt to retake Mecca, and to disperse their forces for the protection of the Hejaz railway. Lawrence's extraordinary personality, resembling in some respects that of General Gordon, his courage and ability as a guerrilla leader, his power of command over Arabs, and, not least, his own vivid account of his activities have given the Arab revolt a more prominent place than is due to it in a general history of the war. Nevertheless, from a military point of view the rebellion became an increasingly important factor in accelerating the Turkish defeat. Early in July, 1917, Lawrence, with a force of tribesmen, captured the port of Aqaba from the land side. Feisal's Arab troops were moved by sea to this port, and thus protected the British right as well as continually harassing Turkish communications along the Hejaz railway.

Allenby had to begin his proposed offensive as soon as possible, since at any time after the end of October the rains might interfere with operations. Furthermore a Turkish force, with strong German support, was already being organised in defence of Syria. Enver Pasha had wanted to use this force for the recovery of Baghdad;[1] the Germans insisted on diverting it to Syria and Palestine because a successful British attack might cut the Turkish communications east of Alexandretta. The concentration of the German force was itself delayed. The German 'Asia Corps' was still on the Asiatic shore of the Bosphorus at the beginning of September, when its main ammunition depot was blown up by British agents.

Allenby followed previous invaders of Syria from the south in deciding (as Murray had intended) to advance along the coastal strip, about five to ten miles broad and everywhere passable by vehicles. This route was open to communication from the sea, but the supply of fresh water was not good, and there was no port suitable for a base. Haifa was a fair anchorage without port facilities, and Jaffa merely an open roadstead. Strong currents and heavy surf also made landings difficult. Gaza, at the entrance to the coastal route, was now very strongly held and difficult to capture. Allenby therefore decided to turn the position by an attack on the Turks at Beersheba. The ground was broken and hilly, and water supplies were a difficulty until Beer-

[1] See above, p. 111.

sheba was taken. Allenby could not hope completely to surprise the Turks – still less the Germans – but he managed to delude them into thinking that the main attack would be delivered against Gaza.[1] Fortunately the British at last had strong air reinforcements, and superiority in machines; the enemy could be kept from close reconnaissance. A further piece of good luck occurred on the day before the attack, when a German reconnaissance plane, which had taken photographs of the area of concentration, was shot down while recrossing the British lines. Hence the Turks were not expecting the attack on Beersheba on October 31; Falkenhayn, the German Commander, was actually in the train between Aleppo and Jerusalem. The success at Beersheba was followed by the capture of Gaza and the whole Turkish line of defence of Palestine. By mid-November the Turks had lost the important junction where the line running towards Gaza and Beersheba left the line running from Damascus and Haifa to Jerusalem. Only strong rearguard resistance, and the difficulty of the pursuers in moving forward their water supplies prevented a complete Turkish collapse. Allenby went on to capture Jerusalem on December 9 before the arrival of Turkish and German reinforcements.[2]

Lloyd George now believed that another offensive would bring about a Turkish surrender. Allenby did not think this likely. The Turkish losses had been heavy but not enough to destroy their fighting power. Moreover the Turkish leaders in Constantinople no longer regarded the loss of Syria as vital; they were more interested in their chances of expansion in the areas now open to them owing to the collapse of Russia. They also expected a German victory in the forthcoming offensive on the Western Front. This victory would regain for them indirectly all that they might have lost in Syria and elsewhere.

In any case Allenby could not take the offensive in the spring of 1918 since, owing to the German success in the west, over 60,000 of his best troops were withdrawn. He was given Indian reinforcements,[3] but

[1] A British officer carrying faked plans of a direct attack on Gaza rode out to make contact with a Turkish patrol. He then feigned a wound, and, as he 'escaped', dropped the wallet containing the plans. The Turks were deceived by this ancient trick.

[2] Unlike the Emperor William II on his bombastic visit to Jerusalem in 1898, Allenby entered the city on foot. To the writer's knowledge, the capture of Jerusalem caused surprise as well as enthusiasm among certain simple Orthodox monks of Mount Athos, who could not understand why the British general had the Turkish name Ali Bey.

[3] They were mainly new recruits, but were brigaded with British battalions, and quickly became of good fighting value.

for a time he could only wait, and try to draw off as many Turks as possible from his ultimate line of attack along the coast by launching small expeditions across the Jordan. Although these expeditions were none too fortunate – one of them was nearly cut off – they had the effect of persuading the Turks to move nearly a third of their forces to the east of the Jordan.

Hence – with Lawrence (known to the Turks as 'al Urans, destroyer of engines') and the Arabs continuing their raids – Allenby was able to resume the offensive in mid-September. The situation in the west was now totally changed. The Turkish armies, ill-supplied, and with no hope of adequate reinforcements, were beginning to break up. They had practically no air support, and Liman von Sanders, the senior German commander with the Turks, expected defeat. Within a fortnight of the opening of his attack, Allenby had broken the Turkish resistance; the speed of his advance was limited only by his own problems of supply.[1] His troops made a triumphal entry into Damascus on October 2. Two days earlier Bulgaria had surrendered. The way to Constantinople through Thrace was now open. There was nothing for the Turkish Government and High Command but to surrender. The Turkish leaders whose policy had brought disaster to their country were replaced, and on October 20 the new government asked for an armistice. The armistice was signed on October 30 on the British battleship *Agamemnon*.

[1] Allenby's decisive victory was won at Megiddo, the modern name for the Hebrew Armageddon where St John (Revelation xvi. 16) saw all the nations of the world gathered in battle. In fact, troops from every Continent fought in this battle; America was represented by a contingent from the West Indies.

PART III

The Western Front in 1915 and 1916: difficulties of the Coalition: death of Lord Kitchener

The western offensives of the spring of 1915: the entry of Italy into the war: failure of the autumn offensive: Haig succeeds French as Commander-in-Chief of the BEF

The principal reason for the delays which ruined the chances of success at Gallipoli was the decision taken by the War Council at the beginning of January, 1915, that the Western Front should be the main theatre of operations for the British army as long as the French required British support. This decision was not, in fact, a real decision upon action – the first necessity in war – but a postponement of action. Moreover the French High Command was given the last word; as long as Joffre considered that the fullest British support was essential in France, the French Government would not take a different view.

The War Council had qualified their decision by saying that, if the result of the next offensive in France showed that no large-scale advance there was possible, British troops might be employed elsewhere. Joffre, however, was convinced that an advance was possible. Sir John French agreed with him; the two commanders, if their offensive failed, were unlikely to conclude that any offensive was almost certain to fail. They would draw the opposite conclusion that with more men, more guns, and more ammunition the next offensive would succeed. Sir John French, who was in closer touch than Kitchener or the War Council with the French High Command knew that Joffre thought British help inadequate; it was therefore very difficult for the commander of the smaller force to refuse co-operation in plans which at this time involved more French than British troops. Joffre, himself, like all Frenchmen, wanted to get the Germans out of France as quickly as possible; since he believed that victory could be won in 1915 he was unwilling to listen to Kitchener's more cautious view that the British armies would not be ready to exert their full force until the spring of 1916.

Hence the War Council, in January 1915, were surrendering their own initiative and committing themselves to the French view that the war could be decided within the next twelve months on the Western Front. Their failure to realise the implications of the French view only added to their troubles. While the British Ministers were considering diversions elsewhere the French and British High Commands were planning offensives in France which would make it very difficult, with the limited supply of men and material available, to support any important diversionary attacks. The general plan adopted by Joffre was an attack on the long lines of communication to the German salient which, at its apex near Noyon, was only fifty-five miles from Paris. Joffre proposed to drive in from the south and west on the flanks of this salient. A British attack eastward at Neuve Chapelle on March 10-13 fitted into this plan.[1] The attack, however, failed; the casualties were 583 officers and 12,309 other ranks. Sir John French reported that he had called off the attack owing to shortage of ammunition. The expenditure of ammunition was far greater than had been expected, but in any case it was clear that the 'break-in' would not have been followed by a 'break-through'.

A French attack in Champagne had also been broken off after gaining a little ground at great cost. Neither Joffre nor Sir John French were discouraged by these failures. They merely thought it necessary to accumulate more ammunition before opening another offensive. Joffre reckoned that the time for this next move would be about the end of April. He asked again for British co-operation, and wrote to Sir John French on March 24 that he was confident of inflicting 'such a blow on the enemy that the greatest results may follow and that our movement may be an important step toward the final victory'. Sir John French replied on April 1 that he hoped to be able to co-operate in a combined offensive at the end of April.

Sir John French at this time knew very little of the general strategic policy of the British Government, if indeed they can be said to have had any policy other than that of postponing decisions. He was, however, giving to the War Council's resolution of January 8 an interpretation which would make it impossible to provide for large-scale operations outside the Western Front, while at this same time the War Council were drifting into an overseas enterprise which would seriously limit the resources available for a large-scale offensive in the west. Before the April offensives opened the Germans themselves took the initiative by attacking in the neighbourhood of Ypres. This attack was

[1] See Map 4.

supported from April 22 onwards by the use of asphyxiating gas.[1] The Allies had received information that the Germans were intending to use gas, but did not believe it.[2] The Germans themselves, fortunately for the Allies, employed their weapon on too small a scale to be decisive. Protective measures – improvised respirators – were devised at once, and experiments made to provide full protection by 'smoke helmets'. The 'second battle of Ypres' continued until the last week of May with important local gains, but no 'break-through',[3] in spite of the

[1] The Hague Convention of 1907 respecting the Laws and Customs of War on Land forbade the use of 'poison or poisoned weapons'. An earlier Hague Declaration of 1899 respecting asphyxiating gases included this veto, and also a veto on 'the use of projectiles the sole object of which is the diffusion of asphyxiating gases'. This wording was interpreted during the discussions at The Hague in 1899 to mean that the destructive effect of the projectile must be greater than the destructive effect of the gas. Thus The Hague Conventions definitely prohibited the use of shells solely for the diffusion of gas; they were intended to cover any other method of diffusing poison gas, but the actual wording did not refer to the diffusion of cloud gas. The Germans themselves appear to have been aware that they were breaking the spirit, if not the letter of these Conventions, since they put out vague and unsupported charges that the Allies had already violated them. The Germans made no allusion to the use of gas in their communiqué announcing the fighting of April 22. The fact is also not referred to in some of the post-war popular German histories of the war.

[2] A German prisoner captured by the Belgians on April 14 had given details of the gas cylinders in position; he also had a respirator. The Allies might well have guessed, from previous German behaviour, that the German allegation that the Allies were using poison gas in their shells meant that the Germans themselves were intending to use it. The Allies did not know that the Germans had already used gas on the Russian front. The Russians themselves may not have known it, since, owing to the extreme cold, the effect was not great. It is, however, more likely, that, with their usual carelessness, the Russian Staff merely forgot to warn their Allies.

The German use of gas was followed, inevitably, by the Allied use of it. As in other spheres, the Germans lost far more than they gained by their adoption of uncivilised practices. They now had the chemical industries of the world against them, while they had given the Allies an additional motive for tightening the blockade. It is even doubtful whether, on balance, they were tactically wise to introduce a weapon which depended a great deal on the prevailing winds; these winds along the Western Front tended to be from the west, south-west, or north-west. Psychologically, the ultimate effect of the introduction of gas warfare was also unfavourable to the Germans. Efficient gas masks reduced gas warfare to an 'unpleasant incident', but meanwhile the Allies were hardened in their view of German behaviour, and, one might say, German guilt.

[3] The situation was for a time serious; the French territorial and African units north of Ypres withdrew in panic under the attack, and the British in the salient were in danger of being cut off. The Germans, however, had not expected a large-scale break-through, and could not exploit it owing to the transfer of troops to the Eastern Front. On military grounds the Allies might have abandoned the

confusion caused by the gas, and in spite also of the much heavier weight of artillery available to the Germans.

The German attack drew off a certain number of British reserves, and made inroads into stocks of ammunition; Sir John French none the less supported Joffre's offensive on May 9 by an attack on Aubers Ridge (toward the southern end of the British front, and not far from the earlier attack at Neuve Chapelle). This attack on a front of two miles was also a failure. The offensive was renewed, on the insistence of the French, in the neighbourhood of Festubert. Kitchener had little hope of success; he thought that, if the French, with at least twice as many divisions in reserve, and ample supplies of ammunition, could not break through, 'we may take it as proved that the lines cannot be forced'.

The French did not break through the enemy lines, and the British attack at Festubert was no more successful than earlier attacks. The British casualties at Aubers Ridge were 458 officers and 11,161 other ranks, and at Festubert 710 officers and nearly 16,000 other ranks. In addition the cost of holding the Ypres salient during the fighting from April 22 to May 31 had been 2150 officers and 57,125 other ranks. The French attacks between May 15 and June 18 had no great results, and were made at the cost of 2260 casualties in officers and 100,273 in other ranks.

In April, 1915, the Allies had won a diplomatic success by securing Italian belligerency on their side. The term 'success' may be used because Italy might well have come into the war to assist her fellow-members of the Triple Alliance. At the beginning of the war she announced her neutrality on the ground that the war of Austria-Hungary against Serbia was an act of aggression, and therefore outside the terms of the Treaty of the Triple Alliance. The Italian defection was not unexpected. Italy did not want to expose herself to a naval war against France and Great Britain. She had just waged a not very glorious campaign in Tripoli and was in no condition financially and materially to take part in a much larger war. She had irredentist claims against Austria and did not wish to further Austrian expansion at the cost of the Southern Slavs. At the same time she was equally opposed to Serbian expansion on the Adriatic coast. Italy, in fact, was open to offers from either group of belligerents. She came down on the side of

---

Ypres salient where the Germans had every advantage of position. For reasons of prestige French would not give it up (Joffre was less unwilling); the Belgians also disliked yielding any territory still left to them. See Map 3.

Great Britain and France because in the early months of 1915 she thought that they were likely to win the war. The German plan to defeat France had failed. The German navy had not attempted to challenge British sea power. The Russian armies had suffered a heavy defeat in East Prussia, but had advanced against Austria. In March, 1915, they occupied the Galician fortress of Przemsyl. The moment therefore seemed favourable for an Italian decision.

In August, 1914, the Italian Ambassador in London had told Grey that Italy might come into the war on the conditions that (i) the British and French fleets joined the Italian fleet in attacking the Austrians in the Adriatic, (ii) Italy should receive in the peace settlement the Trentino and a frontier along the watershed of the Alps, and the port and city of Trieste, (iii) the Albanian port of Valona should be neutral-ised, and, in the event of a partition of the Ottoman Empire, Italy should be allotted a share in Asia Minor. Within a few months Italian demands had risen to include nearly all the Dalmatian coast. Grey thought that the Italians were asking too much, but that it was neces-sary for military reasons to accept their demands. Grey seems to have believed that the number of Italian-speaking people in Dalmatia was greater than it actually was; he also felt that the increase of territory promised to Serbia at the expense of Austria-Hungary could be set off against the concessions to Italy in Dalmatia. The Italian insistence upon a militarily stronger Alpine frontier was also less unreasonable in 1915 than it appeared later after the collapse of the Habsburg Empire.

The treaty of London, embodying nearly all the Italian demands, was signed on April 26, 1915. Russia gave her consent to it reluctantly; she did not want to promise Italy territory which the Southern Slavs hoped to acquire. The treaty was kept secret because a knowledge of the terms would have caused Slav discontent, but the general character of the terms soon became known owing to a Russian leakage, with the result that the Croats and other southern Slavs in the Austro-Hungarian army fought well against the Italians.

It is ironical that the Italian declaration of war against Austria-Hungary (Italy did not declare war on Germany until a year later) took place on May 22, when the Germans had already begun their advance in Galicia which was to drive in the great Russian salient and ultimately to lead to the destruction of the Russian armies in Poland. The Italian entry into the war was of some service to the Russians by holding a very considerable part of the Austrian forces on a southern front, but the Italians failed to make any important advance, and their belligerency did not have much immediate effect upon Anglo-French plans.

After the failures on the Western Front the time would seem to have come for the British Government to return to the previous resolution of the War Council in January, 1915, that, if the results of an offensive in France showed a large-scale advance to be impossible, they would consider themselves free to employ British troops elsewhere. They were in fact already employing British troops elsewhere and on a scale certainly not contemplated six months earlier. Hence, until they had made sufficient provision for victory at the Dardanelles, there were obvious military reasons for remaining on the defensive in the west. Such a defence need not have been merely passive. A continuous local activity, raids, bombardments, and other threats of attack, on different parts of the front would have prevented the German High Command – who were already nervous of their numerical inferiority in the west – from sending more troops away to the east.

The argument for this policy was put very strongly in a remarkable paper submitted by Churchill to the War Cabinet on June 18.[1] He pointed out that the Allied offensives had gained, at very heavy cost, only about eight square miles of territory and that this territory was of little strategic value. We were in the 'unsatisfactory position of having lost our ground [in France] before the defensive under modern conditions was understood, and having to retake it when the defensive has been developed into a fine art'. With these new conditions it was doubtful whether

> the accidents and undulations of ground play so important a part in tactics as formerly. It is easy to speak of acquiring 'the heights which dominate Flanders' . . . etc. In fact, however, the armies have in the main settled down, not in selected positions, but along the actual lines of their chance collision when they came into contact, and both sides are maintaining themselves in all, or almost all, positions, good, bad, or indifferent. Therefore it does not seem safe to assume that particular heights and slopes possess tactical virtues of such supreme significance as to produce strategic results.

Unless it could be shown that the capture of two or three miles of ground would produce such results, a continuance of the offensive was

[1] The positive side of Churchill's argument was that the Dardanelles expedition should be pressed to a successful end. See above, p. 84.

unwise. Moreover we were too readily accepting the view that we could obtain decisive results by the use of vast quantities of high explosive shells. The failure of the recent French offensives[1] did not bear out this view. 'The method is effective for clearing a few miles of ground; but its applicability to the reconquest of Flanders and the advance through Germany is doubtful.'

On the day after Churchill had circulated his memorandum to the War Cabinet, a conference between the French and British Ministers of Munitions opened at Boulogne. This conference, which held three sessions on June 19–20, was presided over by Lloyd George and attended by representatives from British and French Headquarters. The purpose of the Conference was to consider the requirements of the armies in respect of artillery and munitions after taking into account the changed conditions of warfare. The conference reached conclusions of great importance which reinforced Churchill's memorandum and should have been decisive in determining Anglo-French strategy for the rest of the year.

The main factors in the situation were that the recent fighting had shown that field guns were no longer adequate to destroy field fortifications. The Germans were in a better position than the French and British since they had one heavy gun to two field guns; the French had one to four, and the British (though they had a slightly higher percentage of field guns to infantry strength) had only one heavy gun to every twenty field guns. It was therefore necessary to correct this grave deficiency at least to the extent of one heavy gun to two field guns. It was also estimated that in the sector of an attack, the allowance of ammunition should be 1000 rounds for each heavy gun and 2000 rounds for each field gun. In the third place, the experience of previous offensives had shown, though it hardly needed such disastrous failures to reveal so obvious a fact, that on a narrow frontage of attack the enemy guns on the flank could enfilade the greater part of the attacking front. Hence the British view was that the front of attack should be about twenty-five miles. An attack on such a front would require at least 36 divisions, and 1150 heavy guns and howitzers, apart from the normal amount of field artillery.

The British supply position was such that neither the guns nor the ammunition on this scale could be provided before the spring of 1916.

---

[1] I.e. the French were already better provided than the English with high explosives, and therefore the most recent French offensive was a better test than the British offensive.

The French might be able to supply themselves earlier, but certainly not before the end of the ordinary campaigning season of 1915. Moreover, as Kitchener had always pointed out, the new British armies would not be fully trained, in sufficient numbers, before the spring or summer of 1916. Thus it seemed desirable to remain on an 'active defence' for the remainder of 1915; that is to say, to maintain raids, bombardments, mining, and other activities on the Western Front in sufficient strength to make it unsafe for the enemy to withdraw troops eastward, but not to attempt a full-scale 'break-through'.[1]

After the Boulogne Conference Kitchener assumed that the French would give up their plans for an immediate resumption of the offensive. He therefore agreed to send more reinforcements to the Dardanelles. Joffre, however, held to his opinion that an Allied offensive in the west was not only a practicable but an urgent undertaking, since, if it were delayed until 1916, the Russians might be defeated, and might make a separate peace. The Russian position at this time was extremely serious. Since the opening of the German-Austrian offensive in Galicia on May 1 the Russians had been pushed back with immense losses. Lemberg, which the Russians had taken in September, 1914, was lost on June 22, and the whole Russian salient was threatened. Joffre was influenced less by the situation on the Eastern Front than by his own obstinate confidence in success, and by the knowledge that French opinion was becoming war-weary. He had told Sir John French that opinion in France would not understand the postponement of a great effort to turn the Germans out of France; he had also hinted, as before, that the British were not taking an adequate share in the war, and that the French were beginning to doubt the determination and ability of the British Government to fight through to victory. The French did not conceal either their anxieties about their own public opinion or their feelings about Great Britain. Before the Boulogne Conference a member of Joffre's staff had said 'the French people were getting tired of the war'. The effect of these warnings on Kitchener as well as on Sir John French and Haig was to suggest that, unless the British Government gave way to the French demand for early action on the Western Front, the French might make peace in the autumn. The British commanders seemed unaware then, as later, that high military and political opinion in France was far from unanimous in supporting

[1] 'Ordinary' trench warfare between the Festubert and Loos offensives cost about 300 casualties a day.

Joffre's view,[1] and that the French troops themselves, officers as well as men, were far from thinking that another offensive in the west would produce anything more than a continuance of the very heavy losses of the previous attempts. In other words, French 'war-weariness', such as it was, was due more to the uneasiness over costly and premature offensives than to impatience at delay.

The position with regard to an offensive was more difficult because Sir John French had already committed himself, before the Boulogne Conference, to an approval in principle of Joffre's grandiose plan. This plan was – as before – to cut off the immense German salient by attacks northward in Champagne and eastward from the Artois plateau. Joffre would exploit the confusion by sending forward cavalry, and infantry in motor vehicles, through the gaps in the German lines. The last stage would be a general offensive to compel the enemy to retreat beyond the Meuse and thus possibly to end the war.

Joffre asked for British collaboration, and, in particular, for an attack north of Lens. Sir John French agreed in principle with this plan, and promised on June 19 that the British preparations for an attack would be complete by July 10. French then instructed Haig[2] to submit a detailed plan for operations between Lens and the La Bassée canal. Haig replied that the area concerned was unfavourable for an attack. The ground was for the most part flat and featureless grassland, with very little cover; the boundaries were the cottages, dumps, and towns of a coalmining area. Haig also pointed out that, in view of the munitions situation, it was of little use to make plans for offensives.[3] He suggested, however, that if it were necessary to fall in with Joffre's proposals, the main British offensive should be delivered north of the La Bassée canal.

On July 5 Asquith, Balfour, and Kitchener crossed to France to meet representatives of the French Government – Viviani,[4] Delcassé,[5] and Millerand[6] – and the British and French Commanders-in-Chief.

[1] See below, pp. 135-6. Poincaré records in his *Memoirs* that he was informed on July 21 that 'no single general, not excepting Foch, has any more faith in an offensive proving successful' (Eng. trans., iv. 167-8).

[2] Haig at this time commanded the First British army on whose front the attack was to be made.

[3] There is no evidence available to show that Haig at this time knew the conclusions reached at the Boulogne Conference, but it is most improbable that he did not know them.

[4] President of the Council of Ministers.

[5] Minister for Foreign Affairs.   [6] Minister of War.

Kitchener, after a talk with Joffre, came to the conclusion that, for French political reasons, and in spite of the obvious military objections, the offensive would have to be attempted. The British Ministers accepted this view. On the following day an Allied military conference was held at Chantilly. This conference rejected the idea of 'active defence', but was vague about the actual plans for an offensive. On July 11 Sir John French and Joffre met at St Omer. Joffre repeated his absurd view that the area of attack assigned to the British army was 'particularly favourable ground'. French argued that the ground was altogether unfavourable. He agreed, however, to a compromise whereby the British attack south of the La Bassée canal would be undertaken as a main operation only if the advance of the French from the south had neutralised the enemy artillery in the Lens area. Joffre also agreed that the preparations for the offensive could not be completed until the end of August.

The delay was inevitable, but it allowed the Germans time to improve their defences to an extent which lessened still further the chances of a great Anglo-French success. The German plan was to build a strong second line some two to four miles behind the first line, and sited more carefully than had been possible with the front line which, as Churchill had pointed out, had been only the tidal mark of advance or retreat. The Germans also protected this second line with more formidable entanglements than could be set up by night in front of the first-line trenches. Since wire-cutting by field guns artillery was limited to a range of some $2\frac{1}{4}$ miles, the defences of the second line could not be attacked until the first line had been captured. The Germans considered that they would have time to bring up reserves, and construct a third line in a threatened sector before the allies could move forward in sufficient force to attack the second line.

The Germans carried out the work on this second line throughout July.[1] By the end of the month the second line was practically complete. It is, therefore, not surprising that Sir John French should have said, at a conference with his commanders, on July 28, that 'he was practically certain that we should not get beyond our present positions until next spring'. This conference was held after a meeting on July 27 at Frévent between French and Foch, who was commanding the French northern armies. Haig had reaffirmed his view of the unsuitability of the area chosen by Joffre for the British attack; French, however, was

---

[1] They employed, in violation of rules of war agreed at The Hague, French prisoners and civilians on the work.

unable to convince Foch. On July 29, he wrote to Joffre suggesting alternative areas for attack, and stating his opinion that Joffre's plans for an 'all-out' attack were impracticable with the resources available. Nevertheless he agreed to accept Joffre's decision. In a reply Joffre merely held to his original proposal. French then answered that he would agree to Joffre's plan, but that (in accordance with the 'compromise' agreed at St Omer) he would co-operate by artillery fire alone until a French advance from the south had neutralised the enemy artillery in the Lens area.

Joffre wrote back on August 12 that he could not accept this compromise, and that he required a large and powerful infantry attack, regardless of conditions. Owing to this fundamental difference of view Kitchener came to France at Joffre's invitation. Joffre had already asked the French Government to secure greater powers for him. Kitchener agreed with the proposed French formula that

> during the period in which the operations of the British army take place principally in French territory, and contribute to the liberation of this territory, the initiative in combined action of the French and British forces devolves on the French Commander-in-Chief, particularly as concerning the effectives to be engaged, the objectives to be attained, and the dates fixed for the commencement of each operation.

In accepting this formula, to which the British Government assented, Kitchener seems to have had in mind only a temporary arrangement while the British armies were still in comparatively small numbers in France. At the end of the year he told Haig on his appointment as Commander-in-Chief that, while 'the closest co-operation of French and British as a united Army must be the governing policy', his command was 'an independent one', and that he would 'in no case come under the orders of an Allied general further than the co-operation with our Allies above referred to'.[1]

Joffre thus had his way, and indeed used Kitchener's assent to convince the strong party in France which agreed with the British view that a

---

[1] It has been suggested that Haig's instructions gave him slightly less independence than the instructions given to French; the qualifying phrase 'further than the co-operation with our Allies above referred to' does not appear in French's instructions. Too much emphasis, however, should not be placed on the phrase. One of Kitchener's reasons for wanting to delay a full-scale British offensive was his desire not to squander British resources but to harbour them for the last stage

western offensive should be postponed. Kitchener, and the British Government, had surrendered the initiative which they had failed to assert because they had hesitated too long over a definite policy. Kitchener's motive was partly to reassure the French, partly to try to relieve the pressure on the Russians. In his memorandum of June 18 Churchill had suggested that the Russian position would improve, and the Germans find attack more difficult as the area of fighting shifted eastwards from the network of German strategic railways.

In mid-July, however, the Germans had renewed their eastern offensive, and on August 5 had occupied Warsaw. The first Italian offensive in June had failed. A second effort later in July was also a failure. The hope of an early victory at the Dardanelles was fading, and the Allies had not been able to supply the Russians with the munitions in which they were almost incredibly deficient. The British General Staff was afraid of a complete Russian military collapse, and a move by the pro-German and defeatist elements in the Tsar's entourage to make peace before there was a popular revolution. A similar move ten years earlier had brought the Russo-Japanese war to an end when there was no adequate military reason on the Russian side for accepting defeat. In fact, however bad the Russian situation, the pessimistic forecasts of the British War Office were not fulfilled. The Tsar had rejected a German offer of peace. There was no real analogy with the circumstances of 1905. After the treaty of Portsmouth Russia had remained a great military power; she had to give up plans of Asiatic expansion, but her military strength in Europe was only temporarily weakened. A peace with Germany in the summer of 1915 would have allowed the Germans to turn westwards in full force and probably to defeat the western Powers. The Russians would have then been in a situation of permanent military inferiority. There was at this time no need for such a Russian surrender. The Germans themselves, even after their victories, did not expect to do more than break Russian offensive power. They realised that the Russians had immense room for defensive manœuvre, and that the German armies could not be committed too deeply to an

---

of the war and the peace settlement. Kitchener would never have gone as far as Lloyd George in the latter's proposed subordination of Haig to Nivelle. (See below, p. 263.) On the other hand what was needed was a clear assertion of the right of the British Government, in accordance with the increasing magnitude of the total British contribution to the war, to follow the strategy most suited to British resources and therefore most likely to bring a rapid victory. This strategy would not necessarily give priority – as all French commanders were bound to give it – to the liberation of French territory.

advance into Russian territory while Great Britain was rapidly increasing her resources in the west.

Nonetheless, Kitchener told both Sir John French and Haig that the British army must act with the utmost energy in helping the French even at the cost of 'very heavy losses indeed'. On his return to London (August 20) he heard of the fall of the fortress of Novogeorgievsk – the last Russian strong-point on the Vistula. He telegraphed to Sir John French on the following day confirming his conversations in France, and telling him 'to take the offensive and act vigorously'. Sir John French therefore agreed on August 22 to Joffre's proposal that he should attack south of the La Bassée canal.

Joffre then said that, owing to the Russian situation, he wanted to open his own offensive on September 8. He found it impossible, however, to complete his own preparations in Champagne (for the attack in a northerly direction) by this date. He postponed the date twice; the second postponement, on September 4, delayed the opening day of the infantry attack until September 25. It was sufficiently clear by this time that the Germans would not be able to drive the Russians out of the war before the onset of winter. The main argument on which Joffre justified the Allied offensive was therefore no longer decisive. The offensive could have been called off, and the preparations for it would have served their purpose by compelling the Germans to keep in the west divisions which might have been moved to the Eastern Front. Joffre's orders, however, now showed that his real motive was not to relieve the Russian front. He was sure that he would win a great victory in the west. Such was his confidence that he allocated a line in Belgian territory as the objective for the cavalry[1] after the infantry had made a passage for them.

The British offensive opened at Loos on September 21, 1915, with a heavy bombardment. On September 25 the infantry went to the attack.[2] By nightfall 470 officers and 15,000 other ranks – one-sixth of the attacking force – were casualties. Some of the troops had reached the German second lines, but the reserves were not sent forward until too late to be of any use in pressing the attack. This delay caused a bitter controversy between Haig and French, in which Haig accused

[1] Ten cavalry divisions were massed behind the Champagne front for this pursuit.

[2] Haig used gas in this attack. He regarded the allocation of guns and ammunition as insufficient, and was unwilling to attack unless he had this additional weapon. He told his commanders on September 6 that with the use of gas he thought that a decisive victory could be obtained.

French of stating inaccurately, in his report of the battle, the hour at which the reserves were available.[1] Haig thought that, if the reserves had arrived earlier, a victory would have been possible. It is unlikely that the course of events would have been very different – though there might have been more local gains – if the reserves had come up sooner. Two of the reserve divisions were from the New Army, and had recently arrived in France. They had never been under fire, or even seen the front lines; they were marched, with insufficient arrangements for rest and food, directly into battle.[2] The road control was very bad – for this elementary blunder Sir John French's staff were responsible – and the advance thereby made far more difficult. In any case the French attack south of Lens, which was more strongly supported by artillery, was a complete failure, and the British subsidiary attack to the north of Loos had not succeeded in drawing away the German reserves.

The main offensive was continued on September 26, but the German second line was not taken and, although heavy fighting, including strong German counter-attacks, lasted until mid-October, the chance of an important success had vanished; the French had also been held up in Champagne and had suffered in all casualties amounting to 4993 officers and 186,804 other ranks.[3] The British losses from September 25 to October 16 in the main attacks were 2013 officers and 48,367 other ranks. A large proportion of these casualties was incurred because the battle was not broken off after the first failure. In the final attacks on October 13–14 one division suffered nearly 3800 casualties – most of them in the first ten mintues of the fighting. Even so Haig planned

[1] Haig had no army reserve. The general reserve of three divisions was under French's control. The third division in reserve – the Guards Division – was a *corps d'élite*; French regarded it as for use only in a serious crisis.

[2] Sir John French could have used other divisions. He took the extraordinary view that troops engaged for a long time in trench warfare would have lost the 'habit' of attacking in the open, and that it was better to use new, untried troops. The training of these troops in England was carried out largely by officers unfamiliar with the conditions of fighting in 1915 and was based on training manuals written before 1914. Until May, 1916, neither the War Office nor GHQ issued any manuals instructing the new armies in methods of attack.

[3] The total German casualties in the combined Franco-British offensive to October 10 were, according to the official lists (which excluded lightly wounded men), 2700 officers and 139,000 other ranks. The French attack in Champagne came near to fulfilling the conditions laid down at the Boulogne Conference in June. The French employed 35 divisions on a front of 15 miles, and supported the infantry by 900 heavy and 1600 field guns. Not for the first or last time, however, the improvement in the German defence system made the estimate of the attacking side wholly inadequate.

another large attack for November 7, but could not carry it out owing
to the weather conditions.

On September 28, when it was clear that the British and French
offensives had failed in their main objectives, Sir John French said to
Haig that 'we ought to take the first opportunity of concluding peace
otherwise England would be ruined'.[1] It would be unfair to give much
importance to a casual remark, made at a moment of great fatigue and
depression by a man of emotional temperament. Nevertheless, French
had not shown himself an outstanding commander, even when account
is taken of all his difficulties. He was not trusted by his subordinate
commanders, and had not the confidence of Kitchener. Haig had
doubted his capacity from the first, and, after the battle of Loos, had
told King George V that French should be removed from his command.
Robertson had also said to the King that it was 'impossible to deal with
French, his mind (was) never the same for two consecutive minutes'.
French's health was breaking down under a strain too great for a
man of sixty-three who was suffering from heart attacks. The Prime
Minister therefore asked him early in December to resign. The circumstances of his resignation showed his unfitness to retain his command.
He appears to have agreed to resign, and then to have written to the
Prime Minister withdrawing his resignation. King George V insisted
that the resignation should take place, and Lord Esher was sent to
advise French 'to go without further discussion'.[2]

Sir Douglas Haig, who was appointed as French's successor, was a
younger man. He was born in 1861, the youngest child of a Scottish
family of eleven. His parents died before he was nineteen, and left him a
considerable fortune. He was regarded as the dunce of the family, and
incapable of passing the entrance examination to Rugby. He went to
Clifton, and then to Brasenose College, Oxford, where he read for a
pass degree. He lived at Oxford as a young man of wealth and fashion,
rowed, played polo, and spent three pleasant years without showing
intellectual interests or signs of talent. After leaving Oxford, and
working with a crammer, he entered Sandhurst as a cadet in 1884.
Owing to his time at Oxford, he was older than most of the cadets. His
career at Sandhurst was regarded as brilliant; he 'passed out' first of
his year. He joined a cavalry regiment, and, unlike most cavalry

[1] Haig, id., p. 104.

[2] Haig, id., p. 138. Kitchener was away at this time in the Mediterranean. The
decision was thus taken by Asquith, but there is little doubt that Kitchener agreed
with it.

officers, took a serious interest in the technical aspects of his profession. He failed (partly owing to colour-blindness) in his first attempt to qualify for the Staff College, but was admitted in 1896 on the personal nomination of the Duke of Cambridge.[1] He greatly impressed the Commandant of the College, who foretold that he would some time be Commander-in-Chief of the army. He fought in the Sudan campaign and in the South African war. In 1903 he became Inspector-General of Cavalry in India. He had been in close touch with King Edward VII as Prince of Wales, and remained, after King Edward's death, a friend of King George V. In 1905 he married a daughter of one of Queen Alexandra's ladies in-waiting. In 1906 he came to the War Office as Director of Military Training, and assisted Haldane in his plans for the organisation of an expeditionary force. He went back to India for two years in 1909 as Chief of Staff, and returned early in 1912 to take up the Aldershot Command. At the outbreak of war he went to France as commander of the first of the two army corps into which the Expeditionary Force was divided.

Haig's career before 1914 was that of an efficient officer enjoying the advantages of wealth, high social position, and the important 'connexions' which had always been of considerable help in securing military promotion. He might not have obtained this promotion if he had been a fool; the fact that he obtained it did not necessarily mark him out as possessing outstanding qualities of mind or imagination. His knowledge of his profession was sound and solid; he was a man of strong nerve, resolute, patient, somewhat cold and reserved in temper, unlikely to be thrown off his balance either by calamity or success. He reached opinions slowly, and held to them. He made up his mind in 1915 that the war could be won on the Western Front, and only on the Western Front. He acted on this view, and, at the last, he was right, though it is open to argument not only that victory could have been won sooner elsewhere but that Haig's method of winning it was clumsy, tragically expensive of life, and based for too long on a misreading of the facts.

Haig, like French before him, tended, as a cavalryman, to promote other cavalrymen to high command. The war was not a 'cavalry' war, and the solution of the problem of dealing with an unbroken trench system was much more a problem for engineers and gunners.[2] More-

---

[1] The Duke of Cambridge resigned the office of Commander-in-Chief in October, 1895 (see above, p. 26). Haig was one of the last of his nominees.

[2] Another consequence of Haig's cavalry training, as well as of his continued belief in a 'break-through', was that he insisted on keeping the cavalry to follow

over the average of intelligence among British cavalry officers, not-
withstanding their personal courage, was notoriously lower than that
of the engineer and artillery officers. Haig might have realised that he
was failing to take more than a routine approach to a problem which
required new ideas if he had been in closer contact with able men and
especially with civilians of the professional class. He said to a friend,
after more than a year of trench warfare, that generals 'after a certain
time of life are apt to be narrow-minded and disinclined to take
advantage of modern scientific discoveries. The civilian Minister can do
good by pressing the possibility of some modern discovery.' Haig
himself never encouraged any such 'pressing', except in the most
obvious cases, and surrounded himself with men who were unlikely to
attempt it.

Moreover the life of a Commander-in-Chief was necessarily remote
from that of his armies. After the battle of Neuve Chapelle the front of
an offensive increased to such an extent that it was impossible for
the Commander-in-Chief to see for himself what was happening.
Haig's GHQ was an austere and hard-working establishment, but it
was too far away from the battle areas for him to feel, day in day out,
the consequences of the *reductio ad absurdum* of what was formerly, in
the hands of the greatest soldiers, the art of war. Haig – and Sir William
Robertson, the Chief of Staff in London, was as resolute and as unimaginative as the Commander-in-Chief – failed to comprehend that
the policy of 'attrition' or in plain English, 'killing Germans' until the
German army was worn down and exhausted, was not only wasteful
and, intellectually, a confession of impotence; it was also extremely
dangerous. The Germans might counter Haig's plan by allowing him
to wear down his own army in a series of unsuccessful attacks against a
skilful defence. Fortunately the enemy generals were of much the same
'textbook' type of mind as Haig,[1] though Ludendorff was more highly

---

up a success. In November 1916 the War Office suggested that, owing to the
shipping situation and the difficulties of transport in France, part of the cavalry
might be sent home for the winter. Haig refused to send them home, but agreed
to billet them far behind the front where forage could be bought locally.

[1] Haig and Hindenburg were alike confident that they were specially guided
by Divine Providence. The Presbyterian chaplain at GHQ, the Rev. Dr G. S.
Duncan, has written, somewhat oddly, that 'Haig's faith was essentially practical.
There is not the slightest evidence that he ever allowed it to prevent or override
his military judgement.' Nevertheless it gave him 'unshakeable confidence in
victory' and an unclouded 'serenity'. Quoted in J. Terraine, *Douglas Haig* (1963),
p. 173.

strung and had greater tactical originality; the Germans also relied on
'mass' – masses of guns, masses of divisions – and followed the same
plan of setting their troops against British and French machine guns,
but if they had not risked an offensive in 1918, and if the British navy
had not exercised a continuous decisive pressure on German resources,
the war might have ended in a stalemate of exhaustion, as far as all the
European armies were concerned. Even so the Americans could have
turned the scale in favour of an Allied victory. Haig's view of the
working of his own policy was also affected by the absence of first-class
ability in his entourage. He accepted too easily the optimistic views of
his chief intelligence officer, and, every time, believed that the remedy-
ing of the tactical mistakes of past offensives would bring victory.

It is fair, however, to remember that, with all his shortcomings, Haig
was the ablest British commander to be found among the small circle
of high military officers (who, even in war-time, paid close attention to
matters of professional seniority). Haig was at his best in the last six
months of the war. His steadfastness in times of calamity was of the
greatest possible service; so also was his self-effacement when, for the
safety of the British army, he thought it necessary that Foch should be
appointed as *generalissimo* in order to avoid the fatal consequences of
Pétain's defeatism. Haig, rather than Foch, decided the bold strategy
which led to victory after the first counterstroke delivered by the
French army. Haig's confidence in victory had strengthened the
civilian Ministers even before the tide turned in favour of the Allies.
This same confidence led him to believe that at long last, however
heavy the price, he could deliver the final blow.

CHAPTER 10

Allied plans for 1916: Verdun and the battle of the Somme

On December 6–8, 1915, before Haig took over the command of the BEF in France, the Allies held a military conference at Chantilly. Joffre had previously sent to the Allied representatives a long memorandum on the plan of action proposed by the French to their Allies. This plan envisaged simultaneous attacks by Great Britain, France, Italy, and Russia. Until the attacks could be delivered, the enemy forces were to be worn down by vigorous action carried out principally by those Powers which still had large reserves of man-power. The conference accepted Joffre's general plan. They also accepted his view that the process of wearing down – Joffre's term was 'usure' – should be left mainly to the Powers with large reserves of men. Joffre had in mind, obviously, the British army.[1]

Kitchener did not go to Chantilly. Sir Archibald Murray, at this time CIGS, put before the War Committee after his return from the conference a paper by the General Staff on the future conduct of the war. This paper – the first of its kind – shews the re-emergence of the General Staff and, to this extent, the eclipse of Kitchener, or at all events, a partial abandonment of Kitchener's method of action without full consultation with the General Staff. The memorandum recommended that 'every possible division' should be concentrated on the Western Front; that Salonika should be abandoned and other commitments cut down to a minimum. The General Staff also thought that the Germans might decide upon a western offensive since it would give more immediate results than another offensive against Russia.

Before the War Committee discussed the memorandum the change in command in the BEF had taken place, and Robertson had become

[1] The total French casualties by the end of December, 1915, were 50,355 officers and 1,911,332 other ranks. The total number of dead and missing was 1,001,271. The total British casualties up to the same date were 21,747 officers and 490,673 other ranks; the dead and missing were about 200,000.

CIGS.[1] He agreed with the memorandum, and asked that the Committee should accept its main principles. Five days later the War Committee recommended to the Cabinet that 'from the point of view of the British Empire', France and Flanders should remain the 'main theatre of operations'; that every effort should be made to carry out 'the offensive operations next spring in the main theatre of war in close co-operation with the Allies, and in the greatest possible strength'. The 'actual plan of attack' was 'left to the discretion of the commanders in the field'. The Committee referred to Egypt, East Africa, and Mesopotamia, but said nothing about Salonika. French insistence upon remaining in the place had settled this latter question at least for the time.

The War Committee – or certain civilian members of it – were not easy about the main decision. Balfour thought that an offensive in the west should be postponed until the late summer, i.e. until the Germans had weakened themselves by attacks.[2] McKenna and Runciman argued that the resources of the Allies in man-power, shipping, and finance were insufficient to defeat Germany on land, and that the war must be won by economic pressure; their view had no other support, but the idea of postponing a decision was fatally attractive. The War Committee on January 13 altered their resolution of December 28 in one important respect. For the phrase 'every effort is to be made for carrying out the offensive operations next spring' they substituted the phrase 'every effort is to be made *to prepare for carrying out . . .*' They also added a new clause 'although it must not be assumed that such offensive operations are finally decided on'.

This change was yet another case of irresolution. There were four possibilities. (i) To maintain the general policy of an early offensive in the west, (ii) to agree to an early offensive but only on the condition that the new British armies were fully trained and equipped for it, (iii) to give up the idea of an early offensive, on the argument that a complete break-through could not be obtained, and to allow the Germans to wear down their own strength by attack, (iv) to find some other area than the Western Front for the delivery of a grand attack. This last plan could be ruled out since there was now no area of attack which offered any prospect of success on a scale likely to bring about the collapse of Germany or, at all events, likely to do so in time to be of help to the Russians. Moreover the Allies had lost their chance of

---

[1] Robertson's appointment was favoured by Haig. See also below, p. 157.
[2] Esher, *Journals and Letters*, IV, pp. 1-7. Haig, id., pp. 122-4.

moving large forces away from the Western Front while the Germans were fully engaged in the east.

The third plan – which was, in fact, Balfour's recommendation – involved the risk that the Germans might well be satisfied with a period of relative inaction in the west while they completed the destruction of the Russian armies. The second plan – which, in fact, meant postponement – was open to the same objection. Obviously the British armies would be better prepared for an offensive in the late summer, but from the point of view of maintaining Russian resistance, delay might well be fatal. Hence there was no alternative to an early offensive unless the British and French military authorities advised that a decisive break-through – whether Allied or German – was unlikely. In this case it might have been better, whatever the consequences elsewhere, to have held to the defensive in the west. Here again, however, there was the risk that the Germans might take the same view, and, after making an advantageous peace with Russia, and thus greatly strengthening their resources, still refuse to waste them in a western attack. The Allies would then be compelled either to attempt to recover the occupied territory of France and Belgium in the most unfavourable conditions or to come to terms; otherwise the Germans could hold on indefinitely to every square mile of land in their possession.

The French and British military authorities did not think that a successful offensive was impossible. The opinions of Haig and Robertson were well known. Kitchener, though unwilling to attack earlier, had envisaged an offensive in 1916. He told Lord Esher on January 15, 1916, that 'a violent offensive in the spring, followed up by another in the summer, may bring about the crisis of the war'. Kitchener thought it 'possible that about the month of August the Germans will ask us for our peace terms; that we shall most certainly formulate proposals unacceptable to them; that the war will then proceed, but that in November the Germans will, if rightly handled with political aptitude, accept terms that they rejected in August'.[1]

In retrospect – when judgment is much easier – it is open to conclude that the British Government should have accepted the military view that an early offensive was necessary in spite of the advantages of delay – but that they should not have agreed to leave 'the actual plan of attack to the discretion of the commanders in the field'. The civilian Ministers now had sufficient experience to convince them that the

[1] Esher, id., pp. 1–2.

commanders in the field had no 'plan of attack' beyond the accumulation of masses of men, guns, and munitions, and that they had shewn
almost no interest in devising new methods of dealing with the problems
of capturing and advancing beyond a series of strongly defended
positions. In other words, the generals had abandoned the old principles
of victory – economy of force and surprise – and were trusting merely
to mass. The civilian Ministers, most of whom were abler men than the
generals, ought to have remembered that the rifle and machine gun were
mechanical contrivances, and that other contrivances might counter
their effects. If they had accepted, immediately after the autumn fighting of 1915, the lesson that no use of mass could of itself solve this
problem of attack, and that no mere tactical improvement in methods
of advance would enable men to get the better of machine guns, there
would still have been time, before the summer offensive of 1916, to
have produced on a much larger scale the 'tank' surprise which might
have changed the result of the Somme battles. Here was the fundamental error. A second mistake of the British Government was not to
put forward at this stage a stronger claim to determine how and where
their armies should be employed. They had had a lesson in Joffre's
insistence that the British autumn offensive should take place in an area
which French and Haig regarded as unsuitable. It was not unlikely that
Joffre would again make demands of this kind, and that Haig would
find it difficult to refuse them.

Haig did not receive until April 7 the formal approval of the Cabinet
to the participation of the British army in a combined offensive. He
had assumed this approval, and from the beginning of the year had been
arguing, as Sir John French had argued, against the plans which Joffre
wished to force on him. On January 20 Joffre told Haig that he had in
mind five offensives, but that before they were opened he wished the
enemy to be worn down and his reserves exhausted by preliminary
attacks. He therefore asked for a British attack north of the Somme, on
a front at least of 20,000 yards, about the middle of April. Three days
later he proposed a similar attack in May on some other part of the
front.

Haig answered that attacks of this kind, long before the general
offensive and not pressed to a conclusion, would be regarded by the
enemy and by neutrals – as well as by opinion at home – as Allied
defeats, and that they would not prevent the Germans from replacing
their losses and accumulating new reserves. Haig suggested a series of

raids and of small actions some ten to fourteen days before the main offensive. He pointed out that the British army had not enough heavy artillery to carry out a preliminary attack at one point and then a decisive attack elsewhere. After considerable discussion Joffre agreed on February 14 to accept Haig's plan. He also said that he wanted the main combined offensive to be north and south of the Somme. There seemed to be no valid reason for this choice except that, from the French point of view, it ensured British co-operation. Joffre argued – as in 1915 – that the ground was favourable to the attack. In fact, owing to the number of villages in the area, and still more to the ease with which deep dug-outs could be constructed in the chalk, the ground was particularly favourable to the defence. Unless the Allies made a complete break-through their victory would be of little use to them. They might turn a German salient into an Allied salient,[1] but only a victory on a large scale would cut the main German communications. Busigny, the nearest important junction on the lateral railways, was about thirty miles east of the Somme front.[2]

Haig's proposal for a British attack nearer the coast – in the Ypres–La Bassée area – was a better plan, and had greater strategic possibilities; the Germans north of a break-through might have been pushed into the sea or into Dutch territory, and the offensive then turned southward without risk of being outflanked. Joffre, however, would not change his mind. Moreover it was becoming clear that he did not expect even the main offensive to be more than an important stage in the wearing down process. Joffre's plans, however, were soon affected by the German attack on Verdun. This attack opened on February 21. The Germans made it because they thought that the moral effect of the fall of the fortress would convince the French that there was no hope of an Allied victory.[3] The attacks failed to capture Verdun, but, owing to the French neglect of the field defences of the place and their unwillingness to give any ground, the losses of the defenders were slightly higher than those of the German attackers. In spite of the Verdun offensive, Joffre continued his plans for an attack on the Somme. Indeed he took the

[1] The commander of the 2nd German army which had to meet the main British attack on the Somme considered the plan of retreating, and thus enticing the Allies into a 'pocket' from which they could have been attacked on either flank. For the Somme battlefield, see Map 6.

[2] Mézières, a junction of greater importance, was over ninety miles distant.

[3] At the same time the German High Command wanted to begin 'unrestricted submarine' attacks. This plan was postponed, partly through fear of the effect on opinion in the United States. See below, p. 202.

view that the Germans had made their main effort and exhausted a large part of their reserves. He found it necessary, however, to limit the extent of French collaboration. The British offensive, therefore, became increasingly the more important feature of the operation, but Joffre himself still did not expect a rapid and decisive victory. He anticipated a prolonged and continuous struggle, and thought it impossible to settle what was to be done after the three German defensive lines had been taken. With the pressure on Verdun, there could also be no question of delaying the British offensive until August.

Haig indeed was at this time more confident than Joffre – or Foch, or, for that matter, most of his own army commanders – that an offensive could do more than wear down the enemy. He aimed at a definite break-through on a wide front, and hoped to turn northwards and 'roll up' the enemy. The objectives on the first day included a part of the second as well as the first main lines of defence. Haig expected that a week or more would suffice for penetrating the German positions on a scale which would allow this exploitation to take place. As in the Loos offensive, the cavalry were held in readiness for the pursuit.

On July 1, 1916, the first day of the battle of the Somme, more than 1000 officers and 20,000 other ranks of the British Expeditionary Force were killed, fatally wounded, or reported missing; over 1300 officers and 34,000 other ranks were wounded. Most of the casualties were caused by machine-gun fire. The ground gained at this cost was about a mile in depth on a frontage of $3\frac{1}{2}$ miles. The attacks were continued, though on a decreasing scale. After a week of such fighting it was no longer possible to think in terms of a rapid victory which would 'roll up' the enemy line. After four weeks, Haig was still determined to go on with the offensive; he had 'good hope' of forcing the enemy from his 'entrenched positions' before the autumn.

Opinion in England, however, was becoming disquieted. Robertson wrote to Haig on July 29 that 'the Powers that be' were beginning to get uneasy over the heavy losses and lack of 'really great results'. Haig answered this letter on August 1. He said (i) that the pressure on Verdun had been eased, (ii) that the Russians had had successes in the east because the Germans had been unable to move troops from the west, (iii) that the 'proof given to (the) world that (the) Allies are capable of making and maintaining a vigorous offensive and of driving (the) enemy's best troops from the strongest positions has shaken the faith of (the) Germans, of their friends, (and) of doubting neutrals in the invincibility of Germany', and had 'also impressed on the world

England's strength and determination and the fighting power of the British race'. Haig thought that the British attacks had used up 30 per cent of the enemy divisions, and that, in another six weeks, the enemy 'should be hard put to it to find men', and that 'the maintenance of a steady offensive pressure will result eventually in his complete over-throw'.[1]

The arguments were not convincing. The Germans in fact moved five divisions from the Western Front to the Russian front in July, 1916; they moved another four in August,[2] though half of them had suffered heavily in the Somme fighting. The situation had improved at Verdun before the opening of the Somme battle. The 'propaganda' arguments about the battle were futile; the fighting on the Western Front in 1914 and 1915 had already shown 'the fighting power of the British race'. None the less, if Haig's promises revealed lack of general comprehension – almost a total failure – to realise the absurdity that, after two years of war, the High Command was still throwing men against machine guns – his own determination was equally remarkable. So also was his confidence in the troops. He thought that the offensive should be continued; the losses incurred did not make him anxious about the power of the army to continue it. He expected the attacks to go on until the autumn, but concluded that 'it would not be justifiable to calculate on the enemy's resistance being completely broken without another campaign next year'.

Robertson replied to Haig that this letter had pleased the War Committee 'very much indeed', and that it was to be printed and circulated to the Cabinet as a rejoinder to a memorandum by Churchill. Churchill's memorandum was written on August 1, and given to F. E. Smith[3] who circulated it to his Cabinet colleagues. Churchill argued that 'in *personnel* the results of the operation have been disastrous; in *terrain* they have been absolutely barren'. Churchill was not in the Cabinet, and, except for his conclusion that the policy of wearing down the enemy worked disastrously for the Allies, offered no alternative. Meanwhile Haig had put forward in strong terms a definite plan which, in his view, promised ultimate success. Robertson agreed with him. The Prime Minister did not disagree. Indeed on September 6–7 he visited Haig in France and approved of his policy.

Haig therefore went on with his attacks. In any case he could not easily switch them elsewhere since it was not possible to move rapidly

[1] Haig, id., p. 157.   [2] See also below, p. 246.
[3] At this time Attorney-General.

the great mass of guns and ammunition to another part of the line; the situation was an example of the manner in which the generals were already tied down by their own abandonment of mobility for mass. At the end of November the British casualties were over 400,000 and the French casualties nearly 200,000. The Germans had been pushed back over an area of some thirty miles in length, and to a depth, at the maximum points, of seven miles, but there was no break-through, no victory to exploit, no turn northwards towards enveloping the enemy. The German losses, indeed were not far short of those of the Allies; in the later stages of the battle, the Germans suffered more than the attackers, since they stubbornly obeyed their orders never to yield any ground. These German losses, added to those at Verdun, were among their best troops, though probably to a lesser extent than in the British army. In any case the Germans realised for the first time the immense material resources of their enemy as well as the resources in man-power. Moreover the shortages caused by the blockade were beginning to be felt; they were not yet serious enough to affect the morale of the German soldiers, but at least they tended to undermine confidence in victory. The great German successes in the east would be of little value if the Western Front should prove impregnable. For the Germans Verdun was a defeat; the resistance to the offensive on the Somme did not look like a victory.

Nevertheless the Allies were no nearer to driving the Germans out of France. The slight advance in territory had only added to the hardships of the troops and the difficulties of maintaining the line. Haig wrote to Joffre on November 6 that all requirements for the fighting areas had to be 'carried for very long distances over exposed ground, broken up by innumerable shells and rendered almost impassable at present by the continued rain. Those conditions are so exhausting to the troops that all their energies are consumed in bringing forward supplies and munitions – and in the frequent reliefs necessitated by the state of the trenches.'[1] He added what was a significant comment on the battle of 'attrition'.

[1] More precautions were taken than in the previous winter against frostbite and 'trench feet', but nearly 10,000 officers and men were sent for treatment in the last five weeks of 1916. The removal of the wounded and sick from the trenches along tracks of 'duckboards' exposed to shellfire was extremely difficult. In some areas the sea of mud extended for two miles behind the lines. There was an improvement in communications and trench conditions after the offensive had come to an end.

A very considerable proportion of the personnel in my divisions consists now of almost untrained young officers and men, and to bring my units up to strength I have still to receive during the winter a large number of those with even less training. My armies will in fact consist of what I can only describe as raw material, and without intensive training continued throughout the winter they cannot be fit for an offensive next spring.

Kitchener had been drowned in the sinking of the *Hampshire* – which was taking him to Russia – nearly a month before the opening of the battle of the Somme.[1] No one can say whether he would have agreed to the insistent hammering of the German lines after the first few days of failure. Haig and Robertson, however, did not change their views. They attributed failure to all manner of reasons – inexperienced troops, bad weather, insufficient artillery, defective ammunition, improved methods of defence, mistaken methods of attack. It is not easy to know how far they were surprised not only at their failure but at the very heavy cost of the fighting. In the conferences before the battle the commanders always emphasised the importance of the artillery preparation. Rawlinson – an army commander who had at first thought Haig's plans too ambitious – told a conference of corps commanders that 'nothing could exist at the conclusion of the bombardment in the area covered by it', and that the infantry would have only to walk over and take possession of the enemy lines.[2] On the other hand, although he had said earlier that the attack was not to be made until the corps commanders were satisfied that the enemy defences were sufficiently destroyed, Haig noted in his diary on July 2; 'The Adjutant-General reported today that the total casualties are estimated at over 40,000 to date. This cannot be considered severe in view of the numbers engaged and the length of front attacked.'[3]

[1] Kitchener's visit to Russia had been under consideration since the end of April. The western Allies wanted to get into closer relations with the Russian Government and High Command, in order to co-ordinate offensive plans, and also to discuss the immense Russian demands for supplies and credits. Lloyd George had thought of going on a special mission to Russia, but the Cabinet asked him to take charge of policy with regard to Ireland (after the Dublin rebellion). The *Hampshire* appears to have been mined off the Orkneys in rough weather on June 5, 1916.

[2] Rawlinson himself spread his guns evenly along the front without regard to the strength and importance of any particular section; hence many strong points and machine-gun posts were not touched.

[3] Haig, id., p. 154. The figure was an underestimate.

The losses on the first day of the battle might have been less, and the chances of a tactical success greater if the British attack had been made, as Haig had wished, in the mists of dawn, when the assaulting troops would have gained at least a few invaluable moments of surprise. The French, however, on the British right, insisted upon a later time in order to observe the results of the final bombardment. Haig himself must bear the responsibility for the miscalculation that the bombardment would destroy every German in the area covered by it.[1] Even if this estimate had been accurate for the first line of the German defences it could not have applied to the second line. In fact, although the German losses were heavy, there were enough survivors in the deep dug-outs, in some places two storeys below ground – to come out as soon as the shelling ceased, and to direct machine-gun fire from the broken trenches. Furthermore the bombardment did not always clear a passage through the wire entanglements. It was not always possible to locate the enemy wire, for example, in patches of rough grass. In the later stages of the battle the Germans threw out loose wire which was more difficult to cut than wire tautly stretched between pickets.

The issue was, therefore, whether the attackers could reach the trenches, or any available shell-holes, before the enemy had clambered out of the dug-outs. It has been said that the battle of the Somme was lost by three minutes. The factor of speed was overlooked when every infantryman was loaded with 66 lb. of equipment. The men could not easily get out of their own trenches. They had to advance at a slow walk. They could not lie down or rise quickly from the ground. Even if they managed to reach the enemy trenches, their small bombs were inadequate for clearing the dug-outs.

In the later stages of this unequal struggle between men and machine guns, there was one development of great significance. Haig seems to have known nothing about the 'tanks' until Churchill mentioned them to him late in December, 1915. This idea of using mechanism against mechanism – armoured machines against machine guns – had not occurred to him. He was, however, interested in Churchill's report, and

---

[1] Haig was influenced by reports of the effects of the German bombardment at Verdun, but the French field defences at Verdun were known to be defective. Moreover the Germans were able to concentrate more artillery on the front of their attack at Verdun – 700 heavy guns, including 15-inch howitzers on a front of eight miles, or half as many again as the British had on a front of over fourteen miles. (The French had a much larger number of guns on their Somme front of about eight miles.) An additional misfortune was that many of the British shells were defective.

sent a representative of GHQ to keep in touch with developments. He did not regard the 'tanks' as likely to be more than an auxiliary to an infantry assault, or show any special interest in their manufacture on a large scale. During the latter part of July, 1916, indeed, GHQ tentatively suggested that production should be held up until twenty machines had been tried on a definite tactical scheme.

On the other hand, Haig was willing – and indeed imprudently anxious – to use such few tanks as were available. Colonel Swinton, who had been appointed in March, 1916, to command a unit for manning the tanks, regarded this plan as disastrous. He had good reason to complain at the slowness with which the machines were being produced, and at the excessive number of 'demonstrations' which interfered with the training of the crews. He was now faced with Haig's intention to give away the secret of the tanks to the enemy, and to lose the element of surprise. Lloyd George asked Robertson to tell Haig of this obvious objection. Haig replied on July 29 that if the tanks were not used before the autumn, there would be no chance of using them until the renewal of the offensive in the spring. The tanks were therefore employed 'in driblets', and the method of their employment subordinated to the general plan of an infantry assault; the tank commanders were not given an opportunity to determine their own tactics. They could not indeed have done so with much effect, since in all only forty-nine tanks were available,[1] but they were not even allowed to use this small number to the best advantage. The fact that the tanks were distributed in very small numbers over the whole front made control by the commanders almost impossible. In spite of the commanders' objections, four tanks were sent into a wood. The tanks were used on September 15 – only nine days after they had arrived behind the lines, and a month after the first of them had reached France. There had been little study by the corps commanders – and none by the divisional and brigade commanders – of the co-ordination of the tanks with the artillery and infantry; the infantry had not even practised advancing with the tanks.

It is impossible to say how far the mechanical lessons learned from the actual employment of tanks in battle could have been learned as well from continued experiments in training.[2] There can be no doubt

[1] Ten per cent of them remained in reserve.

[2] Especially if the experiments had begun earlier and had been undertaken on a much larger scale, and if the High Command had realised the need for careful study of the tactics which this new weapon required.

that in other respects the secret of a powerful new weapon was thrown away. Fortunately the carelessness of the High Command in this one respect had no serious result. The tanks, in spite of some spectacular exploits, could not and did not have any great success, since they were not employed in the right way. The Germans were not sufficiently impressed by them to suggest the construction of similar vehicles in large numbers and with any great urgency.[1]

On October 5, 1916, the CIGS issued a memorandum stating that in the present stage of their development, tanks were to be regarded merely as accessory to the 'ordinary' method of attack. There was still no imaginative realisation in the War Office that at last some alternative had been found to this 'ordinary' method of putting men against machine guns. Nevertheless, on September 17, 1916 – two days after the tanks had first gone into battle – Haig sent his Deputy Chief of Staff to England to ask for the manufacture of a thousand of them.

[1] On the other hand, one of the German divisions against which the main attack was delivered at Cambrai in November, 1917, had been given at least some instructions about dealing with tanks because the divisional commander had heard of them from his brother who had seen them in action in the Somme.

Difficulties of the first Coalition: compulsory military service: death of Lord Kitchener: Lloyd George becomes Secretary of State for War

At the opening of the battle of the Somme the Coalition Government had been in office for over thirteen months. The lack of any conspicuous military success during this time was in itself likely to lead to criticism of the higher direction of the war. On personal grounds alone a coalition under Asquith would not satisfy Liberals or Unionists. On May 25, 1915, Walter Long had written to Carson that he did not expect the Coalition to 'work when it comes to daily administration. I loathe the very idea of our good fellows sitting with these double-dyed traitors.'[1] At about the same time Birrell, on the Liberal side, was writing to Redmond; 'You cannot imagine how I loathe the idea of sitting cheek by jowl with these fellows.'[2] The first open breach came with Carson's resignation on October 12, 1915; the immediate cause of his resignation was the failure of the Government to send help to Serbia, but Carson and the Unionists had become more and more disquieted by Asquith's procrastination and Kitchener's unwillingness to discuss plans with his civilian colleagues. Carson complained that Kitchener 'did not read' the telegrams and that other Ministers did not see them. Carson was in contact with a group of persistent, self-assured Conservatives, Milner, Amery, Oliver, and Geoffrey Robinson.[3] He also had the support of some 150 members of his party who had formed a 'Unionist War Committee'.

These malcontents, if they can be so called, were dissatisfied with the

[1] I. Colvin, *Life of Carson*, iii, 51.
[2] D. Gwynn, *Life of John Redmond*, p. 52.
[3] Geoffrey Robinson, editor of *The Times*, 1912–19 and 1923–41, took the name of Dawson in 1917 on inheriting an estate. F. S. Oliver (1864–1934) was a successful business man, with an active, though somewhat dilettante interest in politics and political theory, who had advocated a federal solution for the Irish question and for the British Empire generally.

steps taken by the Prime Minister to secure a more efficient conduct of business. The Dardanelles Committee, like its predecessor the War Council, was too large, too argumentative, and therefore too slow in taking decisions. Much business which should have been left to it continued to be discussed also in the Cabinet, and, as before, this duplication led to further argument and delay. Asquith himself realised that the new machinery was no better than the old, and that no plan would work without a change in Kitchener's methods. Discontent with these methods led to the appointment of Lieutenant-General Sir Archibald Murray as CIGS in September, 1915, with the duty of providing in a regular way the information extorted piecemeal and with difficulty from Kitchener. Asquith, in telling Kitchener of the decision, wrote of the importance of having a General Staff 'to guide and advise the Cabinet and its Committees in matters of strategy and of naval and military policy'; one of the duties of the General Staff would be to draw up for the Cabinet a weekly appreciation of the military situation, actual and prospective.

Asquith also suggested the substitution of two smaller committees for the Dardanelles Committee, one of them to deal with the conduct of the war, and the other with financial business. This suggestion had little support, but later in October – this time in the Prime Minister's absence – the Cabinet decided that a smaller committee was essential. The unstated aim of this revolt – a lesser term can hardly be used – was to get rid of Kitchener. Lloyd George said to Bonar Law, apparently at this time, that, as long as Kitchener was at the War Office, 'nothing but disaster' was 'in front of us'. Lloyd George went further with Asquith; he said that he would resign if a change were not made. Asquith, who had no illusions about the purpose of Lloyd George and his supporters, wrote to Kitchener on October 17: 'What is going on now is being engineered by men (Curzon and Lloyd George, and some others) whose real object is to oust you. They know well that I give no countenance to their projects, and consequently they have conceived the idea of using you against me.'[1]

On November 2 Asquith announced in the House of Commons the establishment of a new and somewhat smaller directing committee, consisting at first only of himself, Kitchener, and Balfour. The first act of this committee, or rather of the Prime Minister, was to ask Kitchener to go to Gallipoli to report on the question of evacuation. Kitchener left London on November 4. Some Ministers hoped that he might be

[1] Sir P. Magnus, *Kitchener*, pp. 352–3.

persuaded to stay in the Near East as Commander-in-Chief. Asquith took over the War Office during his absence, and initiated further changes. Murray was not altogether a success as CIGS, and, in the general transfers following the appointment of Haig to succeed French as Commander-in-Chief of the BEF, Sir William Robertson[1] was brought to London as CIGS with increased powers. As a condition of his appointment Robertson demanded that the new War Committee should not be responsible to the Cabinet for the conduct of military operations, and that military advice on these operations should be given to the War Committee through the CIGS. The first of these conditions was, strictly speaking, unconstitutional. Kitchener rejected – also as unconstitutional – a third condition that military operational orders should no longer be issued by the Army Council under the authority of the Secretary of State, but by the CIGS under the authority of the War Committee. Kitchener and Robertson, in fact, worked in complete harmony, though the new status of the CIGS was another stage in the decline of Kitchener's powers and status.

The composition of the new Committee was announced in Parliament on November 11; its members were the Prime Minister, Grey, Lloyd George, Balfour, McKenna, and Kitchener. The First Sea Lord and the CIGS always attended, though their status (members or expert advisers) was not defined. Other Ministers were brought in for special purposes. Curzon, who was one of them, was aggrieved at not being a full member from the outset; Churchill was not included, and resigned from the Cabinet to command a unit on the Western Front.

The new Committee was an improvement on its predecessors. Owing to the reorganisation of the General Staff it was better informed; its work was also better organised. Its greatest weakness was that it was still more or less parallel with the Cabinet which continued to work without recorded minutes and a definite agenda. Moreover, except for the Prime Minister, the members of the Committee were in charge of important departments, and could not give enough time to the general

---

[1] Robertson was a man of great natural ability. He was born in 1860, and enlisted as a trooper in 1877 in the 17th Lancers. He passed the examination for a commission in 1888 and was gazetted a second lieutenant in the 3rd Dragoons, then in India. Here he soon acquired a remarkable knowledge of Indian languages, and was employed on Intelligence work. He was the first 'ranker officer' to enter the Staff College of which he later became Commandant. He went to France as Quartermaster-General at GHQ in August, 1914, and again shewed outstanding competence.

direction of the war without scamping their other duties. In any case, as long as Asquith was in charge, the fundamental grounds of criticism remained; so also did the old party rivalries, the mutual distrust, and private ambitions of the leaders.

The Coalition Government, having survived one crisis, nearly broke down over two grave matters of domestic policy. The most serious of these was the problem set by the failure of the voluntary recruiting system to meet the incessant demands of the army for more men. The weekly intake of recruits, though it was having increasingly serious effects on production, was bringing in only about two-thirds of the number required. Compulsory service was the one possible solution. There was a considerable movement in favour of it as an act of justice to those who had already volunteered. The voluntary system, which at first had provided enough recruits, had now ceased to meet a situation in which some 650,000 unmarried men of military age were in profitable occupations at home, while large numbers of married volunteers were serving with the army. Compulsory service would also make it easier to avoid the haphazard withdrawal of men from 'key industries'. On the other hand, the opposition to any form of compulsion was very strong, especially (though not only) among the working class. Many Liberals regarded compulsion as an interference (as indeed it was) with the traditional liberty of Englishmen. Trade unionists were afraid of an industrial conscription (to the advantage of private profit) in which they might lose their acquired rights and freedom of bargaining. Labour speakers quoted as a warning Briand's action before the war in breaking a French railway strike by calling up the railwaymen as conscripts. They also argued that the conscription of men was inequitable without the conscription of wealth. One simple example of the traditional unwillingness of workmen to give up their freedom to bargain had been shown in January, 1915, in the opposition of merchant seamen to an Admiralty proposal to put the crews of transports under the Naval Discipline Act. The men thought this proposal to be the first stage in the application of the Act to the crews of all requisitioned ships. They were willing to take the risks of serving in these or other ships at sea; they would not surrender their freedom to negotiate their own conditions of service.

The divisions in the Coalition Cabinet on the question were mainly, though not entirely, on party lines; some Liberals – Lloyd George and Churchill, for example – were strongly in favour of compulsory military service. Asquith did not object to it in principle, but wanted to postpone as long as possible the introduction of a measure upon which opinion in the country was divided. Kitchener was also in favour of delaying compulsion; his reason was that he wanted to husband British resources for the end of a long war in which the French and Germans would have exhausted their available man-power. He said to Derby, 'What I am anxious for is that when it comes to peace we shall have the biggest army in the field. It would never do for the French to have more than us.'[1]

The Cabinet agreed upon a last attempt to keep the voluntary system. Lord Derby[2] was made Director-General of Recruiting in October, 1915. He was embarrassed by his duties because he was already convinced that compulsory service was necessary. Asquith promised him that, if his recruiting campaign failed, the Government would introduce compulsion. Derby's plan was to ask all men between eighteen and forty-one on the recently compiled National Register[3] to attest their willingness to serve if and when called upon to do so. The lists thus obtained would be divided into twenty-three age-groups of unmarried, and twenty-three of married men. Asquith pledged himself that the married men would be left until the bachelors had been called up. If sufficient of the latter did not come in voluntarily a bill would be passed compelling them to serve. Few people felt sure that Asquith would be able to keep the public pledge to the married. In fact the Derby scheme brought in only about 340,000 men, including married men, and after deducting the unfit and the 'starred', i.e. men in key industries, about half of the 650,000 available bachelors failed to register.

In December, 1915, the Cabinet decided that they would have to bring forward some measure of compulsion. Sir John Simon resigned on the question of principle. McKenna and Runciman, President of the

[1] R. S. Churchill, *Lord Derby*, p. 192. Kitchener hoped that he might be one of the delegates at the Peace Conference. He told Derby that he was opposed to the return of Alsace-Lorraine to France, or to depriving Germany of her colonies. Hankey has also pointed out (op. cit., i, p. 426) that Kitchener realised (though he shewed little imagination in trying to solve the problem) that it was useless to attempt a large offensive on the Western Front before a very great increase in the supply of artillery ammunition.

[2] Derby was an old-style Lancashire magnate, well known for his interest in local and national affairs, and even more popular as a successful racehorse-owner who in his public speeches often gave excellent 'tips' about his horses. He was a heavy, stupid-looking man, though very shrewd, honest, and sensible in a matter-of-fact way. He had no ambition other than to maintain the status into which he had been born, and was useful in mediating between rival politicians and generals.

[3] See below, p. 469.

Board of Trade, believed that the military demand for an army of nearly seventy divisions[1] was beyond the financial resources of the country and would take more men than could be spared from essential industries. Grey also inclined to this view. The Labour members of the Government came under great pressure from their party; a general meeting of representatives of Labour organisations in January, 1916, described the adoption of conscription as contrary to the spirit of British democracy and full of danger to the liberties of the people. The meeting therefore called upon the Labour party to oppose any form of compulsory military service. Asquith, however, persuaded the party to discuss the question again. At a second conference, held in Bristol, a majority once more voted in general terms against conscription, but deleted from a motion on the Compulsory Military Service Act a sentence binding the party to vote for its repeal.

Meanwhile Asquith had saved the Coalition from collapse, and had been able to pass a Military Service Act on January 27, 1916, applying at first only to bachelors. He also made it clear that compulsion was intended only for the period of the war, and was not a back-door method of introducing a permanent scheme. Soon after the Act came into force there were complaints about the unfairness with which it was being operated. These complaints had substance. The local tribunals administering the Act had neither precedent nor experience to guide them. Some tribunals were too severe; others too lax. Kitchener himself admitted that, owing to the number of extensions of time which the tribunals had been allowed to grant, it had been necessary to call up some of the younger married groups.

The Cabinet appointed a committee to reconsider the whole question. The committee reported on April 14 in favour of extending compulsion to all men who had reached the age of eighteen since August 15, 1915, and of keeping time-expired Regulars and Territorials with the colours; they also suggested a stricter 'comb-out' of men in reserved occupations. The Cabinet would not accept these recommendations, and for a time the Coalition was once more in danger of collapse. At last – early in May, 1916 – they agreed upon a bill extending compulsory service to all male British subjects, married as well as single, between the ages of eighteen and forty-one. Lloyd George throughout the 'crisis' took the line that conscription was necessary, and that the Prime Minister ought to be resolute in enforcing it. Lloyd George told

---

[1] This figure required the immediate enlistment of some 300,000 men, apart from further demands for keeping the divisions at full strength.

Lord Stamfordham that Asquith was not carrying on the war with sufficient 'energy and determination' and that he was too much alarmed at the prospect of opposition on the Clyde and in South Wales.[1] In fact Lloyd George was right. The passing of the bill was not followed by Labour disturbances, and the balance of opinion in the country favoured it. After a meeting between Asquith, Kitchener, Bonar Law, and representatives of the Labour Party and the Trades Unions, the Party Executive agreed to withdraw their opposition.

The differences in the Coalition over compulsory service coincided with the Dublin rebellion, which put a further strain on the unity of Ministers. Asquith thought that nationalist opinion in Ireland might be conciliated if the Home Rule Act were put into operation at once. It was unlikely that Home Rule could be given practical effect during the war, but the good faith of the British Government would be clear. Lloyd George saw Redmond and Carson and obtained their provisional consent to the plan, together with an Amending Bill providing that the six Ulster counties should remain outside the Home Rule area during the war, and that later, an Imperial Conference would be held to consider the future Government of the Empire, including the Government of Ireland. After this Conference outstanding questions such as the permanent position of Ulster would be settled.

The plan was accepted reluctantly by some – not all – of the Conservatives. It broke down mainly over the old dispute whether the exclusion of Ulster was intended to be permanent. There was also the question whether the Irish members of parliament should continue to sit at Westminster. The Conservatives argued that it would be absurd, after the grant of Home Rule, to allow eighty Irish Nationalists to determine – as they might do – the majority in the House of Commons. Redmond insisted on their remaining in the House as evidence that the arrangement was temporary, i.e. that the permanent exclusion of Ulster had not been decided.

Although the breakdown was perhaps inevitable, the general circumstances showed yet again the limitations on the freedom of action of the representatives of the parties in the Coalition. Bonar Law wrote to Asquith during the discussions on compulsory military service: 'I believe that it is easier for you to obtain the consent of your party to general compulsion than for me to obtain the consent of my party to its not being adopted.'[2] About this time Lord Robert Cecil suggested

---

[1] H. Nicolson, *George V*, p. 274. For the industrial unrest, see below, p. 477.
[2] Quoted in J. A. Spender and C. Asquith, *Life of Asquith*, ii, 211.

a reconstruction of the Cabinet with Asquith as Prime Minister, not of a Coalition but of a National Government in which Ministers would be chosen solely for their capacity to do the work in hand – winning the war – and without reference to the balance or affiliation of parties.

After Kitchener's death Asquith gave the Secretaryship for War to Lloyd George. Bonar Law, who, on Asquith's view, had a prior claim, also thought Lloyd George the best choice. Asquith seems to have hoped that close contact with the generals would convince Lloyd George that their objections to his ideas on the strategy of the war were not due to prejudice and obstruction.[1] Lloyd George, however, was very far from being convinced; the failure of the Somme offensive had the opposite effect on him. Moreover there were others, including Bonar Law, in the inner circles of government who agreed with him that some drastic change in the high direction of the war was necessary not only to bring victory but to avoid defeat. The Conservative malcontents were growing in number, and were increasingly anxious to take the control of the war out of Asquith's hands. The group who looked to Milner[2] had brought into their inner counsels Waldorf Astor, an amiable man of no great ability, but the owner of *The Observer*; they continued to have the support of *The Times*. Their difficulty was that they did not agree upon a successor to Asquith or even whether he should be removed altogether or kept as a kind of figure-head. They had no high opinion of Bonar Law. They did not trust Lloyd George (Oliver's nickname for him – 'the Goat' – appears often in their correspondence), and, again in Oliver's words, they did not want to 'kill Charles to make James king'. Anyhow, they were adept at intriguing and pulling strings, but had little understanding of methods of popular appeal. Milner, their source of inspiration, although a most capable administrator, despised and disliked the whole democratic system, and would never be of the slightest use as a political leader.

Lloyd George himself appeared uncertain about his tactics even if he was sure of his ultimate aim. He was in touch with Carson and agreed with the Conservatives that, if Asquith continued to direct the war, the country might be defeated. Bonar Law thought at this time that Lloyd George was 'a self-seeker and a man who considered no interest

[1] Mrs Asquith, however, noted in her diary at the time of Lloyd George's appointment: 'We are out, it is only a question of time when we shall have to leave Downing St.' M. Asquith, *Autobiography*, ii, 245.

[2] For Milner's opposition, see A. M. Gollin, *Proconsul in Politics*, passim.

except his own', and wanted merely 'to put Asquith out and to put himself in'.[1]

This estimate was true at a certain level. Lloyd George was an ambitious man, and conscious of his own ability. Asquith, in 1905, had been no less ambitious and self-confident when he had tried to persuade Campbell-Bannerman to go to the House of Lords and leave him (Asquith) as leader in the Commons. Asquith had given way when Campbell-Bannerman refused to be moved. The situation was now very different. In 1905 Asquith could afford to wait, but in 1916 Lloyd George might well feel that 'putting Asquith out and putting himself in' without delay was in the national interest.

[1] Northcliffe was now attacking Asquith; he might have had less influence even in *The Times*, one of his own newspapers, if Robinson had not agreed with him. Northcliffe's part throughout the crisis leading to Asquith's resignation was less important than he believed.

PART IV

The War at sea to the autumn of 1916

CHAPTER 12

The Grand Fleet in the North Sea: the battles of Coronel and the Falkland Islands: the battle of Jutland

At the outbreak of war the British army, though it provided an Expeditionary Force for the Continent, could not have fought single-handed any one of the Great Powers. The British Navy, on the other hand, was the strongest in the world. As far as the war could be decided at sea, the chances were in favour of a British victory. The Germans had planned for a short war on land in which their success would secure them so great a Continental predominance – including the control of the north French and Belgian coasts – that they could force Great Britain to accept German conditions of peace. If, however, the war on land were prolonged, the Germans would feel increasingly the effects of British sea power, both in cutting off their supplies from beyond the North Sea and in providing a greatly enlarged British army with a freedom of movement which could do much to counter-balance the advantages of Germany's 'inner lines of communication'.

The Germans had spent very large sums since 1900 on the con-struction of a battlefleet. It is true, though hardly credible, that in 1914 the strategic purpose for which they had built the fleet was not clear even to the German Admiralty.[1] The original calculation of Admiral Tirpitz had been that a German battlefleet inferior in strength to that of Great Britain would none the less be an instrument of diplomatic potency, or in plainer language, blackmail, since, in view of the com-bined strength of the French and Russian fleets (against which the

---

[1] In October, 1912, Bethmann-Hollweg told Lord Granville, a senior mem-ber of the staff of the British Embassy in Berlin, that 'Germany required her fleet, not merely for the purpose of defending her commerce, but for the general purpose of her greatness.' He did not attempt to define this 'general purpose'; he added that 'a man would be considered a fool who merely developed his legs and left his arms alone because he was a postman or something of the sort and only required the use of his legs. In exactly the same way Germany must develop her fleet as well as her army'. *British Documents on the Origins of the War*, Vol IX, Pt 2, pp. 36–9.

British 'two-Power' standard was maintained), Great Britain could not risk the losses likely to be incurred in destroying even a weaker German fleet. This calculation was worthless after Great Britain had made agreements with France and Russia, and could reckon the fleets of these Powers as probable allies rather than enemies. Tirpitz thought for a time that by steady building Germany might equal Great Britain in capital ships; this hope was fostered by the introduction of the 'Dreadnought' which gave the British navy a temporary increase in striking-power but rendered semi-obsolete the value of the existing British superiority in older ships. It was clear, however, after 1909, when the British building programme was raised to eight 'Dreadnoughts' in a single year, that there was little chance of overtaking British construction.[1]

The last hope, therefore, of employing the German battlefleet with a reasonable chance of success was to entice the British fleet into waters where it would fight at a disadvantage. The Germans believed that the British Admiralty would fall in with their intentions; they assumed, as the British public also tended to assume, that the British fleet would seek out the enemy and engage his ships regardless of the conditions in which the battle would be fought. On this curious reading of British naval history the Germans apparently based their plans.[2] They had also hoped to weaken the British fleet by torpedo attacks and mines before it had made its expected incursion into the zone of the German defences. They had taken, however, few measures to prepare for attacks of this kind, and, to the surprise of the British, had also done little to organise commerce destruction over the seas of the world. Owing to a chance that the German liner *Kaiser Wilhelm II* of the North German Lloyd Company's fleet put into Southampton for repairs after a collision in the Channel the Admiralty had discovered that the ship had gun mountings. They had expected therefore that a number of armed German liners would emerge from neutral ports to act as auxiliary cruisers. Only one such ship, the *Kaiser Wilhelm der Grosse* left German waters at the outbreak of war; the ship was found

[1] At the outbreak of war the British navy had twenty 'Dreadnoughts' in the North Sea area; the Germans had thirteen. The British margin in battle-cruisers was less – four to three. Four more British and two German 'Dreadnoughts', or rather 'super-Dreadnoughts' were approaching completion. The British margin of superiority was at times dangerously low when a number of ships were in dock for special repair or routine overhaul.

[2] This misreading was also made by the well-known American naval historian Admiral Mahan; he stated (August 3, 1914) his expectation of a great naval battle.

and sunk within ten days of her arrival in South American waters. A few other ships were armed from German warships in foreign stations, but the only serious trouble came from these warships themselves using under skilful leadership the elaborate organisation for coaling and supply built up before the war.[1]

The main strategy of the British fleet was determined by the tasks of keeping the command of Home waters, closing the enemy routes to the oceans, and placing itself in the most suitable position for action if the enemy battlefleet could be induced to leave the shelter of its protected bases.[2] The geographical position of Great Britain in relation to Germany was favourable since the British fleet could carry out these tasks simultaneously; the Germans could reach the ocean only through the Straits of Dover or across the northern waters of the North Sea, where there was a gap of about 190 miles between the Shetland Islands and the coast of Norway. If the main British fleet were stationed in Scottish waters it could protect the British Isles from invasion,[3] secure free access to British ports, keep watch on the German battlefleet, and cut off German oceanic trade. The only advantage on the German side was access to the Baltic through the Kiel Canal. Thereby the German navy protected Prussia east of the Schleswig-Holstein peninsula from invasion by sea and ensured imports of Swedish ore outside the range of the Allied blockade.

The weak point in the British strategical position was that, partly through lack of money, and partly owing to the rapidly changing character of naval war (especially the increases in range and power of torpedoes and in the sea-going capacity of submarines) the Admiralty had been unable to provide the fleet with fortified bases like those on the Channel coast. Rosyth had been chosen in 1903 as a new base; work on it had been proceeding slowly when in 1908 the experts decided that the outer anchorage would be exposed to torpedo attack. Cromarty Firth and Scapa Flow thus became of greater importance

---

[1] See below, p. 172. One auxiliary cruiser – the liner *Berlin* – was specially equipped for minelaying; this ship was sent out from German waters in October, 1914. A mine laid by the *Berlin* sank the 'Dreadnought' battleship *Audacious* on October 26. (See below, p. 175.) The *Berlin* put in at Trondhjem on her way home, in order to escape from some British cruisers, and was interned.

[2] See Map 1.

[3] This protection also covered the north and west coasts of France, and enabled the French to concentrate their capital ships in the Mediterranean. Hence, even if she had wished to do so, Italy could not safely have entered the war on the side of her partners in the Triple Alliance.

as advanced bases; the former was protected before July, 1914, but practically nothing had been done at Scapa. The lack of preparation caused great inconvenience, and some loss, in the early stages of the war; it did not prevent the British fleet from taking its war stations.

By a fortunate chance the Admiralty had decided in March, 1914, to hold a test mobilisation – not on full scale – instead of the ordinary summer manœuvres of the Home fleets. This mobilisation was completed by July 16, and, after a week's exercises, the ships were due to begin their dispersal. Some units had already left on July 26. The Admiralty then ordered that no further moves should take place, and that leave should be stopped. On the morning of July 29 the First Fleet – consisting of a flagship and four battle squadrons – was ordered to Scapa; the ships passed through the Straits of Dover at night, and without lights. Two days earlier the German High Seas fleet, which was cruising off the coast of Norway, had been recalled to its base. The last of its destroyers was entering the shelter of Wilhelmshaven when the main British battle fleet passed far to the north on the way to Scapa.[1]

The contrast between the two fleets – the one seeking hastily the shelter of its defences, and the other moving freely up the North Sea to bar the German route to the oceans – was not altogether as remarkable as it appeared. The Grand Fleet was also taking its station at a protected base: the protection was less adequate than the Commander-in-Chief desired, and his first care was to secure it against attack by enemy submarines. Nevertheless the impression of absolute British superiority at sea was not a wrong one. The Germans began to feel at once the consequences of this superiority; before the end of 1914 the British navy, while keeping its hold on home waters, had also been able to sink or render harmless almost every German cruiser in distant seas.

There was indeed a notable exception to which the term 'render harmless' cannot be applied. In August, 1914, the Germans had in the Mediterranean two modern ships, the *Goeben*, a fast and powerful battle-cruiser, and the *Breslau*, a light cruiser. On August 3 these ships were at Messina. They left the harbour to make a sudden bombardment of Bone and Philippeville. They were seen on their way back to Messina during the day of August 4 by two British battle-cruisers, but

---

[1] The Channel fleet – based on the southern ports – included a battle squadron. There was also a cruiser squadron at Harwich.

the British ultimatum to Germany did not expire until midnight, and the British ships, though within range, did not fire at the Germans.

There seemed little doubt, however, that the two German ships would have to choose between remaining interned at an Italian port, attempting to escape to an Austrian port, or coming out to certain destruction in the Mediterranean where the French had one Dread-nought and fifteen other battleships, six cruisers and twenty-four des-troyers, and the British three battle-cruisers, eight other cruisers and sixteen destroyers. Unfortunately the French dispositions were entirely defensive; their ships were instructed to protect the transport of troops from Algeria to France. The Admiralty, somewhat unnecessarily, in-structed the British Commander-in-Chief, Admiral Sir Berkeley Milne, to assist in guarding the French transports as well as to keep watch on the German ships. Milne assumed that the two German ships would turn west; consequently he left only the light cruiser *Gloucester* to watch the southern end of the Straits of Messina. The *Goeben* and *Breslau* left – shadowed by the British light cruiser – by this way of escape, and soon turned south-east towards the Aegean. Rear-Admiral Troubridge, with four armoured and two light cruisers and eight destroyers off Cepha-lonia, might have intercepted the German ships, but Troubridge had been ordered not to risk his ships in attacking a superior force, and, with some obtuseness, interpreted the order to mean that he could not use his ships to attack the stronger *Goeben*. The captains of the *Gloucester* and her sister ship *Dublin* took a different view, but without support could do no damage. The *Gloucester*, which followed the *Goeben* until the evening of August 7, escaped destruction only because the Germans could not believe that this light cruiser was not being closely supported by the battle-cruisers.

The German ships thus reached the neighbourhood of the Darda-nelles on August 8. The British battle-cruisers were far behind – the Admiralty had given them no indication that the Germans might be making for Constantinople. Even so the two ships might have been caught. A decision to admit them through the Straits implied that Turkey would enter the war on the German side; for two days the Turkish Government hesitated. During this time the *Goeben* and *Breslau* could easily have been overtaken but, again, the Admiralty made a blunder. They sent Admiral Milne a message on August 8 that Austria-Hungary had declared war on Great Britain and France. The report was untrue, but Milne accepted it, and, according to his previous instructions for such an event, began at once to concentrate his fleet at Malta, and therefore called off the pursuit. The message was countermanded too late. On August 10, the Turks allowed the *Goeben* and *Breslau* to pass through the Straits.[1]

The destruction of the only other German squadron outside the North Sea was also preceded by a disaster for which the Admiralty must bear considerable responsibility. On the outbreak of war the Germans had in the China Seas a squadron of two cruisers – *Scharnhorst* and *Gneisenau*, each armed with eight 8·2-inch guns – and three fast light cruisers, *Emden*, *Nürnberg*, and *Leipzig*.[2] Admiral Count von Spee, commander of the squadron, made for the islands of the western Pacific and then for the west coast of South America. The Admiralty had expected von Spee to go to South American waters, and had reinforced Admiral Cradock, commanding the South American station, with an old battleship, *Canopus*. Cradock's squadron, before this reinforcement, consisted of one large cruiser, *Good Hope*, a smaller

---

[1] Turkish feeling had been much aroused because the British Government at the outbreak of war requisitioned two Turkish battleships under construction in British shipyards. These ships, which would have given the Turkish navy an overwhelming naval superiority over Greece, were being paid for largely by private subscriptions in Turkey. The Turks evaded their duty of interning the German ships by buying them, though their transfer, even if *bona fide*, was questionable in law. The transfer was obviously not in good faith; the German crews were retained and the British Naval Mission was refused access to all Turkish ships. The mission was soon recalled from Constantinople. The announcement by the British Admiralty of the escape of the two ships merely stated that 'with the dismantling and internment of these ships, the safety of trade will have been almost entirely secured'.

[2] Three other light cruisers were in distant waters: *Königsberg* off East Africa, *Dresden* and *Karlsruhe* in the West Indies. Before their destruction they had sunk fifty British merchantmen – not much more than a third of the number of German merchantmen captured by the British navy during the first few weeks of the war. The *Emden*, before she was caught in November at Cocos Islands, 500 miles south-west of Java, had cruised for a fortnight in the Bay of Bengal, and destroyed 500,000 gallons of oil at Madras. After this attack the local moneylenders, who financed the Indian traders, took to the hills, with the result that trade was seriously dislocated. This trade included bags urgently needed in Australia for the carriage of the wheat harvest. The *Emden* captured twenty British ships (of which six were recovered). The total losses caused by her attacks on shipping were about £2,200,000, including cargoes. The captain of the *Emden* was careful to observe all the recognised conventions of naval warfare. After the sinking of the ship *The Times* commented that 'had all his countrymen fought as he had done, the German nation would not be execrated in the world today'. The *Leipzig* at the outbreak of war was off California. The ship joined von Spee at Easter Island in October. The *Dresden* also joined von Spee at this time.

cruiser, *Monmouth*, and a light cruiser, *Glasgow*.[1] The Admiralty did
not consider it prudent to detach a battle-cruiser from the Grand Fleet;
the battle-cruiser *Australia* could have been sent as soon as von Spee's
whereabouts were known, but the Australian Government, in view
of their own public opinion, would probably have been unwilling to
allow the ship to go so far from Australian waters. In any case, as long
as Cradock kept his cruisers with the *Canopus*, they would be secure,
since the Germans could not safely come within range of the 12-inch
guns of the battleship. Cradock's instructions were to hold his squadron
together and also to search for the enemy. The Admiralty intended
him to use the cruisers to draw the Germans to the *Canopus* and, above
all, to prevent them from breaking into the South Atlantic, but the
wording of the instructions was not sufficiently precise.

The result was that, on sighting von Spee's ships off Coronel on the
Chilean coast, Cradock, instead of avoiding battle[2] and turning back
his three cruisers towards the *Canopus* some 350 miles behind, decided
to attack. The *Monmouth* and *Good Hope* were soon disabled and sunk.
The *Glasgow* fought on and was able to escape in the darkness. This
unequal battle took place on November 1. The naval position in home
waters and in the Mediterranean was not easy; the *Audacious* had
recently been lost, and Turkey had declared war. Admiral Fisher had
now become First Sea Lord.[3] Fisher was in his seventy-fifth year, but
still had the fierce energy which had brought about such changes in
British naval policy some twelve years earlier. He and Churchill acted
with the utmost speed to prevent von Spee from doing further damage.
The difficulty was that von Spee had a number of choices open to him.
He might pass through the Panama Canal and fall on British shipping
and ports in the Caribbean; he might attempt to break the blockade
and reach home, or go to the South African coast – where the Boer
rebellion had just been suppressed, and Smuts was preparing an expedition against German south-west Africa. Or he might threaten the
Falkland Islands and the River Plate. The Admiralty considered,
rightly, that he would be least likely to go through the Canal. They

[1] The *Monmouth* and *Good Hope* were manned by reservists; the *Scharnhorst*
and *Gneisenau* were not only more heavily armed, but their crews included the
best gunners in the German navy.

[2] Cradock could almost certainly have evaded the pursuit of the German ships.
There were only two hours left before sunset.

[3] Fisher succeeded Admiral Prince Louis of Battenberg, against whom there
had been an unfair and foolish press campaign on the ground of his German
ancestry. Prince Louis himself offered his resignation.

therefore sent two battle-cruisers from the Grand Fleet to bar his passage round Cape Horn, and a third to protect the West Indies.

Von Spee himself was curiously inactive for some time after the battle of Coronel. He did not leave the neighbourhood of Chile until November 26. He then sailed for the Atlantic and, in spite of the advice of his senior officers, decided to bombard installations in the Falkland Islands. He still moved slowly; he spent three days in transferring to his own colliers the coal taken from a captured British collier. Hence Admiral Sturdee, with the two battle-cruisers, one large and two smaller armoured cruisers, and two light cruisers, reached the Falkland Islands on December 7, the day before Spee's appearance off the port.[1] Once the Germans were within reach of the battle-cruisers, there was no escape for them. The whole of von Spee's squadron was destroyed, except for the *Dresden* which managed to get away, and was found, and sunk, three months later.

The battles of Coronel and the Falkland Islands were examples, if such were needed, of the 'absolute' character of superior material strength at sea between two fleets otherwise manned with equal skill, courage, and determination. In defeating Cradock, von Spee had only two men wounded, and suffered no damage to his ships. At the battle of the Falkland Islands the British casualties were only about thirty. The battle-cruisers were soon back again at their station, and the Grand Fleet retained its immense power.

By this time each side also had had sharp lessons in the North Sea. The Germans lost three light cruisers on August 28 off Heligoland Bight after falling in unexpectedly with a British battle-cruiser squadron; three old British cruisers, the *Aboukir*, *Hogue*, and *Cressy*, were torpedoed off the Dutch coast by a German submarine on September 22.[2] The Admiralty had been unwise enough to keep these old ships on a daily patrol within easy reach of German attack; the effect of their loss was to increase the British alarm about the danger to the Grand Fleet in its still unprotected anchorage. For a time the fleet was moved round to Lough Swilly. Here, off the north Irish coast, the

[1] Sturdee's ships were coaling when the German ships were sighted. The Germans seem to have mistaken the heavy smoke clouds from the British ships (as they raised steam) for the burning of oil and coal dumps. (The French had burned their dumps at Tahiti on von Spee's approach.) They did not notice the tripod masts of the battle-cruisers until nearly two hours after they had themselves been sighted.

[2] The *Cressy* and the *Hogue* might have escaped if they had not stopped to pick up survivors from the *Aboukir* and thus given the submarines easy targets.

Audacious, one of the newest battleships, was sunk by a mine which the German liner *Berlin* had laid in the shipping channels. The *Berlin* had escaped detection by a series of chances; she had been laying her mines – illegally – in the hope of catching merchant ships.

This accidental success did not change the main strategy of either side. After the action in the Heligoland Bight, the Emperor, to the great anger of Tirpitz, was unwilling to risk more losses. The British Admiralty and the War Office, especially the latter, were disturbed over the possibility of a large-scale invasion raid. The War Office argued in November that the Germans might be able to spare 250,000 men for a landing.[1] Such an estimate misinterpreted German strategy on land – and was based upon a ludicrous miscalculation of the number of transports and protecting vessels necessary for an expedition on this scale. The Germans were hardly likely to risk the loss of their fleet in attempting so wild a project, but in the long nights of late autumn and early winter they might have tried raids with landings up to the strength of two or three divisions. Although these divisions could not have been maintained or reinforced, they might well have caused immense confusion and great material damage if they had been directed against the north-east coast or Essex estuaries. There were no large minefields protecting these vulnerable areas; the Admiralty had not provided the fleet with an adequate supply of mines.[2] London itself was not fully protected by lines of defence in Essex until February, 1915.

The Emperor, however, wanted to keep the fleet intact as a bargaining-counter for a peace settlement. The military chiefs had no plans for invasion or a large-scale raid, and could not improvise them. The naval authorities continued to protest against the military failure to realise the immense importance to Germany of taking positive action against British sea-power, but for a time there was no change in German tactics. The British Admiralty and Admiral Jellicoe, the Commander-in-Chief, were content with a situation in which the British navy was already asserting superior power; there was no reason to risk the loss of ships by fighting the Germans in unfavourable conditions.[3] John Rushworth Jellicoe (1859–1935) – the only man, in Churchill's well-known phrase, who could have lost the war in an afternoon –

[1] See above, p. 36–7. [2] See below, p. 337, note 3.
[3] A. J. Marder has summed up the matter shortly in the words: 'the Grand Fleet . . . might go through the war without fighting a battle, and yet have been the dominating factor all the time'. *From the Dreadnought to Scapa Flow*, ii, 176.

was by temperament well-suited to a policy of calculated delay and patience. He was far from being timid or sluggish; his mind was quick, active, and observant. He had a full and comprehensive knowledge of his profession. Jellicoe was the son of a captain of the Royal Mail Line; his family, especially on his mother's side, had long been associated with the Royal Navy. He joined the *Britannia* in 1872 and passed out top of his class two years later. His first ship was an iron sailing frigate with auxiliary steam. At the end of the Russo-Turkish war of 1877 he was with the ships sent, if necessary, to force the Dardanelles; he served ashore as a despatch-rider at Gallipoli. He took part later in the Egyptian campaign, and was badly wounded in the expedition to Pekin during the Boxer rebellion. In 1893 Jellicoe, who was ill at the time, was nearly drowned in the sinking of the battleship *Victoria* after she had been rammed in manœuvres. Jellicoe was a short man, stoutly built, and a good athlete. He was quiet, modest in manner, and very popular with the officers and men of the fleet. After taking over the command of the Grand Fleet, Jellicoe had worked out in careful detail what he could and could not do with it. His immense responsibilities did not disturb him; he was not affected by ill-informed criticism – encouraged by German propaganda – about the inaction of the British navy. It is a matter of argument whether he over-rated the risks of torpedo and mine attack on his battleships; the fact that, except for the chance destruction of the *Audacious*, he did not lose any battleships from such attack may well have been due to his precautionary measures, and may not show that he put the danger of loss too high.

Admiral Beatty,[1] who succeeded Jellicoe as Commander-in-Chief in November, 1916, was very different in character and temper, but it was doubtful whether, at least in 1914 and in the early part of 1915, he would have adopted, or whether the Admiralty would have allowed him to adopt, a different policy. In any case, if the Germans refused a fleet action in the North Sea, the British could not compel them to come out.

Fisher, when he became First Sea Lord, had a plan which would have compelled such action, and indeed invited it in circumstances favour-

---

[1] David Beatty (1871–1936), was the son of a cavalry officer of Irish family who had settled in Cheshire, where he bred and trained hunters. Beatty himself might be called a cavalry commander of the Prince Rupert type turned admiral. He had served with Kitchener in the Sudan river campaigns of 1896 and 1897, and was nearly drowned in the capsizing of a boat at the Fourth Cataract. Beatty, like Jellicoe, took part in the operations at the time of the Boxer rebellion. In 1912 he was Naval Secretary to Churchill at the Admiralty.

able to the enemy. Fortunately for Great Britain this plan required long preparation. Fisher wanted to invade Germany by landing an army on the Pomeranian coast. He regarded the plan as his 'main scheme of naval strategy', and set into operation a large building programme of ships of special draught for carrying it out. These preparations were of some use in providing small craft for other purposes, especially anti-submarine warfare; in all other respects they were a waste of resources. The Pomeranian plan never had a chance of success. It was abandoned after the Russian retreat in 1915 had made it certain that the Russian armies could not co-operate in an invasion. The most important effect of the plan was, perhaps, that it occupied Fisher's attention and satisfied his fierce instinct to attack, when otherwise he might have argued for an offensive policy in the North Sea with disastrous results to the Grand Fleet.[1]

The instructions which forbade the commander of the German High Seas Fleet to risk his battleships did not apply to the employment of battle-cruisers in swift raids, without an attempt at landings, across the North Sea. Such raids might cause minor damage by bombardment, and probably greater loss by mine-laying; they were also likely to arouse a good deal of criticism in Great Britain against the supposed inability of the British fleet to protect the coast. In the first of their 'tip and run' raids (November 3, 1914) the Germans shelled Yarmouth. They did no military damage, and lost the cruiser *Yorck* in a minefield at the entrance to their own harbours. The British plans for inter-cepting them, however, entirely failed.

A second raid, on December 15-16, 1914, was on a larger scale. The High Seas Fleet came out to support the battle-cruisers and advanced as

[1] Fisher's project had not been quite as foolish in conception as it seemed in 1914. It meant seizing a North Sea island as a base, destroying or blockading by nets and mines the German High Seas Fleet, and then repeating the process in the Baltic. Even if this second part of the plan had not been feasible, a close blockade of the German coast would have made a German raid or invasion impossible. If the operation had been successfully extended to the Baltic, Germany would have been cut off from indispensable supplies of Swedish iron ore. A plan of this kind had been considered and thought impracticable in 1906-7. Since then the German fleet had become much larger, the islands more heavily fortified, and submarines more dangerous to capital ships. See Hankey, op. cit., i, 241. For an account of the various projects to seize German islands or to invade the Baltic, see Marder, op. cit., ii, 176-98. Churchill for a time supported plans for the capture of Borkum, and, later, Sylt. Admiral Richmond described the Borkum plan as 'quite mad . . . Throwing away troops for the self-glorification of an ignorant and impulsive man.'

far as the edge of the Dogger Bank. The British Admiralty had news of the movements of the battle-cruisers,[1] but did not know that the battle-ships had sailed. They sent Admiral Beatty with a force of four battle-cruisers and Admiral Warrender with six 'Dreadnoughts' to intercept the cruisers. This force might well have been caught up and over-whelmed by the High Seas Fleet of fourteen 'Dreadnoughts' and eight older battleships if the German Commander-in-Chief, Admiral von Ingenohl, had not turned back in the face of torpedo attack. Ingenohl had already gone beyond the limit of his instructions, and, like Jellicoe, felt unable to take the immense risk of losing his fleet. In fact, he had a chance – the only chance in the war – of reducing to nothing the British superiority in 'Dreadnought' battleships. On the other hand, Hipper's squadron of battle-cruisers, which bombarded Hartlepool and the undefended seaside resorts and fishing establishments of Scar-borough and Whitby, ought to have been intercepted, but escaped largely owing to bad signalling in Beatty's squadron.[2]

Hipper made a third raid on January 23–4, 1915. This time he intended to attack the fishing fleet off the Dogger Bank, and probably to carry out another coastal bombardment. He was intercepted by a superior British force, lost the *Blücher* – one of his older ships – and had two others heavily damaged. All four of his battle-cruisers might have been sunk, if the British signalling system had been better. After this raid the Germans gave up risking their capital ships in raids; Admiral von Ingenohl was dismissed, though he had been carrying out his instruc-tions. His successor, Admiral von Pohl, was the least enterprising and least competent of the senior German naval commanders.

Admiral von Pohl resigned through illness in January 1916. His suc-cessor, Admiral Scheer,[3] believed that the unwillingness to risk capital ships, together with the refusal to carry out an unrestricted submarine war, had turned to Germany's disadvantage. The British fleet had not

[1] The Germans were unaware for a considerable time that the signalling codes which they were using had fallen into Russian hands after the wreck of the German cruiser *Magdeburg* in the Baltic, and had been transmitted to the British Admiralty.

[2] After the raid, Churchill wrote a letter to the mayor of Scarborough ex-plaining why it was not possible to prevent incursions of this kind. According to reports in the British press, instructions were then given to German newspapers not to attack Churchill personally since he was useful to Germany owing to his 'happy-go-lucky dilettantism'.

[3] Scheer (1863–1928), like Jellicoe and Beatty, had seen active service of a kind on land. He had taken part in the minor German campaigns in the Cameroons and East Africa.

been 'worn down'; the British people understood Jellicoe's policy, and, although they might complain about raids, were satisfied that this policy was sound. The blockade of Germany was becoming more serious; the military strength of Great Britain was increasing, and, unless the Germans could break British naval power, they would not win the war. Scheer obviously did not think in terms of a great naval battle with a superior fleet; his idea was to be more active in raiding, both by surface ships and Zeppelins,[1] and in setting traps for the enemy until, sooner or later, one of his manoeuvres might succeed to the extent of destroying British numerical superiority in modern battleships and battle-cruisers.

Out of one of these attempts the battle of Jutland developed. Scheer had at his disposition a number of submarines recalled from attacks on shipping after the Germans had given way to the American protests against unrestricted submarine warfare.[2] He sent sixteen of them to lie off Scottish harbours. He then intended to make a raid on Sunderland, with the High Seas Fleet in close support. He expected Beatty to bring his squadrons out from their station at Rosyth. Scheer hoped that the submarines might cut off and destroy some of Beatty's ships, and that the remainder could be caught by the High Seas Fleet before assistance reached them from Scapa.

The plan could not be tried because the weather was unfavourable, and one of the German battle-cruisers was delayed in dock for repairs after striking a mine. Scheer, however, decided to do something before the submarines returned on June 1. He therefore ordered Hipper on May 30 to move towards the Norwegian coast; the battle fleet followed the cruisers northwards. Scheer did not know that the British intelligence was aware of some movement in the German ports, and that Beatty's ships, with the Grand Fleet only seventy miles behind them, were also out in the eastern area of the North Sea in the hope of trapping the Germans.

The British battle-cruisers, having carried out an eastward sweep which had brought them to the south-west of the entrance to the Skagerrak, were just about to turn north on their return when a light cruiser sighted German ships.[3] Beatty now changed his course to the south-east to intercept what he expected to be the German battle-cruiser

[1] For the German use of airships see below, Chapter 25.

[2] See below, p. 202.

[3] Actually the first ship to be sighted was a Danish merchant ship: Hipper had also seen it, and had sent a light cruiser to examine it.

squadrons. Hipper also turned back in order to draw Beatty's squadron into the fire of the High Seas Fleet. If this mutual discovery by the two cruiser fleets had been made an hour later – i.e. when, after Beatty had turned north, the British and German squadrons had been steaming on a parallel course in the direction of the Grand Fleet, Hipper's ships might have fallen into the British trap.

Beatty had his battle-cruisers and four 'Queen Elizabeth' battle-ships, fast ships with 15-inch guns. Unfortunately, he did not keep the battleships and cruisers sufficiently together, and, again owing to a misinterpretation of his signals, the battleships did not turn at once. They were thus too late to take part in the first and – from the British point of view – most damaging part of the cruiser battle. Furthermore, to the surprise of the Germans, the British ships overestimated the distance between themselves and the Germans, and thus by closing in to 16,000 yards lost the advantage of their longer range. They also repeated the mistake made at the Dogger Bank in failing to distribute their fire over all the enemy ships; one of the German battle-cruisers was hardly touched.

Within half an hour the British lost two battle-cruisers. Beatty, however, with great coolness of mind, continued his pursuit, and even came in closer to the enemy. A few moments later he heard from the light cruiser *Southampton* that the whole of the High Seas Fleet was moving towards Hipper. Beatty therefore turned his ships northwards; the battleships again failed to take his signal at once, and had to change their course under heavy German fire. The battle-cruisers were now leading the German fleet directly towards the Grand Fleet; the latter, in six parallel columns of four ships disposed in a great crescent, was steaming at high speed to cut off and destroy the enemy.

Jellicoe's tactics in the next stages of the battle have been a subject of much controversy between experts. The actual course of events was that, unexpectedly, owing to the difficulty of getting exact information, Jellicoe found himself just after 6 p.m. approaching the High Seas Fleet obliquely on his starboard bow. He chose to deploy to port;[1] although this manœuvre would take him away from the direction of

---

[1] His ships had been moving in column – a formation less vulnerable to torpedo attack – but would have to fight in line in order not to mask one another's fire. Jellicoe had previously told the Admiralty (who agreed with his view) that, if a situation of this kind arose, he would deploy away from the enemy's approach, although this move might result in the enemy's escape: he and the Admiralty regarded it as the soundest plan, whatever view uninformed criticism might take of it.

the enemy's approach, he would have the advantage – with his heavier guns – of firing at a long range, and the German ships would show up against the western sky. Furthermore Jellicoe could carry out his deployment out of range of German massed torpedo attack.

Scheer did not know, from his light scouting craft, that he was running into the battleships of the Grand Fleet until just before coming under fire from them. He gave immediately an order to his ships to turn away independently to the south-west. They carried out this difficult manœuvre – which they had long practised – under very heavy attack; bad light and a smoke-screen favoured their escape. They also had the good fortune to destroy another British battle-cruiser. Jellicoe did not follow them. With the approval of the Admiralty he had always laid down that it would be dangerous to pursue the enemy into an area infested with submarines and mines.[1] He now, however, seemed to be well placed between the enemy and their base.

To his surprise he heard, again from the light cruiser *Southampton*, that at 7 p.m. Scheer had turned round again and was making east. On this course the Germans, who hoped to cross astern of the Grand Fleet, drove right into the centre of it, and for six minutes suffered the heaviest weight of bombardment ever delivered at sea. Once again Scheer ordered his ships to turn about independently, and, in order to protect them as best he could, sent his destroyers to deliver a massed torpedo attack against the British ships, and to lay a smoke-screen; he also ordered the battle-cruisers to make straight for the enemy. Jellicoe again in accordance with the principles he had long settled to adopt, now turned his great ships at an angle of 45 degrees from the enemy to avoid the torpedoes.[2] Scheer therefore managed again to escape. Jellicoe has been blamed for this manœuvre, but at the hour – about 7.15 p.m. – it is more than doubtful whether the Germans could not have made away in the fading light, and behind their smoke-screen. As late as 7.50 p.m. Beatty wanted the battle fleet to follow them, but there was now no chance of catching them. Beatty's own ships again had a short and sudden meeting in which they did more damage to the battered German battle-cruisers but had to turn away from the fire of the German pre-'Dreadnought' battleships.

[1] Jellicoe did not know that there were no German submarines near the area of action and that the German battleships did not carry mines for throwing overboard in a retreat.

[2] The enemy could have fired about 224 torpedoes, but Jellicoe heavily attacked their torpedo-carrying craft. Only about 31 torpedoes were fired; no British battleship was hit.

Thus at nightfall Jellicoe had lost the chance of overwhelming the enemy main fleet, but believed that he had cut off the Germans from their base and could take them by daylight next morning. Scheer had three possible ways of return not barred by mine fields (which were known to the British as well as to the Germans). He could return by the Frisian coast to the Ems, or by the west of Heligoland, or by the Horn reefs off the coast of Jutland. He seemed to be making for one of the first two routes, but the Horn reefs was his nearest way. Jellicoe therefore mined the swept channel by the Horn reefs and kept his destroyers behind the main fleet so that he would have rapid inform-ation if Scheer tried to break through astern of him in the direction of the reefs. The main British fleet continued southwards, with the High Seas Fleet to the west, and, for a time, on a roughly parallel course. Scheer, however, turned south-south-east in the darkness towards the Horn reefs – with the intention of passing in the wake of the Grand Fleet or even driving through it if he chanced to meet it. He did in fact meet the destroyers; but they failed to do any damage to his battleships. Two British battleships, less than three miles away, identi-fied the enemy, but, with extraordinary negligence, made no report to Jellicoe. The Admiralty were even more negligent. They had inter-cepted Scheer's order to turn towards the Horn reefs; in sending it to Jellicoe, they gave a manifestly wrong position for the German fleet. Jellicoe mistakenly inferred that the rest of the information was wrong. He would certainly have changed his mind if he had known of another of Scheer's messages intercepted by the Admiralty. In this message Scheer asked for an airship to reconnoitre the Horn reefs at daybreak. This 'intercept' was not passed on to Jellicoe. Hence Scheer reached the Horn reefs at 3.30 a.m. – after losing one old battleship *Pommern* to a torpedo attack in early dawn – and the British Grand Fleet moved through an empty sea to the edge of the German mine-field. At 4.15 a.m. the Admiralty intercepted another message from Scheer revealing his position. They passed his message to Jellicoe who now knew that the enemy had escaped.

The battle of Jutland was the most formidable engagement ever fought at sea. It is a paradox that the question of 'victory' should still be a matter of dispute. On the whole the advantage was with the Germans in the sense that they had been caught in a trap, and had escaped with a smaller loss of men and ships than they had inflicted. In capital ships they had sunk three British battle-cruisers for the loss of one battle-cruiser and one older battleship. Two other of their battle-cruisers were very badly damaged, and in the short meetings with the British battlefleet, four German battleships had been hit some twenty-five times with heavy shell, while only one battleship of the Grand Fleet was hit, and with only two shells.[1] For the British the battle was a lost opportunity. The result made no difference to the general strategical plan for dealing with the German fleet. On the other hand, there could also be no relaxation of control. The ships and crews of the battlefleet could not be released for other purposes; the attendant craft could not be dispersed to attack the German submarines and defend British merchantmen. There was no chance of entering the Baltic, or of undertaking operations against the German river mouths. It is impossible, indeed, to know what effect a heavy defeat would have had on German policy. Such a defeat would not have meant in itself – as defeat must have meant to the Allies – the loss of the war. Yet it may be doubted whether the Germans would have been able, after the casualties in trained men which they would have suffered, to maintain their submarine warfare with such intensity for so long.

On the German side, the battle was at most a defensive victory. It was hardly a victory in that they had done no damage to the twenty-four battleships of the Grand Fleet and could not avoid the conclusion – from their short experience – that they would have no chance of survival if they were caught again in circumstances less favourable to themselves. They had escaped as much by chance and by British mistakes as by their own boldness. Chance indeed played a greater part than the experts were (and still are) inclined to allow. The time for decision was so short; the consequences of the smallest deflection of range over so great a distance were tremendous. A break in the drift of smoke, the loss or advantage of a minute in opening fire, a slight turn away from a torpedo, the interpretation of a signal – when a ship's halyards might be blown away – or the estimate of distance made by a junior officer in a destroyer might bring absolute immunity or complete destruction for a capital ship.

Nevertheless chances tended to 'average out', and the odds remained in favour of the British battlefleet which possessed such great material superiority. Moreover certain accidents which had been to the great advantage of the Germans were unlikely to be repeated. Two at least of the British battle-cruisers had been lost through flames coming down

[1] Out of about 20,000 officers and men on the British battleships of the Grand Fleet, only two were killed and five wounded. The battleships with Beatty's cruiser fleet suffered 190 casualties.

the ammunition hoists and reaching the ships' magazines.[1] This fearful mishap was unlikely to recur, since it was due partly to faults in design – which could be remedied without much difficulty – partly to an acceptance of risks in order to keep up a heavy rate of fire. Again it was found that the British shells with sensitive fuses detonating on impact – sometimes on impact with the water – did not penetrate sufficiently the armour of the German ships. Other technical changes, such as the improvement of range-finding instruments, could be put and were put into effect as rapidly as possible.[2]

The Germans, therefore, had suffered heavy losses without any prospect to themselves of relieving the pressure of British sea power. If the Grand Fleet still had to keep its watch on the North Sea against an unbeaten enemy, the watch was as effective as ever in depriving Germany of the essentials of 'total war'. The only possibility which remained to the Germans was a return to unrestricted submarine warfare; they could not be sure, however, that this plan would succeed, while they knew that it would almost certainly add the United States to their enemies.

It is often said, mistakenly, that, after Jutland, the German High Seas Fleet did not again attempt a sortie outside its bases in the North Sea. In August, 1916, Scheer tried once more the submarine 'trap' combined with an advance of his main fleet. He proposed to bombard

[1] The battle-cruiser *Lion*, Beatty's own ship, escaped a similar fate only because an officer of Marines, Major Harvey, though mortally wounded, ordered the magazine doors to be closed in time. The Germans had had earlier warning of this kind of danger owing to a fire in one of the turrets of the battle-cruiser *Seydlitz* in the Dogger Bank action of January, 1915.

[2] The British armour-piercing shell had been designed primarily for ranges up to 10,000 yards. In fact most naval engagements in the war between capital ships were fought at ranges nearer to 18,000 yards. The angle of descent of a shell at these longer ranges was much steeper, and with such oblique impact the British shells often exploded before penetrating the enemy's side armour. Jellicoe, while at the Admiralty before the war, had put forward designs for improved armour-piercing shells, but the cost had been regarded as too heavy. Even after Jutland there was delay in providing a new type of shell. Beatty reported at the beginning of 1918 that the supply would not be adequate until the summer of that year.

The increased range in naval engagements had another consequence. On the assumption that most of their engagements would be at 10,000 yards or less the British ships were armoured more strongly at the sides than on the decks. The decks were therefore more vulnerable to shells descending at a steep angle. The German ships had more deck protection. Furthermore the armoured protection of the German ships was greater because they were of broader beam. British naval dockyards could not take ships of broader beam, and the Government had been unwilling to face the cost of enlarging the docks or building new ones.

Sunderland with the hope of drawing at least a part of the British Fleet southwards, stationed ten submarines in two lines off the probable course of the British ships, with another nine off the Dutch coast, and used eight Zeppelins as patrols. The Admiralty had information of some movement of the High Seas Fleet, and the Grand Fleet set out to intercept it. Scheer, however, turned back in time owing, in fact, to an error leading him to identify the light forces sent out from Harwich as the van of the Grand Fleet. In October 1916 the Germans made another, though less extensive sortie, but they could no longer spare submarines to set their trap or to act as scouts. Thus, in a different way, though not altogether dissimilar in effect, the deadlock which had set in on the land front at the end of 1914 kept the two great fleets close to their bases after the end of 1916; neither could safely venture across the 'no man's land' of the North Sea. Nevertheless the distinction between superior naval power enforcing its primary aims, and inferior naval power unable to break this supremacy was not lost on the Germans. German morale, not British morale, suffered from the inaction of the two battlefleets. Moreover, in considering the damage done by German submarine attack between the battle of Jutland and the end of the war, it must not be forgotten that, from the enemy side, submarine warfare was only a 'second best'. Two or three battle-cruisers, if they had been free to roam around the approaches to the British Isles, could have done, effectively and quickly, the work which, in the two years of effort, the German submarines failed to do.[1]

[1] There is a large literature about the battle of Jutland. The most recent summary, with an excellent critical discussion, is in *Marder*, op. cit., vol. iii. For a general account of British naval strategy see also S. W. Roskill, *The Strategy of Sea Power*, 1962.

CHAPTER 13

The blockade of Germany: the first German submarine campaign: attitude of the United States towards British and German action at sea

The battleships of the Grand Fleet, before and after Jutland, from the first day of the war until the German acceptance of the Allied terms for an armistice, exercised an indirect but fatal hold on Germany by their control of the routes from German ports to the oceans.[1] The loss of oceanic trade would have mattered little to the Germans in a short war – the war for which they were prepared. In any case the Allies could not bring an effective scheme of blockade into operation until they had persuaded or compelled neutral Powers to accept the consequent interference with their own trade. The legal position was uncertain. There was nothing comparable with the Hague Convention regulating war on land. An international conference had met in London in 1908 to draw up a code comprising the laws of naval warfare in matters such as blockade, contraband, search, transfer to neutral flag, etc. In 1909 the proposals of this conference were issued as the Declaration of London. The Declaration had not been ratified by the belligerent Powers at the outbreak of war and was therefore not legally binding. The United States Government, however, invited all the belligerents to adopt it. Germany and Austria-Hungary agreed on condition that the Entente Powers also accepted it. Great Britain put the Declaration into force by an Order in Council of August 20, 1914, but excluded its lists of contraband.[2] The British Government made further modifica-

---

[1] The British *Official History of the Blockade of the Central Empires, 1914–18* written by A. C. Bell, was completed in 1937, but was not released for general circulation until 1961. The *History* contains valuable information, but is diffusely written and contains much irrelevant matter while leaving a good many important questions unanswered. A separate Ministry of Blockade was not set up until February, 1916.

[2] See below, p. 188. A bill which would have committed Great Britain to a full acceptance of the Declaration had been accepted on a party vote by the

tions later in 1914, in 1915, and in March, 1916. On July 7, 1916, Great Britain and France notified the neutral Powers that, whereas they had adopted the Declaration at the outbreak of war because it seemed in its main lines to state the rights and duties of belligerents as based on the experience of previous wars, they now found that, while it did not altogether improve the safeguards afforded to neutrals, it prevented belligerents from using the most effective means of exercising their admitted rights. Hence the British and French Governments had decided to limit themselves to the application of the historic and admitted rules of the Law of Nations.

Long before this time it was clear that, in spite of their formal assent to the American suggestion, Germany and Austria-Hungary were paying no attention to the Declaration of London in matters where disregard of it was in their interests. There were, however, earlier statements of the rules of war at sea to which all the belligerents were committed. Thus the Declaration of Paris, signed in 1856 at the Peace Congress which ended the Crimean War, had not been abrogated. This Declaration had abolished privateering and declared a blockade to be legal only if it were effective. The Declaration had also laid down that a neutral flag covered enemy goods other than contraband of war.

The binding force of these restrictions was not very certain. The Hague Conference of 1907, in permitting the use of armed merchant-men as auxiliary cruisers, had gone some way towards reintroducing privateering. The meaning of an 'effective' blockade had changed since 1856 when it had meant a line of ships stationed outside the ports of an enemy. In 1914, owing to the invention of torpedoes, mines, and long-range guns, a 'near' blockade was impossible. Since the intention of the Declaration of Paris had not been to abolish blockade as an instrument of warfare, the British Government could reasonably claim that a 'distant' blockade, which closed the northern exits of the North Sea was effective and therefore legal. They were not, in fact, enforcing a full blockade, since the British navy did not close the North Sea to Dutch and Scandinavian ships. They exercised their legal right to search

---

House of Commons in December, 1911, but rejected by the House of Lords. The United States Government put very strong pressure on the British Government in the autumn of 1914 to accept the Declaration without any reservations. The withdrawal of this demand was due largely to the efforts of Mr Page, the American Ambassador, who finally threatened to resign if his Government insisted on the acceptance of the Declaration in spite of four successive British refusals.

neutral shipping, but did not normally enforce the penalty of confiscat-
ing the cargo and the ship if contraband were discovered.[1] The British
Government bought the cargo and returned the ship. They acted in this
way in order to avoid offending or causing loss to neutrals, and especially
to American merchants and shipowners.

Nevertheless serious difficulty arose with the United States over the
definition of contraband. Here also the rules of war at sea were
necessarily vague. The Declaration of Paris, for example, had used the
term 'contraband' without defining it. The interests of States had
differed in the past according to their naval power and the nature and
direction of their trade: the same State might take as a belligerent a very
different view of contraband from the view which it had taken as a
neutral. There was no doubt about commodities such as arms, ammunition, military and naval stores. These were 'absolute' contraband, but,
before 1914, a large category of goods was recognised as 'conditional'
contraband. 'Conditional' contraband included articles which were not
necessarily for use in war, though they might be so used. Such articles
were contraband 'on condition' that they were intended for use in war.
In the days of small armies, employing for purposes of war only a
relatively small quantity of goods, a distinction between 'absolute' and
'conditional' contraband could be made without difficulty. It was,
however, almost impossible, when an offensive in war had become a
'large-scale economic undertaking', to distinguish between 'absolute'
and 'conditional' contraband.[2] The Declaration of London, which
attempted to make this distinction, excluded oil, copper, rubber, and
cotton from the list of 'absolute' contraband; raw cotton and fertilisers
were on the 'free list', i.e. a list of articles either not susceptible of use in
war, or most unlikely to be so used.

Whatever the nature of a ship's cargo, the rules of war at sea did not
allow it to be considered as contraband unless it were destined for the
use of a belligerent. Here again difficulties of application arose. There
could be no doubt about contraband carried on a ship bound for an
enemy port, but a ship might be carrying contraband goods to a
neutral port, and reshipping them thence to an enemy port. Such cases
had arisen during the American Civil War, and the American Prize

---

[1] There had been wide variations of practice in this matter before 1914. The
Declaration of London had allowed the confiscation of all contraband, and also
of the carrying vessel if the contraband, reckoned by value, weight, volume, or
freight, formed more than half of the cargo.

[2] e.g. field glasses, telephone material, heavy boots, horseshoes, and harness.

Courts (borrowing from British and French precedents) had accepted the doctrine of 'continuous voyage', i.e. the whole voyage from the port of first loading to the enemy port of discharge was treated as indivisible. This earlier doctrine had been extended during the Crimean war and was taken in the American civil war to cover cases in which goods were carried for transmission – after arrival in a neutral port – by land or sea (in other ships) to an enemy destination. In other words a neutral address could not protect contraband from seizure if its ultimate destination were an enemy consignee.

At the outbreak of war the British Government, having refused to accept the definitions in the Declaration of London, drew up their own list of absolute and conditional contraband. They also rejected the rule in the Declaration that conditional contraband could not be seized if it were consigned to neutral ports. They laid down that such contraband was liable to capture if there were evidence of enemy destination; in other words they applied the doctrines of continuous voyage or transportation. This safeguard was set aside in October, 1914, to a large extent by an Order in Council restricting seizure of contraband to goods consigned to 'order' or without a named consignee. The British Government in making a concession of this kind to placate American demands had to allow enormous quantities of material which they would otherwise have treated as 'conditional' contraband to reach Germany through 'dummy' consignees. The increase of American trade with Germany through the neutrals shewed the extent to which evasion was taking place. American trade with Sweden and Norway rose sevenfold, and with Denmark almost fivefold; trade with the Netherlands in the two months December, 1913–January, 1914, amounted to 19·6 million dollars, and in the same period a year later to 26·8 million dollars. Moreover the Allies – again out of deference to American opinion – did not put cotton at this time on the list of absolute contraband. They could not interfere, except to a small extent by submarine, with the iron ore traffic to Germany from the Baltic ports, mainly Lulea. This traffic also used Norwegian territorial waters from the Atlantic port of Narvik. At two points ships from Narvik had to leave Norwegian waters, but it was impossible for the British navy to station permanent patrols in these areas on the distant side of the North Sea.

Thus at the beginning of 1915, although German ships had been driven from the oceans, the Allied attempt to deprive Germany of the means of making war was not very successful. The Germans themselves now provided an opportunity for the Allies to enforce a much stronger and more effective control of the neutral trade through which Germany was evading the Allied 'quasi-blockade'. The first step towards this exercise of control followed the illegal laying of mines on the high seas by German ships. At the Hague Conference of 1907 the question of regulating the use of mines at sea was discussed in the light of their extensive use by both parties during the blockade of Port Arthur in the Russo-Japanese war. Great Britain proposed the total prohibition of the use of unanchored mines. Germany and other States objected; they argued that mines were a legitimate means of defence, especially against a pursuing enemy. Great Britain also proposed the prohibition of the use of mines in establishing or maintaining a commercial blockade. This proposal was also opposed. The Conference agreed upon a Convention (No. VIII) prohibiting belligerents (i) from laying unanchored automatic mines which did not become harmless within an hour after they had been laid, (ii) from laying anchored contact mines which did not become harmless on breaking loose from their moorings, (iii) from laying contact mines off the coasts and ports of an enemy with the sole purpose of intercepting commercial navigation.

Great Britain (and the Dominions) signed and ratified this Convention subject to the provision that the mere fact that it did not prohibit a particular mode of action would not debar the British or Dominion Governments from contesting the legality of such action. At the outbreak of war the Germans broke the Hague Convention by laying contact mines in international waters off the Suffolk coast. They repeated this action on a larger scale and again without giving notice of what they had done or ensuring that the mines would become harmless within a limited time. The mine which struck the *Audacious* off the North Irish coast might well have destroyed the liner *Olympic* which was close at hand. On November 2 the Admiralty announced that in view of the danger to shipping caused by these German methods, they were declaring the whole of the North Sea a military area. They gave warning that merchant shipping of all kinds would be exposed to danger in the area 'from mines which it has been necessary to lay, and from warships searching for suspicious craft'. Ships of all countries wishing to pass through the zone to neutral ports were advised to come through the Straits of Dover where they would be given sailing directions. Outward-bound ships would be given similar sailing directions.

This 'deviation of voyage' was necessary on common-sense grounds; it had, from the British point of view, the advantage of directing shipping to an area where it could easily be searched. The United States Government did not protest against the direction of shipping, though they objected, and continued to object to the practice of bringing ships into 'port for search. Three months later, on February 4, 1915, the Germans also proclaimed a 'war zone'. This zone included all waters surrounding the British Isles. From February 18 onward 'every merchant vessel found within this zone would be destroyed without it being possible always to avoid danger to the crews and passengers'.

Such a policy of 'unrestricted' submarine attack had been foreshadowed for some time. Before the outbreak of war the Admiralty had not been much worried over the possible use of submarines as commerce-destroyers. In October, 1914, a French ship was attacked without warning; a British ship was also stopped, and the crew given ten minutes in which to take to their boats. Two more small ships were torpedoed in November. Towards the end of December Admiral Tirpitz, in an interview with the New York *Sun*, suggested an extension of submarine warfare in order to bring about the starvation of Great Britain. The German press took up the idea with enthusiasm; on the other hand the British Admiralty still thought that the Germans would not break the laws of war on so large a scale or risk the hostility of neutrals. The Chancellor opposed the plan on political grounds, and Tirpitz himself seems to have had some doubts whether from a naval point of view it would succeed. The Emperor, as always, vacillated between the advice given by his naval and military experts and the greater caution of the civilians. The naval advisers finally used something like blackmail on him by pointing out the popular demand for 'unrestricted' war. The German declaration, however, was not given full effect owing to a very strong American protest. The submarine commanders were ordered not to attack American (or Italian) shipping in the 'war zone'. The Germans had less reason to be afraid of Scandinavian or Dutch opinion. For reasons of trade, Denmark and the Netherlands could not easily quarrel with Germany; Sweden was already anti-Russian and at least partly pro-German in sympathy.

The German Government attempted to justify their illegal action by counter-charges which it was easy for the British authorities to refute. Their real motive was that, with their failure to take the Channel ports, the British blockade, which was not yet severely felt, might well become in a long war a serious factor – perhaps the decisive factor –

in weakening German power of resistance. The Germans could retaliate, however, only by illegal mine-laying and by submarine attacks. These latter attacks would have to be carried out in areas where a submarine would run great risks if it followed the legal procedure of 'cruiser warfare', that is to say, stopping ships for examination, and sinking them only after due warning and allowance for the safety of the crew or passengers. In other words, while the British action against Germany merely inconvenienced neutrals, the German proclamation openly menaced their ships and crews. The illegality of their threats to neutral shipping did not trouble the Germans. Their difficulty was that they would certainly outrage American and other neutral opinion if they sank neutral or indeed any ships without warning. Hence their attempts to accuse Great Britain of illegal and inhuman practices.[1]

One German allegation was that the British Government was treating all food as contraband. There was indeed nothing illegal in treating as contraband foodstuffs intended for the armed forces of the enemy or taken under control by an enemy Government. On August 20, 1914, after reports that the German Government were taking control of all foodstuffs, the British authorities ordered that food cargoes were to be detained. The order was not cancelled after it was found that the reports were incorrect, but foodstuffs, unless consigned to naval ports, were not confiscated. They were dealt with by pre-empting the cargoes which thus did not reach the enemy, while the neutral consignors suffered no loss. At the end of January, 1915, the German Government announced their intention of taking over all foodstuffs in the Reich. This action enabled the British Government to prohibit the import of food to Germany. The Germans then rescinded their order in so far as it applied to food imported from neutral countries, but, in

---

[1] Another motive at this time was German anger at the American supply of munitions to the Allies. This supply was not illegal; the Germans themselves were buying for war purposes as much cotton as they could get from the United States. They organised a large-scale, though unsuccessful propaganda campaign in the United States at the end of 1914 in favour of an embargo on the export of munitions. In January, 1915, Zimmermann, Under-Secretary at the German Foreign Office, told the United States Ambassador that, if he were to publish a list of the supplies going to the Allies, it would mean war; 'he then spoke of 500,000 trained Germans in America joining the Irish and starting a revolution'. House's comment to Wilson on this outburst was that it shewed 'the necessity of our holding to the friendship of England'. A. S. Link, *Wilson*, iii, 309–11.

It is a curious comment on the German indignation that they had opposed a proposal at the Hague Conference which would have made illegal the supply of war material by neutrals to belligerents.

view of the German announcement of February 4, the British Government maintained their decree.

The Germans now suggested that they might give up their submarine 'blockade' if the British would abandon the food blockade. The United States Administration favoured this proposal and tried to persuade the British Government to agree to it. Grey was willing to consider the plan, but the Germans insisted upon extending it to all raw materials on the 'free list' and also to the list of 'conditional' contraband in the Declaration of London. Obviously the British Government could not allow this wide extension or a further demand that merchantmen should cease to be armed. It was indeed clear that at this time the Germans had little anxiety about food, and were concerned primarily with getting raw materials for industry. There was no food shortage in Germany; talk of a 'hunger blockade' was intended to win over American opinion.[1]

On March 1, 1915, the Prime Minister announced that, in view of German disregard of international law, 'her opponents were driven to frame retaliatory measures, in order, in their turn, to prevent commodities of any kind from reaching or leaving Germany. . . . The British and French Governments will, therefore, hold themselves free to detain and take into port ships carrying goods of presumed enemy destination, ownership, or origin.'[2] This policy was set out in an Order in Council of March 11.

The policy, admittedly, went beyond the accepted rules of war at sea, and could be justified only as a reprisal. As such it was bound to affect neutrals as well as Germany. The Order in Council of March 11, 1915, did not use the term 'blockade', but Grey, in announcing to the United

[1] When House, at Wilson's request, repeated the proposal three months later (see below, p. 216) the Germans again demanded free passage for raw materials. They argued that they were not short of food and that a concession limited to foodstuffs was of little value to them. House wrote to Wilson on May 29, 1915: 'This does away with their contention that the starving of Germany justifies their submarine policy.' As late as January, 1917, the head of the German Food Office declared that, despite the blockade, there was no question of 'starvation' in Germany. This statement had in it a strong element of propaganda; the food situation in Germany had deteriorated since the autumn of 1916.

[2] The order did not proscribe the confiscation of goods or vessels. The intention was merely to prevent vessels from carrying goods to Germany. The British Admiralty at this stage seems to have made the opposite mistake to that of the Germans, and to have underrated the potentialities of submarine warfare. On this view the Germans were playing into British hands by giving them an opportunity for retaliation which would, in fact, harm Germany more than unrestricted submarine warfare was likely to harm Great Britain.

States Ambassador the decision embodied in the Order, said that the British fleet had 'instituted a blockade, effectively controlling by cruiser "cordon" all passage to and from Germany by sea'.

The United States government opposed this 'long-distance blockade'. Although they admitted that a 'close blockade' might no longer be practicable, they complained of the British action on three main grounds. They alleged that (i) the action constituted a blockade of neutral ports, since in order to reach such ports neutral vessels would have to pass through the blockading force; (ii) the action did not even 'bear with equal severity upon all neutrals', since trade between Scandinavian ports and German Baltic ports was not prevented; (iii) the action was not 'effective' since the German coasts were open to trade with the Scandinavian countries and German naval vessels in the North Sea and in the Baltic could seize and bring into German ports neutral vessels bound for the ports of the Scandinavian Powers and Denmark. Thus the British action could not be regarded as a blockade 'in law, in practice, or in effect'.

The British answer to the American arguments was (i) that, if the blockade could be made effective only by extending it to enemy commerce passing through neutral ports, such an extension was defensible and in accordance with principles which had met with general acceptance. The Allies were doing their utmost to distinguish between genuinely neutral commerce and goods intended for Germany, and were imposing, in the case of the latter, penalties less severe than those inflicted in the past for a breach of a blockade; (ii) the passage of commerce to a blockaded area across a land frontier or inland sea had never been held to interfere with the effectiveness of a blockade; (iii) it was doubtful whether there had ever been a blockade in which the ships evading it were so few in relation to the numbers intercepted.

The discussion of points of law with the United States Government lasted many months, and indeed continued until the American entry into the war but the verbal acrimony of the American notes had less significance than might appear. Wilson and his principal advisers did not want the Germans to win the war. In this view they had the support of the greater part of American public opinion. Moreover the United States Government had no cause for complaint that the 'total effect' of Allied belligerency was gravely harmful to American economic interests. In fact, as the Allies felt with some bitterness, Americans were doing very well out of the war, and would have suffered heavily from any restrictions which their government might impose upon trade with

Great Britain and France. They might be exasperated over the high-handedness of British action, but retaliation in the form of an embargo would have brought an economic depression in the United States as well as the risk of an Allied defeat. Furthermore the British Government were right in saying that they were doing all they could do to conciliate the most important American interests. Their treatment of cotton was a good case in point. The cotton exports of the United States to the European neutrals rose from 5 million dollars in the twelve months before June 1914 to 60 million dollars in the succeeding twelve months.[1] British public opinion was so much angered at this indirect supply to Germany of one of the essential constituents of explosives that the British Government would have been compelled – even if they had not felt it necessary to do so for military reasons – to take steps to reduce it. They therefore reached a secret agreement in July, 1915, with the Federal Reserve Board in the United States to buy enough cotton to keep the price at least as high as ten cents a pound. They then put cotton on the list of absolute contraband. For a short time there was an outcry in the Southern States, but the price of cotton continued to rise – owing to the immense Allied requirements – and the demand for retaliation soon died down. The main factor working in favour of the Allies was the inhumanity and political obtuseness of the Germans themselves. The Germans had a case for maintaining that, as the changed conditions of warfare made it impossible for the Allies to maintain a close blockade or to avoid severe and continuous interference with neutral trade, so also the German navy could not keep the old rules of search at sea, and yet could not be expected to renounce all attempt to cut off British trade. They spoiled this case, such as it was, by their deliberate ruthlessness. Moreover they also provided the Allies with a counter-argument to the claim that, if Allied merchantmen were armed, German submarines, in self-defence, were almost compelled to sink them at sight.[2]

[1] Twenty American freighters with cargoes of cotton entered Bremen or Bremerhaven between January 1 and March 15, 1915. Link, op. cit., iii, p. 131.

[2] German attempts at sabotage, etc., in American munitions factories also caused strong feeling in the United States. These attempts were made with a certain clumsiness, and the German organisers, who were acting contrary to their diplomatic status, were curiously inept in allowing their papers, including cheque books, to fall into Allied hands. One of the chief organisers of propaganda and counter-action against the supply of munitions to the Allies left a brief-case full of documents in a New York Elevated Railroad train, where it was picked up by an agent who was shadowing him. A more important organiser of sabotage, etc., von Rintelen, was decoyed by a British message (in a captured German code) to

The German policy of ruthlessness failed even within its particular sphere of operation. The submarine warfare did not at first have any great success. The Germans hoped that by savage action they would deter merchant seamen from going to sea.[1] This attempt at intimidation failed; during March, 1915, 6000 ships (including coastal vessels) entered or left British ports. Only twenty-one were lost. In April the losses were again small. In May the Germans tried to apply the policy of 'frightfulness' to prevent Americans from travelling on British ships. They sank the liner *Lusitania* off the coast of Ireland on May 7 with a loss of 1198 out of nearly 2000 passengers (including 159 Americans) and crew. The ship was carrying 5000 cases of small arms ammunition, and shrapnel, of a total weight of 173 tons, but this cargo was legal and gave no justification for torpedoing her without warning.[2]

---

return to Berlin. He was then taken off his ship by the British *en route* for Germany. On August 30, 1915, an American journalist in the pay of the German Embassy was found by the British authorities to be carrying on a Dutch liner papers including a personal letter from Dr Dumba, Austro-Hungarian Ambassador at Washington, relating to propaganda among foreign workers in American munitions factories. The United States Government asked for Dr Dumba's recall. Wilson was well aware of the illegal activities of Bernstorff, the German Ambassador, and of Captain von Papen (later Hitler's Vice-Chancellor). Papen was expelled from the United States. He was stupid enough to bring back his papers with him, including the counterfoils of his cheques. These papers were also captured by the British authorities, and the most important evidence in them regarding sabotage was published in a British parliamentary paper.

[1] Thus the submarine commander, Freiherr von Förstner, who sank the passenger ship *Falaba* in March, 1915, fired a torpedo while the ship's boats were being launched, and before passengers or crew could leave the ship, with the result that over 100 lives were lost.

[2] The ship sank in twenty minutes. In spite of German allegations to the contrary (i) the *Lusitania* was not armed, (ii) the submarine commander (Schwieger) seems to have fired a second torpedo almost simultaneously with the first (Parl. Papers 1915, Cmd. 8022). Schwieger denied that he fired two torpedoes, and alleged that the second explosion came from a consignment of high explosives on board the liner. The ship had no high explosives on board (their explosion would have blown her to pieces). The rifle cartridges and shrapnel were stowed right forward, and could not have been affected by the explosion of the first torpedo which struck the ship well aft. Some observers maintained that a third torpedo was fired, but missed the ship. Schwieger was drowned in September, 1917, when a 'Q' ship sunk his submarine. ('Q' ships were armed ships disguised as merchant vessels. They were intended to serve as 'decoys' to German submariners. If a 'Q' ship was attacked by an enemy submarine, most of the crew would take to the boats. The submarine, in accordance with its usual practice, would then approach on the surface in order to sink the 'Q' ship. The latter would unmask its guns, and – often at very close range – destroy the submarine.)

The Germans, with their failure to understand why neutral as well as Allied opinion, was rapidly regarding them as savages, struck a medal to commemorate the drowning of these non-combatants, including women and children. The effect of their action was to harden opinion against them. The sinking of the *Lusitania*, which followed closely on the German use of poison-gas, did irreparable harm to the reputation of Germany. It has been said that, in spite of the general wish of the American people to keep out of the war, Wilson could have broken off relations with Germany at once; no single act by the Germans did so much to convince American opinion that the Allies were (as they claimed) fighting a war in defence of human decency, and that the United States might be unable to avoid taking part in it.

The German campaign, however, continued. Another American ship, the *Nebraskan*, was attacked in May, and the submarines now began to operate in the Mediterranean. Indiscriminate mine-laying by submarines also increased. The British Government began the arming of ships to resist attack. By July, 1915, some 250 steamers were permanently armed or fitted to receive a gun. There were not enough guns to go round, and many outward-bound ships left their guns at Gibraltar, Dakar, or Port Said to be used by incoming vessels.[1] The guns gave ships a certain protection, but in August forty-two British ships were sunk by submarines and seven by mines. These figures were serious; after six months, however the restricted submarine war was very far from reducing Great Britain to starvation.

The lack of decisive success – when so much had been promised – the firmness of the American protest against the sinking of the *Lusitania*, and the alarming reports on American opinion sent by Bernstorff, gave the Chancellor another opportunity to state his views to the Emperor. The Emperor now agreed to a secret order that until further notice neutral ships should not be attacked. At the Chancellor's insistence he added that large passenger liners, even if they were enemy ships, must be left alone. None the less on August 19 a submarine sank the 15,000-

---

[1] In order to preserve the non-belligerent status of the ships, from the point of view of entry into neutral harbours, the guns were mounted right aft, where they were of use only for defence, and the ships were forbidden to open fire unless attacked or pursued as the prelude to an attack. The arming of merchant ships for defence was not illegal. The Germans had recognised in their own prize regulations the right of resistance, and had made provision for arming some of their liners. Up to the end of the Napoleonic wars most large merchantmen had carried guns. The practice had fallen into disuse after the Declaration of Paris in 1856 had abolished privateering.

ton White Star liner *Arabic* without warning in St George's Channel.[1] President Wilson, who had previously climbed down a long way from his first indignant demand that the Germans should give up all unrestricted submarine warfare, now asked not only for an apology and an indemnity for the American lives lost in the sinking, but also for an undertaking that no more ships would be sunk without warning.[2] In spite of protests from the German Admiralty, the German Government gave way. On September 18 they stopped submarine warfare against merchant ships in the Channel and off the west coasts of Great Britain. Early in October they disavowed the action of the officer who had torpedoed the *Arabic*, and agreed to negotiate an indemnity.

The German naval and military chiefs were unlikely to accept for long the limitations on submarine warfare. They were pushing on with the building of more submarines, and would soon demand freedom to use them. In a memorandum to the Emperor at the end of December, Falkenhayn pointed out that, even if France were defeated, England might continue the war alone. The German army could not invade the British Isles: the only way of breaking British resistance was by the unrestricted use of submarines. The view of the naval command was that, with freedom of action, they could compel a British surrender in six months. The Chancellor continued to argue that this policy would be the ruin of Germany, since it would bring the United States into the war.

The naval case was strengthened by the fact that the British measures for cutting off German supplies were beginning to have a serious effect upon the resources of the Central Powers. The Allies were taking steps

[1] An unsuccessful attack had been made against a large Cunard liner on July 9.

[2] The German Government protested at this time against the shooting of German sailors by the crew of the 'Q' ship *Baralong* on August 19. This incident had occurred after the *Baralong* had sunk a German submarine which had captured the *Nicosian*, a British cargo ship. Some of the crew of the submarine clambered on to the *Nicosian*; a party of marines from the *Baralong* followed them on board, and, uncertain whether or not they were armed, shot them. (Another version of the incident was that the Germans were thrown into the sea by angry American cattlemen.) The Germans made much of this incident, and asked for the trial of the captain and crew of the *Baralong* on the charge of murder. The British Government replied that they were willing to accept an enquiry if it covered all events at sea during a period of forty-eight hours covering the *Baralong* affair. These other events were (1) the sinking of the *Arabic*, (2) firing by a German submarine on the crowded boats of a collier sunk *en route* from Gibraltar to Barry on August 21, (3) firing by German destroyers on the crew of a British submarine sunk in the Baltic. The Germans, for obvious reasons, refused the British proposals.

to cut off these supplies not only by stopping ships but by a system of rationing and indirect control of the neutrals. The British Government took the leading part in working out and managing this system. The plan of rationing neutrals in accordance with a rough estimate of their own requirements was supported by a decision of the British Prize Court in September, 1915. In October of the previous year four steamers had been intercepted while carrying cargoes of over 5000 tons of lard from New York to Copenhagen. Since lard was normally an export from, not an import into Denmark, the Court decided that all or the greater part of the cargo was intended for Germany, and should be confiscated.

In consequence of this decision rationing committees were set up in London to determine quotas of supply for the Netherlands and the Scandinavian countries, and in Paris to settle similar quotas for Switzer-land. The United States Government protested strongly against the system of rationing and alleged that the Allies, and especially Great Britain, were using it to secure a monopoly of neutral markets for their own goods. The Allied case, however, was so strong that they main-tained and indeed tightened their methods of control. They negotiated in the Netherlands, Norway, Denmark, and Switzerland with associa-tions of importers willing to guarantee that the goods consigned to them would not be exported. The greatest difficulty was with Sweden, where the Government and public opinion was more afraid of a Rus-sian than of a German victory in the war. The Allies could not prevent Germany from trading directly with Sweden across the Baltic, while the Russians were anxious to avoid the stoppage of their own imports from or through Sweden. The Swedish Government refused to allow Swedish subjects to make arrangements on the lines of those negotiated with the other Scandinavian neutrals. In May, 1916, the Allies stopped all copper and oil supplies to Sweden in order to prevent large-scale imports of these commodities into Germany.[1]

The British authorities also developed a very efficient Intelligence service to discover and foil attempts to evade their controls. They instituted a postal censorship – which caused great anger in the United States – to detect transactions with the enemy; they drew up a 'black

---

[1] Grey (*Twenty-Five Years*, ii, 109) mentions an ingenious method by which the Germans evaded the Swedish control of their own exports. After the Swedish Government had forbidden the export of copper to Germany, British agents found that the Germans were importing large numbers of copper statues of Hindenburg, since the Swedish prohibition did not extend to works of art!

list' of firms refusing to accept their regulations, and of traders and shipping companies suspected or convicted of trading with the enemy, and forbade their nationals to have dealings with them. They refused bunker coal to ships on this 'black list'. On the other hand, they did their best to ease the troubles and delays of search. In a long note of November 5, 1915, the United States Government had protested against the practice of taking ships into port for search. The justification of this procedure was (i) that it followed precedents, including those of the American civil war, and that it was impracticable as well as dangerous (owing to the possibility of enemy submarine attacks) to attempt to carry out on the high seas the elaborate search necessary in the case of a great modern ship.[1] From the spring of 1916 the Allies adopted the principle of issuing certificates ('navicerts') to neutral ships. These certificates were given by diplomatic or consular representatives in neutral countries after reference to the home authorities and an examination of the ship's cargo. The 'navicert' testified that the cargo was destined for a neutral port and not liable to seizure; the ship therefore would normally be allowed to go on her way without being brought into an Allied port for examination.

The American protests caused much ill-feeling in Great Britain. Grey wrote to House on November 11, 1915, in terms which summed up the more moderate English view:

> After fifteen months of practical experience of war under modern conditions, I am convinced that the real question is not one of legal niceties about contraband and other things, but whether we are to do what we are doing, or nothing at all. The contentions of your Government would restrict our operations in such a way that Germany could evade them wholesale, and they would be mere paper rights, quite useless in practice.
>
> I cannot help feeling that, if we had done all the things that Germany has done in the war, and if we had instigated, as Germans have apparently instigated, criminal plots on American soil, American opinion would have pushed resentment home against us more than it has done against Germany.
>
> As it is, it looks as if the United States might now strike the weapon of sea power out of our hands, and thereby ensure a German victory.[2]

[1] The examination of a liner with 500 passengers and cargo took a trained staff of 10 officers and 20 men about 18 hours.

[2] C. Seymour, *Intimate Papers of Colonel House*, ii, 79.

Wilson's next move – of which he already had given hints – was even more likely to cause anger in Great Britain. On January 16, 1916, the President issued an informal note to the Allied Governments, and followed it, eight days later, by a circular despatch to the European Embassies of the United States on the question of armed merchantmen. He proposed that the Allies should disarm their merchant ships, if the Germans would agree to observe the established rules of cruiser warfare in all submarine operations against merchant vessels, i.e. before attack a ship should be summoned to stop, and should not be destroyed until all on board had been removed to a place of safety. As far as concerned the Germans, the President was merely asking them to observe the rules of law and principles of humanity which they had been disregarding. On the other hand he was requiring the Entente Powers to give up a long-established maritime right. In Grey's words to Spring-Rice, the American proposal meant that 'the sinking of merchant vessels shall be the rule and not the exception'. In any case the Allies could not trust the Germans to keep to an agreement.

The United States Government hinted that, if the Allies did not accept their proposal, they would treat armed merchantmen putting into American ports as auxiliary cruisers liable to internment. They were in fact unlikely to take a step of this kind. The Allies would certainly not submit to a change in maritime law so obviously to the advantage of Germany; the Americans, on the other hand, would have suffered heavily because they could not have continued their trans-Atlantic trade without the use of British shipping. Bernstorff reported on the situation rightly, but once again, in spite of his warnings, the German military and naval authorities clumsily misjudged what was happening and assumed that the United States Government was intending to 'retaliate' against the British blockade. The German Admiralty on February 8 announced that they were about to give orders to their submarines to return to the former areas of attack, with instructions not to touch passenger ships, but to sink armed merchantmen at sight. They described these orders in terms of a renewal of 'intensified' (but not 'unrestricted') submarine warfare. At the same time the German Ambassador was instructed to try to prevent American citizens from travelling in armed merchant ships.

President Wilson now decided to withdraw, or at all events not to insist upon his proposal about armed merchantmen. It is uncertain whether he changed his mind on hearing of the new German order or whether he realised that the Allies were legally correct in refusing to give up the right of arming their ships and that anyhow his own countrymen could not do without Allied shipping. He issued a general statement on February 15 that merchant ships had a right to arm themselves against attack, and that the United States Government would regard submarine attack against a defensively armed merchantman, with the loss of American lives, as a 'breach of international law and the formal assurances given by the German Government'. In spite of this warning, Bethmann-Hollweg was unable to persuade the Emperor to refuse his consent to a general order that all British merchantmen, other than passenger ships, in the area proclaimed by the Germans as a war zone were to be sunk without warning.[1]

On March 24, 1916, a German submarine torpedoed without warning the cross-Channel passenger steamer *Sussex* with 380 passengers, eighty of whom were killed or injured. The submarine commander made two different excuses for this action.[2] He said first that he mistook the ship for a minelayer, and later that he thought she was a transport. The passengers included American and Spanish citizens. American opinion was exasperated and indeed outraged at this act of defiance at a time when the German Government was supposed to be negotiating with the United States. The President took nearly a month to send a note of protest, but the note was in the strongest terms. He said that 'unless the Imperial Government should now immediately declare and effect an abandonment of its present methods of submarine warfare against passenger and freight-carrying vessels, the Government of the United States can have no choice but to sever diplomatic relations with the German Government altogether'.

The naval and military Chiefs of Staff tried to persuade the Emperor to refuse any concession, but the Chancellor insisted on accepting the American conditions. A note to this effect was delivered on May 4, 1916. Even so the Germans tried to make their promise to observe the rules of war conditional upon the removal of the Allied blockade. They stated that 'should the steps taken by the United States Government not obtain the object it desires, to have the laws of humanity followed by all belligerent nations, the German Government would then be facing a new situation in which it must reserve itself complete liberty of decision'.

[1] The British Government took care to avoid any chance of action by Wilson against armed merchant ships. No armed British merchant ship sailed to American ports until the autumn of 1916. Link, op. cit., iv, 225.

[2] The German Ambassador in Washington at first alleged that the ship had not been attacked by a submarine, but had struck a mine.

President Wilson refused to agree to this piece of effrontery. He notified the Germans that the United States could not

> for a moment entertain, much less discuss, a suggestion that respect by German naval authorities for the rights of citizens of the United States upon the High Seas should in any way or in the slightest degree be made contingent upon the conduct of any other Government affecting the rights of neutrals and non-combatants. Responsibility in such matters is single, not joint; absolute, not relative.

PART V

Great Britain and President Wilson's
proposals for bringing the war to an end,
1914–1917: the entry of the United States
into the war

CHAPTER 14

Great Britain and the diplomacy of President Wilson to
the autumn of 1916: visits of Colonel House to Europe:
Grey's memorandum of February, 1916

The efforts of the United States government to obtain recognition of
their own interpretation of the rights of neutrals at sea against British
and German action would anyhow have brought the maintenance of
good Anglo-American relations into the forefront of the tasks of the
Foreign Office. President Wilson, however, was not content to assert
his own country's view of maritime rights. From the early months of
the war he had in mind the possibility of American mediation between
the belligerents. Except for a short period of exasperation in the winter
of 1916–17 (and even then he was more out of patience with the Allies'
treatment of his proposals to them than he was out of sympathy with
their cause) Wilson wanted the balance of victory to rest with Great
Britain and France. He realised that an Allied defeat would be a grave
misfortune for the world, and not least for the United States. On the
other hand he was afraid that the Allies might misuse a total victory.
He also refused to allocate responsibility for the outbreak of the war to
any one of the belligerents. His plan was to employ American influence
to bring about a 'compromise' peace from which neither side could
claim to have won anything by fighting the war.

Grey, who remained Foreign Secretary until the resignation of
Asquith in December, 1916, was better fitted than any other member
of the Cabinet to deal with President Wilson and his Administration.
Grey himself did not think that the Foreign Office managed Anglo-
American relations very well; he was so much disquieted by the
controversies over the treatment of American shipping that he asked
the Cabinet to appoint Lord Robert Cecil as Minister of Blockade. The
faults indeed were by no means all on the British side. The State
Department, which before 1914 had, on the whole, only minor diplomatic business with the European Powers, was dominated by its legal

section, and tended to treat political questions from a narrowly legal standpoint.[1] There was some truth in the comment of Sir Cecil Spring-Rice, the British Ambassador in Washington during the critical period of Wilson's attempts to stop the war in December, 1916: 'If we regard them (the Americans) as a foreign nation who happen to speak our language, but who by history have been estranged from us, we can only be thankful that their attitude is more satisfactory to us than that, for instance, of Sweden.'[2]

Outside the controversies over maritime rights Grey's attitude towards the war was fundamentally not far removed from the attitude of Wilson. Grey regarded the very fact of a European war as evidence of the collapse of his own policy over many years. He had tried to reconcile the two opposing groups of European Powers. He had failed to do so, and had taken the heavy responsibility of persuading his fellow-countrymen that their interests as well as their obligations required them to come into the war. He did not change his opinion in this matter, though he doubted whether European civilisation would recover from a prolonged war. From the beginning therefore he never ceased to look for some way of ending the war as soon as it was safe and 'honourably possible' to do so. By 'honourably possible' Grey meant accepting terms which did not surrender the principles for which Great Britain was fighting. Grey was the only leading statesman who, in the early days of the war, aimed at 'some collective agreement which would assure every Power, great and small, against the danger of superior power in the hands of one nation'. He hoped at first that, if the Allies could withstand the German attack, American mediation might be possible. He would have accepted such mediation, though not in the form which Wilson persisted in proposing it, that is to say, in the form of a 'compromise peace' which would have allowed Germany, if she chose, to begin the war again at a favourable moment.

At the outbreak of war Wilson had offered his mediation to the belligerent Powers. He cannot have expected them to accept the offer, and they in turn expected him to announce American neutrality. For a

---

[1] One might add that neither the President nor the State Department realised, until the United States entered the war, that naval warfare, in the late Professor Temperley's words (*History of the Press Conference of Paris*, ii, 147), was not just 'a conflict between two opposing fleets without any ulterior purpose', but that it had the definite strategic aim of facilitating invasion and destroying an enemy's trade.

[2] S. Gwynn, *Letters and Friendships of Sir Cecil Spring-Rice*, ii, 359. Spring-Rice did not get on well with Wilson, who called him a 'querulous invalid', Wilson was biased against him owing to his friendship with Theodore Roosevelt.

time, when most Americans thought that the war would be short, Wilson was concerned only with the problems arising out of the interpretation of neutral rights at sea. In the early winter of 1914–15, when the military situation had reached a deadlock, Wilson came back in his mind to the possibility of bringing the war to an end. The Allies, and even Grey, misunderstood his attitude. There was good reason for misunderstanding since Wilson was acting from two different motives – a practical, realist belief that, if the war were to be fought to a finish, the United States might be unable to keep out of it,[1] and an elevated, if slightly self-righteous, idea that the United States alone among the Great Powers, and perhaps the President alone among Americans, could be sufficiently detached to secure peace terms which would make the world safe for democracy. On both grounds, realist and idealist, Wilson wanted to bring about an immediate peace irrespective of the military position of the belligerents – a 'peace without victory'. Wilson inclined always to moralise his policy. He did not comprehend for a long time that his two leading motives might be incompatible; in other words, it might be impossible for Americans to get the right kind of peace without fighting for it. There was also some inconsistency in Wilson's attempt to give to legal neutrality the brightness of a moral principle and in his assumption that by keeping aloof from the war the United States was taking up a stronger moral position than Great Britain and France. Wilson did not really believe, except, perhaps, for a few months in 1916, that there was nothing to choose between the Allies and the Central Powers. He knew that a victory of the latter would endanger American security, while a victory of the Allies would have no such consequence. Whatever faults of intention he might ascribe to Allied diplomacy as tainted with the original sin of entangling alliances, secret arrangements, and imperialist ambition, Wilson thought that the Allies might be persuaded to accept a settlement in Europe on idealist lines. He never supposed for long that the Germans would be willing or even able to do so. The weak point therefore in his treatment of American neutrality as something nobler than the belligerency of the European Powers was that one European group, and not the other, agreed in the large with his principles, and that these principles could not be put into effect without the military victory of the side which

[1] House noted with surprise on September 22, 1915, that Wilson had said to him that 'he had never been sure that we ought not to take part in the conflict, and if it seemed evident that Germany and her militaristic ideas were to win, the obligation on us was greater than ever'.

supported them. Bonar Law, who was not a great maker of phrases, summed up at the end of 1916 the difference between Wilson and the Allies in the words 'What President Wilson is longing for, we are fighting for.'

There was another important consideration. Wilson was an elected President. An overwhelming majority of the American people accepted a policy of keeping out of the war. Wilson had to take account of the composition of the United States electorate. Nearly one third of the population was of foreign stock; $8\frac{1}{4}$ million people were of German parentage at least on one side; another $4\frac{1}{2}$ million were Irish-American, and their views on international questions were determined almost entirely by a traditional hatred of England. The American Jews – a quarter of the population of Manhattan – were anti-Russian (the German Jews by a strange irony were mainly pro-German). The Polish Americans were more hostile to Russia than to Germany; the Swedish Americans of whom there were nearly 2 million in Minnesota and the northern central States – were anti-Russian. Wilson's appeals for complete neutrality of opinion were therefore made largely for domestic reasons,[1] and the danger of violent dissension was more serious because each of the belligerent parties carried on an active propaganda. German propaganda was at first better organised, and always more strident; it was not unsuccessful, particularly in countering the Allied argument that Germany was solely responsible for the war. In the long run, however, the harsh and illegal methods of warfare practised by the Germans nullified much of their propaganda.[2]

In his negotiations with the Allies and the Central Powers over the possibility of American mediation Wilson acted in a way which contrasted oddly with his later insistence on open diplomacy. He worked through his friend Edward M. House[3] rather than through the Depart-

[1] For an analysis of American opinion with regard to the belligerents, see Link, (op. cit., vol. iii. 'Foreign stock' connoted at least one foreign-born parent.

[2] The Bryce report on German atrocities in Belgium – a careful enquiry which was confirmed in its general conclusions by later investigation – had an important influence on American opinion.

[3] E. M. House (1858–1938), came of a prominent Texan family. His health was affected as a child by a fall from a swing, and later by a slight stroke. He did not meet Wilson until 1911. House's father was of English birth, and House himself was for a time at a school in Bath. Among his friends were Dr Charles W. Eliot of Harvard University, Sir Horace Plunkett, and George Lansbury. House disliked the title of colonel which was bestowed on him, against his will, by Governor Hogg of Texas in 1892. The Governor sent him at the same time a full-dress uniform of colonel's rank. House gave the uniform to his Negro coachman.

ment of State and ordinary diplomatic channels. He avoided the usual methods because he distrusted diplomacy and diplomats. He had good reason to consider his own Secretary of State, William J. Bryan, as woolly-minded.[1] He thought Walter Page, the American Ambassador in London, too Anglophil. House was more critical of British policy but not much less sympathetic to the Allied cause than Page; he was, however, in a better position to judge American opinion. Page believed that, if the case were rightly put, the United States could be brought into the war at an early stage; House never took this view. House was a stubborn supporter of what Americans somewhat loosely called the 'freedom of the seas', and therefore – unlike Page – had no occasion to annoy the President by taking, or seeming to take, the British view of the maritime rights of belligerents. House was probably the best 'unofficial' adviser whom Wilson could have chosen. He was a shrewd judge of men and gained their sympathy by his quiet honesty. He knew little at first of the complications of European politics, but Wilson himself knew less, and was always inclined to suspect the European Powers of hidden motives of the worst kind. The difficulty about Wilson's personal diplomacy, carried out through a confidential agent, was that the Allies could not tell how far or how quickly the President would be able to put his policy into effect. On the other hand, as Grey has written, there were advantages in the freedom with which House could discuss questions without committing himself officially about American policy. House was on better terms at Washington with the German Ambassador Bernstorff (until he realised that Bernstorff was deceiving him) than with Spring-Rice, but he had more friends in England than in Germany, and could put his case more frankly to them than to the Germans.

At the end of January, 1915, after earlier enquiries through diplomatic channels, Wilson sent House to Europe again on a mission of investigation. The purpose of this investigation was to discover whether an offer of American mediation would have any chance of success.

---

[1] Bryan resigned in June, 1915. Bryce wrote of him: 'he struck me, when I had dealings with him, as being almost unable to *think* in the sense in which you and I use this term. Vague ideas floated through his mind but did not unite to form any system or crystallise into a definite practical proposition' (quoted in Link, ib., p. 133). Bryan did not believe that a German victory would harm American interests. Lansing, who succeeded Bryan as Secretary of State, was more realist, but equally opposed in 1915 to the entry of the United States into the war. House did not want a sweeping Allied victory since he thought that it would upset the balance of power in favour of Russia.

The President took care to state that he wished merely to serve – with House as his representative – as a channel of communication through which the belligerents might exchange views about the terms of a lasting peace. House went first to London. Grey listened to him with care, and asked whether the United States would participate in a general guarantee of world peace. Here indeed was the weak point of Wilson's action. The Allies could not trust Germany; unless some general guarantee were devised, they could not be sure that the military regime which would remain in power would not treat a peace settlement merely as a truce. The surest method of providing an effective guarantee would be for the United States to join the 'non-militarist' Powers and thus to turn the balance between the two evenly matched European groups into an overwhelming coalition in favour of non-aggression. At this stage Wilson and House were unable to promise such a change in American policy. House, in his report to the President, said that he 'evaded' Grey's question by suggesting another meeting at The Hague for the adoption of rules governing warfare. Grey, so House told the President, 'did not accept this as our full duty'. Grey returned to his question later; House then said 'more directly' that it was 'not only the unwritten law', but also 'the fixed policy' of the United States 'not to become involved in European affairs'.

A second difficulty, which continued until the United States entered the war, was that the Allies strongly resented the way in which Wilson attached a moral lustre to American neutrality. The United States seemed to be concerned with the letter rather than the spirit of international law, and to be straining the interpretation of doubtful legal rules in such a way as to make it difficult for Great Britain to use her naval superiority in depriving Germany of supplies. The Americans stood on the niceties of international law, and talked of the horrors of fighting, while they appeared at the same time unwilling to forego any of their trade profits in order to shorten the war. House's suggestion of a conference to devise means of preventing future aggression looked, to Allied opinion, a little absurd in the face of the American refusal to stop supplying cotton, a prime material of war, to the nation whose army had invaded Belgium and whose navy was breaking the laws of war at sea by sinking passenger ships without warning.[1] Above all,

[1] Grey put the British view to Spring-Rice in a message of January 22, 1915. Grey thought that House should be told before coming to England that 'what is felt here is that, while Germany deliberately planned a war of aggression, has occupied and devastated large districts in Russia, Belgium, and France, inflicts

the British Ministers realised that there was no chance of an agreement between the Allies and the Central Powers. Each group was certain to refuse the terms upon which the other would insist. Grey, in speaking of the British terms mentioned only the evacuation of Belgian territory and the payment of an indemnity to Belgium, but he also made it clear to House that the French would require the return of Alsace-Lorraine and that the Russians wanted Constantinople. Even before he went to Berlin House knew that Germany would not concede the British demands with regard to Belgium.

House therefore undertook his visit to Berlin without much hope. On his way he found that the French intended to get more than Alsace-Lorraine. House was told in Berlin that the Germans would not agree to withdraw from the occupied territory in France without an indemnity, and that they would insist upon the cession by Belgium of Namur, Liège, and the valley of the Meuse. The Germans shewed some interest in House's views about the 'freedom of the seas', but, as Grey wrote to House, 'if Germany means that her commerce is to go free upon the sea in time of war, while she remains free to make war upon other nations at will, it is not a fair proposition'.

The German views of a peace settlement at this time were totally removed from Wilson's idea of a peace without victory and from any terms which the Allies were likely to accept.[1] On September 9, 1914, when German hopes of a rapid and complete victory in the west were still high, Bethmann-Hollweg drew up a memorandum on German policy in the forthcoming (as the Chancellor expected) peace negotiations. The fundamental aim would be the establishment of a central European bloc (Mitteleuropa) under German control, and extending its mastery beyond Europe at the expense of Great Britain, France, Belgium, and Russia. Politically this new order would be secured in the west by the total and final weakening of France, the annexation of

---

great misery and wrong on innocent populations, the only act on record on the part of the United States is a protest singling out Great Britain as the only Power whose conduct is worthy of reproach'. The Germans, on the other hand, since Allied sea power increasingly prevented them from getting war material from the United States, alleged that Wilson's assumption of neutrality was hypocritical unless he imposed a general embargo on the sale of munitions to belligerents. See above, p. 192, note 1. For American complaints to Great Britain in 1914–15 about the use of British sea power, see above, pp. 199–201.

[1] For a study of German war aims, see, in particular, F. Fischer, *Griff nach der Weltmacht* (2nd ed. 1962), H. W. Gatzke, *Germany's Drive to the West* (Baltimore, 1950) and G. Ritter, op. cit. See also below, Chapter 27.

the iron ore region of Briey and, probably, Belfort and the western slopes of the Vosges, and the coast between Dunkirk and Boulogne. Belgium would have to surrender Liège, and possibly Antwerp; she would become a vassal state, with German garrisons at important points. Luxembourg (and parts of the Belgian province of Luxembourg) would become a state within the German Reich, and the Netherlands would be brought into closer political and economic relationship with Germany.

These views were not likely to be modified when the price of victory became heavier. The views were shared not only by the military leaders (their demands were even more sweeping) but also by the majority of German industrialists, intellectuals, and professional men, and by the middle class as a whole. In May, 1915, the six most important German economic organisations representing industry, commerce, and agriculture, presented a petition to the Chancellor asking that Belgium should be held in military and political vassalage to Germany. Germany would control the Belgian coast; France would have to surrender her northern coast from Dunkirk to the Somme, her northern coalfields, the iron ore area of Briey, and the fortresses of Longwy, Verdun, and Belfort. In all Germany would acquire about 50,000 square miles of non-German territory in the west, with some 11,000,000 inhabitants who would lose all political rights and all of the larger and medium-sized units of real property. This increase of German territory and industrial power in the west would be balanced by annexations of agricultural land in the east. A month after this manifesto of robbery, 1347 prominent German intellectuals followed with a petition on similar lines. The petition was signed by 352 professors – including some of the most eminent scholars in Germany – 252 artists, writers, and journalists, 158 clergymen and teachers, 148 judges and lawyers. They too claimed that Belgium should become a vassal state. They supported the industrialists' demand for the annexation of French territory between the Channel coast and Belfort; the 'key enterprises' in the annexed area would be taken over without compensation, and the population which did not quit the area would be allowed no influence in the affairs of the Reich. A high indemnity would be imposed upon France 'without mercy'.[1] She would also lose some of her colonial possessions. As for England: 'if we could get into the position of imposing an indemnity upon England, no sum could be too large'.

[1] This indemnity would include not only the cost of the war, but reparation, pensions, and funds for the restoration and increase of the German army.

Anyhow England would lose her naval stations, her control of Egypt, and much of her colonial empire.

The German Government banned the 'petition of the intellectuals' from circulation because it violated the censorship regulations. None the less it continued to circulate, and similar manifestoes were produced by other groups. In July, 1916, a group of Berlin professors, including the classical scholar Wilamowitz-Möllendorf and the historian Eduard Meyer, put out an appeal in favour of 'strong' war aims. There were a few counterblasts from men of more moderate views, but in general the annexationists held the field. Socialist opinion, though it favoured an early end to the war, was not unwilling to uphold plans for annexation if the opportunity offered. Even the President of the Deutsche Friedensgesellschaft in 1915 wanted for Germany the Belgian Congo and other African territories, naval stations, and an improvement of the German west frontier.

After the failure of the great attack in the west Bethmann-Hollweg became less confident of the possibility of realising the programme of European and world domination. He considered (as well he might) these public pronouncements as inopportune. His own views of the limits which Germany might have to set to her demands varied with the changes in the military situation, but he never gave up regarding the terms which he had outlined in September, 1914, as desirable if they could be realised; few thoughts of right or justice, still less of mercy or ultimate reconciliation, determined his policy. In any case he found it increasingly difficult to resist the pressure of German public opinion. He wrote to Bernstorff in November, 1914, that 'if the luck of the battle is favourable to us, it is highly improbable that we would renounce all idea of booty'. Later, in the spring of 1917, he made an angry complaint to Valentini, the head of the Emperor's private civil Cabinet: that William II himself had demoralised the German people in the past twenty years by arrogance and chauvinism to such an extent that only the humblest classes of society remained truly German.[1] The attempts of Bethmann-Hollweg in 1916 to resist the annexationist plans of the generals when he no longer thought them feasible finally lost him his place.

British and French Ministers had adequate, though not complete, knowledge of German opinion, and were bound to conclude that no peace was possible with the existing regime, and that this regime could not be overthrown until it had suffered complete and obvious military

[1] Ritter, op. cit., iii, 382

defeat. Haldane, who knew Germany far better than Wilson or House – or Grey – put the British point of view in a memorandum to the Cabinet on April 8, 1915:

> This war, unlike some others, cannot be allowed to terminate as a drawn battle, or even as a victory evidenced by mere cession of territory or payment of indemnities. It is a conflict with a power which threatens, should it win, to dominate ruthlessly a large part of the civilised world. It is therefore essential that it shall not in the future be likely to succeed in a second attempt at armed supremacy. To ensure this it is, from the point of view of other nations, desirable that military hierarchy in Germany should be dethroned. Against this dethronement the leaders who are at present supreme in Germany will fight to the last, and no hopes can be built on a refusal of the German nation to follow these leaders, unless a crushing defeat threatens and cannot in any way be averted.

Haldane went on to argue that in any case an Allied success would bring difficulties. The Allies had agreed on September 5, 1914,

> not to make any peace the terms of which had not been agreed on in common. It is hardly likely that any terms will be acceptable to the Allies generally unless they provide for cessions of much territory and the payment of some indemnities. . . . The more these things are demanded . . . the more certainly will Germany and Austria struggle to the last against impending disaster.

Haldane's plan for the future was an Association of Powers on the general line later accepted for a League of Nations – though he realised that vigilance on the part of individual nations would be necessary to ensure that any such organisation maintained its purpose.[1]

Asquith described House's suggestions for peace as 'the twittering of a sparrow in a tumult that shakes the world'. After the sinking of the *Lusitania* in May, 1915, it was clear that, so far from acting as a mediator between the belligerents, the United States might soon go to war. House now repeated the proposal that Germany should give up submarine warfare if Great Britain would allow the free entry of food into Germany.[2] This proposal again came to nothing. Since it had first been put forward in February, 1915, the Germans, as well as killing non-combatants at sea, had begun to use poison gas. It is un-

---

[1] Sir F. Maurice, *Haldane*, ii, 15-16.   [2] See above, p. 193.

likely that, after the torpedoing of the *Lusitania*, public opinion would have allowed the Government to accept the plan even with the addition, upon which Grey was already insisting, that the Germans should abandon the use of poison gas. The Germans made rejection certain by maintaining their demand for the free entry of raw materials. Obviously the Allies would not allow this concession.

House sailed for the United States on June 5. He had accomplished nothing in the terms of his original purpose, but his conversations with Grey were of 'inestimable service'[1] in the maintenance of good personal relations.

The President's next move towards mediation came in the winter of 1915–16. In a letter to House on August 26, Grey had repeated his constant opinion that the victory which the Allies were trying to win would be useless if it were not followed by a general attempt to provide security against future aggression, and that American support in this attempt would be of the greatest value. A month later, on September 22, Grey asked House how much the United States was 'prepared to do in this direction . . . Would the President propose that there should be a League of Nations binding themselves to side against any Power which broke a treaty; which broke certain rules of warfare on sea or land . . . or which refused, in case of dispute, to adopt some other method of settlement than that of war.' He added: 'I cannot say which governments would be prepared to accept such a proposal, but I am sure that the government of the United States is the only government that could make it with effect.'[2]

Grey was thinking of House's proposals earlier in the year. His meaning would have been obvious to any English reader. He was not suggesting immediate mediation to end the war, but was looking forward to the use of American influence after the war in persuading the rest of the world to accept a binding plan to resist aggression. He hoped, and indeed expected that the Allies would win the war, and was also convinced that, unless they won it, and destroyed the machinery of German militarism, there could be no future security. A 'peace without victory' would leave the German military autocracy with its power unbroken.

Wilson and House, on the other hand, thought the Germans likely to win the war. The United States would then be left to meet a German

[1] This term was used by Sir Horace Plunkett in a letter of June 4, 1915, to President Wilson.
[2] Seymour, op. cit., ii, 87–9.

attack ('our turn would come next; and we were not only unprepared, but there would be no one to help us stand the first shock'). Therefore they regarded it as a matter of self-preservation for the United States either to end the war on satisfactory terms or to come into it and assist the Allies while their resistance still held. They failed to see that British war power had not yet reached its height; that Grey's moderate expression of the British hope of victory was an understatement, and that the British Government had no compelling reason to welcome American mediation unless it were on terms which would make it impossible for the Germans to renew the war at a later date of their own choosing. With Wilson's approval House wrote to Grey on October 17, 1915, suggesting that, if the Allies agreed, he would tell the Germans of the President's intention to intervene 'and stop this destructive war, provided the weight of the United States thrown on the side that accepted our proposal could do it'.[1] House told Grey that, if the Central Powers refused, it would 'probably be necessary for us to join the Allies, and force the issue'. House's original draft did not include the word 'probably'; Wilson put this word into the letter. He regarded the addition as 'unimportant', since the British Government knew that he was unable to pledge the United States to definite action in circumstances which he could not foresee.

On the other hand, especially in view of the American attitude towards their use of sea power, the Allies could not commit themselves to Wilson's plan without knowing what his terms of peace were, and without a definite assurance of American intervention if the Central Powers rejected the terms. Wilson could not yet answer these questions, or give any assurances of the kind suggested by Grey. He decided to send House to Europe again to find out the views of the two groups of belligerents.

House began his talks in London on January 6, 1916. The British Government asked for a formal assurance that the United States would combine with the European Powers in the preservation of world peace. Wilson replied, still in general terms, that he would be 'willing and glad when the opportunity comes to co-operate in a policy seeking to bring about and maintain permanent peace among civilised nations'.

[1] Grey had used the term 'elimination of militarism and navalism'. House's reply began with the words: 'It has occurred to me that the time may soon come when this Government should intervene between the belligerents and demand that peace parleys begin upon the broad basis of the elimination of militarism and navalism'. Seymour, op. cit., ii, 90.

House then went to Germany. There, in his stay from January 26 to 29, he found that the German Government were still insisting on terms based upon military conquest.[1] Bethmann-Hollweg maintained that the Germans would require an indemnity in return for the evacuation of France and Belgium.[2] House concluded that a German victory would keep 'the war lords supreme' and imperil democratic governments throughout the world. House next talked with Briand in Paris. Briand did not refuse the American plan, but obviously thought it impracticable; the Germans would not agree to the terms which France would regard as essential. Briand also hoped for a military victory and did not want to commit himself to the acceptance of Wilson's ideas of a 'compromise peace'. House, however, seems to have been satisfied that Briand approved generally of the plan. He told Briand that, if the Allies were successful during the spring and summer, the President would not intervene, but that he would do so 'in the event that the tide of war went against them or remained stationary'. House also said, or the French understood him to say, that the United States would stand by the Allies, if their military position became worse:[3] Briand,

[1] The Emperor's attitude was fantastic. He said to the United States Ambassador: 'I and my cousins, George and Nicholas, will make peace when the time comes.' He made it clear that democracies like France and the United States could not take part in a peace conference. The Ambassador commented to House: 'his (the Emperor's) whole attitude was that war was a royal sport, to be indulged in by hereditary monarchs and concluded at their will'. Seymour, ib., 91.

[2] Bethmann-Hollweg qualified the term 'evacuation' two months later (April 5) by saying in the Reichstag that Germany would not give up the areas which she occupied in the west without gaining complete security for her future. There could be no return to the *status quo ante*. Belgium would have to give real guarantees against becoming an Anglo-French vassal state. Germany also could not desert the Flemings whom the German authorities in Belgium were supporting against the Walloons in the hope of dividing Belgian opinion.

[3] House told Grey that Briand had misunderstood him on this point, and that, if Great Britain and France wanted American assistance, they must not wait until they were in danger of defeat. House said that it would be 'foolhardy for the United States to enter at so late a day in the hope of changing the result in their favour. In these circumstances we would probably create a large army and navy, and retire entirely from European affairs and depend upon ourselves.' There was a certain unreality about this statement. House, who knew the unpreparedness of the United States for war, had already agreed with Wilson that a German victory would not allow Americans any such freedom of action to 'create a large army and navy'. The British Ministers held a similar view. Moreover the fact that Wilson was taking practically no steps to arm the United States for war suggested that he had not thought out what would happen if the Allies accepted and the Germans refused his offer of mediation.

in return, 'agreed not to let the fortunes of the Allies recede beyond a point where (American) intervention could save them'.

After his return to London, House had more talks with the British Ministers. The most important of these talks took place on February 14 when House spoke with Asquith, Lloyd George, Grey, and Balfour at a dinner given by Lord Reading. It was agreed that Grey and House should draw up a memorandum stating the terms which the President might put forward. If the President approved of the terms, the British Government, at an opportune time, would approach the French. This memorandum was accepted by Wilson on March 6 (with the addition mentioned below), and can therefore be taken as authoritative. It was written in the form of a statement by Grey.

> Colonel House told me that President Wilson was ready, on hearing from France and England that the moment was opportune, to propose that a Conference should be summoned to put an end to the war. Should the Allies accept this proposal, and should Germany refuse it, the United States would probably enter the war against Germany.
>
> Colonel House expressed the opinion that, if such a Conference met, it would secure peace on terms not unfavourable to the Allies; and, if it failed to secure peace, the United States would (probably)[1] leave the Conference as a belligerent on the side of the Allies, if Germany was unreasonable. Colonel House expressed an opinion decidedly favourable to the restoration of Belgium, the transfer of Alsace and Lorraine to France, and the acquisition by Russia of an outlet to the Sea, though he thought that the loss of territory incurred by Germany in one place would have to be compensated to her by concessions to her in other places outside Europe. If the Allies delayed accepting the offer of President Wilson, and if, later on, the course of the war was so unfavourable to them that the intervention of the United States would not be effective, the United States would probably disinterest themselves in Europe and look to their own protection in their own way.
>
> I said that I felt the statement, coming from the President of the United States, to be a matter of such importance that I must inform the Prime Minister and my colleagues; but that I could say nothing until it had received their consideration.[2] The British

[1] This word was inserted by Wilson in his acceptance of the memorandum.

[2] The War Committee did not circulate the memorandum to the Cabinet. Towards the end of 1916, when Grey expected to be away for a month in Russia,

Government could, under no circumstances, accept or make any proposal except in consultation and agreement with the Allies. I thought that the present situation would not justify them in approaching their Allies on this subject at the present moment; but as Colonel House had had an intimate conversation with M. Briand and M. Jules Cambon in Paris, I should think it right to tell M. Briand privately, through the French Ambassador in London, what Colonel House had said to us; and I should, of course, whenever there was an opportunity, be ready to talk the matter over with M. Briand, if he desired it.

In accepting this memorandum as a statement of American intention, Wilson safeguarded himself once more by the qualifying phrase, in his note of approval, 'so far as he can speak for the future action of the United States'.

Wilson sincerely wanted peace – so, for that matter, did the Allies – but he was attempting to get it by a 'bluff'. His intention was to keep America out of the war, not to help the Allies to win it. He believed that, at this stage, the bluff might succeed. Hence he was greatly disappointed when the spring and summer went by without an appeal from the Allies. He and House remained more than doubtful about the Allies' chances of defeating Germany. They feared that the Allied military position would get worse, and that, while American pressure early in 1916 might have been enough, without actual belligerency, to compel the Germans to accept a 'reasonable' peace, delay might well mean that the United States would have to enter the war as a belligerent. Wilson's move, therefore, from his own point of view, was turning out very differently from his expectation. The Allies seemed to be taking it as a kind of insurance for themselves. If they came to the conclusion that they could not defeat the Germans, they would appeal for American mediation. The German terms would then have risen, and Wilson would have committed the United States, as far as he could make a commitment, to fight for a compromise which the Germans would be less likely to accept as their military situation improved. Furthermore the Germans, knowing the military unpreparedness of

---

he drew up a memorandum on Wilson's proposal for the Cabinet. Grey did not go to Russia. Before the memorandum was circulated, Asquith's Government had fallen and Grey was out of office. He gave a copy of his uncirculated memorandum to Balfour, but he realised that circumstances had changed, and that Wilson's proposal could not be put forward.

the United States, would almost certainly revert to unrestricted submarine warfare as their sole means of breaking the military deadlock.
In this case also Wilson could hardly avoid war with Germany.

Wilson's exasperation increased during the early summer because,
at least for a time, the Germans seemed more amenable than the Allies.
They gave way, in May, on the question of unrestricted submarine
warfare, though with ominous reservations.[1] The Allies, on the other
hand, aroused American opinion against them by their interference
with mails, their publication, in July, 1916, of a black list of firms
trading with the enemy, and later, their refusal of bunker coal to ships
refusing to accept the British regulations.[2] Irish-American feeling was
greatly affected by the trial and execution of fifteen of the leaders of
the Easter rebellion in Dublin; the Senate passed a resolution in favour
of clemency for the prisoners under arrest. Grey wrote, with some
anger, at this interference, whatever the right or wrong of the case, in
a matter within the jurisdiction of another State; he pointed out that
the Senate had been silent about 'outrages in Belgium and massacres
of Armenians'. Wilson was discovering that he would find it extremely
difficult to bring the United States into the war if the Allies called upon
him to honour his promise of mediation, or even if he thought it
necessary to go to war when, as was likely, the Germans again began
to sink American ships. The Democratic party leaders were also using
as the most popular argument in favour of his re-election the fact that
he had kept the United States out of the war. At the Democratic Party
Convention in mid-June the longest and most excited demonstrations
were on this theme, while the delegates showed little enthusiasm for
the President's measures, inadequate as they were, in the matter of
preparedness for war. By the end of September the phrase 'he kept us
out of war' was the party slogan throughout the Middle West and the
Pacific Coast.[3]

Wilson's own choice of phrases did little to correct this view of his
diplomacy or to reassure Allied opinion. In a speech of May 27, 1916,

[1] See above, pp. 202-3. In fact, the German Foreign Minister instructed
Bernstorff on June 7 to do everything possible to prevent Wilson from approaching Germany with a proposal for mediation, since the German Government could
not accept a peace on the basis of 'an absolute *status quo*', particularly with regard
to Belgium. See Link, op. cit., v, 20-32.

[2] See above, p. 200.

[3] It was easy for the party propagandists to go on from this point to an address
to American mothers that Wilson had 'saved their sons and their husbands from
unrighteous battlefields'.

in which he laid down his general ideas for the organisation of permanent peace, he introduced a sentence that Americans were not concerned with the causes or objects of the war. This sentence was not
relevant to his main argument, but he repeated it in a different form
five months later when he said at Cincinnati, in attacking opinion
favourable to American participation in the war. 'Have you ever heard
what started the present war? If you have, I wish you would publish it,
because nobody else has, as far as I can gather. Nothing in particular
started it, but everything in general.' Wilson indeed during these
months almost refused to take into account the effect in Allied countries
of his public statements[1] or even to listen to the Allied point of view.
He brought Page home on leave from London in order 'that he may
get back a little way at least to the American point of view about
things'.[2] On Page's arrival at the end of July Wilson refused for five
weeks to give him a personal interview. He then told Page that at the
outbreak of war he (Wilson) and his friends were in sympathy with the
Allies, but that public sentiment towards England had greatly changed.

Whatever Wilson might think, the Allies believed that the ultimate
cause of the war was not the 'collision' of rival imperialisms, but the
aggression of Germany; their object in fighting was to defeat this aggression and to prevent its recurrence. If Wilson refused, at least in his
speeches, to draw any moral distinction between the aggressors and
their victims, and if the United States Senate reserved official condemnation only for Great Britain, what guarantee could there be of American willingness to participate in the war in order to enforce terms which
would prevent a recurrence of German aggression? Wilson himself
did not show any understanding of the probable situation in Europe
if the war ended in a 'compromise' peace. The German military autocracy would have strengthened its control of policy in the Reich; the
German people would be told, with pride, that they had defeated one
Great Power, Russia, invaded and held the territories of a second,

[1] House realised the damaging effect of the President's phrases. Wilson might
have been more on his guard in view of the effect of his remark, during the early
stages of the *Lusitania* controversy, that 'there is such a thing as being too proud
to fight'. This comment, from the point of view of domestic opinion in the United
States, was a warning against an emotional rush into war; it had aroused resentment and even contempt in Great Britain, where the decision to go to war had
been taken with the utmost reluctance, and there could be no illusion about
destroying German militarism without fighting.

[2] Link, ib., p. 71. Page, on the other hand, was 'greatly alarmed and distressed
at the mood' in Washington towards Great Britain. 'I find only complaint
about commercial 'cases,' ib. 72.

France, and resisted successfully the attempts of a stronger naval Power, Great Britain, to blockade Germany. The smaller Powers in Europe, observing the fate of Belgium and Serbia, would be terrified of German pressure. Russia would almost certainly collapse in revolution. Great Britain and France would have to continue an immense expenditure on armaments. There would be no sense of security, no guarantee against further German aggression, no chance of reconciliation.[1]

The Allies had no wish to continue the fighting; nevertheless after sacrificing so much, they were bound to go on until they had defeated Germany. Their military advisers told them that they could defeat Germany. On the other hand, if they accepted Wilson's offer, they would be throwing away their chances of complete victory, the only sure hope, or so it seemed, of destroying German militarism. Moreover they would be taking a very serious risk. Wilson had been negotiating through a secret agent, without the approval or even the knowledge of Congress. He was himself prepared, in general terms, to accept the conditions of peace which the Allies regarded as essential. The Allies knew that the Germans would reject these terms. A process of bargaining would then ensue in which American opinion would certainly insist on a drastic reduction of the terms in order to save the United States from taking part in the war. Wilson, even if he had wished to do so (and, from his public statements, and general lack of comprehension of the Allied view of the situation, his wishes were not clear), would have been unable to resist further pressure for a modification of the terms in German favour.

The Allies, on the other hand, could not allow their necessary conditions of peace to become the play of American domestic politics; they could not enter a conference, or even negotiate for a conference, and then refuse terms which American opinion regarded as reasonable. They would thereby lose American support, while they would have encouraged hopes of peace among their own peoples which they could not fulfil, and risked dangerous divisions of opinion among themselves. The Germans would try to exploit these differences of opinion by offering more favourable terms to the least steadfast of their enemies.

---

[1] Haldane pointed out at this time that, after the breach of the treaty of Amiens, the British Government had refused to discuss terms with Napoleon because they knew that 'he would make a peace only to use it for the purpose of maturing his resources in order again, with the lessons he had learned . . . to effect an attack even more terrible'.

Grey was not merely being chivalrous when he pointed out to House that Great Britain, which 'had suffered least from the war, could hardly be the first to suggest ending it without military victory'. The British Government knew that there was an influential party in Russia favouring negotiation, and that a similar party in France would seize upon any chance of alleging that Great Britain was weakening.

It has been suggested that the Allies should have urged Wilson to be more definite, and to assure himself privately of the support of the leaders of Congress for American belligerency if the Germans refused his terms. The Allies could not put such pressure on the President, and Wilson himself, especially in an election year, could not have obtained even provisional approval of a policy likely to lead to American belligerency unless the Germans made another spectacular attack on American rights at sea. Even if the Allies had insisted on a more precise definition of the terms of American mediation, and a more definite guarantee, they could not be certain that the result would be satisfactory. They would still be leaving the decision of peace terms to the United States, with all the possibilities of a reduction in the terms in order to obtain German consent to them.

Grey, as House realised, was more sympathetic than the other Ministers to whom Wilson's proposal for mediation was shewn. Grey was not only less sure about the ability of the Allies to inflict a complete defeat on Germany; he was more afraid that a prolonged war would mean the ruin of Europe. When he wrote his book *Twenty-Five Years* and could look back over the disappointments of the Peace Conference to the proposals of 1916, Grey remained uncertain whether a 'Wilson peace' in that year would not have served Europe better than a continuation of the war for another two years. He thought that the question could not be answered, since it was not possible to say whether the ruling oligarchy in Germany (whose plans for the future depended upon a complete German victory) would have resented Wilson's intervention and would have begun to prepare for another war, or whether the German people would have been 'so disillusioned about war as to depose militarism from control'.[1] Grey's question must remain

---

[1] Grey, op. cit., ii, 131–2. See also below, pp. 231–33. Hankey, who never wholly trusted House, records a conversation of March 16, 1916, in which Grey spoke to him of the 'heavy responsibility' which House's proposal laid on him. 'If he took no notice of it, and the war went wrong, he would have missed a great opportunity either to get a decent peace or to bring in America. If, however, we were

open, but events in Germany after 1925 do not suggest a hopeful
answer.

likely to be completely victorious, it would be better to ignore it. A middle course
was to postpone action, but this would probably be to miss our opportunity.'
Asquith, on the other hand, according to Hankey, seemed 'to regard the whole
thing as humbug, and a mere manœuvre of American politics'. Hankey, op. cit.,
ii, 480.

CHAPTER 15

British Ministers and peace terms in the autumn of 1916:
British and German war aims: the German 'Peace Note'
of December 12, 1916: President Wilson's Note of December 18 and the Allied reply: impossibility of finding the
bases of agreement for a 'peace without victory': the
German resumption of unrestricted submarine warfare
and the entry of the United States into the war

Although there were strong reasons for not accepting Wilson's plan
for bringing the war to an end, the British Cabinet, or at least some
members of the Cabinet, in the autumn of 1916 felt less sure of obtaining a decisive victory.[1] Hitherto the discussion of peace terms had been
somewhat vague and general. The War Committee thought that they
should examine more precisely the conditions upon which it would
be desirable for Great Britain to insist. They invited Robertson, as
CIGS, to draw up a memorandum on the military requirements from
the point of view of British interests. Robertson's answer on August 31
began with a statement of the principles of British policy. These
'principles' were the maintenance of (i) a balance of power in Europe,
(ii) British maritime supremacy, (iii) the independence of the Low
Countries. In order to maintain the balance of power (which Robertson did not attempt to define) British interests required 'a strong
Central European Power. Such a State must be Teutonic, as a Slav
nation would always lean towards Russia.' On the other hand, we
needed to check Germany at sea, while leaving her 'reasonably strong
on land'. Robertson assumed that the British Government intended to
break up Austria-Hungary. He thought it impossible to make independent states out of Bohemia and Moravia and what he called the

[1] Asquith, although unwilling to follow Lloyd George in opposing the plans of
the High Command, was at this time gloomy about the military situation. See
Hankey, op. cit., ii, 558.

'Magyar district' of Hungary. 'Acting on the principle of maintaining a strong Germany, it might be advantageous if Austria proper were incorporated' in the German Reich.

Robertson accepted, though without enthusiasm, the transfer of Alsace-Lorraine to France. He wanted the restoration of Belgium, with the probable addition of Luxembourg and of territory which would secure for Belgium the control of the south bank of the Scheldt below Antwerp. He thought that Schleswig and a part of Holstein should be restored to Denmark. He saw difficulty in giving Danzig to Poland, and thus cutting off East Prussia from Germany, and doubted whether Germany would 'ever be so crushed as to consent to the transfer of Posen' to Poland. Robertson suggested that

> our future relations with our Allies demand as close consideration as our relations with our enemies. What is our policy to be towards the French in Salonika, towards the Italians and French in Albania, towards the Italians in Asia Minor, towards the Russians in the Balkans, and towards the Slav world generally in connexion with the creation of Poland? It is well to remember that the present grouping of the Powers is not a permanency, and indeed it may continue but a very short time after the War is won.

After this somewhat jejune survey, which hinted, or rather said outright, that Great Britain would need Germany as a counterpoise to Russia and France, Robertson referred to the German colonies, and discussed at some length the conditions of an armistice. There was not a word in his memorandum on the questions of disarmament and the extrusion of the military party from the political control of Germany,[1] the effect of the war generally on European and other nationalities under alien rule, or the possibility of any political device such as a League of Nations to enforce future security. The United States was not mentioned.

Since Robertson's reflexions were of little use, and the General Staff could produce nothing more suggestive or enlightening, the civilian Ministers, for better or worse, had to think out for themselves what kind of terms they would offer. Balfour circulated a memorandum to the Cabinet on October 4, 1916.[2] He limited himself mainly to politi-

[1] The only indirect reference was in a comment that the absorption of 'Austria proper' into the Reich would add '10,000,000 South Germans as a counterpoise to Prussia'. Robertson did not enquire how effective this counterpoise would be.

[2] The text of Balfour's and Robertson's memoranda printed in Lloyd George's War Memoirs, ii, 833-43 and 877-88.

cal and territorial questions in Europe and, without mentioning Robert-son's paper, rejected some of the assumptions of the General Staff. He thought that the best way to secure a durable peace would be 'by the double method of diminishing the area from which the Central Powers can draw the men and money required for a policy of aggression, while at the same time rendering a policy of aggression less attractive by rearranging the map of Europe in closer agreement with what we rather vaguely call 'the principle of nationality'.

The second of these methods would secure the restoration of Belgian independence, the return of Alsace-Lorraine to France, the provision of 'some kind of home rule' for Poland, an extension of the frontiers of Italy, and a Greater Serbia and Greater Roumania. Balfour also hoped that careful consideration would be given to the possibility of establishing an independent Bohemia. It was clear also that the application of the second method would greatly facilitate the carrying out of the first proposal – the weakening of the Central Powers.

Balfour then discussed the Polish question at some length. He thought that the best solution would be 'a Poland endowed with a large measure of autonomy, while remaining an integral part of the Russian Empire'. He believed that an independent Poland, 'so far from promoting the cause of European peace, would be a perpetual occasion of European strife'. He wanted the return to Denmark of 'the Danish portions' of Schleswig-Holstein, but pointed out that the Kiel Canal ran through an area which was 'German both in language and in senti-ment'.

Balfour did not think it expedient 'to touch the internal affairs either of Germany or of Austria'. Since an attempt by a victorious enemy to crush German militarism was unlikely to have lasting success, Balfour considered it desirable that a diminished Austria-Hungary should sur-vive as a 'dual monarchy', though it would remain in close alliance with the German Reich. If, however, Austria-Hungary collapsed, the German portion would probably coalesce with the Reich. The result would be a great Germanic State more formidable than the pre-war Reich, even if the influence of Prussia were weakened. In Balfour's view it would be impossible to prevent 'the Germanic Powers, either united by alliance, or fused into a single State, from remaining wealthy, populous, and potentially formidable'. For this reason 'the triumph of the Slav countries' was not

likely to menace German predominance in Central Europe. When we remember that the Slav populations are divided by language,

religion and government, that they fought each other four years
ago; that they are fighting each other at this very moment; that
the only one among them which can count as a Great Power is
Russia; and that Russia, according to most observers, is likely to
be torn by revolutionary struggles as soon as the pressure of war
is removed . . . we shall probably be disposed to think that the
Germanic States will be very well able to take care of themselves,
whatever be the terms of peace to which they may have to submit.

This is a fact (if it indeed be a fact) which is sometimes ignored.
Many of those who speculate about the future of Europe seem to
fear that Germany will be so weakened by the war that the balance
of power will be utterly upset, and Britain will be left face to face
with some other Great Power striving in its turn for universal
dominance. I doubt this. In any case it seems to me quite clear that,
measured by population, Germany – and still more – Germany in
alliance with Austria, will be more than a match for France alone,
however much we give to France, and however much we take
from the Central States. If, therefore, Europe after the war is to be
an armed camp, the peace of the world will depend, as heretofore,
on defensive alliances formed by those who desire to retain their
possessions against those who desire to increase them. . . .

Balfour then pointed out that if the Adriatic coast were to be in
Italian hands, and Salonika to remain a Greek port, the Allies ought to
ensure to the Central Powers access to the Mediterranean. Finally he
raised the question of indemnities. Germany intended, if she won the
war, to ruin her neighbours. The Allies, on the other hand, ought not
to imitate German behaviour in 1871, but 'in the interests of international morality' they should compel the Central Powers to pay for
the damage done by them in Belgium, Northern France, and Serbia,
and to surrender shipping equivalent to the amount sunk in submarine
warfare. 'These are charges which it should be within their power to
meet; and if within their power to meet, then certainly within our
right to demand.'

This memorandum expressed generally the kind of terms which
most thoughtful Englishmen had in mind.[1] As Balfour himself wrote,

[1] The terms were, in fact, very similar to those suggested in the *New Statesman*
on October 14, 1916: (i) a stringent limitation of German armaments in order to
give the Allies an opportunity of reducing their own armaments; (ii) an adjustment of frontiers in accordance with ethnographical facts: Alsace-Lorraine to go
to France; Istria and the Trentino to Italy, Constantinople to be controlled by

the Central Powers would not accept them unless they were compelled to do so by defeat or exhaustion. The immediate concern of Ministers, therefore, was with the question whether the Allies would ever be in a position to enforce their terms, and, if not, whether after all it might be better, in the interests of political prudence as well as of humanity, to attempt to negotiate a 'compromise peace'. The French Government, faced with a suggestion of this kind, had taken a very strong line. On September 19 Briand made one of his finest speeches against peace without victory. He carried his views in the Chamber by a very large majority, and, at the request of the deputies, the speech was placarded throughout France.

A week later Lloyd George, in an interview with Roy W. Howard, President of the United Press of America, also spoke strongly against any peace terms which would not secure the world against further German aggression. Lloyd George directly refused American mediation. 'Britain asked no intervention when she was unprepared to fight. She will tolerate none now that she is prepared.' Grey thought this open refusal both impolitic and unnecessary. He wrote to Lloyd George that Briand's speech had been enough to show the intention of the Allies; that Great Britain would now be held responsible for 'warning Wilson off the course', and that Wilson himself would be more disposed to listen to the Germans, and to give way to the demands of Congress in the matter of British naval measures. The Germans would have an excuse for reopening unrestricted submarine warfare, and Wilson would be less inclined to object to it. Grey ended his letter: 'It has always been my view that until the Allies were sure of victory the door should be kept open for Wilson's mediation. It is now closed for ever as far as we are concerned. I am still anxious about the effect of submarine warfare.' Whatever his personal uncertainties might be,

---

Russia, Austria-Hungary to be broken up into its national components, Poland to be a semi-autonomous State within the Russian Empire, and to include Posen and Galicia, but not Danzig; (iii) the German colonies to be retained by the Allies under a scheme whereby all dependencies which could not be colonised by white men should be governed primarily in the interests of the inhabitants, with equal trading rights for all nationalities; (iv) Belgium to be fully reinstated and indemnified by Germany with 'compensation for disturbance'; (v) no other indemnities to be demanded by the Allies except in respect of actual damage suffered. Damage to merchant shipping to be made good in kind. The *New Statesman* also held the view that 'Prussianism', which had been accepted by the South Germans, could be destroyed only by the Germans themselves. In the previous week the *New Statesman* had approved of the trial of war criminals, but wished to limit the trials to criminals 'in high places'.

Grey made no concessions in public to Wilson's idea of mediation to end the war without victory. Asquith, in the House of Commons on October 11, had said, in grave and measured words, that 'the ends of the Allies are well known; they have been frequently and precisely stated. They are not vindictive ends, but they require that there shall be adequate reparation for the past and adequate security for the future.' Grey spoke in similar terms on October 23; he said that 'if we are to approach peace in a proper spirit, it can be only by recalling, and never for one moment forgetting, what was the real cause of the war'.

Nevertheless behind these public speeches, some members of the Cabinet remained doubtful about the possibility of victory. Runciman gave his colleagues an alarming account of the shipping position and, a fortnight later, forecast a complete breakdown in shipping before the middle of 1917. Lansdowne wrote a long memorandum on November 13 in which he brought together these and other pessimistic estimates, and suggested that the British Government ought not to 'discourage any movement, no matter where originating, in favour of an interchange of views as to the possibility of a settlement'. Lansdowne criticised Lloyd George's interview, and asked that the naval, military, and economic advisers of the Government should be invited to say whether they were satisfied that the 'knock-out blow' could and would be delivered.

The Prime Minister asked Robertson and Haig for their views. They replied in the usual terms that German morale had already been lowered, and that the chances of success on the Western Front in 1917 were most favourable. Even without this confident assertion, a majority of Ministers were convinced, in the words of Lord Robert Cecil, that 'a peace now could only be disastrous. At best we could not hope for more than the *status quo*, with a great increase in the German Power in Central Europe.'

Grey's contribution to this discussion was curiously negative, and seems to have been aimed rather at Lloyd George's flamboyant conclusions. Grey thought that the question of peace should be examined, 'as far as possible, without emotion, certainly without sentiment, and without rhetoric'. Grey submitted for 'observations': (i) As long as the naval and military authorities believed that Germany could be defeated, peace was 'premature, and to contemplate it is to betray the interests of this country and of the Allies'. Grey accepted the views of Haig and Robertson on the military prospects if the Allies could continue the war with full vigour through 1917, or even for the first eight months

of the year. The only matter about which he felt doubt was the submarine attack 'which is not mastered, and, for the present seems to be
getting more and more beyond our control'. Grey thought that the
naval and merchant shipping authorities[1] should give their opinion
whether this attack was likely to defeat the Allies before the latter
could defeat Germany on land. He wrote, plainly, that 'the future of
this country depends upon our giving a correct answer to this question'.

(ii) It would also be premature to make peace 'as long as the military
and naval authorities consider that the position of the Allies is likely to
improve, even though it may not result in the ultimate and complete
defeat of Germany'.

(iii) If the military and naval view were that the Allied position was
unlikely to improve, and that the terms which they could secure a
year hence would not be better than those which could be secured at
once, it would be more prudent to end the war on the best terms
obtainable unless another year of war would weaken the Germans
internally more than the Allies, and thus make their recovery more
difficult.

(iv) If, at any time, the Allied military position were to get worse,
the Allies ought to end the war as soon as possible, 'presumably
through the medium of not unsympathetic mediation; and, if they did
not do so, they would be responsible for future disaster to their
countries'.

Grey then repeated his demand for more information on the naval
and merchant shipping situation. His final words were 'without drawing any conclusions of my own, which, indeed, I have not at present
sufficient data to do, I would venture to say, with all respect both to
Lord Lansdowne and to Sir William Robertson, that Lord Lansdowne
has performed a faithful and courageous act in submitting a paper that
obliges these questions to be examined'.

Grey's reasoning was logical, honest, and intellectually correct, but
it was not the kind of argument which would appeal to the men who

---

[1] Grey was in close touch personally with Runciman (his neighbour in North-
umberland), and knew Runciman's gloomy view of the shipping prospects. (See
below, p. 341, for Runciman's opposition to convoying.) Grey's memorandum is
printed in G. M. Trevelyan, *Grey of Fallodon*, pp. 322–4. In a letter to Balfour
(undated, but written, apparently, in November, 1916) Grey, who very rarely
expressed an opinion on the business of other Departments, wrote: 'the submarine danger seems to me to be increasing so rapidly that unless in the next
two months or so we can do something about it, the Germans will see their way
to victory'.

fought at Agincourt or against the Spanish Armada. Chatham, and his son, and, one might add, Henry V and Oliver Cromwell had not discussed the fate of England in such balanced terms. The Prime Minister and Grey's colleagues took the line which, by temperament, Grey himself favoured. They decided to fight on until victory. Nevertheless the lack of fire in these judicial estimates was among the reasons, good and bad, which led Lloyd George to use every means at his disposal to overthrow the Government.

The conclusions reached by the Cabinet were decisive, and the military plans for 1917 were based on them. The final reason for the collapse of any movement sympathetic to a 'peace without victory' was provided by the Germans. The German Chancellor asked Bernstorff at the end of September to suggest that Wilson should take the initiative in suggesting mediation. Bethmann-Hollweg's motive was plain enough. The fighting at Verdun and on the Somme had convinced him that neither side had much chance of winning a decisive victory solely by attacks on the Western Front, and that, on land as well as at sea, Great Britain was now the leading Power among Germany's enemies. The military and naval authorities believed that they could break down the resistance of Great Britain by unrestricted submarine warfare. Bethmann-Hollweg was not convinced that this attempt would succeed; he was afraid that it would bring the United States and possibly other neutrals into the war, and turn the scales against Germany. In the Chancellor's words, a return to unrestricted submarine warfare 'would place the fate of the German Reich in the hands of a U-boat commander'. Bethmann-Hollweg's influence was weakened at the end of August by the appointment of Hindenburg as Chief of the German General Staff and Ludendorff as First Quarter-Master General.[1] Technically these appointments should have brought no change in the Chancellor's position, but not even the Emperor, if he had wished to do so, could have held out for long against the decisions of the new military chiefs in whom, and especially in Hindenburg, German opinion had a blind confidence.

While Bethmann-Hollweg wanted to save Germany from the fatal mistakes of her military leaders, Wilson was alarmed at the success of his own party slogans. He was now uncertain whether he could get the support of the country for American intervention even if Germany resumed attacks on American shipping. He told House on November 2

[1] In fact Ludendorff was Assistant Chief of Staff, but he disliked a title which emphasised his subordinate position.

that he did not believe that 'the American people would wish to go to war, no matter how many Americans were lost at sea'. It was therefore as necessary for Wilson as for Bethmann-Hollweg to try for a compromise peace before the German military chiefs had their way. Wilson decided that he must wait until after his re-election, but that he would then take the step of demanding, in the interests of humanity, that the war should come to an end; he would invite the belligerents to enter a conference, and would warn them that the attitude of the United States towards them would depend on the frankness with which they stated their respective aims.

Wilson hesitated for some time over the terms of his note. Houes was opposed to Wilson's plan in view of the British and French refusal to consider a peace without victory. In any case he criticised the wording of the note; Wilson had repeated his view, which had already caused great offence to the Allies, that the causes of the war were obscure and its objects not defined by any of the belligerents. Wilson was also affected by the public indignation in the United States at the deportation by the Germans of some 115,000 Belgians for forced labour in the Reich or on the Western Front.

Wilson's delay was too long for the Germans. They decided not to wait for him, but to put forward peace proposals of their own. If the proposals were refused, they would begin unrestricted submarine warfare. The German move was extremely clumsy. The military party seems to have regarded it merely as a prelude to the renewal of submarine attacks, though they hoped that it might divide the Allies; some German civilian Ministers seem to have thought that it might start a movement in favour of peace among the moderates in all countries. The German note, published on December 12 – six days after the German capture of Bucharest – was unlikely to have, and did not have any result except to confirm the Allies in their determination to go on fighting. The note was written in condescending phrases; it spoke arrogantly of German strength, and, while offering negotiation, did not mention definite terms.[1]

The Allies, although they did not know exactly what terms the German Government intended to offer, had a fairly clear idea of them, not only from House's report of his talks in Berlin, but also from the

---

[1] The note was sent to the United States Government for transmission to the Allied Governments. In transmitting the note to the Foreign Office Lansing, on Wilson's instructions, issued a statement that the United States intended shortly to approach both groups of belligerents.

wide public advocacy in Germany of a 'strong' peace. The terms were, in fact, unchanged in essentials, though more elaborated in detail, from the programme put forward when the German rulers were expecting a rapid victory. They included 'guarantees' from Belgium, or, failing Belgian acceptance of the 'guarantees',[1] the annexation of Liège and territory adjacent to it; the annexation of Luxembourg, Longwy, and the Briey iron ore region, 'adjustments of territory' in Alsace-Lorraine, and the payment of an indemnity; the annexation of most of Courland and Lithuania, the establishment of a kingdom of Poland under German control; the return of all German colonies except Kiaochow and the Caroline and Mariana Islands, and the transfer to Germany of all or part of the Belgian Congo. These terms were agreed between Hindenburg and Ludendorff, and approved by the Emperor in November, 1916; Bethmann-Hollweg had already discussed with Baron Burian, Austro-Hungarian Foreign Minister, in October, 1916, the possibility of a peace offer. At this stage the Germans would not have reduced their demands, in the course of bargaining, to anything which the Allies could have accepted.[2]

The Allies thought it useless to ask for a more definite statement from the Germans. Briand said in the French Chamber on December 13 that the Germans were merely trying to divide the Allies. The Russians repeated on December 15 that they would fight on for a peace of victory. Four days later Lloyd George also pointed out that the Germans had not made any definite proposals and were trying to trap the Allies. Sonnino made a similar declaration on the part of Italy. On December 30, after an Anglo-French Conference in London, the French Ambassador[3] presented a Note to the United States Ambassador in Paris on behalf of the Allied Powers. The note accused the Central Powers of forcing the war on Europe, and declared their peace offer to be 'a sham proposal, lacking all substance and provision', and 'merely a manœuvre to encourage their own people, mislead the neutrals, and justify in advance further German illegalities'. The Allies

---

[1] The 'guarantees' which the Germans had in view would have made Belgium economically into a vassal state. William II had told Bülow shortly before this time that he expected the relationship between King Albert of Belgium and himself to be 'rather like that of the Egyptian Khedive to the King of England'.

[2] For the German terms in April, 1917, see below, pp. 402-7.

[3] The War Cabinet considered that American opinion was less suspicious of French than of British views, and less likely, if the French Government spoke on behalf of the Allies, to think that Great Britain was taking the lead in a refusal to make peace. See Hankey, op. cit., ii, 600-1.

could not consider an 'empty and insincere proposal', and would require reparation from Germany and guarantees for the future as the conditions of peace.

It is remarkable that Wilson, also without full knowledge of the German terms, considered that the Allies should accept the offer of negotiation. His own plan, however, was almost wrecked in advance, since the Allies would now think that he was acting in collusion with the Germans. Some German newspapers indeed took this collusion for granted. Nevertheless on December 20 Wilson put out his note – in a revised form which House had earlier suggested. He did not propose mediation; he asked merely that the belligerents should state their war aims. Once again, however, he offended Allied opinion by the phrase that 'the objects which the statesmen of the belligerents on both sides have in mind in this war are virtually the same, as stated in general terms to their own people and to the world'.

To the Allies this phrase was not even roughly true; it was absurd in relation to the public discussions about terms which had taken place in Germany,[1] and fantastic in relation to the conditions which the military authorities and the Chancellor himself had in mind. The Foreign Office realised that the publication of the note would raise so much criticism that they held it back for a few hours until they could warn the editors of the London press to be moderate in their comments. On the other hand the Allies felt bound in reply to state their own terms. The Anglo-French Conference, after considering the wording of the reply to the German note, drew up a joint note to the President. The note denied the President's suggestion that the aims of the belligerents on both sides were similar. The Allies then outlined their conditions of peace:

> the restoration of Belgium, Serbia, and Montenegro, with the compensations due to them; the evacuation of the invaded territories in France, in Russia, in Rumania, with just reparation; the reorganisation of Europe, guaranteed by a stable regime and based at once on the respect for nationalities and on the right to full security and liberty of economic development possessed by all peoples, small and great, and at the same time upon territorial conventions and international settlements so as to guarantee land and sea frontiers against international attack.[2]

The political and territorial settlement was further described, though still in somewhat vague terms.

[1] See above, pp. 213–15.   [2] See also below, pp. 398–9.

The restitution of provinces formerly torn from the Allies by force or against the wishes of their inhabitants; the liberation of the Italians, as also of the Slavs, Roumanes, and Czecho-Slovaks from foreign domination, the setting free of the population subject to the bloody tyranny of the Turks; and the turning-out of Europe of the Ottoman Empire as decidedly foreign to Western civilisation.

The words 'restitution of provinces' could be taken to apply to Alsace-Lorraine. In an explanatory despatch sent by Balfour, now Foreign Secretary, to Spring-Rice for communication to the United States Government, Balfour definitely mentioned the return of Alsace-Lorraine to France and the transfer to Italy of territories within the Habsburg Empire inhabited by Italian-speaking people. This latter condition would enable the Western Powers to fulfil their main pledges under the secret treaty of London, though the complete application of this treaty was bound to raise awkward questions in relation to the liberation of the Slavs. The term 'liberation' was itself ambiguous; the meaning as applied to Italians clearly was 'annexation to Italy', but for the Czechs, 'Slavs, and Roumanes', the word might cover only some form of internal autonomy. The Allies were thus not committed to the disruption of Austria-Hungary. On the other hand, they were intending to break-up the Ottoman Empire; they were also committed by the promise of Nicholas II to set up a 'free and independent Poland'.

Wilson was now more anxious than ever to bring the belligerents into a discussion before the resumption of submarine warfare should make negotiation much more difficult and might well result in drawing the United States into the war.[1] House suggested to him at the end of December that, in a last attempt to bring about a settlement, he should himself propose the main lines of a stable peace. Wilson agreed to the proposal and, significantly, told House that he was 'not so much concerned with reaching the Governments as . . . about reaching the

---

[1] He said to House that it would be 'a crime against civilisation for the United States to enter the war'. House thought that the President was taking grave risks in refusing even to prepare for war. After a talk with the Secretary of the Navy on December 16, House noted in his diary: 'My worst fears as to our unpreparedness were confirmed . . . I am convinced that the President's place in history is dependent to a large degree upon luck. If we should get into a serious war, and it should turn out disastrously, he would be one of the most discredited Presidents we have had . . . We have no large guns, if we had them, we have no trained men who would understand how to handle them. We have no air service, nor men to exploit it; and so it is down the list.'

peoples', a policy which Wilson himself found embarrassing when it was attempted a year later by the Bolsheviks. Wilson's address to the Senate on January 22, 1917, was of great importance in its definition of the conditions of peace. The speech contained proposals, for example, about 'self-determination' which at a later stage were to have a decisive influence. At the time, however, this high-minded exposition of the nature of a 'peace without victory' seemed unreal to the Allies, since they were sure that the Germans would never willingly accept Wilson's conditions.

For some time Wilson, and to a lesser extent House, thought that, if the Allied Governments would not listen to him, he might get more co-operation from the Germans. The Germans merely tried to fool him. They replied in general phrases to his note of December 18 and, without defining their own conditions of peace, suggested that the belligerents should meet in conference. They thus indirectly excluded the President from taking part in their peace negotiations. On January 15, 1917, Bernstorff, on instructions from Berlin, told House that the German Government was willing to sign an arbitration treaty with the United States and to join in establishing a League of Nations and promoting general disarmament after the war.

House thought that at first, in view of the German offer, Wilson would be justified in insisting that the Allies should consider peace negotiations. Wilson soon found, however, not only that the Germans were unwilling to allow him a place at the Peace Conference, but that their promises referred to the future, i.e. after a peace treaty had been concluded. Even so the President still hoped to be able to persuade the Germans to state their terms. He asked the British Government whether they would take part in a peace conference. The British Government let him know that they were willing to begin discussions if the Germans were prepared to negotiate on reasonable terms. Wilson's address of January 22 gave the German Government a last chance of negotiation. They refused it. They had indeed already made their decision. At the end of December Hindenburg and Ludendorff had declared that 'diplomatic and military preparations for the unrestricted submarine war should be begun now' in order that the campaign might open at the end of January. On January 8 the Chancellor went to the German Head Quarters for a meeting with the Emperor and the military chiefs. Before the meeting he told Hindenburg and Ludendorff that, if the military authorities regarded unrestricted submarine warfare as necessary, he was 'not in a position to oppose them'.

Throughout his career as Chancellor he had indeed never found himself at a critical time in a position to oppose military 'necessities' which he regarded as politically calamitous. Bethmann-Hollweg wrote afterwards that he felt he was 'dealing with men who no longer intended to discuss the decisions they had made'. There was little to discuss; each side had already put forward its arguments. The decision was that unrestricted submarine warfare should be resumed on February 1, and that the German Ambassador in Washington should announce the fact on January 31.

In a letter making this announcement Bernstorff, according to his instructions, also gave the President in confidence an outline of the German peace terms. The terms, set out in a somewhat more discreet form by Bethmann-Hollweg, were substantially those agreed earlier between the Chancellor and the military authorities.[1] They included demands for 'a frontier in the east which would protect Germany and Poland economically and strategically against Russia'; the 'restitution of colonies in the form of an agreement which would give Germany colonies adequate to her population and economic interest; the evacuation of occupied France 'under reservation concerning the establishment of strategic and economic boundaries, as well as financial compensation'; the restoration of Belgium 'under special guarantees assuring Germany's safety'; compensation generally for German business concerns and individuals injured by the war, the arrangement of 'reasonable treaties of commerce' and (undefined) 'the freedom of the seas'.

The form of words in which, on February 1, the German Government announced the resumption of unrestricted submarine warfare, gave Wilson no chance of avoiding some positive action. The Germans stated that they would sink all ships in the 'war zones'; they offered to allow one American ship weekly a passage between Falmouth and New York. The offer was in itself a declaration that other American ships would be sunk.

Wilson even now hoped that he could avoid war. He broke off diplomatic relations with Germany on February 3; he did not yet

---

[1] The difference in wording, that is to say, the concealment under general phrases of the German annexationist demands, was not due to any modification of these demands. The military chiefs now wanted 'stronger' terms; the naval chiefs, since the German Note of December 12, were asking (with the Emperor's approval) for the annexation of the Flanders coast. In any case the Germans told Wilson that, as they had had no response to their peace offer, they were not bound by any limits mentioned in that offer.

decide on war. He said that he refused to believe that the Germans would 'do in fact what they have warned us they will feel at liberty to do. . . . Only overt acts on their part can make me believe it even now.' On February 25 the Germans sank the Cunard liner *Laconia* without warning; two American women and an American sailor were among the twelve people lost. Four days later the American public was given an account of a message of January 16 from the German Foreign Office through their Embassy in Washington to the German Ambassador in Mexico. This message instructed the Ambassador 'as soon as the outbreak of war with the United States is certain', to approach President Carranza of Mexico on the subject of an alliance between Germany and Mexico, with the possible support of Japan.[1] The 'bait' offered to Mexico was the return of the 'lost' Mexican territories in Texas, New Mexico, and Arizona.

The British Government had intercepted this message, but held it back until the source of their discovery had been 'covered'. They told Page of it privately on February 23. There was no doubt that the message was genuine; the German Foreign Office admitted its genuineness. Furthermore in sending the message to Bernstorff the Germans had abused a privilege granted them by the President, at House's suggestion, since the end of December. They had been allowed to communicate with their Embassy in Washington in German code through the United States Embassy in Berlin.[2] The German Foreign Office had taken advantage of this privilege to transmit the message to Bernstorff who in turn passed it on to the Ambassador in Mexico.[3]

On March 12 the Department of State announced that armed guards would be provided for merchant ships sailing in the zones in which the Germans had declared unrestricted submarine warfare. Nine days later Wilson called Congress for April 2, a fortnight earlier than the date originally set. Three more American ships had been sunk, one of them with heavy loss of life, on March 18. On April 2 the President asked Congress to agree that the course taken by the Germans

[1] The Germans did not wait for the 'outbreak of war'. On February 5 they sent a special despatch to the Ambassador in Mexico to go ahead with the negotiations. The evidence that the Germans were spending large sums of money in Mexico and were also sending arms to the country went back to 1915.

[2] This permission to use German code was, in fact, a breach of neutrality on the part of the United States.

[3] The German Foreign Office sent the message by two other channels in order to ensure its delivery. All these transmissions were detected by the British Intelligence Service.

was one of war against the United States, and that the United States could reply only by war.[1] The Senate adopted a resolution in favour of war on April 4, and the House of Representatives on April 6. Wilson signed the resolution on the afternoon of April 6. It was characteristic of this strange man that one of his deepest regrets, on the night before he addressed Congress, was that the entry of the United States into the war would make impossible a 'peace without victory'.

[1] In this speech Wilson used the phrase about 'making the world safe for democracy'.

PART VI

Lloyd George becomes Prime Minister:
the Allied offensives of 1917:
mutinies in the French army

CHAPTER 16

The resignation of Asquith: Lloyd George becomes Prime Minister

Before the publication of the German note of December 12, 1916, there had been a change of administration in Great Britain. Criticism and indeed serious anxiety about the direction of the war had become so widespread in the autumn of 1916 that some change was inevitable. The change, when it came, was brought about by methods not creditable to the parties concerned, though it is difficult to see how a certain amount of backstairs intrigue could have been avoided. Asquith was unwilling to resign, and, in the circumstances, a general election was most undesirable. Asquith was too confident of his own rightness and at the same time too hesitant and vacillating in action. He had been in office for nearly eleven years and Prime Minister since 1908; he was tired, and much affected by the death of his eldest son in action in September, 1916. In the words of one commentator, he was too sure that there was 'no presentable alternative' to himself. He did not realise that, although the government still had the support of most of the nation, it was more tolerated than approved, and that, because some press criticism was ill-informed, factious, and irresponsible, all the complaints in the press could not be disregarded. Moreover Asquith was head of a coalition. The Conservatives in this coalition – and especially Bonar Law – felt that they would be disowned by their party if they did not bring about a change in machinery and methods, without necessarily substituting Lloyd George for Asquith as Prime Minister. The central fact, therefore, in the first stage of Asquith's extrusion – the word is not too strong – was that most[1] of

---

[1] Not all. The leading members of the Milner group (see above, p. 155), Carson, and Sir Max Aitken (later Lord Beaverbrook), thought it essential to remove Asquith from the Prime Ministership. Aitken's influence was important, since, although he was not among the Conservative leaders, he was a man of strong determination who knew what he wanted. He was also a close friend of Bonar Law. Aitken's account of the ministerial crisis in his book *Politicians and the War*

the Conservatives, including Bonar Law, wanted to keep Asquith as an insurance against the instability of Lloyd George, and at the same time, to make large changes in organisation. The second stage came when the Conservatives found – partly through Asquith's own action – that they could not get these changes unless they accepted Lloyd George as Prime Minister.

Asquith's hope that closer contact with the military authorities would lead to an improvement in Lloyd George's relations with them was far from being fulfilled. After he had succeeded Kitchener at the War Office in July, 1916, Lloyd George increasingly distrusted the combination of Haig and Robertson; Haig and Robertson – especially the latter – also distrusted Lloyd George. In October Lloyd George asked Robertson whether he had any views on the way to win the war. Robertson produced a memorandum which was, in effect, no more than an assertion that the Allies had more resources than Germany for maintaining the policy of attrition on the Western Front. Lloyd George was dissatisfied with Robertson's arguments and figures. There seemed little justification for the claim that the battle of attrition on the Somme was really turning to the advantage of the Allies. After the withdrawal of nine divisions from the Western to the Russian front in July and August the Germans had been able to send five more divisions between August and October to deal with Roumania. On November 3, in another paper, Robertson himself admitted that 'we shall be well advised not to expect the end (of the war) at any rate before the summer of 1918. How long (the war) may go on afterwards, I cannot even guess.'

Lloyd George knew that these views were also held by Joffre and Haig, and that the military authorities were about to hold a meeting to discuss their plans for 1917. He told the War Committee that, before this discussion took place, a small conference of British, French, and Italian Ministers should meet to consider the general situation, and that a military conference should then be held, not in the west, but in Russia. Lloyd George's intention was clear. He wanted to reassert civilian control over the generals, and also to leave open the question where the main military effort should take place in 1917. If the military conference were held in France, and before the meeting of Ministers,

is the best first-hand record. C. Asquith and J. A. Spender, in their biography of Asquith, give the story from Asquith's side. There is an excellent summary of the events and examination of the conflicting sources in Robert Blake, *The Unknown Prime Minister* (1955). See also R. Jenkins, *Asquith* (1964).

the generals would produce their plans for putting all available resources into another series of costly and futile offensives in the west.

Lloyd George did not get his way. The military conference was held
at Chantilly on November 15, and the meeting of Ministers in Paris
on November 15 and 16. The military conference ended first, and
its resolutions were brought before the Ministers. The meeting of
Ministers produced little more than talk; Lloyd George realised that
Briand would not agree to any plan which interfered with the military
demand for concentration in the west. Moreover Asquith, as usual,
supported the generals, and even deleted from a memorandum drawn
up by Lloyd George a number of passages which might have been
disliked by the French.

Hence one of the consequences of the Paris Conference was to confirm Lloyd George's opinion that, if Asquith remained Prime Minister,
there would be no change in a policy which in his (Lloyd George's)
view was likely to lead to the defeat of the Allies by Germany. There
were other, and serious, grounds of complaint against Asquith's procrastination and indecision, but on this main point the issue was plain.
The Prime Minister sided with the generals: Lloyd George believed
that the generals were losing the war.[1]

The acute period of the political crisis began almost immediately
after the Paris Conference. On November 20 Bonar Law was told of
a plan canvassed by Lloyd George and Carson for a small war committee, of which Lloyd George would be the chairman and Carson
and Law himself the members. This committee would take the place
of the larger War Committee of the Cabinet; Asquith would be,
nominally, president, but in fact the plan relegated him, in a dignified though unmistakable way, to a secondary place. Lloyd George,
Carson – and Aitken – were agreed that, if Asquith refused this proposal, he should be compelled to resign.

Bonar Law went as far as accepting the proposal for a new com-
mittee, but insisted that Asquith should be told at once of the plan.
Bonar Law put it to Asquith on November 25. Asquith refused it.
He thought that the committee could not work properly if it did not

[1] Lloyd George said to Hankey on November 9: 'We are going to lose this
war.' Hankey, op. cit., ii, 557. Derby, as Under-Secretary for War, tried to
mediate between Lloyd George and the generals. Derby thought that Lloyd
George never put his proposals in the right way. 'Most of his suggestions are **very**
sound, and if only they can be put forward in a proper manner, . . . their adoption
would be of great advantage to the Army.' R. S. Churchill, *Lord Derby*, p. 223.

include the First Lord of the Admiralty and the Secretary of State for War. He was unwilling to pass over Balfour, Curzon, and McKenna in favour of Carson; he wrote plainly to Bonar Law that Lloyd George did not 'inspire trust', and that it was impossible to avoid the conclusion that he (Lloyd George) had 'engineered' the plan 'with the purpose, not perhaps at the moment, but as soon as a fitting pretext could be found, of his displacing me'.

On December 1 Lloyd George tried to get Asquith to agree to a War Committee of three, with full powers, subject to the Prime Minister's approval; that is to say, the Prime Minister would not be a member of the Committee, but could refer their decisions to the whole Cabinet. Asquith did not answer at once; later in the day he sent to Lloyd George counter-proposals for reconstructing the War Committee under his own chairmanship, and setting up another Committee of National Organisation to deal with the domestic side of war problems. Most of the Conservatives were inclined to accept this plan. They did not want Lloyd George as Prime Minister, and disliked his attempt – or so it seemed – to force them into supporting his own plan;[1] they also suspected that Bonar Law might be committing himself and the party without proper consultation. On the other hand they knew that Lloyd George, if he broke with Asquith, would lead a movement in the country against the Government. The leading Conservatives met Bonar Law on December 3 and asked him to propose to Asquith that he should tender the resignation of the Cabinet. It is still not clear what the Conservative leaders had in mind by inviting Asquith not merely to reconstruct the Cabinet, but to resign. The Conservative meeting was a somewhat angry one. The leaders were not themselves agreed what they wanted to do; they have left different accounts of the intention behind their message to Asquith. The most likely explanation – given by Curzon in a letter to Lansdowne[2] – is that they expected that Lloyd George would be asked to form an administration, and that he would then have to come to terms with Asquith on a basis which would satisfy both Conservatives and Liberals who wanted a change in the conduct of the war.[3]

[1] The main features of Lloyd George's plan, and the fact that he would resign and appeal to public opinion, if his plan were not accepted, appeared in *Reynolds' Newspaper* on December 3. The Conservatives thought (rightly) that Lloyd George was responsible for the disclosure.

[2] Lord Newton, *Life of Lansdowne*, pp. 452–3.

[3] Mr Robert Blake, in *The Unknown Prime Minister* (p. 317), points out that Austen Chamberlain's account of the meeting 'suggests that the Unionist Minis-

Bonar Law added to the confusion (or at least did not remove it) by explaining the Conservative views to Asquith in such a way that Asquith seems to have believed that the Conservative Ministers were about to desert him. Asquith therefore saw Lloyd George, and agreed, in general terms, upon a smaller War Committee with increased powers; he (Asquith) would keep 'supreme and effective control of war policy'; he could, if he so wished, attend the meetings of the committee – anyhow the chairman would report to him daily. Finally, he could veto the decisions of the committee, that is to say, he could inform the Cabinet of his disapproval.

These terms – leaving out of account the press attacks which put Asquith in a humiliating position – would have been sufficient to secure his real control. As Carson argued later, Asquith could have attended – and presided over – every meeting of the new Committee. Bonar Law indeed thought at this time that the crisis was over. Asquith was less certain, but wrote that it shewed 'every sign of following its many predecessors to an early and unhonoured grave'[1]. Late on the night of December 3–4 he announced that he had advised the King to consent to a reconstruction of the Government.

On December 4 *The Times* printed a leading article giving an account of the negotiations; the writer criticised Asquith, and supported the plan for putting the control of the war in the hands of Lloyd George. Asquith believed – wrongly – that Lloyd George was responsible for the article.[2] Whatever the authorship, this public statement made it much more difficult for Asquith to give way to Lloyd George's demands without complete loss of prestige. He was unwilling to see Lloyd George, but wrote to him that he could not 'go on' unless the impression was at once corrected that he was 'being relegated to the position of an irresponsible spectator of the war'. He summed up, in the following terms, the arrangement to which he had given tentative agreement: 'The Prime Minister to have full and effective control of War Policy. The agenda of the War Committee will be submitted to him; its Chairman will report to him daily; he can direct it to consider particular topics or proposals; and all its conclusions will be

---

ters were influenced not so much by a desire to support Asquith against Lloyd George, as by a feeling that the present state of affairs was impossible and that Asquith and Lloyd George should fight it out between themselves'.

[1] Beaverbrook, *Politicians and the War*, p. 435.

[2] The article was written by the editor on the basis of information from Carson. There was so much talk at this time in London about the crisis that any skilled journalist could have written the article.

subject to his approval or veto. He can, of course, at his own discretion, attend meetings of the Committee.'

Lloyd George replied by accepting Asquith's summary, 'subject . . . to personnel'. Meanwhile the leading Liberal Ministers had read *The Times* article. Grey, Harcourt, McKenna, and Runciman advised Asquith not to accept Lloyd George's terms. Asquith also heard from some Conservative sources that the purpose of the Conservative resolution had been to strengthen his personal position against that of Lloyd George. He still underestimated the support, not necessarily for Lloyd George, but for the changes which Lloyd George wanted in the direction of the war. He decided to insist upon keeping the chairmanship of the War Committee even though he was thereby breaking with Lloyd George. He wrote to Lloyd George on the evening of December 4 that after full consideration he had come to the conclusion that the War Committee would be 'workable and effective' only if the Prime Minister were chairman, and that the arrangement which he had mentioned in his earlier letter was impracticable. He also refused to include Carson in the new Committee.

Lloyd George received this letter on the morning of December 5. He replied that Asquith had gone back on his agreement, and that he – Lloyd George – must therefore leave the Government 'in order to inform the people of the real condition of affairs'. Asquith accepted Lloyd George's resignation. The Liberal Ministers, with the possible exception of Montagu, stood by Asquith.[1] The Conservatives, however, considered that Lloyd George, Bonar Law, and Carson would get so strong a backing that the Coalition Government could not continue against their opposition. Carson had already told Bonar Law that Asquith's earlier proposals for a compromise were unworkable, and that the only solution was for Lloyd George to form a Government. Bonar Law, who had made another attempt to persuade Asquith, decided, on getting a copy of Asquith's letter of December 4, that he must now 'back Lloyd George in his further action'. Curzon, Austen Chamberlain, and Robert Cecil had let Asquith know that they would resign if both Lloyd George and Bonar Law left the Government. Balfour, who, somewhat fortunately for himself, had

[1] Among the prominent Liberals outside the Government Haldane agreed about the desirability of a change. He wrote to Balfour: 'Asquith is a first-class head of a deliberative council. He is versed in precedent, acts on principles, and knows how and when to compromise. Lloyd George cares nothing for precedents and knows no principles, but he has fire in his belly, and that is what we want.' Sir F. Maurice, *Haldane*, ii, 45.

been ill at the time of the Conservative meeting on December 3, wrote to Asquith on December 5 that, in his opinion,

> (a) the break-up of the government by the retirement of Lloyd George would be a misfortune, (b) that the experiment of giving him a free hand with the day-to-day work of the Committee is still worth trying, and (c) that there is no use in trying it except on terms which enable him to work under the conditions which, in his own opinion, promise the best possible results. An open breach with Lloyd George will not improve matters, and attempts to compel co-operation between him and fellow-workers with whom he is in but imperfect sympathy will only produce fresh trouble.

Balfour was 'still therefore of opinion that . . . a fair trial should be given to the new War Council à la George'.

Conclusions of this kind were decisive with the Conservatives. They settled that Bonar Law should insist to Asquith upon the maintenance of the agreement of December 3. Asquith resigned on the evening of December 5. He continued to think that no administration could be formed without him, since Lloyd George would not have sufficient following.[1] Bonar Law, if he had pressed his own claims, might now have become Prime Minister. Most Conservatives would have supported him, though without enthusiasm, against Lloyd George, and there still seemed a chance that Asquith might be willing to serve under him, whereas he (Asquith) would not serve under Lloyd George. Bonar Law, however, and Carson thought that Lloyd George would get enough Liberal and Labour support to form a government. Balfour suggested that the King should call a conference of party leaders. Asquith, Bonar Law, Lloyd George, Arthur Henderson, and Balfour himself, attended this conference at Buckingham Palace on December 6. Lloyd George and Bonar Law said that they were unwilling to serve under Asquith. Asquith would make no statement until he had consulted his Liberal supporters. Finally, it was agreed that, if Asquith would serve under him, Bonar Law should form a government; otherwise Lloyd George would try to do so. Later in the day Asquith refused his support on the grounds that the Liberal party would not accept the proposed arrangement, and that he (Asquith) thought it unworkable. There was a certain element of *amour-propre* in his refusal; he also resented, with good cause, the methods which some of his

---

[1] In fact, 126 Liberals had already promised to support Lloyd George.

opponents had used to get rid of him.[1] Nevertheless there is no reason to doubt the genuineness of his view that, if he joined an administration formed by Lloyd George or Bonar Law, a collision on issues of policy would soon have taken place, and that he (Asquith) could serve the country better by leading a 'sober and moderate opposition'.

Lloyd George had little difficulty in forming a government. Churchill alone among the leading Liberals would have come back into the Cabinet, but the Conservatives refused to allow Lloyd George to take him in. Lloyd George thus had to choose his main supporters from among the Conservative Ministers. Bonar Law became Chancellor of the Exchequer. With his approval Lloyd George offered the Foreign Secretaryship to Balfour. Balfour's answer was: 'That is indeed putting a pistol at my head, but I at once say "yes".'[2]

The Labour party had agreed with much of the criticism of Asquith, but had unanimously condemned the methods by which his extrusion had been brought about. As late as December 1 Henderson had considered Asquith indispensable to any coalition. He too recognised the *fait accompli*, and with five other Labour members, accepted office on the general ground that a German victory would mean the defeat of democratic freedom, and that Labour was therefore bound to support a government which would prosecute the war to a successful end. On the other hand, the *New Statesman* thought that the acceptance of office in the new Government by Labour 'might have destroyed all chances of an independent and influential parliamentary party of labour for another generation'.[3]

---

[1] Asquith was particularly bitter over Lloyd George's use – direct and indirect – of the press to excite opposition against him. He had serious ground for complaint, but, in addition to the fact that Lloyd George was not responsible for the article in *The Times* of December 4, the *Manchester Guardian* and the *Westminster Gazette* – the two Liberal papers of the greatest importance, though not with the largest circulation – and the *Daily News* supported Asquith.

[2] Blake, op. cit., pp. 339–40. There are slightly different versions of Balfour's words, but they agree about the 'pistol'. Asquith's biographers comment (Spender and Asquith, ii, 278) that there were in the end not enough pistols to go round! Lloyd George's administration of thirty-three members, including under-secretaries, contained fifteen Conservatives and twelve Liberals. All the major offices except the Ministry of Munitions went to Conservatives.

[3] On December 9, 1916, the *New Statesman* had a leader entitled 'Had Zimri peace?' – an allusion to 2 Kings ix, 31, which was more easily recognised by readers in 1916 than it would be today. The article appeared with a blank space at the end, and a note to the effect that, on hearing of Lloyd George's appointment as Prime Minister, the paper thought it better, in the national interest, not to print the concluding section.

The ministerial crisis of November–December, 1916, had thus ended in Lloyd George taking into his hands the political direction of the war. The fact that this had been his aim, and that he must have foreseen that he would realise it if he could turn to his advantage the general loss of confidence in Asquith, does not mean that he was merely an ambitious intriguer. Asquith might indeed have remembered his own attitude towards Campbell-Bannerman eleven years earlier.[1] Lloyd George exaggerated his own powers, especially in the field of high strategy; he was also too confident that he would be able to impose his views on the military commanders, but he was convinced that, unless he were in control either as Prime Minister or as a kind of Mayor of the Palace with Asquith removed from the immediate direction of the war, Great Britain would be defeated. The Conservatives, the newspaper proprietors, and the larger section of public opinion which welcomed the change of direction never asked what Lloyd George intended to do in order to win the war. The question was neither answerable nor relevant. It could not be answered because the answer depended on circumstances which no one could foresee. It was not relevant because the discontent in the inner circles of government, and in popular opinion, was based upon the delays, mistakes, and indecision in the past conduct of the war. A new attitude of mind rather than a new programme was necessary.

The Conservatives obtained Lloyd George's consent to certain terms before they finally accepted him as Prime Minister. One condition was that he should exclude Churchill from his government; a second was a promise not to remove Haig from his command. An attempt to bind Lloyd George – in the circumstances of the war – was futile. Within seven months Churchill – whose talents and drive Lloyd George realised – became Minister of Munitions.[2] On the other hand Lloyd George at once, on taking office, abandoned the plan of a War Committee outside the practical control of the Prime Minister. With the consent of the Conservatives he formed a small War Cabinet consisting of himself, Bonar Law, Curzon, Henderson, and Milner. The War Cabinet inherited the secretariat of its predecessors, with the invaluable Hankey to draw up the minutes, circulate them, and carry

[1] See above, p. 163.
[2] Lloyd George brought Churchill into his Cabinet partly because he thought him a more dangerous critic outside than inside it. Smuts was in favour of Churchill's return to office. The Conservatives still distrusted him. The *Morning Post* called him 'a floating kidney in the body politic'.

out the administrative work necessary for giving effect to their conclusions in the departments concerned. Carson became First Lord of
the Admiralty, and, with Balfour and the CIGS, attended the War
Cabinet when necessary. Lloyd George set up new Ministries of
Shipping, Food, and Pensions and an Air Board.

These arrangements continued, with some changes in personnel,
until the end of the war. It would be inaccurate to describe them in
terms of a dictatorship. The establishment of a War Cabinet of which
only one member had departmental responsibilities was the best means
of getting rid of the delays, repetitions, and vacillation which had
hampered the conduct of business. The new system, however, did not
mean that decisions were taken without sufficient investigation into the
facts; the number of interdepartmental conferences, subcommittees
and the like increased. The centralisation of control also did not mean
that the Prime Minister's personal wishes determined the policies
adopted. Lloyd George was too quick, too mercurial to be bound by
rule or to regard consistency as high in the scale of political virtues; his
qualities affected the methods of the War Cabinet, but the charge of
improvisation which later historians have made against his government
is unfair, except indeed as far as the conduct of a war requires continual
adaptation to events. There was nothing 'slap-dash' about Milner,
whose administrative capacities Lloyd George employed to the full.
Lloyd George shewed greater drive than Asquith; he was more unconventional not only in his appointments but in his ways of action.[1]
Thus it is unlikely that Asquith would have done as Lloyd George in
going himself to the Admiralty to find out whether the junior officers
took the view of their seniors that a convoy system was not a practicable
way of meeting the submarine danger.[2] Lloyd George was never able to
'control' the direction of the war in the sense of imposing his strategical
ideas – such as they were – upon Haig. He failed to do so because he
was rarely more than a negative and inconsistent critic of the military
plans which he opposed. He suggested alternatives, but never considered their implications. Moreover the military leaders had strong
Conservative support. Haig was as astute – and in some respects as
unscrupulous – an intriguer as Lloyd George himself, and, for that

[1] One of Lloyd George's innovations was a personal secretariat which he
housed in huts in the garden of No. 10 Downing St. This secretariat, known by
its critics as the 'Garden Suburb', was much disliked by the anti-Lloyd George
Liberals because many of its members were Milner's protégés and admirers. See
Gollin, op. cit., p. 380.

[2] See below, p. 343.

BALFOUR'S VIEW OF LLOYD GEORGE   255

matter, the French military command was opposed to Lloyd George's 'eastern' ideas. Lloyd George was thus unable to change the military strategy which reached a futile climax on the British side in the prolongation of the Passchendaele offensive, while his own effort to keep as many men as he could out of Haig's hands in the early part of 1918 might have led to complete disaster.

Balfour's opinion, in a letter to Lord Robert Cecil on September 12, 1917, is perhaps the best summary of the whole matter. Balfour had joined the administration without illusions about Lloyd George's deficiencies as a War Minister. He now wrote that Lloyd George was

> impulsive; he had never given a thought before the war to military matters; he does not perhaps adequately gauge the depths of his own ignorance; and he has certain peculiarities which no doubt make him, now and then, difficult to work with. But I am clearly of opinion that military matters are much better managed now than they were in the time of his predecessor. . . . (Asquith) never seriously attempted to co-ordinate in one homogeneous whole the efforts of soldiers, sailors, and diplomatists, and the result was disaster.[1] . . . Is there any one of his colleagues in the present War Cabinet you would like to see in his [Lloyd George's] place? Is there any member of the late government you would like to see in his place?

Balfour's answer to his own questions was that there was no alternative to Lloyd George, 'and that being so, the most patriotic course appears to me to provide the man whom we do not wish to replace with all the guidance and help in our power'.[2]

[1] Balfour had in mind the Gallipoli campaign.
[2] B. Dugdale, *A. J. Balfour*, ii, 184–5.

CHAPTER 17

Lloyd George, Haig, and Nivelle

The military commanders at the Chantilly conference in November, 1916, could not take account in their plans of the possibility of American entry into the war at any time, least of all within the next five months. They decided to continue during the winter, as far as conditions allowed, the offensive operations in progress. In order to prevent the enemy from regaining the initiative, they proposed to be ready to undertake combined offensives from the first fortnight in February. These operations on the Western Front were to be synchronised, as far as possible, with attacks on other fronts, 'at dates to be fixed by common accord between the commanders-in-chief'. The situation in the Balkans was to be met by a Russo-Roumanian attack on the Bulgarians from the north and an attack from the south by the army at Salonika. The Salonika force was to be made up to twenty-three divisions, mainly by raising the Serbian army to six divisions. As Lloyd George rightly pointed out, this addition was extremely uncertain. The commanders suggested that it could be secured by the voluntary enlistment of Serbian nationals who had been taken prisoners of war while serving with the Austro-Hungarian armies. Anyhow, in view of the plight of the Roumanians, the reference to a Salonika offensive was somewhat unreal. The main point of the Chantilly decisions was that Joffre and Haig reaffirmed their belief in the battle of attrition on the Western Front and wished to concentrate upon it all their available resources.

It is impossible to say whether the Chantilly plan could have brought victory in 1917. A western offensive in February, 1917, would have caught the Germans as they were retiring to their new positions, and would have been delivered before these positions had been completed. On the other hand it is doubtful whether the Allies themselves would have been ready for a large-scale attack at this time. Haig's account of his own army shews that a longer interval would have been needed for preparation, and that the reorganisation of the French railways was an essential preliminary. The Chemin de Fer du Nord, which carried the British supplies to the forward areas, had lost some of its personnel on mobilisation, and had been deprived of a large amount of locomotives and rolling stock – as well as a number of workshops – by the German occupation of French territory. In the summer of 1916, as the British demands for transport increased, there was a congestion of material at the ports, and something near to a breakdown on the railways owing to the deterioration and shortage of equipment. The situation was likely to get worse, and might endanger the supply of material to the British Expeditionary Force, and hamper gravely the movement of men, guns, and shells during a series of offensives.

Lloyd George – to his credit – had taken the matter in hand almost at once after he went to the War Office. He saw that, as in the case of munitions, the problem was too large and too complicated for the military staff, and that outside help was essential. He chose as his chief consultant Sir Eric Geddes, a former manager of the North Eastern Railway. Geddes was already a Lieutenant-Colonel in the Engineer and Railway Staff Corps which before the war had included many high officials of the British railways. He had served under Lloyd George in the Ministry of Munitions. After a preliminary survey of the problem Geddes was appointed Director-General of Military Railways at the War Office. On October 19, 1916, Haig, who realised Geddes' ability, made him Director-General of Transportation in France. On November 18, 1916 – that is to say, after the Chantilly conference – Geddes discussed his plans with the army commanders. He made it clear that he could not increase the supply of rails and rolling stock to any appreciable extent before March, 1917. The position was aggravated five weeks after Geddes had made this estimate by the grounding of a ship across the entrance to Boulogne harbour. The port was closed for almost a month, and traffic had to be diverted to other ports, including Rouen, Havre, and Dieppe.

The weather in February 1917 was unusually severe. A period of extreme cold was followed by days of thaw and fog which would have prevented a large-scale offensive. The hard frosts in January added to the transport difficulties by stopping canal traffic; the thaws in February did great damage to the roads. Joffre would therefore almost certainly have had to alter his plans. The extent to which these plans would have been changed is merely a question for speculation since on December 13 General Nivelle had taken Joffre's place as Commander-in-Chief of the

Armies of the North and North-East.[1] This change came after the reconstruction of the French Government on December 8-9. The fundamental reason for the ministerial changes and for the change in command was similar to that which led to the changes in England almost at the same time. French political opinion, like English opinion, was dissatisfied with the results of 1916, and wanted better machinery for the conduct of the war.

In other respects, however, the demand for change produced different results. The substitution of Lloyd George for Asquith and the retention of Haig as Commander-in-Chief had the paradoxical effect of setting up a Prime Minister who disagreed with the policy of his military advisers, but had not sufficient personal authority or backing in his own Government to enable him to dismiss them. In France Briand was much more conciliatory than Asquith in dealing with parliamentary critics; he maintained his own position, and indeed did his best to keep Joffre as a military adviser, though not in actual command of the armies. French opinion generally, however, blamed Joffre for the lack of preparations which had led so nearly to disaster at Verdun and for the lack of results in the Somme fighting and earlier offensives. Joffre had made his own defence more difficult by refusing any explanations and indeed any conversations with deputies or ministers, other than the President of the Council and the Minister for War. Furthermore, whereas there was no obvious successor to Haig as British Commander-in-Chief, French opinion had been much impressed by the victory gained at Verdun on October 24 under the leadership of General Nivelle. On this one day the French attacked along a front of $4\frac{1}{2}$ miles, recaptured Forts Douaumont and Vaux, and advanced over nearly two miles of ground which the enemy had taken almost eight months to capture. On December 15 another operation – planned earlier by Nivelle – at Verdun was even more successful.

Nivelle claimed that he had found a new method of attack based on a more scientific use of artillery. His plan was to make use of surprise, overwhelm the defences suddenly with a tremendous bombardment, followed by a 'creeping barrage' much deeper than those hitherto employed; he would then capture in a single attack all the enemy's defence system up to his artillery positions. Nivelle argued that he

[1] Joffre remained in name Commander-in-Chief of the French Armies, but any powers remaining to him were taken away. He resigned on December 26, 1916, and was created a Marshal of France. Briand appointed General Lyautey, who had won a great name in Morocco, as Minister of War.

could apply this plan anywhere – except against the very strongest enemy defences – and to an extent which would allow full-scale exploitation. The weak point in his argument was that the two trials given to the 'new plan' at Verdun had not included a break-through, but only an attack with distant, but limited objectives; even so in the second attack not all these objectives were reached on the first day. It was also unsafe to assume that an operation on a small front, with no more than four divisions could be carried out with equal success on a much larger front with five or six times the number of divisions. The artillery requirements for an attack on a larger scale were much greater; the preparations would take a longer time, and would be much harder to conceal. The chances of local mistakes and failures – which might ruin the whole undertaking – multiplied as the front increased in length.

In 1916 Robert George Nivelle was a man of sixty; at the outbreak of war, he had been only a senior artillery colonel. He had risen rapidly in the war to the rank of army commander; his promotion above the heads of three commanders of groups of armies, Foch, Pétain, and Franchet d'Esperey,[1] was due to the fact that he offered, after the costly failures of more than two years, a sharp and rapid method of ending the war with victory. French politicians, with a few sinister exceptions, had agreed in rejecting the so-called 'peace-offer' of Germany and Austria of December 12, 1916, None the less they, and the French people, were unwilling to face the alternative, or so it seemed, of a long war of 'attrition'. Nivelle appeared to offer a better solution.

Nivelle saw Haig on December 20 and, on the following day, put his views to him in writing. He explained that he wanted to keep the enemy's forces occupied outside the main front of attack, and on this front to concentrate a 'mass of manœuvre' of twenty-seven divisions to allow the full exploitation of the expected break-through. For the purpose of rapid action it was desirable that this 'mass of manœuvre' should be of one nationality – that is to say, French. The British army would occupy the enemy on their front, and, in order to allow the French to find the divisions for the mass of manœuvre, would take over at once a part of the French front. The extension, which would bring the British army some twenty miles further south to the Amiens–Roye road, would require seven or eight divisions.

Haig was favourably impressed by Nivelle, and inclined to accept his

[1] And of Castelnau, who had been a commander of army groups in 1915.

expectation of a great success, though not to the extent of a complete break-through. After the Chantilly Conference, Haig had discussed with Joffre his own plan for an offensive to secure the Belgian ports and drive the enemy out of western Belgium. The Admiralty were becoming alarmed at the increasing successes of the German submarines, and at the chance of raids against cross-Channel shipping. There were three possible methods of attacking the ports: a surprise naval attack combined with the landing of troops at or near Ostend; a local advance, with naval support, along the coast far enough to bring Ostend under the range of heavy artillery; a general advance from Ypres. These possibilities had been considered in 1915 and 1916. A landing at or near Ostend was regarded as impracticable, since the German shore batteries controlled the harbour, and the approaches were defended by mines which could be set off electrically from the shore.[1] An advance along the coast would be handicapped by the narrowness of the front – two miles of sand dunes between the Yser inundations and the sea. This flooding had taken place in October, 1914, when the Belgian army was resisting the German advance, and had let in the sea between the Yser and the embankment of the Nieuport–Dixmude railway.[2] The inundations, covering an area two miles wide, could be drained away, but the ground would remain impassable until it had had some three weeks of good weather in which to dry. The Germans would then have had ample warning of an attack. Haig therefore wanted the third plan: a general attack from the direction of Ypres. He would have tried this plan in the summer of 1916, but the German assault on Verdun, and the drain of the Somme fighting had made it impossible to provide the necessary troops.

Haig returned to the plan, with more hope of a great success, at the end of 1916. Joffre had approved of it. Nivelle regarded it as unnecessary, since he was certain that his own offensive would win the war, or at least compel the evacuation of western Belgium. He was therefore prepared to promise Haig that if his – Nivelle's – attack failed, he would take back enough of the line to allow Haig to carry out his northern plan. On these terms Haig agreed to take over part, though

---

[1] It is, however, remarkable that more study was not given to the possibility of a landing. The Admiralty and the War Office were afraid of repeating the catastrophes of the Dardanelles, and there was no special joint staff for considering amphibious landings.

[2] More than two hundred years earlier Vendôme had flooded the country between Nieuport and Bruges in order to interfere with the communications of Marlborough's army in front of Lille.

not all of the area which Nivelle wanted to transfer to him. Haig and Nivelle discussed their differences at two meetings in London on January 15 and 16. Haig was promised two more divisions from England; he agreed to extend the British front to the point desired by Nivelle and to complete the transfer by the beginning of March. Nivelle agreed to do all he could to relieve Haig if the French offensive failed. Meanwhile Lloyd George had nearly upset the whole plan by suggesting at an Inter-Allied Conference in Italy (held at his initiative) on January 5–7 that 250 or 300 British heavy guns and a number of French guns should be lent to Italy for an offensive to gain Trieste and the Istrian peninsula, with Laibach and the road to Vienna as ultimate objectives. Lloyd George pointed to the failure of the western offensives to win much ground or to help Russia. He wanted to attack the enemy at their weakest point. An offensive could begin earlier in the south than in France, and the guns lent to Italy could be brought back if necessary; on the other hand, they would be of the greatest use to the Italians if the Germans should reinforce an Austrian offensive on the Italian front. Lloyd George agreed that the Allies had not enough shipping to support a large offensive in the Balkans, but thought that the Italians might ease the shipping difficulties by building a road from Santi Quaranta to Monastir.

Briand opposed Lloyd George's plan on the ground that it might interfere with Nivelle's offensive. He said that an offensive was now 'a great industrial operation and could not be improvised'. Cadorna, the Italian Commander-in-Chief, did not welcome the plan. He thought that the arrival of the guns in Italy could not be kept secret, and that it would be impossible to carry out a surprise attack. Cadorna's own suggestion was that British or French troops should be sent to Italy.[1]

Lloyd George now provided a remarkable example of what Esher called his 'instability of vision' which caused such distrust to his military advisers and civilian colleagues. He had found it impossible to persuade either the French or the Italians to accept his proposal for a surprise offensive in Italy. He distrusted Haig's plan for an attack on the Western Front and regarded Haig as merely continuing the negative, wearing-down policy of Joffre. Nevertheless he became converted suddenly to Nivelle's plan. Nivelle's persuasive powers had something to do with this *volte-face*; the main reason seems to have been that Nivelle offered an alternative to the Joffre-Haig methods.[2] Haig was on

---

[1] Cadorna was also uncertain how long he would be allowed to keep the guns.

[2] Nivelle, who had an English mother, spoke English fluently. Lloyd George's *Memoirs* are untrustworthy on his attitude to the Nivelle offensive.

leave when Lloyd George was passing through France on his way back from Rome; Robertson therefore arranged that he (Lloyd George) should see General Kiggell, Haig's Chief of Staff. Kiggell's account of the conversation – in a letter to Haig – was that Lloyd George took the line that each of the Commanders-in-Chief thought only of his own front; that 'we really had not effected much (in the west), and he did not believe we could; that we must strike against a soft front and could not find it in the west; that much of the Somme loss was useless and the country could not stand more of that kind of thing, and so on'.

Lloyd George repeated these views to Haig on the morning of January 15 before the arrival of Nivelle for the meetings in London; he shewed not only his distrust of a western offensive, but also (so Haig wrote in his diary) 'proceeded to compare the successes obtained by the French during the past summer with what the British had achieved. His general conclusions were that the French army was better all round, and was able to gain success at less loss of life.' After the meetings with Nivelle, and a discussion in the War Cabinet, the Prime Minister told Haig that the War Cabinet thought it necessary to agree to Nivelle's proposals and to accept the date suggested by the French – 'their country was invaded, and they wished to clear the enemy out as soon as possible'. Furthermore, by attacking early, the British, in the event of a French failure, would be able 'to launch another attack later in the year at some point further north'.

These were the circumstances in which Haig, against his judgment, gave way to Nivelle. Haig thought that the War Cabinet had been over-hasty in their conclusions; he was too loyal a man not to fulfil his engagement. It is clear, however, that Lloyd George suspected his loyalty. Nivelle also seems to have had doubts.[1] He objected to Haig's inclusion of Vimy Ridge in the area of the British attack, and wanted him to extend his offensive to the south rather than the north; he thought that Haig was using the transport crisis, which reached its height in mid-February, as an excuse for delay. Haig, on his part, considered that, if he attacked solely in the area suggested by Nivelle, he would come up against the Hindenburg line.[2] In any case Haig felt that the transport situation made it absolutely necessary to postpone the opening date of

[1] Colonel d'Alenson, Nivelle's confidential staff secretary, was known to be strongly prejudiced against the English. D'Alenson, as Haig recognised, had a great influence upon Nivelle; his over-confidence in the chances of success of the French offensive was noticed with dismay by his own colleagues. D'Alenson was at this time mortally ill with tuberculosis.

[2] See below, Chapter 18.

the offensive. Haig asked for a conference at which the two Heads of Government and Commanders-in-Chief might settle their differences. Before the Conference met at Calais on February 26 the Commanders-in-Chief had in fact come near to an agreement. Nivelle was behind-hand in his preparations, and ready to accept a postponement of the offensive until April 10. General Lyautey also agreed with Haig about the inclusion of Vimy Ridge in the British area of attack.

Lloyd George now initiated a proposal which did lasting harm to his already strained relations with Haig and Robertson. Without consulting or even informing either of them, he suggested to the French that they should bring forward a proposal at the Calais Conference for the subordination of Haig to Nivelle. The French not unnaturally agreed to do so, and at the Conference proposed that their own Commander-in-Chief should exercise authority over the British forces in matters connected with the conduct of operations, including all plans and their execution, the grouping and boundaries of the armies, and the distribution of resources. The French Commander-in-Chief would have at his headquarters a British Chief of Staff and a Quartermaster-General of the British Forces. The Chief of Staff would be the channel of communication with the British War Office. The British Commander-in-Chief was thus reduced, practically, to an Adjutant-General in charge only of discipline and personnel.

This proposal was not actually made at the meeting, but was given to Lloyd George by Briand in writing after dinner at the end of the first session. Lloyd George then shewed it to Haig and Robertson. He told them that the War Cabinet had decided that, since the French had the larger numbers engaged, and the battle was likely to be their last effort, the British army should be placed under their orders for the period of the offensive. Haig answered that it would be 'madness' to put the British forces under the French, and that he did not believe that they would fight under French leadership. Lloyd George agreed that the French proposal went too far, but insisted that Haig and Robertson should consider how to give effect to the decision of the War Cabinet.

On the following morning Nivelle and Lyautey apologised to Haig for the 'insult offered to him and to the British army' by the paper which Briand had produced. They assured Haig that they had only 'recently' seen this paper.[1] Haig's plain statement to Lloyd George

[1] The facts seem to be that the Assistant French Military attaché in London telegraphed to Nivelle on February 16 that the British Government was ready to give secret instructions to Haig that he should regard himself as subordinate to

made it clear that he would not accept the plan, and Nivelle's apology smoothed the way for a compromise. The terms of this compromise were that the general direction of the campaign should be in French hands; that in the period before the opening of the battle Haig would conform to Nivelle's instructions as regards preparation, but could report to the War Cabinet if he thought that these instructions endangered the safety of his army or were likely to prejudice its success. During the battle Haig would be under Nivelle's orders though he would be free to choose the means and methods of carrying out the orders in the British sector of attack.

Haig signed the document embodying these proposals 'as a correct statement, but not approving the arrangement'. There were further difficulties at first about its execution. Nivelle began by writing to Haig in somewhat peremptory terms, Haig suspected that Nivelle had not altogether abandoned the original plan for the subordination of the British army, while Nivelle thought that Haig was unwilling to give his full co-operation. None the less relations between the two men were not unfriendly, and the final arrangement between them, reached at another conference in London on March 12–13, settled the method of liaison between the two commanders for the execution of the Calais agreement.

---

the French Commander-in-Chief. On the 19th the attaché telegraphed that the British Government wanted a meeting with the French to discuss the question of unity of command. On the 20th Balfour told Cambon that the British Government wanted the Calais meeting primarily for this purpose. Cambon telegraphed that, as far as he could gather, the British Government was perturbed by Haig's behaviour and even thought that his recent promotion to Field-Marshal had gone to his head. They therefore wished to compel Haig to subordinate his views to those of the French Command. On the 24th the War Cabinet met; Robertson was informed that he need not attend the meeting. The War Cabinet agreed that Lloyd George should take measures to ensure the unity of command. Lloyd George's colleagues may not have known fully what he intended to do – Hankey told Haig that Lloyd George 'had not received full authority from the War Cabinet' for what he was doing (see Haig, op. cit., p. 201) but they were fully aware that he (Lloyd George) had not given his own Commander-in-Chief or Chief of Staff any hint of what he was discussing with the French. If Lloyd George was not acting honourably towards Haig and Robertson, Balfour must take some share in the responsibility.

According to French sources, the paper, which Briand, at Lloyd George's suggestion, had produced during the evening of the first day of the Conference, had been composed at Nivelle's headquarters on the 21st. Lyautey may well not have seen it until he was on the way to Calais, but this can hardly have been the case with Nivelle, though there is no reason to doubt the dismay of both French generals when they found that Haig and Robertson were taken by surprise at the proposal. See *Military Operations, France and Belgium, 1917*, vol. 2, 536–8.

The Calais Conference had little immediate military effect; on the other hand its repercussions on the relations between Lloyd George and his military advisers were unfortunate. There was a good deal to be said on Lloyd George's side. He was right in distrusting Haig's optimism, and in regarding his unimaginative confidence in mass attack on the Western Front as likely to lead to more costly failures, and possibly to lose the war – or at best to produce a 'stalemate' in which Germany would be less exhausted than the other belligerents. He also had reasonable ground for complaint that Robertson, who should have been the impartial adviser of the War Cabinet, was in fact Haig's advocate in London. Lloyd George found it difficult to argue with them. They were as unwilling as Kitchener to reveal military information; they could express definite conclusions on paper, but were halting and clumsy in explaining how they reached them. On the immediate issues between Haig and Nivelle, Lloyd George might reasonably insist that, if Nivelle's plan were to be accepted, Haig should be as co-operative as possible.

There was, however, no justification for Lloyd George's assumption that Haig's motives in criticising Nivelle's proposals were mean and contemptible. Lloyd George was temperamentally unable to understand men of Haig's type; he came from a different social milieu, and had made his name largely by attacking the political domination of the class in which Haig moved, and, for that matter, the interests from which Haig drew his private fortune. He might have had more sympathy with Robertson, as a 'self-made' man who had risen from the ranks, if Robertson had not seemed to him to have 'gone over' to the other side. Haig is often said to have disliked all politicians. This judgment is unfair to him. He trusted and admired Haldane, and, to a lesser extent, Asquith. After Lloyd George's two-day visit to him at GHQ in September, 1916, he wrote to Lady Haig that he 'got on with him very well indeed', though he thought him 'flighty – makes plans and is always changing them and his mind'.[1] Even so he was disquieted to find that Lloyd George had criticised his (Haig's) subordinates, though not Haig himself, to Foch and had questioned Foch about their ability. Haig noted in his diary that, unless Foch had told him personally of

---

[1] It is significant, in view of the effect on Lloyd George of Emile Thomas' 'conversion' to the Nivelle plan, that in this letter of September 13, Haig wrote: 'It struck me too that M. Thomas can do what he likes with L. G. so that it seems almost dangerous to allow L. G. to be out alone as he is capable of promising the Frenchman anything.'

these criticisms, he 'would not have believed that a British Minister could have been so ungentlemanly as to go to a foreigner and put such questions regarding his own subordinates'.

The Calais Conference therefore confirmed Haig in his opinion that Lloyd George, as well as being a dangerously changeable 'amateur' in strategy, was ungentlemanly in his acts. Haig himself went far – and not for the first time – in action which might well be called intrigue. He had previously told the King his views about Sir John French. He now wrote, on February 28, a long letter to the King explaining what had happened and offering his resignation, in the knowledge that the King would certainly take his side. Lloyd George might have regarded this letter, if he had known of it, as unconstitutional as well as 'ungentlemanly', but the Prime Minister had put himself in the wrong by withholding from the King any knowledge of the discussions in the War Cabinet until after the Calais Conference had taken place.[1]

Lloyd George's behaviour in the matter made it even less possible for him to dismiss Haig. Derby, as Minister of War, and Curzon as a member of the War Cabinet, wrote to Haig disclaiming the Prime Minister's action; the War Cabinet passed a resolution of confidence in Haig. Haig's own position was strengthened, but neither he nor the Prime Minister was likely to forget what had happened, and, for that matter, neither was likely to forgo backstairs methods, each according to his standards, of defending his own policy. Meanwhile the question of a united command was left, inevitably, until the Anglo-French armies were in a critical position during the German offensive in 1918.

[1] The King's reply – given in a letter from Lord Stamfordham – was a tactful piece of advice to Haig not to resign.

CHAPTER 18

The German withdrawal to the Hindenburg line: the British offensive at Arras: failure of Nivelle's offensive

Any chances of success which Nivelle's plan might have had were already lost before the final arrangements between himself and Haig were settled in mid-March. While Nivelle had been planning a grand offensive, Ludendorff had been considering the best way to counter it. He had come to the conclusion that Germany could not win a decisive victory on the Western Front. He had also accepted the view of the German Admiralty that unrestricted submarine warfare would make it impossible for Great Britain, now the main enemy, to continue the war after another twelve months – perhaps sooner; he knew that a return to unrestricted submarine warfare would almost certainly bring America into the war, but from a military point of view he regarded the American contribution as negligible, even if Great Britain had not been forced to surrender in the autumn of 1917. He did not count on a complete Russian collapse; if he expected it, he could not be sure that it would take place in time to allow Germany to bring back most of her fighting units from the east before the Allies opened another offensive.

Ludendorff therefore decided on a strategic retreat which would be likely at least to delay an Allied offensive until the submarine campaign had made it impossible for an attack to be sustained in full strength. He had begun in September, 1916, the construction of a new line behind the Somme battlefield and the German salients between Bapaume and Arras, and between Péronne and Vailly. This line, known to the Germans as the Siegfried, and to the Allies as the Hindenburg line, was rather a zone of fortified defences; it ran from a point near Arras through St Quentin to the Aisne. The work was on an immense scale – as usual the Germans used the labour of prisoners and impressed civilians contrary to the laws of war; it was unlikely to be completed before March, 1917, and the first intention was to treat it merely as a precautionary measure in the event of an Allied success. During the early winter, however, Ludendorff realised that if he retreated to it, he would shorten his line as well as improve his defences, save thirteen or fourteen divisions, and, if the retreat took place just before the campaigning season, seriously disarrange the plans of the Allies.

Ludendorff obtained the Emperor's consent on February 4 to this retreat. He gave the name 'Alberich' – the malicious dwarf in the Siegfried legend – to the operation and decided to carry it out with complete ruthlessness, that is to say, with complete devastation of the intervening area not already wrecked by battle. By this time the Allies had become almost hardened to German methods of barbarism, but the cutting down of fruit-trees and the pollution of wells were among the acts which intensified the bitter feeling against Germans at the end of the war.[1] The main withdrawal began on March 16, and was planned to last from two to four days. The Allies had been curiously slow to discover what was happening, and did practically nothing to hamper the retreat; a proposal by General Franchet d'Esperey to make an attack in force was forbidden by Nivelle on the grounds that the hypothesis of a voluntary German retreat was wholly unlikely.

The retreat was bound to have the most serious effect on Nivelle's plan to break through the German position on the Aisne, and to advance northwards. Nivelle expected that the subsidiary attacks designed to hold the enemy reserves would develop into a break-through from the west as soon as the German armies were in confusion. With the retreat to the Hindenburg line, Nivelle's main attack would become more difficult because the enemy would have more divisions available for defence. The subsidiary attacks would have to be made over old battlegrounds and a devastated area, and could hardly hope to overrun the new line. Moreover, as in 1915 and 1916, the Germans had learned lessons in defence from their experience of Allied offensives. In addition to giving great depth to his new positions, Ludendorff had applied this principle of depth to the German defences along the whole front, and had ordered the training of troops in accordance with the new conditions.[2] Here again, Nivelle's chances of a complete and rapid 'break-through' were less likely to be realised.

[1] The Crown Prince Rupprecht of Bavaria, whose front was concerned, protested strongly against the methods and the extent of this illegal devastation.

[2] The plan was not new, but it was applied much more thoroughly than in 1916. The front lines were held lightly as outposts; behind them were, as a rule, three defence lines to a total depth of about 8000 yards. Special arrangements were also

Finally, Nivelle's plan depended very much on secrecy. Unfortunately he talked too much about it; he issued operational orders long in advance, and did not take care that they were kept secret. On February 15 the Germans captured a divisional order referring to a great attack planned for the Aisne sector in April. On March 3 a French staff officer carrying a copy of the original French memorandum setting out the principles of the new offensive was taken prisoner in a trench raid. The Germans therefore knew everything except the details, and these they obtained on April 6 shortly before the offensive opened. This last information was of great importance, but the main German counter-measures had already been taken. With the completion of the Siegfried line the Germans had labour available to transform the Aisne front into a very strong fortified zone. They reinforced their heavy artillery, collected large reserves of ammunition, and even set up an additional school for senior officers in the new methods of defence. Their counter-attack divisions were in position in the first days of April, before they knew the actual date of the French attack.

In these circumstances it is remarkable that Nivelle did not call off his attack. The scale of preparations for a mass offensive was such that a commander tended to be imprisoned in his own plans, as the Germans had been tied to the Schlieffen plan in 1914. Nevertheless there was ample opportunity for Nivelle to change his mind. Apart from the German withdrawal to the Hindenburg line, and the obvious activities on their side of the Aisne front, three new facts of the greatest political importance had occurred since December, 1916. Wilson had broken off diplomatic relations with Germany on February 3, after the German reopening of unrestricted submarine warfare.[1] He did not declare war until April 6, but it was clear in February and March that the entry of the United States into the war would not be long delayed. The Allies would thus have immense reserves of man-power, though these reserves would not be available in the summer of 1917. On the other hand the political position in Russia had become much worse, and the most competent Allied observers realised that there was no alternative to collapse or revolution.[2] The revolution took place on March 12. Although no one could foresee its outcome, the Russians would not

---

made for counter-attack troops, trained for the purpose, to be kept close to the positions. The sure and rapid appearance of these counter-attack troops brought confidence to the trench garrisons.

[1] See above, Chapter 15.   [2] See below, Chapter 29.

be of much practical value in immobilising enemy forces during the spring and early summer and the Germans could safely transfer troops from the Eastern to the Western Front. A third factor,[1] the early successes of the submarine war, concerned the French as much as the British; the British Admiralty, rightly or wrongly, urged that the capture of the Belgian ports was essential to the success of their anti-submarine measures.

The situation, therefore, was that, if the Allies had remained on the defensive except in the north during 1917, they might have compelled the Germans to attack them. Whatever their anxieties in May, the British and French Governments in March and early April did not expect the submarine war to be decisive. For the Germans, however, this submarine war was a 'gambler's throw'. If it failed, they must seek an immediate decision on the Western Front. The Allies were in a strong position to meet this offensive if they kept in being their reserves of men and material. The German army had been shaken by the prolonged intensity of the Allied attacks in 1916 and by their own failure at Verdun; the internal situation in Germany was not satisfactory, and the decision to try to win the war by attacks on shipping showed that the High Command did not take a favourable view of the chances of success on land.

Nivelle therefore could allege the strongest reasons for a change of plan. Moreover he would have had little opposition to this change either on the political or on the military side. On March 14, General Lyautey, who had no experience of dealing with parliamentary opposition, resigned after being shouted down in the Chamber of Deputies. Lyautey's appointment had been Briand's master-stroke in reinforcing his Cabinet. The Cabinet could not continue without him. Briand resigned on March 17 and was succeeded by M. Ribot, with M. Painlevé as Minister of War.[2] Painlevé distrusted Nivelle's plan, and wanted anyhow to wait for American help. He consulted, over Nivelle's head, the commanders of groups of armies, and found that they did not believe that Nivelle would obtain the results of which he was still extraordinarily confident. On March 22 General Micheler – whose armies were to make the decisive attack – wrote to Nivelle

---

[1] The Italians were also not ready to synchronise their offensive with Nivelle's attack.

[2] Painlevé had been Minister of Education in the Briand Ministry, and had been in charge of the study of inventions which might be useful to the army. He had made a number of visits to the front and had discussed the military situation with most of the commanders.

that in view of the changed circumstances a rapid break-through was hardly possible, and a rapid exploitation even more improbable.

Nivelle, however, would not give up his plan. On April 3 the French Government agreed that he should carry it out. Two days later the whole matter again came under discussion. Colonel Messimy, an infantry divisional commander, and more important from the point of view of getting himself heard, a Deputy and former Minister of War, wrote to M. Ribot a very strong criticism of the whole plan. Messimy asked that the army group commanders should again be consulted. The President of the Republic therefore held a conference at Compiègne to which he invited MM. Ribot, Painlevé, Emile Thomas, the Minister of Marine, General Nivelle, and the three subordinate commanders concerned in the offensive. General Micheler once more expressed doubts about a successful break-through. General Pétain was in favour of a limited attack. Painlevé put the arguments in favour of postponement, or, at all events, limitation of the offensive. Nivelle offered to resign, but the Ministers were afraid of the effect of his resignation on French public opinion and on the morale of the army. If they maintained him in office, they could hardly refuse to allow him to carry out his military plans. The Conference thus ended without any full examination either of the military chances of success or of the possible consequences on the man-power situation in the event of failure.

The British offensive, on Nivelle's plan, was to occupy the Germans and hold their reserves. The offensive opened on April 9, a week before the French attacked on the Aisne. The immediate objective was the Vimy Ridge north of Arras; Haig hoped for a more far-reaching success if he could reach the new German defence line running from Drocourt, south-east of Lens to the Hindenburg line at Quéant. The attack was made with great skill – except for the failure to understand the proper use of tanks – and succeeded in capturing Vimy Ridge.[1] The victory, however, was not exploited. Allenby, the commander of the Third Army which delivered the main attack, was, like Haig, a cavalryman, and had the cavalry corps ready for an advance. Cavalry, as before, were of little use – tanks might have been much more effective – and merely cluttered up the infantry lines of communication. The weather was unfavourable; a prolongation of winter cold, rain, and snowstorms made it difficult to bring up the artillery. Haig had

[1] This fine feat of arms was performed by the Canadians. Australian and New Zealand troops fighting with equal courage suffered very heavily in the battle.

previously warned the War Cabinet that his troops were not sufficiently trained, and that in taking over so large a portion of the French
line he would not have sufficient reserves for exploiting a victory. The
fault was that the staff work, which was good at preparations for the
attack, failed to secure adequate arrangements for a 'follow up'; the
attacking units complained with some reason that the staff officers were
too much at a distance from and out of touch with the rapidly moving
battle-front.

The later stages of the offensive were more costly, and produced
less result. Haig would have broken off the attacks earlier if the situation had not been changed by the failure of Nivelle's plan. The British
casualties were high – 158,000, of whom nearly 30,000 were killed –
and not on a very much smaller scale than those of the French, but
Haig had not promised a complete 'break-through', and the capture of
Vimy Ridge[1] was an achievement greater and more spectacular than
any of the gains in the Somme fighting of the previous year. Thus, in
spite of the failure of the French on the Aisne front, British morale
remained high.

Nivelle's attack had opened on April 16. The preliminary bombardment had not destroyed the German machine-gun positions, and, once
again, the French infantry were doomed from the start. The expected
break-through did not take place; after five days' fighting the French
had penetrated the German second positions only at one point and
had suffered heavy loss. The Germans had also suffered heavily, but
from their point of view they had won a great defensive victory, while
the French were disheartened and disappointed at the failure of the
offensive which was to have brought a decisive result within two days.
The expulsion of the Germans from France and the end of the war
seemed as far away as ever. The effect of the casualties on the troops
was therefore much greater, and was intensified by a breakdown of the
medical services in the forward zone.[2]

---

[1] It could not be foreseen that the possession of this ridge would be of vital
importance to the British army in the German offensive of 1918. See Map 4.

[2] The French did not even have the encouragement that the tanks might be a
decisive new weapon. Their offensive was supported by 128 tanks, about three
times as many as the British used at Arras. The French High Command, however,
had made the opposite mistake to that of the British Command. They had
realised quickly the potential value of the tank, but had gone ahead too rapidly
with its manufacture, and consequently had produced an unsatisfactory type.
They also, like the British High Command, had failed to make an adequate study
of the conditions under which the tanks could best be used. Twenty-three out of

The French Government had already informed Lloyd George on April 16 that they would break off the offensive within a few days if there seemed no chance of large-scale results. In other words, since Nivelle's plan had failed, they would accept Painlevé's proposal to await the coming of the Americans and the recovery of Russia. Lloyd George seems to have agreed with this view. At all events he decided to discuss the position personally with the French Ministers in Paris. Meanwhile he sent Major-General Sir F. Maurice, Director of Military Operations at the War Office, to ask Haig's opinion. Haig's reply – in a letter of April 19 to Robertson – was that it would be 'most unwise' to cease offensive operations until the Americans and Russians could join in.[1] Haig had not expected an immediate break-through on the French front. He thought that

> 'the results so far attained this year show that we have already reduced considerably, by previous efforts, the enemy's resisting power. Our experiences in the last few days are highly encouraging. The present battle is proceeding very satisfactorily, and to abandon the good prospects of success now would be most discouraging to our armies and encouraging to the enemy, who would be left free to recover and reorganise and to seize the initiative either in this theatre or in another.
>
> Delay in forcing the issue would increase the danger to our shipping from submarines, and might result in the Allies being unable to exert their full strength next year.
>
> I consider that the prospects of success this year are distinctly good if we do not relax our efforts, and that it would be unwise, unsound and probably, in the long run, more costly in men and money to cease offensive operations at an early date.
>
> On the contrary, every effort should be made to induce all the allies to do their utmost now to co-operate with the main offensive in order to keep the enemy fully occupied everywhere.

---

forty-eight tanks employed on one sector of the attack were destroyed by enemy fire before they had crossed the French lines.

[1] Haig's diary for April 18, noting his conversation with Maurice, states: 'I must say at once that it would be the height of folly for the French to stop now, just when the Germans had committed the serious fault of retiring, meaning to avoid a battle, but had been forced to fight against their will.' If, as seems almost certain, Haig's phrase about the 'serious fault of retiring' referred to the withdrawal to the Hindenburg line, this entry in the diary throws a curious light on Haig's general view of the strategical situation on the Western Front.

This letter contains, implicitly, the main arguments on which Haig based his strategy for the rest of the year. He assumed that there was a chance of victory in 1917 and that this victory would be won by the British army, and by the attack in the north for which he had been continuing to plan in view of his disbelief that Nivelle's offensive would be decisive. He regarded his own northern attack as the main offensive, and expected from his allies merely that they should keep the enemy occupied elsewhere.

For the time Lloyd George was convinced by Haig's argument at least to the extent of admitting that an immediate change of policy was undesirable. He met the French Ministers in Paris on April 20; they decided that the offensive should be continued, but that another conference should be held in a fortnight's time. On April 24 Haig saw Nivelle. He told him of his information that the French Government proposed to stop the offensive if an important success were not obtained. He said that it was essential to capture the Belgian ports; that this operation could be undertaken either through an attack from Ypres or indirectly by attacking towards the direction of Charleroi and Liège. Haig was now carrying out the latter plan, and was prepared to make every effort to break the Hindenburg line and take Cambrai, but for this purpose the continued action of the French was essential. Haig therefore asked for an assurance that the French would go on with their attacks, since he feared that, after the British army had exhausted itself in trying to make Nivelle's plan a success, the French Government would call off the offensive, and thus make it impossible for the British army to carry out the alternative plan of reaching the Belgian ports through Ypres.

Nivelle assured Haig that the French offensive would be continued, but Haig soon found that the French Commander-in-Chief was unlikely to hold his position much longer. On the evening of April 25 Haig was asked urgently to go to Paris for an interview with Ribot and Painlevé. He reached Paris on the afternoon of April 26. He found that Painlevé had 'persuaded himself that the French had been beaten on the Aisne'. Such in fact was the case in relation to Nivelle's forecast of victory; the 'whole trouble', as Robertson wrote to Haig, was 'Nivelle's forty-eight hours'. Painlevé and Ribot obviously wanted Haig to suggest Nivelle's dismissal; Haig wisely refused to discuss the question with them. He tried to convince them that the result of the offensive, though falling short of Nivelle's confident forecasts, had not been disastrous. Above all, he wanted to be assured that the French Government did not intend a drastic change of plan which would interfere with his own intention to attack in the north.

Haig came back from Paris on April 27 with some hope that he had persuaded the French Ministers to take a less gloomy view of the prospects of the Allies and to see Nivelle's offensive as a considerable stroke in wearing down the enemy. At all events he had been assured that the French would continue their attacks. On the following day he heard from Lord Esher that the French Government, under parliamentary pressure, had decided to get rid of Nivelle. He concluded that Painlevé's policy would now be adopted, and that, whatever changes were made in the High Command, the French would 'avoid losses while waiting for American reinforcements'. Pétain – almost certainly the successor to Nivelle – had described this policy as 'Aggressive-Defensive'. Haig noted in his diary that 'doubtless in his mind he [Pétain] figures the British Army doing the aggressive work, while the French Army "squats" on the Defensive'.

Haig decided that he must now 'take up in earnest' his own plan, i.e. the northern offensive, but that meanwhile the pressure on the German army must not be relaxed. Haig therefore drew up for the War Cabinet a memorandum giving his views on the general situation. He heard from Robertson that the War Cabinet was also uncertain of the French intentions and that Lloyd George wanted to see him before the meeting with the French in Paris.[1] Pétain's appointment as Chief of the General Staff – with extended powers – was also announced on April 29.

In his memorandum of May 1 Haig assumed that the French did not intend to pursue their offensive. If the British offensive were broken off at once the effect on Russia and Italy, both of whom were at this time assumed to be about to attack, might be serious. Haig therefore proposed to go on with his own offensive, with limited objectives, for two or three weeks, and hoped that the French could be persuaded to do the same. Haig would then press forward with his preparations for the Flanders campaign. Here also he would need French co-operation, both in harassing and pinning down the enemy reserves, and in taking back a sector of the front at least equivalent to that area handed over earlier to the British army in order to allow the formation of Nivelle's 'mass of manœuvre'. Haig said of his own plan that success

[1] i.e. the meeting envisaged at Lloyd George's conversation with the French Ministers on April 20.

was 'reasonably possible, and would have valuable results on land and sea; while even if a full measure of success is not gained we shall be attacking the enemy on a front where he cannot refuse to fight' (i.e. there could be no withdrawal to a distant line of defence), 'and where, therefore, our purpose of wearing him down can be given effect to'.

Haig's argument, which was supported by Smuts, convinced the War Cabinet. Lloyd George himself, in his disillusion over Nivelle, had now veered round to the support of Haig who at least had not promised a decisive victory from a single offensive. He also realised, more strongly perhaps than Haig, the extent to which the French politicians had lost confidence. Anyhow at the Paris meeting on May 4 he took the line that his most important task was to encourage the French Ministers and to point out that both Powers must continue to attack.

On the morning of the conference, before the holding of the plenary session at 3 p.m., Haig and Robertson had met Pétain and Nivelle.[1] They had agreed to continue the offensive during the summer to the full extent of their power. The British army would now make the main attack, and the French would support them both by taking over part of their line and by vigorous 'wearing' and 'containing' attacks. The detailed plans of attack were to be kept secret even from the two Governments.

Robertson's report of this meeting was not wholly clear. He said that the meeting had accepted that it was

> no longer a question of aiming at breaking through the enemy's front and aiming at distant objectives. It is now a question of wearing down and exhausting the enemy's resistance, and if and when this is achieved, to exploit it to the fullest extent possible. In order to wear him down we are agreed that it is absolutely necessary to fight with all our available forces with the object of destroying the enemy's divisions. We are unanimously of opinion that there is no half-way between this course and fighting defensively, which, at this stage of the war, would be tantamount to acknowledging defeat. We are all of opinion that our object can be attained by

[1] Pétain did not supersede Nivelle as Commander-in-Chief until May 15. Foch then took Pétain's place as Chief of the General Staff. Nivelle was nominated Commander of a group of armies, but on June 29 Pétain cancelled this appointment on the ground that no vacancy was likely to occur for some time. After Clemenceau's government had taken office, Nivelle was given the honourable but distant post of Commander-in-Chief in North Africa.

relentlessly attacking with limited objectives, while making the fullest use of our artillery. By this means we hope to gain our ends with the minimum loss possible.

The report said nothing of the understanding that the British army would deliver the main attack. It was indeed obvious that the French at least for some time to come would not undertake any 'main offensive'. Robertson's wording, however, did not suggest a 'main attack' but a number of 'relentless attacks' – a kind of continuous activity with limited objectives. Furthermore Robertson had referred at one point to the employment of 'all our available forces' – which implied the use of reserves – and almost in the next sentence had mentioned 'limited objectives' and 'the fullest use of artillery'. According to Lloyd George Robertson's statement was read to the Conference of Ministers. Pétain agreed with it. Lloyd George then made his speech encouraging the French, and insisting that 'we must go on hitting and hitting with all our strength until the Germans ended, as they always do, by cracking'. He said that the British Government were ready to put their full strength into the attack, but that unless the French did the same, the Germans would 'bring their best men and guns and all their ammunition against the British army, and then later against the French'. Lloyd George also supported the view of the generals that the time, place, and methods of attack were to be left to the military authorities responsible. In other words, there must be no more of Nivelle's imprudence in talking long in advance about military plans.

Ribot promised that the French armies would continue the offensive, provided that their reserves were not squandered on attempts at distant objectives and a general break-through. Pétain repeated his previous opinion to this effect. Since Haig did not disagree, the civilian Ministers assumed that they were giving assent to a series of attacks in breadth rather than depth, and with the shelter of overwhelming artillery fire in order to weaken the enemy and prevent an offensive on his part. They were not expecting victory in 1917, but were reverting to a more cautious application of the 'wearing-down policy'.

CHAPTER 19

The French mutinies: the British offensive in Flanders

If Lloyd George had examined Robertson's report more carefully, and had cross-questioned the generals, he might have seen that, though his own attitude and words had encouraged the French at a most critical time, the Paris Conference had not in fact produced the unanimity which its conclusions recorded. These conclusions were open to wide differences of interpretation. Pétain, even before he was compelled to do so by the state of the French army, wanted to spare the French reserves of man-power, and to fight as little as possible until the arrival of the Americans; Haig, though much more cautious than Nivelle in his statements, and in his plans of attack, wanted to carry out a 'main offensive' which, with French collaboration, might well bring a decision in 1917.

Haig had already told the War Cabinet of his general plan; Lloyd George thus knew of it; he was right in refusing any detailed military discussion at the Paris Conference, but he could have asked Haig privately for more information. If he had made more enquiries he would have found that Haig had gone back to his headquarters, and on May 7 had told his army commanders that the Nivelle offensive had been halted, and that the plan for British co-operation with it was no longer operative; 'the objective of the French and British will now be to wear down and exhaust the enemy's resistance by systematically attacking him by surprise. When this end has been achieved the main blow will be struck by the British forces operating from the Ypres front, with the eventual object of securing the Belgian coast and connecting with the Dutch frontier.'[1] The Arras battle would be continued in the hope of misleading the enemy and wearing him down, but the troops and material employed would be moved gradually to the north. Operations there would be continued in two phases: an attack, about

---

[1] An advance of thirteen miles was necessary to bring Ostend under long-range bombardment. The greatest advance in the Somme area after four months fighting had been only seven miles. See Map 3.

June 7, on the Messines–Wytschaete Ridge, and, some weeks later, a 'northern operation' to secure the Belgian coast. The seizure of the Messines ridge would protect the right flank of the army engaged in the coastal operation. Although this plan, with its reference to a distant objective, was hardly in accordance with the Paris statement, Haig had been keeping it in mind throughout the period of preparation for Nivelle's offensive, and refused to give it up. The original plan, indeed, had been influenced by Nivelle's views. If Nivelle's offensive had succeeded, the Germans would have had to evacuate Flanders. In any case the northern offensive would have been preceded by very heavy attacks on the French front, and on a part of the British southern front. These attacks would have disorganised the enemy and compelled the withdrawal of his reserves from the British northern front. Early in January, 1917, Haig had instructed a special sub-section of the Operations branch at GHQ to work out details for a campaign on Nivelle's principle of rapid action. Haig wrote that 'the whole essence of the new plan is to attack with rapidity and push right through quickly'.

Haig thus had in mind a swift advance, after the Messines–Wytschaete Ridge had been taken, from the Ypres salient to the Passchendaele–Westroosebeke–Staden ridge,[1] followed by a great cavalry sweep through western Belgium, the capture of Ostend and Zeebrugge and the complete destruction of the German armies. Even at this stage Plumer and Rawlinson – the two army commanders chiefly concerned – thought the plan too ambitious, and expected a series of infantry battles of the familiar kind at least until the Passchendaele ridge had been secured. For this reason Haig decided to choose a commander more in sympathy with his own optimistic views.[2] His choice was another cavalryman, General Sir Hubert Gough; Gough was forty-seven, and a younger man than Plumer and Rawlinson. He did not know all the ground over which the attack would be made, but Haig regarded him as more likely to make rapid decisions, and push on with a battle. Furthermore, he expected that the cavalry would take a leading part in the exploitation of victory.

[1] The village of Passchendaele, at the southern end of this ridge, was a little under 4½ miles from the most advanced point of the British positions in the Ypres salient, and 7 miles from the town of Ypres. The capture of the ridge, and of the Gheluvelt plateau to the south, would open the plain of Flanders to an advance. See Map 3.

[2] Gough was even more optimistic than Haig. He had written to Haig on March 10 that 'we can now beat the Germans when and where we like if we have time for a fairly good artillery preparation'.

At the time of Gough's appointment,[1] it was already clear that the plans for the northern offensive would have to be modified. Haig's memorandum of May 1 to the War Cabinet implied that he had given up the Nivelle conception of a swift break-through to a distant objective. None the less, the distant objective remained, and Haig was unshaken in his confidence that he could reach it, though not as rapidly as he had hoped. He had stated, however, certain requirements. The French must come back to the sectors of the line which he had unwillingly agreed to take over; they must also support his offensive by attacks of their own. Within a few days of Haig's conference of May 7 he received information showing that very little, if any, help was likely from the French army.

At the Paris Conference Pétain had made it clear that the French army had lost confidence in victory; he had not told his British colleagues the seriousness of the army discontent. Outbreaks of mutiny did not become widespread until the middle of May. Nevertheless even before the offensive Nivelle had complained that the Government, and particularly M. Malvy, Minister of the Interior, were doing little or nothing to counteract or stop the spread of defeatist propaganda. After Nivelle's failure, this propaganda increased, but the main grievances of the soldiers came from distrust of their own High Command, from insufficient care shown for their own welfare and comfort behind the lines, and from the lack of leave.[2] Acts of indiscipline took place before the offensive came to an end, and, in spite of the efforts of the French authorities to hide the facts, the War Office began to hear of them shortly after the Conference.

On May 12 Robertson telegraphed to Haig that the state of affairs in France, and the possibility of the Russians making a separate peace might have an effect on his (Haig's) plans. Two days later Haig received, by telegram from Robertson, a message from the Prime Minister reminding him that the War Cabinet had laid down as a condition for the support of his plan that the French should take their full part in offensive action. The Prime Minister was anxious that Haig should keep this condition in mind during his discussions with Nivelle and Pétain because the Cabinet 'could never agree to our incurring

---

[1] The appointment was not made formally until May 13; Haig told Gough of his decision on April 30. The change of command was bound to delay the opening of the second (Passchendaele) stage of the grand plan.

[2] The fact that the British armies – owing to the shortage of shipping for cross-Channel transport – were far worse off in the matter of leave made no difference to the French complaints.

heavy losses with comparatively small gains, which would obviously be the result unless the French co-operate whole-heartedly'. Haig took this message as intended to strengthen his hand at a conference with Nivelle on May 15.

The conference was postponed owing to the change in the French command. Haig replied on May 16 to Robertson's telegram of May 12. He said that he felt sure that the French would not fail 'to maintain the degree of offensive activity' which they had promised at the Paris Conference. The Italians were already committed to an offensive, though Haig did not know what results were expected from it. The only question for consideration was a possible peace move by Russia. 'In view of this and other uncertainties,' Haig had already decided to divide his operations for the clearance of the Belgian coast into two phases. The first phase would consist solely of the capture of 'certain dominating positions' on the immediate front of the army. The Russian situation was unlikely to develop rapidly enough to allow the enemy to bring sufficient forces from the east to make this first attack useless. In any case Haig could abandon it, if necessary, at the last moment. The second phase of the operations would not begin until several weeks later, and could be cancelled if the situation were unfavourable.

Haig's reply seems to have crossed another letter from Robertson that he had just received the official French version of the Paris proceedings, and that this version made no mention of the French promise to continue offensive action.[1] On May 18 Pétain and Haig met at Amiens. Pétain spoke plainly about the unrest in the French army, but gave full assurances that it would fight and support a British offensive. He said that he was planning four offensives, one of which would be carried out on June 10 and a second about the end of July. Haig explained his own plans. Pétain questioned their distant aims; he pointed out that they were contrary to the advice which he had given at the Paris Conference in favour of attacks with limited objectives. Haig said that each of his attacks would have such objectives; as the wearing-down process continued, 'advanced guards and cavalry will be able to progress for much longer distances profiting by the enemy's demoralisation until a real decision is reached'.

Pétain wanted a British offensive; he did not consider it his duty to

[1] The date of this letter and of the Prime Minister's message is given in *Military Operations* (*France and Belgium*, 1917, ii, p. 26) as May 16; this date cannot be regarded as certain since the chronology of the correspondence in the official *History* at this time differs from that in Haig's diary.

dictate to Haig how this offensive should be carried out. Pétain indeed had no right to dictate to Haig. The arrangement subordinating Haig to Nivelle had 'faded out' with Nivelle's disappearance. Haig was not bound to accept Pétain's somewhat defeatist attitude; on the other hand he ought to have told the War Cabinet of Pétain's views. Instead he wrote home that Pétain had promised his full collaboration – as was indeed the case – and that he (Haig) expected the French to be able to keep their engagements. Haig was in fact becoming doubtful of the capacity of the French army to carry out any offensive action, though these doubts made him feel that a British offensive on the largest possible scale was essential if only to prevent a German attack on the French front.

On June 2, however, Pétain sent his Chief of Staff, General Debeney, to tell Haig that owing to the state of indiscipline in the army he could not fulfil his promise to attack on June 10. General Debeney explained that the main cause of dissatisfaction was the suspension of leave. Pétain had therefore to grant leave on a large scale; the French army would not be strong enough to launch an attack until late in July. Haig was now in a difficult position. The first stage of his own offensive, the long-postponed attack on the Messines ridge – was due to begin on June 7. Haig was sure that this operation would succeed. If, however, he told the War Cabinet what he knew of the state of the French army, and of the reason why Pétain could not fulfil his promise, he might be instructed to postpone his own attack. He therefore decided to say nothing to the War Cabinet, and to regard the information from Pétain as a military secret. If his own relations with the Prime Minister had been better, Haig would not have gone to this concealment; on the other hand the fact that he had concealed important information, and acted contrary to the instructions of the War Cabinet in risking an offensive without French support, increased the Prime Minister's distrust of him, and added to his own difficulties.

The battle of Messines was, as Haig had anticipated, a complete victory. By retaking the Messines ridge the British army, after two years, held once more at least the southern slopes which dominated the Ypres salient. One of the main factors in the success had been the explosion of nineteen large mines under the German positions just before the assault was launched. The War Cabinet had now to decide whether the larger Flanders offensive should be undertaken. Haig was as convinced as ever that it would succeed. He was much influenced by the views of Brigadier-General J. Charteris, head of the GHQ Intelligence Section. These views, summarised in a report of June 12, were that the

German casualties in the west had amounted to 400,000 since January 1, 1917; that out of 157 German divisions in the west, 105 had lost about 40 per cent of their infantry; that the losses were affecting German morale at home and in the field; that, even if the Russians made peace, the Germans would probably be unable to move more than twenty divisions, at the rate of two a week, to the Western Front. The conclusion of the report was that 'given a continuance of the existing circumstances and of the effort of the Allies, Germany may well be forced to conclude a peace on our terms before the end of the year'.

Haig sent an appreciation of the position to Robertson for submission to the War Cabinet. He pointed out that any relaxation of pressure would encourage the Germans, and have a dangerous effect on the French. Once again he did not feel himself justified in telling the War Cabinet all that he knew about the state of the French army, but he said frankly that the prospect of American assistance was too far distant, and that the French were 'living a good deal on the hope of further British successes'. He admitted that it was 'useless' to expect the French to undertake an offensive or do more than keep the enemy fully occupied.

Haig then went on to give his 'considered opinion' that, if British resources were concentrated on the Western Front, the British armies could effect 'great results this summer – results which will make final victory more assured, and may even bring it within reach this year'. On the other hand a diversion of our resources 'might lead to the collapse of France. . . . The desired military results, possible in France, are not possible elsewhere . . . Given sufficient force, provided no great transfer of German troops is made, in time, from east to west, it is probable that the Belgian coast could be cleared this summer, and the defeats on the German troops entailed in doing so might quite possibly lead to their collapse.' Finally Haig said that without sufficient force he would not attempt to clear the coast but would restrict his efforts to gaining such victories as were within reach.

Haig attached Charteris' report as an appendix to his own statement. This appendix was a vital part of his argument – the premises from which he drew his conclusion. The conclusion was indeed stated almost in Charteris' words. If, however, Charteris' figures were wrong, the inference which Haig had drawn from them was also wrong. The War Office, in fact, considered the figures too optimistic. Their view of the state of the German man-power was very different. Brigadier-General G. M. W. Macdonogh, Director of Military Intelligence at the War Office, had disagreed with the opinions of GHQ, even before he knew the seriousness of the mutinies in the French army. He thought that Charteris exaggerated the depletion of the German reserves; his own estimate was that, if, as was probable, the Russians at least gave up active operations, the Germans could increase their strength on the Western Front beyond that of the Allies. On the basis of Macdonogh's estimates, Robertson had submitted a memorandum to the War Cabinet on May 9 to the effect that offensive operations on the Western Front would obviously 'offer no chance of success, and our best course would be to remain on the defensive, strengthen our positions, economise our reserves in man-power and material, and hope that the balance would be eventually redressed by American assistance'.[1]

Robertson had not been convinced by Haig's arguments before the Messines offensive. On June 9 he had seen Haig, and had put to him the argument in favour of supporting an Italian offensive with heavy guns. Robertson argued that the Austrians, 'if harassed enough', might agree to make peace. Haig told Robertson that his views were 'unsound'; that the Germans were near to their last resources, and that the only 'sound' plan was to send 'every possible man, aeroplane, and gun to France'.

It is uncertain whether Robertson was influenced by the great success obtained at Messines, or whether he was persuaded by Haig that the Flanders plan was likely to succeed or whether Haig merely convinced him that the proposal for abandoning the offensive on the Western Front and assisting the Italians would be a dangerous dispersal of effort. At all events Robertson now changed his view, and changed it to the extent of recommending Haig on June 13 to suppress the appendix to his general 'appreciation'. He suggested to Haig that his argument would be weakened if the War Cabinet had different estimates of the enemy's resources. He advised Haig not to suggest that 'he could finish the war this year or that the German is already beaten'. Haig accepted Robertson's advice.[2] It is extraordinary that, in making a suggestion

---

[1] The general theme of this paper was the military effect of the secession of Russia from the Entente. See also below, p. 306. It should be remembered that in June it was evident that, so far from making peace, the Revolutionary Government in Russia was planning another offensive, though British military observers did not expect it to succeed.

[2] None the less Haig wrote to Robertson on June 15 protesting against a statement in a War Office summary issued to the War Cabinet on June 14 that there was 'no reason to doubt the ability of the Central Powers to continue the war into next year'.

of this kind, Robertson should not have seen that Haig's confidence in the success of an offensive was largely founded upon Charteris' estimates and that, if these estimates were wrong, Haig's conclusions were based upon false premises. In any case Robertson, as the adviser of the War Cabinet, would be failing in his duty if he concealed the fact that the views of the Commander-in-Chief about the state of exhaustion of the German army were not held by the War Office.

The result was that the War Cabinet, though they were disquieted by Haig's optimism, did not know the extent to which it was based on figures which their own military adviser doubted. On June 8 the War Cabinet had appointed a special Committee on War Policy to consider the whole situation. This Committee, consisting of the Prime Minister, Bonar Law, Curzon, Milner, and Smuts held sixteen meetings. Haig was brought to England for discussion, and attended meetings of the Committee on June 19, 20, and 22.[1] The Committee heard from Haig on June 19 for the first time the details of his plan and the distant objectives which he had in mind. He spoke not only of capturing Ostend and Zeebrugge, but of crossing the Scheldt, persuading the Dutch to abandon their neutrality, and, in co-operation with the Dutch army, driving the Germans out of Belgium. Lloyd George pointed out, with good reason, that, when he had supported in Paris the idea of a vigorous British offensive, he had not thought that Haig intended the British army to fight and defeat the Germans single-handed. He therefore proposed either the adoption of Pétain's plan of numerous minor offensives or his own plan of assisting the Italians to deliver an attack on the Austrians with Trieste as its objective. He said that Austria was already making secret overtures for a separate peace, and that a heavy defeat might bring about her collapse, and as a consequence, the isolation of Bulgaria and Turkey, the opening of the Russian Black Sea ports, and the withdrawal of enemy submarines from the Mediterranean. In any case the Germans would have to divert forces to try to save Austria, and would thus be unable to carry out an offensive against the French.

Haig was not to be moved. He repeated Charteris' views about the state of the German army.[2] He said that Germany was within six months of the total exhaustion of her available man-power if the

---

[1] Robertson had already written to Haig that he was uneasy about the Committee. His letter began: 'There is trouble in the land just now.'

[2] The GHQ Intelligence reports at the time of Haig's visit to London were again misleading. On June 20 Charteris estimated that the British attack would have a two to one superiority in infantry, and a greater superiority in guns and

fighting continued at its present intensity. Even Charteris, when he heard of it, thought this forecast beyond the estimate which he had given to Haig. Haig believed that the French army would recover and that anyhow the German counter-attacks on the French were almost as effective in 'wearing out' the enemy as a French offensive. He claimed that his own plan was a series of 'step by step' attacks of the kind advocated by Pétain. As for Lloyd George's idea of 'knocking out' Austria, Trieste was a long way from Vienna, and the Austrians might not surrender. The Germans could reinforce the Austrian front far more quickly – Haig mentioned a figure of five to two – than the British and French could reinforce the Italians. An attack on the Western Front was thus the best way of preventing an Austro-German offensive against Italy; on the other hand the withdrawal of some 300 heavy guns from the Western Front might invite a German attack or the transfer of more troops to the Russian front. Haig ended by repeating his forecast that by concentrating on the Western Front the British armies would make final victory more assured and might 'even bring it within reach in 1917'.

The Committee now knew at least in general terms the premises from which Haig was arguing. Robertson does not seem to have defended the less hopeful estimates of his own Intelligence staff; he said indeed that in his view the War Office was exaggerating the strength of the German artillery. He also expected no difficulty on the British side in providing the men, guns, and ammunition for the offensive. He assumed that the casualties in the whole period of the offensive would not exceed 120,000. In view of the relatively light cost at which Vimy Ridge and Messines had been won, Haig was even more confident of avoiding severe losses.

The most decisive intervention in the discussions came, however, from Admiral Jellicoe. He stated plainly that it was useless to consider plans for 1918 unless the Germans could be driven out of Zeebrugge before the end of 1917. Lloyd George and other Ministers strongly challenged this view of the shipping position, but Jellicoe as strongly persisted in it.[1] The Committee thus found it extremely difficult to come

---

ammunition. In fact the Germans at this time had equal numbers in infantry on the whole front of attack, and had still some weeks in which to strengthen their position.

[1] Jellicoe's general pessimism on the submarine question was already known. In fact, the situation was already showing a slight improvement, and, with the adoption of the convoy system at the end of June, the most critical period had passed. See below, Chapter 23.

to a decision. All the arguments were reviewed in detail at another meeting on June 22. The Prime Minister continued to think that Haig would fail, and that his own Austrian plan would succeed. Milner and Bonar Law agreed with him about the small chances of success on the Western Front; Smuts, who accepted Jellicoe's view of the shipping position, thought that Haig should be allowed to try his plan. Curzon inclined to this view. Balfour, whom Lloyd George consulted, was impressed by Smuts' support of Haig.

The Committee left it that Haig should go on with his preparations, and that the final decision should depend on discussions with the French Government about the extent of French collaboration. Meanwhile the Germans, using their small general reserve of six divisions, easily stopped the last Russian offensive against Austria. On July 18, two days after Haig had opened his preliminary bombardment, Robertson wrote to him that the War Cabinet had not yet given their final approval to the offensive. Robertson had reassured them that Haig did not intend to press his attack beyond the range of artillery support until a break-through had taken place. On July 21 Haig received the authorisation of the War Cabinet to carry out the plan which he had explained in London; he was also warned that, if at any time the results did not seem likely to be commensurate with the losses incurred, the War Cabinet might decide to stop the offensive and try the alternative plan of an offensive against Austria supported by British, and possibly French, heavy artillery. The War Cabinet asked Haig to make the necessary preparations for this alternative action. Robertson wrote to Haig that the War Cabinet wished to know his first objective in order that they might be able to judge the success of his operation. Haig replied that his first objective was the Passchendaele ridge; that he expected several weeks of severe fighting before the whole of this ridge was captured, but that, once the British forces held the ridge further operations would be easier. He complained – not unreasonably – at the refusal of the War Cabinet to allow him to judge whether the operation should or should not be continued, and the extent to which each advance should be pressed. He asked the War Cabinet to say whether they had confidence in him. On July 25 the War Cabinet promised their support, and agreed to consider his views before deciding at any time to call off the attack.

Few British commanders in modern times have had such lukewarm support from a Government. If Lloyd George had been in a stronger political position, he might have dismissed a general with whose plans he now disagreed, though it was not easy for civilian Ministers to set aside plans supported by the naval and military Commanders-in-Chief, the Chief of the Imperial General Staff, and General Smuts. Once, however, the Prime Minister had accepted Haig's plan, it was hardly possible for him to order the offensive to be stopped if the Commander-in-Chief wished to continue it. In effect Lloyd George could not judge how near Haig was to victory or defeat; Robertson should have given him impartial advice, but Robertson, as Lloyd George knew, was on Haig's side. Robertson had written to Haig on June 13 that the War Cabinet 'dare not' reject the advice of the Commander-in-Chief and the Chief of the General Staff. Furthermore there was the grave danger of a German attack on the French army. Haig noted on July 22 that 'the British troops are the only troops in the field at the moment on whose capacity to carry through successful attacks against Germans we can rely'.[1] He expected a French recovery, but only after the French army had been encouraged by further British successes. The War Cabinet could no longer insist upon full French co-operation; the case was that the British must save the French army by acting alone. Pétain, in spite of his previous objections, was now relying upon Haig to carry out his offensive. Here again, once the attacks had begun, the War Cabinet could not easily override Haig's judgment that he must continue them in order to give the French time for recovery.

The results of the infantry attacks on the first four days – July 31 to August 3 – of the renewed offensive were not as tragically disappointing as those of the Somme battle. Nevertheless by nightfall the leading divisions of the main assault had suffered 31,000 casualties and were still less than halfway to their first day's objectives. (Gough had persuaded Haig, who had proposed shorter advances, to aim at a target of 5000 yards.)[2] The British official *History* gives an account of the havoc caused by the intense German barrage. In one important section, where, according to plan, the German batteries should have been destroyed in the last three days of the British bombardment, the enemy fire brought about a complete breakdown in communications; no

---

[1] Haig, id., p. 246.

[2] The delay in continuing the attack – during a period of good summer weather – after the capture of Messines Ridge had given the Germans time to improve their defences. Some two to three weeks of good weather might have been expected in August, but the rainfall for the month turned out to be double the average.

definite information about the progress of the battle reached British divisional or corps headquarters between 5.0 and 10.0 a.m.

> Telephone cables back from forward artillery observers and from the advanced signal stations were cut almost without exception; wireless failed owing to the persistent shelling and damage to instruments; power buzzers were found unworkable owing to the damp ground; and visual signalling was very difficult owing to the bad light. Pigeons and messengers alone remained as a means of communication back from the front line; many of the pigeons sent failed to reach their destination and, although runners did excellent work, some hours necessarily elapsed before they could cover the bad ground back to a telephone headquarters.[1]

After the evening of July 31 the chances of a great success began to fade. Three days of continuous rain made the shelled areas near the front into a swamp more than two miles wide; tanks could not be used until August 17.[2] There was more heavy rain on August 8, and more again on August 14. Digging was impracticable; the artillery could not conceal their gun positions and were terribly exposed to enemy counter-fire; they brought up their ammunition only with extreme difficulty. The infantry were even worse off, and the troops were exhausted before they came to attack.

At the end of August, after four weeks of fighting, and casualties amounting to 3424 officers and 64,586 other ranks, there was still no remarkable success. The Germans remained in possession of most of the higher ground beyond Ypres. Gough had now come to the conclusion that operations should be stopped. He told Haig on August 16 that owing to the state of the battle area a tactical success was not possible, except at too great cost. Haig, however, did not take this view. In a report to the War Cabinet on August 21 he wrote that he was well satisfied, though with better weather more ground would have been gained. He thought that progress would soon be more rapid, and that it was desirable to continue 'to press the enemy in Flanders without intermission'. Haig now put Plumer in charge of the main operations.[3] Plumer asked for three weeks' delay in order to make his preparations. In reporting this delay on September 2, Haig again wrote

[1] *Military Operations, France and Belgium, 1917,* ii, p. 155, note 1.
[2] Even so, the ground was most unfavourable for them. On August 20 six out of ten tanks detailed to assist one division were ditched or hit while circumventing water-filled shell holes on the road to the front line.
[3] This change was welcomed by the fighting troops.

home that the best plan to cover the temporary inaction of the French army was to go on with the offensive.

The Prime Minister was unlikely to be convinced by Haig's optimism. Haig was called to a conference in London on September 4. Lloyd George now suggested to him that, in view of the collapse of Russia, and the state of the French army, it would be desirable to return to the defensive in France, and undertake only minor operations such as the support of the Italians against Austria. Although their demands for Anglo-French assistance on a large scale had been refused, the Italians had opened an offensive on August 17. This offensive met with some success, but General Cadorna reported on August 26 that his advance was held up owing to a shortage of heavy guns and shells. The French were in favour of sending 100 more heavy guns to the Italian front.[1] Lloyd George now proposed that Haig should allow 100 heavy guns from the French First Army in Flanders to be sent at once.

Haig, who had been forewarned by Robertson, put his familiar argument that a suspension of the offensive in Flanders would allow the enemy to attack elsewhere, and that it was better to keep them fighting in an area where the British armies were already established, with their supply services near to the coast, than to be compelled to send divisions to any point where the Germans, released from the Flanders Front, might choose to attack. He agreed, however, to discuss with Pétain the question of sending more guns to Italy. On these terms a majority on the War Committee decided in favour of allowing Haig to continue his offensive.

The next stage of the attack opened on September 20. The weather had improved in September, but the Germans, from the higher ground which they still occupied, were able to cause heavy casualties among the infantry and labour gangs in the forward areas. During the three weeks in which no attacks had taken place the Second Army suffered 299 casualties among officers and 5198 among other ranks. The Fifth Army was even more unfavourably located, and lost 521 officers and 10,135 other ranks in killed and wounded. Haig could not leave the troops in such exposed positions during the winter, and, even if for no other reason, had to go on fighting. The September offensive was more successful; by September 25 the enemy had lost the greater part of the Gheluvelt plateau, and had suffered very heavy casualties.

[1] Ten British 6-inch howitzer batteries had been sent to Italy in April. Six more were sent in July.

Another attack on September 26 increased the British gain of ground, and the enemy counter-attacks were beaten back.

Haig now believed that the armies could reach the Passchendaele–Staden ridge and perhaps get beyond it by the end of October; if the weather held, they might do much more. He told Plumer and Gough on September 28 that the next step, the capture of the east end of the Gheluvelt plateau and the village of Broodseinde, would be followed about October 10 by a much more rapid advance. Once again he looked forward to a break-through which could be exploited by cavalry. Each of the two army commanders wrote to Haig, independently, that rapid 'exploitation' on a large scale was most unlikely. Haig saw them again on October 2, and explained that the opportunity might not come at once, but that preparations must be made for it. Haig said that for this reason he was giving up plans for an offensive elsewhere – in the Cambrai region – and was bringing up more troops for the Flanders operations.

On the evening of October 3 the weather turned again to rain. None the less the assault on the remaining sector of high ground was made on October 4 and succeeded. No exploitation of the victory was possible. The Germans had reinforced their artillery to support their counter-attacks, and the British guns could not be moved quickly across the two miles of mud in the battle area. The bad weather continued. On the evening of October 7 Plumer and Gough advised the ending of the campaign. Haig, however, was still anxious to reach the Passchendaele–Westroosebeke section of the last ridge; the longer he waited, the readier the enemy would be to meet the attack. He was also afraid that, if he stopped attacking in Flanders, the Germans would attack the French. Haig on September 19 noted Pétain's opinion that the French army could not be relied upon to resist a determined German attack.

Hence the offensive went on. The night of October 7–8 was clear, but the rain began again in the afternoon of October 8. From this time conditions, terrible as they had been, became much worse. As Haig had been warned by the Belgians (and the Tank Corps), the shelling had blocked the water courses, and there was no means of draining the dammed up areas. It was almost impossible to move the guns forward to the range necessary for dealing with the German batteries behind Passchendaele. Battery sites had to be within 100 or 150 yards of the main roadways, and the transport of ammunition and supplies from the wagon lines which should have taken an hour required from six to sixteen hours. The shells arrived covered with slime, and had to be cleaned before they could be used. As before, the infantry suffered even more from these conditions. The troops could hardly get to the line for an attack; on the night of October 8–9 five hours were allowed for a move of two and a half miles. Some of the men, struggling in heavy rain, and often knee-deep in mud, had not arrived after ten hours. The wounded and sick could be carried back only with immense labour; sixteen men might be required to take a stretcher across the mud to the duckboard tracks and advanced dressing stations.

In such circumstances the attacks on October 9 made little progress. Haig did not now expect to gain his distant objectives; in a memorandum of October 8,[1] he wrote that he had

> every hope of being able to continue (the offensive) for several weeks still, and of gaining results which will add very greatly to the enemy's losses in men and morale, and place us in a far better position to resume an offensive in the spring. Amongst other advantages, we shall end this year's campaign with practically all the observation points originally held by the enemy in our possession, a very important consideration.

This statement was in fact an admission that the larger aims of the offensive had failed. Haig told a meeting of war correspondents on October 11 that the troops were 'practically through the enemy defences'. In other words, he hoped to reach the line which – earlier in the year – he had regarded as the objective of his first attack.

Another attack on October 12 made a slight gain of ground at heavy cost. On the following day, further attacks were postponed until the weather improved, and roads had been made for bringing forward the artillery. Nevertheless Haig wanted to begin again as soon as possible, although nearly half of the area in front of Passchendaele was under water or deep mud. It was typical of these conditions that the paved surface of the Frezenberg–Zonnebeke road, which was assumed to have been destroyed, was 'rediscovered' far under the mud.

Haig had now decided upon a Cambrai offensive for mid-November, and wanted to keep the German reserves in Flanders. He also expected a French attack in Champagne on October 23. At all events there was a pause until October 26. The rain had ceased for a time, but the Germans continued heavy bombardments, including mustard gas

---

[1] For this memorandum, see below, pp. 309–11. Poincaré (op. cit., ix, 314 and 325) on October 11 found Haig 'plus optimiste que jamais'.

shells, and air bombing. The casualties among the infantry, engineers, and labour battalions engaged in road repairs and other work in the forward areas continued to be almost as many as among infantry engaged in an attack.

The final assault on the Passchendaele ridge was made by the Canadians on November 6. The objective was gained, and held; four days later the position was improved, but it was now too late to attempt to extend the hold on the ridge as far north as Westroosebeke. Haig proposed to open the Cambrai offensive on November 20. He had already been ordered to send four divisions, under Plumer, to save the Italians after their disastrous collapse and retreat.[1] Four more divisions might also be needed for Italy.[2] The bitter fighting in Flanders which, in Haig's view, was to prevent the Germans from moving troops elsewhere had not stopped them from sending to defeat Italy the small reserve army which had brought about the final collapse of Russia in the field.

It is not easy to pass a final judgment on the Flanders offensive which lasted from July to November. Lloyd George was wrong in his fear that the offensive would fail completely. Haig was wrong in his belief that he would win a great and possibly decisive success in 1917. Robertson, in behaving throughout as Haig's advocate, and in allowing and even advising him to conceal relevant data affecting his plans, acted badly, and would have deserved censure even if the campaign had turned out successfully. Jellicoe, as Lloyd George had pointed out, was wrong in his sombre forecasts about the German submarine campaign. The sinkings had fallen to a half of their worst total before the later

[1] A combined Austro-German attack against the left flank of the Italian positions in the Carnic Alps began on October 24 with a break-through at Tolmino and the capture of Caporetto. The attack was then extended, and threatened to cut off all the Italian armies east of the Tagliamento and Piave rivers. The Italians continued to fall back until they reached the Piave. Here the enemy advance was halted with the aid of British and French divisions sent from the Western Front, and also by the flooding of the country between the mouth of the Piave and Venice. The enemy claimed the capture of 275,000 prisoners and 2500 guns. The recovery of Italian morale after this defeat was remarkable.

[2] Haig received on the evening of October 26 the order to send two divisions to Italy. On November 7 he was instructed to send two more divisions, six brigades of heavy artillery, and two squadrons of aeroplanes, and to arrange for Plumer to leave at once to take command of the force. A few days later Haig was told that he might have to send two, and possibly four more divisions, and more artillery, but only one of these four divisions was sent.

stages of the Flanders battle. In view of the Italian collapse the adoption earlier of Lloyd George's plan to send large reinforcements to the Italian front might have led to an even worse disaster than Caporetto. The British or French divisions would have been under Cadorna's command; they would have been interpolated among the Italian troops (whose morale was known to be poor) and might well have been engulfed in the headlong retreat. Italian staff work behind the lines was bad; the English and French in the general confusion might have been unable either to extricate themselves or to go on fighting.

Haig may claim that he was justified in maintaining an offensive in order to save the French from collapse, and to allow Pétain time to restore some measure of confidence and discipline in the French army. It has been said that Pétain deliberately exaggerated to Haig the bad state of his troops, but he was equally pessimistic in his reports to the French Ministry of War. At the end of September a memorandum from French GHQ warned the Ministry that a reverse would again provoke, probably without remedy, the crisis through which the army had passed in May and June.[1] On the other hand it is difficult to justify the prolongation of the Flanders attack in the most unfavourable conditions. As far as the initial stages of the offensive were concerned, and, indeed throughout the campaign, Haig was certainly misled by his own staff, but he had chosen his staff and could have changed them. He knew that the War Office disagreed with Charteris' estimate of the rapid deterioration of the German army and the exhaustion of their reserves. For the persistence in attacking, and especially for the decision to continue the attacks after the beginning of October, Haig's responsibility is greater since he was acting against the advice of his army commanders. These later attacks, with the daily wastage in the exposed areas, caused more than 100,000 of the total casualties (from July 31 to November 10) of 244,897.[2] Apart from the losses, the strain

[1] Joffre's judgment on Pétain was that he was 'trop négatif, trop timide . . . des idées quelquefois un peu fausses, quelquefois de facheuses paroles de pessimisme et de découragement'. Nevertheless it may be doubted whether a man of more resolute temperament could have 'nursed' the French army to recovery more successfully. The troops had lost confidence in 'resolute' leadership, and realised at least that Pétain would not lead them into more disastrous offensives. The price which the British army had to pay for this 'nursing' was heavy.

[2] About two-thirds of the wounded returned to active duty. The casualties and sufferings of the wounded were increased because the Germans deliberately bombed and shelled casualty clearing stations and other medical establishments in spite of their Red Cross markings. The official figures of the British casualties have been challenged as too low and the official historians have been accused of

on the troops in the fighting area was almost unbearable and the loss of material very heavy. The German losses were also extremely severe, possibly as severe as those of the British, but not on a scale sufficient, as Haig had expected, to break the offensive capacity of the German army. Haig underestimated German numbers and morale. Above all, he underestimated the difficulties of the attack. He had not at any time, except in the explosion of the Messines mines, the advantages of surprise. The Germans knew that an offensive was being prepared against them. They could observe the battle zone. They had not to bring their artillery over areas of impassable ground. Their new method of defence – as on the Aisne – increased the difficulties of a 'break-through'. Haig also knew, or should have known, that the attacking army did much to create its own obstacles by destroying roads and tracks and blocking watercourses.[1] No part of the British front was less favourable to the use of tanks than northern Flanders, and yet the value of tank collaboration in attack had already been shown.

Haig could not have foreseen that August would be an unusually wet month, but the average of previous years showed that it was among the wet months. In any case a renewal of the attack in October was almost certain to meet with bad weather. It is difficult to avoid the conclusion, reached bitterly by so many officers and men in the front lines, that Haig himself, and his staff, were not fully aware of the fearful conditions into which they sent hundreds of thousands of men. The Commander-in-Chief and his staff were hard-worked; they had to be located far behind the fighting in a position where information could reach them rapidly from all quarters, but their remoteness had great drawbacks. Haig, obviously, could do little more than visit the army commanders. Too few of his subordinates at GHQ knew what it was like to move forward to an attack across a mile or two miles of mud, or to look for a battery position among a morass of shell holes.

The Passchendaele offensive was less costly than the Somme offensive, and – at the outset – promised better results on the assumption that a

understating them. Other writers, however, have defended the official estimate. See Terraine, op. cit., pp. 371–2.

[1] The official history of the operations, though in general unduly favourable to Haig, admits that 'the British army in this battle, by its bombardments and barrages, created in front of itself its own obstacles – shell craters and mud'. *Military Operations, France and Belgium, 1917*, ii, 126.

break-through was possible, but the Somme battle might have taught Haig the lessons that there was no way, other than by devising better mechanical means, to solve the problem of breaking through positions defended by artillery and machine guns, and that the 'wearing down' policy was merely, as Churchill put it in a remarkable phrase, one of 'exchanging lives upon a scale at once more frightful than anything that has been witnessed before in the world, and too modest to produce a decision'.[1]

[1] Memorandum of March 5, 1918, to the War Cabinet, Churchill, *The World Crisis, 1916–1918*, iv, 402.

CHAPTER 20

Cambrai: the new tactics

Brigadier-General H. J. Elles, commanding the Tank Corps in France, and Lieutenant-Colonel J. F. C. Fuller – Elles' senior staff officer – had been uneasy at the refusal of Haig and the senior commanders to regard the tanks as more than an 'adjunct' to infantry and artillery attack. They also regarded with dismay the choice of Flanders for a main offensive in the early autumn since, as they pointed out, the ground would soon become an undrained swamp in which tanks could not be used. The tank officers were young; they had no senior representatives at GHQ to argue their case. They had worked out new tactical methods based upon the employment of their new arm; they were unable to persuade either GHQ or the War Office that they had at last found a way towards victory. They had protested when Haig and the army commanders seemed in 1916 to be throwing away the first chance of a surprise, but the Germans, fortunately, had not shewn themselves in this respect any less conservative than the British High Command. The opportunity for a great attack with tanks still remained.

If such an attack were made, three conditions were essential in addition to the element of surprise. The ground chosen must be favourable to tank tactics. The attack must be made by well-trained and fresh divisions and supported amply by reserves who could at once exploit a victory. The tank commanders must be allowed to determine the method of employment of their machines. The time of attack was also important. Obviously, if a victory were to be fully exploited, the surprise attack must not be made at the end of the campaigning season, when large-scale exploitation would be difficult, and weather conditions increasingly uncertain, and the Germans might merely be left with a whole winter in which to think out answers to the new methods of assault.

In the belated attempt to make proper tactical use of the opportunity offered by the tanks, only two of the conditions – those of surprise and of favourable ground – were fulfilled, and even so the decision to launch a surprise attack was not taken until the possibilities of extensive success in Flanders were disappearing. The War Office indeed attached such little importance to the new weapon that in August they proposed to stop the expansion of the Tank Corps and even to take away from it, in spite of the need of trained crews, men in the highest medical category.[1] This measure – a *reductio ad absurdum* of the 'wearing down' strategy – was regarded as necessary in order to make good the infantry losses in the Flanders fighting. The plan was not accepted, but GHQ were still occupied with the Flanders battle, and for the time gave little or no attention to Elles' and Fuller's proposals.

They had, however, independent and unexpected support outside GHQ. Brigadier-General H. H. Tudor, who commanded the artillery of the 9th Division on the Cambrai area of the front, proposed to his corps headquarters a plan for a surprise attack to relieve the pressure in Flanders. The main new feature of his scheme was to use survey methods for gun-laying,[2] instead of the preliminary registration of targets which gave away in advance the intention to attack. He proposed that the tanks should be used for wire-cutting; hence there need be no prolonged artillery bombardment to warn the enemy. No gun would fire until the actual moment of assault.

On August 23 Brigadier-General Tudor's scheme had reached Third Army headquarters. Elles was asked to visit the ground. He reported favourably on it, and the plan now went to GHQ where Kiggell pointed out that owing to the Flanders offensive there were not enough troops available. Kiggell does not appear to have asked himself whether it might not have been better to have slackened off the Flanders offensive and supplied the troops for a more promising effort. If the tank commanders had been represented by officers of higher rank at GHQ and if their proposals had reached Lloyd George, it is probable that they would have had more support.

The Cambrai plan was thus held in suspense until mid-September.

[1] See below, p. 301.

[2] This plan, an improvement on 'map-shooting', was the result of a combination of various devices: (i) a careful location of targets by the use of trigonometrical survey methods for every battery; (ii) a careful calibration of guns, and study of the effects of wind, temperature, and barometric pressure on the flight of shells; (iii) the employment of sound-ranging, flash-spotting, air observation and photography in the location of targets. Tanks, like infantry, depended on good counter-battery work to protect them against being knocked out by gunfire. It is of interest to notice once again that the artillery and engineer officers were more inclined to use scientific methods, and to consider their practical consequences, than the cavalry officers like Haig and Robertson.

On September 16, General Byng, who commanded the Third Army, went to GHQ. He had become convinced that the plan was a good one. Haig allowed it to be discussed, and was willing to support it, but refused to fix any date since no troops could be spared for it while the heavy fighting continued in Flanders. Finally, on October 13, he agreed that arrangements should be made for what was now called the 'secret operation'. He promised Byng an immediate reinforcement of four divisions. Byng explained his detailed plans to his own corps commanders on October 26. On this same day Haig was instructed to send two divisions to Italy. He had also agreed, if possible, to take over more of the front line from the French at the end of November. Hence there were not enough troops available for the Cambrai offensive or reserves for the exploitation of success.[1] The Flanders fighting in October had, in fact, gravely diminished the chances of success elsewhere. There was also an insufficient reserve of tanks and of trained crews. Here again the conservatism of GHQ and the War Office were ultimately to blame. Robertson had never changed his view of the tanks as a 'somewhat desperate innovation'. Haig did not take this view; he had ordered 1000 tanks after the battle of the Somme, but had not shown a sense of urgency about their production, or about the expansion of the Tank Corps. Moreover Byng, though he had been willing to try the new methods, still hesitated to give the tank commanders a free hand even in the disposition of their own weapons. They asked that at least as many tanks should be held in reserve as were used in the first assault. This request was refused. Not one tank was held back for the exploitation of the first success. Hence the tank units had no time to reorganise and refit, or even to carry out a proper reconnaissance. Tired crews were sent up 'piecemeal' to work with infantry who often did not know what tanks could or could not do. Thus another condition of success was lacking.

Nevertheless, on November 20, the first day of the battle of Cambrai, an advance of three to four miles was made on a front of six miles, and the two strongly defended trench systems, as well as the outpost defences, of the Hindenburg line had been taken in not much more than four hours; 100 guns and over 4200 prisoners had been

---

[1] Fuller's original plan was not for a break-through on a grand scale, but for a raid which would have lasted about eight to twelve hours, and would not therefore have required the full use of reserves. On the other hand this plan, if put into effect at the end of the campaigning season, would have given the enemy ample time to think out counter-measures to deal with an attempted break-through in 1918.

captured, and heavy losses caused to the enemy at a cost of little more than 4000 British casualties. Here was, within grasp, a victory without parallel. The opportunity was lost. The successful advance was not exploited rapidly. The Germans were allowed time to bring up reserves (which the British Command assumed to be in Flanders); the German counter-attack, which began in force on November 30, succeeded to such an extent by December 3 that the British had lost most of their gains and were driven out of their own trenches on the southern flank of the battle.

The early victory had caused great excitement at home; church bells were rung, and congratulations sent to the armies. The later defeat was the more stinging and caused deeper disquiet. Byng blamed his own troops, or rather attributed the German success in counter-attack to the lack of training of his junior officers, NCOs and men. Haig took full responsibility on himself; he accepted Byng's view, but soon afterwards superseded two of his corps commanders.

It is hardly possible, in the light of detailed knowledge of the course of the battle, to regard Byng's attribution of blame as justified. One important factor was the slowness and excessive caution of the cavalry commanders in exploiting the first success.[1] Almost for the first time since the autumn of 1914 the cavalry fought as cavalry, but the senior commanders had been inactive too long to show initiative or to take justifiable risks. Byng himself was extraordinarily over-confident. He made too little effort to meet a counter-attack. He did not ask for reinforcements or even for the relief of his tired troops. He did not warn his subordinate commanders or bring his own reserves close enough to put them into action at once. He had too few men, asked too much of them, and did not handle them well. If the divisions already sent to Italy had been available at Cambrai, the result might have been very different; if Haig had not wasted men and material in the mud of Flanders, and if he had been more imaginatively aware of the possibilities of the new method of attack, the battle of Cambrai might have been fought before the battle of Caporetto, and might indeed have prevented the Germans from sending their reserves to the Italian front.

The success of the tanks in breaking through the Hindenburg line at

---

[1] The lack of mobility was increased by the heavy weight – 72 pounds – of equipment carried by the infantry. At a time when rapid success was essential, the risk of taking a lighter equipment might have been justified. The lessons of the Somme might indeed have led to earlier experiments in armoured carriers to bring up equipment, and possibly the men themselves. The weight carried at Cambrai was in fact four pounds heavier per infantryman than at the Somme.

last convinced the War Office of their value. In the spring of 1917 the War Office had cut down by two-thirds a building programme of 4000 tanks for the 1918 campaign. After the battle of Cambrai the original figure was restored. In August, 1917, an increased establishment of officers and men for the Tank Corps, though approved by Haig, was postponed owing to the heavy demands of the infantry to replace their losses. This decision was also reversed at the end of November. In mid-April, 1918, GHQ ordered a reduction in the Tank Corps and the transfer of 2600 personnel to the infantry. The senior Tank officers strongly opposed this order, and, two months later, after Pétain and Foch had advocated an increase in the number of tanks, GHQ cancelled the cut.[1]

The failure of the British offensives to produce a decisive result on the Western Front led to the revival, for the most part in private discussion, of the idea of a 'compromise peace' as the only way of escape from the fearful slaughter on both sides. A public formulation of this idea came from Lord Lansdowne. On November 29, 1917, the *Daily Telegraph* published a letter (which *The Times* had refused to accept) from Lansdowne repeating the arguments which he had used in a memorandum to the Cabinet a year earlier. He suggested that an 'immense stimulus' would probably be given to the peace party in Germany if it were understood that the Allies did not aim at the annihilation of Germany as a Great Power or at the ruin of her commerce or the imposition upon her people of any government except that of their own choice. Lansdowne wanted the British Government to say that they were prepared to examine with other Powers questions connected with the 'freedom of the seas' and to enter into an international pact for the settlement of disputes by peaceful means.

Lansdowne had told Balfour what he was intending to write in his letter. Balfour had argued against his proposals, mainly because of their ambiguity, but had not advised against sending his letter to the press. There was indeed nothing new about the proposals. Similar views were being put forward in the press and elsewhere by others. Lansdowne's standing, however, was such that, although he had ceased to

[1] See B. H. Liddell Hart, *The Tanks*, i, Capt. Sir B. Liddell Hart points out the lack of a sense of proportion, in view of the infantry casualties, in deferring the increase in size of a new arm that 'carried the promise of saving much of the sacrifice of life involved in the old style attacks'. An ironical result of the German counter-attack at Cambrai was that their High Command remained unfavourable to 'a further mechanisation' of the battlefield by the introduction of tanks.

be a minister at the end of 1916, his letter might well have been taken as
a sign of weakening on the part of the British Government. Apart from
its vagueness, the weak point of the letter was the assumption that a
military victory was impossible. Lansdowne drew this conclusion from
the deadlock on the Western Front. Other conclusions could be drawn
from this fact without giving up hope of a military victory. In any case
the military chiefs – Allied and German – disagreed with the view that
a decisive victory on the Western Front was impossible. In Germany at
least the generals had the final word. The only effect, therefore, upon
them of Lansdowne's appeal would be to make them suspect that the
Allies had ceased to think that they could win the war. There was not
the least chance, at this stage, of German agreement to a compromise
on Lansdowne's terms.[1] In Great Britain the head of the Government
had not given up hopes of victory, if only he could persuade or order
the military chiefs to adopt a less disastrous strategy. In the United
States, Wilson had come to the view that a lasting peace was not
possible unless the Germans were persuaded or, more likely, compelled
to change their government. Inevitably, the British Government at
once repudiated Lansdowne's letter and Bonar Law heavily attacked
Lansdowne himself at a Conservative meeting.

[1] Hindenburg, on December 11, wrote to the Emperor asking for a restatement
of the German intentions with regard to Belgium as laid down in the resolutions
at the Kreuznach meeting of April 23, 1917. See below, p. 403-4.

PART VII

The establishment of the Supreme War Council: the Western Allies and Russia after the Bolshevik revolution

CHAPTER 21

The establishment of the Supreme War Council: Allied plans for 1918

Lloyd George had become convinced before the battle of Cambrai that the continuation of the Flanders offensive was a grave error, and that, if there were no means of controlling Haig and Robertson, their stubborn adherence to 'wearing down' tactics might lose the war. At every point of controversy the Prime Minister found himself opposed by this military combination. The fact that their forecasts had been wrong did not change their views. They used every turn in the military situation to demand that more men should be sent to the Western Front only to be engulfed – so Lloyd George complained – in useless slaughter. After the battle of Cambrai the War Cabinet insisted that Haig should get rid of Charteris and Kiggell. Kiggell's health was bad, and the War Office – as well as the corps and army commanders – had had more than enough of Charteris' overhopeful reports on the decline in the numbers and efficiency of the German army.[1]

There was, however, still no way open to Lloyd George of removing Haig or even Robertson directly without causing a dangerous political and public controversy, and, possibly, the overthrow of the Government. Lloyd George felt that, if he could not attack Haig and Robertson directly, he might weaken their power to decide future plans, and that he could do so by the establishment of some inter-Allied organisation which would centralise decision as the War Cabinet had centralised it in Great Britain and advise upon the largest aspects of strategy in the war. In any case an organisation of this kind seemed necessary. The

---

[1] It is possible that in the reaction of public feeling after the failure at Cambrai Lloyd George could have substituted Plumer for Haig as Commander-in-Chief. At this time opinion in the army in France would have welcomed the change. Derby wrote to Haig on December 12 that his (Derby's) view of Charteris as a public danger was shared by practically the whole of the army, 'and I feel that if they do not put forward disagreeable facts to you, it is my duty to do so'. Beaverbrook, *Men and Power*, 1956, pp. 370–1.

need for it increased as the military situation deteriorated in 1917 and the western Allies had to act more closely together if they were not to be overwhelmed singly by the Germans. The menacing factor in the situation was now the defection of Russia. In the early months of the year it was clear that little positive help to the Allies could be expected from the Russian armies. The March Revolution staved off a complete collapse, or seemed to have done so, but the last Russian offensive, begun on July 1, 1917, had destroyed the only units in the Russian army willing to go on fighting the enemy. In the period of semi-anarchy preceding the fall of Kerensky, the Germans were able to test – though against a Russian army hardly capable of resistance – the offensive methods which Ludendorff was to apply in France during the following spring. The outbreak of the Bolshevik revolution settled the matter. The Bolshevists asked for peace; they were bound to do so, not only because they could not themselves have survived a prolongation of the war, but also because, on their theory, in the general demand for peace, the governments of all the belligerent countries would be overthrown, and the way opened everywhere for the social revolution.[1]

Early in May Robertson had drawn up for the War Cabinet a paper on 'The Military Effect of Russia Seceding from the Entente'. He concluded that the situation need not lead to the defeat of the western Allies, but that Great Britain would have to economise shipping by keeping her troops as near home as possible, and that she must concentrate upon holding the Western Front in order to prevent the defection of France. Robertson's arguments in this paper were determined primarily by his desire to prevent Lloyd George from scattering the man-power of the British army in campaigns away from the decisive theatre of war. The War Cabinet did not specially discuss the paper, but the position on the Eastern front was one of the matters which affected their attitude toward Haig's plans. An Inter-Allied Conference of July 25 in Paris also did not deal directly with the Russian question; the Allied military representatives, however, held a meeting at which they considered what might happen if Russia made a separate peace, and the Germans were thereby enabled to secure a superiority in numbers on the Western Front in the first half of 1918.[2] One of the recommenda-

[1] See below, Chapter 29.
[2] The Americans planned to have twenty divisions in France by June 1, 1918. The Allied representatives at the July meeting did not think that the German superiority in numbers between January 1 and July 1, 1918, would be sufficient to allow a break-through. Owing to previous lack of preparation the training

tions at this meeting was the unification of action on the Western Front by means of an inter-Allied organisation.

Robertson saw at once that an organisation of this kind would strengthen Lloyd George's position, or at all events, weaken the position of Haig and himself. He wrote to Haig that Foch had made the proposal, and that he (Robertson) would have nothing to do with it. 'You know the meaning of this Allied Staff without my explanation. . . . I can see Lloyd George in the future wanting to agree to some such organisation so as to put the matter in French hands and to take it out of mine.'[1] On his return to London Robertson submitted another paper on the Russian situation and its effects on British military plans. He argued that the most effective way of averting more disasters in Russia was to continue to bring the utmost pressure to bear on the Western Front. He repeated his warning against commitments in secondary theatres of war and on the need for economy of shipping. He made no comment on the proposal about the suggestion for an inter-Allied organisation.

Lloyd George, however, became more anxious to secure such an organisation. He wrote to President Wilson on September 3 that it was 'of supreme importance to establish effective unity in the direction of the war on the Allied side', and therefore to set up 'some kind of Allied Joint Council, with permanent military and probably naval and economic staffs attached to work out the plans for the Allies, for submission to the several Governments concerned'. Lloyd George obviously hoped that this Council would support his own proposals for attacking elsewhere than on the Western Front. He told President Wilson that he wanted to strike at Germany's Allies, and 'to knock away the props upon which the German military power now increasingly depends', rather than to concentrate on attacking the German army in costly and ineffective assaults on the Western Front.[2] The

---

of the American army was much delayed. The training was held up, for example, because the building of cantonments for troops did not get under way for about six months. Congress had appropriated 12,000,000 dollars in 1916 for machine guns, but at the time of the American entry into the war the War Department had not decided on the type to be adopted. In calculating the numbers of American troops an American division should be reckoned as almost double the size of an English division.

[1] Haig, op. cit., p. 251.

[2] Lloyd George committed himself to the remarkable assertion that the 'winter months' were the 'best campaigning season in south-eastern Europe and in Turkey and "Asia" '.

French representatives on the proposed Inter-Allied Council were unlikely to accept Lloyd George's plan to 'knock away the props', or even
to support his proposals for stopping the offensive in the west, as long
as these offensives were being carried out by the British Army. In his
eagerness, however, to break the domination of Haig and Robertson,
Lloyd George was willing to accept French proposals which would
take the control of military policy out of British hands, and thus
prevent Haig from planning more offensives.

On September 25 Lloyd George and Robertson had a meeting with
Painlevé[1] and Foch at Boulogne. At this meeting (which seems to have
been suggested by the French) it was agreed to withdraw the British
and French heavy artillery from Italy, since General Cadorna was
unable to continue the offensive for which the guns were being provided.[2] Lloyd George had been compelled to give up his plan for
driving Austria out of the war, but he was still hoping to destroy
Turkey. Robertson wrote to Haig that he had 'recently' had to argue
against 'a scheme for operations in the Aden hinterland involving the
employment of not less than a division. I have also had to destroy one
for landing *ten* divisions at Alexandretta, all of which would have had
to come from you. Further I have had to fight against sending up more
divisions to Mesopotamia.'

These Turkish plans do not appear to have been discussed at Boulogne.
The French were mainly interested in getting Lloyd George to agree
that the British army should take over more of the French line. They
put the case largely on political grounds; the Chamber of Deputies was
asking for more men to be released for agriculture, and more leave to
be given to the troops. Pétain's reason was that he wanted to keep
forty divisions in reserve in view of the possibility of a German attack
on the Anglo-French front together with an outflanking move through
Switzerland.

Lloyd George, without consulting Haig, agreed in principle, but the
amount of the extension and the time at which it should take place was
left to be settled by the two Commanders-in-Chief. After the meeting
Lloyd George and Painlevé discussed privately the general lines of a
scheme for an Inter-Allied War Council, with an inter-Allied General
Staff as its permanent executive. Foch would be appointed Chief of this
General Staff, and would control the Anglo-French reserves. Lloyd

---

[1] Painlevé had succeeded Ribot as President of the French Council of Ministers
on September 12, 1917.
[2] See above, p. 290.

George and Painlevé hoped that public opinion in England would later acquiesce in the appointment of Foch as 'generalissimo'. Lloyd George proposed to appoint Sir Henry Wilson as British representative on the organisation.

Lloyd George did not mention the new scheme to Robertson; he could be sure that neither Robertson nor Haig would accept it. Haig had already heard from Lord Derby that Lloyd George and Painlevé, for different reasons, were trying to get an Allied General Staff; he did not know until October 3 of Lloyd George's acquiescence 'in principle' to the extension of the British line, though Lloyd George and Robertson came to see him after the Boulogne Conference, and Lloyd George had said that Painlevé wanted the extension.[1] Haig spoke strongly against any such proposal until next year's plans had been settled. Lloyd George asked him to give an opinion on the role of the British forces if the Russians took no further part in the war, and the Italians and French continued to do 'very little'. Haig gave his general view that the Allies should keep to the defensive except on the Western Front, and that the British army should continue to try to clear the Belgian coast.

Haig wrote a considered reply in a long memorandum of October 8 addressed to Robertson. He put the issue plainly: could we, in the conditions postulated by the Prime Minister, base our plans for 1918 'on a belief in the feasibility of overcoming the resistance of the German armies by direct attack before the endurance of the British Empire, and its allies remaining in the field, breaks down'? Haig's answer was two-fold. He believed that, even on the worst hypothesis of a separate Russo-German peace, the British armies in France, assisted by the French and American armies, would be 'quite capable of carrying through a sustained and successful offensive next year', if sufficient provision were made for it. Haig did not think that there was any chance of defeating Germany by indirect means; an attempt to do so by operating against Germany's allies – Austria or Turkey – would have no more than local success, and would prevent an offensive on the Western Front.

Haig argued that the Flanders offensive was having a decisive effect.[2] He showed that he still had some hopes of a larger success, and hinted at 'the possible developments' in the situation on the Western Front 'during the next few weeks'. He was, however, particularly concerned to persuade the War Cabinet against the proposal for an extension of

[1] Haig thought that Robertson 'came badly out of this'.
[2] See above, p. 292.

the British front. He argued that this proposal was both unwise and unfair; unwise because it would interfere with the training of his armies for the offensive of 1918, and unfair because it was putting too much strain on the British troops.[1] The French armies already had much more leave – ten days in every four months – than the British armies; the latter had done much more fighting in the summer of 1917 and would do more in 1918 than the French, and would reasonably complain if preferential treatment in the matter of leave continued to be given to the French. Haig thought that the French demand was due to political and not to military reasons. The British line was shorter than the French line, but mileage was not a fair test. The 'true test' was 'the relative number of enemy divisions engaged by us and still more the role to be allotted to us in next year's campaign'. The French could not 'be expected to admit it officially', but 'the state of their armies and of the reserve man-power behind the armies' was such that 'neither the French Government nor the military authorities' would 'venture to call on their troops for any further great and sustained offensive effort' at all events until it was evident that the enemy's strength had been 'definitely and finally broken'. In these circumstances Haig regarded it as 'beyond argument' that everything should be done 'by our Allies as well as by ourselves to enable the British armies, which alone could be made capable of a great offensive effort', to be as strong as possible; for this purpose they needed 'training, leave, and rest'.[2]

Haig therefore asked that the French request should be refused, 'even to the point of answering threats by threats'. He then made a strong appeal for the support of his general strategical policy by the Prime Minister and the War Cabinet.

One more indispensable condition of decisive success on the Western Front is that the War Cabinet should have a firm faith in its possibility and resolve finally and unreservedly to concentrate our resources on seeking it, and to do so at once. To gain decisive

[1] There was also the important point that the British armies had little 'freedom of manœuvre'. Their bases of supply and of concentration were so near to the front lines that a withdrawal on any considerable scale without disastrous consequences was far less possible than on the French front.

[2] In December, 1917, Haig insisted again on the necessity of leave for the men. He said that they were given at most fourteen days in fifteen months. Over 115,000 had had no leave for a year. In January, 1918, the CIGS told the War Cabinet that there were, at the time, about 350,000 French and only 80,000 British on leave. In July, 1917, the British figures were only 50,000. The main difficulty lay in finding shipping for the cross-Channel transport.

success . . . we have need of every man, gun, and aeroplane that can be provided, and of taking their training in hand as early as possible this winter. To ensure this we must take risks elsewhere and cut down our commitments in all other theatres to the minimum necessary to protect really vital interests. This principle applies equally to our dealings with our Allies. We cannot afford to assist them directly, and it is not in their own interests that the efforts of the only really effective offensive army which will exist next year in the alliance should throw away what is a good prospect and practically the only prospect of a real victory by disseminating its forces. Victory against a strong and determined foe has never been won by such a course and never can be. We must insist that our Allies shall rely on themselves for defence, and the most effective assistance we can give them is by forcing Germany to use up her troops in guarding herself against our blows.

Robertson thought this memorandum 'splendid'. Lloyd George was bound to regard it with dismay. In spite of the relative failures on the Somme and in Flanders, and the failure of Nivelle's offensive, and in spite of the evidence that the German army was not collapsing, and that it could be heavily reinforced from the East, Haig was proposing another great offensive in 1918. Moreover the reasons which he gave for refusing to take over more of the front were, in part at least, that his own army was exhausted and would consist during the winter largely of untrained troops. This view was the more alarming because Haig admitted that the French armies were in a far worse state, and that not much was to be expected from the Italians.

In Lloyd George's view a continuance of Haig's policy would lead to defeat. In Haig's view any other policy would lead to defeat. The War Cabinet considered Haig's report on October 11. Lloyd George summed up the four possibilities open to the Allies: (i) they might accept the views of Haig and Robertson, and reduce to a minimum all their commitments elsewhere; (ii) they might concentrate mainly on the Western Front, but without reducing to any considerable extent their forces elsewhere; (iii) they might accept the French proposals to stand everywhere on the defensive, intensify their 'economic warfare', and await the arrival of the Americans; (iv) they might try to 'knock the props' from under Germany, and to counter the loss of Russia by attacking Turkey.

The Turkish plan was set aside almost at once. Allenby said that he would need at least thirteen more divisions. These divisions could not be found; there was not enough shipping to transport them, and the navy, in view of the immense demands made for the passage of American troops, could not spare the escort vessels. Lloyd George then proposed that the Cabinet should ask the advice of Sir John French and Sir Henry Wilson. The Cabinet agreed, but, if these advisers reported against the views of Haig and Robertson, what was to be the next step? French and Wilson were likely to be critical of Haig. Haig had taken French's place, and was unwilling to give Wilson further employment. Robertson wrote to Haig that he thought of resigning. Haig advised him to protest, but not to resign.

The reports were of little use. French gave most of his space to criticisms of Haig and Robertson, and ended with a recommendation in favour of a defensive policy, with the corollary that the British army should take over more of the line. He also recommended the establishment of an Inter-Allied War Council to survey the situation and formulate plans. Lloyd George had already talked to him about this proposal and French's support of it was not unexpected. Wilson also favoured the War Council project. He did not regard an attack on Turkey as practicable, and pointed out that the Allied superiority in numbers would not be decisively increased until after the arrival of the Americans in full force, i.e. after 1918. Thus the two reports agreed in adjourning a decision, or rather handing it over to another body not yet established, but in each case – and in French's case more definitely – the argument was in favour of a defensive policy in 1918.

On October 14 Lloyd George raised once more with the French the question of a permanent military staff 'to study the war as a whole'. Painlevé discussed the matter again with Lloyd George on October 30 when the Italian situation showed the urgency of some such measure. Lloyd George wanted the organisation to be established at Boulogne or some other town near to the British front. Painlevé suggested Paris; Lloyd George considered that the choice of Paris would associate it too closely with the French Government. Finally they agreed on Versailles. Lloyd George also insisted that no member of the organisation should be at the same time Chief of Staff in his own country. The plans were further considered, and accepted by the Italians, at an Inter-Allied conference at Rapallo on November 4–7. The French nominated Foch as their representative, but Lloyd George continued to hold the view that it was undesirable for a national Chief of Staff to be a member of the inter-Allied organisation. Weygand – Foch's senior staff officer –

was then appointed in place of Foch, and Lloyd George nominated Wilson.

On November 14 Lloyd George announced to the House of Commons the establishment of the Supreme War Council. He knew that the proposal would be strongly criticised by the supporters of Haig. Robertson had opposed it at the Rapallo meeting. On his way to Rapallo Lloyd George had met Haig in Paris and told him of the plan. Haig answered that the proposal had been considered for three years and always rejected as unworkable. Lloyd George also said to Haig that attacks were being made upon him (Lloyd George) in the press, and that these attacks were 'evidently inspired by the Military'. He proposed to reply to them in a speech to the effect that, if his advice had been taken, the military situation would be much better.

Lloyd George made his speech in Paris on November 12. He criticised the army leaders very severely, though only indirectly. He described the Western Front as 'an impenetrable barrier' and said that, although the Allies had won great victories, 'when I look at the appalling casualty lists I sometimes wish it had not been necessary to win so many'. The speech caused much indignation in England; Derby wrote to Haig that he would probably have to show his confidence in Haig by suggesting a peerage for him.[1] Carson, though (since July, 1917) a member of the War Cabinet, repudiated Lloyd George's speech but none the less did not resign because he thought Lloyd George 'the only man to win the war'.[2] Lloyd George, however, in spite of Asquith's opposition, won his case in the House of Commons. He had thus out-manœuvred Robertson. He was indeed, at this time, more concerned to circumvent Robertson – whom he regarded as intriguing against him – than to supplant Haig. He said to Esher on November 12 that he would have liked Haig as CIGS and that he understood Haig's insistence upon getting more divisions for the Western Front.[3] Haig, although he disliked the Versailles plan, had reassured Lloyd George by his frankness and honesty. Haig had told Lloyd George that, if the Cabinet decided to set up a Supreme War Council, he would accept the decision.

Haig, in the meantime, had been further disquieted by a letter of

[1] Derby had already made a proposal of this kind to Haig, and Haig had refused it. Lloyd George's speech was made at a luncheon to which all the Deputies and Senators were invited. Lloyd George himself was uncertain how the French would respond to his plain speaking about the failures of Allied military leadership. Esher, op. cit., iv, p. 159.

[2] Hankey, op. cit., ii, 728.

[3] Esher, ibid.

November 3 from the War Office on man-power. He was told that the reinforcements available to him in 1918 would be far short of his requirements. His infantry was already 75,000 below their establishment. It seemed likely that by October 31, 1918, the deficiency would be about 260,000. Haig's own calculation on the basis of the War Office figures of replacements was that he might be 250,000 short at the end of March, and no less than 400,000 short at the end of October, 1918. Haig gave his figures to the War Office on November 24. He said that 'under such conditions not only will the offensive power of the British armies in France be completely paralysed, but their defensive power will also be curtailed, and they will not be able to hold the same amount of line as heretofore'. Haig was then told that the War Cabinet would shortly come to a decision on the number of men available for military service. He could have little hope that this decision would give him the reinforcements which he regarded as necessary.

The first session of the Supreme War Council had taken place at the close of the Rapallo Conference. The Council had merely instructed the military representatives to report on the situation on the Italian front, and, after a general view of the military position elsewhere, to advise on the amount of Anglo-French assistance to Italy. The second session of the Council was not held until December 1. Clemenceau, now Prime Minister of France,[1] suggested that the military representatives should consider plans for 1918. It was clear that no help would come from Russia. The Council had to estimate how many enemy divisions could be moved to the Western Front. The Italian front seemed now to have been stabilised; should the Allies use the French and British forces on this front for an offensive? Thirdly, there was the question of the transport of American troops, and the measures necessary to secure enough shipping. Finally there was the probability that the war would be won by power of endurance rather than by any military decision. Austria and Turkey were very near to collapse; would it therefore be desirable to adopt Lloyd George's plan and to isolate Germany by destroying her allies?

These questions were not new. The British and French Governments, singly or together, had been discussing them for months past. The new feature, especially for the British Government, and above all for the Prime Minister, was that the discussions were taking place without the presence of the Chief of the Imperial General Staff and the Commander-

[1] Clemenceau took office on November 16 as President of the Council and Minister of War.

in-Chief of the British armies in France. The Supreme War Council was unlikely to devise any new and startling solutions. Robertson, on November 19, had already given the War Cabinet a memorandum on future military policy. He had asked whether it would be better to try to win the war in 1918 or to wait until 1919. Robertson's answer was similar to Haig's answer. The burden of supporting the war in 1918 would rest primarily on Great Britain. If Russia were to rally (Robertson did not expect her to do so) and Italy to recover the power to attack, we should try to force a decision in the spring. If Russia made a separate peace, and Italy still needed the help of British and French troops, we might think it better to wait for the Americans, and to defer our decisive effort until 1919. On the other hand the reasons which might lead us to choose delay might well convince the Germans that they should attempt a decision in 1918.

In any event our policy during the winter should be to concentrate our resources on the Western Front, and to accept the greatest strain on these resources elsewhere in order to make the concentration as strong as possible. We could not know what the general situation would be in the spring of 1918, but even if we were unable to attempt a decisive attack, we ought not to stand merely on the defensive and allow the enemy the initiative in choosing when and where to attack the Allies. Thus the critical question was one of man-power and concentration of resources.

Robertson's memorandum was an attempt to support Haig's view, and also to get the War Cabinet to come to a decision about calling up more men. Two days after the memorandum was submitted, the Bolsheviks put out their demands for an armistice, and on December 3 Russian and German delegates agreed on armistice terms. The Germans had already begun to move troops from east to west. They might now be expected to do so in larger numbers than Haig or Robertson had anticipated. On December 3 also the Cambrai battle came to an end. The possibility of a British offensive on the Western Front in 1918 was disappearing. The initiative must pass to the Germans if they chose to take it; they were likely to do so, since if they waited until 1919 the Americans would have arrived in force to turn the balance against them.

Haig therefore decided that for the time at least his armies must remain on the defensive. He told his army commanders on December 3 that

the general situation on the Russian and Italian fronts, combined with the paucity of reinforcements which we are likely to receive, will in all probability necessitate our adopting a defensive attitude for the next few months. We must be prepared to meet a strong and sustained hostile offensive. It is therefore of first importance that Army commanders should give their immediate and personal attention to the organisation of the zones for defensive purposes and to the rest and training of their troops.

So ended the campaign of 1917 for wearing down the enemy and driving him from the Belgian coast.

The effect of the personal disagreements between the Prime Minister and his military advisers, however, did not and could not end with the closing of the 1917 campaign. The intrigues spread from the chiefs to their subordinates, and resulted in attempts on each side to influence the press and public opinion.[1] Haig and Robertson could not forget Lloyd George's speech in Paris. On the other hand Esher, who had an intimate knowledge of what was happening, and, to a remarkable extent, had the confidence of both parties, told Haig on December 2, 1917, that Lloyd George had spoken to him with 'great bitterness and vehemence' of the 'intrigues' in the army against him and his Government: 'his means of information are varied and go deep into the camp of his opponents. Of this there was ample proof from what he said to me. Conversations with pressmen, communications with critics and wreckers of the Government, all brought to him by agents who have a footing in what he calls "both camps".'[2]

Haig and Robertson, and especially the latter, who was in closer contact with Lloyd George, regarded the Prime Minister not merely as mistaken but as crooked and untrustworthy. Robertson wrote to Haig on December 8, 1917, of 'the impossibility of honestly working with such a man'.[3] Haig noted in his diary on September 24, 1917: 'how unfortunate the country seems to be to have such an unreliable man at the head of affairs in this crisis'. Milner, like Esher, did his best to improve the relations between Haig and the Prime Minister. He told Haig on December 26, 1917, that he was 'more than ever impressed' with Lloyd George's 'ability and power of work'.[4]

[1] Esher, *Journals and Letters*, iv, 165.
[2] Northcliffe, who had hitherto supported Haig, turned against him in December. At the end of the year Northcliffe was promoted to a viscountcy on the recommendation of Lloyd George.
[3] Haig, id., 271.
[4] Haig, id., 274. A month earlier, on November 24, Hankey spoke of Lloyd George as the 'only possible saviour of the country. Lloyd George saw further and had more driving power than Asquith.' Esher, ibid., 159.

One comment, in a letter from Esher, brings out the strange and terrible contrast between the sufferings of the soldiers in the front line and the unpleasing squabbles among the highly placed staff officers. Esher wrote on November 5:

> There were such crowds of people at the Crillon yesterday. All Paris in the tea-room. L.G. came down there and walked about among the people. The soldiers were gathered in groups, representing different 'hates'. Robertson's lot. Henry Wilson's lot. D.H.'s lot. It was comic. Like the *Chocolate Soldier*, and one expected a chorus, – 'Thank the Lord the war is over.' But it is not – alas.[1]

[1] Esher, ibid., 153–4. Great Britain was not alone in suffering from 'hates' and 'lots' in high places. French military (and political) intrigues are conspicuous in Poincaré's memoirs; the 'hates' in Italy, and still more in Russia are equally well known. Fortunately the German higher direction of the war was in no better state. Major-General Hoffmann, possibly the ablest German general, agreed in his diary (*War Diaries*, i, 73) with remarks by Tirpitz in August, 1915, 'When one gets a closer view of influential people, their bad relations with each other, their conflicting ambitions, all the slander and the hatred, one must always bear in mind that it is much worse among the French, English, and Russians, or one might well be nervous.' Later Hoffmann wrote: 'The incompetence of the authorities and of GHQ is greater on the other side than with us, and that is saying a lot' (ib., 97). Hoffmann's view of his own Allies was that 'the Austrians are really impossible. Not content with running away, they lie and send false reports, and with it all they are quite unashamed and make difficulties wherever they can. I should like to go to war with *them*.' ib. 188.

CHAPTER 22

The Allies on the defensive: Lloyd George, Haig, and Robertson

Haig followed his instructions of December 3 to his army commanders with a general memorandum on defensive measures. This memorandum did not exclude the possibility of 'an offensive at some point, as the surest means of assisting the French, should the weight of the enemy's blow fall upon them, or some other portion of our own line'. The offensive was obviously to be limited; there was no mention of victory in 1918. The memorandum then developed the most recent ideas (borrowed largely from the Germans)[1] about a scheme of defence; the organisation of an outpost zone (later called a 'forward zone'), a battle zone, 2000–3000 yards deep, and a rear zone some four or more miles behind the battle zone.[2] This system, with the important reservation that it might break down in conditions of real or artificial fog, was undoubtedly most effective in breaking up an enemy attack, though it

[1] The memorandum was based on a captured German manual of August, 1917.

[2] Churchill has written a vivid account of the new defence organisation in March, 1918, in an area where the necessary works had been fully carried out. 'The system of continuous trenches with their barbed wire networks, their parapets, firing steps, traverses and dug-outs, the first line of which was manned in great strength and often constituted the strongest line of resistance, had vanished. Contact with the enemy was maintained only by a fringe of outposts, some of which were fortified, while others trusted merely to concealment. Behind these, over a distance of two or three thousand yards were sited intricate systems of machine-gun nests, nearly all operating by flank fire and mutually supporting each other. Slender communication trenches enabled these to be approached and relieved by night. The barbed wire networks, instead of being drawn laterally in a continuous belt across the front, lay obliquely with intervals so as to draw the attacker into avenues mercilessly swept by machine-gun fire. Open spaces between important points were reserved for the full fury of the protecting barrages. This was the Battle Zone. Two thousand yards or so farther in the rear were the field battery positions. Strong works to which the long disused word "redoubt" has been applied, and deep grids of trenches and deeper dug-outs elaborately camouflaged, provided for the assembling and maintenance of the supporting troops.' (*World Crisis, 1916–18*, Part ii, 389–90.)

was contrary to a very long tradition that the British army fought in a continuous line, and was not divided up into little pockets or enclosed in 'birdcages'.[1] A note appended to Haig's memorandum was a grim commentary on the offensive of 1917. The note offered guidance on 'the manner of dealing with the Passchendaele and Flesquières (Cambrai) salients.[2] The salients – won and held at such cost – were described as 'unsuitable to fight a defensive battle in'. They were to be held unless they were attacked in great force. In the latter case they were to be used 'to wear out and break up the enemy's advancing troops' before they reached the battle zone of defence which would be 'sited approximately as a chord across the base of each salient'.

There was, in fact, a great deal to be done not only in the training of the armies in defensive tactics, but in the preparation of defensive positions. For more than two years the British armies had concentrated on the attack; the earlier defensive lines had not been kept in repair, and in any case were out of date. Some of them had been filled in by French peasants wanting to get their land into full production. There was not enough labour for the immense work of digging and wiring and building strong posts. Too often the infantry were deprived of rest or training in order to carry out these tasks; in January they were short of barbed wire.[3] Haig was thus unwilling as ever to take over more of the French line. He had promised Pétain, however, in October, 1917, to consider his proposals.

In mid-December Clemenceau, as well as Pétain, pressed very strongly that the French demands should be met. Haig then promised to extend the British front as far as the Oise before the end of January. Clemenceau, at the Supreme War Council on January 30, tried to secure a further extension, but Lloyd George opposed it, and Pétain was satisfied with Haig's concession. On January 10 the Military Representatives at Versailles formally recommended that the point of junction

[1] *Military Operations, 1918, France and Belgium*, i, 256–8. It is difficult to understand why, unlike the Germans and French, the British at first put a considerable proportion of their troops into the forward zone, which was almost certain to suffer very heavily from enemy bombardment. The troops still kept to the old names – 'front', 'support', and 'reserve' lines. For maps of two corps defences in March, 1918, see *Military Operations*, ib., 39–41.

[2] On January 10, 1918, instructions were sent to Fourth Army HQ to draw up plans for a voluntary withdrawal from the Passchendaele salient.

[3] It is hardly necessary to mention that the 'bull-dozer' and many other 'post-war' mechanical devices for digging and clearing sites were not known in 1918. Digging was mainly a matter of hard physical labour as it had been in Roman times.

between the two armies be roughly on the left bank of the Ailette; they suggested that the two commanders should settle the exact place. In fact the point of junction was not pushed beyond the immediate neighbourhood of Barisis, and did not reach the Ailette.

At the end of December, 1917, there seemed little doubt that the enemy was aiming at a decisive attack in the west. The War Office and GHQ agreed that if the Germans withdrew troops from the Italian front as well as from Russia and Roumania they would have 185 divisions in France and Flanders by the end of February, 1918, 195 at the end of March, and 200 at the beginning of May. Thus at this latter date before the arrival of the Americans in force the Germans would have a numerical superiority in fighting troops of some 200,000.[1] The question of man-power was therefore most urgent.

In December, 1917, the War Cabinet had set up a special committee on man-power. The committee consisted of the Prime Minister, Curzon, G. N. Barnes, Carson, and General Smuts. Apart from Smuts, it did not include any soldiers,[2] but the problem before it was not primarily one to be settled by soldiers. The Commander-in-Chief was asking for every man who could be spared. The task of the committee was to estimate how many men were available for every kind of service, and how they could best be distributed. The committee adopted certain priorities; the fighting needs of the navy and air force; shipbuilding and the construction of tanks and aeroplanes; food production, food storage, and timber-felling in order to save shipping space. These priorities were necessary because the survival of the Allies implied not only keeping the armies at the fullest possible strength, but securing the general maintenance of the national life. Moreover the transport of the American troops who were to redress the balance of numbers depended largely on British shipping.

The conclusion reached was that only 100,000 'new' men in class 'A' medical category would be available for the army in addition to the 120,000 youths under nineteen on January 1, 1918, who would reach the age of military service during the year.[3] In other words, the limit of withdrawal of able-bodied men from civilian occupations without

---

[1] The Allied superiority in numbers during their first attacks of 1917 had been greater.

[2] The Director of Military Intelligence and the Adjutant-General were called to the committee to discuss the figures supplied by the War Office.

[3] Parliament had laid down that no youths under nineteen were to be sent overseas except in a grave emergency. In the crisis of March, 1918, the age-limit was reduced to 18½.

grave danger to the 'war effort' as a whole had nearly been reached. The Ministry of National Service put this figure – on the basis of total civilian man-power available – at 150,000, of which 50,000 were required for the navy and the Royal Naval Air Service. They proposed to find the greater part of the 150,000 men by taking 62,000 from the manufacture of munitions, 50,000 from coal-mining, 12,000 from railways and transport, 3000 from agriculture, and 8000 from public utility and other 'certified' occupations.

The War Office, on the other hand, asked for 615,000 new men. The man-power committee found it difficult to understand why this demand was so high. They had been told at least by Haig, and to some extent by Robertson, that German man-power was running out, and that the 'wearing-down' process had had its effect on the German army. It had been known for months past that the Germans would be able to take their best troops away from the Russian front. The Allies were now planning to stand on the defensive or at least to carry out only limited operations, and should therefore suffer fewer casualties. It was also not clear why more of the officers and men in Great Britain could not be sent overseas; the Admiralty, on December 21, 1917, had expressed the view that the navy could deal with an invading force 70,000 strong.[1] Finally the committee proposed that Haig should cut down from twelve to nine the number of infantry battalions in a division, and that he should also reduce the number of his cavalry. The French – and the Germans – had already reduced the infantry strength of their divisions. The troops thus released could be used by Haig to form a mobile reserve, and the infantry of a division would be supported by a higher proportion of artillery.

The Army Council protested strongly against the conclusions of the committee; they described it as 'taking an unreasonably grave risk of losing the war, and sacrificing to no purpose the British army on the Western Front'. In view of the different estimates put forward at different times by the military authorities, and of the fact that Haig's own view of the man-power situation had been more optimistic when he wanted to continue the Passchendaele offensive, the War Cabinet were disinclined to set aside the committee's report. It was indeed hardly possible for them to do so without an equally grave risk of crippling the immense civilian effort upon which the safety of the armies also depended. In any case, a more drastic 'comb-out' of men in industry could have had little effect on the situation in March, 1918,

[1] See above, p. 37.

since none of those secured in January would have been trained by the time of the opening of the German offensive. The only way of reinforcing the British army in France during the early months of 1918 with trained soldiers was by taking more men from the forces at home, or by depleting the armies in other fronts. About 130,000 'A' men were sent from Great Britain to the Western Front between January 1 and March 21, 1918. It is still disputed whether the War Office could not have found a larger number from the army at home.[1] The reinforcement of the Western Front from other fronts was not undertaken to any large extent. One division was brought back from Italy. The War Cabinet, and especially the Prime Minister – with his dangerous enthusiasm for a Turkish campaign – must be regarded as responsible for the policy involved in keeping, at a critical time, so large a number of troops in subsidiary theatres of war.

While the War Cabinet was concerned immediately with the problem of British man-power, they had also to consider general questions of policy and to decide on plans for 1918. The Supreme War Council did not meet between December 1, 1917, and January 30, 1918. though its military representatives circulated a number of Notes to the Allied Governments. Meanwhile the Germans were negotiating with the Bolsheviks, or rather intending to dictate to them conditions of peace. The Germans wanted a separate 'annexationist' peace with Russia. The Bolsheviks, however, at the opening of the conference proposed a general invitation to all the belligerents to enter into immediate negotiations – at Brest-Litowsk – for a peace without indemnities or annexations, and based upon the right of self-determination of peoples. Kühlmann, the German State Secretary for Foreign Affairs and chief German civilian representative at the conference, realised that a general proposal of this kind might have a disruptive effect among the peoples

[1] Lloyd George always maintained that the number of troops kept at home was settled by the War Office in relation to the possibilities of invasion, and that the question never came before the War Cabinet. In 1935 Colonel C. Allanson, who was a GSO I at the War Office in 1918, confirmed to Captain Liddell Hart that the general reserve of 120,000 was kept at home instead of in France on the advice of the General Staff. Their reasons were (i) that it would be better concealed in Great Britain from the enemy Intelligence; (ii) that it could be moved to France during the eighteen days over which Haig said that his existing forces could hold a German offensive; (iii) that its presence at home would be good for public morale which, especially after Passchendaele, tended to regard men sent to France as certain to be killed; (iv) that it would save foreign exchange. Liddell Hart, *Memoirs*, i. 365 and 369.

of the Entente Powers, and that he could safely allow the Bolsheviks to make it because the Entente Powers would certainly reject it. Hence the invitation was issued on December 25, and the conference adjourned to allow time for the delegations from other Powers to arrive. Within a few days the Germans made it plain to the Bolsheviks that Poland, Courland, and Lithuania would be detached from Russia on the supposed ground that the inhabitants of these portions of the former Tsarist Empire wanted to leave it. So ended the German adherence to the principle of self-determination.

The Bolshevik proposals for an immediate general peace were obviously unacceptable to the British and French – and Americans; Lloyd George answered them indirectly in a speech to British Trade Union representatives, and Wilson in an address to Congress which contained his 'Fourteen Points'.[1] The War Cabinet also decided to examine once again what were the prospects of victory. Haig and Robertson were asked to give their views. Robertson answered on December 29 (he had not yet received the report of the committee on man-power) that the Allies should prepare for a German attempt to win the war before the arrival of the Americans. Hence they must act on the defensive in spite of the disadvantages of losing the initiative. The Germans might attack in Italy or on the Western Front. They might aim at Paris or the Channel ports. The British people would have to realise that they were fighting for their existence; the conditions of success were to provide as many men as possible to fight on land and as many ships as possible to carry supplies and American troops. If we could hold out against the German attack, our own opportunity would come later on. The War Cabinet asked Robertson whether he thought that the chances of victory were sufficient to justify a continuance of the war. Robertson's answer, as might have been foreseen, was that victory depended on the establishment of superior numbers on the Western Front.

The next step taken by the War Cabinet – on January 7 – was to invite Haig to London and to enquire whether he expected the position to improve in six months or a year. Haig was never a good speaker. He gave the impression that he did not expect the Germans to attack, since they were likely to realise that, if their attack failed, they would be defeated in the autumn. Next day, however, he submitted an answer in writing to the effect that the Germans might well attempt to force a decision by attacking the British, French, or Italians. Haig regarded

[1] See below, pp. 399–401.

such an attempt 'in the light of a gamble with a determination to risk everything' in order to win quickly. The Allies must therefore prepare to meet the attack and 'to replace the losses which would certainly be incurred'. Haig now knew the limits set by the committee's report to the man-power available for the Western Front. He said that the numbers which the committee proposed to give him were inadequate. As for the future, the military situation would depend on our ability to replace our losses. If we could provide reinforcements, possibly at the rate of 100,000 a month, we could certainly expect an improvement, and look forward to obtaining 'satisfactory terms of peace'.

Haig spoke personally to the Prime Minister in an attempt to explain the contradiction between his two statements. He said that, if the German military authorities had their way, they would attack. If the attack failed, the internal situation in Germany would mean a collapse after 1918. It was thus clear from their reports that Haig and Robertson expected a critical period of some months before the arrival of the Americans in large numbers.[1]

How soon could the Americans arrive, and how soon could they take over a part of the line? On their landing in Europe they would only be partially trained; their senior officers and staffs would be without experience of fighting. One method of using them – at least for some time – would have been to incorporate them in Allied formations. Robertson made a proposal of this kind in January, 1918; the Prime Minister had also suggested it to the United States Government. Whatever the military advantages, there were strong political reasons, and reasons of national sentiment on the American side, against merging, even for a time, United States brigades or battalions with the British or French armies. American opinion, official and unofficial, not unnaturally wished that General Pershing, the United States Commander-in-Chief, should keep his forces together as a separate body under his control. Any other arrangement would have been exploited by German propaganda as a means of arousing domestic discontent in the United States.

On January 21 the Allied military representatives at Versailles circulated a Note[2] containing recommendations for the campaign of 1918. They advised that the Western Front – including Italy – should

---

[1] On December 1 there were in France two regular American divisions, each about 27,000 strong, and two divisions of the National Guard. A fifth division arrived before the end of January.

[2] Joint Note No. 12, signed by Weygand, Cadorna, and Wilson.

be treated as a single strategic field of action, and that the French and British forces on it should be maintained at their existing totals and receive as reinforcements not less than two American divisions a month. They believed that the Allies would be able to withstand a German attack in the west, but that they could not secure a decision for themselves until 1919. There seemed no prospect of any large success in the Balkans, though the defeat of Turkey was not impossible.

The Note thus put forward the French view that victory must await the arrival of the Americans in full force; it took no account of Haig's belief that the defeat of the German offensive would itself open the way to a successful counter-offensive, and that German morale would break down if, after very heavy losses, the great effort of the German army failed. Furthermore the Note ignored the fact that the French and British forces were unlikely to be maintained at their existing strength.

On January 23 the military representatives circulated another Note (No. 14). They asked, as a matter of urgency, for the formation of a general reserve. The British, French, and American Commanders-in-Chief met Foch and Robertson for a discussion of the proposal. Haig and Pétain explained that they had about a third of their troops in reserve; that these reserves were available for either army in case of need, and that their forces, which were already too weak for an offensive or counter-attack on a large scale, must become weaker owing to lack of reinforcements. As Robertson pointed out, the American army was the real reserve on the Western Front.

General Pershing said that he hoped that the four divisions already in France would be in the line or reserve as soon as possible, and that he would have eighteen divisions in France or on their way by the end of July, but that his time-table was being affected by delays in shipping and at the French ports, and by a shortage of equipment, munitions, and aeroplanes. General Pershing repeated his view that the American army must be an independent unit with its own front. All the generals agreed that the British and French troops in Italy should be brought back; there was, however, considerable difference of view on the question of a counter-attack. Haig still argued that, if the enemy were held, the Allies ought to attempt an offensive, and not merely a counter-attack, but that they could not do so with the man-power at their disposition.

The Supreme War Council met at Versailles at the end of January. Lloyd George and Milner represented the British Government. The Council accepted at once the general principle of a co-ordinated defence from the North Sea to the Adriatic with preparations for counter-offensive action wherever possible. Haig and Pétain pointed out that while they agreed with the plan of counter-offensives – Haig had always been convinced of their necessity – they would not have men to carry them out on a large scale. Lloyd George asked for another statement of figures. This statement,[1] which was laid before the War Council on January 31, showed that at the end of January, 1918, the Allies had on the Western Front a numerical superiority of 164,000 – 100 French and 57 British divisions to 171 German divisions. This superiority would soon disappear, since 20 or more German divisions were expected to arrive. The Germans also had nearly a million men available for keeping their divisions up to strength, whereas the British had only 200,000 and the French 170,000. Thirty British and twenty-seven French divisions would have to be broken up before the autumn.

On the basis of these figures Foch complained that the British Government was not making an adequate contribution. Lloyd George replied by showing that since July 1, 1916, the British had suffered heavier losses than the French, and that British man-power was also needed to hold the seas, build ships, produce coal and transport troops and supplies for the Allies generally. Haig – in spite of his own demands for more men – thought that Lloyd George 'answered well'.

Clemenceau then pointed out that the proposals of the military representatives for a 'knock-out' offensive against Turkey were made on condition that the effectives on the Western Front could be maintained. Since this condition could not be fulfilled, the proposals should be dropped. Lloyd George refused to accept this view. He said that the margin of safety on the Western Front was too high. The Germans had held their front against the Allied attacks with an inferiority of 2 to $3\frac{1}{2}$. Lloyd George did not think that the Allies could drive the enemy back to the Rhine; hence they must try to force one of Germany's Allies out of the war. Lloyd George therefore was unwilling to bring back troops from the Near East, and to surrender the conquests made in Palestine and Mesopotamia in order to strengthen the Western Front. Some men might be spared from Salonika, but, even if the Turkish campaign were abandoned, not more than two divisions would be freed. Clemenceau on the other hand, strongly disapproved of the eastern plan and insisted

---

[1] According to (*Military Operations, France and Belgium, 1918*, i, p. 74, note 1) the figures were not printed with the minutes of the meeting. They can be inferred, however, from the discussion. In the absence of the actual tables it is impossible to say how these totals were reached.

that the first consideration must be the security of the Western Front until the Americans were available in full force.

The Council accepted Note 12 as the basis of their policy, with the reservation that no action should be undertaken in the eastern theatre for two months. They also noted that the British Government had made it clear that 'in utilising in the most effective fashion the forces already at its disposal in the Eastern theatre, it has no intention of diverting forces from the Western Front or in any way relaxing its efforts to maintain the safety of that front, which it regards as a vital interest of the whole alliance'.

The Council then discussed probable action on the Western Front. They could not make more than vague recommendations, since it was impossible to forecast what the situation would be, or to know whether a large offensive would be practicable. In any case Pétain and Haig had said that they would not have the men to carry it out. Pétain also argued that there must be some general authority – in the event of a combined offensive – to direct the Commanders-in-Chief when and where to attack. The Council agreed that the co-ordination should be carried out by their own representatives. The most urgent problem, however, was that of co-ordinating not attack but defence, in other words, the provision of an adequate inter-allied reserve. There was agreement about the need of such a reserve in addition to the separate reserves of the armies. Where was it to be found? How was it to be controlled? There were no divisions available on the British and French fronts. The Allied forces on the Italian front were nearly 1,500,000 strong, and the armies – mainly Austro-Hungarian – opposed to them were only 860,000. It seemed safe therefore to recall the 98,000 British and 135,000 French from this front. The Italian Ministers, however, were strongly opposed to any weakening of their front.

The question of control was even more difficult. The obvious solution would have been the appointment of a single Commander-in-Chief. At this time only the French Government would have agreed to this plan, and their agreement would have been conditional upon the appointment of a Frenchman. If the reserve were put under the control of a separate commander or of a committee, should the commander – or the committee – merely decide where the reserve was to go, and then hand it over to the Commander-in-Chief on the front concerned? After considerable debate, Lloyd George proposed – and his colleagues agreed – that the Supreme War Council should delegate to an Executive Committee composed of the permanent British, Italian, and

American military representatives on the Council, and General Foch, certain powers amounting to the control of the reserve. They were to determine its strength and location, and the contribution to be made to it by each national army. They were to decide and issue orders on the time, place, and period of employment of the reserve, and, in the case of a counter-offensive,[1] after deciding on the time, place, and strength of attack, to hand over the necessary troops to the national Commander or Commanders-in-Chief who were to conduct the operation. Foch was to be President of the Committee. In order to facilitate their decisions, members of the Committee were given the right to visit any theatre of war. Their orders with regard to the employment of the reserve were to be 'transmitted in the manner and by the persons who shall be designated by the Supreme War Council for that purpose in each particular case'.

Here indeed was the main point of argument. Haig had asked the pertinent question: 'By what channel am I to receive orders from this new body?' On February 3 the Ministers decided to designate 'the respective Military Representatives on the Executive Committee' to transmit the orders of the Supreme War Council to the armies of their several countries. Haig regarded this plan as extremely unsatisfactory. It was, in fact, from the British point of view, unconstitutional, since it assumed that the Supreme War Council had a right to issue operational orders to the army through a channel other than the Chief of the Imperial General Staff, whereas the Order in Council of January 27, 1916,[2] had expressly given the CIGS the responsibility for 'issuing the orders of the Government with regard to military operations'. More-over the Committee – or Board, as it was immediately renamed[3] – was being given authority over the British armies which deprived the Army Council and the Commanders-in-Chief of their constitutional powers of decision and responsibility.

Lloyd George regarded this objection as merely obstructive. He pro-posed to alter the Order in Council. One of his real aims was to get rid of Robertson. He had nominated Foch, the French Chief of Staff,[4] to

---

[1] The Council clearly intended, though they did not say so, that a similar procedure would be followed in the case of the use of the reserve for defensive purposes.

[2] See above, p. 157.

[3] Apparently from a certain uneasiness about entrusting powers of such im-portance to a 'committee'.

[4] Ferdinand Foch (b. 1851) came from a Catholic family in south-west France. His brother was a Jesuit and his wife a Catholic from Brittany. He received rapid

the presidency of the Committee, but had not given a place to Robertson. He also thought that once he was rid of Robertson, he could more easily control Haig. He was afraid – unnecessarily at this time – that Haig intended to repeat his 'hammering offensives' of the previous year, and that his insistence on getting more reinforcements was for this purpose and not for defence. Haig himself was indeed easier to deal with than Robertson. Haig was less worried than Robertson over the question of the control of an inter-allied reserve. He realised that he and Pétain could check the whole plan by refusing – for reasons of safety – to hand over any of the divisions under their control to form the reserve. Haig was in a strong position for making this refusal, since the Cabinet had already rejected his demands for more men.

Haig also said that Lloyd George's proposals to a large extent gave Foch the position of a *generalissimo*. Here again, he was not inclined to object. Haig – as he was soon to show in a remarkable way – had no jealousy or selfish ambition. He did not grudge Foch his new powers; he realised that, although he and Pétain 'got on well', and had no need of 'co-ordination', the Italian front needed a 'central authority', and that Foch would be likely to exercise this authority by bringing back to the most dangerous area the 'reserve of the British army in France'. Haig was called to London on February 7 to see the Prime Minister. On arriving in London two days later he explained his views to Lloyd George. He pointed out again that the military representatives at Versailles now had powers to commit the British Government – possibly against his (Haig's) own opinion – and 'to take decisions which the British Government ought alone to take'. Haig explained again that only the Army Council[1] or a Field-Marshal senior to himself could give him orders. Haig suggested that Robertson, as C I G S, after consultation with Foch should send him orders with regard to the reserve.

Haig already knew – from Lord Derby – that the Cabinet had

promotion after the Franco-Prussian war owing to the re-organisation of the French artillery. In 1895 he became a professor at the Ecole de Guerre (Staff College), but suffered as a Catholic in the anti-clerical reaction after the Dreyfus case. Clemenceau, however, was impressed with him, and agreed to his appointment as Commandant of the Ecole de Guerre in 1907. At the outbreak of war he was in command of an army corps at Nancy. Foch was a strong believer in the doctrine of the offensive, without much reference to the changed conditions of modern war, but he was not responsible for the exaggerated plan of French attack in 1914. He fell into disfavour after the battle of the Somme, and was relegated to the presidency of a board of military studies. He was brought back to the Ministry of War as Chief of Staff after Nivelle's failure.

[1] i.e. acting through the CIGS.

decided to remove Robertson, and to take from the CIGS the responsibility for 'issuing the orders of the Government in regard to military operations'. In order to give the British military representative at Versailles the necessary authority, he was to be appointed a member of the Army Council with the status of Deputy CIGS Lloyd George now told Haig that he proposed to make Wilson CIGS and to send Robertson to Versailles. Haig warned Lloyd George that Wilson was distrusted in the army, and that his appointment would be unpopular. Lloyd George then suggested that the best solution would be to bring Haig back from France, and appoint him *generalissimo* of all the British forces. Haig thought that – with a German attack impending – it would be unwise to make a sudden change in the command. After further discussion Lloyd George and Haig agreed on a formula that the military representative at Versailles should be 'absolutely free and unfettered in the advice he gives', but that he should report to the CIGS the nature of this advice 'for the information of the Cabinet, and the CIGS will advise the Cabinet thereon'.

Robertson refused to go to Versailles. He also refused an alternative suggestion that he should remain as CIGS under the new Order in Council. Lloyd George then offered the post of CIGS to Plumer. Plumer refused it because he too disapproved of the arrangement about the reserve. Lloyd George therefore appointed Wilson as CIGS, and, with Haig's consent, Rawlinson as military representative at Versailles. Lloyd George thus had his way. He wanted Haig to say that he was 'in agreement' with the changes. Haig said that he did not approve of the new plan, but felt it his duty to try to work it.

The dismissal of Robertson and the controversy over the decisions of the Supreme War Council caused much uneasiness and heated political debate. Lloyd George, however, was able to defend his case and to give Asquith's criticisms an appearance of factiousness.[1] Lloyd George survived the 'crisis', but, as Haig had realised, and Milner had anticipated, the plan for the formation of a general reserve broke down.

---

[1] Lloyd George was helped by the extraordinary indiscretion of Colonel Repington. Repington had been dismissed by *The Times* and was now correspondent of the *Morning Post*. He wrote violent attacks in this paper on the Versailles decisions. It was clear from his articles that he had been shewn the minutes of the Council. Lloyd George, though exonerating Haig from complicity in the attacks, was able to talk of a 'military cabal' and to accuse Repington of revealing military secrets. Repington and the editor of the *Morning Post* were prosecuted, and fined under the Defence of the Realm Act.

Pétain, as well as Haig, refused to contribute divisions to it. Haig stated definitely on March 2 that an enemy offensive appeared imminent on the British and French fronts; that he had disposed of all his troops to meet this attack, and could not hand over six or seven divisions without changing his plans. Since a large change was impracticable, he could not comply with the proposals of the Versailles Committee. Haig explained that the forces in reserve could not be placed in a particular area until the German intentions were known. Any one of the armies might be attacked and might need the whole of its reserves. Haig said that he had made arrangements with Pétain for mutual support. The Supreme War Council met on March 4–5 – a week before the opening of the German offensive. At this time Haig knew that the Germans had eighty-nine divisions in line or reserve opposite the British front, with about another twelve divisions available, whereas the British had forty divisions in line and eighteen in reserve. The Council agreed that for the time neither Haig nor Pétain could be asked to provide a contribution to a general reserve.

The establishment of the Supreme War Council and the discussions over the reserve thus had little immediate effect, but they prepared the way for the appointment of Foch as Commander-in-Chief of all the armies in France, though here also the force of events would have sufficed to persuade public opinion, and the appointment was due to the insistence of Haig who had been unwilling for so long to give up final control of his own forces.

PART VIII

The last two years of the war at sea

CHAPTER 23

The second German submarine campaign and the Allied counter-measures: the effects of the Allied blockade

The first British announcement of the battle of Jutland caused consternation and dismay. Without any attempt to estimate the significance of the battle the communiqué gave a list of British and, as far as they were known, German losses. The result appeared to be very much in favour of the Germans. The German Admiralty, on the other hand, put out a less honest version in which they said nothing of the loss of the battle-cruiser *Lützow*, the grounding of the *Seydlitz*[1] or the sinking of the *Elbing* and the *Rostock*. Within a week the Germans had to admit the loss of the *Lützow* and the *Rostock*; their earlier concealment, compared with the franker British admissions, did them harm. The immediate reactions of public opinion, Allied or neutral, however, were less important than the actual consequence of the battle.

The battle of Jutland was a turning-point in the war at sea. The German naval authorities realised that they had little chance of destroying British naval supremacy in capital ships; their only hope of circumventing this supremacy was by a resumption of unrestricted submarine warfare. Henceforward the issues at sea depended on the success or failure of the U-boats.[2] The German Chancellor, who doubted whether the U-boat campaign would be successful and feared the consequences of bringing the United States into the war, had been able for some months to prevent the naval and military chiefs getting their way, but on February 1, 1917, the new campaign began.

The resumption of unrestricted submarine warfare was not unex-

---

[1] The *Seydlitz* sank in shallow water on her way home, but was raised and towed into harbour a few days later.

[2] This term is used to cover generally all classes of German submarine. There were four main types: (i) U-boats, large craft used chiefly in the Atlantic approaches; (ii) UB-boats, smaller craft used in off-shore attacks, i.e. in the Channel; (iii) UC-boats, minelayers; and (iv) a small number of converted 'mercantile' submarines, capable of crossing the Atlantic.

pected by the British Admiralty. During the previous months the Germans had been extending their field of operations and taking less care to observe their promise to the United States. In September, 1916, nineteen British ships had been sunk in the Mediterranean, eleven in the North Sea, twelve in the Atlantic approaches, the Bay of Biscay, and off the coast of Portugal. The neutrals suffered no less heavily; twenty-six Norwegian ships were lost.[1] In October the Germans, with extraordinary lack of understanding of American feeling, sent a submarine across the Atlantic; this ship, after calling at Newport (Rhode Island), sank five vessels off Nantucket Island.[2]

In October also the British steamship *Marina*, westward bound, was sunk without warning off Cork; six out of fifty-one Americans on board were drowned; another ship, with Americans on board, was shelled while lowering her boats. An American ship, though not carrying contraband, was sunk off Cape St Vincent, and on November 8 the Germans sank the British liner *Arabia*. The increased losses during the late autumn and early winter months of 1916 caused the British Admiralty great anxiety. Jellicoe wrote to the Admiralty late in October that the success of the submarine campaign might compel the Allies to make peace in the early summer of 1917. Beatty took a similar view, and the Admiralty, early in November, warned the Cabinet that 'no conclusive answer has as yet been found to this form of warfare; perhaps no conclusive answer ever will be found. We must for the present be content with palliation.' In view of the seriousness of the problem Jellicoe was asked at the end of November to come to the Admiralty as First Sea Lord. At the same time a special division, under Rear-Admiral A. L. Duff, was formed to deal with anti-submarine measures.

In the last month of 'intensified' but 'restricted' submarine warfare the Germans sank nearly 370,000 tons of British and foreign shipping – more than three times the amount sunk in June, 1916. They calculated that Great Britain was supplied by some $10\frac{3}{4}$ million tons of shipping – including 900,000 tons of captured ships. If they could destroy 600,000 tons a month, and also frighten away some two out of every five neutral ships, they reckoned that in five months they would compel a

---

[1] The Germans wanted to deprive the British coal industry of pit-props, large quantities of which came from Norway.

[2] An American destroyer flotilla was able to pick up survivors. One of the American destroyers was asked by the submarine commander to move out of his way so that he could torpedo a ship. Link, op cit., v, 113.

British surrender. They had certain additional factors in their favour; for example, owing to the comparative failure of the American and Canadian harvests in 1916, British shipping would have to bring more wheat from Australia and Argentina.[1] Moreover the Allied overseas military commitments were very high: all their overseas forces had to be supplied along routes open to submarine attack. The scale of attack might also be increased. In February, 1917, there were 111 German submarines available for active operations; about a third of them were working at any given time. A large building programme had been under way since 1915. In 1916 only twenty-five U-boats had been lost – five by accident or shipwreck, and four in the Black Sea or the Baltic.

The British navy, therefore, was unlikely to destroy more than about twenty U-boats a year, or less than the German intake of new submarines. The Germans had reason to suppose that the Allies had tried every means of defending their own ships and attacking the U-boats. They had used patrols of destroyers and small craft to guard the routes into which traffic was directed and to hunt submarines; they had armed their merchantmen, employed 'Q' boats,[2] depth charges, minefields, nets, and other obstructions, but without much success. Moreover, while the U-boats needed only small crews, the hunting and protecting craft were a vast fleet. In February, 1917, two-thirds of the British destroyers, and all British submarines, mine-sweepers, and other auxiliaries were engaged directly or indirectly in anti-submarine warfare. In home waters and in the Mediterranean some 3000 vessels were employed on this work. The Admiralty could suggest no remedy other than an enlargement and intensification of existing methods of protection and submarine-hunting. More patrols, more minefields, laid with better mines,[3] more and bigger depth charges, the development

[1] The Germans also made the remarkable calculation that a rationing system could not be set up in Great Britain because there were not enough officials to enforce it. For the German failure to allow for the economic counter-measures by which Great Britain could offset the effects of the submarine campaign, see below, p. 497.

[2] See above, p. 196.

[3] Mine-laying was primarily a defensive practice, and therefore likely to have been studied more carefully by a weaker than by a stronger naval Power before 1914. Furthermore the Admiralty had not expected the Germans to lay mines contrary to the accepted rules of war at sea (see above, p. 190). It is, however, impossible to excuse the Admiralty for their extraordinary delay in devising an effective mine. The German mines were based on a design used by the Russians. This design was known to the Admiralty, but was regarded before 1914 as too

of new submarine detectors such as the hydrophone, the use of para-vanes[1] against mines, and heavier armament for merchant ships.

These measures were at first alarmingly unsuccessful in meeting the intensified submarine attacks. In February, 1917, there were thirty-nine encounters in home waters with submarines; only three were sunk, and a fourth destroyed by a mine. The shipping losses – British, Allied, and neutral – were 540,000 tons. In March the Germans sank another 593,841 tons for the loss of four U-boats. With the longer days, and better weather, the Admiralty expected losses to rise to about 700,000 in June. In the third week of April Jellicoe again called the attention of the Cabinet to the seriousness of the position. Nearly 420,000 tons of shipping had been lost in the first fortnight of April.[2] On the other hand the entry of the United States into the war gave some chance of relief. Jellicoe asked that they should send more ships to assist in patrolling and

---

expensive. The Admiralty had provided only 4000 mines of an inferior type at the outbreak of the war. More mines of this type were manufactured, but were found to be so defective that for a time in June, 1915, mine-laying was given up. The strategical importance of mine-laying was now realised, but throughout 1916 there were still no good mines; too much effort was wasted in trying to devise a combination of mines and nets. In the latter part of 1916 more attention was given to research and experiment, and a good type was produced; an adequate supply was not available until September, 1917.

The Admiralty had also neglected before 1914 the study of mine-sweeping. They had indeed organised a reserve of nearly 100 trawlers, which were available at once on the outbreak of war, but the navy had only six torpedo gunboats specially prepared for the work. Another 100 trawlers were taken into use almost at once. In 1914 forty-two merchant ships and a number of warships (includ-ing the battleship *Audacious*) were lost by mine. German submarines began mine-laying in 1915.

Mine-sweeping was carried out during the war almost entirely by British vessels and the work – which was very dangerous – was done largely by fisher-men. At the time of the armistice 726 ships were employed on this work; 214 ships had been sunk or damaged while sweeping, and nearly 24,000 enemy mines had been swept. The total losses of British and neutral ships from enemy mines in 1917 was very little higher than in 1916 although the Germans laid more than twice as many mines. The losses from mines in 1918 were only twenty-eight ships.

[1] Paravanes were invented in 1916. Their use is known to have saved fifty-five warships and at least forty or fifty merchant ships from destruction or damage by mines. Hydrophones were also used, but were not of great value, since their under-water warnings were too often lost in the general noise of water and machinery when a ship was in motion.

[2] The total figure for April was 881,027 gross tons, of which 545,282 tons were British. The May losses were rather less – just under 600,000 tons, but in June the figure rose again to 687,507 tons. The total losses between February and June were nearly 3,300,000 tons of which almost 2 million were British.

escort, and that more merchant shipping should be laid down, including large, unsinkable ships which could carry essential supplies.

Jellicoe's suggestions included extensive mining with the new type of mine, but his main idea was to increase the number of destroyers and light craft available for hunting submarines. There had in fact been a very considerable increase; five cruisers and thirty-seven destroyers had been put into commission since January, 1917; seventy destroyers were at work in the western area; not one of them had sunk a submarine since the start of the unrestricted warfare. Since the beginning of the war to the end of March, 1917, there had been 142 actions between British destroyers and German submarines; only seven of the submarines were known to have been destroyed. Hence, even if the patrolling force were multiplied, the chances of driving the enemy from the shipping routes were still uncertain.

Only two U-boats were destroyed during April. There was no escape from the grim fact that the German plan was succeeding, as far as the sinking of ships was concerned. In one respect alone the Germans were wrong. They had expected their campaign of 'frightfulness' to deter British and neutral merchant sailors from going to sea. The methods had some deterrent effect on neutral shipping, but none on British ships. In spite of the rapidly mounting risks, the ships sailed. During the war over 15,000 seamen of the merchant marine and fishing fleets lost their lives – a higher proportion of the total number serving than in the Royal Navy.[1]

The general conception of anti-submarine warfare adopted by the Admiralty, and accepted by Jellicoe, had been that of searching for and attacking submarines. There was another possible approach to the problem. Instead of concentrating mainly upon attack, the large resources now available might be used primarily in defence. In other words, apart from mine-sweeping and general patrols, the first task of the ships and auxiliary craft of the navy might be the escort and protection of merchantmen. This 'defensive' plan implied the assembling of merchant shipping in convoys, since there were not enough vessels to escort them if they continued to travel singly. The escorts would fulfil indirectly many of the tasks of a patrol. The U-boats would obviously seek out the convoys. If they did not find them, so much the better. If they found them, the escorts would be there to attack.

[1] The losses in the Royal Navy were nearly 23,000, or 4 per cent of those serving; the percentage in the mercantile marine and fishing fleets was about 5·5.

Convoying was, of course, not a new practice,[1] but there was a great difference between the old system of protecting a few convoys, sailing infrequently, against surface attack and the new problem of dealing with an almost continuous flow of world-wide trade which was being attacked by enemies invisible until they delivered their blows. The Admiralty had considered convoys, and were opposed to them on various grounds. They had not enough craft to provide the escorts – their estimate was that these would have to be in a high proportion to the number of ships convoyed. They assumed that a convoy, whose speed was determined by that of the slowest ships, would be too easy a target. They did not think that the average merchant captain would be able to keep station, or that an assembly of ships of different types, sizes, and speeds could manœuvre according to orders in case of attack.

The Admiralty view was not due merely to official 'conservatism'. Naval tradition, going back for centuries, was on the side of convoys, and in rejecting this tradition the Admiralty – though they showed a lack of enterprise and, indeed, of clear analysis – were abandoning an old method because they regarded it as obsolete in the circumstances of the twentieth century. Moreover the German naval authorities took the same view about the impracticability of convoys; they would not have risked war with the United States if they had supposed that the English had open to them a simple and easy method of evading submarine attack, or at least of keeping their shipping losses within bearable limits. The lack of clear thinking on both sides is indeed slightly ludicrous. The Germans suffered most by their mistake, since they brought the United States into the war, depressed the morale of their own people by exaggerated promises of success, intensified public indignation in other countries at their lack of humanity, and enabled their enemies to impose a more effective blockade.

On the other hand, the British Admiralty, in their persistent belief that convoying was no solution of their problem, caused the gravest hazard to the Allied countries. Jellicoe had been too prudent to risk the destruction of the Grand Fleet in a single rash, disastrous action, yet he came near to losing the war in the first half of the year 1917. There was an additional piece of absurdity about the Admiralty view. Only one of their three main arguments against convoying rested on fact. The view that convoys must be especially vulnerable to attack, and that the merchant ships in them could not be kept under sufficient control were hypothetical, and could have been tested only by experience. The

[1] The Tudor term for it was 'wafting'.

statement that the navy could not provide enough ships for escort was a matter of simple arithmetic, and, fantastic though it appears, the Admiralty arithmetic was wrong. The Admiralty took their own total of arrivals and departures – 2500 a week – from British ports as an indication of the number of ships to be protected. They knew that this figure included small coasting vessels, ships moving from port to port, cross-Channel steamers and the like, but they did not analyse the totals or realise how small the number of ocean-going steamers was – in fact between 120 and 140 arrivals a week. The number of escort vessels would therefore be much less than the Admiralty had assumed.[1]

Already in October, 1916, after Jellicoe had sent his warning note about submarine warfare, and had been called to a conference in London, Lloyd George and Bonar Law had asked whether it would not be possible to use the convoy system. The Admiralty answer was that the plan had been tried in the Mediterranean, and that it had been found unsafe to send more than one ship at a time under escort. Runciman, as a ship-owner, did not deny Jellicoe's assertion that a convoy could not be kept in close enough order to enable a few destroyers to protect the ships. Runciman also said that the convoy system was wasteful from the point of view of tonnage, since the fast ships would be kept back by the slow ships, and that the arrival of large convoys would cause delays in unloading at the ports.

In January, 1917, the Admiralty again stated that the method of convoy was impracticable. They laid down as 'evident' that

> the larger the number of ships forming the convoy, the greater is the chance of a submarine being enabled to attack successfully, the greater the difficulty of the escort in preventing such an attack. . . . A submarine could remain at a distance and fire her torpedo into the

[1] Lloyd George's suggestion in his *War Memoirs* that the Admiralty did not know that all these minor shipping movements were included in the total is an instance of his own careless or malicious statements. On the other hand the facts that the Admiralty had not analysed the totals, and that they exaggerated the number of ocean-going steamers shewed that they had not yet understood the full seriousness of the position, i.e. the high proportion of losses to the number of ocean-going ships. The statistics of ocean-going ships were supplied to the Admiralty by the Ministry of Shipping in April, 1917. The Admiralty mistake was first pointed out by junior officers in the anti-submarine division. It is curious that, in a matter of such overwhelming importance, no Minister should have asked for a more detailed analysis of the figures. Anyone living in a port, or who had spent a holiday on the coast near the main lines of shipping could have pointed out that most of the traffic consisted of small coastal vessels and not ocean-going ships.

middle of a convoy with every chance of success. A defensively
armed merchant vessel of good speed should rarely, if ever, be
captured.

Here again, the argument was partly one of fact, partly hypothesis. The
facts were wrong; defensively armed merchant vessels of good speed
unfortunately were being 'captured' in large numbers. There was no
evidence to support the hypothesis that a convoy was really a better
target. Indeed it might be said that a submarine firing at a convoy could
not risk more than a single shot, and that if it came to the surface it
would be attacked not only by the escorting warships but by the guns
of the armed merchant vessels. Moreover it would not be easy to find
the convoys, and, in any case, the change in tactics would probably give
two or three months' respite even if – as was unlikely – the Germans
could devise a reply to meet it. As for the inability of merchant ships
to keep station in a convoy, Jellicoe was supported in his view by a
conference of experienced merchant captains, but here again the experiment had not been tried.[1]

Lloyd George refused to accept the view that the convoy system was
impracticable. He called a meeting on February 13, and gave it a paper
drawn up by Hankey suggesting that the experiment should be made.
He did not ask for an immediate decision, and the Admiralty did not
change their views. They had already agreed, however, to allow
vessels engaged in the short sea trade carrying coal to France to be
organised, in a tentative way, in convoy – the term used was 'controlled sailings'.[2] The results were most satisfactory, and the officer in
charge of the sailings, Commander Henderson, was anxious to extend
the plan to other ships and other routes. On April 3 a conference of
naval officers met at Longhope to discuss possible ways of reducing the
heavy losses in the Scandinavian trade. They reported unanimously in
favour of convoys. The senior admirals to whom the report was submitted differed in their views; some were afraid that German surface
raiders might attack the convoys, but a risk of this kind was not very

[1] Thus it was possible to supply naval officers for training merchant captains
who were themselves not amateurs at their jobs, in keeping station. It was
also possible to make necessary adjustments in engine-room control (a much
shorter task than repairing a damaged ship or building a new one). The difficulties
of varying speeds could be overcome by grouping ships of approximately the
same speed. Ships with the most valuable cargoes could be put in the safest
positions in the convoys, while the fastest vessels could still be left, unescorted, to
rely on their speed to evade attack.

[2] These ships sailed, mainly at night, through closely patrolled waters.

serious outside the North Sea. Beatty, however, did not disagree with the conclusions in the report.

Jellicoe, who had been impressed by the success of the 'controlled sailings' of the coal ships, now consented to try the plan, though he had doubts about it, and anyhow did not regard it as generally applicable. He told the Prime Minister later, on April 23, when his memorandum was under consideration by the War Cabinet, that the Scandinavian experiment had not been altogether successful; two vessels in separate convoys had been lost. Lloyd George, however, had been getting the opinion of junior officers, and was not to be put off by the doubts of their seniors at the Admiralty. On April 25 he obtained the agreement of the War Cabinet to a proposal that he should visit the Admiralty in order to investigate the whole question.

The failure of other methods of protection, the success of the 'controlled sailings' of colliers, the discovery of the mistake in the shipping figures, the possibility of getting escort craft from America, and, not least, the evident intention of Lloyd George to accept the judgment of their subordinates, convinced the senior naval staff that they must give the method of convoys a trial. Lloyd George regarded the matter as settled, but Jellicoe thought it necessary to draw up another memorandum on April 27 in order to warn the War Cabinet that there was no easy solution, and that they must not assume that the establishment of convoys (which Jellicoe now took for granted) would restore to Great Britain freedom of action at sea. He pointed out that Great Britain was carrying on the war as though she had 'the absolute command of the sea, whereas we have not such command or anything approaching it'. If the Government failed to recognise this unfortunate fact, disaster was certain. Jellicoe recommended the immediate withdrawal of the Salonika force, with a drastic restriction of imports. He also said that it would be impossible to bring reinforcements into Great Britain from the Dominions unless they came in ships carrying food and other essentials.

Orders for the arrangement of the first 'experimental convoy' – apart from the coal ships and the Scandinavian convoys – were sent to Gibraltar on April 28. The convoy of sixteen steamers was organised by May 10, and reached British ports without mishap. The fears about station-keeping were shown to be unnecessary; the only trouble was that the slower ships could not maintain even their nominal speed. The Admiralty now proposed to organise an eastbound convoy of sixteen to twenty ships across the Atlantic, under the escort of a group of United States destroyers which were about to leave, but the American authorities – whose views of convoys was similar to that previously held by the Admiralty – objected to the plan. On May 24, however, an experimental convoy of twelve merchant ships sailed from Hampton Roads, and reached Great Britain without mishap.

The Admiralty were now satisfied that the system was at least worth trying on a larger scale. They had already set up a committee to advise on the necessary organisation. The committee reported on June 6. They suggested four points of assembly: (i) New York, for ships from that port, Boston and Portland; ships from Canadian ports would join the New York convoys at sea: (ii) Hampton Roads, for ships from the Panama Canal, the Gulf of Mexico and the Caribbean, and all United States ports south of New York: (iii) Dakar, for the South Atlantic trade, and for ships homeward bound from Australia and the Far East: (iv) Gibraltar, for ships bound from the Mediterranean. In all convoys Allied ships, and neutral ships in Allied employ, would be included if their rate of speed fell within the limits of $8\frac{1}{4}$ and 12 knots.[1] The average size of each convoy was expected to be about twenty ships.

The Admiralty accepted these recommendations, and proposed to put them into effect as soon as the necessary escorts could be made available. Four convoys, with an average of fifteen ships, sailed in June, and arrived safely. By mid-July four homeward convoys were sailing every eight days. Early in August the south Atlantic convoys were started. The homeward sinkings were now showing a most encouraging fall, but the German submarines were turning more to outward-bound shipping. Hence the Admiralty extended the convoy system to outward traffic. The committee had recommended outward bound convoys in June; the Admiralty had thought it impossible to find sufficient escorting vessels, and had exaggerated the number required. An outward convoy actually needed escort only through the 'danger zone' since, once outside, the ships could disperse to their ports. It was also possible to economise in the destroyer escorts through the danger zone by arranging for the escort of an outgoing convoy to meet an incoming convoy. This system put great strain on the destroyer crews, but it was applied with success.

By the end of September the convoy system was in full operation. The results were most remarkable. The British shipping losses fell from

[1] The limit set for the Gibraltar convoys was seven knots owing to the number of old and slow vessels in the coal and iron ore traffic.

a total of over 365,000 tons in July to about 200,000 tons in September. One hundred and seventy-three British and foreign steamers were sunk in June, and only 87 in September; 1306 merchant ships had sailed to British ports up to the end of September in 83 ocean convoys; 1288 ships had arrived safely, and only 10 had been sunk while actually under escort; 55 outward convoys, with a total of 789 ships, had left British ports with a loss of only 2 ships.

These figures were the more striking because the destruction of submarines had been at a slower rate than Germany was building them. Only six were sunk in July, four in August, and ten in September. From this point of view, though convoying had provided a respite of immense value, the anxieties of the Admiralty remained. They could not be sure that the enemy would not devise new tactics for dealing with convoys – possibly by surface raids. The total losses of shipping still exceeded the output of new ships. The anti-submarine measures, taken as a whole, were not defeating the submarines but only keeping them from sinking ships. There were indeed some factors favourable to the Allies: the U-boat losses, though not very large, were large enough to deprive the enemy of many of the most skilled commanders and trained crews. The increase in the anti-submarine devices, such as the kite balloon, the use of aeroplanes,[1] the multiplication of small craft and the improvement in the quality as well as in the number of British mines added to the difficulties of the submarines, kept them longer under water, and affected the morale of the crews.

In October the enemy raided one of the Scandinavian convoys and sank nine ships and two destroyers; the cruiser *Drake* – an old ship – and two other escort vessels were also lost during the month.[2] A second attack was made on a Scandinavian convoy in December, and the submarines increased their attacks closer inshore during November and December in order to catch ships after the convoys had dispersed. Nevertheless after five months the enemy had found no reply to the system of convoying, and the merchant ships as well as the escorting vessels had gained experience in manœuvre (i.e. zigzags) and defence. The shipping losses during October, November, and December were uneven, but the general tendency was downwards. Moreover the

[1] See below, Chapter 24.
[2] The Germans opened fire on a raft and a motor boat carrying some of the survivors after one of the destroyers had sunk. They also treated the merchant crews with great brutality by refusing to allow them any chance of lowering their boats.

Admiralty expected better results from the improved mines. The Dover barrage had been a failure hitherto in keeping U-boats from entering and leaving the Channel. A minefield laid in the Heligoland Bight was hardly more than a nuisance to the Germans, since it could not be kept under continuous British patrol, and the German mine-sweepers were able to sweep channels through it. At the beginning of 1918 Admiral Sir Roger Keyes introduced a new system in the Dover barrage. He increased the patrols, and by the use of searchlights and flares compelled submarines passing the Straits – some twenty-four made this passage every month for the greater part of 1917 – to dive into the minefield. The results were not very remarkable as far as actual losses were concerned – five U-boats were destroyed in the Straits, during the first three months of 1918[1] – but the submarines began to avoid the Channel entrance, and to take the northern passage around the British Isles. Their operating time was thus cut down, in the case of the smaller boats by one-half, and their inshore attacks in home waters rapidly diminished.

In September, 1917, the Admiralty decided, after the Americans had promised to supply most of the mines, to set up an immense minefield across the northern exit of the North Sea, and out of reach of German mine-sweepers. This gigantic plan was not completed until just before the armistice; many of the American mines exploded prematurely, and a number of British mines had to be swept because they were not laid at a sufficient depth to allow surface craft to pass over them. In any case the minefield gave rise to a serious diplomatic problem. The eastern end reached to Norwegian territorial waters. The Germans were known to be evading the minefield by using these waters. The Norwegian Government refused to mine their own waters; the Allied fleets could have laid mines in them, but only in violation of the neutrality of a small State. Moreover the Allies were unable to keep a permanent patrol at this distance from their own bases, and the Norwegians could therefore have swept the mines. Five submarines are known to have been destroyed in the minefield; the passage through it was also a grim test of German morale, but – like other anti-submarine measures – it harassed rather than defeated the enemy.

The turning point, statistically, in the anti-submarine campaign was not reached until July, 1918, when the tonnage of new shipping was greater than the amount lost. There was still no certainty that some new German device would not turn the situation once more against the

[1] Eight more were destroyed between April and September.

Allies. Nevertheless the victory, even though it was only a defensive victory, over the German submarines had been won before July. The Germans had neither compelled Great Britain to surrender nor prevented the transport of a great American army to France. Not one incoming transport was sunk.

During this period of unrestricted submarine warfare, and indeed earlier, the Admiralty had considered the possibility of a direct attack on Ostend and Zeebrugge. Apart from the difficulties of landing, the problems of maintaining a force were regarded as insuperable. These latter problems would not arise in the case of a large scale raid sufficient to hold off the enemy until the naval installations had been destroyed (neither place was a 'natural' harbour) or until a simultaneous land offensive had broken through to link up with the raiders.[1] There were naval officers ready to undertake a raid, but again the Admiralty and the General Staff thought the chances of success too small. Moreover throughout the greater part of 1917 Haig had been hopeful that his own offensive would reach the two ports.

At the end of 1917, when there was no chance of an advance in Flanders, Admiral Sir Roger Keyes persuaded the Admiralty to agree to an attempt to block the entrances to the inner harbours, or rather to the ship canals, in each place. Keyes pointed out that the risks involved were in fact no greater for the attackers than in a major offensive on the Western Front. Keyes' plan was very carefully worked out; it was put into effect on the night of April 22–3 – one of the nights in each month when the tide was full about midnight.[2] The plan at Zeebrugge consisted of a diversionary attack on the curved mole – a little over a mile long – protecting the canal mouth, while ships loaded with cement were sent in to block the canal. At Ostend there was no mole, and the

[1] It must remain an unsettled question whether a closer study of these problems from 1915 onwards – after the experience of Gallipoli – might have produced, with expert civilian advice, a solution not less successful than that obtained in 1944 on the Normandy coast. In other words, the Admiralty seem to have waited far too long before calling upon engineers and other technicians to assist in suggesting means of overcoming the difficulties in the way of an amphibious landing.

[2] Keyes had considered it necessary to choose a moonless night, having a full tide within an hour and a half of midnight. There were only five nights in a month with these conditions. The tide was right on April 22–3, but there was a full moon. The expedition, however, had been twice called off owing to wind conditions unfavourable for a smoke screen, and Keyes was afraid that, in the event of further delay, the Admiralty might cancel the operation.

ships had to try to reach their sinking places under cover of a smoke screen and protective fire.

The operation at Zeebrugge was carried out with wonderful skill and bravery, but the attack was much hampered by a sudden change of wind to the south just before the cruiser *Vindictive* – which was to land the attacking party – reached the mole. Hence the smoke screen which was to deceive the defence only confused the attack. The channel was, however, reached, though it was not entirely blocked. At Ostend, where the wind again shifted at the last moment and – unknown to the attackers – a guiding buoy had been moved, the blockships missed their mark, and became stranded on the shore. Admiral Keyes made another attempt at Ostend on May 10, 1918. The *Vindictive* was brought – again with extraordinary courage – within the entrance to the harbour, but at an angle which obstructed only a third of the channel.

These operations made it clear to the Germans – at a time of disaster to British arms on land – that the enemy whose overthrow they were already proclaiming was very far from losing either initiative or power. Although the actual damage was less than had been hoped, the two ports, and especially Zeebrugge, were less useful as bases for German destroyer raids. This fact may have been the main reason why no raid was attempted on the Straits of Dover; anyhow the improved defences at the Straits were making it increasingly dangerous for German submarines to make the passage. From July onwards fewer submarines attempted this passage.

Meanwhile the Germans had not been able to defeat the Allied blockade. The blockade had been maintained, and indeed intensified throughout the critical months of submarine attack. The entry of the United States into the war had removed most of the political difficulties in the way of Allied interference with neutral trade. The Americans now were most drastic as belligerents in imposing restrictions against which they had protested during the time of their neutrality. By the end of 1917 all imports from overseas to Germany were cut off. So few ships attempted to get through to Scandinavia that the northern patrol was withdrawn in December, and the cruisers used for other purposes; the light forces of the Grand Fleet were enough to keep the entrance to the North Sea closed. The Germans, however, were still getting Scandinavian and Dutch produce. The British Government, in order to check this traffic in food which was now even more valuable to Germany, decided in June, 1917, to stop the import of fertilisers and fodder to

Denmark. American policy was more severe, and aimed at preventing any Scandinavian supplies from reaching Germany. They put an embargo in July on all exports to Scandinavia; three months later the embargo was extended to the Netherlands. The British Government would not go as far as a complete embargo, since they needed some Swedish manufactures, especially ball-bearings, Norwegian fish, food-stuffs from the Netherlands, and Norwegian and Danish shipping. In January, 1918, the British Government reached a *modus vivendi* with Sweden for the import of coal and foodstuffs in return for the use of 100,000 tons of Swedish shipping held up in British, French, and Italian ports. An agreement was also made with the Netherlands for the chartering of 600,000 tons of Dutch shipping to Great Britain and the United States. The agreement was not carried out because the Germans threatened to sink every Dutch ship leaving for the United States. The embargo therefore remained in force.

The United States had meanwhile agreed to send wheat to Norway, and an Anglo-Norwegian agreement had been concluded over fish. The Norwegian embargo was lifted in April when the Norwegians promised to cut off their main exports to Germany. In May Sweden agreed to reduce to 3,500,000 tons a year the export of iron ore to Germany, and to limit other exports.[1]

An estimate of the effect of the Allied naval blockade must take into account that the war itself changed in character as it was prolonged, and that the belligerents, and especially the Allies, came to realise its real nature – a 'total', highly organised effort involving whole populations – only as the months passed. Until they had understood fully the industrial background essential to their military offensives the Allies envisaged their blockade as a measure to prevent the import of military supplies – completed goods or raw material – into Germany, and not as a vast effort to slow down and disarrange German production and transport and all the organised activities of the nation. The Germans, ironically enough, were the first at each stage to take the steps which led to this new conception of war; they were defeated, one might say, by the application to themselves of their own doctrine. They were the first to bring civilians within the operations of war at sea by their illegal mine-laying. They initiated unrestricted submarine warfare – which, if successful, would have starved the civilian population of Great

[1] The United States Government had previously tried to get a complete prohibition of the ore exports.

Britain – at a time when they had no expectation of great difficulty from Allied action against their own food supplies. Their violation of the agreements which they had signed regarding war at sea threatened neutral civilians before Allied interference with neutral trade had much embarrassed the German war effort.

The effects of the blockade were cumulative; as the war lengthened, they pervaded every aspect of enemy war production and civilian life. The shortages had a direct effect on military operations. Lack of fodder, oil, and lubricants hampered the mobility of the army and slowed down the rate of advance during the German offensive of 1918. The standards of military equipment began to deteriorate. The soldiers were worried about the hardships of their families at home. The additional effort required to provide the goods, or the substitutes for the goods which Germany could not import, put an almost unbearable strain on industry. The consequences to civilian morale became more and more serious. The substitution of paper for linen, the general lack of warm clothes, the lack of soap had depressing effects. Above all, the shortage of food bore heavily on the urban population, and led to political discontent and unrest. Much of German agriculture was in areas of poor and sandy soils, and even in summer most German cattle were stall-fed. The loss of fertilisers and feeding stuffs was therefore disastrous. The harvest of 1916 in Germany was bad; the potato crop also failed, and the situation of the 'turnip winter' of 1916–17 was more severe than at any other time during the war.[1]

Matters were worse from the point of view of civilian morale because the hardships and sacrifices were not evenly spread. Difficulties of transport – the industrial regions of west Germany normally drew much of their food from the east – were aggravated by the military demands on the railways in a war of two fronts. The agricultural classes resented the system of price regulation, and the small producers tended to hoard their produce or to sell in the illicit market; the illicit trade in butter was large enough to have a serious effect on the milk supplies in cities. Manufacturers often bought illicit food to keep their work people. There were jealousies between the administrative services of different German States and, in any case, control and rationing were more difficult than in Great Britain where commodities reached the ports in bulk. The Germans, in fact, were less successful than the

[1] As a consequence of diverting large quantities of turnips to human consumption, the meat and milk shortages later became worse.

British in adapting their economy as a whole to meet the drastic adjustments required by the blockade. Unlike Great Britain, Germany had taken precautions before the war to organise her agriculture from the point of view of a possible war and to subsidise it by tariffs to such an extent that a large increase in output was more difficult than in England, where, for example, there was far more good land – much of it formerly under the plough – which had been left to grass.

Even so, German civilian morale might have been less affected if the hopes of the population had not been raised so often, and then disappointed. In the early summer of 1917 Roumanian grain began to appear, and the damage done to Roumanian oil-wells was repaired. The submarine war also seemed to be going sharply in favour of the Germans. Within a few months the Roumanian imports turned out to be less than had been expected. Scandinavian supplies began to fall off, and the sinkings of Allied shipping had been checked. The chances of peace receded, while the prospect of American armies in Europe grew near. At the end of the year the armistice with the Bolsheviks brought hopes of vast supplies from the Ukraine. In this expectation the German Government raised the bread ration, but the supplies did not come. Owing to lack of good seed and implements, and – not less – owing to political disturbance, stocks were lower than the German estimate. The peasants tried to hoard their grain, and would not take Russian, German or Austrian money. Such grain as could be collected was transported only with difficulty.[1]

Once more, in the spring of 1918, the German successes in the west raised hopes, and again, within three months, there was disappointment. Meanwhile the German flour ration fell in June to the lowest figure in the war. The harvest in the Ukraine was not good, and the peasants were no more willing than before to assist the Germans. The Roumanian harvest was almost the worst on record. The German harvest was better than in 1916 and 1917 but much smaller than in the last pre-war years. In Turkey and Bulgaria there were good harvests, but the Bulgarian surrender cut them off from Germany, and also threatened the supply of Roumanian oil; in August the Germans announced that the ration of lighting oil – already low – would be reduced by three-quarters during the winter.

The German armies were in continuous retreat and invasion was likely; the transport system was near to collapse. There were shortages

[1] The Germans also had to assist in supplying Austria where the food position was worse than in Germany.

of everything. The German people had been deceived too long by their Government to hope now for any change for the better. They had no grounds for hope, and no motive for going on. It is is significant that, at the last the sailors of the German navy turned against their officers, refused to sacrifice themselves in a sortie which seemed to them unlikely to affect the issue of the war, and began a mutiny. The mutiny was the start of the German revolution – such as it was – and the final occasion of the German collapse was the indiscipline and revolt of the crews of the battlefleet built up by Admiral Tirpitz to dispute the British command of the sea.

PART IX

The war in the air

CHAPTER 24

The RFC in 1914: air warfare on the Western Front: the RNAS

The failure of the War Office, the High Command of the army, and the Cabinet to ask urgently for all possible help from the engineering industry in breaking the deadlock of trench warfare is the more remarkable because in another and no less difficult sphere – the development of aircraft – collaboration between civilian technical skill and the services was continuous. The aeroplane as an instrument of war was so new that such collaboration was not hampered by military vested interests. Balloons had already been used in war; the problem of attaching engines to them and steering them had long been considered, though it was not adequately solved in the nineteenth century. There had also been experiments in flying machines, but nothing decisive for practical purposes until Orville Wright flew his machine in December, 1903.

For more than five years after this flight neither the Admiralty nor the War Office took much notice of the new invention; pioneer work was left to individuals (who paid for it out of their own pockets, and often risked their lives) and to a few engineering firms willing to make experiments, again at their own cost. Between 1906 and 1908 the War Office refused twice, and the Admiralty once, an offer of Wright's patent. Meanwhile other countries had been less indifferent to the military possibilities of airships and aeroplanes. The French, as earlier with the submarine, had led the way in official experiments. They were concerned primarily with 'heavier than air' machines, though the word 'dirigible' shews their interest in guided balloons. The Germans, owing in part to the remarkable persistence of Count Zeppelin,[1] did more to

---

[1] Count Zeppelin had made his first balloon ascent during the American Civil War, and had fought as a cavalry officer in the Franco-Prussian war. He was about sixty when he turned to the building of airships. The German military authorities began to support his projects about 1906.

develop airships. British official interest was not much aroused until Blériot flew across the Channel in an aeroplane in July, 1909.[1] In this year Asquith set up an Advisory Committee for Aeronautics; seven of the members of the Committee were Fellows of the Royal Society. The Committee was able to use the services of the National Physical Laboratory at Teddington for research into practical questions such as air resistance, strain and stress of material. From this time the chief developments in England were in the construction of aeroplanes. The Admiralty, or rather the firm of Vickers, acting for the Admiralty, built a large rigid airship between 1909 and 1911. The airship collapsed while being taken from its mooring shed. The Admiralty then gave up experiments in rigid machines only to resume them in the summer of 1912.[2]

In November, 1911, the Cabinet asked the Committee of Imperial Defence to make recommendations about the establishment of an air force. The Committee reported quickly; its proposals were accepted, and a Royal Flying Corps came into existence in April, 1912. The Corps had a naval and a military wing, but from the first there was a strong move for a separate naval force; few people at that time thought in terms of an air force as an independent third arm of the services. The demand for a naval air force was not unreasonable. The needs of the navy were different from those of the army. The military command regarded aeroplanes almost entirely from the point of view of reconnaissance, and as a supplement to cavalry. The navy, on the other hand, had in mind from the first the possibility that enemy aircraft might attack coastal installations. In any case members of a naval service would have to know a great deal about ships. Furthermore, owing to the short range of flight of the early machines, the navy wanted a type of aircraft which could operate from a ship. In July, 1914, therefore, the naval wing of the RFC was given separate status as the Royal Naval Air Service.

To contemporaries the technical advances in the few years before 1914 were astonishing. Air photography – at first thought of no value by the military authorities – was being developed by individual experiment; one of the pilots making these experiments provided his own camera. Wireless communication was improving, and the arming of aircraft had begun; the Germans were in this respect taking a lead. There were also experiments on a small scale in bombing, though until

[1] He was very nearly anticipated by a British officer flying a French machine.
[2] See below, p. 370.

the invention of a good bomb sight, and the construction of machines capable of carrying heavier loads, the small bombs were more likely to cause alarm owing to their novelty than (except by chance) to inflict damage.

On the outbreak of war the RFC had only about 150 aircraft of all types, and could send only four squadrons – forty-eight machines, with fifteen in reserve, to France with the BEF.[1] They were armed only with rifles and revolvers. There was as yet no specialisation in machines or pilots; a pilot might be detailed for reconnaissance, artillery co-operation, or fighting. Flying in formation had not yet begun.[2] Most of the repair and maintenance equipment was carried in horse-drawn vehicles; the motor transport consisted in part of hastily requisitioned commercial vans. Some of the machines were damaged before reaching France.[3] Apart from the slowness of their transport, the squadrons found the problems of maintenance difficult during the retreat of the army. They had continually to find or improvise new landing-grounds; the Corps headquarters was at nine different places between August 24 and September 4.[4] Nevertheless, in spite of their troubles – including the risk of being fired at by their own infantry[5] – the pilots soon showed the value of air co-operation, particularly in reconnaissance work. They still had to learn mainly from their own experience. Many of the detailed improvements in their machines and equipment were suggested by the pilots themselves; one of them – in September,

[1] A comparison with the much larger numbers of French and German aircraft is misleading since the armies which these aircraft had to serve were much larger. The overwhelming German superiority – indeed, monopoly – in Zeppelins was a matter of anxiety. Experiments had been made in England in methods of destroying airships by dropping grenades on them, but few such grenades had been manufactured.

[2] Anyhow it would have been impossible with machines of many different types.

[3] One pilot made a forced landing near Boulogne, and was arrested and imprisoned by the French.

[4] The problem of aerodromes and general ground arrangements remained difficult. At first a clear, level field some 300 yards square, free from ridges, and with road communications fit to carry heavy transport was considered enough; with the increase in the number and complication of aircraft, better landing grounds were essential. In these early days there were only portable hangars; steel sheds of French design came into use in the latter part of 1915, though it was not easy to get the fittings for the wire ropes.

[5] In order to provide means of identification the squadrons painted Union Jacks on the undersides of the lower planes. These signs were found not to be sufficiently clear, and at the suggestion of the French, concentric red, white, and blue circles were substituted.

1914 – was the first to propose the use of squared maps for references in transmitting information. Another pilot suggested the 'clock code' instead of the less precise 'left' and 'right' indications hitherto employed by artillery observers. Pilots also suggested the mounting of Lewis guns on their machines. The army authorities continued to disregard the importance of air photography until the value of the trench maps provided for the battle of Neuve Chapelle was too obvious to be ignored; they were also slow in organising even a headquarters wireless unit, and in realising the need to reduce the size and weight of wireless instruments carried in aeroplanes. Kitchener, in December, 1914, doubled the programme of thirty squadrons, with five in reserve, for the new armies, but he had no direct knowledge of military aircraft[1] and did not realise the difficulties caused by the shortage of pilots and machines.[2]

Early in 1915 the Germans began to carry out reconnaissance work and bombing behind the British lines by single machines. Scouts were used to attack them, and, for the first time, the specialised 'fighter pilot' appeared. In the spring of 1915, further specialisation took place for artillery work and long-distance reconnaissance, but machines were still sent out singly. From this time, 'air supremacy', if the term may be used, passed from one side to the other as Allied or German designers produced better types of machine, and pilots developed new tactics in fighting. By July, 1915, every machine which had been in use at the outbreak of war had become obsolete. At first, mainly owing to French initiative, the Allied planes were better than those of the Germans. In October, 1915, the Germans brought into action large numbers of a new Fokker aeroplane.[3] The Allies then had to send out a fighter escort of one machine with aeroplanes doing reconnaissance or artillery work. A single escort was soon found insufficient, so two were sent. The fighters themselves found it better to work in pairs during their own attacks; early in 1916, after the signalling system had been improved, three or four fighters began to act in formation. Single-seater fighter

[1] He once tried to insist on pilots flying in formation although they were using different types of machine.

[2] From the outbreak of war to the end of May, 1915, 530 planes had been taken into service, and about 300 lost or otherwise written off; owing to the prevailing west winds many aeroplanes flying over the enemy lines could not get back after they had been damaged by gun fire. Some 2250 machines were on order in May, 1915.

[3] The Fokker was the first fighter in which machine guns were synchronised to fire through the propeller. Fokker was a Dutchman with factories in Germany.

squadrons were then formed.[1] The German advantage in machines was countered in May, 1916; during the first stages of the battle of the Somme the RFC had almost complete local superiority, though they met heavy losses in more distant operations behind the enemy lines. The Germans soon developed new types – in particular a single-seater fighter with twin guns – and special fighting squadrons.

Trenchard warned Haig at the end of September, 1916, that more and better fighters were urgently needed to counter the German superiority. He asked for twenty additional squadrons[2] for the campaign of 1917, in addition to the fifty-six squadrons in all which he had estimated two months earlier as necessary. Haig supported the demand, but it could not easily be met. The requirements to meet wastage in existing squadrons were heavy. In the first five months of the war the machines of a squadron needed replacement every three months. The period then became shorter (in 1918 it had fallen to two months). Owing to lack of money before the war no reserve of factories or material had been created. For the first six months of the war there were no suitable engines of entirely British make. French help was given on a lavish scale, but one important item – magnetos – had previously been imported from Germany. The supply of British-made magnetos was insufficient before the autumn of 1916, and even at that time some of their component parts were imported. The Government factory at Farnborough was most useful, but furniture or piano makers and other industries had to be brought into the work of making the bodies of aeroplanes and, as in all branches of production, much dislocation was caused by the enlistment of skilled mechanics. A proper co-ordination of supply was also hindered by competition between the naval and military wings of the service. There was considerable public disquiet,

---

[1] Until the summer of 1917 formation flying was done by three to six fighters. A short and interesting account of air fighting was written by Major-General H. M. Trenchard in a memorandum of December, 1917, and is printed in H. A. Jones, *The War in the Air*, iv, 453–6. Trenchard, as Brigadier-General, succeeded Major-General Sir D. Henderson in August, 1915, as commander of the RFC in France. Trenchard, who in his youth had twice failed to pass into Woolwich, and had been rejected twice before obtaining a commission as a militia candidate, had served in India and South Africa. He transferred to the RFC in 1912, when he was nearly forty. Trenchard was a man of strong and somewhat overbearing character, unconventional and insubordinate as a commander, but with immense energy and drive.

[2] In March, 1916, the number of machines in a squadron had been raised to eighteen. A year later the number was increased to twenty-four, but the new figure was not generally reached until 1918.

especially during the period of Fokker superiority, over alleged mis-management of production. In February, 1916, Asquith appointed a committee to co-ordinate matters of supply and design. Lord Derby resigned the chairmanship of the committee early in April on the ground that it had insufficient powers. An Air Board, presided over by Lord Curzon, was set up in May, though still without sufficient executive authority. Moreover the expert members of the Board were repre-sentatives of the Admiralty and the War Office, and merely continued the departmental disputes over priorities. Lloyd George suggested the amalgamation of the two supply departments under the Ministry of Munitions; the Admiralty, the War Office, and the Air Board itself opposed this plan. A second committee on the administration of the RFC reported in August and November in favour of a single depart-ment. Meanwhile in August Curzon had protested against an approach by the Admiralty to the Treasury, without consulting the Air Board, for a programme of construction amounting almost to £3,000,000. Balfour, as First Lord, took the side of the Admiralty.

This dispute was widened when the Admiralty suggested keeping a force of at least 200 long-range bombers at Dunkirk. The military authorities did not believe long-range bombing likely to be effective; Haig said that the diversion of material to meet the Admiralty demands might well 'compromise the success' of his proposed offensive. He now put forward Trenchard's request for an additional twenty fighting squadrons. The Air Board considered it impossible to provide them. Lloyd George increased the powers of the Board and made it, in effect, an Air Ministry: Lord Cowdray, as President, was 'deemed to be a Minister', and the Board had authority to settle the design of machines, the numbers ordered, and their allocation between the two branches of the service. Henceforward there was less wasteful competition, though neither branch was able to get its full demands. In April, 1917, the BEF had only fifty squadrons,[1] including four lent by the Admiralty.

The second period of German superiority in machines, supported by a few fighter pilots of exceptional skill and daring, lasted from the autumn of 1916 to May, 1917. April, 1917, was a month of most serious losses for the RFC.[2] Nevertheless, at great self-sacrifice the pilots kept up

[1] Twenty-seven were fighting squadrons.
[2] Between April 4 and 8 seventy-five British aeroplanes were shot down and fifty-six wrecked in accidents. The accidents were due partly to the heavy strain imposed on the pilots, and partly to lack of sufficient training; pilots were sent

an offensive policy. This policy not only required high standards of personal courage; it was laid down after careful thought and observation. In a memorandum of September, 1916, on future policy in the air,[1] General Trenchard noted that, in raising demands from the ground forces for protection, the moral effect produced by a hostile aeroplane overhead was 'out of all proportion' to the damage which it could inflict.

> The mere presence of a hostile machine in the air inspires those on the ground with exaggerated forebodings with regard to what the machine is capable of doing. For instance, at one time on one part of the front, whenever a hostile machine, or what was thought to be a hostile machine, was reported, whistles were blown and men hid in the trenches. In such cases the machines were at far too great a height to observe the presence of men on the ground at all, and even if the presence of men was observed it would not lead to a catastrophe.

General Trenchard concluded that 'the sound policy which should guide all warfare in the air would seem to be this, to exploit this moral effect of the aeroplane on the enemy, but not to let him exploit it on ourselves'. In other words, offensive tactics were of far greater value than defensive tactics. It was impossible to keep every enemy aeroplane away from the Allied lines, and therefore a waste of force to divert men and machines for this purpose. The only effective way of stopping the enemy from attacking was to attack him.

This offensive policy – on both sides – included short-distance bombing behind the lines, but even after the development of a fairly good bomb sight in the summer of 1915, the material results were hardly commensurate with the losses involved.[2] It was found that the bombing of trains was more effective in blocking railways than attacks on stations and sidings. A most successful raid, however, was made in July, 1916, by four German aeroplanes on a large British ammunition dump on the side of the Calais–St Omer railway at Audruicq. One shed

---

to the front at this time after $17\frac{1}{2}$ hours instruction in the air. Five months later the average was $48\frac{1}{2}$ hours.

[1] The memorandum was written at a time when Trenchard thought that a more aggressive German policy was likely, and that it would bring demands from the British ground troops for more protection. If more fighters were used to escort reconnaissance units, there would be fewer machines for other purposes.

[2] Nevertheless, as Trenchard pointed out, bombing had a considerable moral effect and caused the dispersion of enemy fighters to protect possible targets.

was hit, and the fire spread to twenty-three other sheds; 8000 tons of ammunition were destroyed, and nearly a mile of railway lines wrecked. The damage would have been much less if more care had been taken in the location of the sheds, and in isolating them by ridged banks of earth.

From the middle of 1916 the co-operation of aircraft with artillery became increasingly elaborate, though, with the heavy losses in both arms, the new officers coming out to the front were often insufficiently trained, and the liaison between planes and batteries was not always satisfactory. Furthermore, as their numbers increased, batteries and squadrons moved about a good deal, and the close and friendly contact often established between individuals was less possible. Since slightly different methods were used in different corps or groups, there was need for standardisation. A pamphlet noting the importance of uniform arrangements was issued for the use of officers at the end of 1917.[1] It was also desirable to explain air force tactics to the troops. As Trenchard had foreseen, the German machines had become more harassing to the troops on the ground. The ground forces tended to exaggerate the numbers attacking them; the movements of a single plane over a fairly wide area often gave the impression of a concerted attack. The RFC therefore had to point out once more that the aeroplane was not primarily a weapon of defence; that most of the work of British fliers was done over enemy lines, and that, however continuous the patrols, it was not possible to prevent every enemy aeroplane from crossing the trenches.

Counter-battery work was now of the highest importance. New methods of co-operation between balloon observers and aeroplanes were used in order to lessen the work of the latter.[2] The sound-ranging sections of the Royal Engineers gave useful help, especially in cases where air observers were unable to state the exact position of targets. The number of planes engaged in an offensive had increased to such an extent that at the opening of the battle of Ypres in July, 1917, 508 British machines (230 of them single-seater fighters), 200 French (100 of them fighters) and 40 Belgian machines were allocated to the front between the river Lys to the north-east of Armentières and the sea.[3]

---

[1] A memorandum on co-operation had been circulated a year earlier. In the winter of 1918–19 special short courses on air co-operation were held for senior officers of the ground forces.

[2] A good deal of the preliminary ranging would be observed from balloons, and the aeroplanes would take over in the later stages of firing on the targets.

[3] There were in addition 104 RNAS planes based on Dunkirk.

Low-flying aeroplanes had already been used, both in special attacks and in harassing the enemy behind the lines. They were employed on a larger scale at the battle of Cambrai; they caused heavy losses to the enemy, and affected morale, but the losses to the attacking planes were too costly. About 30 per cent of the machines were destroyed on each day of the Cambrai fighting; in other words, the whole force would have to be replaced after four days. None the less those low flights were of very great value in delaying the German advance during the critical days of Ludendorff's offensive in 1918. It is significant also that, although, after Cambrai, the emphasis of army instructions during the winter was on defence, Trenchard insisted that the RFC must continue an offensive policy.

The German daylight attacks on London[1] convinced the War Cabinet that aeroplane bombing on a large scale had become an important, and perhaps a decisive factor in winning (or losing) the war. Aircraft had thus ceased to be merely auxiliary to the operations of fleets and armies, and could be used for independent action. Smuts, in his second report (September, 1917)[2] to the War Cabinet, even suggested that air attacks might become 'the principal operations of war, to which the older forms of military and naval operations may become secondary and subordinate'. Smuts thought that, with the increasing exhaustion of man-power, the war would become one of arms and machinery. 'The side that commands industrial superiority and exploits its advantage in that respect to the utmost ought in the long run to win.' If full use were to be made of the new factor, it was essential to set up 'a new directing organisation, a new Ministry and Air Staff which could properly handle the instrument of offence and equip it with the best brains at our disposal'.

This line of reasoning led directly to the establishment of an Air Ministry under which the two existing air services could be amalgamated, and an additional force created for the new type of operations. The plan was not carried out without difficulty.[3] Haig disbelieved in the forecast that the war might be won in the air, and feared the diversion of aircraft from the army to new and speculative purposes.

[1] See below, pp. 372-3. [2] See below, pp. 373-4.
[3] There was already considerable support in Parliament for a new policy. The Admiralty, whose special needs were already being dealt with more efficiently than those of the army, was less obstructive than Haig. Admiral Mark Kerr, who had returned to England in August, 1917, from the command of the British Adriatic Squadron, was in favour of Smuts' view.

There was also a risk that, however defective existing arrangements of control might be, the attempt to substitute a new organisation during the war might result in more dislocation. Smuts, however, continued to take the view that preparations for the bombing of Germany were being delayed; Sir William Weir, Controller of Aeronautical Supplies in the Ministry of Munitions, strongly supported the argument that the expansion of the air force could not be realised without a full-scale examination of industrial[1] resources and priorities.

On November 6, 1917, the War Cabinet approved a draft bill for an Air Ministry. The bill was passed late in November, and an Air Council came into being on January 3, 1918. Lord Rothermere was appointed Secretary of State for the Air Force and General Trenchard Chief of the Air Staff.[2] Lord Rothermere resigned in April.[3] Sir William Weir took his place. Meanwhile, on March 7, a new title – Royal Air Force – was announced for the amalgamated services.[4]

These changes in organisation came towards the end of the war, and their practical effect was limited by the delays in carrying out the programme, accepted by the War Cabinet in July, 1917, for doubling the air force.[5] The obstacles in the way of sudden expansion on so large a scale were partly due to circumstances outside the control of the Air Council. The air industry as a whole had been late in the field, and in

[1] Agricultural priorities also had to be taken into account. Thus the Ministry of Agriculture were unwilling to give up 4000 acres of arable land urgently needed for aerodromes (all suitable non-arable land had already been taken).

[2] Haig protested against the withdrawal of Trenchard from the command of the RFC in France. Lloyd George laid himself open to a good deal of criticism because, without consulting Lord Cowdray, the head of the existing Air Board, he approached Lord Northcliffe with a tentative offer of the new Secretaryship of State. Northcliffe refused the offer, and announced his refusal in a letter to *The Times*. The words 'for the Air Force' were changed to 'for Air' in 1919 when the Secretary of State was also given responsibility for civil aviation.

[3] Rothermere did not get on well with Trenchard, and had neither the ability nor the temperament suitable for the post, but it is fair to add that his health was not good, and that he was much affected by the death, from wounds in action, of his eldest son in February, 1918.

[4] The RAF actually came into existence on April 1, 1918. The Admiralty kept control, until October, 1919, of the 'lighter than air' service used mainly for anti-submarine and reconnaissance work. There was some controversy over the designations of the officers of the RAF. The Admiralty objected to the use of naval titles, even with the prefix 'Air'. Fantastic names, such as 'Banneret', 'Reever', and 'Ardian' (from the Gaelic words 'Ard', a chief, and 'Ian', a bird) were proposed. Military titles were, in fact, used until the adoption of the present designations in August, 1919.

[5] See below, p. 365.

the earlier years of the war had not as powerful a backing as that of the Admiralty and the War Office in the struggle for priorities. The military demands which were taking more and more men from industry were especially serious after the opening of the German offensive in March, 1918: any programme of expansion was bound to suffer. Furthermore the immense losses of machines and material during the German advance had to be made good out of 'new' production. Repair facilities had never kept pace with the accumulation of damaged engines; hence new engines had to be used to maintain rather than to increase the size of the air force. The air authorities themselves were, however, much to blame for the shortage of engines. They took too long in settling the types of engine to be put into mass production, and hampered progress by their incessant suggestions for minor changes in design. Even so, the choice of types was unsatisfactory; several of the newer types had to be withdrawn owing to serious faults. The hopes of immediate supply from the vast American programme of Liberty engines were not fulfilled. Lord Northcliffe[1] reported in October, 1917, that this programme would almost certainly meet with difficulties, but he estimated that 5000 machines with Liberty engines would be in France by July, 1918. In fact not one of the machines was in operation on that date, and out of a planned total production of nearly 10,000 by the end of May, 1918, only 1100 had been delivered.[2]

Nevertheless, although the air force was not as large in the summer of 1918 as had been planned, the part played by air warfare was increasingly important. Eight hundred aeroplanes supported the British armies in the battle of Amiens on August 8; nearly 100 were lost or damaged beyond repair.[3] At the end of September, 1058 machines were allocated to a front of three armies in the battle of Cambrai and the Hindenburg line. The losses were again heavy; the German air force was outnumbered, but had received in May and June fighters of a new type better than any on the Allied side.[4] Many of the British losses were incurred

[1] Northcliffe was at this time head of a British War Mission for the co-ordination and supervision of the many separate war missions in the United States.

[2] The British authorities, by the end of 1917, had asked for 3000 Liberty engines, to be delivered at the rate of 500 a month from January, 1918. The first shipment was of 10 engines in March, 20 were shipped in April, 175 in May, 225 in June, and 620 in July. Deliveries then stopped.

[3] During this battle an aeroplane brought an enemy train to a standstill, and then signalled to cavalry in the neighbourhood who captured the train.

[4] A new British fighter outclassing these German machines in speed and climbing power was in course of production, but the first machines did not reach the BEF until after the armistice.

in a relentless pursuit of the enemy; machines were wasted, however, in attacks – at the request of the army command – on strongly defended bridges across the Somme. They might have been used to greater effect in bombing railway centres[1] at a time when comparatively short delays in repair work would have caused great dislocation. Some 2900 tons of bombs were dropped by British aeroplanes between July and October, 1918. The Germans also did considerable bombing, and until mid–August had greater success. One reason for their success was the dangerous overcrowding of British dumps and depots after the spring offensive. Thus on August 11 an attack on Calais wrecked a Mechanical Transport depot containing spare parts for well over half of the lorries, tractors, and ambulances on the British front, as well as 26,000 inner tubes and 16,000 tyres.[2]

At the outbreak of war the Royal Naval Air Service had thirty-nine aeroplanes, fifty-two seaplanes – about one half of them ready for immediate use – and six small airships. This force was intended for coast defence, and for protecting the transport of the BEF to France. There were no large airships, and no arrangements for seaplanes to do reconnaissance work. The German naval bases and their adjacent waters were too far away for distant reconnaissance; the Admiralty also had other means, such as cross-bearings by direction-finding stations, whereby they could discover whether any large number of German warships had put to sea.[3] The responsibility for coastal defence – which the Admiralty kept until February, 1916 – meant the development of fighters, and also of bombers able to reach the Zeppelins or the U-boats in their Belgian bases. Dunkirk became a naval air base from which to make these attacks. One other development – the use of small non-rigid airships for detecting submarines – was of major importance, though fortunately for the Admiralty, the submarine problem was not intense for some months after the outbreak of war. After earlier failures, the

[1] On the other hand, the defence of the bridges cost the Germans a large number of their already depleted force of skilled pilots. One of the most active of the German fighter squadrons – formerly led by the greatest of German airmen, von Richthofen – was under the command of Captain Hermann Göring.

[2] The financial loss caused by the Calais raid – £1,400,000 – was equal to the total material damage done by all the aeroplane raids on Great Britain.

[3] Continuous reconnaissance would hardly have been possible until there were more planes. The few carriers were converted merchant ships, which could not have been stationed, or kept for any length of time, without naval protection in the neighbourhood of enemy waters.

Admiralty – disturbed at the progress made by Germany in the Zeppelins – had started again in 1912 their experiments in airship construction. Two rigid and six non-rigid airships were ordered in July, 1913. The building of the former had not gone far in August, 1914; work had begun only on one of them and little was done during the next twelve months. In July, 1915, a programme of rigid airship construction was authorised, but only one was near to completion by September, 1916, when, by good fortune, a Zeppelin was forced to land, with its structure almost undamaged, north of Mersea Island in Essex. The Admiralty then decided to give up their own design (except for the nearly completed airship which joined the fleet in April, 1917) and to build five airships on the lines of the Zeppelin. Not one of the five was completed by the end of the war. A considerable number of small non-rigid ships were built.[1] There was a rapid improvement in design; the first ships were merely gas balloons with aeroplane engines fastened beneath them. It was found that these small airships could be towed by ships with the Grand Fleet, but until September, 1916, Jellicoe had to rely on aeroplanes and carriers.[2] The practice of towing kite-balloons for observation was of doubtful value, since they could be seen by the enemy while the ships were still below the horizon.

The Admiralty made somewhat slow progress with carriers; the problems of getting seaplanes into and out of the water even in a slight sea or of enabling aeroplanes to take off and land on carrier decks were extremely difficult. The first carriers also were not fast enough to keep up with the Grand Fleet at high speed. The liner *Campania* was adapted as a carrier in April, 1915, and then – in the light of experience – brought back for alteration. She did not return to the fleet until April, 1916. Her aircraft might or might not have made an important contribution at the battle of Jutland, but by some mistake, her captain did not receive the signal ordering him to put to sea with the Grand Fleet. The fleet left Scapa Flow at night, and such lights as were shown were not visible to the carrier. As she had no destroyer escort, and submarines were known to be near Scapa, Jellicoe ordered her return to harbour after she had started out to catch up with the fleet.[3]

[1] Particularly for use by the Dover Patrol or in the Western Approaches.

[2] Jellicoe had been much disturbed by the lack of airship reconnaissance or fire-spotting comparable with that provided by the Zeppelins. In fact the latter took little part in the battle of Jutland – none at all until the concluding phase – and misled Admiral Scheer in his sortie of August, 1916.

[3] The fleet had over two hours start; the *Campania* was slightly faster than the battleships and cruisers, and might have reached them before the opening of the

At the end of January, 1917, a fifth Sea Lord was added to the Board of Admiralty in order that naval representation on the Air Board should be as authoritative as that of the War Office. About the same time Admiral Beatty asked the Admiralty what their policy was with regard to the RNAS. He also appointed a committee of his own officers to consider the future requirements of the Grand Fleet. The Grand Fleet had only three carriers, and only one of them could send up aeroplanes from its deck; a second – the *Campania* – could send seaplanes from the deck. The number of seaplanes carried for reconnaissance and anti-Zeppelin defence was twenty-two, and of aeroplanes only four. By March, 1918, three faster and better carriers – one of them a light cruiser – were in commission. Fighters were also carried in many battle and light cruisers. The problem of sending them up from the decks had also been solved by putting movable platforms on top of the gun turrets.[1] The other problem of landing machines on the decks had not yet been solved. Attempts had been made, but a satisfactory carrier was not ready for her final trials until September, 1918.

After the summer of 1916 the activities of the naval air service were increasingly determined by the German submarine campaign. At the beginning of 1918 Admiral Beatty suggested that British naval strategy should not be based upon attempts to bring the German High Seas fleet into action. These attempts were, in any case, unlikely to succeed; the best policy was to contain the enemy in his bases until the situation was more favourable, and otherwise to concentrate on the protection of shipping. The adoption of the convoy system in the summer of 1917 soon had a decisive effect on German tactics. The U-boat commanders could not attack the convoys without the greatest risks to themselves; they therefore turned to operations close to the British shores where they were able to find ships either on the way to the assembly ports for outward convoys or making for ports after the incoming convoy had dispersed. At the end of 1917 more than 60 per cent of the sinkings took place within ten miles or less from the shore. This change in enemy

---

battle. The small carrier *Engadine* – formerly a cross-channel steamer – was with the fleet. One of her seaplanes made a sortie, but could not get the information that the enemy had changed course back by signal to Admiral Beatty (who, in fact, had received the news from one of his scouting light cruisers). The weather then became too rough to allow the seaplanes to be let down into the water (a cumbrous process which took half an hour even when the carrier was in harbour).

[1] A ship from which an aeroplane was launched thus did not have to leave the line or alter course in order to get suitable wind conditions. All that was necessary was to turn the platform in the desired direction.

tactics gave an increased importance – and opportunity – to aeroplanes working from coastal aerodromes. In March, 1918, the Admiralty adopted a plan of 'protected lanes' of approach. They reckoned that if the lanes were patrolled once every twenty minutes by an aeroplane, the U-boats would be unable to stay on the surface or even to use their periscopes. The object of the plan was not so much to destroy submarines – though, obviously, any chance of attacking them would be taken – as to keep them away from their targets. The patrolling aeroplanes were unlikely to be attacked; hence it was possible to use machines obsolete for other purposes, and pilots not qualified for work against enemy aircraft. Three hundred unwanted training machines were put on these patrols until more and better machines were available. This plan had considerable success; the greatest losses in shipping now occurred at times when, owing to weather conditions, the patrols could not fly.[1] The Germans in 1918 developed instruments enabling them to detect, without coming to the surface, the presence of aircraft; the U-boats could thus more easily avoid discovery, but were still unable to come up to look for targets. The means of detecting submarines were also better and, especially with the improvement in hydrophones after the summer of 1917, an aeroplane flying at a fair speed could discover the presence of a submarine ahead or below before the submarine was aware of it.

[1] Seaplane and aeroplane patrols flew over 860,000 miles in 1917 and over 3,500,000 in 1918. Airships on anti-submarine patrol flew just under 600,000 miles in 1917, and over 1,100,000 miles in 1918.

CHAPTER 25

German bombing attacks on Great Britain: the Zeppelins: aeroplane raids: the bombing of Germany

Before the war German opinion – at least among the population at large – expected much from the bombing of targets in Great Britain by Zeppelins. There was no provision in international law forbidding such bombing in all circumstances; the Germans anyhow showed in other matters how little respect they paid to international agreements when it seemed in their interest to break them. The Hague Conference of 1899 had forbidden the dropping of projectiles from balloons or other aerial vessels. The prohibition was renewed at the Conference of 1907, but the agreement was ratified only by Great Britain, the United States, Portugal, and Belgium, and on the condition that it would cease to be valid in a war in which one of the belligerents was joined by a non-contracting party. Article 25 of the Land Warfare Convention of 1907 forbade the bombardment of undefended places 'by any means whatever'. No definition was given to the term 'undefended'. Article 2 of the Naval Warfare Convention of 1907 allowed the bombardment of military works, military or naval establishments or plant which could be used for the needs of an army or fleet, or ships of war in a harbour. The Convention did not mention bombing from the air, and, therefore, by implication, allowed it if it were limited to the listed type of objective.

The Cabinet in 1908 appointed a committee under Lord Esher to consider how far Great Britain might be exposed to air bombardment. At this time the danger seemed limited to attacks by airships. The committee came to the sensible conclusion that a satisfactory estimate could be made only if the British Government constructed its own airships. After this report the decision was taken to build a non-rigid airship. The attempt failed and for a time was given up. The Admiralty, however, decided to protect their bases against air attack, though little was done except to provide earth shelters for magazines. One reason for the delay was a division of responsibility between the Admiralty and the War Office. This question had not been settled satisfactorily in 1914. At the time of a severe[1] Zeppelin raid on Tyneside in June, 1915, the War Office was responsible for the anti-aircraft guns, and the Admiralty for defence by aeroplanes.

The Zeppelins did not bomb British targets until January, 1915. The heaviest period of raiding lasted for a little less than two years – the last of this series of raids took place in November, 1916. There was then an interval until mid-March, 1917.[2] Five more raids were made between March and October, 1917. Another interval followed, until three raids occurred between mid-March and mid-April, 1918. There were in all fifty-one raids in which the enemy succeeded in dropping bombs on Great Britain; twenty were in 1915, twenty-two in 1916, and only nine in 1917–18. 208 people were killed in 1915, 293 in 1916, and 56 in 1917–18. The material losses were relatively small. Seven raids on London in 1915–16 caused £800,000 of damage by incendiary and high explosive bombs. £530,000 of the damage was in one and £150,000 in another of these attacks; the losses would have been much smaller if adequate precautions had been taken against fire. The total damage was £1,500,000; little harm was done to military and naval installations or munitions factories. The cost to the Germans was eighteen Zeppelins – six of them between September and November, 1916. In October, 1917, owing to unexpected and unusual weather conditions five Zeppelins were lost on their return home from a raid; four of them had drifted across France.[3]

Even when there had been no effective means of defence against them the Zeppelins had been hampered by difficulties in locating their targets; most of their bombs fell in open country or in the sea. The dimming of lights in towns and the illumination of 'dummy' sites added to this confusion. The development of night flying by British aeroplanes soon made the task of the enemy more precarious. The Zeppelins were large targets; the British pilots quickly learned by experience how to attack them with incendiary and explosive bullets. The new

[1] 'Severe' by the standard of air bombardment in the 1914–18 war. It is necessary to remember that no air raids by either side during this war were comparable with those of the years 1940–5 in the Second World War. The total tonnage of bombs dropped by Zeppelins was just under 200, and by aeroplanes 73. On the other hand the experience of air bombardment was entirely new, and the smallest raid had a serious effect on public morale. See below, p. 372.

[2] One Zeppelin crossed the coast in February, 1917, but did not drop bombs.

[3] In January, 1918, four Zeppelins were destroyed in an explosion at their base.

aeroplanes flew faster and higher, and, in order to avoid them, the Zeppelins had to rise to heights from which the location of a target was even harder. On the other hand the airships were also improved; for a time in 1917 they could fly higher than the defending aeroplanes.

Although they did not inflict anything like the damage expected from their bombs, the Zeppelin raiders served the Germans well from a military point of view.[1] They caused widespread alarm, interrupted transport and war production, and diverted men, aeroplanes, anti-aircraft guns, and searchlights from other areas of fighting to the defence of Great Britain. At the end of 1916 twelve squadrons of aeroplanes, and over 17,000 officers and men were allotted to this defence. Many hours of work in factories were lost; in some cases the stoppages affected the safety of blast furnaces. On the day after a raid many workers would stay at home or arrive late. The losses in the production of pig iron in the Cleveland area were estimated at about one-sixth of the annual output. In London the underground railways were at times crowded with people taking refuge from possible attack. In April, 1916, traffic delays during and after a raid had become so very serious that orders were issued countermanding previous instructions for the extinguishing of lights, and the stopping of trains and shunting.

One reason for the decline in the number of Zeppelin raids after 1916 was that the Germans had found a more effective instrument in the bombing aeroplane. Before the end of 1916 twenty-five aeroplane raids had been made on Great Britain. One attack was made on London; the others were in Kent or on the east coast; Dover was raided twelve times. The damage was small; no bombs had been dropped in six of the raids. Only twenty people were killed – fourteen in one raid – and the material damage done was under £12,000.

The raids began again, on a fairly large scale, in 1917 when the new German twin-engined Gotha machine came into service. The first daylight raids, in May, 1917, were made on the south-eastern counties, and extended to London in June and July. A raid by fourteen aeroplanes on June 13 over the City and East End of London killed 162 and

---

[1] After 1916, the Zeppelins were used, as the German navy (though not the army) had expected them to be used, mainly for reconnaissance at sea. Here also their value was much diminished by the British use of flying boats and aircraft from carriers. In 1917 Zeppelins had to fly above 12,000 feet to be out of reach of the flying boats (which had a flying-time of about eight hours); at this height they could not carry out submarine detection. By the early spring of 1918 even the newest Zeppelin could not safely make contact with the Grand Fleet, even in distant reconnaissance, long enough to allow the course of the fleet to be known.

wounded 432 people; 18 children were killed and 30 injured in one school. The military damage was slight, but there was something like a panic demand for strengthening the defences of London. The War Cabinet ordered Haig to send one of his fighter squadrons back to England, and another to Calais. The German attacks were not repeated during the last fortnight of June; the squadrons then flew back to the Western Front. On July 7 London was bombed again by daylight. The War Cabinet asked for the return of the two squadrons, though they hoped to be able to keep one of the two only for a fortnight. Haig pointed out that he badly needed them for his offensive which was opening on July 8 with air attacks. The War Cabinet agreed to recall only one squadron,[1] but they also held back a reinforcement of twenty-four new machines promised to another squadron in France. The War Cabinet decided at once that bombing by aeroplanes was likely to be a major factor in winning or losing the war. They approved a proposal that the number of squadrons in the RFC should be raised from 108 to 200, and that there should also be a large increase in the RNAS. They set up a special committee to consider the arrangements for home defence against aircraft and to advise generally on air organisation and operations. Lloyd George was the nominal chairman of the committee; the actual work was done by Smuts. Smuts presented a first report – on air defence – on July 19.[2] He thought it probable that air raids on London would 'increase to such an extent in the next twelve months that London might through aerial warfare become part of the battle front'. He proposed an anti-aircraft barrage for London, with three single-seater fighter squadrons. The defence organisation was soon strong enough to keep the enemy aircraft away; there were no more daylight attacks on London,[3] but in September the Germans began attacks on moonlit nights with new and more powerful machines. Bombs were dropped in twenty of these night attacks in 1917–18; over 400 people were killed[4] – more than half of them in the London area – and about £1,000,000 material damage was done. The night attacks were a matter of great concern to the War Cabinet, since there seemed to be no adequate means of defence against them. Smuts was asked to give his views. He reported on September 6 that, as the War Cabinet had

---

[1] This squadron remained in England until the end of August.

[2] For the second report – on air organisation – see above, p. 363.

[3] The last daylight attack on Great Britain was on the coast of Kent on August 22, 1917.

[4] One hundred and thirty-two of the fatal casualties were in the naval barracks at Chatham on September 3, 1917.

already realised, the proper defence was an offensive aimed at the enemy's bases. He thought, however, that some defence could be made by installing more powerful searchlights, and by establishing a wire barrage screen suspended from balloons. In fact, the air authorities expected that, given more searchlights, the pilots would soon learn to deal with night raiders as they had dealt with Zeppelins. This forecast was fairly accurate, though for some time the enemy had it their own way. In a raid of May 19–20, 1918, eight German machines were brought down by fighter pilots or gun fire. Henceforward only three enemy aeroplanes crossed the coast; not one of the three dropped bombs. The effects of the daylight and night aeroplane attacks in 1917 and 1918, like those of the Zeppelins, cannot be measured in actual loss and damage; the damage done by anti-aircraft shells was sometimes greater than that caused by bombs. The dislocation and loss of working hours and the effects on morale were greater than in the Zeppelin period. The Germans employed only one squadron in the daylight raids, yet they caused the withdrawal of two fighting squadrons from the Western Front, the formation of three other fighting squadrons solely for home defence, the deployment of a large number of guns which could have been used elsewhere – many of them on merchant ships – and the expenditure of immense quantities of ammunition and labour. The experience of the second war against Germany was to show that attacks in far greater strength would neither destroy British morale nor have a vital effect on production. Even in this first war the effect on morale cannot be judged by the rush of frightened thousands to shelter in the London tubes and tunnels; public morale in general was stiffened to further 'resistance until victory' by these attacks which, even by day, and certainly by night, were a form of war on women and children in crowded urban areas. Nevertheless, from a material standpoint, the attacks were a powerful, though indecisive weapon in enemy hands.[1]

[1] In February, 1918, the British Government were informed that the King of Spain had been in communication with the German Government with the purpose of getting some agreement between the belligerents not to bomb undefended towns. The British Government replied that they had always objected to such bombardment and would consider any proposals put forward by the Germans. No proposals were made officially, but from a statement in the Bavarian Chamber, the Germans seemed to be willing to abandon air attacks on open towns if the Allies also agreed to give them up. This offer appeared to be (and in fact was) due on the German side to the realisation by the High Command that the Allied attacks were having a dangerous effect on German morale, and were likely to become more severe. The Germans had therefore more to gain than to lose by giving up attacks which they had hitherto practised without scruple. Anyhow

They came to an end in May,1918, because the enemy needed all his air force for the Western Front. In any case there was no need, at least for some time, to continue the raids, since the mere possibility of their resumption was sufficient to keep the British home defences at full strength.

From the early summer of 1916, and with increasing force during 1917 and 1918, Allied aircraft were making raids on Germany. A French attack on Karlsruhe on Corpus Christi Day, June 22, 1916, caused heavy civilian losses, and resulted in a widespread demand for more anti-aircraft defence. In the summer of 1916 a British naval air wing was set up at Luxeuil in order to dislocate production in the steel works of the Saar where much of the material for U-boats was made. After the Germans had begun their night attacks on London a special wing of three RAF squadrons was formed to attack German industrial targets; these plans for bombing could not be put into effect on an extensive scale until 1918 owing to lack of aeroplanes and trained personnel. In May, 1918, the Air Council proposed to constitute a strategic bombing force. The name – Independent Air Force – was not happily chosen, since at the very time when the Allies had attained to some unity of command on land it gave an impression that a large bombing force would act independently of the ground forces. Foch wanted, in particular, to be assured that the 'Independent Force' should be at his disposition in battle. An agreement was not reached until late in October, 1918; even then no plan of campaign against distant objectives in Germany was to be undertaken until the requirements of the immediate battle had been met.

---

the old distinction between 'open' and defended areas no longer applied. It was impossible to exempt from attack military targets of the greatest importance – for example, the Saar steel industry or the Badische Chemical works at Mannheim – since their damage or destruction would have a direct and immediate effect on military operations. It was also undesirable, from the point of view of the future, that the German people, after inflicting so much damage on others by air bombardment, should now enjoy immunity for themselves. If air bombardment were limited to areas within twelve or twenty miles from the front, French and Belgian towns would still be open to attack, while German towns would be exempt.

In the late summer of 1918 the Germans were planning large-scale attacks on British and French towns with a new type of small incendiary bomb. These attacks were never delivered. The German Emperor, in August, appears to have forbidden them on 'humanitarian grounds'. It is fairly certain that at this time the Germans realised that such attacks would be followed by Allied reprisals on an even larger scale.

If the war had continued into the year 1919, it is likely that, with the general nervous exhaustion and disillusion of the German people, and the increasing difficulty of the German air force to provide men, machines, and petrol for meeting attack, air bombing would have been a decisive factor in the German collapse. Up to the armistice, however, the German casualties from British and French bombardment of German targets were only 746 killed and 1843 injured, and the material damage about £1,200,000. The Germans themselves, however, admitted severe indirect effects in the loss of man-hours in production, and in the weakening of German resistance. Such weakening was not very serious until the Germans were already faced with certain defeat.

PART X

The German western offensives, March–June, 1918: Allied and German war aims: the defeat and surrender of Germany

CHAPTER 26

The German western offensives, March–June, 1918[1]

The German plans for an offensive on the Western Front were discussed at a conference called by Ludendorff at Mons on November 11, 1917 – the date and place have a curiously dramatic significance. Ludendorff invited to the conference only the Chiefs of Staff of the groups of Armies under the Crown Prince William and the Crown Prince Rupprecht. Neither of these two commanders was present; Ludendorff thought it unnecessary to invite the Emperor (whose formal consent was ultimately given to the plans), or, for that matter, Hindenburg. Least of all did he wish to consult the German Government. The decision to attack was almost inevitable. If Germany had stood on the defensive in 1918, the chances of a 'compromise peace' might have been greater, since, with the arrival of the American army, Wilson would have been in a stronger position to assert his views on the peace settlement. On the other hand, if they were to win the war outright, the Germans could do so only by a decisive attack before the Americans had reinforced their Allies. The submarine warfare had failed to defeat Great Britain; a last 'gamble' in the West was the only chance of German victory.

Ludendorff knew that he was near to the end of his resources; that he must throw the whole of his remaining strength into the attack, and that, if he failed, ultimate and complete defeat was certain. He also realised that he must attack the British army. He thought that the British, though more obstinate and tough in holding on to a position, were less skilful tactically than the French, but his main reason for choosing the British front was that here alone could he hope for his decisive victory. If he attacked the French, he might be attacked in turn by the British in Flanders. If he succeeded in taking Paris, the French – with the prospect of American help – might retreat behind the Loire,[2]

[1] See Map 7.

[2] Here again British sea power, against which Ludendorff fought in vain, and which compelled him to all his desperate decisions, would have enabled the French to be supplied and the Americans to land without interference.

and advance again when the Germans were attacking the British and trying to reach the Channel ports. If, however, he could reach the Channel ports, the greater part of the British army would be likely to fall into his hands. The British were more tied than the French to a single decisive area. Moreover the loss of the Channel ports would cause grave embarrassment to the British navy in the defence of the Atlantic approaches.

Ludendorff considered various points of attack. He could not wait until the middle of April, and an offensive in Flanders might be impracticable earlier. He could not attempt simultaneously two large-scale offensives. He therefore planned a series of violent attacks which would confuse and break' through the 'over-rigid' British resistance in the area south of Arras. As soon as these attacks had been delivered he would turn against the strongly defended area between Vimy and Monchy. Preparations would also be made for a third attack in the north, though Ludendorff hoped that this attack would not be necessary. Fortunately for the Allies the Germans had been too slow in realising the value of tanks; otherwise Ludendorff intended to make full use of the newest methods of attack by small groups of specialised infantry infiltrating the enemy defences.[1] He also took great care to effect a surprise, though, if Haig and Pétain had been more willing to accept the judgment of their local commanders, he would not have succeeded in convincing the British Commander-in-Chief that the main attack was coming further north, and the French Commander-in-Chief that it was to be directed against the French front in Champagne.[2] He secured a tactical surprise by bringing up his assault divisions at night, and by following the new practice of a short but most intense opening bombardment – largely of gas shells – without previous registration.

The first German attack was directed against the British Third and Fifth Armies holding a front of seventy miles from the neighbourhood

[1] One reason for this specialisation was a general fall in the quality of the German army. The drafts sent to replace wastage consisted largely of middle-aged or unfit men, and youths. The obvious way to meet the deficiencies was to choose the better troops for attack, and give them special training, while leaving the less fit to the defensive duty of holding the line. This plan, however, involved a risk that, if the better troops were lost in attacking, the weakness of the rest of the army was increased.

[2] The Germans shewed their usual ingenuity in trying to deceive Pétain. They allowed a captive balloon to fall in the French lines with bogus plans for an attack. They also employed French carpenters to build large numbers of temporary sleeping bunks for additional troops behind the German lines in Champagne.

of Croisilles, some eight miles south-south-east of Arras, to the junction of the British and French forces at Barisis. The greater part – some forty miles[1] – of this front was defended by the Fifth Army under the command of General Gough. Ten miles of the Army's front were covered by the Oise; another four miles, south of the Oise, were in marshy or wooded country over which an attack was unlikely. The Fifth Army consisted of twelve infantry and three cavalry divisions, with about 500 heavy and 1000 field guns. Eleven divisions were in the line, and one in reserve; the cavalry divisions were distributed as reserves along the whole army front. In addition two divisions of GHQ reserves were behind the army.[2]

The Fifth Army front had fewer men and guns per mile than any other section of the British line. The reserves behind it were spaced to provide only one division for every 18,000 yards of the front, whereas on the fronts on the Second and Third Armies there was a division, roughly, for every 8000 yards. The weakness of the Fifth Army front was greater because its defences were dangerously incomplete, especially in the area taken over from the French in January, 1918.

There was some reason for this disproportionate allocation of forces. The northern part of the British line allowed no room for 'elastic' defence; no considerable withdrawals were possible except at grave risk. South of the Scarpe such withdrawals would be less serious if they were made slowly, and if the momentum of an attack were thereby reduced; the reserves could be brought up in time to counter-attack before any 'vital territory' had been lost. It was also desirable to hold the British reserves mainly on the northern part of the line since the French could send reinforcements more quickly to battle areas nearer to their own front. Haig also thought that they would be more willing to do so than to detach their reserves out of easy recall in the event of a heavy attack on their own Champagne front.

Haig's first view had been that the main enemy offensive would come in the north, since the surest way to a German victory would be through the occupation of the Channel ports. At the end of January, however, the evidence tended to show that the Germans were planning to deliver

[1] These measurements follow the front line. The distance in a straight line from Croisilles to Barisis is about 47 miles.

[2] There were three 'reserves': (i) the reserves of each corps; (ii) the reserves of each army; and (iii) the general reserve of eight divisions at the disposition of GHQ. Two divisions of this general reserve were located behind each of the four armies (I, II, III, and V). The numbering of the armies underwent some change during this period. There were only four armies in 1918 until August 23.

their main blow against the southern part of the British line. On February 1 General Gough sent a memorandum to GHQ giving the reasons why he expected to be attacked. He pointed out that General von Hutier, who had carried out a successful offensive against Riga in September, 1917, had been transferred, with the 18th German army under his command, to the area opposite the Fifth Army front. There was also evidence of preparations for an offensive against this front – for example, the construction of aerodromes, and of additional bridges over the St Quentin–Cambrai canal. The Germans wanted an early decision, and would be likely to choose the Oise–Scarpe area since the ground might be suitable for an offensive two months earlier than in the north.

Gough then described his own plan of defence. He thought that, if he had sufficient notice of the German intentions, he could hold their attack with the help of his own reserves and the two divisions from the GHQ reserve. He would need, in all, ninety-six hours' notice, but the more recent German offensives had been carried out after a bombardment of not more than six hours, and with the most careful precautions to ensure surprise. If these methods were repeated, they would 'naturally go far towards ensuring (the enemy) success', especially in view of the state of the defences.

Gough wrote that, in spite of all his efforts, the defences north of the river Omignon would not be 'even satisfactory' before the middle of March or 'in a good condition' before the end of the month. He asked for more labour and stores, more Royal Engineers, and more reports of enemy activities opposite his front. It is difficult not to regard Haig's judgment as badly mistaken in refusing to provide the labour for the construction of a strong defensive line behind the 'devastated area' of the Somme battlefields which the Germans would have to cross before continuing their attack. In the critical period after March 23 it was found possible to construct, within a few weeks, new roads, bridges, and many miles of new trenches and wire entanglements to cover the approaches to Boulogne, Calais, and Dunkirk, and to remove large depots of material to comparatively safer areas. If Haig had been so much disturbed over the shortage of infantry, he might well have considered it a matter of the utmost urgency before the German attack to complete a more modest plan of work. In any case, the strength of the labour companies with the Fifth Army rose from 24,217 to 48,154 between February 2 and March 16; the Army also had available for defence works fourteen entrenching battalions, varying in strength from 650 to over 1000, and most of the men of the divisional pioneer battalions and engineer units. There was, obviously, a great deal of maintenance and other work to be done on roads, railways, camps, water supply, drainage, and the like, but it is hardly comprehensible – in view of General Gough's memorandum to the Commander-in-Chief – that in the two weeks before this memorandum was written, the numbers of men from the labour units employed on defences were respectively 518 and 626, and that for the next three weeks the average was under 1400.[1]

This failure to make up for an inferiority in numbers by adequate defences was especially surprising because the evidence of German intentions became increasingly plain. On February 16 Haig himself came to the conclusion that he would have to meet a severe attack, possibly on a wide front, between Lens and the Oise. From the beginning of March the evidence pointed definitely to the area between the Oise and the Scarpe. On March 10 the GHQ Intelligence summary repeated the view that there were no signs of preparation for a heavy battle in Flanders but that the main attack, of which the Allies would have little warning, would be delivered on the Arras–St Quentin sector of the British front and to the north of Epéhy (about eleven miles north-east of Péronne), and that a large-scale offensive would also be attempted against the French in Champagne.

On March 17 this view was unchanged. Haig was not convinced, in spite of Gough's opinion, that the attack would extend to the Fifth Army front, since he thought that the Germans would have to concentrate on the capture of Arras. A few days before the attack, prisoners and deserters on the fronts of the Third and Fifth Armies confirmed the view that an offensive was about to begin. Gough expected it on March 21. Haig was coming home on leave at this time;[2] he decided on March 20 to wait until March 29. In spite of Gough's anxiety about the weakness of the Fifth Army front, Haig was optimistic about the chances of inflicting a heavy defeat on the enemy. He had told his army commanders on February 28 that he was 'only afraid that the enemy would find our front so very strong that he will hesitate to commit his army to the attack with the almost certainty of losing very heavily'.[3]

---

[1] For the three weeks before the German attack the figures were, respectively, 3120, 7670, and 8830. At the end of December, 1917, GHQ had not made any urgent demand for more labour to construct defence works.

[2] Haig's son was born on March 16.   [3] Haig, op. cit., p. 291.

The offensive opened on March 21 at 4.40 a.m. with a heavy bombardment. Contrary to the German methods, the British forward zone contained about a third of the defending troops; the losses were consequently very heavy. The infantry attack began five hours later in thick fog which did not clear until noon, and on balance favoured the enemy. If the fog hampered the exploitation of the German breakthrough, it also prevented the defence from locating and firing at moving bodies of troops, while the German bombardment was directed mainly on fixed objects whose position was known from the map. By nightfall, and in some cases much earlier, the Germans had come through the forward zone of the Fifth Army and in many places penetrated the battle zone. The rear zone – which might have held them up – hardly existed. On the next day – which also began with fog – the enemy broke through into open country north-west of St Quentin. In the early afternoon of March 22 Gough began to order a retirement behind the left bank of the Somme.[1] By the evening of March 23 the Germans – who had again been helped by fog – were advancing north of Péronne. There was the danger of a gap between the right of the Third and the left of the Fifth Armies which might open the way to Amiens, and an even graver danger that the French – to the south of the Fifth Army – were retreating south-westward and would lose touch altogether with the British. Ludendorff now thought that the whole British front was in disintegration; that he could reach Amiens, and drive the British armies to the Channel while keeping off French assistance from the south.

The British troops – especially those of the Fifth Army – were tired and bewildered. They had been heavily outnumbered; most of them were untrained in open warfare. Reinforcements were a long time in coming. Haig, who had largely misjudged the point of impact of the German attack, did not at once correct his faulty dispositions – he still expected the Germans to attack in front of Arras – or realise the seriousness of the position. He thought on the evening of March 21 that, in view of the heaviness of the German attack, the result of the day was 'highly creditable to the British troops'. In the evening of March 22 he asked Pétain for French support in holding the line of the Somme and the Péronne bridgehead. On March 23 he noted in his diary that he

[1] The destruction of railway bridges had been left to the French railway authorities and was not properly carried out. In any case, owing to persistent dry weather, the river was fordable at many points. Moreover, there was no prepared line behind it.

could not 'make out why the Fifth Army has gone so far back without making some kind of stand'.

Haig saw Pétain in the afternoon of March 23. Pétain was still convinced that the Germans were intending a great attack against his own front in Champagne. Nevertheless he promised to do his best to keep the British and French armies in touch. At this most critical time Haig's nerves were stronger than those of Pétain. He met Pétain again at 11 p.m. on March 24, and found him 'very much upset, almost unbalanced, and most anxious'. Haig explained his plans: he said that he was concentrating to attack southwards if the Germans reached the neighbourhood of Amiens; he asked that Pétain should concentrate as large a force as possible in the neighbourhood of Amiens. Pétain again promised to do what he could, but he was still sure that the main German blow had not been delivered, and that he was about to be attacked between Soissons and Rheims. He told Haig that, if the German advance continued, the French would fall back south-westwards towards Beauvais in order to cover Paris. He showed Haig the order which he had given to this effect.

Haig saw at once that Pétain intended to abandon the British right flank. Pétain agreed that – if he retreated further – this would be the case, and that he had instructions from the French Government to cover Paris at all costs. Pétain's general attitude at this time is still not altogether clear. He appears to have thought on March 24, at all events before his meeting with Haig, that the British were retiring, not westwards, but northwards. He may well have drawn this conclusion if – as he seems to have done – he regarded the battle as lost. He had said to Haig at their meeting on March 23 that, if contact between the two armies were broken, the British armies would probably be driven into the sea unless they drew back their northern flank along the sea coast – a move which would mean abandoning the Channel ports. In the order which he showed to Haig on March 24 he stated (rightly) that the German intention was to drive the principal part of the British armies northwards. On the morning of March 24 he had sent a message to the French President that the British were edging away northwards, and that Haig should be told that he must not compel the French to extend their armies indefinitely in order to keep in touch with the British.

Haig, on the other hand, did not regard the battle as lost.[1] If it had

[1] According to *Military Operations: France and Belgium, 1918,* i, p. 394, on March 23 General Byng, who commanded the Third Army, told his corps commanders that it had not been decided whether a retirement would be made

been lost, he would have been compelled to retire to the north or
north-west, but the Germans had not yet won, and while there was a
chance of maintaining the all-important contact with the French,
Haig regarded it as essential to do so, and not to accept defeat. Haig
had already telegraphed to London suggesting that the CIGS should
come to his headquarters to confer on the situation. He now reported
what he described as the serious change in French strategy, and asked
not only the CIGS but the Secretary of State for War to come to
France. On the morning of March 25 he telegraphed again that he
wanted them to arrange that 'General Foch or some other determined general who would fight, should be given supreme control in
France'.

Before Haig's message was received, the Prime Minister had asked
Milner[1] to go to Paris in order to find out about the situation. Poincaré
and Clemenceau accompanied Milner to Pétain's headquarters at
Compiègne on March 25. Pétain explained the measures which he was
taking to send troops to the British front in spite of his fears of an
enemy attack near Rheims. Foch, who had been called to the conference,
thought that more divisions should be put into the battle. It was agreed
to hold a meeting with Haig on the following morning. Meanwhile
Wilson had reached Haig's headquarters about 11 a.m. Haig told him
that the British army, with a few French divisions ill-supplied with
artillery and ammunition, was meeting the whole weight of the
German attack, and that the French must be persuaded to send more
help. At 4 p.m. Haig went – by appointment – to meet Clemenceau,
Foch, and Milner at Abbeville. He found only General Weygand,
Foch's Chief of Staff; Weygand explained why the other three had not
appeared.[2] Haig gave Weygand a letter for Clemenceau warning him
of the serious consequences if the French did not at once concentrate a
large force north of the Somme near Amiens.[3]

---

north-westwards to cover the Channel ports, or westwards to keep in touch with
the French.

    [1] Milner was at this time Minister without Portfolio. He was appointed to
succeed Lord Derby as Secretary of State for War on April 19. Derby became
British Ambassador in Paris.

    [2] It is uncertain why Haig was not informed in time that Clemenceau, Foch,
and Milner would not be able to come to Abbeville since they were meeting
Pétain at Compiègne.

    [3] Wilson seems to have gone with Weygand to Foch's headquarters. He made
the suggestion to Foch that Clemenceau should be given the duty of ensuring
the co-operation of the two armies. Foch rejected this plan as 'peu désirable'.

On the morning of March 26 Haig and Wilson met Milner, Poincaré, Clemenceau, Foch, and Pétain at Doullens. This meeting was transferred from Haig's advanced headquarters at Dury to Doullens because Haig had already arranged to hold a conference there with his army commanders. The French representatives arrived while the conference was taking place.[1] At this time Pétain, in conversation with Clemenceau, said that he had given orders for the retirement of the French army southwards and away from the British, and that he expected the total defeat of the British army, and, after it, the defeat of the French. Clemenceau answered that a general should not speak, or even think, in such terms; he then repeated Pétain's remark to Poincaré.

There could now be no question of subordinating Haig to Pétain. Haig, on the other hand, showed in the discussion that he would not object to putting himself under the orders of Foch. Clemenceau proposed that Foch should be entrusted with the co-ordination of the British and French armies in front of Amiens. Haig pointed out that these instructions would not be sufficient, and that Foch should be given full authority over all operations on the Western Front. Haig's intention was that Foch should control Pétain; for this purpose he was willing to accept his own subordination. Haig's comment in his diary was that 'Foch seemed sound and sensible, but Pétain had a terrible look. He had the appearance of a Commander who was in a funk and has lost his nerve.'[2] Haig's proposal was accepted. Foch was appointed to co-ordinate the operations of the Allied armies on the whole of the Western Front. Some days later – on April 3 – another Allied Conference was held at Beauvais. Foch had complained to Clemenceau that he had 'responsibility without proportionate authority', i.e. he had authority to co-ordinate action which was taking place but not to co-ordinate preparations for future action. With Haig's full agreement Foch was now given 'the strategic direction of military operations'. The British, French, and American Commanders-in-Chief retained control of the tactical action of their respective armies; each had the

[1] Some had arrived earlier. The hour for the Dury meeting had been fixed for 11 a.m. The hour for the Doullens meeting was changed to midday in order to allow time for Haig's meeting with the British army commanders. It is a sign of the general confusion that the French President was told of the change of place but not of the change of time.

[2] Pétain also made disparaging remarks about the Fifth Army, and compared it with the Italians after Caporetto. Wilson answered him in strong terms. Loucheur told Poincaré on March 27 that Pétain was 'tout à fai défaitiste', and thought that peace negotiations should be opened at once, Poincaré, op. cit., x, 93.

right to appeal to his Government if he thought that Foch's orders endangered the security of his troops.[1]

Haig had explained to Milner before the opening of the Doullens Conference, and had also stated during the discussions, that he did not intend to abandon Amiens; that he hoped to be able to hold on north of the Somme, but that to the south of it, from the neighbourhood of Bray, he must depend on French reinforcements. The position indeed began to improve north of the Somme while the Conference was taking place. The Germans had nearly turned the position of the Third Army at Colincamps, half-way between Amiens and Arras, but were driven back by the New Zealanders with the aid of twelve of the small 'whippet' tanks[2] now coming into action for the first time. Some three hundred of the enemy ran away on the sudden appearance of these tanks. One German writer has written that 'at the last moment, the tank attack had prevented the . . . break-through'. At all events, after this action there was no serious threat north of the Somme. South of it, however, the enemy continued to advance. On March 27 the gap between the British and French was nearly ten miles wide, but no German cavalry attempted to drive through it, since owing to lack of fodder, most of the horses had been taken for infantry transport. In the afternoon of March 27 Crown Prince Rupprecht, on hearing of the refusal of his request for three divisions to push the advance, commented 'Then we have lost the war.' From this time the French began to arrive in adequate numbers, and with their full equipment.

On March 28 Ludendorff ordered the delivery of the expected attacks north and south of Arras. These attacks were beaten back with very heavy casualties to the Germans. They had already lost many of their best assault troops. Their bombardment – though heavy – was less accurate because many of their guns had only just come from the southern area of attack. The weather was clear; the British gunners could therefore fire on moving targets. Furthermore, the British

---

[1] Foch's title was settled by correspondence. On April 14 he became 'Général en chef des Armées alliés en France'. Foch's position was unlike that of General Eisenhower in the Second World War. Foch was not served by an organisation such as SHAEF; he had only a personal staff of about twenty officers. Terraine (op. cit., p. 426) rightly says that 'his appointment was an expedient' (i.e. to overrule Pétain). 'His technique was an outdated reversion to the personal command of earlier centuries. It worked because its function was mainly 'a moral one'.

[2] These tanks were about six feet shorter than the heavier type of tank; they weighed about fifteen tons, and were armed with machine guns. Their speed – eight miles an hour – was nearly twice as fast as that of the latest heavy tanks.

defences in the Arras area were much stronger than on the front attacked earlier; the front lines, though not the whole forward zone, were much more lightly held, and troops were withdrawn from any weak points or salients. The German effort to win through was so great that in some places – after the loss of their assault troops – the enemy infantry reverted to the crude tactics of a shoulder-to-shoulder attack, six lines deep, only to be cut down by machine-gun and artillery fire.

The fighting continued, with decreasing violence, until April 5. Ludendorff then decided that he must order the offensive to be stopped. He dared not risk a battle of attrition, since he could spare neither the time nor the men. He had captured 70,000 prisoners, 1100 guns, and immense quantities of stores, but he had not won a strategic victory. His last attack in the Amiens area had brought him close to Villers-Bretonneux, but this small place was about ten miles from the city. The casualties of the Germans had been as heavy as those of the defenders, and the advance had left them with another dangerously large salient. They could not at once construct adequate defence works for this salient, while behind them their transport was impeded by the battleground of 1916, and – a grim retribution – the area which they themselves had devastated during their withdrawal to the Hindenburg line. The transport difficulties were increased owing to severe shortages of rubber, oil, and grease; here again the German army was being defeated by the unseen British navy.

The great attack, therefore, had broken down, like earlier attacks, because it could not maintain its momentum against a British army which – though at first uncertain about the tactics of a war of movement – never lost confidence. In spite of unnecessary retreats, due more often to bad staff work than to the soldiers' failure of nerve, the troops always rallied when called upon to counter-attack. The units of the Fifth Army which survived the first terrible blows had no sense of defeat. On the other hand, the Germans had expected a decisive victory, and realised that they had not won it. Their great captures of material – especially of food – showed them that the submarine war had been less effective than they had been told.[1] The Germans would

[1] Although German morale was affected by the discovery – on overrunning the British supply depots – that the British armies were far better provided with food than the German armies, there is no evidence to support the legend that the pillaging of these depots (which included immense quantities of whisky) was an important factor in holding up the German advance. This factor, however, slowed down the Flanders attacks in April. Influenza – which took an epidemic form about mid-June – was of greater general importance in its effect on German

fight again, with bravery and determination, but never with the confidence or, indeed, the massed power displayed at the opening of the March offensive.

Ludendorff was now compelled to continue his 'gamble', though the chances of success were less. He decided to carry out the offensive for which preparations had been made in Flanders, though owing to lack of reserves the scale would have to be smaller than he had originally thought possible. He had three advantages which were, from his point of view, a matter of good fortune. In the first place the dry weather had made the Flanders area suitable for battle earlier than usual.[1] Secondly, Haig's Intelligence section believed, as late as April 6, that the main German attack would be delivered against Vimy Ridge, with only a subsidiary attack to the north. The third factor upon which the Germans would not have counted in advance was that some five to six miles of the front upon which they attacked was held by a single Portuguese division. The discipline of the Portuguese troops was known to be unsatisfactory.[2] One of their two divisions had been withdrawn; the second was about to be relieved. The British staff had misjudged – until too late – the direction of the attack; even so the delay in carrying out this relief on a threatened sector was imprudent.

The attack opened on the morning of April 9. The Portuguese broke – taking their artillery with them. Within three hours the Germans had reached open country behind the last defence system. This breach was closed,[3] with great difficulty, by the neighbouring British troops; the 55th West Lancashire territorial division held out for five days against attacks in the fortified village of Givenchy at the south end of the German advance. To the north, however, another strong German attack captured the Messines ridge and by April 12 the Germans were more than half-way to the key railway junction of Hazebrouck. They were held up on the edge of the forest of Nieppe by a mixed force of such men as could be found – including lads of $18\frac{1}{2}$ –

---

morale. The epidemic spread also to the Allied armies, but they were better fed and were more able to resist, and recover from, the disease.

[1] On the other hand, the ground was found to be too soft for the tanks which the Germans hoped to use – though not in very large numbers – in the attack of April 9.

[2] General da Costa, the Portuguese commander, was a very capable soldier. His troops, however, had little interest in the war or understanding why they were asked to fight in it, and complained of insufficient leave.

[3] Among the Germans caught behind it was a band, complete with instruments, which was to have played the victors into Béthune.

and the 4th Guards Brigade; the latter, at very heavy cost, defended a
front of 4000 yards against more than four times their own numbers.

Haig's main concern during these critical days was that the French
were not giving adequate support. He had no doubt that the Germans
were trying to destroy the British army, and were concentrating all
their reserves on the British front. The weight of their attacks was such
that, unless the French provided more help, the British might be over-
whelmed by force of numbers. So far Haig's appeals to Foch had been
of little practical use. When Foch moved French divisions up behind
the British lines, they took no part in the fighting and impeded communications in the back areas.[1] On April 11 Haig had made another
appeal for assistance. Foch's reply was that the British must hold on
where they stood, and must not expect any reinforcement beyond the
'divisions already detailed'. Foch explained to General Davidson, chief
of the operations branch at British GHQ, that he still had to 'nurse'
the French army, and could not rely on it as yet for difficult operations such as entering a defensive battle in which the defenders were
giving ground. Foch also had in mind the offensive which he was
determined to deliver as soon as the situation allowed, but Haig was
afraid that he judged the state of the French army only too well.
When the French at last took over seven miles of the British front they
lost the strong position of Mount Kemmel after less than two hours'
resistance to a German assault.

On the night of April 11–12 Haig wrote an order to his troops:
'Many amongst us now are tired . . . To those I would say that victory
will belong to the side which holds out the longest. The French army
is moving rapidly and in great force to our support. There is no other
course open to us but to fight it out . . . With our backs to the wall and
believing in the justice of our cause, each one of us must fight on to
the end. . . .'[2] Haig, in fact, was none too sure of this French support –

[1] These communications were further impeded by the French insistence that
half the available railway transport should be used for the carriage of coal from
the French mines in the Bruay area. On April 21 the British Government agreed
to provide the coal and also to feed the inhabitants and all French troops in the
British area.

[2] Haig told Mr Speaker Lowther that the night on which he wrote this order
was the only night during which he did not sleep at all owing to anxiety. He
added that he had been more anxious after the failure of the French offensive in
1917 on the Chemin des Dames, and that he considered the Germans to have
realised, after their inability to renew at once their attack at Arras at the end of
March, that they had lost the war. Viscount Ullswater, *A Speaker's Commentaries*,
ii, 256–7.

one reason indeed for his appeal to his soldiers was that he wanted them to hold on without it. He continued to urge that the French should take a more active part in the fighting; he wrote to Foch on April 14 that he 'found it necessary to place on record (his) opinion that the arrangements made by you are insufficient to meet the present situation'. Nevertheless Foch, who remembered the earlier battles of Ypres, thought very highly of the British powers of resistance, and kept to his plans. No French reinforcements came into the line on the most threatened part of the Northern Front until April 19.

Foch's calculation was right. The British army held on, though at very great cost. Ludendorff had hesitated on the most critical days, from April 11 to 13, because he too expected French reinforcements to be coming up in strength. His attacks continued for another fortnight; the capture of Mount Kemmel on April 25 was the last outstanding success. On the night of April 29 Ludendorff decided that he had not the men to carry out any more successful attacks. He needed ten or twelve fresh divisions if he were to capture and get beyond Poperinghe, but these divisions were not to be found. So he decided, for the time, to remain on the defensive along the British front. He had compelled the Allies to concentrate more than half their total reserves on this front. He would now make the attack on the French which Pétain had expected in March. After he had dealt a very heavy blow against the French, he would resume the offensive in Flanders.

Ludendorff had begun preparations for this attack in Champagne, but only on a large scale in the middle of April. Even so, he could not deliver the attack for another month; during this time the Allies had a certain respite. Moreover the German position was worse than at the end of the first offensive. The Germans had not reached the Channel ports; they now had a second salient to defend as well as the salient in the Somme area. They had suffered as heavily as the British whom they had attacked. They could still reckon on reinforcements, but whereas they were drawing on the last resources of their man-power, the troops reaching the British line included excellent divisions from Italy and Palestine. Above all, the Americans were arriving at an increasingly rapid rate. Already on March 25 General Pershing had offered to give up, for the time, the formation of an American corps, and to send four divisions wherever they could be of use. Three of them, with a fourth in reserve, took over quiet sectors on the French front. On April 24 Pershing, with the approval of the United States Government, agreed that the infantry, machine gun, engineer, and signal units of six American divisions should be brought over as soon as possible without waiting for their artillery. The total number of American troops transported in March was 64,200 and in April, 93,128. In May the figure rose to 206,287, of whom nearly two-thirds were infantry. The increase in the numbers was due largely to the use of British as well as American shipping; one-half of the arrivals in May and June and nearly two-thirds of those in July came in British ships.[1] This transport continued without loss from submarine attack; once again, therefore, Ludendorff's defeat was being hastened, inexorably, by Allied, and especially British sea power. When the Germans attacked on the French front at the end of May, two American divisions – apart from the three already in the line – were at the disposal of the French in Picardy; three other complete divisions and a depot division were in France. Every week in which Ludendorff was compelled to delay his next attack allowed more time for the battle training of these American troops.

Ludendorff had one piece of good fortune in attacking the French on the Chemin des Dames. After the offensive expected by Pétain had not taken place, the French High Command began to assume that the Germans thought the French position too strong to be attacked. Foch even persuaded Haig – against his own wish not to disperse his armies – to send five exhausted British divisions to 'rest' in the French front line, and thereby free five French divisions for the area near Amiens. The French positions generally on the Champagne front were weakly held; the defences were not kept in good condition, and the French army commander made matters worse by holding far too many of his men in the forward zone, in spite of the recent experience of German methods.

Until twelve hours before the attack on May 27 Ludendorff was able to conceal his preparations.[2] The American Intelligence Staff had warned Foch a month earlier of the probability of an offensive against the Chemin des Dames, but Foch did not accept their conclusions.

---

[1] British shipping carried in all a slightly higher number of American troops than American shipping. About 82 per cent of the escort vessels were American.

[2] The noise of the dumping of material – especially bridging material – in the forward zone was drowned at night by the croaking of frogs in the marshes of the Ailette which ran through no-man's land. Dust clouds observed on the roads leading towards the front in the early mornings and later in the evenings of May 22, 23, and 24 were in fact caused by the movement of heavy artillery, but the French did not take the precaution of investigating further in order to discover their significance.

394 GREAT BRITAIN AND THE WAR OF 1914-1918

Only in the afternoon of May 26 two German prisoners gave away the plan. It was, however, too late to do more than warn the divisions in the line, and to start at once the transfer of reserves from the north. The German bombardment before the attack was of the usual 'concentrated' type – heavier indeed than in the earlier offensives of the year. It was followed by the longest advance made in a single day since the beginning of trench warfare. The centre of the attacking force crossed three rivers – including the Aisne, which averaged about fifty yards across, and reached Fismes, thirteen miles from its starting point. This success – though it was due mainly to overwhelming artillery and mortar fire, and to great local superiority in numbers – encouraged Ludendorff to go on, and to postpone the renewal of the northern offensive for which the Chemin des Dames attack was only a diversion. By May 30 the Germans had reached the Marne, and were within fifty miles of Paris. Once again there was anger – and some panic – in the French Chamber, but Clemenceau stood firmly by Foch. Within a week the danger was over, at least for a time; the Germans had only repeated the cycle of their March and April offensives. They were held on the flanks; the centre slowly lost momentum as the Allied reserves came up. The result was that the Germans had made for themselves another great salient: their position was insecure, since this new salient was thirty miles deep and served by only one main railway close to its western end.

Ludendorff was therefore committed to another attack in order to broaden his front, since he could not abandon the area over which he had advanced. He attempted this attack on June 9. He had some success, but the French – under General Mangin – counter-attacked, and drove the enemy back two miles. Furthermore the Germans met, for the first time, an American attack near Chateau-Thierry. They regarded the attackers as inexperienced and wasteful in their methods, but had great difficulty in holding them back. It was necessary once again to postpone the renewal of the northern offensive. Ludendorff decided to attempt another diversion before delivering his final blow in the north. While he was waiting for his immense train of heavy artillery to be brought into position the Allies won a number of small successes which were ominous for the future of the German armies. Moreover, when the German attack opened on July 15 the French had had full warning of it. The Germans had not been able to conceal their preparations and, for propaganda reasons, the High Command had let it be known that the 'offensive to gain peace' was about to be opened. Hence Allied reserves had been brought down from the north; the defence was organized in great depth, and the French did not waste men in holding their front positions.

The attack was made on either side of Rheims. To the east of the city the Germans failed entirely, with very heavy losses. On the west – between Chateau-Thierry and Dormans – they had more success. They crossed the Marne, stormed the wooded hills on its south bank, and advanced three miles beyond the river, before they were held by the French and Americans. They had, in fact, been halted after their last victory in the war. On July 18 Mangin carried out a surprise attack on the right flank of the Germans in the salient between Soissons and Rheims, and compelled them to bring up reserves which they had intended to use in Flanders. By August 3 the Germans were back on the Aisne and the Vesle. The French attack had been boldly planned; Haig was somewhat alarmed at the moving of troops from the Flanders front. Pétain had thought the plan too risky, and had wanted only to cut off the Germans south of the Marne. Ludendorff, who had left his headquarters on July 17 to make final arrangements for the Flanders offensive, again postponed it for a fortnight or three weeks.

Ludendorff – though few other German commanders shared his opinion – still hoped that this offensive would be carried out. On August 8, however, the British Fourth Army[1] delivered a well-planned surprise attack, with strong tank support east of Amiens. At the end of the day they had advanced about seven miles, and captured 15,000 prisoners and some 350 guns. The attack was not pressed after the second day; the British commanders, with some reason, were cautious in dealing with the enemy. The old trenches, with much wire intact, and the mass of shell craters in the area of retreat, favoured the German rearguard defence. The Tank Corps Staff would have used their 'whippets' to go on through the gap in the line, but the High Command refused, although the battle spread south as far as the Aisne. The Germans thus had time to bring up reserves, and to re-establish themselves on a new line. None the less Ludendorff's well-known

---

[1] The main attack was delivered by the Canadian and Australian Corps. The former had not taken part in the earlier defensive fighting, and its sudden appearance was itself disconcerting to the Germans. The tanks – over 500, including 120 supply tanks, each capable of carrying ten tons of supplies or fifty men – were of immense value. The cavalry, who had been brought up from reserve, were, as usual, held up by machine guns and difficult ground.

description of August 8 as the 'black day' in the history of the German army during the war has some truth.[1]

It has been said that in each of his offensives Ludendorff went either too far or not far enough. Thus, if he had stopped the first offensive as soon as the British reserves had been brought to the St Quentin area, and if he had opened the northern offensive earlier, he might have taken Hazebrouck. On the other hand, if he had exploited his success at the southern end of the British front, he might have captured Amiens and attacked Arras from the rear. In the northern offensive, after he had taken Mount Kemmel, he might have pressed on to Haze-brouck if he had not been so nervous of a British counter-attack. This argument must remain conjectural. What was and is clear is that the initiative had now passed to the Allies. This decisive fact could not be concealed from the German soldiers or from the German people.

[1] Ludendorff regarded the tanks as 'decisive for the issue'. After August 8 the German High Command decided – too late – to include tank production in the 'urgent' class of war material. Liddell Hart, op. cit., i, 185.

CHAPTER 27

The definition of Allied war aims in 1918: President Wilson's Fourteen Points: German war aims in the West

The failure of the German western offensive and the passing of the military initiative to the Allies meant that Germany could no longer expect a complete victory in the West. There was another consequence which the German High Command took a surprisingly long time to realise. They had rejected Wilson's ideas of a compromise peace as long as they thought that they could extort their demands for annexations and indemnities from the Allies. It was now too late for the Germans to go back to Wilson's earlier proposals. Whatever Wilson might say, the European Allies were determined to destroy, as far they could do so, German power of aggression. The war was 'to end war'. Wilson himself had been compelled by events to give up the idea of a return to the *status quo*; he was also no longer in the morally stronger position (or so he thought it) of a neutral. Nevertheless the President still regarded himself as outside the rivalries and intrigues of the European Powers, and destined to compel them to accept his more dispassionate view of the future peace settlement. He now took the line that the German Government, not the German people, were responsible for the war, and that, if the Germans repudiated their Government, they should be treated without vindictiveness. This argument, which the President brought out in his speeches, may have been of some use in separating the German people from their military and civil leaders, though the fact of utter defeat after promises of unlimited victory was enough in itself to drive even the most docile people against their government. To the European Allies (Wilson was careful to maintain that the United States was not an 'Allied' but an 'Associated' Power) there was something dangerous in assuming that all the Germans had to do in order to escape the consequences of defeat was to get rid of the Emperor and to alter their constitution. The English and French, who had suffered immense losses of men and material in the war, could not allow such an easy evasion of responsibility.

The President, however, continued to think almost solely in large and somewhat vague terms of a future from which a wise peace settlement would have eliminated the causes of war. He was also aware of American power, and, with a curious mixture of realism and idealism, proposed to use Allied exhaustion as well as German defeat to impose upon Europe his plans for a world order. He wrote to House in July, 1917, 'England and France have not the same views with regard to peace that we have by any means. When the war is over we can force them to our way of thinking, because by that time they will, among other things, be financially in our hands.' Wilson was careful not to attempt this forcing process too early, since he did not want disagreement among the Allies before Germany had been defeated, but in the early autumn of 1917 he authorised an American 'Inquiry' into Allied war aims 'in order that we may formulate our own position either for or against them and begin to gather the influences we wish to employ – or at least, ascertain what influence we can use; in brief, prepare our case with a full knowledge of all the litigants'.

Before the end of the year Wilson had tried – and failed – to secure an Allied-American public statement of war aims.[1] He then decided to make a statement himself. On January 5, 1918 – before Wilson had made his statement – Lloyd George gave an account to the British Trade Union Congress of the war aims of the British Empire. Lloyd George had consulted Asquith, Grey, and Lord Robert Cecil as well as the Labour Party leaders and certain overseas representatives.[2] He therefore claimed to speak with authority in assuring the Germans that the British Government and people did not aim at the 'break-up' of Germany, though they would support the French demand for the return of Alsace-Lorraine. They were also not fighting to destroy Austria-Hungary, but would support the grant of 'genuine self-government on true democratic principles . . . to those Austro-Hungarian nationalities who have genuinely desired it'. Similarly, while the British were not fighting to turn the Turks out of Thrace, they accepted

[1] See below, p. 437.

[2] Including Sir William Wiseman. After being gassed on active service, Wiseman was attached to the British Embassy in Washington in 1915. He became a close friend of House, and lived in the same apartment building. House had a private telephone to the White House, and Wiseman a private code for telegrams to the Foreign Office. (There was at this time no transatlantic telephone.) Wiseman's position was of special importance owing to Wilson's suspicions of Spring-Rice. Lord Reading, when he succeeded Spring-Rice, also saw little of Wilson, and worked through Wiseman and House.

the right of the 'subject lands' of Turkey – Arabia, Armenia, Mesopotamia, and Palestine – to a 'recognition of their separate national
conditions'. Lloyd George said, somewhat vaguely, that Russia could
be saved only by her own people; he spoke of an independent Poland
as an 'urgent necessity for the stability of Western Europe'. He declared that the German colonies should be 'held at the disposal of a
Conference whose decision must have primary regard to the wishes
and interests of the native inhabitants'. He asked for the complete
restoration of Belgium, and the payment of reparation – though not
of a war indemnity – by Germany. He laid down three conditions of
a permanent peace: (i) re-establishment of the sanctity of treaties, (ii) a
territorial settlement based on the right of self-determination; (iii) the
creation of an international organisation 'to limit the burden of armaments and diminish the probability of war'.

On reading Lloyd George's speech Wilson thought at first that his
own address was unnecessary. He decided, however, not to give up his
plan, and on January 8 delivered to Congress the address containing
fourteen points essential to a settlement. This address – the most important of Wilson's speeches – was drafted after much care and consultation.[1] The basis of the address was the finding of the American
'Inquiry'. The general arrangement was largely suggested by House,
but the wording was almost entirely Wilson's own choice. The only
paragraph shown to an Allied representative concerned the Balkans.
M. Vesnitch, head of the Serbian Mission in the United States, was
asked his opinion of the paragraph: his view was that the President
should have required the break-up of the Habsburg Empire.

The 'Fourteen Points' differed little in their territorial requirements
from those put forward by Lloyd George. Wilson asked for the
'restoration' of the invaded areas of France, and the return of Alsace-
Lorraine; the evacuation and restoration of Belgium; a readjustment
of the frontiers of Italy; 'the freest opportunity of autonomous development to the peoples of Austria-Hungary'; Roumania, Serbia, and
Montenegro were to be evacuated and restored, and Serbia given
access to the sea. 'Secure sovereignty' was to be assured to the Turkish
portions of the Ottoman Empire, and an opportunity of 'autonomous
development' to other nationalities under Turkish rule. An 'independent Polish State' would be established for 'the territories inhabited

[1] The address was drafted before Wilson had read Lloyd George's speech.
Wilson was not altogether pleased that Lloyd George had anticipated him. He
made no change in his draft except to approve of Lloyd George's 'candour'.

by indisputably Polish populations, which should be assured a free
and secure access to the sea, and whose political and economic independence and territorial integrity should be guaranteed by international
covenant'. All Russian territory was to be evacuated, and the Russians
given full opportunity to determine their own political development
and national policy. Finally – in Point XIV – the President asked for 'a
general association of nations . . . formed under specific covenants for
the purpose of affording mutual guarantees of political independence
and territorial integrity to great and small States alike'.

The President's statement established him as the principal Allied
spokesman. He was speaking with the authority of the strongest Power
on the Allied side, even though American resources had not yet been
fully deployed. He was also a greater orator – in this particular kind of
public speaking – than Lloyd George. Nevertheless the effect of his
speech was due mainly to his emphasis on the future, and on the conditions necessary for the maintenance of world peace. His proposal for
a general association of nations came at the end of his Fourteen Points,
as a guarantee of the territorial settlement; on the other hand he had
begun with certain large general requirements: 'open covenants of
peace openly arrived at'; 'absolute freedom of navigation upon the seas
outside territorial waters'; 'the removal, so far as possible, of all
economic barriers and the establishment of an equality of trade conditions'; 'adequate guarantees . . . that national armaments will be
reduced to the lowest point consistent with domestic safety'; 'a free,
open-minded, and absolutely impartial adjustment of all colonial
claims'.

Within the next nine months the President made three other speeches
on the principles of a permanent peace. On February 11, 1918, after
saying that there must be 'no annexations, no contributions, no punitive damages', he laid down four principles: (i) each part of the final
settlement must be based on the essential justice of that particular case;
(ii) peoples and provinces were 'not to be bartered about from sovereignty to sovereignty as if they were mere chattels and pawns in a
game, even the great game, now for ever discredited, of the Balance
of Power'; (iii) 'every territorial settlement must be made in the interest
. . . of the populations concerned'; (iv) all well-defined national elements to be accorded the 'utmost satisfaction without introducing new
or perpetuating old elements of discord and antagonism'. On July 4
Wilson repeated his views in slightly different language. Nearly three
months later, on September 27, when the defeat of Germany was

certain, the President added 'five Particulars', amplifying for the most part, his previous statements; he was now definite about the part to be taken by the United States in the proposed League of Nations.[1]

In view of the remarkable effect of Wilson's speeches the Allies left the public definition of war aims largely in his hands. In July, 1918, Lloyd George said in a speech that the German Emperor could 'have peace tomorrow', if he would accept the President's terms. Lord Lansdowne, in a letter to the press of July 31, pointed out that Wilson's speech of July 4 was not 'an outline of peace terms, but a very loosely worded description of the things for which the associated peoples of the world were fighting', and that the acceptance of these premises 'would place us at the beginning, and not at the end of a very complicated negotiation'. Wilson himself had described the Fourteen Points (on February 11) as only an American 'provisional sketch of principles and the way in which they should be applied'.

One of the most skilful, though dangerous, features of Wilson's oratory was his capacity for giving the impression of preciseness to a statement which was, in fact, vague. The Fourteen Points, for all their appearance of clarity, were far from being well defined. Thus Point VI required 'the evacuation of all Russian territory', and Point XIII the establishment of an independent Polish State including the territories inhabited by 'indisputably Polish populations', but a great deal of this area had been Russian territory – held in full sovereignty – before 1914, and there were also very large areas in which the population was neither 'indisputably Russian' nor 'indisputably Polish'. Point IV, again, asked for 'the removal, so far as possible, of all economic barriers'. What was meant by 'so far as possible'? Clearly Wilson could mean only 'as far as the electorate in democratic countries would vote for such removal'. What would happen if American and other electoral supporters of high tariffs continued to regard economic barriers as necessary to secure 'an equality of trade conditions'?

The main purpose of Wilson – and of Lloyd George – in January, 1918, was not to put forward terms to the Germans – the Allied military position was by no means favourable to a peace offer – but to counter the propaganda of the Bolsheviks. The negotiations between the

[1] On the other hand, Wilson's attitude towards Germany was very different from the 'peace without victory' of his former views. Early in April, 1918, he talked of 'force, force to the utmost, force without stint or limit' as necessary in dealing with Germany.

Germans and the Bolsheviks reopened on January 7, 1918, after a delay during which the latter had issued their appeals to the proletariat in all the belligerent countries to stop fighting a 'patriotic war' and to concentrate on world revolution and join in the conference to achieve a general peace without annexations or indemnities.[1] Wilson's sixth point was a counter appeal – a bid for a liberal and democratic Russia, and an offer of definite American support.

The Bolsheviks took no notice of Wilson's appeal to Russian democracy except to denounce his 'imperialism', but a chain of events led the Germans to accept the Fourteen Points as the basis of a treaty of peace in spite of their vagueness, and of the particular circumstances in which they were laid down. Wilson had begun to realise after the spring of 1917 that, as the British and French had long insisted to him, the ruling class in Germany would not concede 'Wilsonian' terms, and indeed could not concede them without the loss of the dominating position in Europe which Germany had held before 1914. A large section of German opinion – including a majority of the middle class and sections of the working class – agreed with the demands of their rulers. The minority could make no headway against this view until the military situation was so unfavourable that the High Command had to insist on an immediate armistice. They then asked for an armistice to be followed by a peace on the basis of the Fourteen Points, but they no longer had either the time or the power to safeguard themselves by a more precise interpretation of the conditions of their surrender.

So far from thinking in terms of a 'peace of compromise', the military leaders of Germany throughout 1917 were still planning annexations and would not even consider giving up their hold on Belgium. The early successes of the submarine campaign, the military collapse of Russia, and the failure of Nivelle's offensive encouraged hopes of getting their full programme; their terms, indeed, in their own words, were even 'stronger' than a few months earlier.[2] On April 23, Bethmann-Hollweg, at a conference with the Emperor and the military chiefs at Kreuznach, accepted the military demands for direct control of Belgium until the country was ready to accept an offensive and defensive alliance with Germany. During this 'intermediate' period – of which the German Government would determine the length – Germany would have the right to occupy Belgium and to supervise Belgian communications. In any event Liège, its surrounding

[1] See below p. 437.   [2] See above, p. 236.

territories, and the Flanders coast were to remain in German hands or to be leased to Germany for ninety-nine years. The south-east corner of Belgium – near Arlon – was to be ceded either to Germany or to Luxembourg, and Luxembourg was to be embodied as a federal state in the Reich. France was to surrender the Longwy-Briey area and to accept 'frontier rectifications' elsewhere. A month later, the military rulers of Germany – again with Bethmann-Hollweg's reluctant assent – put forward a programme for a Great German Empire in Central Africa – a Mittelafrika to supplement a Mitteleuropa – with the necessary naval stations. These stations included some, if not all of the Azores, and Dakar. Finally, on May 15, in a speech to the Reichstag which aroused immense applause, Bethmann-Hollweg said that 'Time is on our side . . . We can be completely confident that we are reaching a conclusion favourable to us. The time will then come when we can negotiate with our enemies about our war aims, in regard to which I find myself in full agreement with the Supreme Military Command.'

Bethmann-Hollweg, as the Supreme Command well knew, was not in agreement with them; for this reason they were trying to get rid of him. In spite of his public statements, he was not sure that time was on the side of Germany. He refused to regard the Kreuznach resolutions as more than a statement of German maximum demands. If the military situation allowed their realisation, he would have no scruples about enforcing them. If the military situation were less favourable Germany might have to be content with much less. Bethmann-Hollweg had been discussing, unknown to the German Supreme Command, terms on this more tentative basis with Count Czernin[1] who insisted that Austria must have peace before the end of the year. Nevertheless, the only limit which the German Chancellor set to the joint territorial demands of the two Allies was the extent of their military victory, though, with a characteristic German addition, Bethmann-Hollweg pointed out that acquisitions of territory must be proportionate to the respective military efforts of the two Powers. Germany would thus have a greater claim than Austria-Hungary.

The Emperor Charles, who had succeeded Francis Joseph in November, 1916, could have no illusions about the desperate need of his own subjects for peace. After the rejection of the German 'peace offer' of December 12, 1916, Charles made more than one attempt to get

---

[1] Count Czernin succeeded Baron Burian as Austro-Hungarian Foreign Minister in December, 1916.

in touch with the Western Powers. The most important of these approaches had been made through his brother-in-law, Prince Sixte de Bourbon,[1] to Poincaré. Poincaré had told him that France required the return of Alsace-Lorraine, the Saar territory, and Landau (i.e. the French frontier of 1814), the restoration of Belgium and Serbia (with the grant to the latter of a port on the Adriatic), and the cession of Constantinople to Russia. The Emperor, unwisely from his point of view, sent a letter in his own handwriting on March 20 to Prince Sixte, promising to support the 'just claim' of France to Alsace-Lorraine, and accepting all Poincaré's demands other than the cession of Constantinople.

Poincaré now consulted Lloyd George. Lloyd George had always hoped that Austria might be detached from her German Ally. There was, however, little chance at this time of making her an acceptable offer unless the Italians would give up the purpose for which they entered the war, that is to say, the military weakening, if not the destruction of Austria-Hungary as a Great Power. The Italian Government would not withdraw their claims to a part of the Tyrol, the Trentino, and Istria, guaranteed to them under the secret Treaty of London. Charles was willing to agree to the surrender of territory by Germany, but there were limits to the amount of his own dominions which he would concede. He also refused to declare war on Germany or to take back Silesia from Prussia as compensation for the lands to be handed to Italy.[2]

Meanwhile Czernin, who did not know the extent to which Charles had committed himself in writing, drew up after his meeting with Bethmann-Hollweg a memorandum for the Emperor to send to the Kaiser. Czernin stated plainly in the memorandum that Austria-Hungary was in danger of collapse, and that, whatever the German High Command might think, if the monarchs of the Central Powers did not make peace, their peoples would do so over their heads; both Germany and Austria-Hungary would then be submerged in a revolutionary storm. Charles next offered to hand over Galicia (not without compensation from Roumanian territory!) if the Germans would agree to the surrender of Alsace-Lorraine to France. Obviously the

[1] Prince Sixte de Bourbon was an officer in the Belgian army. As a member of the family of Bourbon he was legally debarred from serving in the French army.

[2] The Emperor would not commit himself about Constantinople until the Russian political position had been 'stabilised'. In April, 1918, Clemenceau published the Emperor's letters to Prince Sixte. Charles attempted to deny their authenticity, and compelled Czernin to do so, but no one believed the denials.

German military authorities would not give up Alsace-Lorraine unless they were forced to do so by defeat, and at this time – the end of April – the military position did not suggest a German defeat. Czernin himself came to Germany in mid-May, only to return with bitter comments on the German attempts to get world domination.

Two months later, and even before the adoption of convoying had brought down Allied shipping losses, it was becoming clear to the German people that their submarine campaign had not broken, and was unlikely to break, the resistance of Great Britain, at least within the promised time, and that Germany would be faced with another war winter. In two speeches of July 3 and 6 to the General Committee (*Hauptausschuss*) of the Reichstag Erzberger, a prominent politician of the Centre party, proposed that the Reichstag should recognise the facts, and should pass a resolution in favour of a 'peace of understanding'. Erzberger had obtained, through Austrian court circles, a copy of Czernin's memorandum, and had told its content to the leaders of the Centre party. Erzberger not only doubted whether the submarine campaign would win the war; he was afraid, like Czernin, that unless peace were made before the winter, revolution would break out in Germany and Austria-Hungary.

Erzberger's proposal had a sensational effect because he had ventured to say outright what many Germans were beginning to think. The sequel to the speech, however, was an absurd and not altogether honourable anti-climax. On July 19 Erzberger introduced into the Reichstag a resolution in ambiguous terms containing a number of generalities that 'forced territorial acquisitions, and political, economic or financial means of coercion' were 'incompatible with a peace of understanding and the permanent reconciliation of peoples'. The resolution was passed, but Erzberger himself was in favour of the annexation of the Longwy-Briey area; he also hoped to keep Alsace-Lorraine and did not oppose plans for the post-war domination of Belgium by Germany or for German expansion in the east.[1] Moreover Erzberger and his supporters had already taken a step which was fatal to any chance of a 'peace of understanding'. They had demanded the resignation of Bethmann-Hollweg mainly on the ground that, having brought the country into the war, he was not the right man to negotiate an early peace.

[1] Erzberger, who had connections with German industrialists (especially Thyssen) had been a consistent supporter of an annexationist peace, and an advocate of unrestricted submarine warfare and Zeppelin attacks on London.

After the failure of the German note of December 12, 1916, Bethmann-Hollweg had opposed the idea of a 'peace resolution' as useless
and as likely to encourage the Allies. On the other hand, the Chancellor was now a 'moderate'; he was resisting in a weak and devious
way the intransigence of the military chiefs, and might have been in a
stronger position to do so after the passing of the Reichstag resolution.
In any case the overthrow of Bethmann-Hollweg was an act of folly –
or worse – since the politicians of the Reichstag were unable to determine the choice of his successor.[1] The High Command were only too
happy to see Bethmann-Hollweg go; the occasion of his dismissal –
though he concealed the fact, as he had already concealed so much –
was an ultimatum to the Emperor from Hindenburg and Ludendorff.
The military chiefs were careful that the new Chancellor should be
their willing as well as their obedient servant. They wanted Bülow,
but the Emperor refused to accept him. They were content with the
choice of an official, Dr Michaelis, who was at the time Food Commis-
sary for Prussia. The views of the Reichstag were not even asked.
Michaelis himself was as much surprised at his elevation as were most
of his countrymen. He took the post out of a sense of duty, and at once
surrendered to the military leaders and the annexationists. He qualified
his adherence to the peace resolution with the gloss 'as I understand it'.
There was indeed no doubt about the manner in which Michaelis
understood it. He wrote to the Crown Prince that 'the notorious
Resolution' had been passed by 212 votes to 126, with 17 not voting.
'Through my interpretation of it I have exorcised its chief danger.
With the Resolution we can ultimately conclude any peace we
like.'

The Emperor, in his own manner, shewed the kind of peace which
the military party 'liked'. He still held that the submarine warfare
would bring about the collapse of England. On July 20 – the day after
the passing of the Reichstag resolution – he received (for the first time
in almost twenty years) delegates from all parties except the Independent Socialists. He told them that a peace of 'adjustment' – a term used
by Michaelis but not by the supporters of the resolution – meant that
Germany would take what she chose from her enemies. He then spoke
of his plans for a 'Second Punic War' against England in which he

---

[1] A committee of the Reichstag, with the exception of representatives of the
Social Democrats, supported the Chancellor's refusal in answer to a papal 'peace
note' of August 1, 1917, to commit Germany before the opening of negotiations
to the unconditional return of Belgium.

would unite the whole Continent against British world domination. He also made the egregious remark: 'Where my guards appear, there is no room for democracy.' Behind this bombastic talk of a weak and frightened man there was one obvious fear. The supporters of a moderate peace were also, for the most part, the supporters of a real parliamentary regime in Germany. It seemed likely – with the example of the Russian revolution – that such a regime might throw over the whole military party and its attendant paraphernalia, including the Hohenzollerns.

Henceforward indeed in Germany the question of peace became increasingly linked with that of domestic reform. The conservative elements could not accept an end to the war which might affect their control of the German state; they dared not risk the reaction of public opinion when the Germans realised that the war had not brought victory. The parties of the left, on the other hand, wanted an immediate peace, on 'compromise' terms, not only because they wished to end the miseries of war but also because an 'annexationist' peace would enable the military, undemocratic regime to maintain its hold. Herein lay the great difference between Germany and her enemies, and, in a final analysis, the justification of Great Britain and France for insisting upon an Allied victory. The 'Second Punic War' was just what the Allies, and Wilson, hoped to prevent.

It is unnecessary to follow in detail the manœuvres in German politics which led to the resignation of Michaelis and the appointment of the Bavarian Count Hertling as Chancellor, and, later, when Ludendorff had given up hopes of victory, and was afraid of utter defeat, the substitution of Prince Max of Baden for Hertling. The weakness of the moderates still lay in their unwillingness to oppose an 'annexationist' peace as long as it seemed obtainable. Thus the Treaty of Brest-Litovsk took from Russia the Baltic provinces, the Ukraine, and Russian Poland, and put those vast areas under the direct control of the Central Powers. The 'moderates' in the Reichstag acquiesced in these terms; Erzberger described them as 'entirely within the bounds of the resolution of July 19 . . . wherever it deviates from those principles, it represents only temporary police measures'. In the spring of 1918 the moderates began to feel uneasy at the treatment of the provinces 'liberated' from Russia, but, as usual, they were too late, and their protests were ineffective. The protests might have carried more weight if the moderate parties had passed a resolution in favour of the full restitution of Belgium, but here again, as long as there seemed a considerable chance of a military victory, they hesitated to lose the possibility of territorial and economic gains.[1]

The military party was therefore opposed only by the left-wing Socialists who wanted an immediate end to the war as the indispensable condition of the overthrow of the existing regime in Germany. The army and navy chiefs were as obstinate as ever about the need to control Belgium; the navy wanted to secure the Flemish ports Ostend and Zeebrugge, and the army asked for the occupation of Liège. They reaffirmed these conditions in every discussion with the political leaders. As late as July 3, 1918, at a conference presided over by the Emperor, the Chancellor agreed with Hindenburg and Ludendorff that in order to keep Belgium under German influence the conditions of peace must secure the division of

> Flanders and Wallonia into two separate states, united only by personal union and economic arrangements. Belgium must be brought into the closest relation with Germany through a customs union, common railways, etc. For the time being there must be no Belgian army. Germany must obtain a long-term occupation of Belgium with a gradual withdrawal in such a way that the Flanders coast and Liège would be evacuated last. Final evacuation would depend upon the closeness with which Belgium attached herself to Germany.

In particular the Germans would have to be fully assured about Belgian measures for the protection of the Flanders coast.[2]

Thus until the last days before the chances of victory turned with ironic suddenness into the certainty of defeat, the German Government as well as the military and naval chiefs were resolved upon the one condition which above all made a negotiated peace impossible. Even after the German military *dégringolade* had begun the military authorities refused to allow a statement on the unconditional restoration of Belgium.[3] In the talks between Hindenburg and Ludendorff on September 27, 1918, before the military chiefs insisted that Germany must ask for an armistice, Hindenburg still considered that the German annexation of the Longwy-Briey area should be one of the conditions.

---

[1] After the early successes of the German offensive, the German liberal press began to edge away from the idea of a peace with the Western Powers on the lines of 'no annexations'.

[2] Fischer, op. cit., p. 800.

[3] A German writer has compared the discussions on the subject between Ludendorff and the Vice-Chancellor in the latter part of August and early September with 'two men playing a leisurely game of chess on board a rapidly sinking ship'.

CHAPTER 28

The military defeat and surrender of Germany: the military terms of the armistice[1]

The German army, after their defeat in the second week of August, lay sprawled over a front some seventy miles longer than that of the previous winter. The salients created by the great attacks were difficult to hold; there had not been time in which to build adequate lines and, indeed, no men could be spared for the work. Ludendorff's 'gamble' had failed; his army knew it, and there were already instances of indiscipline and talk of peace. The case of Germany's Allies was no better. The last Austrian offensive against Italy – in mid-June – had been a failure, and only the unwillingness of the Italians to strike back energetically had saved the Austrian army from complete disaster. Since the capture of Jerusalem on December 9, 1917, Allenby's army in Palestine had been unable to carry out large-scale offensive operations because more than 60,000 of its best men had been sent to the Western Front. Reinforcements, however, were being provided from India, and meanwhile the Turkish army was falling to pieces owing to neglect.[2] The Germans could have no doubt that Allenby would resume the offensive, and that the Turks would lose Syria as well as Palestine. In any case the Bulgarians were unlikely to resist for long when the Allies were strong enough to break out of their fortified lines beyond Salonika. Turkey would then be cut off from direct land communication with the Central Powers.

The balance of opinion among German political leaders had been in favour of attempting a negotiated peace while Germany still held the initiative on the Western Front. Even if the Germans had been willing to negotiate on terms which the Allies could have accepted,

---

[1] See Map 7.
[2] The Turkish Government were more interested in looking for gains in the Caucasus – as a result of the Russian collapse – than in saving Palestine. They would lose Palestine anyhow, but the Allies were unlikely to make them surrender prizes taken from the Bolsheviks.

Ludendorff's promises of victory had prevented this opportunity from being taken. At a Crown Council held at Spa on August 14, under the presidency of the Emperor, Ludendorff now admitted that the enemy could not be brought to ask for peace by an offensive. The war must be ended, and ended by diplomacy. At this stage Ludendorff and Hindenburg still argued that, although Germany could not win the war, she had not lost it, and need not lose it. The allies of Germany might fail, but the German armies could maintain themselves in France until 'war-weariness' compelled their opponents to make peace. The French, in spite of Clemenceau, would become increasingly anxious for peace; the American President was unlikely to hold out for severe terms. The English, whose obstinacy was most to be feared, could not go on without the French and Americans. The Emperor thought that negotiations should be opened at a suitable time through neutrals – the King of Spain and the Queen of the Netherlands. The 'suitable time' was left, somewhat vaguely, as 'after the next success in the West'. A tentative approach seems to have been made to the Queen of the Netherlands, but no serious initiative was taken, in spite of the fact that on the afternoon of August 14 the Emperor Charles, with his Foreign Minister and Chief of the General Staff, arrived at Spa to say that 'somehow or other' the war must be ended, and that the Austro-Hungarian forces could not hold out over the winter.

Meanwhile a decision had to be reached on military policy. The Crown Prince was in favour of an immediate retirement to the Hindenburg line. Ludendorff argued that a rapid retreat would be too dangerous, since the enemy might advance in strength to the new positions before the winter. Ludendorff believed that he could move back slowly and that the Allies could not force the pace.

On the Allied side the first objective was to prevent this orderly retreat. Foch and Haig differed on the method of preventing it. Foch wanted a series of frontal attacks; Haig believed it safe to take the risks of attempting a great turning movement. In this last phase of the war Haig was at his best. Whether his earlier arguments were right or wrong, his conclusion had turned out to be correct. He had said at the beginning of 1918 that the Germans would be unwise to attempt an offensive; that they would fail, and that after their failure, their defeat would be rapid. He now believed that the war could be won in 1918.[1]

[1] On July 20, two days after the 'turn of the tide', Haig spent an afternoon playing golf at Le Touquet for the first time since he had come to France. Lloyd George, on the other hand, at this same time, had recalled Lord Cavan, who was

At this time neither the War Cabinet nor War Office took so hopeful a view. Shortly after July 25 Haig had received from the War Office a memorandum of thirty-three pages, signed by Sir Henry Wilson, on 'British Military Policy, 1918–19'. Wilson did not think that the main Allied offensive could open before July 1, 1919. A month later – on August 21 – Churchill came to show Haig his programme of munitions for the following year. Haig told him that 'we ought to do our utmost to get a decision this autumn'.

Haig was able to persuade Foch to accept his plan. He struck the enemy almost continuously between August 21 and September 3. Péronne was recaptured on September 1. Next day the Canadians broke through the Drocourt–Quéant line linking the Hindenburg line with the Lens defences. Each of these blows, together with French advances, and a successful American attack at the Saint-Mihiel salient on September 15, brought great captures of prisoners and material; their purpose was to disintegrate the enemy forces. Haig wanted to attack them on the Hindenburg line between Cambrai and St. Quentin before they had time to organise their defence. At the beginning of September the War Cabinet still failed to understand the extent of the change in the situation. The Prime Minister, remembering Passchendaele and Haig's earlier offensive, was afraid that he would waste his reserves in a premature attack. No word of congratulation was sent to Haig on his victories. Instead he received a private warning from Wilson that the War Cabinet would become anxious if there were heavy losses in an unsuccessful attack on the Hindenburg line. Haig went to England on September 9. He persuaded the Government to allow him to carry out the attack, but even Milner – his strongest supporter – was anxious; he told Haig later in September that, if he lost his army, there were no men to replace it.[1] Haig, on the other hand, was now sure that the enemy morale was breaking, and that a decision could be obtained 'in the very near future'.

The anxiety of the War Cabinet was not altogether ill-founded. The German defences on the Hindenburg line between Cambrai and St Quentin were immensely strong, and covered over most of their

in command of the British force in Italy, to London with the possibility that he might be given Haig's command in France. Lloyd George appears not to have been satisfied that Cavan would do for the post. After Haig's victory on August 8 Lloyd George gave up any idea of a change in the command.

[1] In the attack of August 21 50 per cent of the British infantry were youths of 18 to 19. The British casualties on the Western Front between August 8 and September 26 were 189,000.

area by canal lines impassable by tanks. The general strategic plan in
which the British attack had an important place aimed at the 'distant
objectives' which had been so disquieting a feature of Haig's earlier
attacks. The objective was now to reach the German lateral railway
communications behind the front, and to compel a retreat to the
Antwerp–Meuse line. A British advance in the north would secure
Lille; thirty miles beyond Cambrai lay the junction of Aulnoye where
the line from Lille met the line running through Mons into Belgium.
Forty-five to fifty miles beyond the Rheims–Verdun sector was
the junction of Mézières–Charleville where the main railway south
from Namur followed the valley of the Meuse into France. If the
British attack on the Hindenburg line and a Franco-American attack
on the Rheims–Verdun sector succeeded, most of the enemy divisions
would be cut off from their main retreat into Germany.

The plan was not wholly successful. The attack opened on September 27. The Belgians in the north advanced eight miles and recaptured
Passchendaele; once again the advance in this area was held up by
mud. The French and Americans also had great initial successes, but
the Americans crowded too many troops into a small area, and were
inexperienced in the method of dealing with fortifications in depth.
The French were held up after their first advance. The British armies
on September 29 broke through the southern part of the Hindenburg
line; four days later they were in open country behind the last German
defences. They had accomplished a superb feat of arms; they had not
enough men to push on to the main lateral railways. They were
hindered by the difficulty of bringing up supplies in a devastated area,
and, although the Germans were now surrendering in large numbers,
their machine gunners fought tenacious rearguard actions.

None the less, the breach of the Hindenburg line had one all-
important effect. Ludendorff lost his nerve – there is some evidence
that he had a slight stroke – and insisted, on September 29, upon an
immediate request for an armistice, and an offer to make peace on the
basis of President Wilson's Fourteen Points. He had discussed the
matter with Hindenburg on the previous night. His main reason –
before the disaster on the Hindenburg line – had been that the collapse
of Bulgaria would enable the Allies to advance through Austria-
Hungary and take Germany in the rear. In fact, such an invasion –
which could not have been undertaken for some months – would
hardly have been necessary; the shortest way to victory would have
been to cut off German oil supplies from Roumania. Without these

supplies Germany could not have continued the war for more than two or three months.

The Bulgarian collapse had taken place within a few days of the opening of an Allied offensive from Salonika on September 15.[1] The small number of Germans on the front fought well, but the Bulgarian army marched home. A new Government had already determined on peace. King Ferdinand was forced to abdicate, and on September 30 the country surrendered. Meanwhile Allenby had opened a final offensive in Palestine on September 19, and by September 21 had destroyed the two Turkish armies west of the Jordan.[2]

On September 28, however, Ludendorff was in a panic over the possibility of an immediate German collapse in France. He told a Council of War held at Spa on the morning of September 29 that the situation of the army allowed no delay; not an hour must be lost in demanding an armistice. Ludendorff had not read President Wilson's Fourteen Points. He seems to have thought them a vague statement of principles about which Germany could argue once the army had been brought back across the German frontier; the immediate requirement was to get the troops back, and give them some rest in a secure position. He talked of resuming the fight in this more favourable situation if the Allies' terms of peace were unsatisfactory.

Ludendorff's misconceptions were indeed extraordinary. It was fantastic to suppose that the Allies would allow an armistice except on terms which would make it impossible for Germany to begin fighting again, or indeed to think that the German army as a whole could be brought to fight once a cease-fire had sounded. In other respects, however, Ludendorff and his fellow officers kept their heads. If there were to be a surrender, the responsibility for it must be shifted from the military oligarchy which was controlling Germany. The bait to attract the Socialists into accepting a share of this responsibility would be a grant of responsible government – a 'revolution from above'. The Kaiser was persuaded to carry out this revolution. Ludendorff insisted that the new government must be formed within two days. On October 1 he and Hindenburg telegraphed to Berlin that, if Prince Max of Baden, who had been hesitating about taking the Chancellorship, formed a government at once, the announcement of the demand for an armistice could be delayed until the following morning; otherwise publication was to be made on the night of October 1.

On October 2 Major von der Bussche, liaison officer between G H Q

[1] See above, p. 98.   [2] See above, p. 122.

and the Reichstag, told the Reichstag party leaders that the war was lost, and that every twenty-four hours might make the situation worse and allow the enemy to see clearly the German weakness. The Emperor and the army chiefs also met in conference. Hindenburg said that he expected a full-scale attack within eight days, and could take no responsibility if a catastrophe (here he corrected himself, and added, 'or the gravest consequences') ensued.

Prince Max of Baden – a pleasant but somewhat ineffective aristo-cratic liberal – still objected that a demand for an immediate armistice would itself disclose the weakness of Germany. He asked that the High Command should state their demand in writing. Hindenburg gave him a note stating that the High Command maintained the demand of September 29 for an immediate peace offer. Prince Max then put five questions in writing to Hindenburg: (i) How much longer could the army hold the enemy beyond the frontiers? (ii) Did the High Com-mand regard a military collapse as certain, and, if so, within what limit of time, and would this collapse mean the end of all power of military resistance? (iii) Was the military situation so critical that steps must be taken at once to secure an armistice or peace? (iv) If the answer to (iii) were 'yes', did the High Command realise that a peace offer under the pressure of the military situation might lead to the loss of the German colonies and of German territory, and, in particular, Alsace-Lorraine and the purely Polish districts of the Eastern provinces? (v) Did the High Command agree to the draft text of an appeal which was included with these questions?

Hindenburg gave a vague reply. He evaded an answer to the first four questions, and said only that the High Command maintained its demand for the immediate issue of a peace offer. On October 3 Prince Max of Baden formed a new government with the support of the so-called Majority parties (Centre, Progressive, and Majority Socialist). On October 4 the German Government sent the request – dated October 3 – for an armistice to the Swiss Government for transmission to President Wilson. The request, which was received in Washington on October 6, was worded in terms which, in comparison with previous German offers, left no doubt about the German view of the military position.

> The German Government requests the President of the United States of America to take steps for the restoration of peace, to notify all belligerents of this request, and to invite them to delegate pleni-potentiaries for the opening of negotiations. The German Govern-

ment accepts as a basis for the peace negotiations the programme laid down by the President of the United States in his message to Congress of January 8, 1918 [i.e. the Fourteen Points], and in his subsequent pronouncements, particularly in his address of September 27, 1918. In order to avoid further bloodshed the German Government requests the President to bring about the immediate conclusion of a general armistice on land, on water, and in the air.

President Wilson replied to the German note on October 8. He asked two questions, and laid down an important preliminary condition. The questions were (i) Did the Germans accept the Fourteen Points, and therefore intend to limit themselves in any discussions merely to the practical application of those points? (ii) Was the German Chancellor speaking merely on behalf of the constituted authorities of the Empire who had so far conducted the war? The preliminary condition of negotiation was the immediate withdrawal of the German and Austro-Hungarian armies from occupied territory.

This 'condition' put an end at once to Ludendorff's hope that the Allies would allow Germany a respite after which she could begin the war again on more favourable defensive conditions. The Germans recognised, obviously, the significance of Wilson's request. The Minister of War described the evacuation of occupied territory – apart from the danger of a disorderly return of the troops (the Germans might well remember what had happened in Russia) – as 'the signing and sealing of our inability to defend ourselves; it is unconditional surrender'.

The position of the German army was temporarily more favourable. There had been no 'catastrophe'; the German lines of retreat had not been cut off, and the French and American offensives in the south were held. Nevertheless Ludendorff knew that this respite would be short. He therefore thought it necessary to accept the President's condition, and also to agree to renounce any right to negotiate over the principles of the Fourteen Points. Here again the Germans were giving way on a question of great importance. The vagueness of many of the 'points' left room for argument. The German Government had now agreed to allow their enemies to determine what the 'points' meant.[1] The

[1] The Chancellor did in fact prepare a memorandum on the Fourteen Points. The memorandum was not sent to Wilson because the military authorities could not risk further delay in the armistice negotiations. The Chancellor was not even allowed to make a speech reserving rights under the Fourteen Points. He wrote later: 'my speech would have aroused Germany to the startling consciousness that

President's second question seemed easier to answer. The Chancellor said that he was speaking in the name of the German Government and people, and that this Government had the support of a majority in the Reichstag.

The German reply to the President was sent on October 12. On this same day occurred one of the worst German offences at sea against international law. A German submarine torpedoed, without warning, the Irish mail boat *Leinster* in the passage between Dublin and Holyhead. A second torpedo was fired at the ship after she had begun to sink; more than 400 lives were lost.[1] Wilson's note of October 14 to the Germans after this outrage was rightly severe. He said that

> neither the Government of the United States nor (he is quite sure) the Governments with which the United States is associated as a belligerent will consent to consider an armistice as long as the armed forces of Germany continue the illegal and inhumane practices which they persist in . . . the nations associated against Germany cannot be expected to agree to a cessation of arms while acts of inhumanity, spoliation, and desolation are being continued which they justly look upon with horror and with burning hearts.[2]

The President also made it clear the process of the evacuation and the military conditions of the armistice were matters to be left to the judgment of the Allies, and that no arrangements would be considered which did not provide the fullest guarantee of the maintenance of their 'present military supremacy'. Finally, the President warned the rulers

---

it had never considered what Wilson's programme really meant', Prince Max of Baden, *Memoirs* (Eng. trans.), ii, 41. It is clear indeed that Ludendorff never intended to honour his agreement to Wilson's conditions. The essential need for him was to gain time, during which he would bring his army intact to the frontiers of Germany. He could then use it as an instrument of pressure in further negotiations. Hence, in accepting the demand for the evacuation of France and Belgium, the German note made the apparently harmless suggestion that a mixed commission should meet to draw up necessary arrangements.

[1] On October 4 a German submarine torpedoed and sank in the Irish Sea the Japanese passenger steamer *Hirano Maru* with a loss of nearly 300 lives.

[2] In addition to the submarine outrages, the President mentioned the wanton acts of destruction by the German armies as they were retreating in France. There were many acts of cruelty and pillage, but the German Supreme Command does not appear to have issued orders – as in their retreat of 1917 – for systematic destruction contrary to the laws of war. They had neither the time nor the men to carry out a systematic devastation of the countryside; they were engaged beyond the capacity of their depleted transport in trying to withdraw their own material. They were also now a defeated army, and had to consider the likelihood of reprisals when the Allies entered Germany.

of Germany that their 'revolution from above' was not enough. In order that there might be 'no possibility of misunderstanding' on this point, he reminded the Chancellor of his address of July 4, 1918, in which he had called for the destruction of 'every arbitrary power' capable of disturbing the peace of the world. He said that 'the power which has hitherto controlled the German nation' was of 'the sort . . . described' in his speech. 'It is within the choice of the German nation to alter it. . . . The whole process of peace will . . . depend upon the definiteness and satisfactory character of the guarantees which can be given in this fundamental matter.'

The German Government took six days to answer this note. The Chancellor described its terms as 'terrible'. Ludendorff, who had recovered for the time from his panic, and who realised that acceptance of the note meant the downfall of the military regime in Germany, now asked for resistance to the last. He said that a break-through was unlikely; that the campaigning season would be over within four weeks, and that, if he had reinforcements, he could retire to the Meuse and fight again in the spring. So little did he comprehend the significance of Wilson's references to the German conduct of the war that he asked for the continuance of submarine warfare. As late as October 25, he ordered that Belgium must be made into a military base. No more food was to be sent into the country; the inhabitants were to be told that peace was a long way off, and that they might yet suffer the horrors inseparable from war to an extent that '1914 will be child's play compared to it'.

Other army leaders, and the civilian government of Germany, were less blind to the facts.[1] They had suggested, and Ludendorff had refused, on September 29 a last appeal to the nation for resistance to the end. It was now too late. Hence they agreed to give up submarine warfare – while protesting against the charge of inhumanity on sea or land. They accepted also the President's statement about the armistice terms, though they tried to safeguard themselves by the vague statement that the 'actual standard of power on both sides in the field' should form the basis of the terms. They also trusted that the President would disapprove of any demands incompatible with the honour of the German people and with a peace of justice. They explained that the changes

[1] Crown Prince Rupprecht, in a letter of October 18 to the Chancellor, wrote that he did not believe that there was any possibility of holding out over December; that a catastrophe might occur at any time, and that Ludendorff did not realise the seriousness of the situation.

now taking place in the German constitution provided the safeguards which the President required.

President Wilson answered this note on October 23. He said that, in view of the assurances of the German Government that it 'unreservedly' accepted the terms of peace laid down in the Fourteen Points and the 'principles of settlement enunciated in (the President's) subsequent addresses', and that it desired 'to discuss the details of their application', and that this wish came

> not from those who have hitherto dictated German policy and conducted the present war on Germany's behalf, but from Ministers who speak for the majority of the Reichstag, and for an overwhelming majority of the German people; and having received also the explicit promise of the present German Government that the humane rules of civilised warfare will be observed both on land and sea by the German armed forces, the President of the United States feels that he cannot decline to take up with the Governments with which the United States is associated the question of an armistice.

The President, however, repeated that 'the only armistice he would feel justified in submitting for consideration would be one which should leave the United States and the Powers associated with her in a position to enforce any arrangements that may be entered into, and to make a renewal of hostilities on the part of Germany impossible'. The President had therefore transmitted to the associated Governments his correspondence 'with the present German authorities', and had suggested that if those Governments were

> disposed to effect peace upon the terms and principles indicated, their military advisers, and the military advisers of the United States be asked to submit to the Governments associated against Germany the necessary terms of such an armistice as will fully protect the interests of the peoples involved, and ensure to the associated Governments the unrestricted power to safeguard and enforce the details of the peace to which the German Government has agreed, provided that they deem such an armistice possible from the military point of view.

The President then went further in his demand for constitutional change in Germany. He had good reason for doing so because there were few signs of any real change of control. The Reichstag was not even in session. It had been adjourned on October 5, and had not met again until October 22, when it adjourned once more, after a short sitting,[1] until November 9. The Emperor still retained all his prerogatives as Supreme War Lord. The Bundesrath, or Federal Council, in which the Prussian vote was strong enough to defeat any proposals for an alteration of the Constitution, had not been touched. The President therefore pointed out in his note that the guarantees of responsible government were insufficient, and that 'the heart of the present difficulty' had not been reached. 'It is evident that the German people have no means of commanding the acquiescence of the military authorities of the Empire in the popular will; that the power of the King of Prussia to control the policy of the Empire is unimpaired; that the determining initiative still remains with those who have hitherto been the masters of Germany.' If the United States had to deal with these 'military masters' and 'monarchical autocrats of Germany', they 'must demand, not peace negotiations, but surrender'.

The Chancellor now initiated rapid legislation to give the Reichstag full control over all the machinery of state.[2] He also secured the removal of Ludendorff. On October 25 – without consulting the Government or even asking for the approval of the Emperor – Ludendorff issued an Order of the Day rejecting the President's terms. The German Government described this order as a 'stab in the back' – the first use of the term in 1918[3] – and the Emperor told Ludendorff on October 27 that the difficult political situation had been created by the military situation. He ordered Ludendorff to send two senior generals to report on the military situation. At this obvious withdrawal of confidence, Ludendorff offered his resignation; the Emperor accepted it and appointed General Groener as his successor.[4] On the same day the German Government sent another note to the President stating

[1] During this short session a suggestion was made that 'the defeated Commander-in-Chief' – Ludendorff – should resign.

[2] The Chancellor was at this time in bed with influenza and unable to attend the conferences at which the President's note was discussed.

[3] The Kaiser's comment on September 29 came near to using this phrase: 'So the war has come to an end and, really, quite differently from our expectations. . . . Our politicians have let us down pitiably (haben erbärmlich versagt).' *The Kaiser and his Court*, Diaries, etc., of Admiral G. A. von Müller, ed. W. Görlitz (Eng. trans.), pp. 397–8.

[4] General Groener had been Chief of Field Railways, and was chosen as a transportation expert in view of the imminent breakdown of German communications in the west. Two other considerations were probably of greater importance in determining the choice: (i) Groener was the son of an NCO in the Württemberg army, and thus did not belong to the Prussian military caste, (ii) in 1916–17 Groener, as Director of the military programme of increased war production, had been in contact with the German Labour leaders.

that the negotiations would be conducted by a People's Government to which the military power would be subject, and that this Government awaited the proposals for an armistice which would introduce a peace of justice on the lines laid down by the President. It is significant that the original wording of the note – that the German Government expected proposals for an armistice, not a demand for laying down arms – was modified in order not to offend the President.

On the evening of October 27 the German Government had news of the collapse of Austria-Hungary. The Emperor Charles had sent a peace note to President Wilson on September 15 suggesting a conference of all belligerents in a neutral country.[1] The President had replied on September 16 that the United States Government had already announced the terms upon which it would consider making peace, and that no purpose would be served by a conference. The Emperor sent another note on October 7 on the lines of the German note. The President did not reply to it until October 15. On October 16 the Emperor announced the transformation of Austria into a federal state. Even this announcement was incomplete, since the Hungarians would not allow autonomy to the subject races under the rule of St Stephen's crown.[2] In fact the whole Empire was already in dissolution. On September 3, 1918, President Wilson had recognised the Czecho-Slovak National Council as a belligerent government; only two months earlier he had said that American policy aimed at the liberation from German and Austrian rule of 'all branches of the Slav race'. Hence his answer to the Austrian note of October 7 was to call attention to the right of the Czechs, Slovaks, and Southern Slavs to decide their own future. On October 24 the Italians – after long delay – opened a final offensive. If they had waited any longer, they might have prejudiced their claims at the peace conference. They were just in time. The offensive was not as successful as they had hoped; the survivors of the Austrian army, half-starved and ill-equipped, fought extremely well against greatly superior numbers, but were defeated within three days. The Emperor Charles now asked for an immediate armistice. The defeat precipitated a revolution in Vienna which could not have been long delayed. On November 3 the Allies accepted the capitulation of the army; one of their conditions was that they should have free passage through the Tyrol to attack Bavaria.

[1] The note was also sent to the Allied Powers, to neutral countries, and to the Pope.

[2] i.e. the territories ruled by the Habsburg Emperor as King of Hungary.

President Wilson's notes to the German Government had been sent on his own responsibility. He had not consulted the British and French Governments about the text of the notes, and they had been afraid, at first, that the Germans might be attempting to manœuvre them into negotiating a 'peace without victory'. Lloyd George and Bonar Law were in Paris on October 6 at the time of the announcement of the first German note. They had come for a meeting of the Supreme Council to consider the armistices with Turkey and Bulgaria. They now had to deal with this unexpected German move. Lloyd George and Clemenceau agreed that they could take no decision until they knew Wilson's reply to the Germans. They discussed, however, in general the terms which they would require, and asked for the opinion of Foch and of the military representatives at Versailles. On October 8 Foch, at Clemenceau's request, submitted his views in writing. He laid down three indispensable conditions: (i) the evacuation by the enemy of Belgium, France, Alsace-Lorraine, and Luxembourg within a fortnight; (ii) the occupation by the Allies of bridgeheads on the right bank of the Rhine as 'bases of departure' in the event of the resumption of fighting; (iii) the occupation by the Allies of German territory on the left bank of the Rhine as a pledge for the reparation which the Allies would demand in the Peace Treaty.

Foch believed that the Germans would accept any military terms offered to them. The British Ministers were less inclined to take this view. They thought that, although the Germans had obviously lost the war, their position was not yet so desperate that they would agree to demands equivalent to unconditional surrender. On October 9 the Council considered the text of the President's reply to the German note. They were reassured to notice that the President had laid down as a preliminary condition for negotiation the withdrawal of the Germans from occupied territory. Clemenceau was inclined to await the German answer. Lloyd George pointed out that the speech of the German Chancellor to the Reichstag explaining the German Peace note was an admission of defeat, and that the Germans might well agree to the evacuation of occupied territory, and accept the President's terms of negotiation. The Allies, however, were not prepared to take the Fourteen Points as a basis of negotiation without further discussion of their meaning. If they did not safeguard their position, the Germans might also interpret their silence as implying that they regarded the evacuation of occupied territory as the only military condition of an armistice.

The Supreme War Council therefore decided to send a note to the President pointing out that the evacuation of occupied territory might place the enemy in a better position for resuming hostilities, and that the terms of an armistice could be fixed only after consultation with the military experts and in accordance with the military situation when the fighting came to an end. This note dealt only with the immediate question of an armistice. The Allied Ministers sent a second telegram on the larger question of co-operation in the conduct of peace negotiations. They suggested to the President that decisions of supreme importance with regard to the war might have to be taken up at very short notice. They therefore proposed that the President should send to Europe an American representative possessing the full confidence of the United States Government 'to confer, when occasion arose, with the other associated Governments so as to keep them accurately and fully informed of the point of view of the United States Government'. The President designated Colonel House for this purpose. House arrived in Europe on October 26.[1] Meanwhile the British and French Governments had to formulate their military and naval terms for an armistice. The President's second and third notes had safeguarded their freedom to ask for more than the evacuation of occupied territory.

Neither the British Government nor their Commander-in-Chief agreed at first with Foch's view that the Germans would be compelled by military necessity to accept any terms offered to them. Sir Eric Geddes, who was at this time in the United States, reported that the President was afraid that the military and naval authorities would put forward demands which the Germans would 'reject as unduly humiliating'. Whatever his views about Foch's demands, however, Wilson had no cause to be anxious about Haig. Haig indeed at this time underestimated the weakness of the enemy. Foch had complained to Pétain of the lack of enterprise and determination in the Franco-American offensive; Clemenceau had even suggested that Foch should ask for the dismissal of Pershing.[2] The British advance had been more successful, but the Germans, although defeated, were not a broken army. The season was late, and the difficulties of supply and maintenance over devastated territory increased with every day and every mile of the advance. A breakdown in the negotiations would have a bad effect

[1] For the political discussions with House, see below p. 428.

[2] Smuts had thought earlier that Pershing was not suited for his post. On June 4 Smuts had suggested to Lloyd George that he (Smuts) might be given command in the field over the Americans, while Pershing remained in charge of all organisations in the rear. Sir K. Hancock, *Smuts*, i, 482–3.

on the morale of the British troops. They knew – as Haig knew – that they were bearing the heaviest burden of the fighting.

Furthermore the Prime Minister had accused Haig of wasting the lives of his troops in unnecessary and unprofitable offensives. There is no evidence in his letters or diaries that Haig's judgment on the armistice terms was affected by a wish to defend himself against this charge, but he may have remembered that only a year earlier he had underestimated the strength and tenacity of the enemy. In any case Haig was not a man of vindictive temper. If Great Britain could now secure the aims for which she had been fighting, there was no justification for spending more British lives in humiliating the Germans or enforcing demands put forward by the French – so Haig suspected – for political rather than military reasons. On military grounds Haig regarded an advance to the Rhine, and across it, as unnecessary.

One fact is also clear. The Allies were now sure of winning the war. The Germans indeed had admitted that they had lost it. The German armies since July had suffered the greatest defeat in history. There was no thought on the Allied side that this army would invent a legend that it had not been defeated at all, and that its surrender was due to betrayal by the civilian government and population. Haig, in his wish not to goad the Germans into a useless prolongation of resistance, and Wilson, when he insisted upon a real constitutional change in Germany, could not have supposed that they were giving the beaten German army an *alibi* for defeat.

Lloyd George did not ask at once for Haig's opinion. He waited until October 19 before inviting him to give his views on the armistice terms to the War Cabinet. Haig then said that the nature of the terms depended on two questions. (1) Was Germany so much beaten that she would accept any terms, i.e. unconditional surrender? (2) Could the Allies continue to press the enemy sufficiently during the winter months to withdraw so quickly that he would be unable to destroy the railways and roads? Haig thought that the answer to these questions was 'No'. The German army was capable of retiring to the German frontiers and of holding them if there were an attempt to touch the honour of the German people. Meanwhile, on the Allied side, the French army was worn out, and latterly had not been really fighting. The American army was not yet properly organised. The British army was never more efficient, but it had fought hard, and lacked reinforcements. The French and Americans were not at the time capable of making a serious offensive. The British army alone could do so, but why spend more British lives? Haig therefore thought that our terms should be such as the enemy would accept at once: the immediate evacuation of Belgium and occupied France, a withdrawal from Alsace-Lorraine, and the return of Belgian and French rolling-stock and of all the population which had been removed.

Lloyd George asked Haig what would be the attitude of the army if the Allies held out for stiffer terms which the enemy refused. Haig said that the Prime Minister had stated our war aims about a year earlier. The British Army had done most of the recent fighting, and wanted to be finished with the war as soon as these aims were secured. Haig thought the troops would not fight keenly for anything beyond the aims we had laid down. According to Haig's diary, Balfour spoke 'about deserting the Poles and the people of Eastern Europe', but the Prime Minister agreed with Haig, and gave the opinion that 'we cannot expect the British to go on sacrificing their lives for the Poles'. Milner suggested, as a middle course between the views of Haig and Foch, that the Allies should occupy the west bank of the Rhine as a temporary measure until the Germans had complied with the peace terms.

On October 25 Foch held a conference of the Allied Commanders-in-Chief at Senlis to consider the military terms of an armistice. He asked Haig to give his views. Haig could not state plainly what was in his mind, but he repeated as closely as possible the opinion which he had given to the War Cabinet. Foch then asked Pétain and Pershing to say what they thought. Pétain supported Foch's plan, with the requirement that the German withdrawal should be so rapid that they would have to leave most of their material behind them. Pershing, who two days earlier had agreed with Haig, was now even more drastic than Pétain.

Foch invited Haig to comment on the views of Pétain and Pershing. Haig said that the German army was still capable of withdrawing to a shorter front and making a stand against equal or greater forces. If they held out to the last point of resistance, the Allies might take as long as two years to enforce surrender unless the internal state of Germany compelled the enemy to accept any terms. Since the Allies did not know very much about the state of Germany, the attempt to impose unnecessarily severe terms was too much of a gamble. Haig also described Foch's demands as inexpedient from a military point of view. He agreed that the Allies must occupy Alsace-Lorraine and its fortresses of Metz and Strasbourg, but considered that, if the Germans attempted to renew the war, the Allies could deal with them more easily if they were entrenched behind the frontier of 1870 rather than on the right bank of the Rhine.

Foch answered that the German army had been defeated. The Allies did not know its exact condition, but they had been attacking it for three months, and were now delivering blows on every part of its front of 250 miles. This army had lost a quarter of a million men in prisoners alone, and over 4000 guns since July 15. Physically and morally, it was thoroughly beaten. 'When one hunts a wild beast, and finally comes upon him at bay, one faces greater danger, but it is not the time to stop.'

Foch's view – supported by Pétain and Pershing – prevailed over Haig's view. The German military collapse became so much more rapid in the last days of October that Haig himself began to think that the 'gamble' was justified. He had seen Lloyd George in France on October 29, and had recommended insistence upon strong naval terms; he had not then changed his opinion about the military terms, although the situation was now more favourable to the Allies. Three days later Haig attended a meeting of the Supreme War Council at Versailles. He heard the terms of which the Prime Minister had approved. He noted in his diary that Austria and Turkey had now abandoned Germany 'so probably the Allied Governments are justified in demanding stiff terms. On the other hand, the determined fight put up by the enemy today shows that all the Divisions in the German Army are not yet demoralised.' On November 4 the British army broke through the enemy lines of defence between the Schelde and the Sambre. They captured 20,000 prisoners and 450 guns. Haig now described the Germans as 'capable neither of accepting nor of refusing battle'. From November 1 the Americans had begun to advance rapidly along both sides of the Meuse, and were threatening from the south the last German line of retreat.[1]

The Allied doubts about the likelihood of sustained German resistance to their proposed armistice terms were now removed. These terms, as finally agreed between the British, French, and United States Governments, amounted in fact to an unconditional military surrender. They included the evacuation of Belgium, France, Luxembourg, and Alsace-Lorraine within fifteen days; the surrender of 2500 heavy and 2500 field guns, 25,000 machine guns, 3000 trench mortars, and 1700 fighting and bombing aeroplanes; the evacuation, within thirty-one days, of the left bank of the Rhine, and the surrender of

[1] For the German position at the time of an armistice, see Map 7.

three bridgeheads, each with a radius of thirty kilometres on the right bank of the Rhine opposite Mainz, Coblenz, and Cologne. The Germans were also to hand over 5000 locomotives, 150,000 trucks and 5000 lorries. German troops in territories formerly belonging to Austria-Hungary or Turkey, and all troops in former Russian territory were to be withdrawn as soon as the Allies ordered such withdrawal.

The naval terms of the armistice required, even more obviously, the complete surrender of the German fleet. Here again, however, the decision to exact the most severe conditions had not been made at once. During the Allied discussions about these terms, the roles of Haig and Foch were curiously reversed. Foch, who had argued against Haig for harder terms on land, did not want to risk the German rejection of the armistice by demanding severe terms with regard to the German fleet. Foch had therefore drawn up and submitted to the Supreme War Council a draft asking for much less than the Allied Naval Council considered necessary. The latter had decided on October 28-9 to demand the surrender of all German submarines, ten 'Dreadnought' battleships, six battle-cruisers, eight light cruisers, and fifty destroyers. In submitting this draft to the Supreme War Council the British and French admirals said that they had based their demands on the assumption that the Germans would now accept conditions which could be imposed only on a completely defeated enemy. If this assumption were wrong, the terms would have to be revised.

When the Supreme War Council discussed the draft on November 1 Foch objected strongly to the terms. He said that only the German submarines need be surrendered, since they alone had done real damage to the Allies. It would be sufficient to occupy Heligoland and Cuxhaven and to send the German battlefleet to the Baltic. In spite of his statement that the Germans would accept any terms on land, he argued that they would refuse the demand for the surrender of the main units of the fleet, and the Allied armies would thus have to continue the fight. The British representatives pointed out that, if Marshal Foch had not been troubled by the German High Seas fleet, the reason was the British fleet had held it in the North Sea for four years. On Foch's plan the Allies would not be able to enter the Baltic, and the British fleet would have to remain fully mobilised. The relationship between the two fleets would be similar to that of two armies ready for battle across their lines of trenches. The Supreme War Council rejected Foch's proposal, but at the same time thought that the Allied

Naval Council were asking for too much, and that it would be unwise to demand more than the disarming and internment of the battlefleet.

The Allied Naval Council met again on November 1 to consider this suggestion. The British and French representatives thought it possible to secure the surrender of the fleet, and dangerous to reduce their demand. The Allies intended to set the most drastic limits on the German fleet at the peace settlement. The Council had been told that the armistice terms were to be as close as possible to the final terms; why then should the Germans be left with an interned fleet which they would certainly try to recover by bargaining at the conference? The American representative, Admiral Benson, however, thought that the sole purpose of the armistice terms was to make it impossible for Germany to reopen hostilities, and that disarming and internment would therefore be sufficient.

The Supreme War Council accepted this view, though Foch tried once again to substitute his own plan. In the final discussion, on November 4, the Supreme War Council decided, for practical reasons, to change the proposal that the internment should take place in a neutral port or ports. It was not certain whether any neutral country would be prepared to accept the plan; in any case there were obvious legal difficulties in the way of keeping an enemy fleet interned under Allied supervision in neutral harbours. The armistice terms therefore were drawn up to allow internment 'in neutral ports, or failing them, Allied ports'.[1] The terms also included the continuance of the blockade. On this point there was no difference of opinion among the Allies. The civilians as well as the naval and military chiefs agreed that it was impossible to allow the Germans to improve their chances of reopening hostilities – in the event of a breakdown in the negotiations – by restocking during the period of the armistice.[2]

During the last stages of the Allied discussion on the naval terms, the sailors of the German battlefleet had ceased to obey the orders of their commanders. After the German Government had agreed to give up submarine warfare Admiral von Scheer planned a large-scale naval

[1] After the signature of the armistice, the Allied Governments agreed upon Scapa Flow as the most suitable place.

[2] Erzberger, the chief German representative on the armistice commission, protested that the continuance of the blockade would bring suffering to women and children in Germany. He asked whether this was 'fair'. He was told that the Germans had sunk Allied passenger ships without any heed for women and children. The Allied delegation, however, undertook that the Allies would make provision for the feeding of Germany. See below, pp. 571–2.

action which – if successful – might influence in German favour the negotiation of an armistice.[1] Two cruiser squadrons were to raid the Straits of Dover and the mouth of the Thames. The Germans then expected the Grand Fleet to move south from Scapa. All the available German submarines now withdrawn from commerce destroying would harass its course southward, and the German battlefleet would engage it – after it had suffered considerable loss – off the Dutch coast.

It is impossible to estimate the degree of success which this bold plan might have had. It depended to a large extent upon secrecy in the early stages, but the Admiralty had discovered that the German battle-fleet was about to come out (and had forecast that it would move towards the Dutch coast) some days before the main operations were planned to begin. In fact, the fleet never came out. The crews muti-nied, and on November 4 the port of Kiel was in the hands of revolu-tionaries who were raising the red flag. From Kiel the revolution spread to Hamburg and Bremen and thence inland; a separate outbreak at Munich on November 6 brought about the abdication of the King of Bavaria.

Meanwhile the Allies had discussed with House the larger political question of accepting the German surrender on the basis of the Four-teen Points. The discussion was not easy, since the Fourteen Points and Wilson's other pronouncements were open to wide differences of interpretation. House insisted that, unless the Allies would accept Wilson's general conditions, the United States Government might conclude a separate peace. The Allies, however, made two reservations. The first of them was due to Lloyd George. With French and Italian support he refused to commit the British Government to the American interpretation of the 'freedom of the seas'.[2] The second reservation

---

[1] The official *History of Naval Operations* points out (v, 369) that Admiral Scheer's plan resembled that of the Dutch attack on the Medway which influenced the negotiations at Breda at the end of the second Dutch war.

[2] Sir E. Geddes, who had just come back from the United States, where he had discussed the question with the President, thought that Wilson's views were still vague and undecided. The insistence that the Allies should accept the 'prin-ciples' without any discussion or exact definition of the terms seemed to come more from House. The Allies replied on November 1 reserving their right to discuss the terms at the Peace Conference. Wilson's answer on November 3 recognised the need for discussion, but still wished the Allies to declare their agreement in 'principle' to the freedom of the seas. Lloyd George refused a declaration in advance, though he repeated his willingness to consider the question 'in the light of the new conditions which have arisen during the present war'. In

was rather an interpretation – also in general terms – of the President's declaration that the territories invaded by the Germans must be restored as well as evacuated and made free. The Allied Governments stated that by this declaration they understood that 'compensation will be made by Germany for all damage done to the civilian population of the Allies and to their property by the aggression of Germany by land, by sea, and from the air'.

Subject to these qualifications, the Allied Governments, in a note of November 5 to the United States Government, declared themselves willing to 'make peace with the Government of Germany on the terms of peace laid down in the President's Address to Congress of January 8, 1918, and the principles of settlement enunciated in his subsequent Addresses'.

The President was therefore able to inform the German Government of this reply, and to say that the United States and the Allied Governments would authorise Marshal Foch to receive German representatives and to communicate to them the terms of an armistice. He repeated that these terms must necessarily be such as would 'fully protect the interests of the peoples involved, and assure to the Associated Governments the unrestricted power to safeguard and enforce the details of the peace' to which the Germans had agreed. In communicating to the Germans the terms of the Allied Governments' reply to him, the President stated that he accepted their reservation with regard to the freedom of the seas, and their view that the 'restoration of the invaded territories implied the payment of compensation for all damage done to the civilian population of the Allies and their property by the aggression of Germany by land, by sea, and from the air'.

The Germans thus had before them a statement committing the United States and the Allied Governments to a peace upon the basis of Wilson's Fourteen Points and other declarations. They could also see that the European Allies had asked for and obtained an important interpretation of Wilson's words on the question of German obligations after the war. They did not themselves raise any question of interpretation, even with regard to this immense and undefined obligation of compensation for damage. They did not repudiate or protest against the Allied statement – endorsed by the President – that this

---

his reply of November 3 the President said that, 'if the Allies and the United States reached agreement after discussion, and before the Peace Conference, the matter need not be discussed with the German Government'.

claim to compensation was due to German 'aggression'.[1] They did not question the President's statement that the Allies would have 'unrestricted power to safeguard the details of the peace to which Germany had agreed'. They had previously spoken of a discussion of details. They did not now safeguard their right to any such discussion.

These facts have an important significance for the history of the Peace Conference, and indeed for the whole fateful history of Germany and the world in the next quarter of a century. The reason for the German surrender without an attempt at bargaining is that they dared not wait. The German Government received Wilson's communication – transmitted, as before, through the Swiss Minister at Washington – on the evening of November 6. Earlier in the day General Groener had left for the German headquarters at Spa.[2] He had told the Chancellor that even five days' delay might be too late, and that 'painful as it is, we must take the step of asking Foch for terms, and meanwhile retreat behind the Rhine'. He had therefore settled with the Chancellor the composition of a German armistice commission. The commission included General von Gündell as the representative of the High Command. The General's name was withdrawn at the last moment, so that, technically, it could be maintained that the civilian Government, not the army, had asked for the armistice.[3] In view of Ludendorff's action at the end of September, and Groener's decision on November 6, this pretence did not seem, at the time, likely to deceive anyone.

At 12.30 a.m. on November 7 Foch received a wireless message from the German Headquarters asking for a meeting place, and requesting a suspension of hostilities as soon as the German plenipotentiaries reached the Allied lines. The Germans were told where to present themselves. They arrived at the place designated – the outposts of the French First Army – on the evening of November 7, and were taken by car and train to the railway station of Rethondes in the Forest of Compiègne. Here, on the morning of November 8, they were brought before

[1] The absence of any German protest at this time is relevant to the subsequent controversy over article 231 – the so-called 'war guilt clause' – of the Treaty of Versailles.

[2] At the time of his appointment Groener was with the German armies in the East. He had reached Spa on October 30. He found that no reserves were left, and that the fortress guns – even from Metz and Strasbourg – had been taken into the field. He left Spa to visit the front, but was called to Berlin on November 5.

[3] The naval command was less wary, and did not remove the naval representative from the commission.

Foch. They said to him that they had come to receive the Allied proposals. Foch answered that he had no proposals to make. The Germans then said that they had come to ask the conditions of an armistice. Foch answered again that he had no conditions to propose. The Germans then read Wilson's note. Foch said to them: 'Do you ask for an armistice? If so, I will make known to you the conditions on which you may obtain it.' When the Germans answered 'yes', Foch gave them the Allied terms, with a time-limit of seventy-two hours. The Germans again asked for an immediate suspension of hostilities; they used the argument that every day's fighting increased the risk of bolshevism sweeping over Europe. Foch replied that bolshevism was 'a disease of the vanquished'.

The delegates sent the terms to Berlin. While they were awaiting an answer, the Imperial regime had fallen. The increasing severity of Wilson's attack on the regime had had its effect, but the reason for the turbulent demand throughout Germany for the abdication of the Emperor was that the nation – long-suffering and resolute as it had been – was suddenly and hopelessly disillusioned at the military collapse, and turned in anger against the leaders. The Government requested the Emperor on November 8 to abdicate. He refused, and, although he would not risk coming to Berlin from his headquarters at Spa, asked the army chiefs to plan the suppression of what was now becoming a general insurrection. Hindenburg pointed out that his proposal was impracticable; the troops would no longer obey the Emperor's orders, and certainly would not shoot down their fellow citizens. By the morning of November 9 William II had decided to abdicate as German Emperor but to keep his title of King of Prussia. The Chancellor telephoned to him, and was told that he was writing out his act of abdication. Prince Max announced it at once – without any reference to the kingship of Prussia.[1] The Chancellor himself then resigned in favour of the Socialist Ebert. In the early afternoon, a Republic was proclaimed from the steps of the Reichstag. Next morning the ex-Emperor left for the Netherlands.

These events left it uncertain at Compiègne whether there was a Government in Germany with power to sign or carry into effect the Allies' terms. Hindenburg – the army, not the civilians – settled this question by telling the delegates that, even if they could not get the amendments for which they were being instructed to ask, they 'must sign nevertheless'. They signed at 5.00 a.m. on November 11.

[1] This reservation had not been mentioned on the telephone.

PART XI

The Western Allies and the Bolsheviks

CHAPTER 29

The western Allies and the Bolsheviks, 1917–1919

Apart from the immediate task of defeating the enemy the greatest political and military problem with which Lloyd George's Government had to deal during the latter part of 1917 and the first half of 1918 was that of their relations with Russia. The Allies had made heavy sacrifices on behalf of Russia. The war had broken out over an Austro-Russian dispute of no vital concern to France and Great Britain. The Russians had done their Allies valuable service in the first phase of operations by an invasion of East Prussia which had turned out disastrously for themselves. The Russian armies, doggedly brave, but badly led and as badly supplied from the rear, continued to engage large numbers of German and Austro-Hungarian troops; their general military position, however, had worsened as the months passed. A Russian political veto, at a critical point in the development of the Gallipoli campaign had lost the chance of Greek co-operation which might indirectly have saved Russia from ultimate collapse.[1] Russian demands for every kind of military material and for large loans were a drain on Allied, and especially on British, resources and shipping.

The British Government knew of the incompetence and corruption which were ruining the military chances of the Russian army and reducing the internal administration to chaos. They were also aware that revolution would certainly break out, if the Tsar took no steps to get rid of the court clique and the evil types whom, under the influence of the Empress and the monk Rasputin, he continued to keep in office. The British Government did everything possible to warn the Tsar what would surely happen if he failed to use his authority in favour of more competent and honest advisers. Sir George Buchanan, British Ambassador at St Petersburg, had spoken plainly to Nicholas II in February, 1916, and again in January, 1917, about the urgency of making concessions to satisfy public opinion, and of clearing out the court favourites. After the inevitable revolution took place in March,

[1] See above, p. 73.

1917, the British and French Governments misread the situation. They hoped for a strong government which would restore discipline in the army and order in the home administration, and thus enable Russia to continue to fulfil her obligations as an Ally in the war. The mistake of the western Powers was that they failed to realise that the revolt of the Russian people was far more profound than a wave of resentment against the autocracy.

The Russian people had lost the will to continue fighting. The western military commanders, who were the strongest influence in determining policy towards Russia, too long refused to face this disturbing fact. They knew nothing about Marxist theory; the matter, however, was not one of theory. The Russian soldiers who drifted back from the armies to their homes were not acting as class-conscious proletarians; they had reached the limit of endurance. The Russian Provisional Government was itself divided; the left wing wanted to abandon 'imperialist' war aims, such as the acquisition of Constantinople, and to get in touch with Allied socialists for the purpose of ending the war. The right wing Ministers wanted to continue fighting the enemy, but were afraid to strengthen the army in case it might turn against the revolutionary government. They ordered an offensive which had considerable success against the Austrians, and was then defeated easily and completely by the Germans. The final collapse of the army and the lack of vigorous action by the government enabled the Bolsheviks to carry out a second revolution in November.[1] The Bolshevik leaders cared nothing for the western alliance. For some time they and the Allies were under opposite delusions. The Allies hoped that by a restatement of war aims they might prevent Russia from making a separate peace. Lenin and Trotsky hoped that by appealing to the Allied and German peoples – the workers and soldiers – they might bring about revolutions and establish governments on communist lines in every belligerent country.

On November 8, 1917, the Bolshevik leaders announced proposals for general peace negotiations. Even if they had not wished to give up fighting, they had no option, since they no longer had an army. They addressed themselves especially to 'class-conscious workers' in England, France, and Germany. Later, in another appeal which ignored the Allied Governments, they suggested an immediate armistice on all fronts; they had already asked the Germans for an armistice. When the Allies

[1] The Russians, owing to their use of the Julian calendar, called it the 'October Revolution'.

protested and referred to the agreement of September, 1914, not to conclude a separate peace, Trotsky published the secret treaties of which the Tsarist Government had been a signatory; on November 29 he invited the Allied Governments to join in peace discussions.

Buchanan at this time thought that the only way of getting the Russians of their free choice to continue fighting with the Allies was to release them from their engagements. A public release of this kind would counter the Bolshevik propaganda that the Allies were trying to force Russia to continue an 'imperialist' war. Even if the French had not vetoed Buchanan's suggestion it would have had no effect in recreating in Russia a willingness to continue a war which seemed hopelessly lost. Buchanan then issued a statement on his own authority disclaiming 'imperialist' motives in the war, and warning the Russian people that the Germans would not agree to a 'proletarian peace'. Wilson and House wanted a presentation of Allied war aims in a form distinct from the secret treaties. Again the French (and Italians) would not agree, and Lloyd George was not inclined to give the proposal much support.

Meanwhile the Germans, in their negotiations with the Bolsheviks at Brest-Litovsk, began by claiming that they were willing to accept a 'peace of no annexations and no indemnities'. Wilson's formula could thus be turned against the Allies. Wilson continued to think – and to say – that, if the Allied war aims had been better, the Bolsheviks would never have won over the Russian people; he failed as completely as the western Allies to realise that the Russians were not interested in a 'democratic' peace. Hence Wilson's appeal in the Fourteen Points to the Russian people over the heads of their latest leaders was as futile as Lenin's appeal to the peoples of Germany and the Allies.[1]

The Bolsheviks were soon disillusioned about the prospects of an immediate proletarian revolution in the Allied countries and also about the kind of terms which they would get from the Germans. The Germans maintained that Russian Poland, Courland, and Lithuania wished to be separated from Russia, and that the future of these territories and of the Ukrainian lands further south must be settled between representatives of the peoples concerned and the German and Austro-Hungarian Governments. After more inconclusive discussion Trotsky announced on February 10 to the German delegates at Brest-Litovsk that the Bolshevik Government would neither agree to the German terms nor continue the war. The Germans then denounced the armistice

[1] For Wilson's and Lloyd George's speeches in reply to the Bolshevist general appeal at the opening of the Brest-Litovsk negotiations, see above, pp. 401–2.

and resumed their advance into Russia. Lenin now persuaded the other Bolshevik leaders that they must accept the German terms or submit to the overthrow of the Bolshevik Government by German force. The treaty of Brest-Litovsk was signed on March 3 and ratified by the Bolsheviks on March 16; neither side, as the other side well knew, intended to honour their signature. The Germans would ask for more concessions after victory in the west; the Russians would repudiate their surrender as soon as they were able to do so, that is to say, as soon as revolution (which they still confidently expected, though its outbreak was delayed) had begun in Germany and western Europe.

On January 19, 1918, the Bolsheviks had forcibly dissolved the Russian Constituent Assembly formally elected under a democratic franchise after the March revolution.[1] This action lost them any legal claim to be recognised as a government; they were only one among a number of rival factions disputing for power in Russia. There was no legal or moral reason why the Allied Governments should not support one or more of the anti-Bolshevik groups. The Bolsheviks had repudiated Russian international engagements. They had left their military allies in a dangerous position. They continued to abuse and denounce these allies. They boasted that, if they were forced to accept temporary help from the western Powers against the Germans, they would do so merely to preserve the Bolshevik regime until the inevitable downfall of every 'imperialist' government before the onset of proletarian revolution. They regarded themselves as free to use every kind of propaganda – including the 'indoctrination' of prisoners of war – to hasten the coming of this revolution. The only argument, therefore likely to restrain the Allied Governments from active support of the enemies of Bolshevism was the risk that they might drive the Bolsheviks completely over to the Germans. The Foreign Office was aware of this danger, and for the time refused to recognise openly a counter-revolutionary move by the Cossack general Kaledin, though they were willing to give him and other anti-Bolsheviks sums of money in secret.[2] The Foreign Office also maintained unofficial contact with the Bolshevik Government through agents – Litvinov in London and Bruce Lockhart in Russia.[3] Lockhart was a 'regular' consular official,

[1] The assembly was convoked for January 18, 1918, and dissolved on the following day.

[2] Kaledin committed suicide in February, 1918, after failing to get adequate support for his movement.

[3] Sir G. Buchanan left Russia owing to a breakdown in health on January 7, 1918.

young, clever, and self-confident. He stayed in Petrograd and later in Moscow until October, 1918. During the first part of his time, although he provided valuable information, he was of little positive help in framing British policy because he was sure that the Germans would soon renew the war on the Russian front, and that the Bolsheviks would then accept Allied help.

Lockhart thus thought it unwise to support any anti-Bolshevik movement, but the British Government could hardly avoid intervention in Russian affairs. In north Russia there were at Archangel some 12,000 tons of munitions and about 200,000 tons of other war material, most of it British, which, if not removed from Bolshevik control, might fall into German hands. British naval personnel had left Archangel in the early winter of 1917-18 while the harbour was still ice-free; a naval detachment was being maintained at the newly created port of Murmansk. Here the local Soviet was willing to accept Allied help against a likely attack by 'White' Finns with German support; the Allies could not allow this valuable base, recently and precariously linked by railway with Petrograd, to be open to the Germans, whose submarines were already active in the Barents Sea. The Bolsheviks were also reported to be considering the cession of Petsamo to the 'White' Finns, who would admit the Germans into it.

There appeared to be a serious danger in the south. With the melting away of the Russian armies, distance, the mutual distrust of the two Powers, and the increasing disintegration of the Turkish armies were the only obstacles to a joint German-Turkish advance through Transcaucasia. If they were able to control the Caspian, they might move along the railway from the port of Krasnovodsk to Merv; they would then be close to the frontier of Afghanistan, and could stir up trouble in India. Sir Henry Wilson, as CIGS, regarded as most 'urgent' the establishment of British control on the Caspian, and of a secure line of communication to it from Baghdad.[1] Baghdad was over 400 miles from Enzeli, the nearest port on the Caspian, and the 'line' to it was

---

[1] The British Government – and the Government of India – felt a certain anxiety at this time about a Turkish-sponsored political movement known as Pan-Turanianism ('Turan' was a Persian word applying to the peoples of the Central Asiatic steppes) and aiming at the political unity of all peoples of Turkish 'race'. Apart from the military collapse of Turkey there was never much chance of creating a sense of political unity among the populations of this wild and backward area. Pan-Islamism, which might have had more appeal, was no more successful. The 'reform' of Turkey came only after these larger ambitions had been abandoned for a more practical consolidation of Turkish power in Anatolia.

across mountain passes ranging from 5000 to 8000 feet and through country inhabited by Kurdish and other tribes of uncertain attitude.

A small British force under Major-General Dunsterville was sent from Baghdad to Enzeli in January, 1918, with the almost impossible task of organising a coherent body of resistance out of miscellaneous and often mutually hostile groups of anti-Bolshevik Russians, and anti-Turkish Georgians, Armenians, and Assyrians. This British detachment reached Enzeli in mid-February. They found the place occupied by a fairly strong body of troops under the direction of a Bolshevik committee which would not allow Dunsterville to go on to Baku. Later on, however, with the help of some reinforcements, and naval guns sent from Baghdad, Dunsterville was able to enter Baku and to secure a partial and precarious command of the Caspian with some captured Russian ships, while an even smaller detachment of Indian troops took possession of Krasnovodsk. The local Bolsheviks, however, refused to let Dunsterville move on into the Caucasus on what would anyhow have been an impossible task of consolidating local resistance. In September, 1918, a large part of Dunsterville's local levies refused to fight, and the British force had to be withdrawn from Baku in face of a Turkish attack. By this time the Germans were in no position to attack British interests in the Near or Middle East; the Turks were within a few days of their final defeat by Allenby and their surrender at the end of October.[1]

If the War Office exaggerated the threat to India from a German or Turkish advance through Central Asia, they were equally wrong in their estimate of a possible extension of German influence and control in the Russian Far Eastern territory, and especially in the Maritime Province with its capital and port of Vladivostok. The Far Eastern problem was of special interest to the United States and Japan. Japan had been alarmed for some time at the likely consequences in the Far East of a German victory in the west. The Japanese had been supplying Russia with munitions in the hope of maintaining her resistance; they had exacted a good price in the form of an agreement of July, 1916, with secret arrangements for the transfer to Japan of seventy miles

[1] General Dunsterville wrote an account of his almost incredible expedition in *The Adventures of Dunsterforce*, 1925. A small Indian force was sent into Transcaspia mainly because the Indian government thought that some 35,000 German and Austrian prisoners of war in the area might stir up trouble. For German designs east of the Caucasus in the event of victory, see Fischer, op. cit., Chapter 20.

of the Chinese Eastern Railway from Harbin to Chang-chun.[1] The Japanese knew that the United States would strongly oppose any increase of their power at Russian (or Chinese) expense. On the other hand, after the Bolshevik revolution the Allies were much afraid that the Germans might get possession of some 660,000 tons of military stores which had accumulated at Vladivostok. There was in fact very little real danger that the stores would fall into German hands; the disorganisation of the Trans-Siberian line, especially after the Bolsheviks had seized power, was such that the stores could not have been transported to the west for many months.

The question of a landing at Vladivostok to protect the stores seemed urgent to the Allied military authorities when the Bolsheviks were about to make a separate peace.[2] But who was to land? The Americans would not agree to a landing solely by the Japanese; the Japanese would not accept a joint landing by the Allies. Any landing, and particularly one by the Japanese, would unite Russian feeling against the Allies. The British Government at first favoured, tentatively, a joint Allied operation, though for a time they gave way to American objections. After the breakdown of the negotiations at Brest-Litovsk appeared certain, the War Office developed much wider – and wilder – ideas of intervention. They suggested that Japan, on behalf of the Allies, should be invited not only to land troops at Vladivostok to safeguard the stores, but also to advance along the Trans-Siberian railway in order to deprive the Germans of the vast agricultural resources west of Lake Baikal. The War Office thought that in any case the Japanese would probably insist on landing at Vladivostok, but that they would not go past Chita without an Allied mandate.

The Foreign Office was much less ready than the War Office to support this ill-considered proposal. Wilson rejected it on the familiar and sensible ground that it would set Russian opinion against the Allies. Later the Americans somewhat changed their view, but the Japanese themselves hesitated until they could be sure of American approval. Early in April, 1918, the Japanese naval commander at Vladivostok

[1] The Chinese Eastern Railway provided a shorter route than the Trans-Siberian Railway from Vladivostok through Manchuria to a point just east of Chita on the line running wholly through Russian territory. The strip of territory through which the Chinese Railway ran was practically a Russian enclave.

[2] The question of British intervention in Russia in 1918 is well treated in R. H. Ullman, *Anglo-Soviet Relations 1917–1921, I, Intervention and the War*, 1961. G. F. Kennan, *Soviet-American Relations, 1917–20* (Vols. I and II), is authoritative for American policy.

took the initiative in landing a small force to protect Japanese nationals against attack. The British naval commander also landed a detachment but both forces were withdrawn at the end of the month.

After the ratification of the treaty of Brest-Litovsk the situation in the Far East was further complicated by the release of some 800,000 German and Austro-Hungarian prisoners of war east of the Urals. The Allied military authorities were afraid that these ex-prisoners might get arms, and use them to serve German ends. This fear was as little based upon fact as the belief in the possible transfer of vast quantities of military stores from Vladivostok to European Russia. Most of the ex-prisoners were Austro-Hungarian subjects from non-Germanic parts of the Habsburg empire; they were concerned only with trying to make their way home. A more genuine problem came from the Czechs and Slovaks who had been recruited in Russia, again mainly from among prisoners and deserters, to form a national Czecho-Slovak army. Masaryk went to Russia early in 1918 to arrange for the removal of this force from Russia. In March Lenin agreed that it should return at once through Vladivostok. The Bolsheviks, however, became nervous about the passage of a fairly large organised army through Siberia. The French wanted the men to be sent to the Western Front; the War Office thought that they would be more useful if they were left in Siberia, where they would be less likely than a Japanese force to alienate Russian opinion. It was agreed, as a compromise, that all the Czecho-Slovaks west of Omsk should go for evacuation to north Russian ports, and all those east of Omsk should continue on their way to Vladivostok.

The Bolsheviks, however, attempted to disarm the contingents east of Omsk and prevent their journey eastward. In May, 1918, the Czechs decided to fight their way to Vladivostok; by early June they were in control of the Trans-Siberian from a point west of Samara to a point west of Irkutsk. Another contingent of 15,000, which had already reached Vladivostok, seized and held the place against the Bolsheviks as a preliminary to return westwards along the railway to help their compatriots. At the end of May the Germans let the Bolsheviks know that their military operations on Russian territory (they had sent troops to the Ukraine, the Crimea, and Georgia) had come to an end, and that they did not propose to occupy Moscow or Petrograd.[1] The Bolsheviks therefore had no more need to consider what was for them the desperate expedient of an appeal to the Allies to save them from the German

---

[1] Secret agreements of August, 1918, included a German promise to turn the Allies out of North Russia if the Russians themselves were unable to do so.

armies; the Allies, on the other hand, if they decided to intervene in Russia, would have to do so against Bolshevik opposition. The British and French still feared a German exploitation of Russian resources; hence they were more anxious than ever to use the Czechs and the Japanese in Siberia, and to secure for themselves Murmansk and Archangel from which (without much consideration of the distances involved) they hoped to link up with the anti-Bolshevik forces east of the Urals.

At the beginning of June Wilson had been persuaded to agree in principle to the despatch of an American contingent as part of an Allied force in North Russia. He refused to regard Murmansk or Archangel as bases for further intervention, or to consider an expedition from Vladivostok into Siberia. He was willing to send a civilian commission to assist in reorganising the Siberian railways and the supply of food. He would have nothing to do with the far-reaching French and British plan to try to establish, with Japanese help, a new eastern front or at least to prevent a German exploitation of Siberia. The European Allies were exasperated by Wilson's veto. They asked the Japanese whether, if the United States consented, they would intervene and advance as far west as possible 'for the purpose of encountering the Germans'. The intervening force would take no part in Russian domestic politics, and would respect Russian territorial integrity. The Allies suggested Chelyabinsk as the western limit of the Japanese advance, though the nearest Germans were 1000 miles further to the west and shewed no intention of moving eastwards. The Japanese answer was that they could make no decision until they knew that the United States agreed with the plan, and that anyhow they could not engage themselves to go beyond Eastern Siberia.

The western Allies made another appeal to Wilson. They supported it by a reference to the Czechs who appeared to be in danger from concentrations of Bolsheviks and armed prisoners of war near Irkutsk. Wilson admitted an obligation to aid the Czechs but continued to regard the establishment of a new front, east of the Urals, as physically impossible and politically undesirable. He was willing to allow a mixed body of 14,000 Americans and Japanese to assist the 15,000 Czechs already at Vladivostok who wanted to go to the rescue of the larger Czech forces west of Irkutsk. The United States Government, somewhat tactlessly, sent their reply to the Japanese before informing the Allies and said nothing about the possibility of British or French contingents joining the American-Japanese force.

Lloyd George thought the American plan 'preposterous'; the small force which it envisaged would be likely to meet the fate of Gordon's rescue expedition to Khartoum. The question at issue was a 'race between the Germans and ourselves for the control of Siberia'. Lloyd George considered that the Japanese should be invited to take their share in the 'Allied plan of campaign against Germany'. Balfour also described the American proposals as 'indefensible' from a military point of view. Milner, on the other hand, believed that once the President had committed himself to intervention, he would be led on by events to carry out the whole of the Allied policy.

Finally, after more controversy, the United States Government stated in an aide-memoire of July 17 (drafted by Wilson himself), that they regarded the chance of reopening an eastern front as unlikely, and that even if it were possible, it would be of no decisive value against Germany, but would add to the confusion in Russia. The United States therefore would not go beyond aiding the Czechs and protecting the stores at Vladivostok and in North Russia. The United States Government could not prevent the Allies from trying to do more; they reserved the right to withdraw their troops from any further action.

The Japanese now agreed to advance as far as the junction of the Chinese Eastern and Trans-Siberian railways. They said nothing about the Anglo-French idea of forming a new eastern front, though they refused Wilson's appeal to set an upper limit to the size of their force. Wilson did not want this limit to be above 12,000; within a month there were 70,000 Japanese soldiers in Manchuria and eastern Siberia. Few of them ever went beyond Irkutsk. On the day before the American commander arrived at Vladivostok the Czechs to the east and west of Lake Baikal met at Chita, and by September 10 the Trans-Siberian was under their control as far as the Urals. The original purpose of the American expedition had thus been fulfilled, though there was no shipping to take the Czechs back to Europe. The Czechs on the Volga were waiting for help from the north which never came.

The Allied force sent to North Russia occupied Archangel on August 2, 1918, after a local *coup d'état* had turned out the Bolsheviks. A week later the British Consul at Helsingfors reported that the Germans were leaving Finland. There was thus no likelihood of a German attack on Murmansk; the Allied force there, about 15,000 strong, had nothing to do. The force at Archangel was smaller, but its original *raison d'être* had also disappeared; there were no stores left in the place because the Bolsheviks had removed them. The chances of this small expedition to North Russia getting in touch with the Czechs through Vologda were very small. From about this time the Czechs began to be hard-pressed by the Bolsheviks. At the end of October they made a general retreat eastwards along the railway.

The whole situation had indeed changed with the imminent defeat and surrender of Germany. The Allied intervention had caused bitter anger among the Bolsheviks, though the Allies might reasonably claim that their own victories in the west had saved the Russians from the consequences of the treaty of Brest-Litovsk. (In fact, the Bolsheviks would not make an admission of this kind.) The Allies could also claim that they had a right to protect their own military property and to fight the Germans wherever they were to be found. On the other hand, if Allied forces were to remain in Russia, they could not now maintain a pretence of neutrality between the contending Russian factions. The British Government did not want to be associated with counter-revolution, but there seemed no hope of restoring order except by means of a military dictatorship. Military dictatorships, once established, were not inclined to surrender power, and a permanent military despotism in Russia might well become a danger to the peace of the world. For a short time the British Government had hopes of a united anti-Bolshevik government at Omsk; a coup by Admiral Kolchak, however, dissolved this government before it had established itself.

The intervention in North Russia and Siberia had already brought about a complete diplomatic breach between the Bolsheviks and the western Powers. The Bolsheviks exaggerated the size of the western forces, but it was clear that while these forces were on Russian territory Allied consular representatives could not remain in the country. The attempted assassination of Lenin on August 30, 1918, by one Dora Kaplan, a Social Revolutionary, led to an invasion of the British Embassy at Petrograd by a mob and the murder of a British official. (The British had no connection with the assassination.) The British Government held the members of the Soviet Government personally responsible for the murder of the official, and threatened that they would be treated as outlaws if there were more acts of violence. In fact the attack on Lenin had started a series of mass murders by the Bolshevik Cheka which Chicherin, now Soviet Commissar for Foreign Affairs, was unable to stop. Lockhart was arrested, and with other officials exchanged later for Litvinov, Soviet representative in Great Britain, and Russians in London.[1] Even so, the Soviet Government continued to hold British civilians of military age.

Lockhart was now in favour of Allied intervention on a large scale. He thought that, although by leaving the Bolsheviks alone we should avoid the charge of supporting counter-revolution, we should be deserting our friends in Russia who had been given reason to expect help from us; we should also be allowing the Bolsheviks a free hand to spread their movement in Europe. Lockhart saw no solution in the middle course of intervention on a small scale by supporting anti-Bolshevik movements with money and arms and by trying to form a ring of small states on the western frontier of Russia. The anti-Bolsheviks were not strong enough to defeat the Bolsheviks without outside help, and the small 'barrier' states were more likely to be overrun by Bolshevism than to contain it.

Lockhart wrote his views in a memorandum of November 7, 1918, to the Foreign Office. Balfour noted that the memorandum was 'a very able document, whatever one may think of the conclusions'. The British Government did not yet accept the conclusions. They were more hopeful than the French, and less hopeful than Wilson of the possibility of some plan of pacification in Russia which would remove Bolshevik extremism without giving a free hand to counter-revolution of an equally extreme kind. Before the opening of the Peace Conference in Paris the Bolsheviks themselves made a temporary *volte-face*, and on December 26, appealed to the western Powers. The appeal was addressed primarily to Wilson. The State Department in return sent a member of the United States Embassy in London to see Litvinov early in January. Litvinov was conciliatory to the extent of admitting the possibility of a recognition by the Bolshevik Government of Russian foreign debts, and of an undertaking to give up propaganda against the western Allies. He made the excuse that this propaganda was merely a form of retaliation. Litvinov's overtures seemed insincere especially in view of the fact that the Bolsheviks were known to have interpreted the German revolution as the first stage in the collapse of 'imperialist' governments everywhere, and in the movement for social revolution.

Nevertheless the Allies did not refuse discussion. On January 16 Lloyd George proposed a meeting of all the contending factions in Russia. Clemenceau would not allow this meeting to take place in

---

[1] The British Government had been on the point of returning Litvinov to the Russians as a gesture of good will.

France, so the island of Prinkipo, near Constantinople, was suggested as a meeting place. The Bolshevik Government accepted the invitation, but the anti-Bolshevik groups refused to attend; their refusal encouraged the strong anti-Bolshevik feeling in England, especially among the Conservatives. During the absence of Wilson and Lloyd George, Churchill went over to Paris to try to persuade the Council of Ten to give arms to the anti-Bolsheviks. This proposal was refused. Wilson, with Lloyd George's approval, sent another American diplomat to enquire what terms of pacification the Bolsheviks would accept. The emissary – William Bullitt – returned with a list of terms. The terms, accompanied by a time-limit for acceptance, were the cessation of all hostilities in Russia on lines corresponding with the territory occupied by the various fighting groups, the withdrawal of all Allied troops and Allied assistance in kind, and a resumption of diplomatic and economic relations between the Allies and the Bolshevik Government. In return for this recognition of themselves the Bolsheviks offered to recognise Russian foreign debts. Neither Wilson nor Lloyd George was prepared to submit these terms to the Conference. The French, and probably the Italians, would certainly have opposed them; Lloyd George would have found it difficult to persuade his own Cabinet colleagues to agree to them, especially at a time when Admiral Kolchak was advancing successfully against the Bolsheviks and seemed likely to take Moscow. In any case the western Powers, as before, had good reason to doubt Bolshevik sincerity. At this time – March, 1919 – Lenin was still talking of war to the death between the Soviet regime and the 'imperialist' states. Just before Bullitt's arrival in Moscow a conference had been convened to found the Third International – the 'Comintern' – as a nucleus for the organisation of revolutionary communist parties outside Russia. A Communist government set up in Hungary by Bela Kun, a returned prisoner of war from Russia, was also causing the Allies much embarrassment.

A last attempt at a settlement with the Bolsheviks was suggested by Herbert Hoover who had been directing food relief for the Allies in Europe. At the end of March, 1919, Hoover proposed that the Allies should offer to provide food for Russia on condition that fighting between the factions ceased and that all transportation in Russia should be under the direction of the Relief Commission.[1] These conditions

---

[1] Hoover obtained the support of the well-known Norwegian explorer Dr Fridtjof Nansen. Hoover himself was totally out of sympathy with the Bolsheviks whom he described as 'murderers'.

were obviously unacceptable to the Bolsheviks. They pointed out that the demand for a general cease-fire meant that they were being asked to give up the opportunity, which they thought favourable, of securing a military victory over people whom they regarded as rebels.

The Allies did not take this view of the military situation. They believed that Kolchak would defeat the Bolsheviks. They asked him to give assurances that he would call a constitutional convention and permit free elections, and that he would not try to restore the old regime. The Allied note to Kolchak was sent on May 26, 1919. Kolchak gave a satisfactory, and for himself, a sincere answer, but it was already clear that without active military help – a large Allied contingent as well as supplies – he was unlikely to escape defeat.[1] No one of the Allied Governments would provide an army to fight in Russia; no one of them could have provided it, since their troops would have refused to fight and there would have been strong political opposition at home. Labour opinion in Great Britain, though not Communist in sentiment, was much affected by the institution in Russia of a working-class regime, anyhow in name, and resented attempts to interfere with it. For this pressure on official action they received no thanks from the Bolsheviks who continued to treat all non-Communist socialist parties as lackeys of the bourgeois, but the pressure had its effect.

With the Bolshevik defeat of their rivals for power, the British and American contingents on Russian territory disappeared without *éclat*. The Allies never had adequate information about the situation in Russia. They did not realise that the anti-Bolshevik forces had neither solid organisation nor administrative bases from which to act and that, though the leaders might be honest, the behaviour of a great number of their supporters was likely to lose them the support of the peasantry. British and American troops in fact took little part in the early stages of the fighting and none in the final stages. British money and supplies delayed the Bolshevik victory but not for very long. Even if the western Powers had never attempted intervention, their relations with the Bolsheviks would hardly have been any less unfriendly; the gulf between Lenin and the parliamentary democracies which he held in

[1] Kolchak's overthrow of the Omsk government was typical of the political errors of the anti-Bolsheviks. This action had lost him the support of the West Siberian peasants, who thereafter would not provide him with recruits. Kolchak began impressment, and thereby turned the peasants even more strongly against him. Kolchak received £15 millions out of a total British subsidy of £100,000,000 to the anti-Bolsheviks He was killed by the Bolsheviks in February 1920.

such foolish contempt was impassable. Later years have shewn the difficulty of bridging this gulf; one cannot suppose that greater foresight and a cooler judgment on the part of the 'imperialist brigands' would have eased the position for their successors.

PART XII

The organisation of British resources for total war

The transition from peace to war: 'business as usual': the beginnings of control: the supply of arms and munitions: the Ministry of Munitions

The war was won by the men who fought at sea, on land, and in the air. Without their steadfastness and self-sacrifice no political leadership, no organising skill would have availed. It is therefore not enough to say that victory came to the side which possessed the greatest material resources and employed its productive power to the greatest advantage. On the other hand the fighting men depended for the instruments of victory upon the merchant seamen and upon the work of non-combatants at home. The production of these instruments of victory compelled a break from existing habits and methods and a redirection of labour, management, and capital in almost every branch of the national economy. The adjustments had to be made in the face of increasing shortages and increasing restriction of civilian consumption. All this interference required organisation and controls which could be put into effect only by the supreme authority of the state.

In retrospect the remarkable feature of such a vast transformation might appear to be not that it came about, but that it did not come sooner. The Ministry of Munitions was not established until May, 1915, the Ministry of National Service until March, 1917. There was no Shipping Control Committee before January, 1916, no Ministry covering shipping and ship-building until the end of that year. A coal Controller, in charge of a Mines Department, was not appointed until February, 1917. Lloyd George appointed a Food Controller in December, 1916, and, two months later, set up a Food Production Department with its own Director-General; local rationing schemes began towards the end of 1917 and increased in size and scope, but rationing on a national basis did not come into full effect before July 8, 1918. The national organisation of resources was thus a piecemeal affair in which every step was taken *ad hoc*; there was neither a consistent philosophy nor an 'over-all' plan of control. The real paradox, however, is not the slowness and somewhat haphazard nature of the change to the conditions of 'total war', but the fact that under the pressure of events the extension of state control was accepted so readily by a government and people still disinclined to state interference in, or state management of economic life. The Cabinets which imposed the controls were, by a majority, neither socialist not protectionist. The civil servants who devised most of the schemes of control realised the inadequacy of their own departments to regulate the economic life of the country. The industrialists who took a large part in working the schemes disliked arrangements which interfered with the conduct of their own businesses and in many cases put some of their number in a position of authority over their trade competitors and gave them inside knowledge which they might use later to the detriment of their rivals. The feeling against control of labour by an omnipotent state was strong among workpeople, including those who wanted the nationalisation of particular industries. Skilled men resented the loss of privileged status in the interest of rapid production. The surrender of freedom was eased for capital and labour by increased profits and wages, but the gains were offset to a considerable extent by increased taxation and rising prices. For all these reasons the government took care to keep within the bounds acceptable to a somewhat illogical public opinion. The state interfered hardly at all with ownership and as little as possible with detailed management. The powers of directing labour were used sparingly, and even abandoned in the face of strong resistance. The state took over the railways and, later, the mines; it did not nationalise them. It controlled milk supplies, and brought nearly three million additional acres of land under tillage; it did not nationalise farms. It encouraged the co-operation of businesses in the interest of more efficient production; it did not require their amalgamation.

If there had been more thought for war conditions in peace-time, if the length and duration of the war could have been foreseen, many of the mistakes and hesitations about the imposition of controls might have been avoided, and on the financial side much money could have been saved. There had been little industrial preparation for a large-scale and long war because neither the Government nor the public had expected it, and when it came had no experience enabling them to cope with it. The Imperial Defence Committee had produced a valuable book of instructions for immediate departmental action on the outbreak of a war; these measures did not go much beyond certain administrative steps required for military reasons. They did not even include proposals for averting a banking and financial crisis. It was known, or perhaps it would be better to say it had been forgotten, that in the Napoleonic war, the work of two men at home was needed to supply one soldier in the field; with the elaboration of armaments, and a much higher expenditure of ammunition, it might have been guessed that the work of three men would have become necessary a century later, yet the Committee of Imperial Defence had no plans or standards for the allocation of man-power between industry and the armed forces. Kitchener, with a foresight shewn by few of his military or civilian colleagues, began at once to ask for recruits for a war lasting at least three years. It is a curious example of the limited outlook of the ablest professional soldiers that Kitchener should have taken no account of the industrial man-power required to sustain these new armies. Skilled engineers, miners, and 'key' craftsmen of all trades were allowed to enlist without regard to the needs of the industries they were leaving.[1]

In the first weeks of the war there was a general and sensible wish – expressed in the term 'business as usual' – to avoid hardship likely to be caused by any sudden fall in demand leading to widespread unemployment. On the day of the outbreak of war, the Cabinet set up a committee, under the chairmanship of Herbert Samuel, President of the Local Government Board, to deal with measures for the prevention and relief of distress. Samuel appointed four sub-committees, one for London, one for agricultural districts, one for urban housing, and one for women's employment. He asked local authorities to form representative committees in their own areas. The various departments of state also took their own measures. The Local Government Board advised local authorities to go on with all work in hand and to decide what new works could be undertaken. The Board of Trade drew attention to the Labour Exchanges, and the Board of Education arranged for an extension of the feeding of school children.

In a few cases state interference was accepted at once. The Government took over the railways. They gave a guarantee to banks and discount houses. They controlled very early the purchase and import of sugar. These three measures did not involve an elaborate mechanism of interference. The take-over of the railways had been planned in advance to ensure the rapid mobilisation and despatch of the British Expeditionary Force. It did not mean the substitution of outside officials for

[1] See below, p. 464.

the railways staff in the working of the lines. The control of traffic was given to an Executive Committee of Railway Managers, and the Government agreed to maintain the companies' average profits during the three years immediately preceding the war on the condition that rates were not raised.[1] The decision to take over the purchase and import of sugar was an emergency one, but not at this time connected with any shortage of shipping. Two-thirds of the British supply of sugar normally came from Germany and Austria-Hungary. The sugar refiners themselves wanted to get their raw material with the least disturbance in the world market. The Government began at once to buy sugar in Cuba and the East and West Indies.

The guarantee to the banks was also necessary. Asquith's comment on the London bankers as a pack of 'old women' was unfair, especially from a former Chancellor of the Exchequer who should have understood the risks of a serious financial collapse.[2] London was the centre of a world system of credit which worked on the assumption of continuity in trade and business, that is to say, on the assumption of international peace. If this continuity and free circulation were interrupted by war between the leading Great Powers, a breakdown was likely. If foreign debtors could not honour their bills, the London houses which had accepted them might be unable to meet their own liabilities, and would not be in a position to give further credit. If, on the other hand, foreign centres tried to raise money by selling securities, they would send down the prices of these securities, and thus affect the dealers who held them on short term loans from banks. The joint stock banks would be unable to recover their loans, while they might be faced with demands for cash, in excess of their reserves, from their depositors.

The Government had made no preparations for meeting a crisis in credit in the event of war. The crisis indeed began, not in London, but in Vienna, with the delivery of the Austrian ultimatum to Serbia on July 23. On July 27 the Bourses in Vienna, Budapest, and Brussels were closed, and there was heavy selling pressure on the security markets in London, Paris, and New York. The French banks drew on large balances held by them in London, and brought about extensive withdrawals of gold. Most financial centres, however, were in debt in

[1] Any loss due to increased working expenses would be made good by a government guarantee.
[2] There is, however, evidence that firms and individuals with interests favourable to Germany deliberately exploited fears of a financial collapse in order to influence British opinion, official and unofficial, in favour of maintaining neutrality. See above, p. 20, note 2.

London, where they had drawn bills, as usual, in anticipation of the movement of goods; they were now in difficulties about payment. Foreign dealers in securities were also in debt to London brokers. Since gold could not be shipped quickly, if at all, to relieve the pressure, the foreign dealers began to sell securities. This upset prices, at first on the Continental Bourses, then in London and New York. An account on the London Stock Exchange ended on July 29. The Stock Exchange was closed on July 31 in order to allow time for the difficulties of settlement. The London discount houses had already, on July 27, ceased to give new credits.

In addition to the sudden paralysis of ordinary business transactions, there were anxieties about the future. British trade with the belligerents was a large factor in the total of world trade. This British trade would now cease; trade with neutrals would be affected by blockade, and the movement of gold stopped or greatly hampered. Many traders and manufacturers, having lost their markets, would be unable to meet their debts or continue their businesses. As in previous times of temporary financial crisis, the London bankers turned for help to the Bank of England. The Bank did its best by granting credit freely to bill-brokers and by continuing to pay out gold for its own notes. On August 1, however, Lord Cunliffe, Governor of the Bank, told the Chancellor of the Exchequer that he could not meet the demands on the Bank unless he had authority to issue notes against securities in excess of the amount laid down in the Bank Charter Act of 1844.[1] The Chancellor gave this permission, but it was not used. There was no run on the banks.

The first positive step towards preventing the loss of some £300,000,000 to £350,000,000 outstanding bills was a proclamation of August 2 postponing for a month the payment of bills accepted before August 4. On August 3 this moratorium was extended to other payments; a further extension, announced a few days later, covered payments (other than wages) due under contracts entered into before August 4. The joint stock banks agreed to cash cheques for wages, but otherwise to 'ration' their customers' withdrawals. The immediate danger of a rush for currency was averted by extending the August

[1] The act had been suspended in the financial crisis of 1847, 1856, and 1866. Lloyd George was assisted on the technical side of these measures by the Lord Chief Justice, Lord Reading, who had practical experience of the working of London financial arrangements. For a good short account of the crisis, and of the measures taken to meet it, see Sir Henry Clay, *Lord Norman*, pp. 76–83.

GREAT BRITAIN AND THE WAR OF 1914-1918

Bank Holiday to the following Thursday, and by printing currency notes.[1]

These measures were not enough to set going a working system of payments, that is to say, to make it possible for accepting houses to resume giving credits and holders of bills to sell them or borrow on them. Hence on August 13 the Bank of England, under Government guarantee against loss, offered to discount at bank rate, without recourse to the holders, all approved bills accepted before August 4; the acceptors of such bills discounted at the Bank might postpone payment at maturity by paying interest at 2 per cent above bank rate. Three weeks later the Bank offered to lend acceptors funds to pay all pre-moratorium bills at a similar percentage above bank rate, with an understanding not to claim repayment of sums not recovered by acceptors from their clients until a year after the end of the war. The general moratorium ended on November 4; on January 4, 1915, the Stock exchange re-opened. Henceforward there was no 'credit crisis', though the Bank of England primarily, and other banks indirectly, were concerned with the problem of dollar exchange due to immense Government purchases in the United States.

After the immediate crisis caused by the outbreak of war trade and business continued for a short time not entirely 'as usual' but much nearer to normal conditions than had been expected. The ocean routes were soon clear; there was no shortage of food. Measures against general unemployment turned out to be unnecessary. The demands of the armed forces occupied all available labour. Many of these demands were specially urgent; they could be met only by governmental interference with the ordinary channels of trade. This interference of an *ad hoc* kind to meet particular emergencies developed into a more general control of raw materials, production, and prices to an extent which no one in the first few months of war had foreseen. The emergency measures were taken in the provision of military supplies not only owing to the size and suddenness of the demand but also because the existing military arrangements for meeting it were necessarily cumbrous. These arrangements were designed to avoid waste and to keep down prices while providing safeguards to maintain a high standard of quality. They were worked largely by professional soldiers

---

[1] Known at first as 'Bradburys', since they were signed by Sir John Bradbury as Joint Permanent Secretary to the Treasury.

without business experience, untrained to improvise and indeed lacking statutory powers to do so.

One early case was the provision of sandbags after trench warfare set in on the Western Front.[1] Sandbags were made of jute, and jute was used for commercial packing. When the military authorities requisitioned supplies of jute, and also required manufacturers to sell their output of sacking to the War Office, meat importers complained that, if they could not get their wrappers, they would be unable to carry on their business. The sudden increase in demand for jute also sent up prices. In order to get some measure of price stabilisation the War Office had to take more steps in interference. They appointed one large firm of jute importers as their agents for the purchase of jute goods and began later, with the help of the India Office and the Government of India, to negotiate directly with the manufacturers and merchants in Calcutta. India was the world centre of the jute industry. The War Office could not requisition jute mills in Calcutta, but could secure supplies at a reasonable price by getting the Government of India to prohibit the export of jute except under licence and also by persuading the Allied Governments to make their purchases through British channels.

The demand for sandbags was of special urgency, and literally a matter of life or death. Other requirements were not much less urgent. The manufacture of tents was an example of the way in which attempts to secure raw materials at a reasonable price led to methods of 'distant control'. The raw material of tent canvas was flax, normally imported from Russia through the Baltic ports. The German navy cut off this Baltic trade, and the only route open – except a long overland journey through Finland and Sweden – was from Archangel (during the months when this port was ice-free). The flax had to be brought to Archangel over several hundred miles of a single-track railway. There was a shortage of rolling-stock on the railway; Russian speculators were able to buy an option on the use of railway wagons, and then let them at a high figure to flax merchants who were themselves making large profits out of their flax. In order to check this method of forcing up prices the War Office developed early in 1916 a system of purchasing flax in the interior of Russia through buyers who dealt directly with the

[1] For an excellent general account of the early application of state control, see E. M. H. Lloyd, *Experiments in State Control at the War Office and the Ministry of Food* (Economic and Social History of the World War, Carnegie Endowment for International Peace), 1924.

peasants. They arranged with the Russian Government for an allocation of wagons, and obtained tonnage from the British Admiralty for the transport of the flax from Archangel to the United Kingdom. These plans required the prohibition of private trading in flax by British firms. The monopoly (and very largely the control of the price) of an important Russian export obviously needed the collaboration of the Russian Government not only in allowing the purchase and facilitating the transport of the flax but in providing roubles since the ordinary foreign exchange market was almost closed. The Russian Government welcomed the plan since they wanted sterling for their own large purchases in England.

The supply of boots was urgent for the troops already in the field and the new armies in training. Here was a case in which the civilian demand could not be cut beyond a certain point. Boots and shoes might be 'rationed', and economies made by reducing the number of types, but a large minimum demand had to be met. After some early delays by the War Office in putting out contracts the problem was solved with remarkable efficiency owing to the goodwill and co-operation of the leading manufacturers, and the excellent organisation of the industry.[1] The manufacture of standardised[2] military types was arranged as quickly as possible, though the supply did not fully catch up with the demand for some eighteen months. There had been no 'stockpiling' of leather, and, in addition to the requirements for boots, large quantities were needed for harness and saddlery.[3] Hence direct negotiations were undertaken, first with the tanners, and then with their suppliers of hides.

The demand for uniforms, blankets, shirts, socks, and other woollen requirements was on an even vaster scale. The supply proved to be less difficult at first owing to abundant supplies of wool.[4] Manufacturers,

[1] In order to meet American competition in the years before the war, the boot and shoe industry had been equipped largely with American machinery.

[2] 'Standardised' was a relative term. There were 'regulation' infantry boots (different in each of the Allied armies). The British army also required cavalry boots, gum boots (for the trenches, horse-lines, etc.), mosquito boots, hospital shoes and slippers, women's boots for the W A A C and so on. Some sixty different patterns, in different sizes, were manufactured for the British army alone. Early in 1916 the Russians ordered 7 million pairs of boots, and 6000 tons of sole leather, and the Italians 1,500,000 pairs of boots. Nearly all of the 300 or so boot and shoe manufacturers in the United Kingdom were employed on some form of military order. The repair of army boots became an industry in itself.

[3] Most of the artillery was horse-drawn.

[4] The supply of clothing was held up for a time owing to a shortage of buttons.

especially spinners, made large profits which the War Office could not easily control, but the demand was met. In 1916, however, the position changed. Wool supplies fell by 20 per cent. A severe drought in Australia during 1914–15 had reduced the number of sheep; wool production in South America was less owing to the competition of cattle-raising and wheat-growing. The Japanese were importing large quantities of wool from Australia and New Zealand, and the import into the United States was rising rapidly. Meanwhile the British and Allied military demand was continuing to increase until it reached, in 1917, a level almost equal to the total pre-war consumption of the United Kingdom. In June, 1916, the British Government forbade dealings in British wool and set up arrangements for buying the clip. To the astonishment of the traders they also made secret arrangements with the Australian and New Zealand Governments to purchase the whole of their annual supply. These arrangements were continued until the summer of 1920.[1]

A survey of almost every article in a soldier's equipment or in the furnishing of a camp would give a similar story of demand outrunning supply and of measures taken first to regulate sales and manufacture and then to control the raw material used in production. The widest ramifications of state control were in the production of arms and ammunition. The slowness with which these manifold demands were met caused much public criticism, some of which was well founded, though not enough allowance was made for the difficulties and inevitable delays before plans for the expansion of output could be put into effect. The first open attack upon the higher direction of the war came over the shortage of shells on the Western Front. The Coalition Ministry of May, 1915, was formed partly as a result of this attack,[2] and one of its earliest measures was to set up a Ministry of Munitions with Lloyd George as Minister.

In peace-time the responsibility for the supply of munitions for the army rested with the Master-General of the Ordnance. He had control of the Government munitions factories at Woolwich Arsenal, Waltham Abbey, and Enfield. These factories kept a reserve of machinery, but for financial reasons the personnel employed in peace-time was not

---

[1] This plan brought complaints from the middlemen who talked of the extravagance of engaging 'hordes of officials' for the purpose. In fact the plan saved a great deal of money; the administrative expenses of distribution were one-fifth of one per cent of the sales.

[2] See above, Chapter 6.

more than about half the number required to work the plant necessary for an estimated daily expenditure of ammunition by the Expeditionary Force; there were no reserves of machinery for the supply of the Territorial Force. The only other sources of manufacture in the United Kingdom were the commercial armament firms which in peace-time worked mainly for the British and foreign navies. Without foreign orders these private firms could hardly have kept going; the Birmingham Small Arms Company, one of the chief manufacturers of rifle ammunition, maintained itself by making sporting guns.

The supply and reserves of ammunition for the army were based upon a report in 1904 of a committee set up three years earlier. The scales laid down were sufficient for a force of seven divisions in a campaign on the lines of the South African war. No change was made after the Russo-Japanese war, or after the British field artillery had been armed with a new quick-firing gun which used more ammunition. The reason was, as usual, lack of money, but the General Staff do not seem to have pressed strongly for larger reserves and wider sources of supply. If they thought of a Continental war, they envisaged it as lasting only for a short time. The Master-General of the Ordnance in 1914 was Major-General S. von Donop, a competent officer without much imagination or drive. Within a few days after the fighting began it was obvious that the existing scales were insufficient. The French and German armies had also greatly underestimated their needs, but had more facilities for meeting them. The problem for Great Britain, apart from maintaining supplies for the navy, was to increase at least five-fold the rate of replacement allowed for the Expeditionary Force, and at the same time to provide on this enlarged scale the guns, rifles, and ammunition required for a new army ten times larger than the old.

This task would have been too much for General von Donop and his staff, even if they had been less routine-minded. Kitchener was unable to give it adequate attention. The problems set by it could not be solved without the collaboration of almost every department of State and of representatives of capital and labour. The failure to deal adequately with so vast a matter cannot altogether be blamed on the administrative officers of the Regular army, though they often obstructed efforts to help them. The Admiralty were in less difficulty; the fleet was better supplied in peace-time, and used in the early part of the war less ammunition than had been expected. The Admiralty staff also set about the work of expansion with more imagination. The War Office failed in every respect. They went on underestimating their needs and made only feeble efforts to meet them even on their own inadequate scale. They handed over the work of expansion to the Superintendent of the Government Ordnance factories and to the seven most important private firms, and left them to do all subcontracting. On September 30, 1914, these firms were asked to increase their plant; a Government subsidy of £20,000,000 was allocated for the purpose. According to Lloyd George, General von Donop thought it undesirable to tell the firms of this large figure. On October 12 the Cabinet appointed a committee to consider the whole question of munitions requirements and supply. The committee was composed of Kitchener, Haldane, Lloyd George, Churchill, McKenna,[1] Runciman,[2] and Lord Lucas.[3] Lloyd George had already come to the conclusion that the military authorities themselves were the greatest obstacle in the way of a rapid increase in production.

The committee on munitions met five times before October 23 and then, after another meeting on January 1, was considered to have fulfilled its duties. They sanctioned large sums for the expansion of manufacture at home and for the placing of contracts in the United States. They found at their first meeting that, in addition to heavy artillery, of which the army had very little, General von Donop had ordered just under 900 18-pr. field guns – a supply sufficient for twenty-four divisions; nearly all of these guns were to be delivered by June 15, 1915. The committee thought that the number should be increased to 3000, and the date of delivery put back to May 1, 1915. They called together representatives of the Government factories, and of the largest private firms – Vickers, Armstrong, Beardmore, and the Coventry Ordnance Company. These firms, on being told of the offer of financial help, promised to increase their output. Kitchener had already secured for Great Britain and her Allies the output of the Bethlehem Steel Corporation in the United States for five years. The committee telegraphed to the British inspecting staff in America that they should try to secure not less than 1500 field guns and 500,000 rifles by July, 1915. After some negotiation the Bethlehem Steel Corporation promised 200 18-prs. by July 1. The committee also initiated arrangements for increasing the supply of cordite. They found that von Donop had ordered 781,000 rifles by July 1, 1915; they asked him to increase the order by another 400,000. Finally the committee decided not to maintain the policy of centralising orders with a few large firms, and

[1] Home Secretary.　　　　[2] President of the Board of Trade.
[3] President of the Board of Agriculture.

leaving these firms to make sub-contracts. They set up an Armament Firms Committee with power to distribute munitions orders to all firms judged competent to execute them.[1] By the spring of 1915 War Office orders for munitions involved some 2500 firms in the United Kingdom. In the United States Messrs J. Pierpont Morgan had been appointed agents for the British Government and, to a large extent, for the other Allied Governments, and were thus preventing a scramble for orders.

It was, however, already clear that only a quarter of the contracts placed in the United Kingdom were likely to be fulfilled. One reason was a shortage of labour caused by the indiscriminate recruiting of skilled men. At a time when there was an acute demand for rifles, guns, and shells, 16 per cent of the employees in small arms factories and 23 per cent of those in chemical and explosive works had been allowed to enlist. On September 8 Kitchener had issued a notice that skilled men were wanted for munitions work, but Kitchener himself disliked any interference with recruiting. Some effort was made to bring back men who had already enlisted; the results were small.

The Government tried to increase the supply of labour by calling on private firms not engaged on war work to release for munitions factories skilled men in their employment. Neither masters nor men responded easily to this appeal. The smaller firms objected to the advantages thus gained by the larger firms; the men did not like to be moved, and there were no arrangements for housing them if they left their own localities. A rough census of production in March, 1915, shewed that of the machinery available for the manufacture of munitions only about one-fifth was being used for night shifts, and that most of the remainder was worked for eight hours out of twenty-four.

On March 15, 1915, an amendment of the Defence of the Realm Act of 1914[2] gave the War Office powers to compel manufacturers to undertake Government work if they had the necessary plant; otherwise they had to allow the transfer elsewhere of their skilled labour. One solution – already adopted by the French – was to employ women; another plan was to extend the use of unskilled labour. Between the outbreak of war and March 15, 1915, only 2000 women and unskilled

[1] Towards the end of 1914 the Board of Trade suggested that the War Office might show in the principal engineering centres types of the simpler fuses and shells, so that firms would be able to judge whether they could make them. The War Office did not act on this suggestion until March, 1915. W. H. Beveridge. *Power and Influence*, pp 122–3.

[2] This Act, known and disliked as 'Dora', gave the Government wide regulating powers, including in certain areas control of the supply and sale of drink.

men had been taken on for armament work. During the next two months nearly 80,000 women applied for such work; only 1815 were accepted.

The question of employing women and unskilled men on work hitherto done by skilled men touched the Trade Unions at a most sensitive point; War Office officials were not competent to deal with it. The Government set about looking for a solution in the only practical way. They called a conference of employers and trade union representatives. They obtained – with difficulty – agreements on the suspension of many restrictive practices limiting output, on so-called 'dilution' whereby unskilled men could be brought in to do the work of skilled men, and on the submission of industrial disputes to arbitration.[1] These agreements, if observed, would remove the most serious obstacles on the labour side to increased production.

The Government were now well on the road to taking full direction of the rapidly expanding munitions industry out of the hands of the War Office. In April, 1915, they appointed a strong committee, known as the Treasury Munitions of War Committee. Lloyd George, who had earlier threatened resignation if something of this kind were not done,[2] was chairman; Balfour and Arthur Henderson were among the members. Lloyd George asked von Donop to supply him with statistics; von Donop gave the revealing answer that he would have to spend some days getting them ready, since he alone knew the facts.[3] The War Office, under the critical eyes of the Treasury Committee, attempted a compromise between their original plan of expansion through the agency of a few recognised firms and the method of 'spreading' contracts. They divided the country into 'A' and 'B' areas. An 'A' area was within twenty miles of a Government Ordnance factory or a recognised private firm; this area was treated as a reservoir of labour for such factory or firm. All other areas were rated as 'B', and in them contracts were distributed among individual firms or groups of firms. It was soon clear that this plan was impracticable. There was not enough skilled supervision to deal with the 'B' areas and the system of distributing work over twenty or thirty small factories in widely separated towns was uneconomical. In any case the thirteen 'A' areas

[1] See below, pp. 472–4.
[2] Balfour was a less impetuous critic, but he wrote to Lloyd George on March 25, 1915, that he 'could not help suspecting that Kitchener has only an imperfect grasp of the problem with which he has been faced for seven months'.
[3] Beveridge, op. cit., p. 124.

included a very high proportion of the surplus engineering capacity of the country, and therefore left too little for the 'B' areas.

In mid-April Lord Kitchener asked the advice of Colonel Sir Percy Girouard, an engineer officer who had been Director of Railways in the Sudan and South Africa, and, at the age of forty-eight, had been appointed managing director of the Armstrong works at Elswick. He recommended setting up new factories in all the important manufacturing areas and concentrating in them men and machinery under one staff and management. They were to be State factories, though, for convenience, they might be built and staffed under the supervision of recognised armament firms, and located, where possible, in their immediate neighbourhood. The Cabinet accepted this scheme, and also realised that it carried with it implications beyond the competence of the military authorities. Only a large governmental organisation specially set up for the purpose could ensure the provision of raw material and tools, allocate labour in relation to other war industries and the export trades, and so forth. In other words, a Ministry of Munitions would have been created within a short time, even if there had been no pressure of public opinion urgently demanding a better use of the national resources.

The Coalition Government created such a Ministry on May 26, 1915, with Lloyd George as Minister. A Munitions of War Act provided the new Ministry with more extensive powers over 'controlled establishments', that is to say, all factories doing armament work which the Minister thought fit to place under control. The Act also gave legal sanction to the agreements reached in March with the Trade Unions over the suspension of restrictions. Strikes and lock-outs were prohibited, and a system of arbitration laid down for disputes. The profits of controlled firms were limited to the average net profit of the firm concerned during the two financial years preceding the war. The powers already given by the Defence of the Realm Act to compel manufacturers to take Government work and to permit the transfer of workmen were extended to allow the compulsory transfer of skilled men and machinery to the State-owned factories.

The new Ministry began work as an organised body on July 15, 1915. Deliveries of shells under its first contracts did not begin until the following year; there was also at first some risk (as von Donop had pointed out) of sacrificing quality for quantity. Much of the ammunition produced during the first year of the Ministry's work was defective, with serious consequences in the battle of the Somme. Nevertheless, although Lloyd George took too great credit to himself, there is no doubt that the establishment of the Ministry was necessary, and that it should have been set up sooner. No other arrangement would have been adequate to provide munitions on the immense scale with which they were used in 1916, 1917, and 1918. During its existence the Ministry spent over £2000 million, and its staff rose to more than 65,000.[1]

[1] Lloyd George has described the Ministry as solely a 'business organisation'. On the labour and administration side, it was begun by civil servants and reinforced to a considerable extent with professional men, especially from the senior ranks of the universities. The Ministry also owed a great deal to regional organisations through which it obtained local knowledge of the potential capacities of an area.

CHAPTER 31

Labour questions: conflicting demands on man-power:
the Ministry of National Service: the suspension of restrictive practices and the 'dilution of labour': women
workers

One of the main problems of the Ministry of Munitions, and indeed
of the British economy during the war, was an increasing shortage of
man-power. This shortage, especially in the field of skilled labour, was
aggravated by the lack of a considered labour policy on the enlistment
of men in trades essential to war production. The War Office was not
alone in overlooking the probable consequences of indiscriminate recruiting. The Committee of Imperial Defence had made no plans in
the matter and the Cabinet had not asked them to do so. There was
no single Ministry dealing with the general question of labour. The
Local Government Board was concerned with what might be called
the catastrophes of the workers – unemployment, poverty, old age.
The Home Office dealt with factory inspection and conditions of
work and the Board of Trade with the administrative regulation of
railways, shipping, and the new Labour Exchanges. No department was responsible before 1914 for the organisation of labour in a
war.

Early in 1915, after the heaviest period of voluntary enlistment was
over, the War Office began to realise what they had done, or rather,
what they had allowed to happen. In May, 1915, they issued an order
that men from certain industries producing material for the forces
should not be accepted for military service. The Admiralty (which
needed fewer recruits) had begun to 'protect' men earlier. The War
Office list of protected workers was drawn up narrowly; it included
neither miners nor steel workers. The system of 'protection' also
worked unevenly. The Admiralty by July, 1915, had given some
400,000 badges to men working in industries essential to the navy; the
War Office had 'protected' only 80,000 men, three-quarters of whom

were in government factories or in the five largest armament firms. In any case local recruiting officers tended to ignore the order not to accept reserved men. The newly formed Ministry of Munitions took over and extended the granting of exemptions, but no adequate survey had yet been made of the labour force available in the country. A National Register of men and women between sixteen and sixty-five was ordered. The results could not be known or classified for some time. An estimate at the end of October put as 1,500,000 the number of men of military age already in reserved occupations.[1] Meanwhile the War Office needed this number for the campaign of 1916.

The Military Service Acts of 1916 changed the character of the labour problem.[2] So also did the heavy losses in the offensives of 1916 and 1917. After the battle of the Somme the problem of man-power was no longer one of keeping back skilled workers from enlisting; the difficulty now was to prevent the War Office from making excessive and dangerous demands for the army. More was known about the facts; there was general agreement that a limit had nearly been reached to the numbers of skilled men who could be taken out of the industries essential to the fighting forces. The question was whether too many exemptions were being given to men whose civilian work was not essential. Thus at the end of 1916, out of over a million men allowed exemption, and working for some 12,000 firms, no less than 400,000 were unskilled. Obviously some 'comb-out' was possible and necessary.

Lloyd George, on becoming Prime Minister, set up a Department of the Director-General of National Service; this department was not able to devise the local organisation required to settle the exemption of many thousands of individuals. A scheme, known as the Trade Card Agreement, which gave the Trade Unions authority to issue cards of exemption, was unlikely to be of much use; Union officials elected by their fellow-workmen could not be expected to undertake the task of deciding who was and who was not to be sent into an army which was losing men at an appalling rate.

A schedule of protected occupations issued early in 1917 covered, primarily, men in Admiralty, War Office, munitions or railway work, and also gave protection of a less absolute kind to men in 'scheduled occupations' outside the four main categories. Local committees were

[1] The total number of men of military age was about 5,000,000.
[2] See above, p. 160. For the question of labour supply, see H. Wolfe, *Labour Supply and Regulation* (Economic and Social History of the World War).

formed to hear appeals. In August, 1917, the War Cabinet reformed the new Ministry of National Service with instructions (i) to review the whole field of man-power, (ii) to arrange for the transfer of men from other occupations to urgent national work, (iii) to determine the relative importance of occupations, and to reserve a sufficient number of workers in the industries outside war production to maintain essential public services and 'preserve a nucleus of civil occupations and industries', (iv) within these limits to secure men for the army in numbers laid down by the War Cabinet. The Ministry had the assistance of a Cabinet Committee under General Smuts in deciding upon the most urgent industrial needs.

At last recruiting for industry and the services had come under a single control, though the problem was far from being solved, and indeed never could be solved, since it was determined by a military strategy which had accepted 'wearing down' the enemy in a series of costly offensives as the only way to victory. The Ministry was able to take 70,000 men from 'scheduled industries' for the army without lessening the production of food and munitions. If the war had lasted longer, the task of finding more soldiers would have been progressively more difficult. As things were, the age of military service was raised in April, 1918, to fifty-one. The arrival of American reinforcements, however, would in any case have eased the strain, though with the inevitable result of cutting down the size of the British army.

Even if there had been no conflict between the demands of the army for more soldiers, and those of industry for more labour, there would still have been difficulty in finding workers for the new factories and for increasing the production of the existing large and innumerable small firms which had undertaken to work for government orders. The Labour Exchanges set up in 1909 and multiplied under the Insurance Act of 1911 were of great value; if they had not existed – there were over 400 of them in 1913 – it would have been necessary, and difficult, to improvise them in order to prevent a chaotic search by employers for workers, and something like a stampede of workers without direction or knowledge where to go. The additional labour force available consisted of men or women employed on unessential private work, older men who had left off working, boys, women who had never previously done factory work, and a certain number – never very large – of workers from the Dominions or elsewhere who were brought into the country. As time passed, there were also prisoners of war, though these were employed mainly in agriculture. The most important newcomers to the labour force were women; boys would have entered it anyhow in due course. In July, 1914, the total number of women workers employed in commerce and industry was 3·2 million; in July, 1918, the figure was a little under 5 million. More than a third of these new workers came in without government intervention, except by way of public appeal. 168,000 women joined the civil service as clerks; 220,000 went into government factories, and about 420,000 into the metal trades.

At first the Trade Unions opposed the invasion of men's jobs by women. The Government had appealed to women at the end of 1914 to enrol for war service. 79,000 were enrolled in March, 1915, in a Women's War Register; after three months only 2000 had been placed.[1] The immediate need was not for unskilled women, but for skilled men. Some early agreements were made with a few unions; no general progress was possible until the difficult question of the 'dilution[2] of labour' had been settled. This question, from the trade union point of view, was most serious. In effect, it meant putting unskilled or semi-skilled labour to do, with the help of new machinery, and after short training, work hitherto done by skilled men. At the same time, in order to speed production, the unions were asked to give up so-called restrictive practices.

The problem indeed was not a new one. The engineering trade was already in a difficult state of transition. For a long time past manufacturers in many industries had been installing machinery which did not require highly skilled workers; the process had gone further in the United States than in Great Britain. To the skilled men these new machines seemed a threat as serious as similar innovations had appeared years earlier to the Luddite rioters. The maintenance of standards of living by restrictive rules was an out-of-date method, which was bound in the end to harm the working class, but to the skilled worker there seemed no other way to protect himself against a fall in wages or against unemployment. The restrictions limited the number of apprentices taken on in a trade, excluded women from men's work, regulated output of work and the class of job done by each category of tradesmen, prohibited working with non-union men, and forbade the employment

[1] These figures are a little misleading because in the early part of the war many women workers lost their employment. The Labour Exchanges rightly gave precedence to these regular workers in filling vacancies.

[2] This word was not used until after the agreement of March, 1915. There was something euphemistic or, at all events, neutral about it.

on machines of semi-skilled workers under a skilled operator. The regulations went into great detail. They laid down

> what machines should be used for particular jobs; how the machines should be placed in relation to each other, and the speed at which they should be worked; whether an operative should complete a whole job, or attend only to one machine, or form part of a team of specialised operatives each doing a different process; what wages, if any, should be paid in the intervals between jobs, or whilst waiting for material.[1]

This code had been built up slowly, and often with hard struggle. The men were asked to give it up without being sure that it could be restored at the end of the war. They were also being asked to make the surrender when the employers were gaining large profits, and, as the workers saw it, were not being required to give up anything.

Early in February, 1915, the Prime Minister set up a Committee on production in engineering and ship-building establishments employed on Government work, with instructions to report on methods of making a fuller use of the productive power of these establishments. The committee attempted to deal with the men's grievances; as a result of its report representatives of thirty-eight Unions[2] went to a conference at the Treasury on March 11, and appointed seven delegates for further discussion with officials and representatives of the employers. Two agreements were concluded. In the first of them the unions promised (i) to forego during the war stoppages of work on production essential for victory, and in their place to accept arbitration, and (ii) to relax trade union rules and practices subject to their restoration after the war and the safeguarding of permanent standards of wages. In the second agreement the Government undertook to assist in the restoration of pre-war conditions, and also to restrict the profits of firms in which the relaxation of trade union practices had taken place.

The abolition of practices restricting output had immediate results. 'Dilution' met with more resistance, and anyhow could not be brought into effect at a stroke. By definition, the unskilled workers, especially the women new to industry, did not know how to do the skilled jobs. If they could not fit the work, the work had to be fitted to them.[3] It could be fitted to them, in the large, by substituting machines for

---

[1] S. Webb, *The Restoration of Trade Union Conditions*, pp. 10-11.

[2] The Parliamentary Committee of the TUC was also represented.

[3] In certain industries, coal-mining, for example, 'dilution' was impossible. There was little scope for it in ship-building. In the ship-building industry, how-

craftsmen; the unskilled workers thus became machine-tenders.[1] The machines, however, had to be made, and as a preliminary, the machine tools had to be provided for making them, but tool-making itself was perhaps the closest preserve of the skilled worker, and the introduction of 'dilution' into the industry most difficult to accomplish. In any case, as new machines, easily worked by unskilled labour, were introduced into factory after factory, the skilled men might well wonder whether it would be possible to restore the old state of things after the war. All in all, 'dilution' was not really effective before the spring of 1916; even then it was causing discontent. The employers, on their side, also required much persuasion to accept it, since they were at first afraid that it might reduce output. A special staff of 'dilution officers' was appointed to go round from factory to factory, and to deal with local difficulties and grievances.

Apart from the general problems of dilution, the introduction of large numbers of women into industry was in itself less difficult than the transfer of men from one occupation to another. Most of the women were new-comers; very few were skilled, and not many were even semi-skilled workers. There were few women's unions[2] and for this reason few questions of 'restrictive' practices. The agreement of

---

ever, trade union limitations on the allocation of work to this or that craft were extremely rigid; the relaxation of these rules was a matter of serious disquiet to the workers. 'Dilution' was also not very practicable in the metal manufacturing trades. For a special study of the problems of 'dilution', see G. D. H. Cole, *Trade Unionism and Munitions* (Economic and Social History of the World War).

[1] The method of substitution was largely one of sub-dividing the processes of manufacture, and using machines which could perform automatically much of the work done previously by the skilled craftsmen. This method of sub-division was continually pushed forward. Thus the 'semi-skilled machinist' came to need less and less skill, and the functions of the skilled worker became more and more limited to 'setting-up' the machines for a particular job. The munitions industry lent itself easily to these methods of standardisation and automatic repetition.

[2] In 1914, the only 'general' women's union – the National Federation of Women Workers – had a membership not larger than 20,000. A few other 'general' unions included women workers. In the textile trades women were organised in the men's unions. The number of 'new-comers', in the sense of workers totally new to industrial work, has been exaggerated. Many women workers just changed their jobs, and many married women – including soldiers' wives – who had worked before marriage, re-entered industry. The soldiers' wives tended to be 'anti-strike'. Of the new recruits to factory work, domestic servants were, on average, highest in physique and intelligence. It is typical of British social conditions before 1914 that many women – especially in country districts – had no adequate outdoor clothes – coats and shoes – and had to be provided with them.

March, 1915, safeguarded the men's unions from wage-cutting owing to competition from women workers, though detailed arrangements about wages were not always simple. The formula 'equal pay for equal work' was a rough rule, but what was 'equal work', and did 'equal pay' cover war advances and bonuses on the 'basic' rates of men's wages? On the whole, women doing work previously done by men came off better than women who were doing work previously done by women. In general, however, the rates of women's wages in industry went up by 50 per cent more than the rise in the cost of living, and all women workers gained in the long run from the demonstrated fact that they could soon acquire proficiency in jobs altogether new to them. Indirectly the contribution of women's work in the auxiliary armed services and industry had an important political consequence in that it could no longer seem fair or reasonable to refuse women the parliamentary vote.

CHAPTER 32

Wages: strikes: the reasons for labour unrest

The 'dilution' of labour added greatly to the difficulty of settling disputes about wages during the latter part of the war. For some time wages had remained fairly constant. After considerable rises in the cost of living 'war bonuses' of all kinds began to be paid, and the armament firms were competing for labour. The Munitions Act of July, 1915, laid down that wages in a 'controlled establishment' should be changed only with the consent of the Ministry of Munitions. The purpose of the order was, primarily, not to fix any general rates of wages, but to prevent employers from 'poaching', that is to say, from dislocating the smooth running of factories by enticing workers away with promises of higher pay. This practice was easier for the employer when he was paid for the product of his factory on a basis of cost of production plus a fixed percentage of profit.

With the introduction of the war bonus there arose the problem, almost insoluble from the point of view of equity, of deciding upon the method of its application. Should a bonus be on a flat rate for all workers or should it be graded according to existing rates of pay? The trouble was greater because there was no uniform system throughout industry for the calculation of wages even among trades where the unions had been able to enforce negotiations on a national level. Rates in the coal industry were based on weekly output (subject to a minimum wage), and in the iron and steel trades on a sliding scale determined by the sale price of the product. The main textile trades had national wage agreements, but most of these trades were localised in certain areas; there were no cotton mills in the south. The railway workers had fixed scales with a large number of grades. Again, one industry differed from another in the relative importance of time or piece work. In some industries the employers had to deal with a very few unions; in other trades, such as ship-building, there might be a score of unions. Agriculture – a large industry dispersed throughout the country – was in a category of its own. Wages generally were higher in London than elsewhere, and otherwise higher in the north than in the south. Finally it became clear that an increase granted in one branch of industry brought demands from allied or similar industries, and that these demands soon spread to other trades and occupations.

The unions had insisted that the influx of unskilled and semi-skilled workers into the carefully guarded preserve of the skilled should not bring with it a reduction in wages. The actual problem was very different, and had not been foreseen. The workers had been guaranteed that, where payment was by piece work, an increase in output would not be followed by a cut in piece rates. This promise, which was made in September, 1915, was regarded as a part of the bargain over 'dilution'. Soon afterwards, with the increase in automatic machinery, and with simplifications in design – especially of shells and fuses – there was a very rapid rise in output. The new workers also became familiar with their machines and worked them more quickly. Unskilled workers tending machines now began to earn higher wages than skilled workers. In many cases a foreman was paid less than the workers whom he supervised. The Government could not go back on their promise, while the cost of raising the wages of all skilled and all time-workers to, or above, the level of the favoured piece-workers was impossibly high. The grant of bonuses at a flat rate to all workers in order to meet the high cost of living was an additional source of grievance to the skilled worker. The unrest was so dangerous that in October, 1917, against the advice of the Minister of Labour, the War Cabinet granted a $12\frac{1}{2}$ per cent increase to certain classes of skilled time-workers. The Ministry of Labour wanted this grant to be conditional on the acceptance of a plan for payment by results, but the unions would not agree.[1]

The $12\frac{1}{2}$ per cent bonus, though it added to the financial burden of the war, and raised the cost of living, obviously did not settle the grievances of the skilled men. All classes of skilled and semi-skilled time-workers at once asked for the bonus. Unskilled time-workers then put in claims, and finally piece-workers demanded their inclusion. The

[1] The objection to 'payment by results', i.e. assessment of wages on the basis of output, was not universal. More than half of the shipbuilding workers were paid on this basis. Many unions were opposed to it on the ground that it led easily to wage-cutting by employers. Opposition in other unions was due partly to the unsuitability of piece rates for certain kinds of skilled workers, e.g. supervisors or tool hands.

army needed the munitions, and in the mood of war-weariness and general discontent among the working class, refusal would have meant large-scale strikes. The $12\frac{1}{2}$ per cent bonus was thus given to all munitions workers.

Labour discontent had become serious before the autumn of 1915. The first six months of the war had been almost clear of strikes in the engineering, ship-building, and metal trades; a certain unrest had developed early in 1915 over increases in the cost of living, and over reports, largely, though not always exaggerated, of immense profits made by employers working on government contracts. The first open trouble came on the Clyde in February, 1915, over a wage demand which had been postponed – by agreement – on the outbreak of war. The strike was brought about by 'unofficial' leaders; the executive council of the Amalgamated Society of Engineers did their best to get the men back to work. They soon went back, but there was an end to the 'industrial peace'. If, however, the stoppages of work are considered against the background of the bitter disputes in the years immediately preceding the war, and against the nervous strains and difficult adjustments of the war years, the surprising fact is not that there were strikes as the months passed but that there were so few of them. In 1916 76,000 men in the engineering, ship-building, and metal trades went on strike and 346,000 working days were lost. In 1917 386,700 workers lost a little under 3,000,000 days.[1] On the other hand no less than 8000 awards made by arbitration tribunals set up under the two Munitions Acts were accepted by the workers. At a serious strike of July, 1918, in Coventry Churchill, then Minister of Munitions, warned the men that, if they did not go back to work by a certain date, they would be called up for military service. The men went back to work. This was the only case in the munitions industry in which the Government threatened to use their powers of compulsion. No strikes took place during the critical weeks of the German offensives on the Western Front. The Coventry strike did not start until the Allied counter-offensives were under way.

The attitude of public opinion and the press was not always helpful in calming industrial unrest. Before a strike took place, the newspapers tended to ask for strong measures, and then later to blame Ministers and officials for delay in reaching a settlement – that is to say, for a refusal to make immediate concessions. In fact the 'dead

[1] The totals for all trades in 1916 were 338,376 workers on strike, over 2,500,000 days lost; in 1917, 820,726 workers on strike and over 5,500,000 days lost.

hand of bureaucracy' was neither as lifeless nor as heavy as opinion believed. There was some truth in the charge that the Ministry of Munitions, though it gave great attention to labour disputes and to negotiations on a national scale, was less ready to consider the 'un-official' representation of local grievances. In June, 1917, the War Cabinet appointed a number of Commissions to enquire into the causes of industrial unrest. They reported their general view that war condi-tions, and not official blunders or revolutionary feeling – with the in-tention of overthrowing the Government and ending the war – were the real reasons for the strikes. They listed fourteen contributory causes; among them were high prices and unequal distribution of food, overlong hours of work, restrictions on personal freedom, especially the regulation preventing workmen who left their jobs from getting work elsewhere without a certificate from their previous employer permitting their withdrawal,[1] delays in settling minor disputes, doubts about the restoration of 'trade union conditions' after the war, the operation of the Military Service Acts, the skilled men's pay grievance, lack of housing facilities,[2] the raising of the income tax exemption level, and, particularly in South Wales, a 'lack of communal sense'. The last item in the diagnosis was vague, but real, though in a final analysis one might consider whether the 'lack of communal sense' among certain classes in certain areas was not due to past neglect and lack of education.

To this general analysis one might add two important considera-tions. A remarkable feature of the war-time industrial unrest was the emergence of a new form of leadership from the ranks, and by-passing to a large extent the existing machinery of the established Unions. Most of the Glasgow strikes were sponsored by shop-stewards. The shop-steward movement, or, as G. D. H. Cole has called it, the 'work-shop movement', was 'a spontaneous growth, the outcome of circum-stances common to many different areas rather than the creation of any mind or group which made itself the master of circumstances'.[3]

---

[1] This was one of the main grievances of the Clyde workers in the early autumn of 1915. The workers regarded it as a step towards 'industrial conscription'.

[2] Housing conditions in Glasgow and the neighbouring urban areas were especially bad. The immigration of workers into the region during the war added to these housing difficulties. Large numbers of people already working long hours had to spend an undue time getting to and from their work.

[3] G. D. H. Cole, *Workshop Organization* (Economic and Social History of the World War), p. xi. This book, written primarily from the workers' standpoint, is the best account of the shop-steward movement.

It was primarily a movement among the rank and file, with local not national leaders. The local leaders and their most active supporters came largely from the left wing of the politically conscious working class; many of them used the movement for political ends, but the opportunity for such use was provided by events outside their calculation.

The shop-stewards were minor union officials, or rather, union members with minor administrative duties, such as checking membership cards, and reporting to the regular union officials on any workshop matter affecting members' interests. They were to be found mainly in the engineering and ship-building trades. They had no official powers in the processes of collective bargaining, but the coming of dilution gave them a sudden importance. Dilution in the workshops, especially in its earlier stages, meant a number of detailed changes which had to be discussed and arranged in each shop and for each job. The shop-stewards were the only people who could deal with these detailed negotiations. Their numbers therefore increased, and the employers found it necessary to recognise them and to work through them. Much of the shop-stewards' work was thus a valuable smoothing over of difficulties, tending to reduce, and not to create friction and unrest. There were, however, factors which did not make for agreement. The shop-steward movement was something of an innovation in British trade unionism, since it introduced organisation on a workshop, not a craft basis. During the years of industrial unrest before the war the left-wing critics of the parliamentary Labour party and the large craft unions had advocated this form of organisation. The supporters of 'direct industrial action' had given the plan wide currency as a means of getting rid of capitalism and substituting workers' control. The Syndicalists and Guild Socialists had similar ideas about the importance of workshop organisation. The extremists tried to use the special circumstances created by the war (towards which many of them took the left-wing ILP attitude)[1] as an opportunity for putting their plans into effect. They regarded the official acceptance of dilution by the unions as an act of surrender.[2] The Clyde Workers Committee – an unofficial body brought into existence as a 'Labour Withholding Committee' by the shop-stewards during the strike of February, 1915 –

[1] See above, p. 47.
[2] G. D. H. Cole himself called this acceptance a 'disarmament' of the unions, without reference to the reasons why dilution was essential if Great Britain were to avoid military defeat through lack of munitions.

described the acquiescence of the unions in the Munitions Act of July, 1915, as 'an act of treachery to the working classes', and announced their intention of 'forcing the repeal of all the pernicious legislation that has recently been imposed upon us. . . . We will support the officials just so long as they rightly represent the workers, but we will act independently immediately they misrepresent them.'[1]

From this time the relations between the regular union officials and the shop-steward committees became sharper. The shop-stewards also began to be chosen directly by the workers in the shops, not by the district committees of the unions or with the latter's approval. The shop-steward movement spread rapidly to other industries and areas, and, as always, the extremists pushed out the more moderate men. The opposition of the left-wing to compulsory military service and the success of the Russian revolution added to the enthusiasm of the militants, and encouraged their hopes of establishing full workers' control in British industry.

The authorities took action against the extremists, though not very effectively. In March, 1916, some of the members of the Clyde Committee were deported to other areas (where they assisted in the spread of their ideas). *The Worker* had already been suppressed – only to reappear later – and the editor and printer sent to prison for advocating something like sabotage in the factories. The official commissioners of enquiry, however, were right in affirming that the great majority of the workers were neither revolutionary nor defeatist, and that they did not strike for political reasons. The support of demands for workers' control was a practical way of expressing practical grievances. After the war, when the shop-steward movement faded out in conditions no longer favourable to it, the demand for a greater measure of workers' control continued and was brought forward through normal union channels, while the extremists of the Clyde and similar committees drifted away to the newly founded and uninfluential British Communist party.

This judgment on war-time strikes needs to be qualified by a second feature in the handling of industrial disputes; the failure of the Government to improve the relations between workers and employers in the coal industry. There were no severe coal strikes in the war; but the reason was that the Government gave in to many, though not to the

---

[1] The Clyde Committee's Journal, *The Worker*, wrote of the Munitions Act as 'having started on its enslaving career'. See U. R. Scott and J. Cunnison, *Clyde Valley Industries* (Economic and Social History of the World War).

most significant, of the miners' demands. The mining industry was already organised on a local basis with a single pit or small group of pits as a unit; 'pit meetings' included all the workers employed in the unit. Ideas of a greater control by workers developed easily in this kind of environment. Relations between employers and employed in the industry were notoriously bad, especially in South Wales. The Miners Federation had failed in a strike of 1912 to obtain a wages settlement on a national basis; their declared objective was the nationalisation of the industry with a large measure of workers' control. They had been preparing to put forward their demands again in conjunction with their partners in the so-called 'triple alliance' of miners, railway, and transport workers. Hence they objected to proposals for wage increases to meet rises in the cost of living which did not accept the idea of a national agreement. The Federation took little part in the negotiations over dilution; there could not be much substitution of unskilled for skilled labour in the mines, and women could not take the place of men in underground work.[1] The Federation also refused to agree to compulsory arbitration for the settlement of disputes, though they offered to refer disputes to the chairmen of the Coal Conciliation Boards set up in the various areas in 1910. In March, 1915, the Federation asked for a uniform national advance of 20 per cent in wages. The employers, as usual, refused a settlement on a national rather than a district basis. After long negotiation the Prime Minister persuaded both sides to accept his arbitration. He ruled in favour of a wage increase by districts.[2] The Federation accepted the ruling under protest, and an unofficial strike broke out in July, 1915, over the terms of a new wages agreement. The Government proclaimed the strike as illegal under the Munitions Act; they could not take proceedings against 200,000 miners. After six days they gave in to most of the men's demands, and promised that the employers would accept them.

The immediate occasion for controlling the industry was the question of wage agreements. An Order of November 29, 1916, imposing

[1] Production in the mines had been much affected by the policy of unrestricted recruiting. During the first seven months of the war over 191,000 miners joined the forces; another 75,000 enlisted between March and August, 1915. In the first year of the war 75,000 workers entered the industry; most of them were young men under military age or older miners returning to work.

[2] Wage rates in the industry were complicated and cumbersome. Before the war there were eleven 'districts' in Great Britain; systems of working and methods of payment were often not uniform in a single district; basic rates went back to a standard fixed in 1879, with later percentage additions.

control in the South Wales area, was made just before Lloyd George became Prime Minister. The purpose of the Order was described in Parliament as the elimination of war profits, the avoidance of industrial disturbance, and the furtherance of the best productive results. Lloyd George let it be known that he would extend control throughout the industry. Some Labour representatives seem to have had the impression that he intended the nationalisation of the mines.

A Coal Controller, in charge of a new Mines department, was appointed in February, 1917. As in the case of the railways, the employers were left to manage the industry, subject to the control of profits and to any action which the Coal Controller might take with regard to the production, sale, and distribution of coal.[1] The owners were guaranteed a standard rate of profit based upon the profits of any one of the three years preceding the war, on condition that output reached the annual average of the period taken for the calculation of profits. 80 per cent of any additional profit went to the Exchequer; 15 per cent was retained to form a pool from which the guaranteed profits could be made up in any given case. The remaining 5 per cent was allowed to the owners. The imposition of national control, with a profits pool and unified financial arrangements, made it easier for the miners to insist on national rather than district settlements in any further wage increases to meet rises in the cost of living. A national advance at a uniform rate was granted in September, 1917, and another in July, 1918. The Miners Federation at their annual conference in July, 1918, put forward a programme for a National Wages Board, a five-day week, and a six-hour working day. A month later the Scottish miners carried unanimously a motion in favour of nationalisation, with a large share in management for the workers. Thus, while in other industries, economic demands with political implications tended to disappear (with the exception of a strong movement in favour of leaving the Russians alone to work out their economic and social

[1] The Coal Controller did much to promote economy in the distribution of coal. Thus he found that the North Wales area, which imported considerable amounts from other areas, was exporting to these areas 40,000 tons of its own production. The Controller took in hand the supply of material for the mines. Canadian lumber-men and German prisoners of war who were woodmen by trade were brought in to assist in felling home-grown timber. Maintenance in the mines was reduced to the minimum necessary for safety; the rations of pit-ponies and colliery draught horses were reduced. At the end of 1918 the Technical Adviser to the Controller reported that five to seven years' work would be needed in some mines to restore pre-war output.

experiments), the coal-mining industry came out of the war, and soon had to face a difficult fall in demand, with the relations between employers and employed as unreconciled as they had been before 1914.

After the Coventry strike of July, 1918, Churchill, then Minister of Munitions, appointed another committee to enquire into the causes of industrial unrest. The committee made two reports – the second and longer was submitted after the armistice. The diagnosis of the causes of unrest was little changed, but the situation had now become different, and, except for its recommendations on measures for easing the transition of industry from war to peace, the report had mainly a historic or at all events a retrospective interest. From this point of view the December report summed up what was, in fact, the main background to the labour problems during the war:

> At the commencement of the war the Government had two courses open to it: first, the bold but logical course of general conscription, both combatant and industrial; or second, combatant conscription with a limited measure of industrial regulation. The first course would, if practicable, have involved a decision by the nation that every man of suitable age and health was definitely enlisted in the national service and subject to orders as to the task best suited to him. Soldiers and civilians would then have stood on a substantially similar footing, each civilian would have been regarded as a temporarily exempted combatant, and discipline and the obligation of allotted service would have been universal.
>
> The traditional antagonism of the nation, however, to conscription prevented the adoption of this course. We [i.e. the Commission] have observed the unanimity with which the great body of witnesses before us have expressed a resentment not only of the substance, but even the appearance of industrial conscription or the control of the State over the right of the workman to employ himself where he will at the best wages he can obtain.
>
> The second course was adopted. A large measure of freedom was left to the worker and such a degree only of regulation was made as was necessarily required by the national interest.

The report added: 'It is obvious from the evidence before us that the great body of workers are anxious to reduce, and, as soon as possible, to remove the war-time regulations of labour conditions which at present exist.'

CHAPTER 33

Shipping

The exigencies of the war and the extension of governmental control affected most people in Great Britain not only as producers but as consumers. In the shortest definition the problem was how to get essential supplies of food and raw material to the ports in the face of enemy action at sea and, when there were increasing shortages, how to settle priorities and to distribute what was available with the greatest advantage to war production and the least hardship to individuals. The economic history of the war could be written from the end of 1915 largely in terms of the shipping shortage.[1] This shortage was the more serious because Great Britain was not only providing the shipping for her own needs but was also supplying nearly half of the tonnage for French and Italian requirements – almost twice as much as the French and Italians supplied for themselves. In addition, she found most of the ships for the transport of American troops to Europe. In the last year of the war only 57 per cent of British shipping was being used for imports to Great Britain, and, even so, a large proportion of British imports consisted of raw material for the manufacture of goods to be delivered to her Allies. This diversion of British ships to Allied service added greatly to the hardships of the British people; food restrictions would have been less if more British ships had been available to meet domestic requirements. The magnitude of British shipping aid was never realised by her Continental Allies, and never employed, as it well might have been, to justify a greater claim for Great Britain to decide the high strategy of the war.

The need to allocate ships to the common advantage led to the whole of British shipping coming under governmental control. This extension of control was difficult because the transport of persons and goods by sea before the war was not 'planned', in any wide sense of the term. The adjustment of the supply of carrying capacity to the

[1] See A. J. Salter (later Lord Salter), *Allied Shipping Control* (Economic and Social History of the World War).

demand was left to a free market. There was no 'comprehensive survey' of needs. Hence when such a survey became necessary during the war even for one country, there were no experts who could give a ready answer, since the facts were not known. It was known, indeed, that there were in existence some 8000 ocean-going steamships manned by some 450,000 men, and built and maintained by another 250,000. The capital value of these ships was about £300,000,000 – less than that of the two largest British railway companies. About half of the ocean-going ships were British, with a gross tonnage of 18 million.[1] Germany had between 700 and 750 ocean-going ships, with a gross tonnage of about 4 million; the United States had about 500 ships, with a tonnage a little over 2 million.[2]

Since there were enough ships to meet the average annual demand, traders had no reason to lock up capital in the storage of supplies unless governments made it worth their while to do so. The British Government had taken no precautionary measures of this kind. At the outbreak of war the country had, for example, only one to two months' supply of imported foodstuffs, about the same reserves of iron ore, and two to three months' supply of wool. The cabinet, however, had not entirely overlooked the possibility of a dislocation of shipping in time of war, whether Great Britain was or was not a belligerent. It was realised that ship-owners would hesitate to send their ships outside British and other strongly protected waters if they had to pay the high premiums which insurance brokers would have to impose in order to cover war risks. In May, 1913, Sir Hubert Llewellyn Smith, of the Board of Trade, had suggested to the Prime Minister the appointment of a sub-committee of the Committee of Imperial Defence to consider the question of war risks at sea. This sub-committee reported at the end of April, 1914. They were able to provide approximate estimates of costs, since the ship-owners themselves had formed 'clubs' or associations to cover war risks, though only for a war in which Great

---

[1] This tonnage was almost equally divided between 'liners' and 'tramps'. There were about 6000 British coastal steamers under 1600 tons. (Gross tonnage is a total measurement reckoned at 100 cubic feet per ton. Net tonnage is gross tonnage less space for engine-rooms and crew; the ratio of gross to net tonnage is about 8 to 5. The term 'deadweight' is applied to cargo and bunkers in a fully laden ship.) For an account of the British merchant shipping industry in 1914, see C. E. Fayle, *The War and the Shipping Industry* (Economic and Social History of the World War), Chapters 1 and 2.

[2] Owing to the boom in overseas trade in 1912–13 most ship-building yards in Great Britain and elsewhere had large construction on their stocks.

Britain remained neutral. The Government had not accepted any plan of state insurance, but the facts were available for immediate decision.

Such a decision was necessary in the last week of July when insurance rates rose steeply. On July 25 the chartering of ships for Black Sea cargoes – mostly of wheat – was suspended; four days later Austrian and Russian ships were almost uninsurable, while the premium on British ships calling at Continental ports rose to 5 per cent. The market closed on July 31 until after the August Bank Holiday. On the night of August 2–3 the three main associations were promised a guarantee, and on August 4 the Government announced a scheme for reinsuring ships to cover war rates.[1] This measure, together with the steps taken for the safeguarding of credit,[2] had an immediate effect. The effect was greater because, contrary to expectation, German raiders did not come out in large numbers to attack British ships. On August 12 the Admiralty announced that traders need not hesitate about sending their ships to sea. Within a short time the Atlantic liners resumed their ordinary sailings, and there was a fall in insurance rates (i.e. in market rates outside the government guarantee).

The effects of war, however, were soon felt in a rise in the costs of freight. The pre-war figure for chartering a tramp steamer was about 3s. a ton deadweight per month. By December, 1914, this rate had doubled. For the second half of 1915 the figure averaged 15s. These increases led to much public criticism and to charges of profiteering. A good deal of this criticism was unfair.[3] The rise was not caused by shipping losses. British ocean-going tonnage in June, 1915, was very little lower than twelve months earlier. The cost of buying space on ships went up for three reasons; the redistribution of traffic, the requisi-

---

[1] The rates were 1½ per cent for hulls, and five guineas per cent for cargoes.

[2] See above, Chapter 30. Owing to the general credit and discount arrangements most cargoes in fact 'belonged' to banks and discount houses. Until the spring of 1915 the State made a profit on its war insurance of ships; the insurance of cargoes was profitable for a longer time.

[3] High profits were made, but, on the whole, not through deliberate attempts to force up prices by cornering a market. The increase in cost was based not on the British demand alone, but on world demand for shipping. The shortage of supply was thus real, not artificially contrived. On the other hand there was full justification (i) for taking the additional profits in the form of special taxation, and (ii) for extending control as far as was possible, so that the additional profits would not go to the ship-owners. If individual ship-owners had not accepted the market prices open to them, the profits which they would have refused would merely have gone to merchants importing the cargoes.

tioning of ships, and congestion at the ports. The closing of so many Continental ports to British traffic meant that imports had to be fetched from longer distances, and therefore took up shipping space for longer times. There were fewer available ships owing to government requisitioning. Some arrangements had been made before the war to hire ships for the transport of the British Expeditionary Force. These arrangements were on a small scale; the department of the Admiralty concerned with the hiring was also small.[1] In October, 1914, when freights had begun to rise, arrangements were made by a joint committee of ship-owners and officials for the hire of different classes of ship at fixed rates. These rates, which were published,[2] ultimately saved the taxpayer very large sums, but were a matter of considerable grievance to ship-owners until requisitioning was extended to cover nearly all British ships. As freight rates for 'free' shipping rose to immense heights, owners whose ships had been taken at Blue Book rates made far less profit than they could have obtained in the ordinary market.

The chief reason at the end of 1914 for the increased competition for shipping space was the immobilisation of so many ships for long periods owing to congestion in the ports. This possibility had been considered before the war, but no detailed plans had been made to avoid it. Such plans could not be easily devised because there were so many causes of congestion. The diversion of much traffic from east coast ports north of London would anyhow have brought a strain elsewhere, and the more so because ports had tended to specialise in facilities for particular kinds of cargo. Thus coal and ore ports had no silos for wheat, and little or no cold storage space. At the coal ports much accommodation was taken up by colliers for the use of the fleet and auxiliaries. The demand for raw materials of every kind connected with war production rose very rapidly; warehouses and transit sheds – where mixed cargoes

[1] The requisitioning of ships began early, since the Admiralty and War Office wanted to avoid a repetition of the high charges paid during the South African war. One difficulty, which was not fully overcome until the establishment of a Ministry of Shipping, was that there was no single authority competent to deal with a shortage of shipping. The Marine Department of the Board of Trade supervised only the condition of ships, not their supply or use. The Transport Department of the Admiralty had assumed that they would always find ships available for their special needs.

[2] The table of rates was published officially. Hence the use of the term 'Blue Book rates'. The Government hired the ships, provided fuel, and paid war insurance premiums and any additional cost in wages above pre-war rates. In some cases the hiring extended only to a part of a ship – e.g. insulated space.

were sorted – became choked.[1] There was not enough dock labour; many skilled and reliable dock workers had enlisted. The railways were also crowded with traffic and short of trucks. Other factors had an indirect effect; thus the prohibition of any increase in railway rates encouraged traders to send by rail goods which might otherwise have been carried to smaller ports in coastal ships. Congestion also affected French and Italian ports, and was soon to spread to trans-oceanic ports. According to an estimate in January, 1915, about 1,500,000 tons of British, French, and Italian shipping was held up in this way, and the total carrying power reduced by some 20 per cent.

The requirements of the Mesopotamian, Gallipoli, and, later, Salonika expeditions put a heavy strain on shipping. The military authorities had at the time little or no sense of the importance of economising sea transport, and indeed economy was not always possible. The shipping for the Gallipoli expedition had to be requisitioned suddenly, to the dislocation of other traffic. Ships were loaded in haste, often as the material arrived in the docks; many had to be brought to Alexandria for reloading. If they went directly to the base at Mudros, they were delayed for weeks because there were no piers, quays, or warehouses, and not enough tugs, lighters, or labour for discharging colliers. A number of ships were kept indefinitely as warehouses or for military headquarters.[2]

From the middle of February, 1915, the German submarine attacks[3] added greatly to the shipping difficulties, not merely owing to the shipping losses (the number of sinkings, though serious, was not yet enough to cause grave alarm), but owing to delays caused by deviations of route, or holding ships in port when U-boats were known to be in the neighbourhood. Measures were taken in home ports to deal with this congestion. The situation soon became a little more in hand, though matters grew worse at French and Italian ports. At Genoa in Novem-

[1] Sugar imports increased by about a third between October, 1914, and January, 1915. During this time the Sugar Commission – having no storage accommodation elsewhere – kept most of the supply at the ports.

[2] e.g. one large steamer at Mudros was used as a Headquarters base, and another as an Ordnance Depot. The military authorities did not insist on the provision of port equipment because they were hoping for a move to the mainland. For this same reason, a large number of motor lorries, though they were not wanted at Gallipoli, were held on board ship at Alexandria for immediate transport in the case of an advance. (For the congestion at Basra, see above, p. 101.) A speaker in the House of Commons early in 1916 claimed that some eighty ships had lost over 7000 'ship-days' through government mismanagement.

[3] See above, Chapter 13.

ber, 1915, some 700,000 tons of cargo were held up in warehouses or in ships awaiting discharge.[1] Italian demands, especially for coal, were absurdly high, Russian requirements were an even greater problem. The only ports now available in European Russia were on Arctic waters.[2] The harbours on the Murman coast were ice-free; there were, however, no railways connecting them with St Petersburg; one was in course of construction, but the work was going very slowly. Archangel was not ice-free in the winter, and had not enough cranes or quays; it was linked with the south, as far as Vologda, only by a narrow-gauge, single line.[3] Ships going to Archangel were vulnerable to submarines and mines, and Russian patrol work was very inefficient. Owing to a miscalculation by the Russians in 1915 about the date to which the port would remain ice-free some sixty to seventy ships, including eleven colliers, were held up at Archangel until May, 1916.

The ever-rising cost of freight led to increasing public demand for some form of shipping control. The difficulties in the way of control were serious. If maximum charges were laid on cargoes carried in British ships, the Government would also have to determine the cargoes. If they insisted on applying these charges to cargoes of British goods or destination carried in neutral ships, they would certainly lose the use of neutral shipping which would go to more profitable employment elsewhere. The use of neutral shipping was, however, essential to British and Allied purposes.

A first step towards control had been made with sugar imports, when the Government had requisitioned – at Blue Book rates – ships to carry the Cuban crop. This first step in requisitioning tonnage for purposes not directly or indirectly military was followed almost at once by a similar measure dealing with the transport of coal to French ports; the purpose here was more directly military, since the coal was largely for the use of French railways. The plan was then applied to the requisitioning of insulated space on cargo liners importing South American and Australasian meat. In November, 1915, a Ship Licensing Committee was set up to requisition ships for the carriage of foodstuffs and other commercial goods. Even so, the demand for tonnage and the cost of freights continued to rise.

[1] The British Government refused to allow sailings to Genoa until these arrears had been cleared off. At the end of January there were still 350,000 tons.

[2] See above, p. 62.

[3] A broad-gauge line was being built, but had not passed the half-way point in the summer of 1915.

At the end of 1915 it was clear that some more general form of control of imports would be necessary. The Liverpool Shipowners Association had made proposals of this kind, but had realised that the working of a system of control was beyond the competence of the shipping companies. A Port and Transit Committee set up in 1915 had made similar suggestions; an obvious example was the curtailment of bulk imports of paper for advertising purposes. The committee also agreed upon the difficulty of deciding what were, or were not, essential imports and upon the need of a comprehensive survey of the total requirements of the country. They thought a licensing system preferable to complete prohibition, since it could be applied with the least interference with ordinary trade, and could take account of the indirect consequences of a drastic cut. Lord Salter mentions, as one of these 'indirect consequences', that prohibition of the import of furniture might well have increased the demand for home manufactures, and therefore for home-grown timber, and thus, by lessening the quantity of home-grown timber available for other purposes, have resulted in larger imports of foreign timber. There was also the risk of trouble with the Dominions, whose financial stability depended on exports to Great Britain, and with neutral exporting countries who might retaliate by refusing essential supplies.

The Government appointed a Shipping Control Committee[1] in January, 1916, to advise upon the allocation of British shipping to meet the essential needs of Great Britain and her Allies. In fact the real problem was already not to allocate ships but to make good an existing deficiency in shipping, and, if this were impossible, to distribute the inevitable 'cuts' fairly between all concerned. The Committee estimated that British imports would have to be cut by 4 million tons; the Board of Trade was unwilling to accept a reduction of more than 2 million tons. The shipping situation grew worse as the months went by. In January and February, 1916, most of the sinkings by submarines were in the Mediterranean, but there were heavy losses from minelaying in home waters. The mines were laid in groups; their constant renewal shewed that submarine minelayers were passing through the Dover barrage. Two surface raiders now appeared. One was captured on her way out; the other – the *Moewe* – did great damage and also caused much delay owing to the diversion of shipping; Australian and Far Eastern traffic was diverted to the longer Cape routes, and therefore

[1] The Committee consisted of a Cabinet Minister as chairman, two shipowners, and a financial expert.

took up more shipping. Meanwhile the demands of the Ministry of Munitions for heavy cargoes of iron ore, nitrates, vegetable oils, and ammunition from the United States, continued to increase.

New enemy submarines, with a wider cruising range, began to appear. Nearly 500,000 tons of British shipping were destroyed between January and June, 1916 – two and a half times the output of the shipyards in those months. During the last quarter of 1916 British losses averaged 160,000 tons and neutral losses 100,000 tons a month. In the month of December the Norwegians lost 160,000 tons. Even so the sailors went to sea. Only 2 per cent of the cargoes were lost, and the total British imports in 1916 were only 5 per cent less in tonnage than those of 1915. The arming of merchantmen was a considerable defence. U-boats were vulnerable on the surface, and owing to longer absences from home had to rely more on gunfire than on torpedoes. On the other hand there were not enough guns.[1]

One of Lloyd George's first acts as Prime Minister was to appoint Sir J. Maclay, a ship-owner, as Shipping Controller in charge of a Ministry covering both shipping and ship-building. In announcing the new department Lloyd George said that, for the period of the war, shipping, like the railways, would be 'nationalised in the real sense of the term'. Lloyd George, after his manner, did not explain what he meant by 'the real sense of the term', but he made it clear that his chief motive was to cut down the cost of freight and the extravagant profits of ship-owners. The working of the control – as in the case of most other industries – was carried out largely through the leading representatives and organisations of the shipping industry. The requisitioning or direction of shipping was merely a generalisation of procedures already begun; the new feature was that the Ministry had power to build or buy ships and to run them as a Government enterprise.

The measures necessary to put the Ministry into operation were not fully implemented until the beginning of April. Meanwhile the shipping position had become critical. At the end of January, 1917, the Germans had announced their renewal of unrestricted submarine warfare. They knew that they were risking war with the United States; the risks seemed justified by the early successes of their campaign.

---

[1] Early in 1916 owing to agitation at home, the Government diverted a number of guns for anti-aircraft defence of towns – many of which were never even attacked – while sailors were left to man slow tramp steamers without protection. For the anti-submarine measures, see above, Chapter 23.

313,000 tons of British ships were lost in February, and 353,000 in March. The losses in the second fortnight of April were nearly 400,000 tons.

The Germans did not frighten the British merchant marine, but for a time the neutrals almost withdrew their sailings. The British Government had to insist upon a 'ship for ship' principle, that is to say, they refused shipments of necessary imports to neutral countries unless these countries sent an equivalent in exports to Great Britain. This policy was not altogether successful. Swedish, Danish, and Dutch trade with Great Britain was almost suspended. The 'ship for ship' plan could not be applied to Spain owing to the extreme need to maintain in full the import of Spanish ore, but no Spanish ship arrived in a British harbour during the first three weeks of March.[1] The total entry of Spanish, Dutch, and Scandinavian shipping during February and March was about a quarter of the figure for those months in 1916, and would have been very much less if the Norwegians had not continued their sailings.

Even if the terrible losses in April had represented the 'peak' of the German effort, British and Allied imports would have had to be reduced beyond the limits thought practicable only a few months earlier. Not much relief could be expected in the immediate future from new construction. At the end of 1916 ocean-going shipping under the British flag was nearly a million tons below the figure at the outbreak of war. Although a large number of new ships were on the stocks, building was slow. The yards had to do a great deal of repair work to ships damaged by enemy attack, and also to make good breakdowns caused by the use of inferior coal and the lack of efficient crews; many masters, engineers, and firemen had been taken for naval service. Steel was short; there was not enough labour, and at this time work was too often interrupted by strikes.[2] Orders had been given in 1916 for the release of trained ship workers from the army. 3816 out of 6470 men for whom application had been made were released by the end of November; there was little hope of getting more releases, though in January, 1917, the Ministry of Shipping had obtained exemption from military service for all workers already in the industry. Towards the

[1] The withdrawal of the Spanish ships affected the supply of British coal to France, since the ore ships on their return voyages from Great Britain took cargoes of coal to French Atlantic ports.

[2] One reason for setting up state building yards was to overcome the suspicions of the workers that they were being asked to augment the profits of ship-building firms.

end of 1916 the Government decided to build 'standard' ships of three main types; the largest type was 8000 tons gross. The programme was delayed, partly owing to a foolish newspaper agitation for an 'unsinkable' ship, but over 125 of the standard types had been ordered by the end of May, 1917. Only 85 were completed before the armistice.[1] There was practically no building in French or Italian yards. On the other hand much help was expected from the United States. Those expectations were not realised. The United States Government in July, 1917, took over the large building programme (900,000 tons) which American ship-builders were carrying out for Great Britain, and decided upon an immense programme of ships under their own flag. There was at first – as in Great Britain – considerable delay owing to discussions about types; two months were spent in deciding whether to concentrate upon steel or wooden ships. If the war had lasted through the winter of 1918-19 the American construction would have been of the greatest value, but from the shipping point of view in 1917, and for most of 1918, American entry into the war added to the problems of transport.[2]

The introduction of the convoy system[3] saved a situation which in May and early June seemed almost desperate. It was, of course, impossible to foresee whether the Germans would find some way of defeating this system; nevertheless in and after July, 1917, the Allied problem was not so much one of absolute survival, but of tiding over an extremely difficult six or twelve months until relief came from the ship-building programmes. In fact, British losses for the rest of the war were less than were expected. They remained above 300,000 tons a month until September, 1917, when they fell to 200,000 tons. Even so, until June, 1918, the amount of monthly losses was greater than that of new building.

The period of 'tiding over' was in itself most difficult. Every instrument – shipping control, rationing, prohibition of non-essential

[1] The total British output of mercantile shipping in 1917 was a little over a million tons.

[2] A certain amount of enemy shipping in American ports was taken into use in 1917. On February 1, however, the crews on these ships interned in United States harbours had received orders from Germany to render their ships unusable. The United States put guards on the ships, but in general acted too late to prevent damage which cost several months of repair work. The Brazilian Government also delayed seizing nearly 250,000 tons of enemy shipping; meanwhile the crews damaged the ships, and repair work was a much more difficult matter in Brazil than in the United States.

[3] See above, Chapter 23.

imports – was used to the fullest extent. Shipping control indeed was almost complete before the opening of the second period of 'unrestricted' submarine warfare. All British ships – including liners – were requisitioned at 'Blue Book' rates. The requisitioning of liners was a more serious matter than that of tramp steamers because it interfered with the regular sailings by means of which British shipping lines had built up a large trade over many years. Some liners were taken as troopships or hospital ships; in other cases, whenever it was possible, the owners were allowed to use for 'private' cargoes the space not required for imports on government account. Considerable economy was also secured in the use of military and naval transport – 335 ships of 1600 tons or over were being employed in March, 1917, in the service of the forces in Egypt, Mesopotamia, Salonika, and E. Africa. The reorganisation of the railway transport arrangements of the BEF in France carried out after October, 1916, by Sir E. Geddes was now bringing results, and lessening delays at the ports.[1] The tonnage taken up by the army and navy was reduced in July, 1917, by about a sixth, but the total was still about a quarter of the tonnage of British shipping.

More steps were taken to lessen the congestion in British ports. A Transport Workers battalion, of some 600 men, had been organised in 1916 to be sent where there was special need; this force was increased in April, 1917, to a strength of 10,000.[2] The problem of railway traffic from the ports was now greater than ever; in 1917 the Great Western Railway carried 25,000 trains on Government account. There were not enough engine drivers, firemen, guards, and maintenance men. Large numbers of engines and wagons had been sent overseas, and railway shops were being used for munition-making. All private goods trucks had been pooled in 1916, but the number of insulated vans and wagon sheets fell far short of the demand.[3] At the most dangerous period of the submarine attacks it was impossible to close the port of London, since the railways could not carry more traffic from other ports. Although most of the output of lorries was taken

[1] See above, p. 257. Colonel C. W. Paget, in charge of railway operating troops in Boulogne, had earlier suggested the formation of inland depots to which ammunition could be sent, on arrival, from the ports for sorting and assembly. It was impossible to do the work completely at home, since the cargoes had to be stowed with regard for the safety and stability of the ships.

[2] The men were organised on military lines, and were classed – and trained – as soldiers when not engaged on dock work. When they were doing dock work, they were paid at current civilian rates.

[3] The Ministry of Munitions refused to allow linseed oil for their manufacture.

by the army, 10,000 tons of traffic were diverted in April, 1918, from the railways to the roads; a very much larger amount – 67,000 tons in a single month – was carried on inland waterways.

These improvements in organisation could not solve the main problem; there were too few ships to carry the full amount even of 'essential' imports. The complicated system of import controls, which for the latter part of the war changed the ordinary conditions of living and modes of economic life, was mainly due to this shortage of ships. Meat shipments, arranged by Great Britain for her Allies as well as herself, were down in 1917 by 30 per cent on the previous year.[1] The imports of wheat were slightly higher than in 1916; home supplies were larger in Great Britain, but the harvests in France and Italy in 1917 were poor. There was no margin for 'non-essential' imports, and a heavy fall in the export of 'miscellaneous' manufactures. An estimate of the position likely in 1918 shewed that there might be a reduction of 8 million tons in British imports without allowing for the diversion of more British ships to carry American troops.[2] The reduction would have to come in food and munitions.[3]

In November, 1917, the British Delegation to an inter-Allied conference in Paris submitted a memorandum on the shipping position and prospects. They pointed out that Great Britain was providing France and Italy with nearly 2 million tons of cargo space and Russia with a quarter of a million tons and that another quarter of a million was being used for the smaller Allies. If these ships had been kept by the British for themselves, Great Britain could have maintained her imports at something like their pre-war level. The British people were suffering considerable hardship; most of their imports were of food and munitions, and no further reduction seemed possible. In spite of this large-scale British effort, serious deficiencies were expected unless the United States provided more shipping. The United States Government had said that no American ships could be withdrawn from their present uses, but the American delegation were being asked to reconsider their refusal in the light of the reductions made by Great Britain – a country more dependent than any other of the Allies on imports.

[1] 46,000 tons were lost at sea. The fall in imports was more serious owing to the number of domestic cattle slaughtered to provide fresh meat for the army.

[2] Allowance was made, however, for 2 million additional tons of cereals for France and Italy.

[3] A good deal of space was saved by taking North American wheat imports in the form of flour, though this economy meant losing the valuable by-products of milling.

The delegation then put forward estimates of the tonnage to be provided for the transport of 400,000 American troops to Europe by April
30, 1918, 800,000 by September 30, or a million by December 1.

The Paris Conference accepted a British proposal for an Allied
Maritime Transport Council which would suggest the most economi-
cal use of the available shipping and allocate it to the different needs of
the Allies in a way most likely to assist their common cause; the
programme of each Ally would then be adjusted – in fact, cut down –
to the allocation of ships. The idea of a general pool of shipping was
thought impracticable. The Americans would not have accepted it;
the British Government, which was finding most of the ships, did
not want to lose the power of refusing to meet unreasonable Allied
demands.[1] Anyhow, since the ships could not be concentrated like an
army reserve in one place, an arrangement for a common pool was
not workable.

The Allied Maritime Transport Council did not begin operations
until February, 1918. By this time an exceptionally severe winter had
caused a 'freeze-up' of shipping in American harbours, and congestion
on the American railways had brought a shortage of bunker coal. In
January, 1918, 100 British and Allied ships were held up in the port of
New York alone, and cargoes of coal had to be sent out to the United
States and Canada.[2] In March the German offensive brought a serious
risk that French coal supplies from the Pas de Calais mines might be
cut off; there was also an urgent demand for the transport of American
troops to Europe in greater numbers. During the four months from
April to July 519,000 American soldiers were transported in British
ships which otherwise might have carried at least a million tons of
imports. In July the decision was taken to give priority to the transport
of troops and munitions, and to delay the import of cereals until after
the end of the year; Great Britain and the Allied countries meanwhile
could live on the 1918 harvests.

The need to make good as rapidly as possible the vast quantity of
material lost in the German offensives also diverted resources from
ship-building. There could be no certainty that after the experience
of more than twelve months the Germans might not be devising some
means of attacking convoys. At the beginning of 1918 there were more

---

[1] Italian demands were especially high.

[2] The explosion in December, 1917, at Halifax of a ship loaded with munitions
wrecked the harbour installations and a good deal of the town. For a time shipping
had to be diverted elsewhere.

U-boats than in the opening month of 'unrestricted' warfare. The Germans were breaking up old battleships and cruisers in order to provide the steel for larger and more heavily armed submarines, with a longer cruising range. The armistice therefore came none too soon from the point of view of British and Allied shipping problems.

It has been argued[1] that British action in cutting down imports, increasing domestic food production, rationing consumption, allowing capital assets, e.g. buildings, to run down, and Anglo-American co-operation in substituting supplies from North America for those drawn from more remote areas were sufficient in themselves to defeat the German submarine campaign even if the convoy system had not been adopted with such success. This argument is valid up to a point. The Germans aimed at destroying 600,000 tons of shipping a month; they estimated that after five months, i.e. after the loss of 3,000,000 tons, Great Britain would have to sue for peace. The German average of sinkings for six months was over 640,000 tons a month – but it did not bring surrender. It is, however, much less certain that Great Britain could have held out or that victory could have been won if the shipping losses had continued at this high rate for another six months. There were limits to the British economic counter-measures and at the end of July, 1917, the limits were within distance of being reached. If shipping losses had not fallen, the large number of American troops could not have been transported without loss – or even transported at all – and the shortages of war supplies as well as food would have become critical.[2]

[1] The most recent statement of this view is in M. Olson Jr, *The Economics of Wartime Shortage*, Duke University, U.S.A., 1963.

[2] On the other hand the contrary view that, if the Germans had resumed unrestricted submarine warfare earlier, they might have won the war, is also unlikely. The British and American economic counter-measures would have begun earlier; so also would the use of convoys.

CHAPTER 34

Food production and rationing

In view of the gravity of the shipping shortage the surprising fact about food rationing in Great Britain is that it began so late. The control of certain foods came earlier, and by the end of 1917 some local authorities had introduced rationing schemes for sugar, butter, and margarine. At the end of February, 1918, a more comprehensive scheme, including meat, was put into operation for London and the home counties – a scheme so large that it could hardly be called 'local'. Rationing on a national basis developed out of this and other schemes in July, 1918.

Direct control of food production also came fairly late in the war. There was little interference with farmers until the latter months of 1916. No plans had been made either for maintaining an adequate supply and distribution of food in the event of war or for producing more food in the United Kingdom. These problems might well have been given more attention. British home-produced food in 1913 supplied the country only for 125 days of the year, or, as the historian of food production[1] has put it, over each weekend from Friday night to Monday morning. The acreage of land under corn in England and Wales had fallen since 1871 by nearly $2\frac{1}{2}$ million acres. The fall was not due to the unsuitability of the land for the production of corn, but mainly to the competition of cheap wheat from the American continent. The area lost to arable could be brought back again.

The fact that even after war had broken out no important steps were taken at once either to increase the production of food or to ensure economy in consumption shewed how great was the confidence in the ability of the Royal Navy to keep open the sources of supply, and how strongly the Government and the public felt that interference with private trading and the normal processes of production and dis-

[1] T. H. Middleton, *Food Production in War* (Economic and Social History of the World War), 1923. See also, in the same series, W. H. Beveridge, *Food Control in War Time*, 1928.

tribution would do more harm than good. On this question of interference with trade in foodstuffs the Government was perhaps more
nervous than the public and more bound by orthodox liberal economic
theory. Walter Runciman, President of the Board of Trade, was a
liberal 'non-interventionist' of an old-fashioned kind; he disbelieved
in 'government trading', and, in spite of Kitchener's warning that the
country should prepare for a war of at least three years, thought it
unnecessary to include in the 'preparations' of his own department
anything which would disturb the free play of private enterprise.[1]
The Prime Minister's acquiescence in this refusal to provide against
dire emergency may be regarded as typical either of his general failure
to give a lead in his Cabinet or of his cool-headed unwillingness to be
pushed into over-hasty measures before the necessity for them was
apparent.

The Cabinet indeed did not overlook the matter entirely. At the
beginning of the war they set up a Committee on food supplies; in
view of Runciman's policy, the Committee had little to do, and soon
faded out. The Board of Trade was given powers to requisition stocks
of food 'unreasonably withheld'; here also action was not needed because there was little or no 'withholding'. The President of the Board
of Agriculture and Fisheries appointed a Consultative Committee on
Agriculture in the first week of the war. This Committee suggested
an increase in the production of cereals; the Cabinet decided on September 9, 1914, not to offer a 'financial inducement' to farmers to
plough up more land. They advised the farmers to sow as much wheat
as was 'conveniently possible'; they were prepared to assist them in
getting manures, feeding stuffs, and labour, but they would not take
even the first steps towards compulsion.

None the less, in some directions the Cabinet was compelled to act
contrary to the principle of non-interference with the machinery of
private enterprise. In addition to the purchase of sugar they had begun
to buy meat. One-fifth of the total meat consumed in the United
Kingdom came from South America. Owing to the disorganisation of
the exchanges the meat companies early in August, 1914, could not buy
cattle or even pay wages in South America; the cost of freights also
rose. The Board of Trade intervened both to secure lower freight

[1] Runciman came to the Board of Trade on John Burns' resignation immediately before the outbreak of war. Burns' negative policy at the Board of Trade
was possibly one of the reasons why the problem of maintaining food supplies
in war had received so little consideration.

charges and to make contracts with the South American producers. At first the Board acted as mediators between the War Office – who came forward as very large purchasers – and the meat companies; they soon found it necessary to act as principals, though, in order to remove the fears of the Argentine Government that their neutrality might be compromised by negotiations between Argentinian producers and a British Government department, the nominal purchaser of the meat was the Orient shipping line. The buying of meat was soon extended to supplies from Australia and New Zealand. Moreover the French Government, which had been much impressed by the fighting qualities of the British Expeditionary Force, and by the size of their meat rations, increased the rations in the French army. For a time the French made their own contracts, and thus forced up the price of meat and the cost of freights. The Board of Trade persuaded them to get their supplies through the British purchasing organisation. This plan was later extended to the Italians. The British Government also began in November, 1914, to buy cereals in order to build up a reserve. They made their purchases secretly through a single private firm. The facts became known in the spring of 1915, but the operation was repeated in the autumn, and in November, 1916, the co-operation of other Allied Governments was secured in a 'Wheat Executive Agreement'.

With these important exceptions the policy of *laissez-faire* was continued, and indeed justified itself as far as present supplies were concerned. Private enterprise provided the food. The British harvest in 1914 was excellent; the harvest of the 'cereal year' 1915–16 was good in North and South America, and reached the British Isles. The British acreage under corn had increased in twelve months by 251,000 acres; 76,000 acres had been ploughed up from grass. The wheat crop in 1915 was nearly a third greater than the average for the years 1904–13, and there was an increase of more than 14 per cent in potatoes. Prices in June, 1915, were only 32 per cent above pre-war levels. The food question was not much discussed, and, apparently, caused little official anxiety.

The change of policy, and the public demand for a change, came slowly. Lord Selborne, President of the Board of Agriculture in the Coalition Government of May, 1915, was alarmed at the success of the German submarines, and at the consequences to British food supplies if the war lasted into 1917 or longer. He appointed a committee, with Milner as chairman, to consider what should be done to maintain, and, if possible, increase domestic food production on the assumption that the war might be prolonged beyond the harvest of 1916.[1] Milner's committee reported in July, 1915, that at least a million acres in England and Wales should be turned back to arable in 1916, and more in later years, and that farmers should be guaranteed prices for corn over the next four years. The Scottish committee, on the other hand, thought that such a guarantee would be wasteful since it would lead to the ploughing of unsuitable land.

Once more – on August 15, 1915 – the Cabinet decided against a guarantee. They regarded the submarine danger as 'under control' (such was the Admiralty view at this time). The increase in arable during the past year had been satisfactory. Another increase on a larger scale would need a considerable diversion of labour; buildings, implements, horses or tractors, and in many cases roads and stronger bridges would have to be provided. The general demand for labour set a limit to the amount available for agriculture, and the menacing situation on the Russian front suggested that there would be heavier calls on British man-power for the army.

The submarine danger was not 'under control', but the public demand for action over food supplies came less from forebodings of a serious shortage later in the war than from irritation at the rise of retail prices. In June, 1916, prices were 59 per cent above the level of July, 1914. The reasons for this rise were not generally understood. Public opinion was inclined to disregard the hard facts of reduced supplies, increased demand, and currency inflation, and to attribute rising prices to 'rings', 'profiteering', and speculation. The Government instructed Runciman to set up a departmental committee on prices. The committee issued its first report in September, 1916. The report was largely negative; it gave the reasons for the increase in prices and pointed out that reduction was unlikely. The committee found little evidence of 'profiteering', and noted that, with the general rise in wages, there was a larger demand for food.

Before and after the publication of the report Winston Churchill had asked in Parliament that the question of food prices should be put on a 'war basis'. Runciman, however, in a speech on the committee's report, had opposed proposals for a Ministry of Food and a Food Controller. He said that 'the thing . . . we ought to avoid in this country is . . . to put ourselves in the position of a blockaded people. Bread tickets, meat coupons, all these artificial arrangements are harmful, and

[1] Similar committees were appointed for Scotland and Ireland.

they are harmful to those who have least with which to buy . . . We want to avoid any rationing of our people in food.'

It was, however, already clear that owing to bad weather the British harvest of 1916 would be below the average, and the North American crops generally less than those of the previous year. In spite of Runciman's declaration the Government had taken action in regard to wheat. On October 10, they set up a Royal Commission on Wheat Supplies with executive authority. This step meant the disappearance of large-scale private trading in wheat; there could be no half-measure. As Runciman himself put it, 'It was inevitable that we should go the whole distance. . . . The merchant cannot go on with the great block of Government action hanging over his head.'

The purpose of this measure was the control of prices; it was also part of the general plan to secure co-ordination of purchasing with the other main Allies. Nevertheless, although he still refused to draw the obvious conclusions from the figures, Runciman startled the House of Commons on October 17 by disclosing the shipping losses through submarine action as 2,000,000 tons. Within a month the seriousness of the shipping position and, for that matter, of the military situation generally, had brought a change in Runciman's attitude. He acknowledged this change in a speech to the House of Commons on November 15. He said that 'the strain which we shall all have to bear next year will fall primarily on food supplies'.[1] He felt compelled, therefore, to give up 'the voluntary principle'. He proposed an extension of the Defence of the Realm Regulations to include food control – the regulation of prices, the reservation of particular articles for human consumption, the prevention of waste and 'harmful speculation', the regulation of flour milling[2] in order to allow the introduction of 'war bread'. Runciman explained that the Government intended to appoint a Food Controller of high standing to exercise the new powers and to co-ordinate the work of the different departments concerned with food.

The House welcomed this speech. The main criticism was that the proposals should have been more drastic and that they should have come much earlier. Churchill put the case against the Government's delays in very strong terms:

I believe that before the end of this war, unless it comes to an

[1] It was also evident by this time that, owing to bad weather, the potato yield would be much below normal.

[2] i.e. a reduction in the amount of 'offals' (much of which could be used, as in brown bread, for human consumption) left over in flour milling.

unexpected end, all shipping will certainly be taken over by the Government and regulated in one form or another, no doubt through its existing owners. I believe that all important employments will be regulated by the State for the purposes of the war. I believe that ration tickets for everything that matters will be served out to every one of us. . . . that prices will have to be fixed. . . . that we shall come to a national organisation of agriculture. . . . All this will come . . . and more than we can think of now will be done by the desperate resolution of the British nation. . . . But why not do them now while there is time? No one is stopping the Government except themselves.

It is remarkable that, after their own *volte-face*, and after the indication that the House of Commons and public opinion wanted immediate and strong action, the Government allowed three weeks to go by without announcing the appointment of a Food Controller. The Board of Trade indeed became more active, particularly in regard to the milling of flour. The Wheat Commission had already been given authority to deal with other grains as well as with wheat. The Sugar Commission had been compelled to reduce supplies, and a committee was considering the problem of distribution. Milner, to whom the appointment of Food Controller was offered, appears to have refused it because he was already convinced that a change of government was necessary; the failure of the Prime Minister to follow up words by deeds in meeting the food situation was among the counts which decided many people to support Lloyd George against Asquith. The new Government made their appointment at once. Four days after Lloyd George became Prime Minister Lord Devonport's name appeared among the list of new Ministers in the office of Food Controller. At the same time R. E. Prothero became President of the Board of Agriculture, with a mandate to increase the production of food, and especially of wheat.

The two men whom Lloyd George had put in control of the production, supply, and distribution of food were very different in type and training. Lord Devonport (H. E. Kearley, 1856–1934) had left school at the age of fifteen, and after working in a firm of tea and coffee merchants had built up a large grocery business;[1] he had sat in Parliament as Liberal member for Devonport from 1892 to 1910, and was

[1] The International Stores.

Parliamentary Under-Secretary to the Board of Trade in 1908. In the following year he had been appointed the first Chairman of the Port of London Authority. R. E. Prothero (later Lord Ernle, 1851–1937) was the son of a clergyman; he had given up practice at the bar owing to eye trouble. After complete recovery he turned to literature, and was from 1893 to 1899 editor of the *Quarterly Review*. In 1898 he became agent-in-chief for the town and country estates of the Duke of Bedford. He had entered Parliament as a member for Oxford University at a by-election in June, 1914, and had been a member of the Milner committee in 1915.[1]

Prothero was faced with great difficulties. Large numbers of agricultural workers had been and continued to be taken for the army or had gone into munitions factories; more than a third of the skilled labour force had been lost in this way. Machines and vehicles were unrepaired and horses unshod owing to the lack of blacksmiths and wheelwrights. Makers of agricultural machinery and implements were working on munitions; fertilisers were scarce, and hitherto had no priority of transport. The amount of winter-sown wheat had fallen and a general decline in the cultivation of arable seemed likely.

Prothero started too late to get very large results in 1917, but he obtained an additional 3 million tons of wheat, barley, oats, and potatoes, partly by the ploughing of nearly 200,000 acres of grassland, partly by a 50 per cent reduction of the area under hops. Prothero also encouraged the cultivation of allotments. He summed up his programme for 1918 in the slogan 'back to 1870'; in other words, he planned to bring 3 million more acres in the United Kingdom under tillage. He was not thinking only of war measures, but of the re-establishment of British agriculture in the position which it held before the long depression of the nineteenth century. He set up a Food Production Department[2] which worked locally in England and Wales[3] through seventeen and, later, twenty Agricultural Executive Committees, small in membership, with extensive powers. Owing to the shortage of labour the programme of 3 million acres had to be cut down to 2·6 million. The risks taken by the farmers in turning over so much

---

[1] See above, p. 500.

[2] The Food Production Department of the Ministry was given separate status in February, 1917, with Sir Arthur Lee (later Lord Lee of Fareham) as Director-general. Lee resigned in July, 1918, but by this time the main work of the Department was done.

[3] For administrative reasons the procedure was different in Scotland and Ireland.

land to arable were obviated by a five-year guarantee of prices; at the same time the labourers – for whom new tillage meant increased hours of work – were guaranteed a minimum wage to be fixed by wages boards. The difficulty of finding labour was also lessened by the employment of women – a Women's Land Army was started in 1917, and was 13,000 strong in 1918 – and by the use of prisoners of war. It is typical of the English countryside that, whereas the prisoners were made welcome, and were soon on a friendly footing with their employers, an attempt to use 'conscientious objectors' on agricultural work failed because very few farmers were willing to receive them.

Although the Department was promised help by the War Office, only 26,000 of the 43,000 men who were to have been made available at the end of August, 1917, were provided. 21,500 of them were to have been skilled ploughmen – or at least accustomed to the use of horses. In fact only 2500 could plough, and the Department had to set up ploughing schools for men who could be trusted with horses. The supply of horses was not easily arranged, yet the shortage turned out to be in harness rather than in animals. The Department hoped for nearly 5500 tractors before the end of the year; in November the number available was only 1500.[1] The tractors were new to most farmers and indeed to most members of the Agricultural Committees; at first tractor units had to be managed directly by the Department. Even at the end of 1918 it was not always easy to find firms – generally motor engineers – who could repair them. As with all new schemes, the Department and its committees had to consider minor as well as major shortages which might have hampered their plans; bindertwine for harvesting, as well as supplies of seed.

The results were more satisfactory than the critics of the 'ploughing up' scheme had expected. Nearly 3 million more acres than in 1916 (1·7 million in England and Wales) were under tillage in 1918; in spite of bad weather about a million tons of wheat and not far short of 1·5 million tons of potatoes above the 1904–13 average were gathered.[2] The milk supply was not much affected by the decrease in inferior or average grass lands, since one of the aims of the 'ploughing up policy' was to get more winter fodder for cows and other livestock. There may have been a loss in the supply of meat; the loss in any case was not more than about 60,000 tons, and as a set-off to it, the 1918

[1] 500 were in hand earlier in the year; less than one-fifth of the additional number asked for was received.

[2] In addition 330,000 more acres than in 1908–13 were under potatoes.

harvest provided an equivalent in stocks of food and fodder of some 4 million tons of shipping space.[1]

While the Food Production Department was at work on increasing the supply of home-produced cereals, the Food Controller had an even more complicated task in securing that a diminishing supply of food-stuffs was adequately distributed at a fair price. This work was more difficult in the sense that it was novel. The Agricultural Committees were engaged on a change-over which, to a large extent, might have been carried out in peace-time. They were asking the co-operation of farmers in growing more food and in ploughing up land most of which had once been ploughed; they were not 'taking over' the agricultural industry or establishing State farms. Devonport, however, had no precedents to guide him in the control or rationing of food. Prothero could feel hopeful that his war-time measures would bring a permanent improvement in British agriculture and the status of farmers and labourers. Devonport could have no such hopes about his work. He was doing something which he and almost everyone in the country regarded as economically unsound and justified only by extreme necessity.

Devonport resigned owing to ill-health at the end of May, 1917. The best part of his work was in his steady support of the proposals of the Wheat Commission, and in the preparation of a scheme which, although directed primarily towards the rationing of sugar, could be applied to other commodities. This plan was based on the establishment of Food Control Committees by each of the 2000 local authorities of Great Britain, and the division of the country into a dozen or more areas under divisional food controllers. In dealing with the public, however, Devonport was less successful. His colleagues in the Government made his work harder because they still hesitated to introduce compulsory rationing in spite of the fact that they had promised a more rigorous prosecution of the war. Voluntary rationing proved as unsatisfactory at this stage as voluntary enlistment. Devonport's own measures were not always well-considered. His plans for distribution took insufficient account of the shift in population, and therefore did not prevent serious local shortages. He asked for the voluntary rationing

[1] A programme for the harvest of 1919, aiming at a further increase, was drawn up in the early spring of 1918. At first the military demand for more man-power – 30,000 men from agriculture – made it impracticable; with the sudden change in the military situation later in the year the programme was withdrawn.

of bread, meat, and sugar – 4 lb. of bread, $2\frac{1}{2}$ lb. of meat, $\frac{3}{4}$ lb. of sugar per head per week – without reckoning that the working class in general consumed less than $2\frac{1}{2}$ lb. of meat – owing to its cost – and ate much more than 4 lb. of bread.

Lord Rhondda (against the advice of his doctors) took over the post of Food Controller after Devonport's resignation. Rhondda (David Alfred Thomas, 1856–1918), one of the seventeen children of a prosperous grocer in South Wales who had made money by colliery speculation, entered Parliament as a Liberal in 1888; although he was in the Commons until 1910 he was never noticed by the Liberals. Lloyd George recognised his ability in 1915, sent him to the United States cn munitions business, and gave him a peerage in 1916.

Rhondda had the advantage of learning from Devonport's mistakes and profiting by the organisation which he was building up. He was an abler man, of wider judgment, and much readier to work through carefully chosen subordinates. Even so the strain of the office was too much for him; he died of overwork in July, 1918. Before his death he had devised and set into operation a vast system of rationing which, as far as any such arrangement could be popular, satisfied the public because it was based on the principle of fair shares for all, and because it performed what it promised. The first step in planning was to bring under one department the scattered agencies dealing with food. Rhondda found the Ministry of Munitions in control of oils and fats, including the materials necessary for the manufacture of margarine. The Board of Trade managed the imports of meat and cheese and was beginning to take over the purchase of frozen fish. The Board also had arrangements with the Home and Foreign Produce Exchange to set maximum prices for provisions,[1] and with a committee of traders to deal with tea. The Admiralty, War Office, and Army and Navy Canteen Board were making very large purchases of foodstuffs without reference to any other department. The Board of Trade and the War Office shared the control of oats; the Board of Agriculture was responsible for food preservation, and most of Lord Devonport's food economy campaign had been carried out by the War Savings Committees. The Ministry of Food, with the collaboration of the Wheat and Sugar Commissions, gradually took over these various duties until it controlled almost everything except the supply of frozen meat. In 1921, when the Ministry was dissolved, its trading turn-over had amounted to £1,200,000,000.[2]

[1] These maximum prices had, in fact, no legal validity.
[2] The Ministry made a profit of about ·5 per cent on its total transactions.

Rhondda, like Devonport and Runciman, regarded state control as a misfortune which had to be endured in war-time. Runciman would have agreed with his public comment that 'no student of economic law would lightly interfere with the operation of supply and demand at any time. . . . I hold strongly that the less government interferes in business in ordinary times, the better.' On the other hand, the bridge had been crossed. Rhondda was in office to undertake this interference. He realised that it would have to be drastic and far-reaching. 'If the Food Controller is to set aside economic law and arbitrarily fix prices, it can only be in those articles over the supply of which he can secure complete control and obtain a virtual monopoly, and even under these conditions he must not overlook the effect his action may have in discouraging supply and increasing consumption.' In other words, if the work of the Food Ministry were to be done effectively, it must reach out into the whole of the organisation and distribution of supplies. As Runciman had said earlier about the purchase of wheat, there was no half-way point.

On the other hand, if it were essential to treat the economy of the country on the analogy of employing dangerous drugs to tide a patient over a critical but temporary illness, the mischief could be lessened by making the process as un-bureaucratic as possible – that is to say, by decentralising a great deal of the work, and using local knowledge and voluntary help. Rhondda put into effect Devonport's scheme for local food committees. Their membership was, roughly, limited to ten or twelve, and included at least one woman and one representative of labour. The committees were appointed by the local authorities, but were independent of them. The central authority was represented by fifteen divisional food controllers; here also men of local standing and administrative experience were chosen. Finally, the central authority was organised, with a staff reaching 4350 in June, 1918, under divisional controllers. No one of the heads of divisions had had previous experience in the wholesale buying of food; a civil servant from the Board of Education was in charge of fish, fresh fruit, and vegetables, while bacon, tea, and dried fruit were controlled by a former chief of criminal investigation in the Government of India. In addition, the Wheat Commission, which was now buying also for the Allies, had its own large overseas organisation, with agencies in all the export markets; two members of the Commission went to North America, one to South America, and another to Australia. Rhondda did not neglect technical advice; each division had its experts, and the Ministry kept in touch with an advisory committee of the Royal Society. Even more important, from the public point of view, was the establishment of a Consumers Council and the publication in September, 1917, of a *National Food Journal*.[1]

Rhondda himself took the greatest care to keep in touch with 'consumers' opinion'. He was readily accessible, sometimes, in the opinion of his staff, too readily accessible to journalists. The Ministry dealt skilfully with a mass of parliamentary questions, and went out of its way to invite meetings and conferences for the discussion and criticism of its policy. The *National Food Journal* informed the public of the orders issued by the Ministry, and of the reasons for them. The first number expressed the facts, which the Government had taken so long to recognise, that

> there can be no question of the willingness of the public to endure petty discomforts, and even to suffer actual pecuniary loss, once it is understood that the discomfort and loss involved are really necessary. People must first of all be convinced that the Department is honestly tackling, with greater knowledge than is possessed by themselves or the newspapers, the problems which the war has brought in its train.

In one important respect Rhondda's position was better than he knew. The most serious threat to imported supplies had come before July, 1917, and, although no one could foresee the course of shipping losses, and, although the effect of these losses was felt increasingly as the months went by, the peak of danger at this time had been passed.[2] In the spring of 1917 the position with regard to wheat and sugar had been extremely serious. The North American harvest had been short, and that of the Argentine a failure. The wheat crop in Great Britain, and in France and Italy, had also been below the average. The Australian harvest was good, but there were not enough ships to bring it to Europe. The shipping losses were more than three times higher than

[1] The Council was not constituted until the beginning of 1918; its original members were six persons nominated by the Parliamentary Committee of the Co-operative Congress, and three each by the Parliamentary Committee of the TUC, the 'War Emergency Workers National Council' and the National Organisation of Industrial Women Workers. The Chairman was J. R. Clynes, a Labour MP and Parliamentary Secretary to the Minister of Food. Rhondda later nominated four other members to represent the 'unorganised consumers', and those not of the working class.

[2] See above, Chapter 23.

the average for the last two years of the war. 80,000 tons of sugar – nearly one-sixth of all the cargoes at sea – were lost between February 4 and June 23. On one day in April the stocks of sugar in the United Kingdom represented only four days' consumption, and about the same time, the stocks of wheat and flour were sufficient only for nine weeks.

The Ministry had troubles of a different kind over many of the home-grown 'staples'. Potatoes, for example, could not easily be imported in case of shortage, or disposed of in the case of a glut or stored for very long. Hence the Ministry had to deal with an almost intractable problem in deciding on variations of price. In 1917 they guaranteed too high a price, and the Exchequer had to pay over a million pounds in fulfilling guarantees to producers. In 1918 the Ministry took over the whole crop, and promised also to bear the cost of any 'abnormal' wastage, with the result that the farmers had little interest in seeing that wastage was avoided. Price-fixing indeed was a matter of endless ramifications as well as of hazards. It was, for example, useless to control the price of food in one form if the same food were not controlled in other forms; thus the control of milk made it necessary also to control cheese and butter, since otherwise milk would have gone into cheese- and butter-making. Similarly control at any one stage between producer and consumer implied control at all stages; otherwise the advantages would be secured by middlemen at some link in the chain. In the most important of all foodstuffs – bread – the Government went beyond the control of prices and introduced a subsidy. This subsidy was recommended in June, 1917, by a Commission on Industrial Unrest. The decision to subsidise bread was announced in general terms at the end of June. The price of a 4 lb. loaf, which had risen since 1914 from $5\frac{1}{2}d$. to $1s$. was to be reduced to $9d$. The cost of the subsidy from September, 1917, to December, 1920, was £162,500,000.[1]

Lord Beveridge has described the bread subsidy as 'the price of content', but, as the Commission on Industrial Unrest had pointed out, from the point of view of the public the control of prices was a benefit only if it were accompanied by an efficient system of distribution in the case of food which was in short supply. Here also the Ministry was able to make use of earlier experience. The Sugar Commission had begun by supplying wholesalers, who in turn supplied retailers, with a percentage of the supplies which each had taken in 1915. This principle was inconvenient for a number of reasons. It did not allow for shifts in

[1] The subsidy was carried into effect through the control of flour mills.

population or changes in shopping habits, and therefore did not prevent local shortages. It secured neither the retailer nor the customer. The retailer had no accurate list of customers or of the quantities which each of them bought; he could not know how many customers were buying in more than one shop. The customer, on the other hand, had no assurance that he would actually get his quota of supplies. In any case a proportionate reduction in the consumption of essential foods was not fair in itself, since the poorer customers had less margin from which to reduce their consumption.

The only sure and equitable solution was rationing, that is to say, a system in which money alone would not suffice to buy food. The Cabinet, however, still hesitated to introduce ration tickets.[1] The first stage was to assist distribution by requiring customers to register with a retailer. A decision to apply this system was adopted for sugar in June, 1917. The method at first proposed was one of registration by households, but before the end of the year the plan was changed to individual rationing (from January 1, 1918) and a more general scheme of rationing was hurried on owing to the new trouble of 'queueing'. Food queues, especially for margarine, butter, bacon, and tea spread from London to all the larger towns in November, and grew snow-ball-wise in December.[2] The need for haste settled the mode of rationing. Towards the end of November, plans had been drawn up, on expert advice, for grading the population into five different categories for rationing purposes. There was considerable discussion whether the method to adopted should be on a local or a central basis. Local rationing came to be accepted because a centrally based scheme would have taken too long to prepare. Some local Food Committees indeed had already taken the initiative in their own areas, and had begun to ration sugar, butter, margarine, and tea. Before the end of December the Food Committees generally were asked to draw up plans for local distribution which would include, if necessary, rationing as well as registration.

The local schemes were put into effect rapidly, and, as might have

[1] One reason for hesitation was a desire not to encourage the Germans by an admission that the submarine warfare had driven Great Britain into rationing. The Germans, on the other hand, believed that there were not enough British officials to make possible the introduction of rationing. See above, p. 337 n. 1.

[2] On December 17 *The Times* stated that during the past week it had been difficult in London to buy sugar, tea, butter, margarine, lard, dripping, milk (fresh or condensed), bacon, pork, rice, currants, raisins, spirits, and Australian wines.

been expected, led to co-operation between adjoining areas. The most important of these areas included London and the Home Counties. During the month of January and the early part of February the representatives of the twenty-eight Food Committees in the London area drew up plans for rationing meat, butter, and margarine. These plans were accepted by the neighbouring Home Counties, and the scheme was put into operation on February 28, 1918. No one could foretell how it would work. In fact, it worked remarkably well. The food queues disappeared at once, and their disappearance shewed that the problem at this stage was not one of increasing supplies – the supplies for London and the Home Counties were not increased – but of restoring public confidence by an equitable system of distribution. As soon as consumers realised that their ration coupons would be honoured, they had no reason to stand in queues. Between the end of February and mid-July the local schemes were generalised into a uniform national system devised and controlled centrally but administered under the local Food Committees.[1] The national scheme provided for supplementary rations of bacon to boys between thirteen and eighteen and also to certain categories of agricultural and industrial workers; this discrimination between classes of workers was strongly opposed by the Parliamentary Committee of the Trade Union Congress – though some unions supported it – as well as by the Consumers Council. The supplementary rations were introduced, but were soon unnecessary owing to the increased supplies of bacon.

Rationing, and food control generally, worked better in Great Britain than in most countries where it was introduced. There was less strain, since bread was not rationed. The distribution of supplies was easier since so much was imported, and could be controlled on arrival at the ports or through 'bulk' purchases in the countries of origin. The success of the British plan was also due largely to its excellent balance between centralised and decentralised administration. The local committees, and the local officials, knew the needs of the neighbourhood, and in most cases secured popular confidence. They also had popular support behind them in imposing penalties for breaches of the food regulations. In comparison with Germany, where there

---

[1] The meat ration was about 1 lb. a week per head, the sugar ration about ½ lb. Bacon and ham were also rationed. Tea was not rationed nationally, but a national distribution scheme in July, 1918, in fact laid down a ration of 2 oz. weekly. Jam was rationed nationally only between November, 1918, and April, 1919. Cheese was not rationed on a national basis. Bread was never rationed.

were more than ten times as many convictions, the British figures were light, but they amounted to over 45,000 in the two years 1918 and 1919.[1] Such a total shews that the majority of citizens were law-abiding, and also that even at the critical point in the war (the prosecutions fell after 1918) there was a minority which refused to respond to the general will. It may be added that the law-abiding majority made very considerable efforts at self-help. Allotments – obtained through the use of land in public parks as well as the turning over of private gardens to food production – added some 800,000 tons of food, mainly in fresh vegetables, to British supplies in 1918 and saved a great deal in railway transport. Most of these plots were cultivated by the unpaid labour, in 'leisure' hours, of middle- and working-class householders and their families.

[1] In Ireland there were nearly 23,000 prosecutions for a population one-eighth of that of Great Britain. The percentage of convictions was about the same, but the punishments were ludicrously small; in many cases fines of under 1s. were imposed.

CHAPTER 35

Paying for the war

The diversion to war purposes of the productive labour and resources of a modern industrial society, the employment in the armed forces of a large proportion of able-bodied men, the wastage and destruction of immense quantities of capital goods – particularly, for Great Britain, ships – involved a cost beyond the most extravagant expenditure of earlier wars. How was this expenditure met?[1] The precedents of past wars were of little use in planning the organisation of the national resources between 1914 and 1918. The war-time financial policy of the younger Pitt, however, had set an example which was still relevant. After some floundering for a few years the nation had paid for nearly half of its war expenditure between 1799 and 1815 out of taxation. Pitt, and Gladstone after him, regarded the income tax as a 'national taxation reserve' for a time of war. Lloyd George's last peace-time budget, which increased the higher ranges of income tax,[2] was criticised by the Opposition as undermining this taxation reserve. Some critics quoted Asquith's statement as Chancellor of the Exchequer in 1906 that income tax at a uniform rate of a shilling in the £ in time of peace could not be justified, and would tend 'to destroy or at any rate to contract a readily available source on which the State can draw in a sudden or unforeseen emergency'.

It is therefore a little surprising that so effective an instrument was not used more firmly until some time after the outbreak of war. There was no really heavy increase in taxation until the third war budget of September, 1915. One reason for this delay was a general feeling that the war would not last long. In any case governmental action was concerned at first with meeting the risks of a breakdown in the

[1] Sir J. Stamp (later Lord Stamp), *Taxation during the war*, 1932 (Economic and Social History of the World War) remains the best book on the subject.

[2] The rate on earned incomes above £1500 was 9½d. in the £, and rose by stages until it reached 1s. 4d. in the £2500–£3000 range. Tax on unearned income was raised from 1s. 2d. to 1s. 4d. Supertax began at 5d. in the £ after £3000. The purchasing power of the £ in 1914 was about six times greater than in 1967.

mechanism of credit. Efficient measures were improvised,[1] with remarkable skill, but they did not, and could not include a drastic increase in taxation, still less anything like an 'excess profits' duty, when the immediate problem seemed to be a severe fall in the amount of domestic and foreign trade.

Parliament thus accepted, on August 6, 1914, a vote of credit of £100,000,000 without discussing the sources from which the money would be drawn. A second credit of £225,000,000 was voted on November 29. Meanwhile Lloyd George had introduced the first of the war budgets. The cost of the war was now between £900,000 and £1,000,000 a day. The government proposed to double the income tax for the last third of the financial year, and to increase the taxes on tea and beer. They intended to raise a loan of £350 millions at 95 to meet an expected deficit of £321 millions at the end of the financial year.

The second war budget was introduced at the normal time of year and passed in July, 1915. From the point of view of taxation it was still somewhat tentative, and covered only six months. Lloyd George had made two estimates of expenditure during the year – the first of them assumed that the war would last for another six months, the second that it would last for another year. Lloyd George also considered the possibility that the war might go on much longer. He thought that, until the prospects were clearer, he ought not to lay down a policy for more than six months. The cost of the war was now a little over £2 millions a day, and was rising. The National Debt had already been increased by £458 millions to a total of £1165 millions. Lloyd George raised the duties on alcoholic drinks – mainly in an attempt to cut down consumption; he did not propose any new taxes, or a further increase in income tax or supertax. When Snowden wanted more taxes on the rich, Lloyd George answered that the total of incomes over £3000 a year reached only £220 millions, and that if he took three-quarters of this sum he would not thereby be 'financing the war'.

There was already much criticism of the profits being made out of the war by many industrialists, and not merely by those engaged in the manufacture of munitions. One firm whose profits in 1913 had been £90,000 had a profit of £367,000 in 1914.[2] Lloyd George promised

---

[1] See above, pp. 456–8.
[2] This case was much quoted. The profit had been made by buying American wheat before a rise in prices. If the British firm had not made the purchase, the profit would have gone to the Chicago wheat dealers.

to consider taxing the profits of armament firms; McKenna, who
succeeded him as Chancellor of the Exchequer, widened the consideration to include all war profits, but before the next budget Lloyd George
himself – now Minister of Munitions – had limited the profits of munitions firms to an additional 20 per cent on pre-war earnings.

When McKenna introduced the third war budget in September,
1915, there was a more general belief that the war would last a long
time. It was therefore essential to raise more money by taxation.
Income tax was increased by 40 per cent to 3s. 6d. for the last half of
the year, and the exemption limit reduced from £160 to £130. This
latter measure brought a large number of wage-earners into the class
of income tax-payers. Supertax on incomes above £8000 was raised,
and postal charges and indirect taxes increased. McKenna also broke
the long tradition of free trade by imposing a number of protective
duties on clocks, watches, films, and other articles. The purpose of the
duties was to restrict consumption rather than to bring in revenue,
but they mark a change not only in policy but in the world position
of Great Britain as a trading nation. McKenna, as he had forecast, also
introduced an excess profits duty[1] from which, in a full year, he expected about £30 millions. For the half year all the new taxes were
not expected to produce more than about £33 millions, or a little over
a fortnight's cost of the war. On the other hand McKenna was working on a principle, which his successors followed, that the new taxation
should be sufficient to cover the interest on the new debt incurred
during the war.

At the time of the introduction of the fourth war budget in April,
1916, the war had cost nearly £1560 millions; £1222 millions had
been borrowed, and the National Debt was now £2140 millions.
McKenna estimated the gross cost of the war for the next twelve
months at £1825 millions or £5 millions a day. A part of this sum
was made up of advances to the Dominions and the Allies; the actual
war expenditure of Great Britain was £3,750,000 a day. The figure
seemed likely to remain fairly constant, since, although prices were
rising, the organisation of war production was now more or less complete. The revenue was estimated at £502 millions, of which about
£86 millions would come from excess profits duty. The rate of duty
was raised from 50 to 60 per cent, and income tax was also increased.

---

[1] The term 'excess profits tax' seems to have been used first in July, 1915, by
Hartley Withers, in a memorandum written by him as Financial Adviser to the
Treasury.

A new tax on tickets for entertainments was introduced. The amount brought in by this tax, though not negligible, did not come to a great deal – £5,000,000 – but, as with the excess profits duty, there was a certain moral connotation to it. The excess profits duty was working adequately, in spite of a certain amount of evasion, and, on the other side, not a little hardship. It was not easy to define 'excess profits' in many thousands of marginal cases. The inclusion of personal profits was too difficult, and indeed income tax and supertax were already dealing with individual gains, but even in the case of firms, there were wide differences in the source of high profits. They might come directly from the demand, e.g. for armaments, clothing, timber. They could come from indirect causes such as the movement of population to certain districts; breweries, for example, gained when their area of trade suddenly included large military camps or new factories. Profits could also arise in trades unconnected with war production which had previously had to meet severe competition from Germany or other belligerent countries; toys, dolls, pianos were cases in point. The most troublesome decisions about high profits concerned firms which had spent large sums before the war in installing new plant or slowly building up a business from which an adequate return had not been expected for several years. The revenue authorities tried to cover hard cases without at the same time providing ways of escape for tax-evaders. They allowed a business to take the average profit of the best out of three pre-war years, or to choose as a standard 6 per cent interest on their capital.[1] No tax, especially in war conditions, can be wholly 'fair' and on the whole, the excess profits duty was the least unjust method of taking differential gains due to circumstances outside the normal expectations of business.

Bonar Law had succeeded McKenna as Chancellor before the fifth war budget of May, 1917. He was less of a financial expert than McKenna, but had practical experience of business and was quick to adapt himself to a situation. He tended, however, to judge proposals too readily by his ability to get them through the House of Commons. He raised the excess profits duty to 80 per cent, with retrospective effect from January 1, 1917. He did not make any important new tax

[1] Rates of profit had always varied in different industries. In the mining industry, where the extraction of minerals diminished the total capital value of the profit-producing asset, a higher rate was justifiable than in engineering, where, except for a higher rate of wear and tear and replacement of machinery, high profits were not necessarily relevant to, and did not diminish the capital value of an undertaking.

proposals.[1] Taxation was now so heavy that its effect could hardly be otherwise than to diminish the amount of capital available at the end of the war. The country was paying 26 per cent of its war costs out of revenue. Bonar Law maintained the principle, laid down by McKenna, of providing in taxation for the interest on all loans up to date.[2] The National Debt had now risen by £1714 millions to £3854 millions. On the other hand the entry of the United States into the war was likely to bring relief, especially in regard to the British shortage of dollars.[3]

The last war budget – brought forward in the critical month of April, 1918 – was on similar lines. Full allowance was made, as before, in the calculation of revenue to ensure that interest on the increased debt charges would be covered, and that no new taxes for this purpose would be required after the war. The total revenue for the coming year was estimated at £840 millions; the balance was to be met by borrowing £2130 millions. Just under £2000 millions had been borrowed in the financial year 1917-18, so that the total gross debt at the end of the financial year 1918-19 would be about £7980 millions; in April, 1918, the war seemed likely to go on at least until the summer of 1919. Bonar Law made no allowance in his calculations for the return of the money lent to Russia, but thought it reasonable to deduct one half – £1124 millions – of the advances made to the other Allies and the Dominions. With this deduction the net total of post-war British debt would be £6856 millions;[4] £380 millions would therefore

[1] One difficulty about imposing new taxes was that the Inland Revenue Department, which had already released 3000 men for the army, was so much overworked with existing business, including Excess Profits Duty, that it could not cope with anything new.

[2] Until the latter half of 1916, when the Government began to appeal to small savers by means of war savings certificates, etc., a great part of the money raised by loan came from the extension of bank credit due to Government borrowing from the Bank of England or selling bills.

[3] The difficulty of finding dollars to pay for purchases in the United States had led at the end of 1915 to an official appeal to owners of dollar securities to sell or lend them to the Treasury. In 1916 interest from such securities not offered to the Treasury was subjected to an additional tax. In January, 1917, the Government decided to requisition certain classes of securities, but large American loans after the entry of the United States into the war eased the dollar position. £332 millions out of £623 millions of requisitioned securities were later returned to their owners.

[4] About £500 millions could also be deducted for stores, land, buildings, ships, etc., of which the Departments concerned would wish to dispose after the war. Munitions costing £325 millions were valued in this estimate at £100 millions.

be necessary for the debt service. Bonar Law raised the standard rate of income tax to 6s., added 1s. to the maximum rate of supertax, and lowered from £3000 to £2500 the level at which it was imposed. He also hoped to bring in £5,300,000 by a better assessment of farmers' profits – always a difficult source to tax since only about one farmer in ten kept accounts. He increased the liquor, tobacco, and sugar taxes, and proposed a 'luxury' tax. This proposal was popular. The amount spent on 'luxuries' was a visible offence to others; the expenditure tended to be blatant, and also concentrated in certain areas; hence public opinion greatly exaggerated the total.[1] Such a tax was not impossible – the French had imposed one – but a 'luxury' was not easily defined, and the cost of collecting the tax and preventing evasion might well have been found too great. A Select Committee of the House of Commons was authorised to draw up a list of 'luxuries'. They had not finished their work when the Finance Bill passed into law. The project was not continued after the armistice.

The British nation paid by taxation a higher proportion (nearly 30 per cent) of their war costs than any other European belligerent. The amount of taxation per head in Great Britain rose from £3 11s. 4d. in the last year of peace to £22 at the end of the war.[2] None the less the burden of interest on war debt was likely to be heavy, and would increase if prices fell. Hence there were proposals for getting rid of the burden once for all by a capital levy. Snowden had suggested this plan early in the war but rather from a partisan point of view. 'Making the rich pay' was a good cry. By 1918, however, the argument for a levy had considerable support. This argument was put in the Budget debates of 1918 by Mr (later Lord) Arnold[3] in a speech which impressed Sir Josiah Stamp as a 'masterful performance'. Arnold thought that the payment of interest on the debt would mean, after the war, a permanent rise in income tax to 7s. 6d. He assumed the taxable capital of the country to be £24,000 millions. He proposed a levy in two stages, the first immediately after the war, the second two years later. The levy would begin above the £1000 level; it would rise to

---

[1] Opinion also tended to overlook the fact that existing taxation at a very high level was in itself a check on large-scale spending. Certain 'luxuries', such as drink and tobacco, were already highly taxed.

[2] Before 1914 57·5 per cent of the revenue was obtained by direct, and 42·5 by indirect taxation. At the end of the war the figures were, respectively, 72 and 28 per cent.

[3] Arnold had been a junior Minister before 1914. In 1922 he joined the Labour Party.

4½ per cent in all at £5000, and more steeply in higher income ranges. The total amount raised would be about £4000 millions. The levy would be met by handing over war stock, by credit facilities, or by cash payments. The strongest argument for the plan was that, on the whole, the owners of capital would be relieving themselves of the burden of income tax and supertax.

PART XIII

The Peace Settlement with Germany

CHAPTER 36

The Peace Conference: the Council of Ten: the Council of Four

The Conference of Paris was called – so the Allies announced – 'to lay down the conditions of peace, in the first place by peace preliminaries, and later by a definitive Treaty of Peace'. This formula was somewhat vague; it did not explain what form the 'preliminaries' would take, or whether, after they had been 'laid down', they were to be imposed without discussion on the enemy.[1] Before the armistice Lloyd George seems to have had in mind an Allied Conference which would agree upon the terms of peace and then present them to the enemy. He did not expect much discussion with the Germans. He told House on October 29 that the 'preliminary Conference' could be finished in three or four weeks, and that the 'peace Conference' need not last more than a week. Wilson seems at first to have expected German representation at an early stage, since in a telegram to House about the number of delegates from each country he said that he had in mind that 'Germany should also have five places'. Wilson, however, either at this time or a little later, agreed that the Germans should not be brought into the meetings until the terms had been drawn up, and that it would be dangerous to allow them in earlier because they would certainly try to take advantage of any disagreement among the Allies.

The exceptional character of the armistice negotiations made it less necessary to consider German representation. The Germans had already accepted the 'principles' of the Fourteen Points as the basis of a treaty of peace; they had also admitted, at least tacitly, the right of

[1] The vagueness of the term led to a certain confusion of ideas among the delegates themselves. The French term 'Préliminaires de Paix' would have been translated more accurately as 'Preliminaries to Peace'. As the British Foreign Office pointed out, 'a state of belligerency cannot be brought to an end more than once'. Nevertheless it would have been possible to draw up a treaty in sections and later to combine these sections, as at Vienna, in an 'Acte Général'. For a discussion of the question, see F. S. Marston, *The Peace Conference of 1919: Organisation and Procedure* (1944).

the Allies to interpret these principles; hence all that remained to be done, or so it seemed, was to draft a document on lines agreed in advance by all concerned. In these circumstances there also seemed no reason for any delay in assembling the Conference; every practical consideration was in favour of a rapid settlement after which the process of European recovery and reconstruction could begin.

The plenipotentiaries, however, did not meet in Paris until January 12, 1919. Wilson was unable to come to Paris before the middle of December. Lloyd George was then occupied with the British general election and the formation of a new Cabinet. The delay allowed more time for 'expert advisers' to prepare material (much of it was, in fact, submitted at too great length) and for the Governments of the States established on the ruins of Austria-Hungary to set up some kind of administration. The leading statesmen – Lloyd George, Wilson, Clemenceau, and Orlando – did not think it necessary to commit themselves in advance to any plan for the conduct of the Conference; neither the British nor the American experts had made recommendations about procedure and organisation. The French had drawn up at the end of November a somewhat elaborate form of procedure, including an order of debate, a list of subjects to be discussed, and the order in which these subjects should be arranged. Lloyd George and Wilson accepted a good deal of this French plan without binding themselves to a fixed order of discussion. The leaders agreed about keeping the control of business in their hands. One of the reasons why they had chosen Paris as their meeting place[1] was that the Supreme War Council already held its meetings there, and thus provided a nucleus for the organisation of the Conference. The Council would have to meet anyhow to discuss, for example, business connected with the renewal and execution of the armistice, and to act, for all practical purposes, as a high governing body for Europe in many questions, large and small, which needed immediate settlement. The first meeting between Wilson and the three European Heads of Governments on January 12, 1919, was in fact a meeting of the Council. The Council drew up rules for acceptance by the Conference, and ensured thereby that it kept control of matters to be put before the general sessions, and

[1] Lloyd George had been in favour of Geneva as a meeting-place. Wilson at first thought that Geneva (or Brussels, which had also been suggested) would give more opportunity for German or Bolshevist intrigue. The French wanted Paris; the choice of London would have caused suspicion of an Anglo-American attempt to dominate the Conference.

that nothing was submitted to these sessions until the Great Powers were in agreement about it. The Great Powers also secured representatives on all Committees and Commissions set up by the Conference. They distinguished between themselves as 'Powers with general interests' and the smaller Allies as 'Powers with special interests'; they described themselves not only in the discussions but in the Treaty as 'the Principal Allied and Associated Powers'.

In addition to President Wilson and the three Prime Ministers of Great Britain, France, and Italy, the meeting of January 12 included the Foreign Ministers of the Four Powers; two Japanese representatives were then invited to join them. This body, known as the 'Council of Ten' thus became the controlling authority of the Conference. Technically, when they were discussing the business of the Conference, and not sitting as the Supreme War Council, the members of the Council of Ten were 'holding conversations'; in fact they were taking all the important decisions. Only six meetings of the plenary Conference were held before the delivery of the terms to the Germans; at the second session, on January 25, Clemenceau, as President of the Conference, asserted the authority of the five Great Powers, in answer to an attempt by the smaller Powers to obtain representation, by pointing out that at the time of the armistice they had 12,000,000 men in the field. The full text of the treaty was not submitted to the smaller Powers until a meeting of the plenary conference on May 6. The treaty was thus 'dictated' to the smaller Allies hardly less than to the Germans, though these minor Allies had more opportunity to state a case. They chose to do so orally as well as in writing; the Great Powers found it expedient to give way to their wishes in this matter at the cost of much expenditure of time.[1]

There was something curiously haphazard about the abandonment of the plan for a preliminary peace. The plan was indeed not changed formally. The Conference remained a 'preliminary Peace Conference', and turned into a Congress when the Germans attended to receive the terms, and again when they signed the treaty, but Tardieu, in summarizing the treaty at the plenary meeting on May 6 – the day before the appearance of the Germans – spoke of the 'text of the Preliminaries

---

[1] One representative of a Syrian delegation (though he had not been in Syria for thirty-five years) made a speech to the Council of Ten (on February 13) lasting for two and a half hours. Long before the end of the speech Wilson left his seat, walked to the other side of the room, and looked out of the window.

of Peace' with Germany.[1] One reason for the change was the slow progress made by the Council of Ten. On January 30, during a discussion of the Roumanian territorial claims, Wilson came to the conclusion that much time was being wasted because the 'experts' did not bring agreed proposals to the Council, and the plenipotentiaries had therefore to listen to long discussions on matters of detail. Wilson suggested that the British, American, and other experts should meet before the meetings in order to settle any differences of view. On February 1 Lloyd George made a similar proposal. Five territorial commissions were appointed to clear the way for the decisions of the Council. The establishment of a Supreme Economic Council on February 9 to consider questions of finance, food, shipping, etc., also relieved the Council of much administrative business.[2] Nevertheless the advance towards the first stage in the proceedings of the Conference – agreement among the Allies about the main terms – was disappointingly slow, and public opinion, which had been led to expect quick results, was becoming restive.

Meanwhile the Council was getting anxious over the evident facts that the Germans were not carrying out the military terms of the armistice, with the consequence that, as the armistice came up for renewal, the French in particular wished to stiffen these terms, and, if necessary, to take steps to secure their enforcement. Neither Wilson nor Lloyd George wanted a renewal of the war, especially over what were, after all, comparatively minor breaches of faith by the Germans. On the other hand the American troops were already going home; there was unrest in the British and French armies over delays in demobilisation and, if the preliminaries of peace were not settled quickly, the Germans might well think it safe to refuse the Allied terms. Hence the Council appointed a special military and economic commission, under the presidency of Foch, to consider the whole matter. This commission reported on February 12 that, in order to 'obtain as rapidly as possible a final result, and to put a stop to the difficulties which are constantly raised by the Germans . . . naval and military terms of peace should be drawn up immediately by a

[1] At the meeting with the Germans, however, Clemenceau made no reference to 'preliminaries', but spoke of the 'Second Treaty of Versailles'. Similarly on June 28 the treaty then signed was described as 'the Treaty of Peace between the Allied and Associated Powers and Germany'. Nevertheless the minutes of the 'Plenary Sessions of the Preliminary Peace Conference' continued until May 31 – the last meeting dealt with the Austrian Treaty.

[2] The Council held its first meeting on February 17.

Commission appointed for the purpose' and should be 'imposed on the enemy'.

Balfour (in Lloyd George's absence) supported this recommendation. Clemenceau opposed it because he was afraid that if Allied demobilisation followed the German acceptance of the naval, military, and air terms, it would be much more difficult to deal with any resistance to the economic and political terms. Balfour pointed out that the purpose of the naval and military terms was to secure that Germany was disarmed and physically incapable of resistance. Wilson said that, according to the experts, these terms could be drafted in forty-eight hours; he was prepared to allow them to be decided in his absence in the United States.[1] The Council then authorised a Committee under the chairmanship of Foch to submit a draft of the naval, military, and air terms. Balfour and House wanted to do more; they hoped to complete all the articles of a preliminary peace, and to have them ready for presentation to Wilson on his return. Wilson agreed in general with this plan, though he told House that, while he was willing to allow the military and naval terms to be considered while he was away, he did not want any other matters, such as transfers of territory or 'questions of compensation' to be presented for discussion. This limitation did not mean that the political or economic clauses should not be prepared. Balfour in fact proposed on February 22 that the Commissions dealing with the non-military terms should send in their reports by March 8. House approved of this suggestion. For several reasons this plan broke down. Clemenceau was wounded by a young anarchist on February 19, but insisted on going back to his work within a few days. On the other hand, in spite of Foch's forecast, the military experts were unable to prepare their terms quickly; hence the French came back to the view (which Clemenceau had given up somewhat unwillingly) that all the main terms of the German treaty should be presented simultaneously. House and Lansing now agreed with the French view. At this point the Italians objected that concentration on the German treaty would postpone a settlement of the Austrian and other treaties, and thus cause great difficulties in Italy. As a compromise it was agreed that proposals for these treaties might be drawn up simultaneously with those for the German treaty, but on February 24 the Council had not altogether ruled out the possibility of a separate military treaty with Germany. On this same day House telegraphed to

[1] Wilson left Paris for the United States on February 14. He arrived back in France on March 14.

Wilson that the reports of the Commissions would be available on his return to Paris. They could then be submitted, after Wilson's approval,[1] to the 'Peace Conference' as a whole not later than in the first week of April. On March 1 House telegraphed that Lloyd George agreed with him that it might be possible to 'settle the preliminary peace terms with Germany by the 23rd and name a day for the regular Peace Congress in which the Central Powers are to participate'. House suggested April 2 'tentatively' as the date 'for the assembling of the Congress'. The military terms were not agreed by the special committee until March 3. The Supreme Council sent them back for redrafting on March 7, and considered them again on March 17, that is to say, three days after Wilson had landed at Brest.[2]

Wilson, however, seems to have thought that House had conceded too much.[3] On his return to Paris he told Baker to issue a statement that there would be no preliminary peace excluding the Covenant. It appears probable that, before leaving Paris, Wilson had not realised that a preliminary peace treaty containing the military and naval clauses would require the approval of the Senate. Anyhow Wilson found in the United States that there was likely to be more opposition to the Covenant than he had expected. He did not want to double his labours and risks by submitting two treaties to the Senate; he was even less willing to allow the opposition a chance of rejecting the Covenant while accepting the other clauses of a treaty. He could not state his difficulty openly, but at the Supreme Council on March 17 he explained that he had assumed that the 'preliminary Convention would only be temporary until the complete Treaty was prepared, and that it would have the character of a sort of exalted armistice, the terms being reincluded in the formal Treaty. If this preliminary Convention had to be submitted to the Senate for a general discussion there, he knew from the usual slow process of legislatures that it would be several months before it would be ratified.'

Balfour realised at once the implications of Wilson's statement. He pointed out that 'the policy accepted was that a Preliminary Treaty should be made, each clause of which should be a part of the Final Act, so that by the settlement of the Preliminary Peace a great part of the final Permanent Peace would actually have been covered. It now

---

[1] It is of interest that House used the words 'After you have approved them, they should be submitted to a Plenary Session.'

[2] The military terms were not finally settled until April 25.

[3] The beginnings of a breach between Wilson and House date from this time.

appeared that the American Constitution made that full programme impracticable.' Although Wilson would not commit himself – he said that he wanted to consult 'the constitutional lawyers' – the idea of a preliminary peace was in fact dropped, or rather faded out. No statement was made about it; nothing could be said without causing Wilson more difficulty.

If, however, there were to be only one treaty with Germany, the need for rapid action was even greater. The first requirement was a change in procedure. The Council of Ten was too large for working out the compromises which were now seen to be necessary on the most important issues. House had suggested to Clemenceau on March 12 that it would be a good thing to cut out the 'Quai d'Orsay meetings' and to hold a private conference with Lloyd George and Wilson on his return. This meeting was held on March 14, and similar meetings followed. It is fairly clear that the four leading plenipotentiaries regarded their meetings at first as an *ad hoc* procedure likely to last only for a short time. Lloyd George had arranged to go back to England on March 18. On March 17 his colleagues asked him to stay in Paris; he agreed to do so for another fortnight if they would write him a letter. They wrote in these terms: 'It seems to us imperative, in order that the world may wait no longer for peace than is actually unavoidable, that you should remain in Paris until the chief questions connected with the peace are settled. . . . If you can arrange to remain for another two weeks we hope and believe that this all-important result can be attained.'

Lloyd George stayed in Paris, but the 'all-important result' was not attained in a fortnight. The 'Big Four' continued to meet without the presence of the Foreign Ministers. On March 24 Wilson realised that this combination of informality and centralised decision was essential. The smaller Powers, however, resented it, and, again for obvious reasons, no formal statement was made about the change in procedure. The complaints about over-centralisation were less than they might have been if the new procedure had not been adopted, at first, as a temporary expedient. Furthermore, in spite of their attempts to delegate work, the Council of Ten had continued to spend a great deal of time on executive business. Much of this business could now be handed over by the 'Big Four' to the Foreign Ministers. The latter could also work as a separate body on a number of lesser problems, and thus save time in drafting, with the help of an extremely competent Drafting Commission, many of the clauses of the treaty.

The decision to combine all the German terms in a single document was not followed by any change in the decision that the Germans should not be brought into the discussions before the Allies were in agreement about the terms. The principal Allied Powers were as yet far from unanimous about the main issues in the treaty. If they invited the Germans to oral discussion before their own minds were made up, the German delegates would soon discover and exploit these Allied differences. There was indeed no difficulty about discovering them. In spite of efforts to maintain secrecy practically all the main terms of the treaty, and the Allied differences over them, were revealed in the press; journalists had every inducement to report and exaggerate the points of difference since they had more news value than the points of agreement.[1] The truculent attitude of the Germans since the armistice showed that oral discussion would lead to long delays terminable only by Allied dictation. The Allies had no doubt that the Germans would object strongly to a treaty which was bound to register the consequences of German defeat, and that they would not feel bound by their surrender of the right of interpretation of the 'principles' of the Fourteen Points. It was impossible to carry out the transformation of Europe envisaged broadly in the Fourteen Points without causing deep resentment among those who did not want such changes and were politically, militarily, and economically, the losers by them. The Germans themselves, in an uproar of criticism over the terms as reported in the press, made it clear that they would accept the treaty – if at all – only under compulsion.

The Germans indeed over-reached themselves in the violence of their threats that they would refuse to sign the treaty. They were trying to evade the armistice terms; they had in fact been deprived of the power to renew the war with any chance of military success, even if the war-weariness of the German people had allowed a renewal. The Allies, however, were also demobilising rapidly, and were hard put to it to deal with anarchy or defiance in the Baltic area or central and south-eastern Europe, but they were never without complete superiority over the Germans.

Lloyd George, who was, as usual, less inclined to trust the judgment of his own military advisers, was more worried than Clemenceau or Wilson about the consequences of a German refusal to sign. The

---

[1] President Wilson's promise of 'open covenants openly arrived at' gave the minor Allies as well as the journalists an argument against any kind of secret discussion. The details of the proposed naval, military, and air terms, as well as the facts of Allied disagreement over Poland, appeared in the newspapers.

American military commanders did not think the Germans capable of resistance. Clemenceau did not believe that they would resist; if they attempted to do so, the French could hammer them still harder, and in the end exact more severe terms. In any case the 'Big Four' agreed that there was need for haste, and, as they hurried on with their own decisions, so they were less ready to allow a long and desultory discussion with the enemy. On April 12 the 'Big Four' thought that the Germans would need 'several days' to examine the text given to them.[1] As the arrival of the Germans drew nearer, the Allies were inclined to give them more time for considering the terms; there was never any suggestion that they should be allowed to talk with the 'Big Four' – still less with the whole conference.

Meanwhile Wilson had been compelled to face the necessity of compromise. His own position was less strong because he had come back from the United States with the knowledge that, if he could not secure some changes in the Covenant of the League, he would have great difficulty in getting the United States to accept it. The most important of the American demands were for a recognition of the Monroe Doctrine, and for an explicit statement that the League had no power to deal with matters of domestic jurisdiction. In return for changes in the Covenant to meet these demands Wilson had to give way on other issues.[2] He conceded the French demand, which was supported by Lloyd George, that no definite sum should be stated in the treaty as the total German liability for reparation, and that this liability should include charges for pensions and separation allowances. He agreed to a special regime in the Saar, and to a limited occupation of the Rhineland. He promised to join with Great Britain in a treaty guaranteeing French security. He accepted the Japanese demands about Shantung.

Wilson – and House – felt uneasy about these concessions, and made them unwillingly. On April 7, when the French seemed determined to refuse a compromise over reparation, the President sent a private message to Washington asking how soon the *George Washington*, which had brought him to Brest, could be available if he decided to break off American participation in the conference and go home. He tried to justify to himself his concessions to the demands of his Allies

---

[1] As late as April 28 the 'Big Four' intended to tell the Germans that they would be given fifteen days in all within which to submit written observations, but that their observations on certain questions, e.g. frontiers, reparation, must be delivered within a shorter time. Lloyd George pointed out the difficulties of this plan from the German point of view.   [2] See below, Ch. 37.

by the argument that, once the League had been established, the mistakes of the treaty could be revised. It is, however, fair to remember that Wilson did succeed in reducing to a considerable extent the demands of his European Allies, especially the French, and that where the latter insisted on their case they were not necessarily in the wrong. Clemenceau was merely asserting facts when he said that the Germans had shown that they would not submit willingly to terms which deprived them of their former dominant position, and that the French could not be sure in advance that the League of Nations would provide France with security. The British and French Ministers were again stating facts when they said that public opinion in their respective countries would insist on the Germans paying reparation to the limit of their capacity; American public opinion, with less justification, from an Anglo-French point of view, was equally insistent upon the repayment of money borrowed from the United States for the purpose of carrying on the war. Wilson's unyielding attitude on this latter question was very different from his views on the need to avoid placing too heavy a burden on the Germans. Thus Lloyd George pointed out to Wilson at a meeting of the Council of Four on May 8 that the United States had made 'large profits out of the belligerents during the early part of the war, when she had not herself been a belligerent'. Wilson's answer was not very convincing. He said that 'the wealth which the United States had drawn from these sources had not gone to the Government, but to particular financiers and to particular classes of the nation. Congress would take the view that the Government ought not to accept on behalf of the nation any obligations because certain interests in the nation had made profits.'

It is also significant that, while Wilson was asking the European Powers to put their confidence in the League, and to accept a clause advocating disarmament to the limit of national security, the United States Government was unwilling to give a pledge to cut down the large American naval programme decided in 1916. This programme involved at least parity with Great Britain in capital ships. From the British point of view acceptance of parity meant an absolute change in naval policy. On the other hand, if the Americans refused to accept anything less than parity, the consequence might be a new and ruinously expensive competition in ship-building which the British Government could not afford. Hence behind Wilson's idealist assurances, there seemed to be a hard realism as far as American interests were concerned. Wilson himself put the matter frankly in conversation with a neutral on November 20: 'I want to tell Lloyd George certain things I can't write to him. I'll tell him, Are you going to grant the freedom of the seas? If not, are you prepared to enter into a race with us to see who will have the larger navy – you or we?' The British representatives raised this question of naval competition, but obtained nothing more than an explanation that the American programme had been sanctioned by Congress, and was being put into effect, and that the President could not interfere with its execution.[1] On the other hand the Americans maintained that they were not building in competition with Great Britain;[2] they would regard an increase of armaments as inconsistent with the spirit of the Covenant, and would agree to exchange information with the British Government about naval programmes.

The Council of Four was itself in serious disagreement not over the terms to Germany, but over the Italian claims in the Adriatic. After Wilson had issued (April 23) a statement of his views on this question, the Italian Delegation withdrew from the Conference. The withdrawal had no effect[3] on the work of the Council. The Covenant of the League was accepted by the Allies in a plenary session of the Conference on April 28 and, on April 29, the German Delegation, led by Count Brockdorff-Rantzau, arrived at Versailles.

[1] Wilson did not raise the question of the freedom of the seas which had caused the British Government anxiety at the time of the armistice (see above, p. 428). Wilson's own explanation why he did not insist on a matter which was included in the Fourteen Points, and upon which he had expressed strong views, was that there would no longer be any wars other than those undertaken by members of the League against a recalcitrant State. Hence there would be no neutrals, and no interference with neutral trade.

[2] The Germans had given similar assurances before 1914.

[3] Except for the insertion of a clause that ratification by three of the Principal Allied and Associated Powers would be sufficient to bring the treaty into force. This clause was of the greatest importance later in regard to the refusal of the United States Senate to ratify the Treaty. The Italians came back again on May 5.

CHAPTER 37

The Treaty of Versailles: the Covenant of the League of Nations: the territorial settlement: German reparation: the mandatory system

The four main features of the Treaty of Versailles were the establishment of a League of Nations, the compulsion laid upon Germany to surrender territory which she or, earlier, Prussia had forcibly annexed in spite of the wishes of the inhabitants, the arrangements for the payment of reparation, and the transfer of German overseas possessions from German sovereignty to a newly created system of trusteeship under the League. Since the evacuation of Belgium had already taken place under the terms of the armistice, the most important single act of the Conference, as far as British interests and opinion were concerned, was the establishment of the League. The recovery of Alsace-Lorraine by France repaired a historic wrong, and at the same time strengthened the French military and economic position in relation to a possible recurrence of German aggression. The return of North Slesvig to Denmark was, like the return of Alsace-Lorraine to France, not directly a British interest. The restoration of an independent Polish State and the recognition of successor States on the ruins of the Habsburg Empire, were matters affecting Great Britain only to the extent to which they were likely to promote peace and economic recovery in Europe.

A proposal for a League of Nations 'binding themselves to side against any Power which broke a treaty' had been made by Grey to House in a letter of September 22, 1915.[1] Wilson was impressed by Grey's idea, and mentioned his proposal favourably in a speech of May 27, 1916, though from the first there was a difference between his

[1] See above, p. 217. Grey was strongly influenced by his belief that, if the leading neutral State in 1914 had been willing to say that they would take sides against a State refusing a conference to settle the Austro-Serbian dispute, the war might have been avoided. Grey hoped that the United States would propose a plan on the lines of his suggestion to House.

(Wilson's) view of a League and the plan envisaged by Grey. Grey thought in terms of an improved Concert of the Powers; Wilson had in mind something more like a general application of the Monroe doctrine as a means of safeguarding democracy. Wilson, however, said that the United States would take part in an association of nations for the realisation of the rights of self-determination, equality among the Powers, and freedom from military aggression. The speech had less influence than might have been expected because Wilson also said in it that the United States was not concerned with 'the causes and objects of the present war'.[1]

Meanwhile in Great Britain the advocacy of a League of Nations was left mainly to private individuals and societies. In the autumn of 1916 Lord Robert Cecil submitted to the Cabinet a memorandum on plans to prevent a recurrence of war. The Entente Powers also included a project for a League in their answer to Wilson's Peace Note of December 18, 1916.[2] A Committee of the Cabinet in April, 1917, recommended that the signatories of a Peace Treaty should agree not to resort to war with one another until they had submitted the matter in dispute to a conference. The last of Wilson's Fourteen Points referred to a 'general association of nations ... under specific covenants for the purpose of affording mutual guarantees of political independence and territorial integrity to great and small states alike'.

No official study of the matter had yet been made either in Great Britain or in the United States. In March, 1918, an official British Committee was appointed to consider the organisation of a League. The Committee, which consisted of three members of the Foreign Office and three historians, with Lord Phillimore as chairman, drew up a draft convention on the lines of the recommendation to the War Cabinet. The Committee thought that only an agreement or alliance for co-operation was possible. They suggested that, before a resort to war, a dispute should be taken to arbitration or conciliation; that all parties to an agreement should combine against any violation of its terms, and should apply economic sanctions – a boycott or blockade – and in the last resort should go to war with the violating party. The War Cabinet adopted the suggestions of the Committee. A French scheme, put forward in June, 1918, and going beyond the Phillimore plan, proposed an International Council with the duty of applying diplomatic, economic, and, ultimately, military sanctions. Wilson still thought public discussion of detailed plans undesirable, but asked House

[1] See above, pp. 222–3.   [2] See above, p. 237.

to provide a revise of the British proposals. A Foreign Office memorandum of November, 1918, suggested something like a permanent
Conference of the Great Powers prohibiting recourse to war, but not
offering any territorial or political guarantees. The British and American
Governments opposed the French idea of an international force to uphold the agreement; Wilson said that American opinion would not allow
the United States army or navy to be under any kind of foreign control.

A pamphlet issued by General Smuts in December, 1918, was also of
great importance in influencing official and public opinion. Smuts'
view was that a League should take the form, not of a 'super-State', but
of 'a permanent conference between the Governments of the constituent States for the purpose of joint international action in certain
defined respects'. The organisation would have a permanent secretariat
and would consist of (i) a general conference in which all states would
have equal voting power, and which would make 'recommendations
to the national governments', and (ii) a Council, or executive committee
on which the Great Powers would have a bare majority.[1] Wilson was
impressed by Smuts' draft, and, in a draft of his own on January 10,
1919, accepted the principle that a State violating the agreement should
be at war *ipso facto* with other signatories. Wilson's advisers pointed
out to him that an agreement on these lines was incompatible with the
constitution of the United States which left to Congress alone the
power of declaring war. For this reason the American draft was
changed to read that a State breaking the agreement 'shall *ipso facto* be
deemed to have committed an act of war against all the members of the
League'.

The first British official draft was published on January 20, 1919.
From this time there were close Anglo-American discussions. On
January 25, 1919, Wilson obtained the consent of Lloyd George and
Clemenceau to the inclusion of the Covenant in the Treaty of Peace,
and also submitted to a plenary session of the Peace Conference three
resolutions regarding the establishment of the League. The Conference
accepted the resolutions and appointed a Commission on the League of
Nations. The Commission was very strong. Wilson was chairman; the
British representatives, Smuts and Lord Robert Cecil, gave him full

---

[1] Smuts suggested that the new territorial settlement resulting from the break-
up of the Russian, Austro-Hungarian, and Turkish Empires should be decided
by the League. He also proposed compulsory arbitration in justiciable disputes,
the abolition of military conscription, and the nationalisation and inspection of
armament factories.

support. The first session was held on February 3; on February 14 the first draft of a Covenant was brought before the Conference. The Commission had worked on a draft drawn up by C. J. B. Hurst,[1] and the American David Hunter Miller.[2] The President at first wanted to change the draft for one of his own, but agreed to take the joint Anglo-American draft. The Commission had little to do except improve the wording of this latter draft; the main decisions of principle had already been settled. The most serious differences of view on matters of substance were over the French proposal that the League should have an international force under its control,[3] and the Japanese proposal that the Covenant should include a clause recognising racial equality.[4] The French proposal was rejected absolutely by the President on the ground that it was incompatible with the constitution of the United States. Wilson would not go beyond a permanent military committee to advise the League. The Japanese proposal was opposed by Australia, with the backing of the British Delegation.

After the plenary session on February 14 a committee of revision prepared a redraft, but the most important change in the text came from the American side. Wilson had found that opposition in the Senate was concentrated upon securing a special reservation regarding the Monroe doctrine, and upon the exclusion of domestic questions from the control of the League. There was also a wish to make withdrawal easier if American interests seemed to require it. These demands were of great importance. If the Americans asked for a special sphere of influence in the western hemisphere, Japan might make similar requests for herself in Asia. In any case the Japanese would understand that the demand for the exclusion of domestic questions from the control of the League referred in fact to immigration, and that this demand was in direct conflict with the Japanese proposal for a statement on the equality of nations. Acceptance of the request for easier withdrawal would lessen the confidence of the French in the League as a guarantee

---

[1] Later Sir Cecil Hurst, Principal Legal Adviser to the Foreign Office.

[2] A legal member of the American Delegation who worked in collaboration with Wilson.

[3] Another important difference was over the question of mandates. See below, pp. 555–9.

[4] The wording of the proposed clause was as follows: 'The equality of nations being a basic principle of the League of Nations, the High Contracting Parties agree to accord, as soon as possible, to all alien nationals of States members of the League, equal and just treatment in every respect, making no distinction, either in law or of fact, on account of their race or nationality.'

of security, and was again in sharp contrast with the French wish to create some permanent form of military machinery under League control.

None the less Wilson's colleagues did their best to help him. Lord Robert Cecil and Orlando were willing to agree on the drafting committee to a clause that 'nothing [in the Covenant of the League] shall be deemed to affect the validity of international engagements such as treaties of arbitration or regional understandings like the Monroe doctrine for securing the maintenance of peace'.[1] A new clause was also added on matters relating to domestic jurisdiction, and a new sub-clause allowing withdrawal from the League after two years' notice. The French agreed, with much reluctance, to the American proposals. On April 28 the revised draft was approved at a plenary session of the Conference.

The speed with which this work was done was remarkable. The reasons were the drive and energy of the President, the general know-ledge that he intended to get his plan through the Conference, the collaboration of the three Great Powers – and particularly the United States and Great Britain – and the amount of previous discussion and canvassing of drafts. Furthermore the purpose of the League was to solve a practical problem. The existing diplomatic machinery and engagements of the Great Powers had not prevented war in 1914. It was thought that a new kind of machinery, including a permanent Council of Nations, served by a permanent international secretariat, might prevent at least the drift, or rather the catastrophic descent into war which had taken place in the last fortnight of July, 1914. Any arrangements which allowed time for reflexion and for the considera-tion of disputes would help to secure a settlement without war.[2] Similarly the violation of Belgian neutrality by the Germans had shown that the pre-war system of treaties between single Powers or groups of Powers was not enough to secure the independence of small States. Hence the guarantees in the Covenant of the territorial integrity and political independence of the Members of the League, and the common obligation to enforce the maintenance of peace.

[1] The British representatives had suggested naming the Monroe doctrine without defining it. Wilson (at the suggestion of Taft) had proposed to define it without naming it.

[2] The amount of administrative work carried out during the latter part of the war by inter-Allied organisations outside the traditional sphere of diplomatic action was a new and, as it appeared, a hopeful sign of the extent to which such international machinery might be developed.

The powerful advocates of the League were therefore able to get their plan through quickly. They had every reason to do so, since a long discussion might have given the impression that the most urgent problems of the peace settlement were being subordinated to vague proposals – which could be considered later – for preventing future aggression. Protracted debates on the Covenant would also have allowed sectional or regional views to assert themselves more strongly than the 'general will' for common action to prevent war. The policy of 'pushing' the Covenant was therefore justified since without it there might well have been no League, but it was not finally successful. It did not prevent the United States Senate from rejecting the Covenant, or the defeated enemy States from regarding it as a barely disguised trick of the Allies for the maintenance of the allegedly unfair terms of the Peace Treaties. In any case the acceptance of the obligations of the Covenant after such short discussion by the Conference as a whole was not secured without a price. This price was paid in the omissions, vagueness, and 'silences', as well as the imperfect drafting of the Covenant, and, above all, in the early attempts made by some of the members to give a minimal interpretation to the obligations which they had undertaken.

Since the first purpose of the League was to prevent sudden aggression and to allow time for the settlement of disputes, the members, under Article XII of the Covenant, agreed to submit disputes to arbitration or enquiry by the Council, and to refrain from resort to war, in any case, 'until three months after the award by the arbitrators or the report by the Council'.[1] The Covenant thus did not establish the principle of compulsory arbitration, though the members were pledged, under Article XIII, to submit to arbitration 'the whole subject-matter' of a dispute 'which they recognise to be suitable for submission to arbitration and which cannot be satisfactorily settled by diplomacy'. They agreed to carry out an award in good faith, and not to 'resort to war against any member of the League which complies therewith'. They also decided (Article XIV) to establish a Permanent Court of International Justice for the determination of disputes submitted to it by the parties concerned, and for advising the Council or Assembly on any points referred to it by them. In the case of disputes not submitted to arbitration, but to enquiry by the Council, the Members were pledged (Article XV) not to go to war with the party to the

---

[1] The delay was in fact longer, since the Council was allowed six months in which to make its report.

dispute which complied with a unanimous recommendation by the Council.[1]

What was to happen, however, in the event of a breach of the Covenant by one of its Members, that is, in the event of a refusal to accept an arbitral award or a recommendation of the Council, and a resort to war? Here – in Article XVI – the Covenant laid down 'sanctions'. The Members undertook (i) to regard a Member resorting to war in disregard of Articles XII, XIII, or XV as having committed 'an act of war against all other Members of the League'; (ii) to subject such a defaulting State to 'the severance of all trade or financial relations, the prohibition of all intercourse between their nationals and the nationals of the Covenant-breaking State, and the prevention of all financial, commercial, or personal intercourse between the nationals of the Covenant-breaking State and the nationals of any other State, whether a Member of the League or not'.

This action was likely to bring armed resistance from the Covenant-breaking State. What then? Here was the crux of the matter. The duty of the Council did not go beyond making 'recommendations' to the 'several Governments concerned what effective military, naval, or air force the Members of the League shall severally contribute to the armed forces to be used to protect the covenants of the League'. The Members had a moral obligation to accept these recommendations. They had no legal obligation to do so. Furthermore, the League, as such, depended wholly on the forces of its members for the execution of sanctions. Apart from the American objections to the French proposals for a permanent International force with fixed contingents from the Members, and for an International staff to deal with all matters relating to the organisation of the International force and the 'eventual conduct of military operations', it was impracticable to draw up plans in advance against an unknown enemy in unknown circumstances, or to keep in being a force sufficient to deter any but the smallest Powers from aggression. The purpose of the League, as its founders regarded it, was not to wage war but to prevent it, and to do so by providing machinery which, if it had existed, might have prevented war in 1914.[2]

[1] If the Council did not make a unanimous report, the Members were free to act as they might choose. The parties to a dispute were excluded from voting on the Council's recommendations.

[2] Wilson himself had set a fashion of regarding the deeper causes of war as due to the defective nature of international machinery, or, more specifically, a 'bad system' of interlocked alliances and secret military engagements. Neither Wilson nor the chief English protagonists of the League took account of the fact that, as

The proposals for the prevention of war and for possible action against an aggressor laid down in Articles XII–XVI were unlikely of themselves to seem sufficient to the smaller Powers. Wilson realised that they required some more positive guarantee of their independence. He was therefore responsible for the so-called guarantee in Article X: 'The Members of the League undertake to respect and preserve as against external aggression the territorial integrity and existing political independence of all Members of the League.' Here again, however, the obligation was moral rather than legal. 'In case of any such aggression or in case of any threat or danger of such aggression the Council shall advise upon the means by which this obligation shall be fulfilled.' The President – though he had previously described Article X as 'the very backbone of the whole Covenant' – told the United States Senate that Congress was 'absolutely free to put its own interpretation' on the duty of Members under the article 'in all cases that call for action'. He also explained that 'territorial integrity' meant immunity from forcible annexation, not from 'armed intervention'. The first draft of the clause by the President (and also, in different terms, the British draft of January 20) included a further qualification that

> such territorial readjustments, if any, as may in the future become necessary by reason of changes in present racial conditions and aspirations, or present social and political relationships, pursuant to the principle of self-determination, and also such territorial readjustments as may in the judgment of three-fourths of the Delegates be demanded by the welfare and manifest interest of the peoples concerned, may be effected if agreeable to those peoples.

Neither this qualification (which hinted, incidentally, at the future break-up of colonial Empires) nor the simpler and vaguer British proposal[1] was maintained in the draft. Instead, Article XIX laid down

---

far as 'machinery' was concerned, the method of informal conferences of Ambassadors in London could have been as effective in 1914 as they had proved effective under Grey's direction in dealing with the crisis of 1913. The trouble was that the Germans and Austro-Hungarians refused to use the machinery.

[1] This proposal ran: 'If at any time it should appear that the boundaries of any State guaranteed . . . do not conform to the requirements of the situation, the League shall take the matter under consideration, and may recommend to the parties affected any modification which it may deem necessary.' Any State not accepting the recommendation would lose the guarantee provided by the League.

in general terms only that the Assembly could advise the 'reconsideration by Members of the League of treaties which have become inapplicable and the consideration of international conditions whose continuance might endanger the peace of the world'.

The procedure for delaying recourse to war and finding peaceful solutions of disputes was also to be buttressed by a reduction of armaments. Article VIII of the Covenant recognised that 'the maintenance of peace requires the reduction of national armaments to the lowest point consistent with national safety and the enforcement by common action of international obligations'.[1] The Council, therefore, 'taking account of the geographical situation and circumstances of each State, shall formulate plans for such reduction for the consideration and action of the several Governments'. It was assumed that these plans would be formulated at once, since a further stipulation required that they should be reconsidered and revised every ten years. Here again, however, the phraseology was novel; no previous treaty had ever committed the victors to their own disarmament. On the other hand the commitment was dangerously vague. It was unlikely, for example, that any country would regard the League as in fact competent to decide the point at which its armaments reached or went beyond the requirements of national safety. Wilson himself was not prepared to accept a standard of naval armament for the United States lower than that of any other naval Power.

A League of Nations without an armed force of its own did not satisfy the French demand for security against a renewal of German aggression. The French, with the support of Foch, put forward a claim to the Rhine frontier which Wilson regarded as morally wrong and Lloyd George as politically dangerous since it would lead to another 'Alsace-Lorraine question' between France and Germany. The British delegation proposed as a compromise a temporary French occupation of the Rhineland, a temporary administration of the Saar territory by the League of Nations, and an Anglo-American guarantee to France. Lloyd George raised this latter proposal with House on March 14, and Wilson agreed to it two days later. Clemenceau, however, would accept a guarantee only on the conditions of a thirty years occupation of the Rhineland and of a permanently demilitarised zone of fifty

---

[1] The limitations on German armaments were described as being enforced in order to render possible 'the initiation of a general limitation of the armaments of all nations'.

kilometres east of the Rhine. On March 25, after conferring at Fontainebleau with Smuts, Sir Henry Wilson, Hankey, and Kerr,[1] Lloyd George produced a memorandum warning against the risk of driving the Germans into a Bolshevik alliance if the terms imposed on them were unjustly harsh, but accepting the idea of a permanently demilitarised zone and repeating the offer of an Anglo-American guarantee.[2] The President held the same views, but did not issue a statement jointly with Lloyd George. Wilson and Lloyd George were now not on the best of terms; in any case, Lloyd George may have thought that a joint statement would irritate the French. Clemenceau gave a contentious answer, and Lloyd George replied to it in sharp words. Meanwhile there was opposition in the French delegation to the proposed guarantee. The French held out for the annexation of the Saar, and Wilson announced publicly that he had ordered the *George Washington* to be ready to take him back to the United States.[3]

Wilson had put the establishment of a League of Nations and the prevention of future wars as the primary task of the Conference, but he understood that the prospects of the League depended first of all upon a satisfactory territorial settlement in Europe. This settlement had therefore to be considered as a whole and not merely in relation to Germany. The return of Alsace-Lorraine to France and the fulfilment of a pledge given by Prussia half a century earlier for a plebiscite in North Slesvig were accepted by the Germans, bitterly enough, as a consequence of defeat. Germany was as much pledged as the Allies under the Fourteen Points to re-establish an independent Polish State and to allow the constituent nationalities of the former Habsburg and Tsarist Empires a right of self-determination, though the Allies realised that the Germans would protest violently when they had to carry out their engagements. The recognition of an independent State of Czechoslovakia was bound to involve keeping a large number of German-speaking subjects of Austria-Hungary as a minority in a predominantly non-German State,

---

[1] P. H. Kerr (later Marquis of Lothian) was Lloyd George's private secretary.

[2] For this important memorandum, see Parl. Papers, 1922, Cmd. 1614. See also below, pp. 546 and 553.

[3] A compromise solution was finally accepted according to which the Saar was put under a Governing Commission appointed by the League of Nations, for fifteen years. After this time the inhabitants would decide by plebiscite their political allegiance. The Saar coalfield was given outright to France and Germany was pledged to buy it back if the plebiscite went in favour of union with the Reich.

and also to make it impossible on strategic grounds to permit the union of German Austria with the Reich.[1] Even without their pledge the Allies could not have done otherwise than re-establish an independent Poland after the break-up of Austria-Hungary and the temporary eclipse of Russia. An independent Poland consisting only of the former provinces of Austria-Hungary and Russia would been have an absurdity. In fact, for reasons outside their control, the Allies were able to enforce a much more satisfactory line, from an ethnographical point of view, on the western than on the eastern frontiers of Poland; the harshest treatment was given to the Ruthenians whose claims to self-determination were ignored in spite of efforts made by the British Delegation on their behalf. The most important consideration, in fact, for the Germans was not what they lost but what they retained. Of the three great Continental monarchies Germany alone had survived defeat and revolution; the non-German nationalities on the borders of the Reich could be detached from it without breaking up German unity even if this detachment involved transferring a large number of Germans in 'mixed areas' to alien rule. The economic hardships, and the break with old habits of which the Germans complained with well-organised reproaches were less than those in other areas of central and eastern Europe. Vienna was much more affected than East Prussia by the economic consequences of territorial change, and the administrative problems which the new States had to solve were more difficult than those caused to Germany by her territorial losses. The population of Germany remained, after the treaty, greater than that of France; and, the real value of German foreign trade in 1929 came very close to the record figure of 1913.

The 'Big Four', contrary to reports which were too easily believed, gave much care and attention to the question of the Polish frontiers, and modified in a sense favourable to Germany the recommendations of their own experts. Among the experts the Americans went further than the British in support of the Polish claims, and Lloyd George was readier than Wilson to make concessions to the Germans. The Fourteen Points were vague in assigning to the new, or rather the revived state of Poland, 'territories inhabited by indisputably Polish populations',

[1] The Sudeten territory included in Czechoslovakia had been part of the Habsburg dominions and was separated from the German Reich by a range of mountains. The territory had been administered from Prague and was linked economically to Czech markets. Lloyd George agreed that it should form part of the Czechoslovak State, though he described this State as 'polyglot and incoherent'.

and in promising Poland access to the sea. The Polish Commission suggested that (i) Danzig and the whole length of the Danzig–Mlawa railway should be included in Poland; (ii) that in Posnania and West Prussia the westernmost limit of the Polish frontier should follow, with certain modifications, the Polish ethnographical majorities; (iii) that all regions in Upper Silesia with a Polish ethnographical majority should be assigned to Poland, and a small area in the south to Czechoslovakia; (iv) that a plebiscite should be held in the region of Allenstein.

The Commission pointed out that owing to the mixed character of the areas a large number of Germans would have to be included in the Polish State. Before the partitions of Poland there had been German minorities permanently settled on Polish territory. Since the partitions, and especially since 1871, the German Government had done everything in its power to increase the German population. The German minority was not merely in the western borders but was scattered over Polish territory; hence it was impossible to give to Poland these 'indisputably Polish' provinces, containing two million Poles, without bringing in about a million Germans.[1] The question of Upper Silesia was complicated by the fact that the landowners, and mine and factory owners, were largely German, and the working class Polish,[2] but this state of things had come about to some extent owing to the deliberate policy of the German Government; in any case the principle of self-determination was not intended for application merely in the interest of the well-to-do.

The case of Danzig was especially difficult because there was no suitable 'access to the sea' for Poland except the estuary of the Vistula. Danzig had remained predominantly Slav until 1307. Although the population had been opposed to their annexation by Prussia in the second partition of Poland (1793) there was no doubt that in 1918 they did not wish to be reincorporated into a Polish State. On the other hand it would have been politically impracticable to have left the Polish outlet to the sea in the control of the German Reich. The proposal to restore to Danzig the status of a Free City within the Polish Customs Union was made by the British Delegation;[3] the appointment of a High Commissioner (under the authority of the League) to decide questions

[1] In addition to measures of colonisation in former Polish territory annexed by Prussia, the Germans had excluded Poles from posts in government employment (including workers on the State railways).

[2] The population of 2,000,000 was, roughly, ⅔ Polish and ⅓ German.

[3] The first British proposal was that Danzig should be made a 'free port'.

at issue between the Free City and the Poles seemed the best way of meeting the political differences likely to arise in spite of the common economic interests of the parties concerned.[1]

In the first discussion of the report of the Polish Commission on March 19 Lloyd George said that he was concerned over the proposal to put 2,100,000 Germans under Polish rule. He thought that this decision might cause trouble for Poland in the future, and that the German Government might refuse to sign a treaty containing such a plan. Lloyd George also thought that it was unfair and imprudent to settle the Polish-German frontier without hearing the German as well as the Polish case. Wilson defended the recommendations of the Commission, but agreed with Lloyd George 'about the danger of German irredentism'. The whole question was therefore referred back to the Polish Commission, and discussed again by the Council of Ten on March 22. The experts maintained their previous conclusions. Lloyd George said that he was 'not as convinced as at the previous meeting' that there was no need to include so many Germans in Poland, but that he was still worried about the possibility of a German refusal to sign the treaty. Lloyd George accepted the report on the condition that the Council 'reserved the right of revision when it came to consider the total effect of all these proposals'. Lloyd George repeated his views in his memorandum of March 25.[2] He wrote that the proposal to place 2,100,000 Germans 'under the control of a people which is of a different religion, and which has never proved its capacity for stable self-government throughout its history, must . . . lead sooner or later to a new war in the east of Europe'.[3]

At the opening of the Peace Conference neither the leading statesmen nor the leaders of political opinion in the Allied countries could have foreseen the extent to which the question of German reparation payments and inter-Allied debts would dominate the field of inter-

---

[1] The separation of East Prussia from Germany was not due only to the decision to give Poland access to the sea. A belt of territory with a predominantly Polish population extended from the main Polish territory to the sea west of Danzig. The Germans alleged that the inhabitants of this territory spoke only a dialect of Polish, and were not properly Poles, but not even German statistics suggested that they were German. The German Government before 1914 had been developing the trade of Königsberg at the expense of Danzig.

[2] See above, p. 543. Lloyd George thought that Wilson was influenced by the fact of the large Polish vote in the United States.

[3] Wilson also agreed to a plebiscite in the Marienwerder area.

national relations for more than a decade after the war. No one of the Heads of Governments was a trained economist, but each of them knew well enough that there was a practical limit to the amount which Germany could pay and possibly to the amount which the Allied countries could receive without damage to their own economies. The trouble was that expert opinion differed very widely in its estimate of these limits, while popular opinion in the Allied countries had expectations far beyond the most optimistic figures proposed by the experts.

There were two further considerations. French fiscal arrangements had been less satisfactory than those of Great Britain in meeting a considerable part of the cost of the war by direct taxation; French ministers were aware that, without large contributions from Germany, France could not find the capital to restore the devastated areas and restart the exhausted French economy. The case of Italy was even more serious; the chances of recovering anything from the successor states of the Habsburg Empire were very small. Above all, there was the question of inter-governmental debts. Great Britain and France had borrowed large sums from the United States, and France was heavily in debt to Great Britain. Neither France nor Great Britain could hope for a long time, if at all, to recover the sums owed to them by the former Tsarist Government of Russia. If Germany were not required to make payments on an unprecedented scale, France and Great Britain would find themselves liable to heavy debt charges, while the Germans would be free to re-establish their own economy and perhaps to prepare for aggression. If Wilson had been able to offer a cancellation of Allied debts to the United States, the problem of German reparation would have been manageable. To British and French opinion such a cancellation would have seemed equitable. The United States had come out of the war richer than she had gone into it, and her losses in men had been far less than those of her European associates. Wilson, however, could not make an offer of this kind, since American opinion would not have supported it.

On the precedents of earlier wars – including the Franco-Prussian war – the Allies would have been justified in demanding the cost of the war from Germany and her allies. They would have had to assert this claim against Germany alone. The Austro-Hungarian Empire had disappeared. Turkey and Bulgaria were incapable of paying anything. It was, however, obvious that the Germans could not make good the total war expenditure of the Allies. Until the end of 1916 the Allies had maintained their right to exact, in the words of their reply of December 30 to the German Peace Note of December 12, 'penalties, reparation, and guarantees'.[1] Wilson, however, on political rather than economic grounds, was strongly against the exaction of penalties or indemnities; his Fourteen Points limited reparation for damage to Belgium, the invaded territories of France, Roumania, Serbia, and Montenegro. In his address of February 11, 1918, Wilson said directly that there should be 'no annexations, no contributions, no punitive indemnities'. Lloyd George, in his speech of January 8, 1918, on war aims, had asked for the 'political and economic restoration of the invaded countries, and for reparations for injuries done in violation of international law'. He did not put forward demands for a punitive indemnity or for the cost of the war.

The Allies did not regard Wilson's statements as sufficiently clear or, in as far as they were clear, adequate to meet what seemed to them their just claims. In their acceptance of the Fourteen Points as the basis of an armistice the British and French Governments wrote to Wilson that 'no doubt ought to . . . exist' about their demands. These demands were for 'compensation . . . by Germany for all damage done to the civilian population of the Allies and their property by the aggression of Germany by land, by sea, and from the air'. The Germans did not contest this interpretation of the 'principles' of the Fourteen Points or ask for any closer definition of 'compensation' and 'damage'.

The British Government, at the end of 1916, had asked the Board of Trade to report on the probable effect upon British trade of 'an indemnity (whether in money or in kind) paid by the enemy at the conclusion of the War, or within a reasonable time afterwards, to make good damages in the territory overrun'. The report concluded that an indemnity would not be harmful to British interests, but that it would not go far towards meeting the costs of the war. Professor Ashley and J. M. Keynes added a note that an indemnity in kind would be preferable to money payments, and that any cash payments should be spread over a period of years, and should thus involve a charge 'not so much on wealth already accumulated as on future accumulations'.

On October 17, 1918, the War Cabinet asked the Board of Trade for a more general report on the economic considerations affecting the terms of peace. This report was submitted on November 26. It suggested that since the total claims under the head of reparation would be very high, and would 'take precedence over an indemnity proper . . . no

[1] In their note of January 10, 1917, to President Wilson the Allies used the phrase 'compensation and equitable indemnities for harm suffered'.

useful purpose would be served by putting forward a claim' for the latter unless it were thought expedient to do so for bargaining purposes. The claim for reparation would not be less than £2000 million; this sum could probably not be exacted without spreading payment over 'so long a time that a long period of occupation of German territory would be necessary to enforce it'. The Board of Trade considered that only about £400 million could be secured in kind (ships, railway material, coal, potash, gold, etc.), and that another £400 million might be obtained from German (and Austro-Hungarian) external investments. The remainder would have to be paid in interest-bearing securities.

A Treasury Committee appointed by Bonar Law, as Chancellor of the Exchequer, and including Keynes[1] among its members, suggested a higher maximum – £3000 million. This sum could be found (i) by an immediate levy – applied ruthlessly, and with the consequence of ruining German overseas development and trade for many years to come – followed by small payments over a term of years, or (ii) by less drastic immediate treatment, and a higher level of payment for a long period of years. In either case it was difficult to make an estimate without a more detailed examination. Lloyd George appointed a committee to make this examination. The financial experts on the committee were Sir G. E. Foster,[2] Canadian Finance Minister, W. A. S. Hewins, a well-known economist, Lord Cunliffe, Governor of the Bank of England, and the Hon. Herbert Gibbs, a leading city banker. To the embarrassment of Lloyd George and Bonar Law, these experts concluded that the total direct cost of the war to the Allies had been £24,000 million; that the enemy Powers, after the restoration of 'normal' conditions, could well pay £1200 million in annual interest on this sum, and that there was no reason to fear any ill effects upon Allied trade from these payments.[3] On the contrary, 'the enforcement of an Indemnity will operate as a deterrent to future aggression, and be a substantial guarantee of the world's peace'.

[1] Keynes told the American Norman Davis that the British Government would make a claim for shipping tonnage illegally destroyed. Keynes thought £2000 million might be a safer estimate of German capacity of payment, but he did not rule out the higher figure.

[2] At a meeting of the Imperial War Cabinet when the report was discussed, Sir G. E. Foster said that he had signed the report with certain reservations since he did not consider that the committee had had sufficient time or information to make definite estimates.

[3] These estimates were accepted by the Federation of British Industries and the Associated Chambers of Commerce.

Lloyd George and Bonar Law did not publish these estimates, but they became generally known. Bonar Law was careful in his election speeches not to commit himself to any extravagant hopes. Lloyd George, however, and others of his colleagues were much less guarded. Lloyd George realised that popular feeling was convinced that Germany could and should 'pay for the war'. In a speech at Bristol he said that the British Government proposed 'to demand the whole cost of the war', and believed that it could be exacted, and that the exaction would not do harm to the countries receiving it. He hedged his statement with a few cautionary comments, but to the audience his words must have seemed a promise. Asquith, on the following day, said merely that he agreed with the Prime Minister's statement that Germany ought to pay for the war. There was no general election in France, but French opinion was even more persuaded than British opinion that Germany must and could pay for the whole cost of the war and not merely for the restoration of the devastated areas.

On January 22, 1919, the Council of Ten appointed a Commission to enquire into reparation. The British representatives were Mr W. M. Hughes, Prime Minister of Australia, Lord Cunliffe, and Lord Sumner. The original terms of reference of the Commission were that it should enquire into the amount of 'reparation and indemnity' which Germany should and could pay. Wilson asked that the word 'indemnity' should be taken out, since 'bodies of workpeople all over the world' had protested against 'indemnities'.[1] Lloyd George agreed on condition that the term 'reparation' had the widest application, though he did not explain what application he intended to give to it. The first business of the Commission was therefore to ascertain what was and what was not 'reparation for damage'.[2] Bonar Law and Sir Robert Borden had

[1] An Inter-Allied Conference in London on December 2, 1918, had agreed to a proposal for a Commission on 'Reparations and Indemnities'. House had then wanted the words 'and Indemnities' to be excluded. Wilson himself, in a note of May 26, 1917, to the Russian Provisional Government, had said that 'no indemnities must be insisted on except those that constitute payment for manifest wrong done.' The American 'Inquiry' (see above, p. 398) into the conditions of peace assumed that the Allied demands would be limited to the repair of actual damage.

[2] The use of this term in public and private discussions of the question of German payments had somewhat confused public opinion. Arthur Henderson, for example, had used the word in his election speeches, and had defined it as exacting from Germany the fullest possible restitution for devastation and wrong-doing outside legal warfare. A short outline of a proposed agenda for the Peace Conference submitted by the United States technical advisers to Lansing on

already mentioned to the War Cabinet their doubts whether the Allied reservations to Wilson on the Fourteen Points could be taken to include a demand for repayment of the full cost of the war. Lloyd George had then said that unless Wilson was prepared to pool with the Allies the whole cost of the war, he (Wilson) was not in a position to reject claims for an indemnity. The American representatives on the Commission maintained that reparation could be exacted only in accordance with accepted principles of international law or with the Fourteen Points as qualified by the Allied memorandum and that the Allies had debarred themselves from asking for an indemnity. The British representatives and those of the European Allies argued that they remained free to claim the whole cost of the war. The Commission had reached no agreement on the question by February 24. They then referred the question of principle to the Supreme Council.

Meanwhile it was clear that the question itself was largely academic. The claims for which the Allies could undoubtedly make demand were so high, and the estimates of German capacity to pay so much reduced from the figure suggested by Lord Cunliffe, that there was not the least chance of any surplus payment towards the cost of the war.[1] Lloyd George now shifted his ground.[2] He gave up the claim for full repayment of war costs, but included a demand for the cost of war pensions and separation allowances. Wilson opposed this inclusion as going beyond the Armistice terms. Lloyd George realised that in fact the inclusion of the cost of war pensions would only add to a total sum which was already beyond German capacity of payment; on the other hand its inclusion would make a great difference to the British share in the distribution of the amounts which Germany was able to provide.[3]

December 30 used the term 'indemnity' to cover all payments by way of restitution, reparation, etc., to be made by the Central Powers.

[1] J. F. Dulles, a member of the American Delegation, suggested the inclusion in the treaty of a clause stating German responsibility for the costs of her aggression but renouncing the Allied right to claim them in full on the ground that Germany could not pay the sum. See below, p. 555.

[2] In his book *The Truth About the Peace Treaties*, Lloyd George says that he was definitely of opinion (early in March, 1919) that 'we were committed by the Armistice terms not to demand an indemnity which would include the cost of prosecuting the war' (i, 490). Lloyd George does not say when he reached this opinion.

[3] In Lloyd George's words 'Unless . . . Britain could include pensionable injuries, her share of the total compensation received from Germany would be insignificant in comparison with that received by other Allies, whose real financial burdens were no greater . . . and some of which were considerably less per head

Lord Sumner produced a legal interpretation in favour of the British claim. He argued in a memorandum of March 31 that the soldier was

> simply a civilian, called to arms in the cause of justice; his uniform makes no difference; his true position is that he quits civil life only to defend the Commonwealth, and, if he survives, to civil life he will return. I think that History will not find in his case anything to deprive him of civilian rights. Will it really be contended that [the Allied 'reservation'] actually intended . . . to stipulate the benefits for unenlisted men from which they consciously designed to exclude the uniformed soldier.

The argument was sound from the point of view of equity and common sense, but it did not answer the question whether, by inadvertence, the Allies had not made this exclusion.

Wilson would probably have held to his objection to the British demand if Smuts had not submitted on March 31 a more cogent memorandum arguing that the Allies had included in their note of November 5 a general principle 'of far-reaching scope', i. e. 'compensation for all damage to the civilian population of the Allies in their persons or property which resulted from the German aggression, and whether done on land or sea or from the air'. Smuts argued that 'the plain commonsense construction of the reservation' led to the conclusion that while 'direct war expenditure' (e.g. soldiers' pay and equipment, guns, etc.) 'could perhaps not be recovered from the Germans, yet disablement pensions to discharged soldiers, or pensions to widows and orphans . . . were all items representing compensation to members of the civilian population for damages sustained by them, for which the Germans are liable'. A shop-keeper who suffered wounds and disablement was thereby as much entitled to compensation as he would have been if his shop had been destroyed by the Germans. Lloyd George put the matter with his usual vividness. He said that he 'wanted equal treatment for damage of all kinds; he could not acknowledge that damage to houses was more important than damage to human life'.

After defining the nature of their claims the Allies had to estimate the total amount which they would ask Germany to pay and – here were the decisive questions – the amount Germany could pay and the methods of payment. The French held for a time that Germany could

of their population than those sustained by the British Empire.' Lloyd George, op. cit., i, 491.

pay £40,000 million. Lord Cunliffe and Lord Sumner came down to £12,000 million – half their original estimate. The Americans thought that within about two years the Germans could pay £800 million to £1000 million, and another £5000 million over a period of years. Keynes' estimate was now about £2000 million. There was, however, general agreement about the impossibility of making anything more than an approximate estimate of German capacity of payment after what was assumed to be her 'recovery'. Furthermore, apart from the difficulty of deciding upon the limits of German capacity to make payment, the Allies had to settle whether they would secure what they could from Germany at once, without any consideration of the effect of their action on the German economy, or whether they would wait to take larger sums after this economy had recovered from the dis-organisation of the war and the loss of territory. The Allied needs were immediate; on the other hand, apart from reasons of humanity, they could not risk putting forward demands which might lead the Germans, in desperation, to resume fighting, or which might result in driving the German working class to accept Bolshevism. If they were to obtain reparation without severe damage to the German economy, the Allies would have to wait until Germany again had an exportable surplus; they would also, in all probability, have to assist in providing her with food and raw material. Finally there was the dilemma which was never out of the minds of the French. If Germany were kept weak and poor, she could not afford to pay reparation, while if she were allowed to regain her economic strength, she might well refuse to pay it.

Since the Commission could not agree on a total figure, this question also went back to the Supreme Council who appointed their own committee. The committee suggested a figure of £6000 millions. Lloyd George and Clemenceau appeared to accept the figure, but in fact no agreement was reached. Lloyd George now contested the estimate put forward by his own experts; in another of his familiar quick changes of view, he was afraid that, if the figure were too high, the Germans would refuse to sign the treaty. The final decision was that no total figure should be named, but that the categories of pay-ment should be stated, and a definite total sum calculated by a Repar-ation Commission within two years.[1] Lloyd George and Clemenceau

---

[1] The United States Delegation wanted to secure a time-limit for German reparation payments (and thus, indirectly, to ensure that the assessment of liability was not impossibly high). British and American experts suggested thirty years.

realised that this solution would ease matters in dealing with popular and parliamentary demands in the Allied countries. Wilson accepted this plan, and gave way on the question of including pensions in the categories of payment; he assumed that, in view of the limited German capabilities of payment, this inclusion would effect only the apportionment and not the amount of the total sum to be exacted.

The Supreme Council therefore appointed a Reparation Commission with the task, among other duties, of producing an estimate by May, 1921. They considered that, by this time, the German economy would have recovered to an extent which would allow a reasonable estimate of Germany's capacity for payment. They also laid down that by May 1, 1921, the German Government was to hand over £1000 million in gold or its equivalent (commodities, ships, securities, or otherwise), and also to deliver, on the ratification of the treaty, gold bearer bonds to the amount of £2000 million, which would bear interest after 1921. The German Government was also put under an obligation to issue another £2000 million of bonds which would bear interest at a date to be fixed by the Reparation Commission. The first obligation included as payment in kind practically the whole of the German mercantile marine and a quarter of the fishing fleet, quantities of live stock, machinery, etc., similar to the amounts removed from occupied territory, and deliveries of coal and coke to assist in reconstruction.

The two main clauses in the treaty defining German liability were thus an amplification of the Allied statement at the time of the armistice negotiations. Article 231 repeated that Germany and her Allies were responsible for all the loss and damage to the Allied and Associated Governments and their nationals 'as a consequence of the war imposed upon them by Germany and her allies', and stated that Germany accepted this responsibility. Article 232 then limited the extent of the claims which the Allies proposed to make.

M. Klotz, the French Finance Minister, opposed any escape clause. Lloyd George was willing to accept thirty years with an additional thirty years if German recovery during the first period had not been 'normal', i.e. if the assessed liabilities had not been met. In Wilson's absence House accepted this compromise. Article 234 of the Treaty allowed the Reparation Commission 'to extend the date and modify the form of payment after taking into consideration the resources and capacity of Germany,' and giving her representatives 'a just opportunity to be heard'. Wilson said later: 'We instructed [the committee] to find a definite sum. And then we got Klotz on the brain'. F.R.U.S, *Paris Peace Conference*, x, 205. For Wilson's volte-face, see P. M. Burnett, *Reparation at the Paris Peace Conference*, i, 775.

The Allied and Associated Governments recognise that the resources of Germany are not adequate, after taking into account permanent diminutions of such resources which will result from other provisions of the present Treaty, to make complete reparation for all such loss and damage. The Allied and Associated Governments, however, require, and Germany undertakes, that she will make compensation for all damage done to the civilian population of the Allied and Associated Powers and to their property during the period of the belligerency of each as an Allied or Associated Power against Germany by such aggression by land, by sea and from the air, and in general all damage as defined in Annex I hereto.

These two articles in the treaty, and especially Article 231, caused the greatest indignation in Germany, and the Allies themselves, in a curious way, forgot the reason for the wording of the so-called 'war-guilt' clause. In fact, although the Allies had good cause to hold to the moral implications of the clause, the statement of German responsibility was based upon J. F. Dulles' earlier suggestion[1] that the Allies should make a formal claim of right to recover the cost of the material loss and damage caused by German aggression, and that they should then recognise the inability of Germany to make good the whole of such loss and damage. In spite of German protests, Lloyd George and Clemenceau insisted upon the German acceptance of this affirmation of their responsibility.

President Wilson's fifth point had referred to 'a free, open-minded, and absolutely impartial adjustment of all colonial claims, based upon a strict observance of the principle that in determining all such questions of sovereignty the interests of the populations concerned must have equal weight with the equitable claims of the government whose title is to be determined'. Lloyd George had spoken earlier, on June 29 and December 20, 1917, and on January 5, 1918, in similar terms. It was clear at least that the Allies were going to discuss at the Conference the future of the German colonies. At the time of the armistice all these colonies were in Allied hands. Prince Max of Baden had told Hindenburg on October 3 that 'the initiation of a peace offer under the pressure

[1] See above, p. 551 n. 1. Similarly worded statements of responsibility were included in the treaties with Austria and Hungary without protest from these countries.

of military necessity may lead to the loss of the German colonies' as well as to territorial losses in Europe.[1] Nevertheless, the Germans did not ask at that time for any clearer definition of Point V or of the Allied intentions.

The German case was not strong. German colonisation had been an economic and political failure before 1914 largely because it had neglected 'the interests of the populations concerned'. There was no part of Africa from which the removal of German control was not welcome to the inhabitants other than the native soldiers drawn from the warrior tribes and allowed special privileges. The debates on the colonies in the Reichstag between 1912 and 1914 provided grim evidence of cruelty, exploitation, and depopulation. In south-west Africa the Hereros had been driven to a desperate rebellion, which was then suppressed with hideous savagery. The Cameroons were known throughout West Africa as the 'land of the twenty-five' – the twenty-five lashes by which even minor offences were punished. The result of German heavy-handedness was to cut down productivity. Thus the total annual production of cocoa in 1912 in the Cameroons was 4550 tons of which $\frac{6}{7}$ came from European-owned plantations. The production in the neighbouring British Gold Coast Colony was over 50,000 tons and came almost entirely from native growers. The whole of Germany's imports from her African colonies supplied less than 2 per cent of her total imports of colonial produce; the total German trade with these colonies was only one-third of 1 per cent of Germany's foreign trade. The number of German settlers was only about 10,000. Whatever the prospects for the future, therefore, it could not be argued with much cogency that the loss of her colonies was depriving Germany of an element essential to her economic life.

There had been a change for the better in German policy just before 1914; the revelations in the Reichstag of misgovernment were one reason for the change, but there could be no certainty that the new democratic government in Germany would be strong enough to insist upon more humane and more sensible methods of colonial administration; the German treatment of natives, other than their soldiers, during the war had been very harsh. For that matter there was no certainty that the new democratic government would survive. Hence, on the tests which the Allies had announced, the Germans had weak claims to the return of any of their lost colonies. Even if the German record had been less unsatisfactory, the Allies would have been unwilling to allow the

[1] See above, p. 414.

Germans back. During the war German surface raiders had destroyed about 600,000 tons of shipping. The British Admiralty did not want to let the Germans regain harbours in the Cameroons, German East or South-west Africa or Samoa from which raiders might set out in another war.[1]

The solution adopted for the future administration of the German colonies was the application of a system of trusteeships. This 'mandatory' plan had been suggested in more than one quarter. The term had been used in a memorandum drawn up by a member of the American 'Inquiry' at the end of 1917; the context was the disposition of the non-Turkish provinces of the Ottoman Empire. On his way to Europe in December, 1918, Wilson had suggested that the former German colonies and the territory to be taken from the Ottoman Empire should be handed over to the League for administration, not by any of the Great Powers, but by the smaller States. Smuts, in his pamphlet on a plan for a League of Nations, had proposed a form of trusteeship under the League for the territories formerly belonging to Russia, Austria-Hungary, and Turkey.

Smuts did not include the German colonies – the Union of South Africa wanted to secure German South-west Africa in full sovereignty[2] – but his plan was approved by Wilson. The alternative of international administration was much less satisfactory. Previous experience, though on a small scale, had shown the difficulty of fixing responsibility for acts of policy upon any of the Powers participating in such an administration. On the other hand the tragic fate of the Congo Basin under the administration of Leopold II of Belgium was a warning against leaving the holder of a trusteeship without adequate control. In the discussions over the draft of the Covenant there was practically no suggestion that Germany should receive back her colonies, but the question of mandates gave rise to great difficulties. Lloyd George was favourable to the plan. Clemenceau accepted it with some reluctance; the French were afraid that it might lead to difficulties similar to those which Germany had put in the way of France in Morocco. The strongest opposition came from the Dominions. The South African case with

[1] German writers themselves as late as July, 1918, had advocated a German Mittel-Afrika from which British trade routes in the Atlantic and Indian Oceans could be threatened. See above, pp. 236 and 403. A force from the Union had occupied S.W. Africa by July 1915. Enemy resistance in E. Africa, ably led by General von Lettow Vorbeck, was prolonged until November, 1918.

[2] Hughes claimed for Australia the German colonies in the Pacific.

regard to German South-west Africa was that the area concerned was very large – about one and a half times the size of Germany – but most of it was uninhabited; the native population was about 250,000. Since the territory adjoined that of the Union, a separate administration, with its own fiscal, native, and general economic policies, would have been wasteful and might have led to great practical difficulties. The objections of Australia and New Zealand to the application of the plan to the former German colonies south of the equator were based partly on nationalist feeling, partly on misunderstanding – the mandatory system was confused with a system of international administration – partly on a fear of the risks of interference from outside Powers in matters affecting Australasian interests.

Lloyd George, in the discussions about the drafting of the Covenant, thought that the demands of the Dominions were reasonable. The question was argued with some heat between the President, Lloyd George, Clemenceau, and the Dominion Prime Ministers. Finally a compromise was arranged, on January 31, which took account of Dominion wishes. This solution was (i) to give 'mandates' to particular Powers, (ii) to require the mandatory Power to report to the League on the exercise of its mandate, and (iii) to set up a permanent Mandatory Commission of the League to examine the reports and advise the Council on all matters connected with the mandates.

There were three classes of mandate: Class A applied to territories of the former Ottoman Empire. Here it was agreed that 'certain communities' had reached a stage of development 'where their existence as independent nations can be provisionally recognised, subject to the rendering of administrative advice by a Mandatory Power until such time as they are able to stand alone'. Class B mandates applied in particular to East and West Africa. Here the Mandatory Power was required to administer the territory under certain conditions, but nothing was said about the provisional and temporary nature of the mandate. Class C applied to territories which owing to their position or other geographical features could be best administered by the Mandatory Power as integral parts of its territory.

One of Wilson's reasons for objecting to the Australian claims was that they carried with them acquiescence in the claims of Japan. In January, 1917, Great Britain had accepted the help of Japanese destroyers as escort vessels in the Mediterranean on the condition of British support for Japanese claims to the German islands in the Pacific north of the equator and to the rights formerly exercised by the Germans in

Shantung. In return Japan promised to support British claims south of the equator. The United States navy in December, 1918, wanted to get the Marshall, Caroline, and Mariana Islands as naval bases. The Japanese prudently allowed Great Britain to go ahead in pressing the Australian claims south of the equator. Wilson ultimately gave way to these claims, and Japan obtained the northern groups of islands as Class C mandates.

There was also a dispute over the French claims to a mandate over the whole of Syria and not merely to the coastal region assigned to France under the so-called Sykes-Picot agreement.[1] Lloyd George wanted to exclude Damascus, Homs and Hamadan; Aleppo had already been promised to the Arabs. Wilson said that he was indifferent both to French and British claims, and that he was concerned only with the wishes of the inhabitants. He suggested sending an Allied Commission to Syria to report on the matter. After some delay a Commission – without British or French representation – went to the area. The Commission reported on July 10 that the population wanted either an American or a British mandate, and were opposed to a French mandate. No action was taken on the report because neither the United States nor Great Britain would accept the mandate. Lloyd George told the Supreme Council on September 15 that the British troops in Syria would be withdrawn and replaced by French troops in accordance with the Sykes–Picot agreement. He suggested that Wilson might appoint an arbitrator if the British, French, and Arabs could not agree on the boundaries between Syria, Mesopotamia, and Palestine. The French, however, seized Damascus and other areas reserved for an independent Arab State.

The Syrian Commission also reported that Moslems and Christians alike in Palestine were opposed to Jewish immigration and to Zionist plans for the country. The report suggested a greatly reduced programme of immigration and the incorporation of Palestine in a single mandate with Syria.

NOTE TO CHAPTER 37

The peace treaties with Austria, Hungary, Bulgaria, and Turkey

For obvious reasons public interest in Great Britain was concentrated during and after the Peace Conference on the treaty with Germany.

[1] See above, p. 119, n. 1.

Treaties were signed with Austria (St Germain-en-Laye, September, 1919), Hungary (Trianon, June, 1920), Bulgaria (Neuilly, November, 1919), and Turkey (Sèvres, August, 1920). The first three of these four treaties affected Great Britain only indirectly; the British people had forgotten that Austro-Hungarian intransigence had been one of the main causes of the war, and that Bulgarian war atrocities in occupied territory had been particularly bad.

Although there were no pre-armistice agreements with these smaller States, the Allies followed as far as possible Wilsonian principles in dealing with them. Thus all the treaties included the Covenant of the League; the United States signed the treaty with Bulgaria, though she had not been at war with her. The details of the treaties are outside the scope of this *History*. Some of the more important territorial questions – the western frontiers of Poland, the inclusion of the Sudetenland in Czechoslovakia had already been settled in the treaty of Versailles. The mixed character of the populations – including a number of enclaves – as well as important strategic and economic considerations made complete self-determination on ethnographical lines impracticable. For this reason the Great Powers imposed clauses in the treaties safeguarding the rights of minorities. In order to be fair to the minorities within the states accepted as allies similar safeguards were assured in special 'minority treaties' between the Great Powers and Poland, Czechoslovakia, Yugoslavia, Greece, and Roumania.

Great Britain had a more direct interest in the treaty of Sèvres with Turkey, but this treaty was never ratified by Turkey and never came into effect. The signature of the treaty was delayed because the European Allies were waiting to know whether the United States would accept a mandate for Constantinople. Meanwhile a military revolt in Turkey under the leadership of Mustapha Kemal changed the situation. Kemal refused to recognise a Greek mandate for Smyrna. The ensuing Graeco-Turkish war is again outside the scope of this *History*. After the total defeat of the Greeks, and a narrowly averted collision between the victorious Turks and a British force holding Chanak on the Asiatic side of the Dardanelles, peace was signed with Turkey at Lausanne in July, 1923.

CHAPTER 38

The German observations on the Treaty and the Allied reply

The Germans were given the terms of peace on May 7, 1919, and informed that they would be allowed fifteen days in which to submit any observations which they might wish to make. Their attitude was unlikely to encourage the Allies to offer further concessions. When they heard that there would be no discussion of the principles of the treaty, they decided at first merely to send secretaries to Versailles to receive the document and bring it to the German Government. The Allies refused this procedure. The Germans then sent a delegation. If this delegation had shewn even a dignified reserve, there might have been a revulsion of feeling, especially among the British and American delegates, in favour of a German Government and people suffering the penalties of defeat. Such a revulsion of feeling did take place at the final ceremony when the peace was signed, but it was too late to affect the terms of the treaty. On May 7, 1919, however, the Germans merely angered their enemies. Brockdorff-Rantzau, the leader of their delegation, behaved with deliberate rudeness at the formal session of the conference in which the text of the treaty was handed to him. After a short statement by Clemenceau, who, as usual, rose from his chair to speak, Brockdorff-Rantzau made or rather read a speech. He did not stand up while he was speaking or even attempt to conceal his hatred.[1] He accused the Allies of killing 'with cold deliberation' hundreds and thousands of non-combatants through the blockade since November 11,[2] and asked that a neutral commission should be appointed to consider the question of responsibility for the war.

[1] At Balfour's suggestion, the Conference had stood on the entry of the Germans. Brockdorff-Rantzau's speech was translated, sentence by sentence, first into French and then into English.

[2] This particular charge, for which Brockdorff-Rantzau produced no evidence, was especially outrageous not only in view of the negotiations which had taken place with the Germans over the supply of food, but also in regard to the fact that,

The effect of Brockdorff-Rantzau's speech was – as might have been expected – to stiffen the attitude of the Allies.[1] Their first reaction was to consider more definitely what steps they would take in the event of a German refusal to sign the treaty. Lloyd George said at a meeting of the Council of Four on May 9 that he would like consideration to be given to the forces necessary for an occupation of Berlin. He thought that there was much to be said for such a move if the Germans refused to sign the treaty. 'It would be the outward and visible sign of smashing the Junkers. They would never be convinced otherwise. He felt sure of this after hearing Brockdorff-Rantzau's speech.' Wilson said that 'the hope rested on the remainder of Germany ridding themselves of the Junkers. Apart from Brockdorff-Rantzau, the other German delegates had looked reasonable men.' Lloyd George pointed out that 'none the less they had allowed the Junker to take the lead. They could not free themselves from the sense of servitude to the Junkers.'

The Germans did not send their full reply until May 30.[2] The reply consisted of a document of 443 pages with a covering letter. While they were drawing up these documents the Germans made a number of requests to the Allies. Some of these requests were absurd. They asked, for example, that all prisoners of war detained for offences other than those against discipline should be returned at once. It was easy for the Allies to reply – quoting a specific case of the murder of two French civilians by a German prisoner – that they could not send back prisoners who had been guilty of crimes or penal offences dealt with by legally constituted authorities irrespective of the nationality of the guilty party.

The German protests against the attribution to them of responsibility for the war were also in the nature of special pleading. In a letter of May 13 the Germans claimed, first, that they were not chiefly or solely responsible for the war, and asked the Allies to produce proof of German responsibility.[3] Secondly, they argued that in any case the

---

at this very time, contrary to their engagements, the Germans were still refusing to carry out the surrender of merchant ships in Spanish ports. See also note at the end of this chapter.

[1] After hearing the speech Wilson said to Lord Riddell, 'The Germans . . . always do the wrong thing. They always did the wrong thing during the war. That is why I am here.' Riddell, *Intimate Diary of the Peace Conference*, p. 74. While Brockdorff-Rantzau was speaking, Lloyd George pressed his paper knife on the table with such vigour that it broke. Riddell, and others, *The Treaty of Versailles and After*, p. 20.

[2] They asked for, and received, an extension of the time-limit.

[3] It is remarkable that the Allies did not take this opportunity to ask the Germans to make their State archives accessible to Allied investigators.

German people could not accept responsibility for the action of their former Government. Here again the Allies gave the obvious answer. They pointed out in a reply of May 20 (i) that the Germans, at the time of the armistice, had not protested against the statement in the Allied memorandum of November 5 (submitted to them by the United States Government) that the obligation to make reparation arose out of 'Germany's aggression by land, sea, and air', and (ii) that the Germans had

> never claimed, and such a declaration would have been contrary to all principles of international law, that a modification of its political regime or a change in the governing personalities would be sufficient to extinguish an obligation already undertaken by any nation. She [Germany] did not act upon the principle she now contends for either in 1871 as regards France, after the proclamation of the republic, nor (*sic*) in 1917 in regard to Russia after the revolution which abolished the Tsarist regime.

The German answer – sent on May 24 – was unlikely to commend itself to the Allies. The Germans asserted that they had understood the memorandum of November 5 as applying only to aggression which they admitted against Belgium and Northern France.[1] They denied that the wording of this memorandum committed them to an acceptance of responsibility for the war. They admitted that a nation could not cancel by a change of government or of personnel an obligation once incurred by its government, but they claimed that the Allies had promised that 'Germany's lot would be fundamentally altered if it were severed from the fate of its rulers'. They did not wish to consider this promise merely 'as a ruse of war employed to paralyse the resistance of the German nation'. They also admitted that the term 'peace of violence' could be applied to the treaties of Frankfurt and Brest-Litovsk; they argued, however, that the Allies had already debarred themselves from using these acts of violence as a precedent for the treatment of Germany. Finally they repeated their challenge to the Allies to prove German responsibility for the war. Four days later

---

[1] Apart from the general context of the Allied statements about German responsibility, from which it was clear that the Allied Governments regarded German responsibility as applying to the war, the wording of the Allied memorandum could not bear the limited interpretation which the Germans now put on it, since (i) it referred to aggression by *sea*, as well as by land and by air, and (ii) it mentioned generally 'the civil population of the Allies' and not merely the population of Belgium and Northern France.

they presented another note in which they reported the result of an 'independent' enquiry of their own into published Allied documents.

The full German reply, like the preliminary notes, was not well-composed or even accurate. It was drawn up partly with a view to a propagandist effect, and did not lessen Allied mistrust. The Germans would have been wiser if they had concentrated on those points of the treaty upon which their case for revision was strongest. Instead they protested against every clause which was at all to their disadvantage, and abused the Allies generally for what they called a manifestation of imperialist and capitalist ideas. They complained that the Allied terms took no account of the establishment of democracy in Germany; they themselves showed no sign of understanding why the governments and peoples of the Allied countries regarded the German people with deep anger, and were unwilling without further experience to trust a German Government which had been established only under the compulsion of defeat and had as yet provided no evidence of anything more than self-pity for the calamities brought by Germany on the world. Their arguments gave the impression that they would do everything possible to evade the fulfilment of the treaty, and that the Allied lack of confidence in them was therefore justified.[1]

The Germans claimed that 'scarcely a single stipulation of the Treaty corresponded with the conditions of surrender'. They also quoted more than once statements by Wilson and other Allied leaders which had no connexion with the Fourteen Points and the terms or circumstances of the armistice. They alleged that the terms involved 'the complete annihilation of German economic life' and the reduction of the German people to a state of financial slavery. They asked for immediate admission – on the signature of an agreed Treaty of Peace – to the League of Nations, subject to negotiation ensuring that the Covenant was modified to meet their wishes. Their acceptance of the disarmament clauses in Part V of the Treaty was also conditional on their immediate entry into the League.

Lloyd George held a meeting of Dominion Prime Ministers and British Ministers in Paris on June 1-2 to consider the German reply.

---

[1] On January 18, 1919, the *New Statesman* printed an article from 'a correspondent lately in Germany'. This correspondent noted 'hardly any recognition of the crimes Germany has committed. . . . The German people as a whole do not in the least understand why they are hated. They realise the fact, only to be bewildered by it. Never having been a democratic country, they have not that sense of common responsibility for the acts of their government which with us is instinctive.'

Smuts was most critical of the treaty; his objections were mainly (i) to the military occupation of a large area of Germany for fifteen years, (ii) to the refusal to admit Germany to the League on the signature of the Treaty, (iii) to the frontiers allocated to Poland, (iv) to the internationalising of German rivers, and (v) to the omission of any definite figure of German reparation obligations.[1] The general outcome of the discussion was to authorise Lloyd George to suggest (i) a delimitation of the German-Polish frontier more favourable to Germany, with a plebiscite in doubtful cases, (ii) an earlier admission of Germany to the League, subject to the condition that she was loyally attempting to carry out her obligations, (iii) a reduction in the size of the occupying forces and in the period of occupation, and (iv) an offer to Germany to propose within three months a fixed sum for the total discharge of reparation obligations.

The Allies made considerable concessions to the Germans, notably in regard to holding a plebiscite in Upper Silesia, and – as it seemed at the time – the British proposal to allow the German Government to suggest a fixed sum in payment of reparation. The importance of these concessions was, however, lost in the extreme vehemence of the German protests, and the anger – one might say the angry surprise – with which the Allies received the German attempt to disclaim responsibility for the fact of the war and for the illegalities which they had committed during its course. The Allied reply to the German observations followed the German form of a memorandum and a covering letter. The letter stated that the Germans seemed to think that Germany had only to 'make sacrifices in order to attain peace, as if this were the end of some mere struggle for territory and power'. The Allies therefore considered it necessary to 'begin their reply by a clear statement of the judgment passed upon the war by practically the whole of civilised mankind'. They then repeated in the most serious language their judgment that Germany was responsible not only for the war but 'for the savage and inhuman manner in which it was conducted', and that 'her conduct is almost unexampled in human history'. They stated that 'justice is what the German Delegation asks for, and says that Germany had been promised. Justice is what Germany shall have. But it must be justice for all. . . . Somebody must suffer for the consequences of the war. Is it to be Germany, or only the peoples

[1] Smuts' criticisms might have had greater weight if he had not held out for the full demands of the Union of South Africa with regard to the former German South-West African territory.

she has wronged? . . . Not to do justice to all concerned would only leave the world open to fresh calamities.' If the rule of law were to be established, and the Germans and other nations 'deterred from following in the footsteps of Prussia, . . . if there is to be early reconciliation and appeasement, it will be because those responsible for concluding the war have had the courage to see that justice is not deflected for the sake of a convenient peace'. The Allies welcomed the German Revolution, but this revolution 'was stayed until the German armies had been defeated in the field, and all hope of profiting by a war of conquest had vanished. Throughout the war, as before the war, the German people and their representatives supported the war [and] obeyed every order, however savage, of their government.' They shared the responsibility for the policy of their government: they would have acclaimed its success, and could not 'now pretend, having changed their rulers after the war was lost' to escape the consequences of their actions.

The German objections in detail, after referring to the League of Nations, began with the territorial settlement. The German memorandum argued against the cession of Alsace-Lorraine without a plebiscite though the demand for this cession in Point VIII of the Fourteen Points did not contain any suggestion that a plebiscite was necessary. The Germans overlooked the fact that the Allied plan for the Saar was merely a temporary arrangement for fifteen years after which the inhabitants would be given the right of choosing their allegiance. They stated that they had no intention of forcing the union of Austria with the Reich but that they could not pledge themselves to oppose a move for union coming from the Austrians.

The strongest German objections to the territorial settlement in Europe concerned the surrender of territory to Poland. The Germans had agreed to the inclusion in an independent Polish State of 'territories inhabited by indisputably Polish populations'. They objected that the treaty did not keep to this principle, but transferred to the Polish State large parts of East and West Prussia, Pomerania, Posen, and Silesia which were not inhabited by 'indisputably Polish populations'. The rest of East Prussia was to be cut off from Germany and 'condemned to a lingering death'. The Hansa town of Danzig was to be put under Polish suzerainty. Upper Silesia had had no political connexion with Poland since 1163.[1]

[1] This statement was misleading. The Upper Silesian principalities did not become part of the Habsburg dominions until the sixteenth century. Silesia was taken from the Habsburgs by Frederick the Great in 1740-2.

The Allied reply to the Germans stated two 'principles': (i) They (the Allies) had a 'special obligation' to use their victory for the re-establishment of Polish independence which had been unjustly suppressed over a century earlier. 'The seizure of the Western provinces of Poland was one of the essential steps by which the military power of Prussia was built up . . . To undo this wrong is the first duty of the Allies.' (ii) The Allies had also proclaimed, and Germany had accepted, that the restored Poland should include those districts now inhabited by an indisputably Polish population. As far as Posen and West Prussia were concerned the application of this latter principle modified the first principle only to a small extent. At the time of the partition of Poland these areas were completely Polish, except in some towns and districts where German colonists had settled. If the Allies had 'applied the strict law of historic retribution, they would have been justified in restoring to Poland these two provinces almost in their entirety'. They had, in fact, 'deliberately waived the claim of historic right because they wished to avoid even the appearance of injustice'; they had left to Germany those districts in which there was an undisputed German predominance in immediate contiguity to German territory. It was impossible, however, to avoid leaving certain enclaves, such as Bromberg, in Poland. 'There must be some sacrifice on one side or the other.' It was also necessary to remember that German preponderance in certain districts had been established by dispossessing the original population. 'To recognise that such action should give a permanent title . . . would be to give an encouragement and premium to the grossest acts of injustice and oppression.' Nevertheless the Allies 'in order to eliminate any possible injustice' had reconsidered the question of the western frontiers of Poland and made certain modifications in detail 'with a view to bringing the frontier into closer harmony with the ethnographical division'.

The Allies pointed out that East Prussia had not been included in the political frontiers of Germany before 1866; that it was conquered territory, and that the interest of less than 2,000,000 Germans in maintaining a land connexion with Germany was much less vital than that of the whole Polish nation in securing direct access to the sea. Danzig was not being transferred to Poland, but was being restored to a status similar to that which it had possessed for many centuries before it was annexed, contrary to the wishes of its inhabitants, to the Prussian State. The Allies agreed that Poland might be said to have no legal claim to Upper Silesia; the majority of the population, however, was indisputably Polish in the area now to be ceded to Poland, and the Allies were prepared to hold a plebiscite in the area in order to test the German contention that the inhabitants did not want to be transferred to Poland. They also conceded that if, as they expected, the plebiscite went in favour of Poland, the coal of Upper Silesia should be available to the Germans for fifteen years on the same terms as to the Poles.

In their objections to the surrender of their overseas possessions the Germans argued that the Allies were acting 'in irreconcilable contradiction' to Point V of the Fourteen Points. They denied the Allied charges that German colonial rule had been harsh and unjust to native populations. They claimed that they needed colonies for economic reasons, and that their claims should have been given a hearing before any decisions had been taken. The Allies in their reply affirmed that they had given first consideration to the interests of the native populations formerly under German rule. There was sufficient evidence from German sources alone to establish German 'dereliction in the sphere of colonial civilisation'; the Allies could not take the responsibility of making 'a second experiment and . . . again abandoning thirteen or fourteen millions of natives to a fate from which the war has delivered them'. They did not consider that the loss of the colonies would hinder German 'normal economic development'. The Allies added that they also were 'compelled to safeguard their own security and the Peace of the world against a military imperialism which sought to establish bases whence it could pursue a policy of interference and intimidation against the other Powers'.

The German argument against the reparation clauses of the treaty was that the terms imposed were both contrary to the armistice agreement and unworkable. The Germans maintained that their memorandum of November 5 had admitted responsibility only for the invasion of Belgium, and therefore that they were responsible only for reparation to Belgium. The German Government was, however, willing to acknowledge responsibility for the damage done in Northern France, but not to the occupied territories of Italy, Montenegro, Serbia, and Roumania, or to Poland. The Germans then implied that their liability, thus limited in area, extended only to the destruction of property. In any case, apart from the legal argument, the Germans objected that

> the sum to be paid is to be fixed by our enemies unilaterally, and to admit of subsequent modification and increase. No limit is fixed, save the capacity of the German people for payment, determined

not by their standard of life, but solely by their capacity to meet the demands of their enemies by their labour. The German people would thus be condemned to perpetual slave labour. . . . Even in internal affairs we are to give up the right of self-determination. The International Reparation Commission receives dictatorial powers over the whole life of our people in economic and cultural matters.

The Allied reply began by a refusal to enter into a discussion of the 'principles' underlying the reparation clauses, and by quoting the memorandum of November 5. This reference was, in fact, a sufficient answer to the German legal argument in favour of a more limited area of liability. The Allies then turned to the German objection to the undefined extent of their obligations and to the functions and powers of the Reparation Commission. They pointed out that the problem of reparation was so large and complex that a 'continuing body . . . with broad powers' was necessary to deal with it. The Commission was, however, instructed by the Treaty itself to ensure an early and complete discharge of German obligations, and to take account of German economic interests. 'It is not an engine of oppression or a device for interfering with German sovereignty.' The matters at issue were 'bare questions of fact, namely the amount of the liabilities'. It was impossible to fix the liability at once, since 'the extent of damage and the cost of repair' had yet to be ascertained. The Germans had hitherto made no definite offer. The Allies were willing to accord them facilities to survey the devastated and damaged regions, and 'to make proposals thereafter within four months of the signing of the Treaty for a settlement of the claims under each of the categories of damage for which she [Germany] is liable. If within the following two months an agreement can be reached, the exact liability of Germany will have been ascertained.'

The Allies recognised that the reparation demands were severe. They came back to the argument that the German people could not throw off responsibility by a change of government, and that Germany must undertake to make reparation to the very uttermost of her power, 'for reparation for wrongs inflicted is of the essence of justice'.

Finally, the Germans objected to the Allied occupation as a guarantee for the fulfilment of the Treaty. They argued that no further security was necessary against possible German aggression; Germany was now too weak to be a menace to any Power. The occupation could not be a guarantee of the fulfilment of German reparation obligations, since it would in fact render such fulfilment 'either most difficult or absolutely impossible'. Germany had now become a democracy and a republic, and, as such, deserving of confidence, and with a right to a place in the League of Nations. German membership of the League 'would in itself alone constitute the most inviolable guarantee for the good faith of every German Government'. The Germans then made a general appeal, 'in the very moment of founding a new commonwealth, based upon liberty and labour', with a view to Labour and Socialist sympathies elsewhere. 'The working people of Germany have always desired peace and justice . . . Only a return to the immutable principles of morality and civilisation, to the sanctity of treaties, would render it possible for mankind to continue to exist.'

The Allies took up this last sentence in their reply. They answered it shortly. 'After four and a half years of war which was caused by the repudiation of those principles by Germany, the Allied and Associated Powers can only repeat the words pronounced by President Wilson on September 27, 1918: "The reason why peace must be guaranteed is that there will be parties to the Peace whose promises have proved untrustworthy." ' The Allies agreed, however, to a declaration that, if before the end of fifteen years Germany had shown goodwill and had provided satisfactory guarantees with regard to the fulfilment of her obligations, the occupation of the Rhineland might be shortened. Similarly, German admission to the League might come sooner.

The Allied reply was given to the Germans on June 16. They were told that they must accept or reject the terms, as modified, within a week. Lloyd George, who continued to be afraid that the Germans might refuse their signature, had been more inclined than his colleagues to make concessions. Clemenceau did not believe in the possibility of serious German resistance. Wilson took the view that, unless the Allies were convinced by the Germans of the injustice or impracticability of any of their decisions, they should not change them merely because the terms were hard.

The offer of a plebiscite in Upper Silesia had some effect on opinion in Germany, but the German Government fell, and Brockdorff-Rantzau was replaced by Hermann Müller as Foreign Secretary on June 22. The Germans offered to sign if the Allies would not insist on Article 231 and on the Articles (227–230) which provided for the surrender of the Kaiser and of other war criminals. The Allies rejected both demands, and the Germans gave way shortly before the expiry of the time-limit. The treaty was signed, as the world knows, in the great Galerie des Glaces at Versailles on June 28. The German delegates appeared, signed, and disappeared. They showed nothing of the truculent rudeness of Brockdorff-Rantzau, yet no one present at the ceremony of signature could regard the conclusion of peace as a step towards European reconciliation.[1]

NOTE TO CHAPTER 38

The maintenance of the blockade of Germany after the armistice

One of the most widespread themes of German propaganda against the Allies after the armistice was that they deliberately maintained the naval blockade at the expense of starving German women and children. The facts are as follows: (1) The blockade was maintained after the armistice for the obvious military reason that the Allies could not allow the Germans to stock up with provisions in order to enable them to refuse to sign the treaty of peace, to denounce the armistice, and to recommence hostilities.

(2) In November, 1918, the Allies were faced with a serious shortage of shipping (owing to German submarine attacks) for all purposes, including the supply of food for their own peoples and those of Central Europe where the situation was in many areas worse than in Germany. The German mercantile marine in home or neutral ports amounted to about three million tons. The Allies would have been wise to have included in the original armistice a demand for the temporary surrender of this shipping, without prejudice to its ultimate disposition.

(3) In the renewal of the armistice on December 13 an agreement was reached that the Germans would place their merchant marine at the disposal of the Allies for the duration of the armistice, with compensation for its use, in order to facilitate the provisioning of Germany and Europe generally.

(4) After a further renewal of the armistice on January 10 the Allies promised a first instalment of 270,000 tons of food if the ships were

---

[1] Sir William Orpen painted an 'official' picture of the statesmen and generals in the Galerie des Glaces at the signing of the treaty. Within a year he painted another picture of the Galerie des Glaces. This picture had neither statesmen nor generals; only, in an otherwise empty hall, a draped catafalque guarded by the wraiths of two soldiers from the trenches. The second picture was inscribed: 'To the Unknown British Soldier in France.'

handed over. The Germans then refused to surrender the ships without a definite guarantee that the food would be delivered. Further delays took place over the terms of payment for the food; the French would not agree to let Germany pay in gold which would otherwise have been available for German reparation. On March 8 Lloyd George argued strongly against further delay. Six days later an agreement was reached. The blockade was then relaxed, and the import of 370,000 tons of food a month from overseas was permitted (the import overland of food from the Scandinavian countries and the Netherlands had not been interfered with). With the German ratification of the treaty the blockade was entirely removed on July 12, 1919, and no restriction remained on German food imports.

CHAPTER 39

The attitude of British opinion to the Treaty of Versailles

The Treaty of Versailles was first debated in the House of Commons on July 3, 1919. Lloyd George described the terms as 'in many respects terrible terms to impose upon a country', but justifiable owing to the acts of Germany in planning, preparing for, and provoking the war. He dealt with the main headings of the treaty, and also with the criticism that, while its clauses were 'individually . . . quite fair', the 'cumulative effect' was too severe. The House did not raise many objections to the treaty. The Leader of the Labour Party disapproved of some of the territorial changes; he regretted the postponement of the admission of Germany to the League, the absence of a general abolition of conscription, and of sufficient provision for disarmament. At a second debate, on July 21, there was again little substantial criticism, though a few members made 'extreme' speeches for or against the terms. Nevertheless, from the time of the first German protests British opinion began to move against the treaty, and, in spite of occasional sharp criticism of German evasions and of the more preposterous German complaints (such as fastening the responsibility for the collapse of the mark upon the Allies), intellectual opinion in Great Britain became, one might say, ashamed of the treaty as unjust and as missing an immense opportunity for a peace of reconciliation.

There was no single reason for this rapid change. It can be understood, perhaps, fundamentally as part of a more general reaction from the nervous strain of the war. The reaction shewed itself in a widespread mood of disillusion and even of cynicism. For a time people turned away from the grim and exhausting emotions of the war, and were willing out of sheer weariness to repudiate the moral indignation which they had genuinely felt against their enemies. Furthermore, the British people had as little understanding of what might be called a 'post-war situation' and, more directly, the difficulties of making peace, as they had had, before 1914, of the experience of a great European war. They had lost all memory of the political confusion, the stubborn conflicts of national interests and ambitions, the missed opportunities which had characterised the peace settlement after the fall of Napoleon. They expected the reconstruction of Europe to be rapid and comparatively easy; they wanted a return to normality. In a sense they were embarrassed by the four years of fighting as a period of collective madness. When their hopes of an easy return to pre-war conditions were disappointed, they looked for an explanation, and found it too easily, not in the inevitable complications and shortcomings of human politics, but in a lack of imagination and statesmanship in their leaders responsible for the treaty of peace.

Somewhat ironically President Wilson must take a good deal of the blame for the discredit with which he and his European collaborators were soon regarded. At the end of October, 1918, he had told House that there could be no real difficulty about the peace terms, 'if the Entente statesmen will be perfectly frank with us and have no selfish aims of their own which would in any case alienate us from them altogether'. On his voyage across the Atlantic Wilson said to the experts who were travelling with him that 'Americans will be the only disinterested people at the Peace Conference', and that 'the men with whom we are about to deal do not represent their own people'. There was, in fact, very real difficulty in a solution of problems such as the promised outlet to the sea for Poland, or the viability of the Czecho-slovak State with its large number of German-speaking citizens. American disinterestedness very soon reached its limits when it came to a generous settlement of inter-governmental debts, and at the end, whoever represented the views of the electorate in his own country, Wilson could hardly claim to do so. Wilson indeed was extraordinarily insensitive to public feeling in Great Britain and France. At a dinner in his honour at Buckingham Palace he did not refer to the part played by Great Britain in the war.[1] He refused a French invitation to make

[1] Lloyd George suggested that Lord Reading, with whom Wilson was on sufficiently friendly terms, should give the President a hint that he might make good his omission at a later speech in the Guildhall. Reading gave the hint, but Wilson's Guildhall speech contained only a perfunctory reference to the Allies. Wilson was not alone among the American representatives in what Lloyd George called his 'pervasive suspiciousness'. Lansing wrote to General Bliss, in December, 1918, that the American delegation was 'face to face with jealousies which have drawn the map of Europe in the past, and will be attempted again'. House had told Wilson that, if he appealed to the Liberals and labouring classes in Europe, 'he might possibly overthrow the governments in Great Britain, France, and Italy', though House thought that the responsibility for such action was too great for any man to take.

a tour of the devastated areas. He visited Rheims and Chateau-Thierry, but told a Swiss friend that the French had pestered (tourmenté) him about their devastated regions.

Wilson's somewhat contemptuous attitude towards the European statesmen with whom he had to work tended to lower their standing with their fellow-countrymen, and turned, ultimately, to his own discredit. The President soon found conditions in Europe more complicated than he had supposed and much less amenable to clear-cut solutions based upon large, high-sounding principles. It was not easy, however, for him to convince his idealist supporters that he was neither being tricked by Europeans nor giving way to them out of weakness. Lloyd George and Clemenceau in fact were less rigid than Wilson. Lloyd George was quicker to suggest concessions to the Germans: Clemenceau, in spite of his intransigence, accepted his failure to obtain what his military advisers regarded as necessary for the future security of France.[1]

In addition to depreciating the moral position of his colleagues, Wilson's attitude of superiority gave public opinion a misleading view that the decisions of the 'Big Four' were taken, if not *ex nihilo*, on the basis of certain principles in which considerations of selfish interests were the main factors. In fact every question had been studied by experts; many of the decisions merely registered the conclusions reached in this study, but the 'Big Four' had also to reckon with political facts – the actual situation in Europe – and often to make a compromise between conflicting demands. In some subjects the experts failed them. This was especially the case in regard to estimates of German capacity to pay reparation. The British experts themselves, though the business men and bankers were less guarded than the

[1] It can be argued that Wilson made a mistake in coming to Paris. House, Lansing, and the British and French Ministers considered that he would have been wiser not to have taken a personal part in the Conference. Smuts, on the other hand, thought him right in coming. Wilson would have done better to have included Senators Taft or Root in the American Delegation; Henry White, the only Republican delegate, carried little authority in his own party. Wilson in Paris did not use White as a liaison with the Republican party leaders. Even the Democratic members of the Delegation did not have his full confidence; he did not trust Lansing, and saw General Bliss only five times. Wilson's greatest mistake had been an appeal before the American Congressional elections to the electorate to return only Democratic candidates. This appeal angered the Republicans who had supported his peace programme. The elections gave the Republicans a small majority.

economists, admitted that they were working in a field upon which neither they nor anyone else could offer firm conclusions.

It is, however, fair to remember that the clauses in the treaty dealing with reparation were expressly subject to revision, within large limits, by a special body set up for the purpose. The establishment of the Reparation Commission, and the refusal to fix at once a total figure of German liabilities were – as events turned out – not as unfavourable to the Germans as they alleged them to be. The fact that Lloyd George was hampered by his election speeches and Clemenceau even more hampered by French opinion made little difference in the matter. Lloyd George indeed slipped away from his commitments to the electorate. Clemenceau prudently asserted that he knew nothing of financial affairs, and left the discussion of figures to his subordinates. At this stage neither Prime Minister could have changed the tide of public opinion. As the victors turned to the vast and difficult problems of reconstruction, and of meeting their own huge financial obligations, they would certainly look to Germany to pay reparation to the uttermost limit of her capacity. They would also exaggerate this capacity. The Allied decisions, though they too exaggerated the possibility of obtaining adequate payment, at least allowed for a revision of their estimates when public opinion had become more realist or, one might say, more disillusioned about the facts. It would have been impossible to have gone far beyond public opinion in acknowledging that the 'force of things' would enable Germany to elude a burden which, on moral grounds, the Allied peoples felt that she should bear.[1]

What should be said of the charge that, whereas nearly every one of the clauses, territorial or economic, involving the Germans in some loss of burden, could be justified in itself, their cumulative effect was far too severe, and that the treaty showed no sense of magnanimity? The critics of the treaty on this score do not suggest where the conces-

[1] On November 16, 1918, less than a week after the armistice, the *New Statesman* had commented that some of the terms in the armistice might have been more severe if the Allies had drafted them only a week later. The paper added that 'the new Germany must in various ways bear the burden of the old'. Even without penal indemnities 'the bill for the actual damage done by the Germans on land and sea to non-combatants will probably take more than a generation to pay. And if other nations did not insist that this bill should be paid by the German people, there would be in that no magnanimity; there would be only gross injustice to Belgium and France. For the bill for restoration has got to be paid by some one.' Six months later, on May 10, 1919, the *New Statesman* thought it 'impossible to approve the wisdom of a scheme which proposes to make [Germany] pay tribute for such a period as thirty years'.

sions should have been made or at whose expense magnanimity should have been exercised.[1] One possibility existed; the United States had suffered far less from the war than any of the European belligerents. An American offer to cancel the debts owed to the United States by these Powers might well have changed their demands on Germany. Wilson did not make such an offer, and could not have made it.

Two other general considerations are worth notice. The attitude of the Allies towards the punishment of war criminals was not just a surrender to mass hatred and vindictiveness. Such hatred existed, and was inevitable after more than four years of savage fighting. Inevitably again this hatred was directed against the ex-Emperor; his own exhibitionism, as well as his constitutional position had drawn attention to his responsibility as the 'All-Highest War Lord' – the title in English had an air both satanic and ridiculous – for all that had been done in his name.[2] The views of the Allied governments, however, marked a real

[1] Magnanimity indeed is rarely found in decisions reached at large international meetings on matters affecting the vital interests of the states concerned. Such decisions, historically, have almost always conformed more to the French saying 'les nations n'ont pas de cousins'.

[2] The question of trying the Kaiser was first suggested, on the British side, according to Lloyd George, by Lord Curzon who seems to have been impressed by Clemenceau's advocacy of the proposal. Curzon brought the matter before the War Cabinet. The latter asked the Law Officers of the Crown to consider charging the Kaiser (and possibly the Crown Prince) with 'the crime against humanity of causing the war' and with offences against international law during the war. On November 28, 1918, Sir F. E. Smith, Attorney-General, reported to the War Cabinet in favour of proceeding against the Kaiser either by a political act such as the Allies had employed against Napoleon, or by trial, not on the wide question of responsibility for the war, but on the count of breaches of international law. In their reply to the German objections to the treaty, the Allies stated that 'the public arraignment under Article 227 framed against the German ex-Emperor has not a juridical character as regards its substance but only in its form. The ex-Emperor is arraigned as a matter of high international policy, as the minimum of what is demanded for a supreme offence against international morality, the sanctity of treaties, and the essential rules of justice. The Allied and Associated Powers have desired that judicial forms, a judicial procedure, and a regularly constituted tribunal should be set up in order to assure to the accused full rights and liberties in regard to his defence, and in order that the judgment should be of the most solemn character.' The Emperor's responsibility was indeed not light, though it rested more upon fundamental flaws of character than upon positive evil intentions. Since the Dutch Government refused to hand over the ex-Emperor for trial, the feasibility of the proposed Allied procedure was never put to the test.

The Allies were on stronger ground in insisting (Article 228) to try in their own tribunals Germans accused of atrocities in the course of the war. The Germans successfully evaded this clause. They brought twelve alleged war criminals before

change in the attitude of civilised societies towards war. 'Responsibility' for war was assessed for the first time in terms of punishable guilt. The Allied reply to the Germans shews the change of opinion: the Allies

> regard this war as a crime deliberately plotted against the life and liberties of the peoples of Europe. They therefore regard the punishment of those responsible for bringing these calamities on the human race as essential on the score of justice. They think it not less necessary as a deterrent to others who, at some later date, may be tempted to follow their example. The present Treaty is intended to mark a departure from the traditions and practices of earlier settlements which have been singularly inadequate in preventing the renewal of war ... The trial and punishment of those proved most responsible for the crimes and inhuman acts committed in connexion with a war of aggression is inseparable from the establishment of that reign of law among nations which it was the agreed object of that peace to set up.

In the second place those who, like Smuts, regarded the treaty with misgiving because it seemed to offer stern justice without at the same time providing measures of appeasement always had in mind that the League of Nations would offer a general opportunity of revision. The difficulty, however, was that no revision was likely until Germany's enemies in the war were convinced that she intended to fulfil the treaty as a whole and that they had no reason to be afraid of her. The German attitude towards the treaty, and the extent and violence of German propaganda against it were wholly unfavourable to the growth of confidence. Smuts, himself, in a remarkable statement issued on June 29, 1919, warned the Germans that they must 'convince our peoples of their good faith, of their complete sincerity through a real honest effort to fulfil their obligations'. The German failure to produce any conviction other than that they intended to disavow and undo the treaty was, perhaps, a reaction which might have been expected, but the responsibility for the consequences does not lie wholly with the Allied statesmen.

Nevertheless, in spite of a total failure to comprehend why the Allied nations felt such indignation against Germany, and such deep sus-

---

the German Supreme Court at Leipzig, where the accused were either acquitted or given light sentences. An Allied juridical commission of enquiry recommended that other accused men should be handed over for trial in accordance with the treaty, but, wisely or unwisely, no steps were taken to enforce the demand.

picion and fear of a renewal of her aggression, the clamorous and efficiently organised self-pity of German propaganda had a very considerable effect in Great Britain. German views reached Great Britain more easily than French views. In spite of the pre-war Entente and war-time Anglo-French collaboration, there was far less contact between French and English than between Germans and English. The French took little trouble to influence British public opinion; the Germans used every means of impressing the English with their grievances. Moreover they had unexpected support from a powerful quarter in England. J. M. Keynes' two books, *The Economic Consequences of the Peace*, and *The Revision of the Treaty*, accepted and even exaggerated the German case. The first of these two books appeared in the autumn of 1919, at a time of general malaise and disappointment. The book was brilliantly written, and the writer's over-confidence, and indeed arrogance, were noticed less than the savagery of his attacks. Keynes was one of the most remarkable younger economists in England. He had attended the Peace Conference not as an independent expert, but as the representative of the Chancellor of the Exchequer. He was more familiar than any of the leading statesmen with the economic problems involved in German reparation. His argument, in the simplest terms, was (i) that the claims against Germany were too high for payment, (ii) that an attempt to enforce payment might well ruin Europe, (iii) that the claims were themselves based on an exaggerated estimate of the damage, and (iv) that the inclusion of pensions and allowances was a breach of the terms under which Germany had surrendered. It is possible to argue against every one of these points.[1] Keynes not only gave an impression – to a public not yet accustomed to the fallibility of economic forecasts – that his case was unanswerable; he attacked Wilson, Lloyd George, and Clemenceau for incompetence and dishonesty because they did not take his advice. He also extended his condemnation from the economic to the political clauses of the treaty. Here he was writing outside his competence, and, by a not unfamiliar paradox, carried opinion because his caricatures were more titillating and amusing than the facts. Keynes used Wilson's attitude of superiority first to destroy Lloyd George and Clemenceau, and then to ridicule Wilson himself. Wilson had given the impression

[1] No detailed examination of Keynes' economic arguments was made in English by a trained economist until the Second World War. M. Etienne Mantoux's book *The Carthaginian Peace* was written in the United States between 1941 and 1943, and published after his death in 1945.

that he alone was capable of keeping the treaty settlement on the right lines and resisting the selfishness and shortsightedness of the Europeans. Keynes argued that Wilson was a mere ranter who had given way, through ignorance and incompetence, to Clemenceau and Lloyd George. Wilson had been right in his suspicions, but had done nothing to support them.

Keynes' first book thus set a fashion which his second book continued. The treaty of Versailles, like the monarchy of July in France, became an object of contempt as well of dishonour. From a psychological point of view it is remarkable that Keynes should not have realised that his slapdash methods and cocksureness were defeating his purpose. Keynes hoped that the League of Nations would secure the revision of the Treaty of Versailles, and also that the United States would assist in saving Europe from collapse by agreeing to a general cancellation of inter-Allied war debts and by a large loan. At the time when Keynes was writing his book, and at the date of publication, it was clear that Wilson alone could obtain American acceptance of the first condition of treaty revision, that is to say, the participation of the United States in the League. Wilson was already fighting a very difficult battle for such participation. Keynes not only did his best to discredit Wilson himself, but to show that he – and with him the people of the United States – had been 'bamboozled' (this was Keynes' word) into accepting a treaty which was dishonourable and unworkable.

The American edition of Keynes' book appeared in January, 1920. It had a very large sale; on February 10 Senator Borah read long extracts from it in the Senate and commented, in the light of Keynes' accusations, that the plenipotentiaries at Versailles had 'lightly wrecked the economic system of an entire continent and reduced to starvation millions of people and perhaps prevented the world peace from coming at all ... The Treaty in its consequences is a crime born of blind revenge and insatiable greed.' The treaty was rejected, and Keynes' description of the European governments as all equally immoral remained year after year to reinforce American isolationism and distrust.

It is possible to push a step further the historical analysis of Keynes' motives. His real target was Lloyd George; his anger against Lloyd George went back before the Peace Conference to the general election in which Lloyd George's adroit vindictiveness, as Keynes would have put it, completed the political shipwreck of the 'dissident' Liberals. The attack on Wilson – though it was the most unfair and, in its consequences, the most harmful part of Keynes' book[1] – was incidental to the indictment of Lloyd George; Wilson had his own experts, but Keynes was, after all, attached to the British Delegation, and the rejection of his advice by Lloyd George filled the cup of his wrath. Keynes, though he wrote later about his duty to destroy the idols of the marketplace, was in fact taking a popular side. The reaction to Lloyd George's Government had begun before the end of the Peace Conference and, rightly or wrongly, became increasingly bitter. The opposition was also increasingly personal; Lloyd George himself dominated his Government, and was open to attack from enemies outside the two wings of his coalition. As his own personal credit fell, so also did esteem fall for his work, and criticism of the Peace Treaty became as much a target as criticism of the Irish policy of his Government, or of his failure to fulfil his promises of domestic betterment.

The Germans on their side did all they could to exploit the Allied sense of guilt about the treaty. Their main objective was to destroy the basis of the Allied case by demonstrating that Germany and her Allies were not responsible for the war. Here again, circumstances worked in their favour. Wilson's sweeping condemnation of pre-war diplomacy and international relations in Europe had covered the Allies as well as the Germans. Wilson himself had refused at first to discriminate between the Allies and the Central Powers in the matter of responsibility. He took the view later that the responsibility for the actual outbreak of war lay with Germany, but his Fourteen Points, with their emphasis on open diplomacy, and open agreements, and their implied criticism of pre-war methods and aims, did not fit the thesis that the German responsibility was total. The publication of the secret treaties by the Bolshevists, and the whole Bolshevist attack on imperialism helped the German case that the responsibility for the war was shared more or less equally by all the Great Powers. It was therefore

[1] Twelve years later Keynes himself did not appear to have felt any regret or uneasiness about the effect of his book. In a paper – written for a private audience, probably in the summer of 1931 or 1932, but published later at his expressed wish by his executors – Keynes describes how he read the manuscript of his chapter on Wilson to Dr Melchior (a German banker who had resigned political office rather than be a party to the treaty) and to a German-American banker Paul Warburg. Keynes noted that 'Warburg, for personal reasons, hated the President and felt a chuckling delight at his discomfiture; he laughed and giggled and thought "it an awfully good hit".' Melchior took a different view. *Two Memoirs*, J. M. Keynes, 1949, pp. 70–1. Even if the rejection of the treaty by the United States Senate was practically certain before the appearance of Keynes' book, there can be no doubt about the effect of the book on American opinion for the next two decades.

easy to influence opinion among the Allies by general talk about an international anarchy in which Germany was as much a victim as a criminal. The establishment of a League of Nations seemed of itself evidence that something had been badly wrong with the conduct of international affairs before the war. A good many of the academic supporters of the League talked in terms outside their own knowledge of matters such as the 'balance of power' without understanding the meaning of the term, or realising that the League itself was another attempt to secure the kind of international relationship – an equilibrium of satisfied States, each with an interest in maintaining the general peace – which had been envisaged a century earlier in the Treaty of Vienna after the defeat of Napoleon, and over two and a half centuries earlier in the Treaty of Westphalia.

One may accept at least in part the view that no one Power can take the whole blame for the collapse of the imperfect system of international relations existing before 1914: at the same time one may hold that Germany and Austria-Hungary share the greater responsibility for the outbreak of war. Such a view would have justified the Allies in requiring the payment of reparation; Germany was not required to pay an indemnity. The Allies in this matter were curiously indifferent to the defence of their own good name. The Germans had asked for an impartial investigation into the charges of war-guilt. The Allies thus had an opportunity (though they might well have taken the initiative themselves) to demand access to the German archives and to open their own documents to study. The Allies were so confident of the rightness of their cause that they did not take this opportunity. The Germans on the other hand began as early as 1919 to produce a collection of documents which they hoped would clear their people of responsibility for the war. The first collection of this kind was made by Karl Kautsky, a socialist journalist, and one collaborator. Their work was incomplete; they spent only six months on it. After some hesitation – they were not quite sure whether the results would be sufficiently favourable – the German Government brought in two more collaborators. They added very little to Kautsky's work, and published in 1919 four volumes on the 'Outbreak of the War'. The German Government then decided upon a much larger plan – a publication reaching back to 1871. This collection extended ultimately to fifty volumes of which the first was published in 1922. It is typical of the change in general opinion and the lack of critical attention to recent history in Great Britain after (as before) 1919 that these volumes were accepted at their face value in Great Britain and in the United States, and that a corresponding series of British documents did not begin to appear until 1926. Even before the publication of their documents, the Germans had begun to issue a mass of apologetic literature in which it was often impossible for anyone without expert knowledge to detect misinterpretation and even falsehood.[1] The average opinion in Great Britain was indeed not concerned with a *post mortem* enquiry into pre-war policy, but the lack of adequate replies to the spate of German propagandist literature on the subject added to the general impression that the Versailles Treaty was based on a totally unjustified view of German responsibility. Thus by 1925, the legend of the infamous treaty of Versailles had not only taken shape, but was accepted without question by large sections of conservative as well as progressive opinion in Great Britain. The legend was believed more easily because, in the average British view, the greatest obstacles to European peace and recovery came not from Germany, but from France, and from the so-called client states of France in central and eastern Europe. On April 4, 1925, the *New Statesman* wrote that the German case with regard to the Polish Corridor and the industrial towns of Upper Silesia was 'overwhelming in all save Polish eyes. . . . the problem which deserves attention is not whether Germany is entitled to recover these territories, for that is a *chose jugée* amongst the informed public of western Europe, but the question of [*sic*] how she is to recover them without precipitating a new war which neither she nor anyone else desires'.[2] In the same article the paper denied that Czechoslovakia had anything to fear from Germany, or that Great Britain ought to undertake any obligations east of the Rhine. So far

[1] The late Professor R. W. Seton-Watson has pointed out the turns taken by the Germans in their efforts to find a scapegoat. They first put the blame on Grey. When their attacks on Grey proved merely absurd, they shifted the responsibility to Poincaré and Isvolsky. The evidence did not sustain this 'second choice', so the German apologists next based their case on the Russian mobilisation order. Again the evidence shewed that this order was not the immediate cause of the outbreak of war. The Germans then found that the 'guilt' lay with the Serbian Government. When it was clear that this charge was not valid, the Germans began to put the responsibility on Austria-Hungary.

[2] This article followed an earlier article by a correspondent on the Polish question. The correspondent, with some naïveté, said that he had stayed with 'a German baron', from whom he seems to have drawn his information. On March 14, 1925, the *New Statesman* declared that 'it is absurd to imagine France being dragged into a conflict with Germany, and dragging England with her to determine the colour of letter boxes in Danzig; it is so absurd that, in fact, it could never happen'.

did this confidence in Germany and distrust of France go that at this time – in the spring of 1925 – the *New Statesman*[1] attacked the 'nebulous futility' of Austen Chamberlain's view that the future stability of Europe depended on the closest Anglo-French co-operation. Chamberlain had said that British as well as French security depended upon restricting the 'effective military frontier' of Germany to the right bank of the Rhine. The *New Statesman* commented that the idea of a war with Germany was as grotesque as that of a war with France, but that 'if it were necessary for us to be afraid of the armaments of any foreign Power it would naturally be of the aeroplanes and submarines of France, not of Germany'.

This view did not mean that the *New Statesman* had in fact accepted the German thesis about responsibility for the war. In an article on the subject[2] – *à propos* of the German attempt to raise the question before Locarno – the paper still held that Germany had the major share – 75 per cent – of responsibility, but the whole question now seemed irrelevant. At the end of 1926[3] the *New Statesman* thought that any attempt to continue the 'supervision' of Germany was also irrelevant. Germany could in fact do as she pleased.

> We all know that Germany can . . . go a very long way . . . in repudiating the restrictive conditions imposed upon her by the Treaty of Versailles without running the slightest risk of recreating a militant European coalition against her. She can be fairly sure of the support of Signor Mussolini in almost any rational policy she chooses to pursue; and she can be absolutely sure that she will not encounter the active hostility of Great Britain or America by any policy which falls short of definite territorial aggression. If she should choose explicitly to repudiate . . . every form of supervision, and all the disarmament clauses of the treaty, she could probably do so with almost complete impunity.

The war was over and done with. 'We have no longer any feelings either of hatred or of fear in regard to Germany.' French armaments indeed were more of a concern to us. From our point of view there was no reason why Germany should not have as many aeroplanes as France. 'There is certainly not going to be another European war in this generation at least.' If there should be such a war, who could say whether we should be the enemy or the ally of the Germans?

If these views, which represented a good deal of Conservative as

---

[1] March 7, 1925.   [2] October 3, 1925.   [3] December 11, 1926.

well as Liberal and Labour opinion in England, are set against the views of important groups in Germany during the year of the Weimar Republic, it is not difficult to understand the ease with which soldiers like von Seeckt, with the connivance of the civilian authorities, laid the foundations of German rearmament, and the long period of British indifference – one might almost say, deliberate blindness – to the danger until too late.[1] A French comment that the Treaty of Versailles was 'too mild for the severity of its contents' is perhaps the best general verdict on it.

[1] It is a curious and forgotten fact that, as early as September, 1914 – after the battle of the Marne – an American newspaper quoted a high German diplomatic authority as saying that, if the world hoped for disarmament after the war, the 'crushing of Germany' would be 'the poorest way to accomplish it'. A 'crushed Germany', would 'repeat the era after the Prussian defeat by Napoleon', and would 'arm every man, child, cat, and dog in the Empire for the day of revenge'.

In this same context one might notice the last two chapters – 'The Army in the Future' and 'Still Ready for War' – of General H. von Freytag–Loringhoven's *Deductions from the World War*, a widely read book written when the German military leaders still expected victory.

For a fuller treatment of the change in British opinion with regard to the Treaty, see R. B. McCallum, *Public Opinion and the Lost Peace*, 1944.

Maps

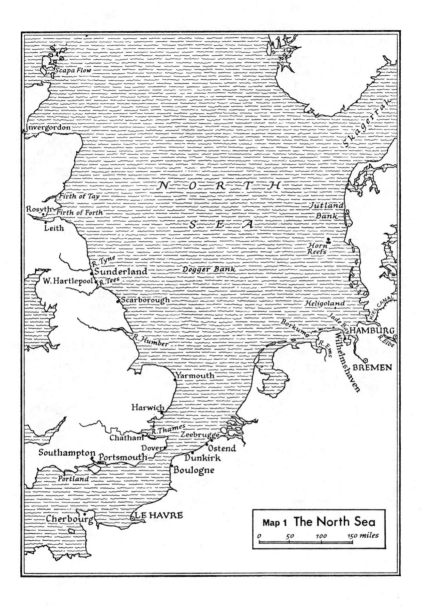

Scapa Flow

Invergordon

N O R T H

Firth of Tay
Rosyth — Firth of Forth
Leith

Jutland
Bank

S E A

Horn
Reefs

R. Tyne
Sunderland
W. Hartlepool R. Tees

Dogger Bank

Heligoland

KIEL CANAL

Scarborough

Borkum

Jade R.

HAMBURG

R. Ems

Wilhelmshaven

R. Elbe

R. Humber

BREMEN

Yarmouth

Harwich

R. Thames

Chatham

Zeebrugge

Dover

Ostend

Southampton   Portsmouth

Dunkirk

Boulogne

Portland

Cherbourg   LE HAVRE

Skagerrak

Map 1 The North Sea

0   50   100   150 miles

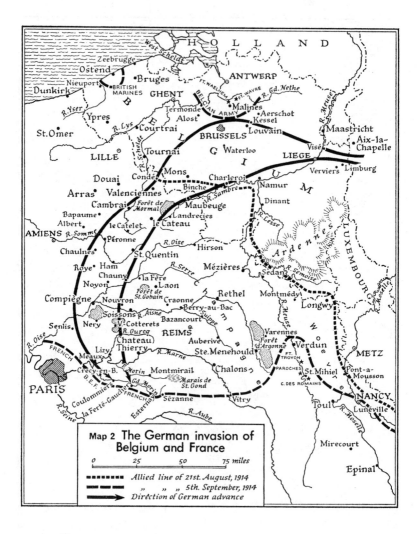

Map 2 The German invasion of
Belgium and France

0   25   50   75 miles

-------- Allied line of 21st. August, 1914
— — —   "   "   "   5th. September, 1914
——➤   Direction of German advance

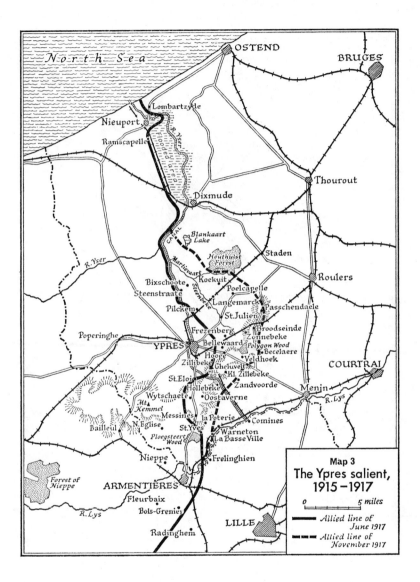

North Sea

OSTEND
BRUGES
Lombartzyde
Nieuport
Ramscapelle
R. Yser
flooded area
Thourout
Dixmude
CANAL
Blankaart Lake
R. Yser
Houthulst Forest
Staden
Martevaart
Bixschoote
Koekuit
Poelcapelle
Roulers
Steenstraate
Steenbeke
Langemarck
Pilckem
St.Julien
Passchendaele
Poperinghe
Frezenberg
Broodseinde
Zonnebeke
YPRES
Bellewaard
Polygon Wood
Hooge
Becelaere
Zillebeke
Gheluvelt
Veldhoek
St.Eloi
Hollebeke
Kl.Zillebeke
COURTRAI
Wytschaete
Oostaverne
Zandvoorde
Mt. Kemmel
Messines
Menin
R. Lys
Bailleul
N.Eglise
la Poterie
Comines
St.Yves
Warneton
Ploegsteert Wood
La Basse Ville
Nieppe
Frølinghien
Forest of Nieppe
ARMENTIÈRES
Fleurbaix
Bois-Grenier
R. Lys
LILLE
Radinghem

Map 3
The Ypres salient,
1915–1917

0   5 *miles*

⎯⎯⎯ *Allied line of June 1917*

– – – *Allied line of November 1917*

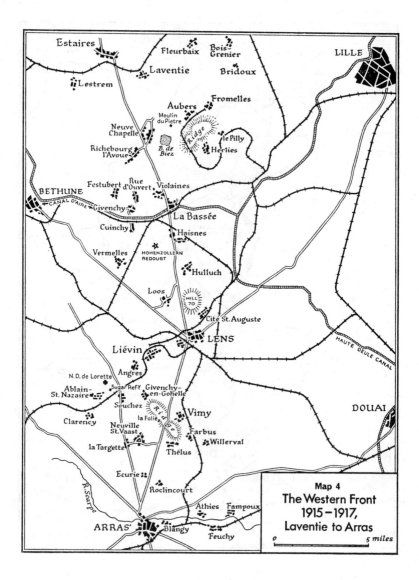

Estaires

Fleurbaix

Bois-Grenier

LILLE

Lestrem

Laventie

Bridoux

Fromelles

Aubers

Moulin du Pietre

Ridge

le Pilly

Neuve Chapelle

Richebourg l'Avoue

B. de Biez

Herlies

Festubert

Rue d'Ouvert

Violaines

BETHUNE

CANAL D'AIRE

Givenchy

La Bassée

Cuinchy

Haisnes

Vermelles

HOHENZOLLERN REDOUBT

Hulluch

Loos

HILL 70

Cité St. Auguste

HAUTE DEULE CANAL

LENS

Liévin

N.D. de Lorette

Angres

Ablain-St. Nazaire

Sugar Ref.y

Givenchy-en-Gohelle

DOUAI

Souchez

la Folie

Vimy

R.d.e

Clarency

Neuville St. Vaast

Farbus

Willerval

la Targette

Thélus

Ecurie

Roclincourt

R. Scarpe

Athies

Fampoux

ARRAS

Blangy

Feuchy

Map 4
The Western Front
1915–1917,
Laventie to Arras

0   5 miles

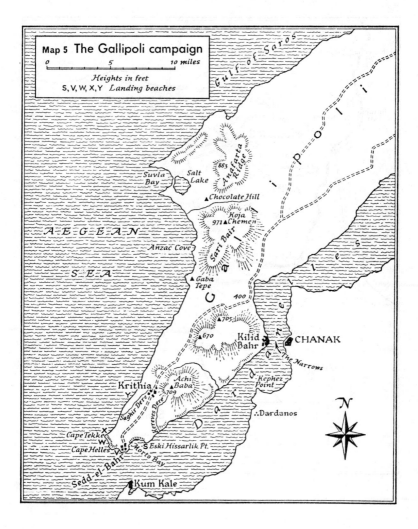

Map 5 The Gallipoli campaign

0   5   10 miles

Heights in feet
S, V, W, X, Y   *Landing beaches*

Gulf of Saros

885 ▲

Anafarta Ridge

Suvla Bay

Salt Lake

G a l l i p o l i

▲ Chocolate Hill

Koja
971 ▲ *Chemen*

A E G E A N

Sari Bair

Anzac Cove

S E A

▲ Gaba Tepe

G a b a

400

▲ 705

▲ 670

Kilid Bahr ◼

◼ CHANAK

The Narrows

Krithia

Achi Baba
▲ 709

Saghir Dere

Gully Dere

Kephez Point

∴ Dardanos

D a r d a n e l l e s

Cape Tekke X
W
Cape Helles V ◼
S Eski Hissarlik Pt.
Sedd-el-Bahr
Morto Bay

N

▲ Kum Kale

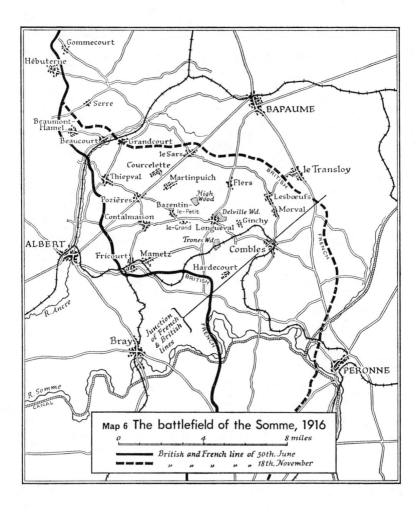

Map 6 **The battlefield of the Somme, 1916**

British and French line of 30th. June
" " " " " 18th. November

Map 7 The German and Allied offensives, 1918

0	25	50	75 miles

1 ——————— Allied line on 21st. March
2 ▪▪▪▪▪▪▪ Positions reached by German offensives
3 Same as 1 Line reached by Allies in July–August
4 ━ ━ ━ Armistice line 11th. November

North Sea

HOLLAND

Ostend
•Bruges
GHENT
⊚ ANTWERP
Dunkirk
Ypres
R. Lys
R. Schelde
⊚ BRUSSELS
Hazebrouck
•Armentières
⊚ LILLE
R. Dendre
Béthune
Valenciennes
Charleroi
Namur
R. Meuse
R. Sambre
Arras•
Cambrai
•Maubeuge
Albert•
Avesnes
Chimay
•Péronne
AMIENS
•St.Quentin
Montdidier
•la Fère
Mézières•
Sedan
Luxembourg
Compiègne
Laon
R. Aisne
Stenay•
Thionville•
R. Oise
Soissons
REIMS•
Verdun
R. Meuse
METZ•
R. Marne
•Chalons
St. Mihiel•
PARIS

Map 8 Mesopotamia

Map 9 Palestine and Syria

0   25   50   75 miles

- - - - - - British line

Index

608 INDEX

Russia—*contd.*

rejects German peace offer (1915), 136, March revolution (1917), 269, 306, 435–6, 284, 287, 306, Bolshevik revolution, 306, 436, Allies consider effects of Russian collapse, 306–7, 309, 311, allied attitude towards (1918), 400–2, Brest-Litovsk negotiations, 401–2, 437–8, 445, allied relations with Bolsheviks and intervention in Russian territory, ch. 29

Saar, 375, 531, 542–3, 566
St Quentin, 382–4, 396, 411
Salonika, 62–4, 67, 70–1, landings at, 88–94, 96, BEF, 97–8; 144, 256, 343, 413
Salter, Lord, 484 n.1, 490
Samuel, H., 455
Sarrail, General, 87, 98
Sassoon, S, xxv, xxvi
Scapa Flow, 169–70, 179, 427 n.1, 428
Scheer, Admiral, 178, Jutland, 179, 181–2; 184–5, 367 n.2, 427–8
Schelde, river, 425
Schlieffen Plan, 8, 21, 31–3, 269
Selborne, Earl of, 83, 500
Senussi, 114–15
Serbia (also Servia), relations with Austria, 3–5, Austrian ultimatum to, 9–11, Austria declares war on, 12, repels Austrian attack, 70, 88, Bulgarian attack on, 90–2; 128–9, 256
Seton-Watson, R. W., 583 n.1
Shipping, insurance of, 485–6, rise in freight costs, 486–7, 489, 491, requisitioning of, 487, 489, 494, congestion at ports, 487, 494–5, Ministry of Shipping, 491, shipbuilding and repair, 491–3, transport workers' battalions, 494, Inter-allied Shipping Conference (Paris), 496, Inter-allied Maritime Council, 496 (see also Convoying, Ships, Shipping Losses)
Shipping losses, British (1916), 336, 490–1, (1917), 338, 345, 492–3, allied and neutral (1917), 338, 345, 490–1
Ships, British (War), *Aboukir*, 174,

Audacious, 169 n.1, 175, 337 n.3, *Campania*, 367–8, *Canopus*, 172–3, *Cressy*, 174, *Drake*, 345, *Dublin*, 171, *Engadine*, 367 n.3, *Glasgow*, 173, *Gloucester*, 171, *Good Hope*, 172–3, *Hampshire*, 151, *Hogue*, 174, *Inflexible*, 74, *Lion*, 184 n.1, *Monmouth*, 173, *Queen Elizabeth*, 68, *Southampton*, 180–1, *Vindictive*, 348
Ships, British (Merchant), *Arabia*, 336, *Arabic*, 198, *Baralong* (Q ship), 198, *Falaba*, 196 n.1, *Laconia*, 241, *Leinster*, 416, *Lusitania*, 196–7, 216, *Marina*, 336, *Nicosian*, 198, *Sussex*, 202
Ships, German (War), *Berlin*, 169 n.1, 175, *Blücher*, 178, *Breslau*, 60, 170–2, *Dresden*, 59, 172 n.2, 174, *Elbing*, 335, *Emden*, 172, *Gneisenau*, 172, 173 n.1, *Goeben*, 60, 170–2, *Kaiser Wilhelm II*, 168, *Kaiser Wilhelm der Grosse*, 168, *Karlsruhe*, 172 n.2, *Königsberg*, 172 n.2, *Lepzig*, 172, *Lützow*, 335, *Magdeburg*, 178 n.1, *Moewe*, 490, *Nurnberg*, 172, *Pommern*, 182, *Rostock*, 335, *Scharnhorst*, 172, 173 n.1, *Seydlitz*, 184 n.1, 335, *Yorck*, 177
Silesia, Upper, 545, 566, 568, 570, 583
Simon, Sir J., 24, 159
Slesvig, North, 543
Smith, Sir F. E., 24 n.1, 577 n.2
Smith, Sir H. LL, 485
Smuts, General, 253 n.2, 276, 285, 287–288, 320, 363, 373–4, 422 n.2, 470, League of Nations, 536, 543; supports inclusion of pensions in reparation, 552, mandates, 557, criticism of treaty, 565, 578
Snowden, P., 47, 515, 519
Sonnino, S., 236
Spee, Admiral Count von, 9, 172–4
Spring-Rice, Sir C., 201, 208, 211, 212 n.1, 238, 398 n.2.
Stamp, Sir J., 514 n.1, 519
Stokes mortar, 44
Stopford, Hon. Sir C., 85–6, 90
Strikes, 477, Clydeside, 477–9, Coventry, 477, 483, mines, 481, Commissions of Enquiry into labour unrest, 478, 483
Sturdee, Sir F. C. D., 174